Christian Perspectives on Social Problems

Edited by
Charles P. DeSanto
Zondra G. Lindblade
Margaret M. Poloma

Wesley Press
P.O. Box 50434
Indianapolis, IN

Christian Perspectives on Social Problems
Copyright © 1992 by Wesley Press

Wesley Press
P.O. Box 50434
Indianapolis, Indiana 46250-0434

ISBN 0-89827-087-1

T his book is dedicated to David O. Moberg, Professor of Sociology Emeritus, Marquette University, Milwaukee, Wisconsin.

Dr. Moberg clearly stated in his 1972 book, The Great Reversal, the need for the contemporary evangelical church to again recognize and cope with social evil, as well as personal sin. It is in this tradition that this present book is written.

Christian Perspectives
on Social Problems

Edited by
Charles P. De Santo
Zondra G. Lindblade
Margaret M. Poloma

PREFACE FOR STUDENTS

INTRODUCTION

PART III THE FAMILY AND RELATED ISSUES

PART IV INEQUALITIES AND RELATED ISSUES

PREFACE FOR STUDENTS

Although sociology seeks to be value neutral, a careful reading of different sociological works makes it clear that this desired neutrality is an illusive goal. Each writer, whether aware of it or not, is influenced by personal background factors, cultural milieu, as well as assumptions made in various sociological theories. The approach sociologists use to uncover some of the biases is known as the sociology of sociology, a branch of the sociology of knowledge which aims to demonstrate the effect various factors have on the kind of sociological knowledge produced. For example, a wealthy stockholder who has an advanced degree in economics may analyze the appropriate role of economics in society very differently from a professional social worker. Both may live in the same society, be equally observant, and be well educated, but both may have irreconcilable differences about the workings of the government. Sociologists, too, have these background assumptions about social life that stem from personal life histories.

A sociologist of sociology is also aware that different sociological theories may rest on incompatible assumptions about the nature of person and society, the appropriate role of a sociologist, as well as the nature of the problems facing modern society. Professor De Santo's introductory article discusses some of the differences among sociologists — even Christian sociologists — in approaching social problems. There frequently is not an agreement about what constitutes a social problem or about the appropriate ways to resolve perceived social disorders — even once agreement is reached in their identification. Part of the difficulty stems from background assumptions stemming from personal factors, but much of the disagreement also rests on differing sociological perspectives, each of which contains certain inherent assumptions. Since assumptions are necessarily at the base of each theory, and since they can neither be proven nor disproven, the application of a particular theory to a reputed social problem will not readily find consensus.

In order to alert the reader to some of the inevitable bias, we have written brief introductions to each article. The introductions are intended not as a criticism of the author's work, but to encourage the student to consider alternate points of view. Although both the introductions and the articles have been written within a broad Christian framework, there is much room for differing opinions within their perspective. As Professor De Santo's article emphasizes, there are absolute truths set forth in God's Word, but our understanding and application of the truths are often tenuous. Human beings are not omniscient. Our knowledge as human beings is clouded by both personal biases and by cultural norms.

The introduction to each article on a particular social problem will point out some of the assumptions underlying the particular sociological framework employed by the author. For example, some sociological theories stress consensus or agreement between people; others stress conflict or disagreement. Usually it is not a matter of one sociological perspective being correct and the other being wrong. It is rather analogous to two people looking out of an open doorway after a fierce storm. One sees the mud and debris left by the rains; the other sees the rainbow and the clear skies.

Being alerted to alternate perspectives before reading the article will hopefully encourage the reader to recognize there are no simple answers to the problems facing modern society. As Christians and as citizens, it is important for us to learn to weigh proposed arguments, to recognize underlying assumptions, and only then to take a position that is in accord with one's Christian convictions.

The Editors

THE INTRODUCTION

THE SOCIOLOGY OF SOCIAL PROBLEMS
Charles P. De Santo

Virtually everyone is affected by some contemporary social problem that pervades all our major institutions: the family, education, business and industry, religion and government. Our mass media bombard us with problems dealing with drug and alcohol abuse, prejudice and discrimination (race, sex, or age), poverty and homelessness, religious cult activity, single parentage, spouse and child abuse, health care and crime and delinquency, to name a few. While some are interested in analyzing the causes and effects of various problems, virtually everyone is ready to suggest solutions. Sociologists have engaged in the scientific study of social problems for decades, and their services have been employed by private and government agencies at every level. Because young and old are concerned about social problems, sociology courses that deal with social problems are among the most popular in colleges and universities across the country. Since social problems have been viewed from various sociological perspectives, students can profit from examining these views as they attempt to understand and construct their own eclectic perspective that is consistent with Christian values.

Why a Christian Perspective on Social Problems
While there are many excellent social problems texts on the market today, this book meets the need of those who desire one that evaluates social problems from a Christian perspective.

Sociology as a science seeks to understand the forces operating in society—forces that hold it together, as well as those that tear it apart. If one hopes to gain a complete understanding of society, one must begin by examining societal values. This means that we must examine the basic assumptions that inform sociologists' analyses, for these assumptions are related to what they believe to be a "social problem." When dealing with social problems, we are thrust immediately into the whole question of the place of values (Holmes, 1987). For while sociologists work diligently at being objective and value free, it is now generally agreed that this is an impossibility. It is impossible because our values enter the picture at several stages, both consciously and subconsciously — first, when one selects social problems for research, then when variables are chosen to use in analysis, and finally when suggestions are made as to how a problem may be solved. Furthermore, value judgments are inherent in statements that are made about social issues. For example, "Abortion and contraception must be employed in reducing overpopulation." "STD's (sexually transmitted diseases) are destroying the youth of our nation." "A national health plan is a must because adequate health care is a right." "Alcoholism, prostitution, and drug abuse are 'victimless crimes'." "Homelessness is the result of our economic system that values profits more than people." Behind such statements is a standard informing us as to what ought or ought not to be. For Christians, the standard or "plumbline" used to judge personal behavior and societal problems is the principles set forth in the Bible (Amos 7:8; Micah 6:8; Matthew 7:12 a; 22:39).*

* Unless otherwise stated, quotations are from *The Revised Standard Version* of the Bible.

SOCIAL PROBLEMS AND THE IDEAL SOCIETY

Definitions

Sociologists have defined social problems in different ways. For example, Kornblum and Julian (1989:2) say: "When most people in a society agree that a condition exists that threatens the quality of their lives and their most cherished values, and also agree that something should be done to remedy that condition, sociologists say that the society has defined that condition as a social problem." Balswick and Morland (1990, p.16) however, define a social problem as "any situation which the members of a group consider to be undesirable and which they think should be remedied by cooperative action." Robert Merton (1976, p.7) says: "Basically, a social problem exists when there is a sizeable discrepancy between what is and what ought to be." H. E. Freeman, et al, (1979, pp.18-21), who prefers the "social policy approach" to social problems (because it "does not favor certain types of behavior over others, or one research method over another") uses as his criterion for identifying social problems the existence of discontinuity between the ideal (community norms) and the real (behaviors contrary to those norms). The current community norms, therefore, constitute the ideal.

Finally, Horton, Leslie and Larson (1991, p.2), who also have in mind a community ideal inherent in their definition of a social problem, state: "A social problem is a condition affecting a significant number of people in ways considered undesirable, about which it is felt something can be done through collective social action." While all of the above are valid definitions of social problems, I prefer the following definition: anything that is destructive to humans and tears down a system is dysfunctional and, therefore, constitutes a social problem. Whereas, anything that builds up a social system and enhances personal lives is functional and, therefore, not a social problem.

One other important point needs to be made, namely, the distinction between a *personal* and a *social* problem. Lauer (1989) succinctly clarifies the difference between them. He says that when we define problems as *social*, we identify the *causes* as lying primarily outside of the individual, rather than within the person. For example, while he would not deny that personal choices play a part in determining our condition (in such things as unemployment, divorce, single parenthood, and homelessness) the primary causes lie in the social structure of the society in which one lives (in plant closings and relocations, permissive divorce laws, and the unavailability of low income housing). This distinction determines the causes of the problem we identify, the consequences of the problem, and the ways we attempt to solve it.

The "Ideal" or Utopian Concept

While some sociologists (e.g., Moore and Moore, 1982, pp. 30-31) reject some approaches to the study of social problems because they believe the perspective is biased by implying "a normal state," it seems obvious that any consideration of a phenomenon as a social problem assumes some ideal or utopian state. This fact is made clear by sociologists who work in the area of social problems. For example, Kenneth J. Neubeck (1991) straightforwardly sets forth a vision or ideal against which he measures the status quo. In all of the definitions of social problems listed above, therefore, we find two common ideas. *First*, each explicitly or implicitly identifies some objective standard against which the status quo — things as they are in society — is measured. *Second*, each assumes that change is constant — that what may be considered a problem at one time may not be one at another.

Christian sociologists agree with the above. We readily acknowledge that change is constant even though many both inside and outside of the church resist and reject change. Change is constant for several reasons. For one thing, human knowledge is growing at an exponential rate. Technological and scientific knowledge, as well as creative output in the humanities and the social sciences, have been growing so rapidly that there are few, if any, "renaissance" persons. Inevitably, therefore, this results in some changes in our beliefs, values, and norms.

Secondly, change is constant because as finite creatures who grow with increased knowledge and experience, our perception of reality is altered. Furthermore, because we are limited in our grasp of an issue, we need input from colleagues within and beyond our discipline or sphere of competence to enlarge our knowledge and understanding. Therefore, Christian sociologists, like their secular colleagues, approach problems open-endedly, realizing that our description and analysis might be incomplete, in error, and/or in need of modification. For this reason, premature closure on any subject is unwise.

Christians, however, differ from their non-Christian colleagues in that the ideal of society against which they measure things as they are is one based upon the principles set forth in the Bible. And this difference is crucial. The basic Christian principles that serve as our guide are: "You shall love your neighbor as yourself" (Mark 12:31), and "Do to others as you would have them do to you" (Luke 6:31 NRSV).

Christian assumptions about persons and society combine the concepts of *absolutes*, *tentativeness*, and *relativity*.

Absolutes exist in the eternally relevant and unchangeable teaching in Scripture about relationships and responsibility to God, persons, and society. These serve as appropriate guides for personal and corporate rights and responsibilities in society, regardless of social conditions. Yet our understanding of absolutes is tentative because humans are *not* omniscient. Therefore, we must change our perspective and understanding of social issues and problems as societal conditions change, and as new knowledge and insights are acquired. Finally, because human cultures vary, human traits are generally relative to the central theme of each particular society. Many of these traits are neither right nor wrong, but merely a matter of preference — such as whether one eats with fingers or with utensils. As we learn about other cultures — their ways of feeling, acting, and thinking — we can adapt and enrich our own culture. However, some cultural traits are ruled out from the outset because they are both inhumane and contrary to teachings of Christ, such as the former Indian practice of *suttee* (in which the living wife of a deceased husband was burned upon his funeral pyre), or the lingering practice of cannibalism in some primitive tribes.

For Christian sociologists, therefore, some things never change. The ideal remains the ideal, regardless of how behavior and values in secular society may change. The basic principles set forth in the *Ten Commandments* and the *Sermon on the Mount*, that are applied in the prophetic writings of both the Old and New Testaments, remain constant. It is still as wrong today to bear false witness against our neighbor, to pervert justice, and to exploit others for sensual and economic gain as it was thousands of years ago. It is still wrong to steal, kill, and commit adultery as it was in Moses' day when the commandments were chiseled out on tablets of stone at Mount Sinai.

ASSUMPTIONS THAT INFORM A CHRISTIAN PERSPECTIVE

Since most people in the United States and Canada are affiliated in some way with the Judeo-Christian religious tradition, their religious assumptions and value system merit serious consideration (Horton, Leslie and Larson, 1991). Just what are these basic assumptions that inform our perspective? While we may not be conscious of these assumptions at all times, we have internalized them just as non-Christians have internalized a set of beliefs and values. They serve to inform and guide us in our life and work, and when we operate contrary to these principles, the Spirit of God convicts us of sin and judges us (John 16:8-11; Romans 2:12-14). Except for minor differences, all who have contributed to this volume would subscribe to the following statement about the implications of commitment to Christ.

The theological statements of the faith have been set forth in the historic creeds of Christendom. We do not propose to reproduce them here. As sociologists and social scientists who are Christians we believe that Christian humanistic beliefs and values should inform and direct our response to social problems. There is only one kind of faith, a personal faith in Jesus Christ as Savior and Lord that acts to establish and maintain justice in the social order (Micah 6:8; James 2:18; Matthew 7:21).

It is no accident that Jesus summed up the commandments by stating that we must love our neighbor as we love ourselves, and that to do so is comparable to loving God (Mark 12:30-31; Matthew 25:31-46). Furthermore, Jesus explicitly stated that we should do for others just what we would like others to do for us (Luke 6:31). Christians are to play the servant role in both church and society (Mark 10:43-45; Matthew 5:43-48). We are to be "salt" and "light" in the world (Matthew 5:13-16). We are to lose our lives in service for Christ; i.e., others (Matthew 10:38-39; 25:35-46). In the struggle for a just and equitable society, Christians are not to fear those who may kill the body, but rather to fear God who has power to destroy both body and soul (Matthew 10:28).

We acknowledge that the Church in the past, as well as in the present, has often reneged on its servant role. There have been individuals, groups, and "Christian nations" that have done irreparable damage to the cause of Christ. But, for the most part, the Church has aspired, with varying degrees of success, to play the servant role. We who have contributed to this book believe that as Christians we must accept Christ's call, responding to the challenge to work for justice and peace in the world (Matthew 23:23; 5:9). But above all, in our attempt to apply Gospel principles to the restructuring of society, we believe Christ calls us to show mercy and compassion to those who have been victimized by the system — by others (Luke 10:25-37; Matthew 9:13; 25:31-46).

These basic assumptions, beliefs, and values, therefore, provide a frame of reference for viewing societal problems. Most sociologists who are Christians believe that there is no such thing as Christian sociology — only sociology. They do believe, however, that our Christian perspective comes into play when deciding *what* to do, *when* to do it, *how* to do it, and *why* one should do it. While so-called Christian monarchs and others have acted shamefully from time to time throughout history, we reject the idea that all of those who professed to act in the name of Christ were Christians. Instead, we identify with that faithful remnant who have sought to follow Christ in a servant role for the alleviation of pain and suffering and the establishment of justice and peace in the world.

Let us now move on to consider common fallacies about social problems, and then briefly examine various perspectives that sociologists have developed and employed to understand them.

WHAT SOCIOLOGISTS DON'T BELIEVE ABOUT SOCIAL PROBLEMS

There is always the danger of being deceived by those who advocate some simplistic, single solution to complex problems. Merton (1967, pp. 5-7) cautions us to be on guard against those who are ready to offer a single theory or single cause for understanding and solving social problems. He would concur with H. L. Mencken's statement: "For any social problem, there is an easy solution which is feasible, plausible, and wrong." As long as humans are human, and as long as we live on earth, there will be social problems. This is not to say that we should throw up our hands in despair and do nothing. That would be irresponsible and cowardly. We have a choice. Either we become a part of the solution, working to turn injustice into justice, making the dysfunctional functional, or through inactivity and default contribute to the growth of the problem.

Because there are many mistaken notions about social problems, let us consider some of them before moving on to various sociological perspectives. Horton, Leslie, and Larson (1991, pp. 6-10) identified nine common fallacies that people hold about social problems. *First, it is fallacious to believe that there is consensus or agreement as to what the social problems of our society are.* While corporate executives and others profit from unrestrained capitalistic practices favored by former President Reagan's economic policies, those who suffer from unemployment and from inadequate wages do not. Reducing money allocated to higher education for loans and grants might be hailed as a good way to reduce the national debt, but needy students and university administrators view it as a shortsighted policy that will reduce the pool of educated and trained leaders in our nation. Furthermore, it is obvious that each socioeconomic class, ethnic group, religious group, political group, and age group perceives and interprets problems differently. Indeed, what may be a problem for one, is not a problem for another.

Second, it is believed by many that *"social problems are natural and inevitable."* While social problems are endemic to the human condition, there is no "law of nature" that decrees they should be. Many of our health problems have been eliminated by medical advancements and through improved health care and nutrition, although about 20 percent of Americans still do not have adequate health care and the number of homeless is increasing (Kornblum and Julian, 1989). The *extremes* of poverty and malnutrition at least by comparison with third world nations — have been greatly reduced by our enlightened social welfare/health programs. Horton and Leslie (1981, p. 9) state that "in only one sense are social problems inevitable; namely, that certain social arrangements make certain outcomes inevitable." But as noted above, by changing the social structure many problems have been and can be eliminated.

Nonetheless, historical realism compels us to accept the fact that, given the human propensity to selfishness and greed, "There will always be poor in the land" (Deuteronomy 15:11; Matthew 26-11). We say this, not to foster despair and inactivity on behalf of the poor, but to foster better social welfare programs. As Moses said, "Therefore I command you to be openhanded toward your brothers and toward the poor and needy in your land" (Deuteronomy 15:11 b).

Third, many hold the mistaken notion "*that social problems are abnormal.*" While Horton, Leslie, and Larson (1991) readily admit that problems develop from a breakdown in the established order due to rapid social change or deviant behavior, they contend "that many problems are the product of normal behavior, not of ineffective or outmoded norms or deviations in social behavior." They cite environmental pollution and overpopulation as two things that are due to normal growth and development. "*The traditional, normal, and acceptable behavior of decent people contributes at least as much to the development of social problems as does abnormal, deviant, anti-social behavior . . . . In short, social problems are usually the logical, normal, and inevitable products of present social values and practices*" (1991, p.7).

Here again, the Christian understands what the authors mean, but we would say that while we realize that normal people do not have the ability to predict the future (See Walker's chapter, "The Future as a Social Problem"), thereby correcting for negative latent consequences, nonetheless we are responsible. Can those involved in the chemical/nuclear industry honestly say they were completely unaware of the consequences of their production?

Fourth, it is commonly believed that "*social problems are caused by bad people.*" Horton, Leslie and Larson (1991, pp.7-8) note that "nice people move to a pleasant suburb, carefully zoned to keep out the poor . . . . Some social problems persist, then, because nice people tolerate and support the conditions that produce them." Unfortunately, school integration and open housing have often been opposed by "good" people who discriminate on the basis of race, religion, and socioeconomic class.

At this point the Church is also guilty! While the Church through its various arms — organizations and agencies — has done and is doing a phenomenal amount of development and relief work, it has too often not been at the forefront of social reform. Like the "priest and the Levite," it has walked by quietly on the other side of the street (Luke 10:31-32), or remained quiet (Mark 14:51, 66-72). All manner of evil flourishes because "good people" do nothing!

Fifth, many believe "*that problems are created by being talked about.*" In actuality, problems usually exist for a long time before they finally are brought to light, and public sentiment is aroused to do something about them. The plight of the homeless, the oppression of women, blacks and other minorities, was not created by talk. Quite the contrary, their conditions were improved by healthy criticism and litigation. If there were no NAACP or Dr. Martin Luther King, Jr. to lead the nonviolent black revolution, would blacks have made any significant strides for equal rights? Those who chant, "America, Love It or Leave It!" are enemies of democracy. For only by sustained, open, and free debate can we preserve American democracy.

Sixth, it is naively assumed "*that all people would like to see the problem solved*" (Horton, Leslie, and Larson 1991, p. 8). This is a patently false assumption. Pimps, the Mafia, and other ethnic organized gangs that deal in drugs and pornography vigorously fight all who seek to eliminate them, just as many "respectable" people who avail themselves of their services covertly support them. Likewise, those whose jobs depend on racial discrimination or unequal treatment of women have a vested interest in

8

preserving the status quo.

Whether or not society wishes to eliminate social evils, it is one of the functions of a prophet to warn the people of impending doom. While we seldom build monuments to "living prophets," the prophetic role is a function the Christian student of social problems must perform. Ezekiel warns that unless we call attention to the inequities of life in our society, God will hold us accountable (33:1-6).

Seventh, Horton, Leslie, and Larson (1991, p. 9) suggest that many believe "*that problems will solve themselves*" if given enough time. While some may become less acute over time (e.g., unemployment might diminish due to the seeming inevitable rise and fall of the economy), most problems, if untreated, become worse. Certainly, this has been true of the AIDS epidemic, crime and delinquency, wife and child abuse, the homelessness, poverty, and the threat of nuclear war. Unfortunately, these problems in society are more like venereal diseases — if unchecked, they reach epidemic proportions.

Eighth, some believe that "*if people only get the facts social problems will be solved.*" But if people do get the facts we have no guarantee that they will be interpreted properly. For example, knowing the divorce rate is over fifty percent, that over twenty percent of our families are headed by single parents, and that the teenage illegitimacy rate is rising will not necessarily cause the problems to go away. What do we mean by right people? Usually, we mean "people who share my values." The problem will get attended to only if we can rouse public sentiment in support of our cause, and what is more important, channel the sentiment into action. We must change public policy.

Finally, the ninth fallacy is "*that problems can be cured without institutional changes.*" Unfortunately, many believe that all we have to do is change the individual, not the structures of existing institutions. *Unfortunately, changed people do not always change structures.* If we hope to reduce the percentage of those in poverty, sweeping changes will be necessary "in our educational, economic, and governmental institutions. ... Likewise, to provide more low cost housing for the poor, we will have to drastically reduce the cost of materials or increase government subsidies to the poor" (Horton, Leslie and Larson 1991). Weinberg and Rubington (1981, p.11) observe: "It is much easier to muster sentiments than soldiers in the battle against a social problem." Merely changing people without organizing them to help restructure societal institutions is really a manifestation of practical atheism — faith without works, which is really no faith at all (James 2:17-19). The literary Hebrew prophets of the eighth to sixth centuries B.C. identified institutions as corrupt and in need of reform — political, business/economic, social, and religious (Micah 7:3; Isaiah 1:10-20; Amos 8:4-6; Jeremiah 2:8; 5:31; Malachi 2:16). In fact, Jeremiah (1:10) said that God had commissioned him to lead a *revolution*: "see, today I (God) appoint you over nations and kingdoms, to uproot and tear down, to destroy and overthrow, to build and to plant."

SOCIOLOGICAL PERSPECTIVES ON SOCIAL PROBLEMS

Before we propose aspects of a Christian perspective with which we can examine social problems, let us briefly identify perspectives that sociologists have developed.

These not only offer keen insights but they form an integral part of a Christian perspective.

The Social Pathological Perspective

Weinberg and Rubington (1981, p. 20) say that "social pathology . . . refers to unhealthy social conditions and processes caused by disease." This perspective uses the organic medical model, viewing society as a system of interrelated parts that must work together for the healthy functioning of society. Horton and Leslie (1981, p. 35) object to this perspective because it uses emotive terms such as "sick." "Analogies are useful literacy devices that should be viewed as colorful prose, not scientific descriptions." But from a Christian perspective, *sickness* is used as a synonym for that which is dysfunctional — a condition that is injurious to the organism, as well as to others. It is a reality to groups, organizations, and institutions. It is a legitimate, descriptive term used in Scripture to describe a system or aspect of a system that is dysfunctional and in need of rectification (Isaiah 1:5; Hosea 5:13-14; Jeremiah 30:12-15; compare Nehemiah 9:33-34; Jeremiah 5:5, 31; Zephaniah 3:1-4).

Early pathologists such as Charles Henderson (1909) and Samuel Smith (1911), located the sickness in the individual. As we saw earlier, this is where much of the responsibility belongs, although as Furfey (1978) and Menninger (1973) rightly point out, *social sin* is a significant factor.

While there are innumerable environmental and economic factors that predispose one to deviate from the norms of society, the pathological perspective attributes the primary cause of deviance to the individual. The solution, therefore, lies in resocializing deviants, teaching them the proper rules of social interaction and fitting them for society. Later pathologists transferred the "blame" from the individual to the structures of society.

Christians, while not denying the profound influence of social sin on the individual have a tendency to blame individuals who are often suffering from various forms of oppression. While we readily admit individuals often are partially responsible for their plight due to unwise decisions, Christian sociologists believe that if the situation is going to be improved, change must occur at both levels — the structural corporate level, as well as the personal level. We would acknowledge, however, that rather than sit idly by, we should take steps to improve their situation. Nonetheless, all the blame cannot be laid at the door of the "establishment" (Jeremiah 31:20-30), for it is often the individual, regardless of socioeconomic class, who is in a state of rebellion against God and Christian norms, who must repent and accept God's offer of forgiveness. But having said that, we must recognize that faith in God does not automatically change all things. The genetic and social consequences of past personal and social sins often have far-reaching consequences (Exodus 34:7; Numbers 14:18, 33). When we experience the "new birth" it does not turn us into geniuses. It does not make us well educated, socially adept, or skillful, nor does it reverse the ravages of cirrhosis of the liver! However, a serious commitment to Christ as Savior and Lord will certainly markedly improve our total well-being and go a long way towards making us more responsible, productive members of society. Any local cleric, Catholic or Protestant, can identify those who have not only been personally transformed by the grace of God in Christ, but also have improved their familial situation. Christians, therefore, can identify with early pathologists who saw the problem and the solution in a "resocialized" individual. But we also agree with later pathologists who identify the root cause of deviant personal and social problems with elements of the corporate structure that are plagued by the effects of social sin.

The Social Disorganization Perspective

The central theme of this perspective is that life is orderly and there are rules by which all must live. When, for some reason, the rules do not seem to fit the situation, or when various rules contradict one another, or if people follow the rules and they are not rewarded, social disorganization occurs. This approach assumes that society operates by value consensus. That is, there are legitimate goals in society and there are agreed upon means whereby one achieves those goals.

This perspective sees social problems accelerated during periods of rapid change — economic booms and busts, military crises (such as the invasion of Panama and the Middle East conflict), revolutions, and population changes. Disorganization results when societal norms are not clear or no longer apply — when a state of *anomie* exists. It also results from culture conflict and from "breakdown" — when conformity to the rules does not result in the promised reward.

The solution is found in reestablishing a consistency between ideas and actions. When a new set of rules develop that people can follow which will lead to rewards, people will proceed towards their goals and find satisfaction. Normlessness, culture conflict, and breakdown will then disappear; organization will replace disorganization. Another suggested solution is to slow down the rate of change and/or prepare people for it so that stress and frustration are minimized.

The Christian sociologist recognizes change as constant, but contends that change need not always be disruptive. Often disorganization results from changes that are too precipitous. When new technology and other innovations are introduced without adequate social planning, this usually results in *cultural lag*. For example, the impact of the automobile itself has forced changes in dating practices, family life, leisure activities, and the location of business and industry. And now, the introduction of micro-chips, computers and robots into the already automated car industry has resulted in significant reduction in the workforce. This cultural lag — society's inability to rapidly make the social changes necessary to accommodate to these changes in technology — has had a disorganizing effect at all levels in society.

Furthermore, it seems almost inevitable that in a pluralistic society such as ours — with competing religious, political, and philosophical ideologies — disorganization is bound to occur in various segments of society.

So long as we operate on a subjective, relativistic basis — especially with reference to morality — anomie, conflict, and breakdown are bound to occur. The Christian sees the solution in working for value consensus based upon basic biblical principles for personal and social morality. Society cannot operate when "every person does what is right in his own eyes" (Judges 17:6; 21:25). While we must fight against the attempt of any one segment in society that pushes for conformity on nonmoral issues, we need a moral consensus based upon Judeo-Christian ideals to maintain a viable sense of community. While we work towards this end, however, our ardor is somewhat dampened by the inability of the different Christian denominations and independent groups to reach any kind of consensus on many issues.

The Value Conflict Perspective

Richard C. Fuller (1937) coined the title "value conflict" that views the rise of social problems from a clash of values between various groups within our pluralistic society. Whenever one has a difference based on age, sex, religion, socioeconomic class, political ideology, or ethnicity, inevitably one finds a clash of values. This conflict of values often results in social problems. For example, strikes are viewed by management as an unfair leverage but as the ultimate weapon by labor.

All groups have values. There are no neutral ones. As Saul Alinsky (1971, p.10) said: "All of life is partisan. There is no dispassionate objectivity."

Unlike the functionalists who assume that consensus is the norm in society, the values conflict perspective believes that conflict is the norm. Social order prevails only when conflict "is bound up in a socially sanctioned system of compromise" (Weinberg and Rubington, 1981, p.139). But following Marx and C. Wright Mills (1959), the conflict school contends that it is the "power elite" that controls society. It is the affluent, powerful elite minority in control who not only are least compromising but who are also most oppressive, expressive, exploitive, and calloused toward the disadvantaged minorities and the poor.

Problems caused by conflict of values can be solved by reaching a new consensus, by trade-offs (each group giving up something), or by exerting power (force), enforcing a solution (Kornblum and Julian, 1989, pp.10-12).

There is much in the conflict approach that has merit (Yoder, 1980). The prophets (Jeremiah 5:20-31), Jesus (Luke 6:24; 16:19-31; 18:23; Matthew 19:23-24; Mark 10:42-45), and the apostles (1 Timothy 6:10; James 2:14-17; 5:1-6) all caution about the diabolical consequences of avarice (greed) which corrupts both the avaricious person and group. Non-Christians, as well as "fat" affluent Christians (Psalm 73:3-12), who work the capitalistic system to the hilt and disregard the casualties the system produces, often turn a deaf ear to Christ's teaching cited above. All too often we take refuge in the false interpretation of Jesus' hyperbole (Matthew 19:24): "Again I tell you, it is easier for a camel to go through the eye of a needle than for a rich man to enter the kingdom of God." He did not have a literal gate in mind. Christ's meaning is plain: "You cannot serve both God and money" (Matthew 7:24 NIV).

It is common knowledge that most of the wealth is controlled by a very small percentage of the population (Macionis, 1989). The wealthiest 20 percent of the families in our society own 78.7 percent of the wealth. There is no way these people who live socially isolated lives can view life the way the lowliest 20 percent do who own 0.4 percent of the wealth. It is not only questionable how long developed nations can merely hand a "sop" to third world countries, but also how long the rich and super-rich in America can ignore the plight of the poor. As the rich become increasingly richer and the poor poorer, and as the middle class continues to shrink, this is bound to cause a crisis (Center on Budget and Policy Priorities, 1990). Should not Christians become more actively involved in the struggle of minorities and the homeless and other poor as they struggle for "a fairer share of the action"? Should not blighted urban areas, as well as the desolate lot of the rural poor be declared the "new mission frontier"? Is it not time to include some kind of a national health plan in our human welfare program? Should not every American have the "right" to good health care, as well as a good education, and a decent job? Values conflict - yes! From a Christian perspective, identifying with the radical program of Christ is the only safe way to avoid the extremes of the radical right and the radical left.

The Deviant Behavior Perspective

The deviant approach recognizes cultural norms to which the majority in society adhere as the acceptable standard of behavior. Those who do not conform to these standards are called "deviants." The basic assumption of this perspective is that deviant or unacceptable patterns of behavior are learned in much the same way we learn acceptable patterns. Every culture transmits unique ways of feeling, acting, and thinking to its members through the process of socialization. Once these beliefs, values, and behaviors are internalized, they constitute a sense of *oughtness* within us. When there is a discrepancy between what *is* and what *ought to be*, we have a situation conducive to deviance.

This perspective assumes that the role of societal expectations needs to be changed, not the person. "A given behavior occurs under given conditions; therefore, if conditions change, then behavior changes" (Weinberg and Rubington, 1981, p.182). Merton (1938) argued that deviant behavior results when the legitimate *goals* of society are not open to some members of society because the legitimate *means* for achieving them are blocked. But not all people in the so-called disadvantaged sectors of society become deviant. Why not? E. H. Sutherland's (1939) response was that this was due to "differential association." He stated that deviance resulted from a preponderance of associations with nonconforming individuals. A. K. Cohen (1955) argued that because working class youth are denied access to middle class means they develop their own means which middle class society labels deviant. Cloward and Ohlin (1966) added that for deviance to develop, there must be a deviant subculture in the community to socialize individuals into a deviant lifestyle.

One solution suggested by the deviant perspective is that the deviant individual must be resocialized. Another suggests that if we identify and change the dysfunctional and inequitable structures within society, as Merton might suggest, we might reduce deviance. Or, if we change the individual's primary group association from nonlaw abiding to law-abiding, then we might successfully resocialize the individual into the mainstream of society (Weinburg and Rubington, 1981).

The deviant behavior perspective provides helpful insights for the solution of problems. Christians agree that behavior is learned. We often hear the proverb, "Train a child in the way he should go, and when he is old he will not turn from it" (Proverbs 22:6). The Apostle Paul confirms Sutherland's conviction that if individuals associate with "deviants" they will probably become involved in deviant behavior. Paul (1 Corinthians 15:33) says: "Bad company corrupts good character." Therefore, it is essential that the church and parachurch organizations provide a supporting fellowship for its members and also for new converts. New Christians not only need to be nurtured spiritually, but they also need a supportive community (1 Peter 2:2-3; Matthew 18:5-6; Acts 4:42, 46; 1 Thessalonians 5:14; Hebrews 10:25).

Also, Merton is correct in pointing out that the opportunity to achieve is *not* open to all. While we recognize that social stratification is inevitable, abilities and contributions to society will vary with the individual's innate endowment and performance. We, therefore, insist that society's opportunities must be open to all. Christians must do all they can to tear down the numerous "walls" that divide people (Ephesians 2:14; Acts 2:26), and affirm Christ's teaching that all are brothers and sisters (Matthew 25:31-46).

We contend, however, that while all are obviously not aware of God's grace in Christ, there is a natural revelation of God of which all persons are aware. The Apostle Paul argues that God's righteous standards — are known by all (Romans 1:18-32, 2-3). The very fact that deviant acts are perpetrated in "the dark" or when "the law" is not present indicates that all, to some degree, have an inner sense of what is "right" (John 3:19-21; Romans 2:14-15). The solution is not only to work for justice in societal institutions, but to work to change the human heart by offering salvation in Christ (Ezekiel 36:26-27; Matthew 28:19-20; 2 Corinthians 5:17-18).

The Labeling Perspective

Although E. M. Lemert (1951) did not use the term "labeling theory," he set forth the postulates that form the basis of the labeling perspective. The theory became popular when Howard Becker (1963) wrote his book *Outsiders*. Labeling theorists call attention to the fact that the label *deviant* is placed on certain practices by the elites in society, or by the dominant groups who control the money and power. They insist that the establishment is not only selective in what it labels deviant, but also selective in enforcing the law.

Labeling theorists maintain that it is not the act, *per se*, that is necessarily deviant, but how a given society reacts to the behavior that determines whether or not it constitutes deviance and is labeled a problem.

Kornblum and Julian (1989, p.14) contend that when a segment in society believes it can profit by labeling something deviant, it does so. He contends that society suffers from labeling in two ways. First of all, by labeling, one group gains power over another. Secondly, by labeling persons (e.g., delinquents) they accept the label "as part of their social identity and self-concept, leading them to fulfill the expectations of others . . ." (Macionis, 1989). Subsequently, they become more firmly entrenched in the deviant subculture. It is the secondary stage that is the most devastating to individuals and their subsequent lives. Labeling gives individuals a "master status," a status that overrides all others.

Some suggested solutions are (1) stop labeling behaviors as deviant; (2) change or redefine what is illegal as legal (e.g., decriminalize marijuana, legalize prostitution); (3) diminish the power of those who label; and (4) remove the profit motive from those who label (Kornblum and Julian, 1989, p.14).

The Christian sociologist cannot but agree that labeling places a stigma on certain behaviors, and that these labels are difficult to remove. In many cases, the Church and Christian groups do work to reduce "secondary deviance." Both Catholics and Protestants, through their various outreach programs do much more than many other voluntary organizations to assist those in need of help. Unfortunately, because of the secular bias of most social problems texts, the Church's efforts go largely unnoticed. (If one examines texts dealing with the subjects of delinquency, crime, and social problems, very little, if any attention is given to the topic of religion and the positive force it plays in rehabilitating offenders, or the constructive force it exerts in society.)

But we are not comfortable with the suggested solution of some who suggest that labels must go. Labeling is pervasive, and in many cases it is helpful, but every effort must be made to protect the individual against being labeled unjustly, since labels have a way of sticking long after individuals have paid for their crime. Christians object, also, to the suggestion that labels should be removed by legalizing so-called victimless crimes, or crimes without victims. Many Christians object to these being labeled "crimes," while they do believe that they are "sinful." To legalize drug abuse or prostitution is unconscionable. We believe that any behavior that injures an individual also injures others. From a Christian organismic perspective there can be no victimless crime. While some evangelical Christian groups are quick to emphasize personal sins and vices (such as excessive drinking, smoking, and sexual aberrations), thankfully an increasing number of Evangelicals, Catholics and Protestants are addressing social sins/ crime (such as the exploitation of developing nations, the crass materialism of our society, the arms race, environmental pollution, the plight of children in third world countries, and the AIDS crisis).

Let us now move on to consider a Christian model of society, keeping in mind that much of what other sociologists have already contributed in the perspectives discussed above are essential to a full understanding of societal problems and their possible solution.

A CHRISTIAN MODEL OF SOCIETY

When discussing a model of society, we must of necessity begin with our concept of personhood. We discussed this earlier when we mentioned our Christian assumptions, but let us carry the discussion a bit further.

Human Nature

Christian sociologists differ with their non-Christian colleagues in their definition of human nature. They do not identify with Rousseau and humanistic sociologists who believe in a *tabula rasa* — that the human mind is uncontaminated, a clean slate that is only later contaminated by an evil society. They feel greater kinship with Hobbs who emphasizes the depraved state of humans (Poloma, 1980). Most sociologists assume that humans are born amoral and acquire a conscience through the process of socialization, but Christians also believe that humans are born with an innate weakness — more accurately, an innate selfishness, a perversity that seeks to exalt and satisfy self at the expense of others. The empirical evidence for this assumption is all around us, as past history and present experience testify. Whereas social pathological theorists identify humans as the problem, later pathologists and conflict theorists locate evil in the institutions people construct in society. Christian sociologists believe that *both* humans *and* the structures they create are flawed (Gaede, 1980).

Organic Model of Society

So while men and women were created by God and were originally "good," they chose to sin, allowing sin to enter in and affect and infect all relationships. While many sociologists adopt a functionalist perspective that grew out of the earlier organic model of society, I prefer the term "organic" because it is a wholistic concept and because it is biblical (Poloma 1979:15-30). Paul (Romans 12:5; 1 Corinthians 12:1-31; Ephesians 1:22-23) used this ideal organic model, the human body, to symbolize the Church. By using this model to view the Church, Paul was able to show the relevance of each part to the whole. By inference, therefore, I use the organic model to refer to the whole of human society — individuals, groups, organizations, institutions, and nations all dynamically related to one another. It, perhaps more than any other analogy, demonstrates the symbiotic relationship that exists among the various elements in society. As Paul (1 Corinthians 12:26) said, "If one part suffers, every part suffers with it; if one part is honored, every part rejoices with it." While this is not true in many cases (e.g., when a guilty rapist is acquitted he rejoices; when the Nazis exterminated the Jews and when Iraq soldiers occupied Kuwait and captured hostages, raped Kuwait women, they cared little for their victims), generally "in community" it is.

Societal Institutions

Christian sociologists view the major institutions of society as constituent parts of one system, each interfacing and impacting others. Of these institutions in contemporary Western society, most sociologists would probably identify the economic and/or the political institution as the most important. These two seem inseparably interrelated. While many Christians agree that the occupations parents hold have a significant effect on the family's socioeconomic status, they would insist that the institution of the family exerts the most profound influence on its members. For it is in the family that we are socialized — that we acquire our F.A.T. — our ways of feeling, acting, and thinking. It is through the family that we internalize these beliefs and values that provide motivation and direction for life. It is in the family that we feel loved and secure — at least where we should. In addition to the family, most Christians view the Church or Christian community — the religious institution — as one that runs a close second to the family. However, because of our belief in the separation of Church and state, and the apparent lack of religious influence in the formulation of much of our economic, political, and social policy, its pervasiveness may not be apparent. But religion — a belief system that informs and results in attitudes and behaviors — is indeed most influential. It is just that the secular surrogate religions that pervade American culture do not use symbols that most would interpret as "religious." There are, nonetheless, many secular religious surrogates such as materialism, humanism, hedonism, and Marxism. While we stoutly defend human freedom in every sphere of life in our democratic society, Christian sociologists work for the implementation of Judeo-Christian values in American society (Psalm 33:12). For it is God, Christ, the Spirit and the Word that give life (Luke 12:15, 23; Matthew 16:26; John 1:1-4; 5:26; 6:35,63; 7:37-39; Hebrew 4:12). All other worldly systems are found wanting and are doomed to pass away (1 Corinthians 8:1-6; I John 2:15-17).

Individual and Social "Sin"

The social problems that arise in society, therefore, arise because of individual and social sin; i.e., individuals, groups, and organizations that refuse to abide by standards of personal and corporate morality set forth in the Bible — and this includes the Church. For while the Church was founded by Jesus Christ, not only the prophets (Jeremiah 14:14; Ezekiel 34:1-10; Hosea 4:4-6), but both Jesus and the apostles readily admit and caution the faithful that not all who serve within the Church are true servants of God. (Matthew 7:15; 1 Corinthians 3:10-15; 2 Corinthians 11:12-15; Philippians 3:17-19; 2

Peter 2:1; 2 John 4:1). As Margaret Poloma reminds us, "Christianity first was called *The Way*; it was to be more than an institution; its institutionalization in itself is a kind of problem" (Poloma, 1982). For the Christian, therefore, the root cause of social problems is to be found in the sinfulness of individuals — non-Christian and Christian alike (Menninger, 1973) — *and* the imperfect social structures created by them. Menninger (1973, p.19) interprets sin as follows:

> The wrongness of the sinful act lies not merely in its nonconformity, its departure from the accepted, appropriate way of behavior, but in an implicitly aggressive quality — a ruthlessness, a hurting, a breaking away from God and from the rest of humanity, a partial alienation, or act of rebellion.
>
> Standing on one's head is nonconforming, and it is neither aesthetic nor congenial behavior nor expressive of a moral ideal, but it is not likely to be considered sinful. Sin is a willful, defiant, or disloyal quality; *someone* is defiled or offended or hurt. The willful disregard or sacrifice of the welfare of others for the welfare or satisfaction of the self is an essential quality of the concept *sin*. St. Augustine described it as a turning "away from the universal whole to the individual part .... There is nothing greater (i.e., more important, more desirable, more worthy) than the whole. Hence, when he desires (seeks, devotes himself to) something greater, he grows smaller." And sin is thus, at heart, a refusal of the love of others.

The Westminster Shorter Catechism (1951) defines sin as "any want of conformity unto, or transgression of, the law of God." But what motivates one to violate the law of God, or the sense of wholeness that Menninger and Augustine refer to? While the Scriptures uncover many motives, the Church historically has identified Gregory the Great's list of seven deadly sins (desires) as the root causes. They are: *pride* (the source of all others), *covetousness, lust, envy* (jealousy), *gluttony, anger,* and *sloth* (Swanson, 1980). The Apostle James (4:1-2) put it this way: "What causes wars, and what causes fightings among you? Is it not your passions that are at war in your members? You desire and do not have; so you kill. And you covet and cannot obtain; so you fight and wage war." Scripture will not allow us to project the blame from one to another. Each person (group, organization) is guilty and responsible because of choices made to yield to inordinate desires (Jeremiah 31:29-30; Ezekiel 18:19-20). Paul (Romans 6:13) emphatically states that the choice is ours, and so is the responsibility. "Do not offer the parts of your body to sin, as instruments of wickedness, but rather offer yourselves to God, as those who have been brought from death to life; and offer the parts of your body to him as instruments of righteousness." This applies equally to the board of directors of corporations as it does to individuals.

But people do not live in isolation. We are social beings and we form groups and organizations and we establish institutions. Long before Walter Rauschenbusch (1917) emphasized the corporate nature of evil in his book, *A Theology for the Social Gospel*, the Mosaic legislation of the book of Leviticus spoke of social sins and the corporate nature of evil. The book of Leviticus (4:1-3, 13, 22, 27) not only makes provision for sin offerings for the common person, but also for leaders (kings and priests), and for groups (the congregation). Furthermore, the social legislation of Israel touched on every conceivable social sin. Of the Ten Commandments the last six are "social commandments." And they apply to every aspect of life — business, social, judicial, and familial

(Leviticus 19:35-36; Exodus 21:28-32; Micah 7:3; Amos 8:4-6; Jeremiah 7:1-10). Paul Hanley Furfey (1978, pp.15-19) rightly points out that most social problems do not merely involve the sins or law violations of one, two or three persons, but many — various groups and collectives. Because social problems are social and complex in nature, Christians must engage themselves in change above and beyond the personal level. Structures need to be changed, and this means changes in economic, political, and social policies. The standard against which we measure all practices that we deem unjust is the Word of God, especially the teachings of our Lord Jesus Christ. These are best summed up in three basic statements in the Gospels: (1) "... do to others what you would have them do to you ..." (Matthew 7:12); (2) "Love your neighbor as yourself" (Mark 12:31); and (3) "A new commandment I give to you. Love one another. Even as I have loved you, so you must love one another" (John 13:34 NIV).

We believe that the organic model is one that is uniquely suited for Christians to use as they look at society, because it sees not only individuals but also institutions as part of the problem, as well as the solution to social problems. It enables us to see every part of society as a constituent part of the whole. None is more important than the other. All of life is viewed as sacred "for in Him we live and move and have our being" (Acts 17:28). This is not to say that the perspectives we discussed earlier are non-Christian, they are not. Each has a contribution to make within the organic model — as will subsequent perspectives that will be developed. Therefore, we acknowledge our indebtedness to all those scholars in the discipline who have enabled us to get a better understanding of social problems and suggested solutions. We join with them in working for a just society.

Study and Discussion
Questions

1. "It is impossible to be value free!" Do you agree or disagree? Why? Elaborate.

2. Several definitions of a "social problem" have been presented. Which do you prefer and why? Write your own. Does Lauer's distinction between "personal" and "social" problems necessarily remove individual responsibility for one's condition? Discuss.

3. What is your Christian concept of the "ideal society"? In the light of that definition, what do you see as the serious problems today?

4. How do you relate the concepts of absolutes, tentativeness, and relativity in your Christian sociological approach to social problems? For example, how do you relate them to the changing gender roles of women and men? What is the basic kernel of truth in Scripture, and what reflects the sociocultural context in which it was written?

5. What basic assumptions does the author make from which he evaluates society? How do yours differ from his? Be specific in your answer.

6. List the common fallacies that Horton, Leslie and Larson enumerate. In what ways do you agree/disagree from your Christian perspective? Why don't "knowledge" and "changed" individuals necessarily eliminate social problems?

7. The author presents several sociological perspectives on social problems: the pathological, value conflict, deviant behavior, labeling. What are the strengths and weakness of each? How would you critique them from a Christian perspective?

8. What are the essential components of the author's Christian Organic Model of society? In what way does Scripture support this model? Discuss fully.

9. Evangelicals generally feel that faith in Christ is the answer to social and societal problems. While this is often true in many ways, it would not eliminate all problems. Why? Discuss fully.

10. Scripturally speaking, what possible solutions would you suggest towards solving societal problems? What part ought Christians play towards solving these problems, on both a personal and a corporate or societal level?

References

Alinsky, Saul, *Rules for Radicals*. New York: Random House, 1971.

Balswick, Jack O., and J. Kenneth Morland, *Social Problems: A Christian Understanding and Response*. Grand Rapids: Baker Book House, 1990.

Becker, Howard, *The Outsiders: Studies in the Sociology of Deviance*. New York: The Free Press, 1963.

Burton, C. Emory, "Humanism and Religion." *The Humanist Sociologist* (June) Vol. 7, No. 2, 1982.

Center on Budget and Policy Priorities, Washington, D. C., 1990.

Cloward, Richard A. and Lloyd E. Ohlin, *Delinquency and Opportunity*. New York: The Free Press, 1966.

Cohen, A. K., *Delinqent Boys*. New York: The Free Press, 1955.

Freeman, H. E., C. Jones Wyatt, and Lynne G. Zucher, *Social Problems: A Policy Perspective*. Third Edition. Chicago: Rand McNally, 1979.

Fuller, Richard C., "Sociological Theory and Social Problems." *Social Forces* 15 (May): 496-502, 1937.

Furfey, Paul H., *Love and the Urban Ghetto*. Maryknoll: Orbis Books, 1978.

Gaede, Stan, "Functional and Conflict Theory in Christian Perspective: Toward an Alternative View of Order and Conflict," in *A Reader in Sociology: Christian Perspectives*, edited by C. P. DeSanto, Calvin Redekap, and Wm. L. Smith-Hinds, Herald Press, 1980.

Horton, Paul B., and Gerald R. Leslie, *The Sociology of Social Problems*. Seventh Edition. Englewood Cliffs: Prentice-Hall, 1981.

Horton, Paul B., Gerald R. Leslie, and Richard F. Larson, *The Sociology of Social Problems*. Tenth Edition. Englewood Cliffs: Prentice-Hall, 1981.

Holmes, Arthur F., *The Idea of a Christian College*. Revised Edition. Grand Rapids: Eerdmans, 1987. See chapters 2 and 3 for an excellent discussion of the theological foundations and the biblical concept of the person.

Kornblum, W., and J. Julian, *Social Problems*. Sixth Edition. Englewood Cliffs: Prentice-Hall, 1989.

Lemert, E. M., *Social Pathology*. New York: McGraw-Hill, 1951.

Lauer, Robert H., *Social Problems and the Quality of Life*. Dubuque, Iowa: Wm. C. Brown Publisher, 1989.

Macionis, J. J., *Sociology*. Second Edition. Englewood Cliffs: Prentice-Hall, 1989.

Menninger, Karl, *Whatever Became of Sin?* New York: Hawthorn Books, 1973.

Merton, Robert K., "Social Structure and Anomie." *ASR*, 3 (October); 672-682. 1938. *Contemporary Social Problems*. Fourth Edition. New York: Harcourt Brace Jovanovich, 1976.

Mills, C. Wright, *The Power Elite*. New York: Oxford University Press, 1956.

Moore, Joan W., and Burton M. Moore, *Social Problems*. Englewood Cliffs: Prentice-Hall, 1982.

New International Version of the Holy Bible. Grand Rapids: Zondervan Publishing Co., 1984. Unless otherwise stated, Scripture quotations are from the NIV.

Newbeck, Kenneth J., *Social Problems: A Critical Approach*. Third Edition. New York: McGraw-Hill, 1991.

Poloma, Margaret M., *Contemporary Sociological Theory*. New York: Macmillan, 1979. "Theoretical Models of Person in Contemporary Sociology," in DeSanto, et al., *Reader in Sociology: Christian Perspectives*. Scottdale, PA: Herald Press, 1980.

Is There a New Pentecost? Boston: Twayne Publishing Co., 1982.

Rauschenbusch, Walter, *A Theology for the Social Gospel*. Nashville: Abingdon Press (1978), 1917.

Smith, Samuel, *Social Psychology*. New York: Macmillan, 1911.

Sutherland, E. H., *Principles of Criminology*. Philadelphia: J. B. Lippencott, 1939.

Swanson, Stephen C., *The Double Cross: Messages on the Seven Deadly Sins and the Seven "Deadly" Virtues*. Minneapolis: Augsburg Publishing Co., 1980.

Weinburg, M. S., and Earl Rubington, Editors. *The Solution of Social Problems: Five Perspectives*. Second Edition. New York: Oxford University Press, 1981.

Westminister Presbyterian Standards. Richmond: John Knox Press, 1951.

Yoder, Michael L., "Coming to Terms with Karl Marx," in DeSanto, et al., *A Reader in Sociology: Christian Perspectives*. Scottdale, PA: Herald Press, 1980.

PART I

SOCIO-ECONOMIC ISSUES

CHAPTER 1
THE CITY: INTRODUCTION

Professor Hillery's thought-provoking article is an appropriate lead for our discussion of specific social problems. In writing about the Christian in the city Hillery sets a context for other problems treated in subsequent articles. We live in an urban society, and the problems addressed in this text are framed in an urban context.

As noted in the Preface and in Professor De Santo's introductory article, however, all authors make certain assumptions that can neither be proved nor disproved. Hillery's article is no exception, and it reflects one side of a long-standing debate over the inherent "goodness" or "badness" of the city. Two classic works on modern society, one by French sociologist Emile Durkheim and the other by his German contemporary, Ferdinand Tönnies, may be used to demonstrate the assumptional bias of Hillery's discussion.

Emile Durkheim is usually numbered among the founding fathers of sociology. His discussion of how social cohesion changes as we move from simple societies (with their "mechanical solidarity") to complex ones (characterized by "organic solidarity") is known to every serious student of sociology. The choice of terms "mechanical" to discuss simple society and "organic" to refer to the modern world, however, is a clue to the pro-modern bias found in Durkheim's theory. Although he recognizes the problems that accompany change, his bias toward "progress" found in modern society is readily evident. This bias is one that has fit well with an American "scientific sociology" that has viewed science and technology itself as an indicant of progress.

The assumptions about social progress and its bias toward the modern are clearer when contrasted with a classic sociological work having a different assumptional base. Durkheim's contemporary, Ferdinand Tönnies, preferred the life of a simple village to that of a modern cosmopolitan area. Although he knew that it was futile to try to turn the clock back to the Gemeinschaft, based on affective relations, he was hopeful that humankind would move beyond the Gesellschaft, or society based on rational contract. Tönnies' theory of Gemeinschaft and Gesellschaft, like Durkheim's on organic and mechanical solidarity, is known to all sociologists. The major difference is that Tönnies is more critical of modern development and is thus less compatible with scientific sociology's progress bent than is Durkheim. Tönnies' work is deemed interesting and even useful, but it is Durkheim's contribution that remains basic to the field.

Hillery's article is in the tradition of Tönnies. Following contemporary French sociologist and lay theologian Jacques Ellul, it is colored by an anti-urban bias. Although Hillery has questioned the biblical foundation of Ellul's categorical assertion that the city is "cursed by God," he modulates the position only to the extent of noting that "one may still conclude that the city is a source of spiritual difficulty, if not danger." Hillery traces the problem in a Tönnies-like fashion to the city's resting on the limited cooperation of contract, rather than the open-ended cooperation of family.

Although Hillery identifies a set of urban problems and traces their cause in part to contractual relations, the relationship between "urban" and "social problem" is not always that clear. For example, crime is identified as a social problem, and Hillery notes that it is "particularly evident in cities." Yet the crime rate is much higher for New York City than for London, Tokyo, or Toronto, but lower than many Latin American nations where violence has become a way of life. Japan, perhaps, provides the most interesting illustration of the difficulty in simply correlating higher crime rates with urbanization. In spite of Japan's rapid industrialization, Akira Fukushima reported that not only does Japan have a low violent crime rate, but that the rate of violent crime and industrialization has decreased remarkably since 1950 — "during the years when urbanization and industrialization have increased substantially" (*Begun Institute Newsletter*: Vol 6 No.1, 1980). Clearly there must be other factors besides urbanization that are linked with the crime rate. In addition, Hillery fails to note or explain why crime is increasing in rural areas in the United States.

Hillery's assumption that God has ordained two institutions, the family and the congregation (church) is questionable, as is his assumption that the city is "man-made." Surely God "works for good" (Romans 8:28) in all human institutions and organizations where people look to God in faith and obedience to the great commandments (Mark 12:29-31). Paul himself states that the powers that be are ordained of God (Romans 13:1-7) — this includes the complex structures of urban life that are designed, however imperfectly, to provide an orderly, peaceful place for people to live.

Hillery unfortunately equates "the city" with "the world" (John 17:15-18; 1 John 2:15-17). The "world" that Christ tells His disciples not to be a part of is not the city, per se, but those philosophical/political systems of personal and corporate life and organization that are not based on the great commandments and the Golden Rule. Christ did command us to be the "light" of the world and the "salt" of the earth (Matthew 5:13-16) — and this includes a mandate to be salt for and light to the city, with all of its problems. As members of the kingdom of God, we are to be as leaven, leavening the whole lump of dough, including society (Matthew 13:33; 1 Corinthians 5:6).

For many, Hillery's failure to emphasize more forcefully the responsibility of Christians to be agents of change, working for economic and social justice, will be perceived as a serious flaw in his Christian perspective. Many Christians believe that we are to wrestle with the forces of evil in society (Ephesians 6:10-20), striving to overcome them by the power of Christ (2 Corinthians 2:14-17), following the noble example of Christ (Hebrews 12:1-4). Furthermore, Hillery sees the contract as something less than Christian, yet there is nothing in Scripture that says the Gospel does away with the need for law (the contract). In fact, many see it as essential, one factor that helps to insure justice in a world of sinful, finite persons.

Hillery's interpretation of biblical passages on the family also may be questioned in light of differing opinions about male headship being a biblical mandate. Although this issue will be considered again in the articles found in Part IV of this reader dealing with family problems, a question may be worth posing here. What exactly did Jesus have to say about the family? Jesus announced that all who do "the will of my Father in heaven is my brother and sister and mother" (Matthew 12:46). Earlier Jesus said that He had come to turn "a man against his father, a daughter against her mother" (Matthew 10:35-36). In one passage Jesus calls us to honor and care for parents (Matthew 15:4-6), yet paradoxically in another, Jesus states, "and everyone who has left houses or brothers or sister or father or mother or children or fields for my sake will receive a hundred times as much and will inherit eternal life" (Matthew 19:29). Could it be that the paradox of

Jesus' call to honor parents, while at the same time urging followers to leave them, is actually a challenge for believers to become a new kind of family — what Hillery refers to as "congregation" in this article? Could it be that Jesus was more radical than many contemporary church leaders who long for a family of yesterday that was just as problem-ridden (albeit with different problems, but still problem-filled) as the contemporary family? Could it be that the integrated family and church that Hillery calls for is actually a call for Christians to become a radically different family of God, as Jack and Judy Balswick call for in their chapter on the family?

Furthermore, Wayne Meeks of Yale suggests that Galatians 3:27-28 was probably a pre-Pauline baptismal formula that proclaimed a "new humanity" in Christ — a kind of androgynous new being that embodied both the attributes of a male and female. Or to put it more sociologically, Paul was probably going beyond cultural definitions of female and male gender roles (cited by J. Dart, *The Christian Century*, Feb. 1983:16-23). Paul himself seems to equivocate saying, "Be subject to one another out of reverence for Christ" (Ephesians 5:21), and then a couple of verses later that the husband is head of the wife (5:23). De Jong and Wilson (*Husband and Wife*, 1979), who discuss the concept of headship at length, suggest that it does not mean what many traditionalists believe. They insist that "in Christ" we become "new beings" since the results of the Fall were overcome by God's redemptive work in Christ. Therefore, Christians are to strive to regain the original equality that existed before the Fall.

These are only a few thoughts for reading not only Dr. Hillery's excellent article but for many of the other readings as well. Hopefully they will be useful in stimulating the reader to think further about the relationship of Christians to their urban world. Some of these ideas as well as those presented by Hillery, will be raised again as we deal with specific social problems throughout this text.

THE CITY

George A. Hillery, Jr.

Nowhere do the social problems of today come to a more visible focus than in the city. Not only is the city a place where social problems are localized; the city itself is a problem. If we examine the Bible as an historical document, we find there are many negative references to the city, and so apparently the city has had numerous social problems throughout recorded history. Nevertheless, the only thing modern observers can agree upon is that there are problems. There is no unified perspective. The following analysis will first present the viewpoints of the modern social scientists. Then the Scriptures will be examined in order to discover the meaning of the city and to identify a Christian solution to urban problems.

PROBLEMS OF URBANIZATION

The kinds of social problems existing in the city are seen by those who write in this area as extremely varied. Of the authors specifically surveyed (Coleman and Cressey, 1980; Freeman et al., 1979; Merton and Nisbet, 1976; Wright and Weiss, 1980) there is a disagreement, not necessarily about the problems that exist but about which problems are important. Although all writers mention crime and housing as problems of urbanization, some do not include them as among the leading problems, though most do. Some instead mention education, government, financing, unemployment, and race or ethnic relations as major problems, while fewer mention population density or over-crowding, transportation, and environmental deterioration. As can readily be seen, the lack of agreement is as impressive as the diversity. One may go further and say that not all writers even mention the city in a discussion of social problems. Accordingly, what little consensus there is about the presence of social problems in the city can by no means be considered as universal. To some extent arbitrarily, three of the problems selected for more extensive discussion are crime, housing, and education.

Crime is particularly evident in cities. Indeed, James S. Coleman calls it "the most severe problem faced by urban residents" (Merton and Nisbet, 1976, p. 570). Sociologi-cally speaking, the reason for increased crime in cities stems in part from two sources. One, as Coleman points out, is the lack of informal controls found in the smaller towns and rural communities. An additional factor is sheer size. For example, 7,706,753 arrests were made in the United States in 1979. This amounts to 3.1 percent of the population. For a town of 100 persons, this means an average of three arrests for the year, almost not enough to warrant having a police force. For a town of

---

* Acknowledgements for critical reading and suggestions for this chapter are made to Mark Andrus, Marie Lou Bautista, Pearl Katz, Joseffino Magallanes, George B. Telford, Jr., and the editors. Special mention is given to Phyllis K. O'Neil (1981) for assistance in preparing the section on "A Christian Solution." I alone, however, am responsible for the way in which this good advice (not always heeded) was used.

10,000, this amounts to slightly more than 300 arrests, or somewhat less than one arrest per day. But in a city of one million persons, the same percentage would total 31,000 arrests, or approximately 85 arrests per day. Even more, if one equates arrests with criminals (an underestimate, since not all criminals are arrested), it is easy to see that in a town of 100, three criminals would hardly have the opportunity to do much mischief, especially if the forces of informal control are added. But in a city of one million persons, we have tens of thousands of criminals, who are also much more likely to come together and commit crimes.

Thus, the larger the city, the more crime one can expect. Evidence confirms this probability. Statistics show that large cities have four times more crime than suburban areas and more than six times the crime in rural communities (Coleman and Cressey, 1980, p. 470). With few exceptions, the smaller the city, the lower the crime rate. However, the rate of crime is increasing, and it is generally increasing faster in the smaller than in the larger cities, probably because the smaller towns (including the suburbs) and the rural areas are becoming more like the larger cities.

Housing is another of the frequently mentioned problems of the city. The immediate cause is, of course, senescence (see below), but the contributing causes are more varied. Two in particular may be mentioned: government management (or mismanagement) and the continual movement of the upper and middle classes out of the older areas.

The original intent of the government was laudable: to provide housing for the poor and to enable the middle classes to own their own homes. But the efforts to house the poor were left to local officials, and corruption often reduced the housing quality, leading to rapid deterioration. In addition, as Wright and Weiss (1980, p. 400) point out, housing was built without considering the development of communal organization among the poor, and thus the social controls needed to ameliorate vandalism and other forms of delinquency were absent.

Again, in a well intentioned effort, the Federal Housing Authority and the Veteran's Administration subsidized efforts of the middle class to leave the city for the suburbs. Consequently, instead of putting money and energy into maintaining their older housing, the housing in the central city was abandoned to the poor, who lacked the means to maintain it.

Other causes could be mentioned, but enough has been said to show that the central cities are deteriorating physically as well as socially. Further, the outlook for the future is not bright, as will be shown.

Education is one of the most important community functions. It ensures that the child will participate not only in the values and skills imparted by the family but in those of the larger community as well. Thus, deterioration in the schools is also deterioration in the community, especially as far as the future is concerned. The problem of education in American cities involves at least three areas: authority, finance, and desegregation (Coleman, in Merton and Nisbet, 1976, p. 572).

At one time, the principal was the primary authority figure in the school. Now, this authority is being contested by the federal and state governments, by school boards, by the teachers (through unionization), by parents, and even by the students through such things as the students' "bill of rights." One teacher has expressed her view of the problem as follows:

Trust between administrators and teachers has become a thing of the past. Students laughed openly if a teacher threatened to send them to the office. Principals began to place the problems . . . in the schools, on teachers. Some principals even went so far as to state at faculty meetings that only . . . poorly prepared teachers sent students to the office. Teachers were told not to report fights between students, being cussed at [etc.], and sometimes were advised not to notify authorities outside the school system of being attacked (Anonymous, 1981).

In addition, costs of public schools have risen drastically, while at the same time, confidence in public schools has decreased. As a result, bond issues and tax increases have been repeatedly rejected (Merton and Nisbet, 1976, p. 572).

Finally, racial desegregation has contributed directly to increased racial violence. This development has been aggravated by efforts to create "racial balance" in the schools by extensive busing, especially in large cities. Such busing has been opposed by both a majority of whites and a majority (though smaller) of blacks. Coleman (in Merton and Nisbet, 1976, p. 575) quotes the remarks of one white parent that are especially revealing:

I am against forcing my children into high crime neighborhoods that I worked so . . . hard to get out of as fast as I could. I used to be responsible for some of those crimes, gang fights, etc. I don't want my children taken from me and transported into slums with the dangers and defeatism that thrives there. I don't care if that slum neighborhood is black . . . or like the white section I lived in while a youth.

CAUSES OF URBAN SOCIAL PROBLEMS

There appears to be virtually no agreement on the causes of these problems. Technically speaking, not all writers specifically mention causes at all. Thus, Wright and Weiss (1980, pp. 386-387), in speaking of their "conceptual orientation," maintain: "To understand the problems facing American cities we must understand the concept of *senescence*" by which they mean "the process of aging, physical deterioration, and a corresponding decline in vigor and dominance." As important accompaniments of senescence, they mention the shifts of various segments of the population — the more affluent moving to the suburbs and a major movement of disadvantaged persons into the cities. But strictly speaking, these authors do not identify causes of urban social problems.

Similarly, Freeman, Jones, and Zucker (1979, p. 31) do not speak of causes. They agree on the importance of demographic shifts of status groups but do not mention senescence. Instead, they speak of economic relocation of industry. More important, urban problems are themselves seen to be at the heart of all social problems. Their view of social problems places primary emphasis upon the discrepancies between the social behavior that actually exists in the community and those that the various standards or norms say should exist.

Even when made specific, however, not all are clear about causes. Coleman and Cressey (1980), for example, cite Wirth (1938) on the supposed influence that size and density of population have on urban life. Then they qualify Wirth's position by citing

Gans (1970), who showed that cities could also support homogeneous, stable, and well-integrated ethnic communities. Toward the end of their discussion, however, they note: "Economically and socially, the population [of America} has been fused into huge metropolitan units; politically, no such fusion has taken place. As a result many cities do not have an adequate financial base from which to draw tax money" (Coleman and Cressey, 1980, p. 482). But there are other products of urbanization, too, which do not stem from this population fusion, and for which no cause is offered.

One of the most sophisticated efforts in discerning the causes of urban problems is that of James S. Coleman (in Merton and Nisbet, 1976, p. 600). Coleman identified four basic causes, ranging from quite abstract to very concrete ones. First, an historical shift has taken place from common activities to interdependent activities. This lack of common activities and common dependence on the same events provides in itself a basis for community disorganization, generating conflicts of interests. Second, centralized decision-making is less attentive to problems of community organization, especially in housing, education, transportation and crime prevention. Third, "locality specialization provides fewer supports for community organization" which may in turn remove "some of the supports for the raising of children. Community disorganization and family disorganization feed on each other. . . ." Finally, the mass media invade the community with values and norms from outside the community, and thus provide stimuli that are not responsive to the community's culture.

PROPOSED SOLUTIONS TO URBAN PROBLEMS

As might be expected, in view of the general lack of agreement on causes, there is no agreement on solutions. One writer said nothing about solutions at all. Another specifically maintained that no solutions were visible. Another claimed that what was needed was a "new national consensus . . . that will literally move mountains of garbage, rechannel rivers of sewage, raise acres of houses, and rebuild a promised land" (Freeman, Jones, and Zucker, 1979, p. 215). The problem is, of course, that we do not know how to achieve this consensus.

To be sure, more specific solutions are mentioned, but as noted, there are no agreements. Further, most solutions are merely statements of what has been attempted or recommended by others. For example, Coleman and Cressey (1980, p. 474) mention government reorganization as a solution, meaning, generally, the creation of larger governmental units. But on the next page they note that other "experts on metropolitan government reject the whole idea of centralization." And indeed, we have seen that James S. Coleman (Merton and Nisbet, 1976) has listed centralization itself as a *cause* of social problems.

In brief, therefore, though there is general agreement that such things as housing and crime are serious urban problems, there is little agreement on what else constitutes urban problems, and there is no agreement on solutions.

One of the reasons for this confusion is that there is no agreement on the meaning of community (Hillery, 1982, pp. 28, 53, 95-96). There are well over a hundred different definitions of the word (Willis, 1977). The effect of this lack of agreement is particularly evident in understanding causes, and in view of the situation, one is hesitant to recommend new theories. Of those that have been advanced here, Coleman seems most adequate (Merton and Nisbet, 1976), but one should also point out that inhabitants of the city have not yet learned to live with the contradictory functional requirements (Sjoberg, 1960) of the family and the contract (Hillery, 1968). These two features are central to any city. In spite of the position of theorists such as Wirth (1938), the family is very much a central component of even the most modern city. Equally important is the contract, which may be defined as a limited form of cooperation (Hillery, 1968). Contractual cooperation permeates urban life. It is found not only in the job and the market, but also in such institutions as education, recreation, and government. This limited cooperation is in contrast to the older form of open-ended cooperation found in the family.

The family and the contract are basic requirements of any city; thus they are functional for cities. Yet they oppose each other, the demands of each impinging on the demands of the other. Accordingly, we have conflicts of interest between the family and virtually all other institutions, since the contract is so pervasive. For example, the contractual requirements of the job require that we treat customers or employees on the basis of the limited agreements required by the relationship. Yet the contract may well be ignored if the customer is one's son, or the employee is one's wife or husband. Similarly, for teachers to have their own children in class produces many difficulties, because the parent-child relationship is open-ended, and the teacher-student relation is limited (or closed). We have developed a modus vivendi with this contradiction by sharply dividing the location of the family from the other institutions: one's residence is not usually the place where one works, worships, gets an education, etc. In this way, the conflict is reduced, not eliminated.

A CHRISTIAN PERSPECTIVE

When one reads of the various proposals for causes and solutions to urban problems, one is reminded of the Tower of Babel. Everyone has something to say, but no one seems to be listening to anyone else. However, all is not chaos. As with the Tower of Babel, there is a reason for the confusion, to be found in the relation of man to God (or lack of a relation), for in the city, people become more concerned with limited ends.

Jacques Ellul, the French lay theologian, offers an extreme interpretation of the reason for the existence of urban problems. (For another Christian interpretation, see Schriver and Ostrom, 1977.) The basic point Ellul (1970) makes is that the city as portrayed in Scripture is a product of the sinful nature of human beings and consequently the city is under a curse. Although it is difficult to sustain the thesis that God (or Jesus) cursed the city, much of Ellul's interpretation is useful. Let us first present his thesis in detail. He offers five major points: (1) The city was founded in the absence of God. (2) Thus, God has condemned the city. (3) Jesus Christ, as the Son of God, also condemns the city. (4) Because of the redemptive act of God in Jesus Christ, we are freed again from the curse of the city. (5) Finally, there will be created a new city, the New Jerusalem, and it will be perfect because it will have been constructed totally through God's power.

The first city, Ellul points out, was built by Cain. After Cain had killed his brother, God put a curse on Cain: "Then Cain went away from the presence of the Lord, and dwelt in the land of Nod, east of Eden . . . and he built a city, and called the name of the city after the name of his son, Enoch" (Genesis 4:16-17). First, note that it was when Cain was away from God's presence that he built the city. Furthermore, the building of the city was in defiance of God, since Cain was supposed to be a wanderer. The city may be interpreted as an effort to settle down. Thus, the very creation of the city is an effort by human beings to do things their own way, apart from the reliance on the will of God:

> For when man is faced with a curse he answers, "I'll take care of my problems alone." And he puts everything to work to become powerful, to keep the curse from having its effects. He creates the arts and the sciences, he raises an army, he constructs chariots, he builds cities (Ellul, 1970, p. 11)

In reference to Ellul's second and fourth points, it should be noted that Ellul claims that God cursed the city, not necessarily the inhabitants of the city. Nevertheless, by being in the city, people expose themselves to spiritual risks:

> The man who disappears into the city becomes merchandise . . . And thus man's triumph, this place where he alone is king, . . . where there are no traces of God's work because man has set his hand to wiping it out bit by bit, where man thinks he has found all he needs, where his situation separated from Eden becomes intolerable — this place becomes . . . the very place where he is made slave. And a remarkable slavery it is since . . . we see him subject to the power of money and luxury (Ellul, 1970, p. 55).

Third, Ellul believes that not only does God condemn the city but so does His Son. It is not so much that Jesus condemns the city, per se. It can be shown that what Jesus condemns is at the very heart of the city — the contract. Compare the limited cooperation of the contract — I do this for you if you do that for me — with the open-ended behavior of the Sermon on the Mount:

> You have heard it was said, "An eye for an eye and a tooth for a tooth." But I say to you . . . if any one would sue you and take your coat, let him have your cloak as well; and if any one forces you to go one mile, go with him two miles. Give to him who begs from you, and do not refuse him who would borrow from you (Matthew 5:38-42).

Finally, Ellul places the earthly city, including of course the modern city, in the clearest perspective of all when he says that God will create a new city. The reference is to the New Jerusalem, as depicted in the book of Revelation:

> Then I saw a new heaven and a new earth; for the first heaven and the first earth had passed away, and the sea was no more. And I saw the holy city, new Jerusalem, coming down out of heaven from God, prepared as a bride adorned for her husband; and I heard a great voice from the throne saying, "Behold, the dwelling of God is with men" (Revelation 21:1-3).

The new city, the new Jerusalem, will be perfect because God created it, not humans.

The most important point to be gained from Ellul's study, for the purpose of this chapter is that the city is a monument to humanity's self-will and to that extent is a rebellion against God. The social structure on which the city is based is one that, because of concerns with efficiency, leads people to choose limited instead of open-ended cooperation; that is, people behave contractually. And the contract is at the heart of the city.

Though one can agree with much of what Ellul says, it should be pointed out that nowhere in the Bible does God (or Jesus) curse the city, per se. Further, there are too many instances where God in some sense blesses the city. Only three points here need be mentioned (we have already noted the New Jerusalem). First, Jerusalem at least at times, was holy. It contained the ark of God (2 Samuel 15:29) and was chosen of God (1 Kings 11:13). Second, when the Israelites came into possession of Canaan, the Levites were awarded various cities as part of their inheritance according to the commandment of God (Leviticus 25:32-33, Numbers 35:1-8). Certainly, God would not give his priests something He had cursed. Third, some cities were actually designated sanctuaries, where one could flee if he killed someone unintentionally (Numbers 35:9-11). A city that is made a sanctuary by God is not under a curse. One could continue, but the point is established: Ellul's judgment that God cursed the city is too categorical.

Nevertheless, one may still conclude that the city is a source of spiritual difficulty, if not danger. For example, we are expected to ask a tooth for a tooth in the city, to resist giving even our coat if sued, to go no more than the distance required. One may offer the hypothesis that the social problems in the city arise because of the gaps in social relationships that are left by these limited agreements (contracts), and as long as people are not willing to go the extra mile, the social problems will remain.

To be sure, there is hope, but the hope is spiritual, not physical.

A CHRISTIAN SOLUTION

What then is to be done? We cannot completely solve, nor can we totally eliminate all of the problems of cities. And yet more and more people are living in them. In fact, most of the readers of this book will be urban dwellers.

If there is no hope for the cities, there is hope for the people who live in them. This hope is to be found in Jesus Christ. In the midst of the corruption that we call urban social problems, Jesus offers us a personal salvation and deliverance. But the problem does not stop there. There is the further problem of the nature of our surroundings. In the parable of the sower, Jesus says:

> A sower went out to sow. And as he sowed, some seeds fell along the path, and the birds came and devoured them. Other seeds fell on rocky ground, where they had not much soil, and immediately they sprang up, since they had no depth of soil, but when the sun rose they were scorched; and since they had no root they withered away. Other seeds fell upon thorns, and the thorns grew up and choked them. Other seeds fell on good soil and brought forth grain, some a hundred fold, some sixty, some thirty (Matthew 13:3-8).

The question is how to prepare the good soil.

We find some directives in Scripture. If the city is a creation of humans, there are two groups that one can identify as ordained of God: the family and the congregation. Let us first establish this point.

Of the family, we read in Genesis (2:18): "Then the Lord God said, 'It is not good that man should be alone. . . .' " But no other creature was suitable for this companionship. So God created woman, and the two were designed to be partners, such that . . . a man leaves his father and mother and joins himself to his wife, and they become one body" (Genesis 2:24, *Jerusalem Bible*). We are not told directly that the married pair was created to be holy, but we are told that man and woman are designed by God to be together as one body, and therefore the married pair is a creation of God, ordained by God. The married pair, as the foundation of the family, is the first group created by God. This ordination, further, is confirmed by Jesus.

> And the Pharisees came up to him and tested him by asking, "Is it lawful to divorce one's wife for any cause?" He answered, "Have you not read that he who made them from the beginning made them male and female, and said 'For this reason a man shall leave his father and mother and be joined to his wife, and the two shall become one?' So they are no longer two but one. What therefore God has joined together, let no man put asunder" (Matthew 19:3-6).

The argument is not being made that the family is perfect. Families are composed of sinners, and thus the family, like any human institution, becomes corrupted. But the *form* of the family, based on a husband and a wife committing themselves unreservedly to each other, is a form ordained by God, and this form is holy.

The Bible is not as explicit about the ordination of the congregation, but the evidence is still there. The first mention of the congregation is in the book of Exodus at the institution of the Passover. On that day, the Lord said, each man shall take an animal from his flock, one for each family. It shall be chosen ahead of time and kept until the Passover,

> "When the whole assembly of the congregation of Israel shall kill their lambs in the evening. Then they shall take some of the blood, and put it on the two doorposts and the lintel of the houses in which they eat them. They shall eat the flesh that night, roasted; with unleavened bread and bitter herbs they shall eat it" (Exodus 12:6-8).

Therefore, the first congregation arose from the confrontation with Pharaoh. But note that God's response to Pharaoh was not to create another kingdom. God's response was to create the congregation, the initial duty of which was to celebrate a religious festival, the Passover, which in turn initiated the salvation of Israel out of Egypt by the Lord God.

Both of these groups therefore were ordained by God. Further, we may add that these are the only two groups ordained by God. Other groups were *permitted* by God, but that is a different thing. For example, Samuel anointed Saul to be king, but only after he had warned Israel, "Consider then and see what a very wicked thing you have done in the sight of Yahweh by asking to have a king" (1 Samuel 12:17, *Jerusalem Bible*).

In addition, both the family and the congregation may be legitimately called communities. The communal organization may be contrasted with the formal organization in the tradition of Tönnies, Durkheim, and Parsons, as highly institutionalized groups which do not give primacy to specific goals (Hillery, 1968, pp. 76-85, 142-152). The full implications of this definition are too extensive to be explored here, but at least three things can be observed: (1) Formal organizations are devoted primarily to things and tasks, whereas communal organizations are primarily devoted to people. (2) It follows from the first observation that communal organizations are more free than formal organizations (since people are of primary concern). Indeed, empirical data show this to be so (Hillery, 1982, pp. 181-203): A collection of 46 communal and formal organizations showed that communal organizations were more free than formal organizations in four different measures of freedom. (3) The definition is a general one, including not only the family and the congregation but also, and especially, the village and the city.

Thus, these two groups God has ordained are communities, just as the city is a community. If we were to rely on the two ordained communities primarily, instead of relying primarily on the city, we would be in a better position to do God's will. Not that we are to ignore the city. We are to be in it, to work in it, to change it as we can, to win people for Christ, but we are not to be of it.

There is no hope of doing away with the city, for the city will remain until the end times and the second coming of Christ. The Book of Revelation makes that quite clear. There Babylon is used as the archetype of all cities, and her fate will also be the fate of all cities:

> "Fallen, fallen is Babylon the great! It has become a dwelling place of demons, a haunt of every foul spirit, a haunt of every foul and hateful bird, for all the nations have drunk the wine of her impure passion, and the kings of the earth have committed fornication with her, and the merchants of the earth have grown rich with the wealth of her wantonness" (Revelation 18:2-3).

So the kings and nations and the merchants are all part of Babylon. As kings and nations and merchants have always found their principal home in cities, so they will find their homes in Babylon. And Babylon was only destroyed just before the New Jerusalem came. So the city will remain until the end times.

If there is no hope of doing away with the city, so is there no hope in fleeing the city, for the modern city is so pervasive that its influence can be felt in the most isolated parts of this country. Farmers watch the evening news on television and sell their crops on the world market. No matter how small the town, it is under the influence of Babylon.

What, then, are we to do? We have in fact been granted ample resources, if we will but use them. The very groups God originally ordained, the family and the congregation, are yet with us. To be sure, they have been corrupted, but in spite of their corruption, the forms are still available. And in spite of our own corruption (from whence these groups have received their corruption), we still have the Lord Jesus Christ, our salvation from our sin.

Thus, though we are in the midst of corruption, we must, through Jesus Christ, turn to the basic form of human communities given us by God and strengthen this. The blueprint for this strengthening is the Bible. If we follow this blueprint, it means a radical return to an essentially more conservative position. In reference to the family, note only three points: First, divorce is to be avoided: if not completely, certainly to be used only as a last resort. Second, parents should exercise authority and a leadership role in their homes. And third, within the framework of mutual servanthood, the man is to be the head of the house (Ephesians 5:21-33). The last point, particularly, may seem reactionary, but here the Bible is especially clear. I am not saying that women should not develop their full capabilities. I am only saying that these capabilities have a framework, just as the capabilities of men have a framework. As Christ is the head of the church, so should the husband be head of the household. The family must have some authority or one literally encounters a state of anarchy. (The definition of anarchy is absence of authority.) But the responsibility of the husband goes further: "Husbands, love your wives, as Christ loved the church and gave himself up for her" (Ephesians 5:25). In other words, the woman is not to be the man's vassal or sexual playmate. She should be loved as Christ loved. This love does not exclude sex, by God's own decree (Genesis 1:27-28; 2:18; Song of Solomon; 1 Corinthians 7:2-6). But the love is certainly not limited to sex, and marriage is not simply for the man's or woman's gratification. Biblically, the love of the husband and wife should be mutually sacrificial (Ephesians 5:21).

When these biblical passages are examined carefully, it can be seen that both the husband and the wife in the Christian family have reciprocal responsibilities (Lehmann, 1980). Both are to give up their rights to themselves in favor of the other and the family as a whole.

The recommendation for the church is again strictly biblical. Jesus Christ is to be proclaimed Lord. He is to be lifted up, so that He can draw all people to Him. To be sure, the church is to be a source of agapic love, but most of all, it is to be a place of worship. Social welfare programs and almsgiving are of course necessary. But unless these things are done in love under the direction of the Holy Spirit and in the name of Jesus, they are spiritually worthless (Matthew 7:21-23; 1 Corinthians 13:1-3).

But it is not simply the strengthening of the family and the church that is being called for. A third and necessary point is that the two groups should work together. When integrated, the family and the church become a basis for operating amidst the corruption of the city. Notice that the family and the church are not being depicted as a *refuge* from corruption, but a *base for operating* in the midst of the corruption.

We come to the church to receive the Word that strengthens us for service in the city. The family, in turn, provides a more physical basis for nurturance, for we are, after all, physical beings. One further point needs emphasis. The family, alone in the city, no matter how pious, is fragmented and extremely vulnerable. It is fragmented because it is cut off from support, and it is vulnerable for the same reason. The family in the congregation strengthens both. Together, they become truly the salt of the earth, preserving to some degree whatever they touch from corruption, and perhaps averting the anger of God from a sinful world.

One should also note that the above prescriptions do not constitute idle speculation or wishful thinking. The Jews have followed these prescriptions to some degree since the Babylonian captivity more than 25 centuries ago. Though not all Jews have been urban (many Polish and Russian Jews, for example, have been rural), and though Jews have been constantly involved in the process of assimilation, enough have lived in strong families and well-integrated synagogues such that they have been able to withstand the even greater hazards of urban life that have plagued the city in earlier times. For example, Jews have remained an urban people even though, for perhaps most of its existence, the city has sustained higher death rates than birth rates. As urban people, the Jews should have died out long ago, but probably because of biblically founded health practices (upheld by the synagogue and maintained in the family), they have survived. Moreover, they survived as educated people and a people of low delinquency; education and delinquency are two of the more important urban problems of our day.

What is being recommended is that we build our lives on communities ordained by God, rather than on communities initiated by humans. Dietrich Bonhoeffer (1963) offers a penetrating comment on this point:

> The community which is from God to God, which bears within it an eschatological meaning — this community stands in God's sight, and does not dissolve into the fate of the many. It has been willed and created, and has fallen into guilt; it must seek repentance, it must believe . . . and experience grace at the limits of time. It is clear that this can happen only 'in' the individual. Only thus can the hearing of the call be concretely comprehended, and yet it is not the individuals, but the collective person . . . who in the individuals, hears, repents and believes (Bonhoeffer, 1963, p. 83).

In other words, the salvation of the individual must come through the individual. But the individual also needs the community, and it makes a great deal of difference to which community the individual is committed.

We may conclude, then, that our concern in solving the problems of the city is not with the city. Though we must deal with urban problems, the city can be redeemed only by God. Our concern is with the family and the congregation, already ordained by God, as a means by which we can work in the city. The solution to urban problems proposed here is to strengthen the family and the congregation in the light of the blueprint given by God. In this manner, the family and the congregation can provide the necessary nurturance for Christians, and Christians in turn will be enabled to carry the word of God into the city, by word and by deed. Our task, therefore, is to live in the light of God's ordination: to keep the family as God intended it and the congregation as the body of believers, worshiping God and God alone.

Study and Discussion
Questions

1. What are the most frequently mentioned social problems in the city? Are these the most important? From whose viewpoint? Explain.
    (Rationale: The student should know what is generally agreed on and the existence of the disagreement.)

2. What are the causes of urban problems? Can you be sure? Why?
    (Rationale: Again, there is no agreement on the causes.)

3. Are the causes of social problems in the city related to the kinds of social problems mentioned by researchers? How?
    (Rationale: Of course, they are, because often the cause is part of the problem.)

4. What is meant by "contradictory functional requirements" and how are they important in understanding urban social problems?
    (Rationale: The intent of the question is to remind the students of the dynamics and tensions of the city and to have them be aware of two of the most central institutions in city life: families and contracts.)

5. What are the strong and weak points of Jacques Ellul's reasons for the existence of urban problems?
    (Rationale: Though Ellul has developed an interesting thesis, and a spiritually oriented one, it has its drawbacks, and the student should be cognizant of these.)

6. What are some of the spiritual dangers encountered in the city?
    (Rationale: The central point of the answer is that the city encourages individual self-seeking rather than the sacrificial love taught by Jesus.)

7. Which human groups have been ordained of God? Why is this important in attempting to solve urban problems?
    (Rationale: In working through the family and the congregation, we are in a better position to seek a spiritual direction in solving urban problems, and the thesis of this chapter is that at heart the basic problem of city life is spiritual.)

8. Which is more important in today's world, the solution to urban problems or the effort toward solving them? Why?
    (Rationale: Since the solution to the city's problems will not come until the New Jerusalem, we must do the best we can here and now.)

9. What objections would the secular world have to the proposed solution to the problems of the city?
    (Rationale: The chief objection would come from feminists, I feel, although there are points on which feminists would agree, such as allowing women to develop their full capabilities.)

10. What are the advantages and limitations to using the Jews as a model for solutions to urban problems?
    (Rationale: First, the Jews have survived and they have done so largely in terms of the model I propose. But they have survived by turning in on themselves. My model proposes a reaching out.)

References

Anonymous, "A Segregation Odyssey." Unpublished manuscript, 1981.

Bonhoeffer, Dietrich, T*he Communion of Saints*. New York: Harper & Row, 1963.

Coleman, James William, and Donald R. Cressey, *Social Problems*. New York: Harper & Row, 1980.

Ellul, Jacques, *The Meaning of the City*. Grand Rapids, Mich.: W. B. Eerdmans, 1970.

Freeman, Howard E., Wyatt C. Jones, and Lynne G. Zucker, *Social Problems: A Policy Perspective*. Third edition. Chicago: Rand McNally, 1979.

Gans, Herbert J., "Urbanism and suburbanism as ways of life: A re-evaluation of definitions" in Robert Gutman and David Popenoe, eds. *Neighborhood, City and Metropolis*. New York: Random House, 1970.

Hillery, George A., Jr., *Communal Organizations: A Study of Local Societies*. Chicago: University of Chicago Press, 1968.
A Research Odyssey: Developing and Testing a Community Theory. New Brunswick, N.J.: Transaction Books, 1982.

Jerusalem Bible, The, Garden City, N.Y.: Doubleday & Co., Inc., 1966.

Lehmann, Paul, "The Commandments and the Common Life." Interpretation, 1980.

Merton, Robert K., and Robert Nisbet, *Contemporary Social Problems*. Fourth edition. New York: Harcourt Brace Jovanovich, 1976.

O'Neil, Phyllis K., "The unique perspective of Jacques Ellul." Unpublished manuscript, 1981.

Shriver, Donald W., Jr., and Karl A. Ostrom, *Is There Hope for the City?* Philadelphia: Westminster Press, 1977.

Sjoberg, Gideon, *The Preindustrial City*. Glencoe: The Free Press, 1960.

Willis, Cecil L., "Definitions of Community II: An examination of definitions of community since 1950." *The Southern Sociologist* 9:14-19, 1977.

Wirth, Louis, "Urbanism as a way of life." *American Journal of Sociology* 44:1-24, 1938.

Wright, Wright, and John P. Weiss, *Social Problems*. Boston: Little, Brown and Co., 1980.

CHAPTER 2
ECONOMIC SYSTEMS: INTRODUCTION

In his critique of existing theory, German sociologist Ralf Dahrendorf wrote a classic essay entitled "Out of Utopia." Dahrendorf's assertion was that sociology had been so fascinated with the consensus of the social world that it had neglected to study social conflict. Its emphasis on cultural norms described an ideal society or a utopia, but it failed to deal with the real world.

Dahrendorf's criticism was leveled against structural functional theory, a perspective that describes institutions and institutional norms in terms of what they contribute to the larger society. Structural functionalists assume that society is a whole unit with all its component parts serving the maintenance of the larger social structure. The danger in using this model is one of inadvertently focusing on the ideal culture (i.e. utopia) rather than the real culture.

Professor Hunt has utilized a structural functional approach in his discussion of the economy. As such he describes the manner in which the capitalist system is supposed to work, but fails to discuss its actual shortcomings. The positive functions (those factors that build up the social system) are stressed while the dysfunctions (those consequences that work against the system) are downplayed.

Most economists would agree that we do not have a pure capitalist system governed by Adam Smith's "invisible hand." That may be an ideal, but the reality is quite different. In reality we have a mixed economy, with principles of capitalism intertwined with those of the welfare state, and he sees this development in a negative light.

Moreover, personal values are reflected by the labels chosen to describe our American economy, especially its welfare facet. A labeling theorist commenting on the economic order of the United States might quip: "We may have a mixed economy, but it is characterized by giving subsidies to the rich and welfare to the poor." Being subsidized has a better ring to it than being supported by welfare; yet wealthy farmers, recipients of corporate tax benefits, and poor inner city dwellers all receive government benefits.

Professor Hunt's discussion tends to emphasize the positive functions of the ideal capitalistic system while simultaneously stressing the real dysfunctions of communism. The works of Karl Marx are overly simplified and presented in a negative light to contrast unfavorably with the capitalistic perspective. Furthermore, the writings of Karl Marx are equated with the pre-1990 Soviet socialist economic system, a system that would have probably pleased Marx no more than lassez faire capitalism. Marx would have been no more impressed with the contemporary communist societies that failed to implement many of his basic ideas than he would have been with capitalistic countries. In discussions it is important to compare the ideal philosophical writings of communism with the ideal philosophical tenets of capitalism. Similarly the real economic situation of capitalism needs to be assessed in light of the real economic issues of communism.

Hunt's discussion seems to focus, as we have noted, on the ideal model of capitalism in which voluntary cooperation is the norm. A conflict theorist would make very different assumptions in attacking the system that Professor Hunt praises. Conflict theory, particularly Marxist strains of it, views capitalism as an exploitive and coercive system that is unstable (see E. M. Schur's discussion of "Corporate Crime" in *The Politics of Deviance*, 1980). Those who favor conflict theory, moreover, often see capitalism as extremely irrational — as a system in which people go hungry at the same time that food rots in storage bins and where people in poverty die prematurely at the same time hundreds of thousands of dollars may be spent to keep a more affluent person alive on life-support systems.

Immanual Wallerstein, a historical Marxist theorist, would contend that in fact there has yet to be a true communist or socialist economy anywhere in the world. Taking what is known as a "world systems approach," Wallerstein argues that the capitalist system dominates the globe. Even in the height of the Soviet Union's so-called socialist economy, the USSR competed in the global capitalistic system, playing the same economic game as capitalistic countries. His theory emphasizes a basic premise of Marxism: namely, those in power (the "haves") tend to exploit others (the "have nots"). The major difference is that Wallerstein's unit of analysis deals with the world as a single system and nations (rather than individuals representing particular classes) as the actors. Countries that have the power and resources ("core countries") exploit both the natural resources and cheap labor of their less powerful neighbors ("peripheral countries").

Not only are secular conflict theorists in disagreement with some of Professor Hunt's basic assumptions, so are many Christian sociologists. Rather than focusing on the ideals of freedom, equitable distribution of goods and services, and serving as a work incentive, these writers have looked at the reality of economic coercion, poverty, and human despair. The arguments and facts presented in Ronald Sider's *Rich Christians in an Age of Hunger* (1977) or Donald Kraybill's *The Upside Down Kingdom* (1978) cannot be summarized here. What is important to note is how easily a theoretical perspective, in this case functional theory, can present a biased appraisal of a social problem. It could be effectively argued that theistic communism, such as that practiced by the Christian Hutterites in response to their interpretation of Acts 2:44, is more in accord with biblical principles than is capitalism.

While Hunt mentions "the innate selfishness and corruptibility of every human being," unfortunately he applies it only to Joseph Stalin and Russia. Again there is a confusion of the ideal and real cultures. Numerous secular sociologists, as well as Christian writers, have demonstrated that we are governed in the United States by a ruling elite whose primary concern seems to be maintaining their own status, wealth, and control (See G. William Domhoff, *The Powers that Be: Processes of Ruling Class Domination in America*, 1978). If those in leadership roles in national and multinational corporations took a long-range view of things, rather than the short-range view bent on maximizing profits, would not the developed and developing nations both be better off?

Finally, some might wonder why Professor Hunt did not say something about Christ's teachings about the damning power of wealth (Matthew 13:22; 19:23-24; Luke 6:24; 12:13-21; 1 Timothy 6:9-10)? Why did he not deal with the concept of "just price" more critically? Certainly the reader should ask if the results of our economic system demonstrate that the system is just — fair to all concerned?

In order to prompt creative questioning of Professor Hunt's article, we would like to conclude these introductory comments with a quotation from Donald B. Kraybill's award-winning book, *The Upside-Down Kingdom* (1978, p. 305).

The people of God are continually tempted to accommodate and assimilate the values of their surrounding cultural environment. It's easier to temper the scandalous nature of the gospel by making it palatable and acceptable to the majority. Before they know it the people of God borrow the ideology, logic, and bureaucratic structures from their worldly neighbors. They put a little religious coating on top, but underneath the mentality and procedures are often foreign to the way of Jesus.

ECONOMIC SYSTEMS
Chester L. Hunt

Academic fields are too complex to define in a short passage. However, Jules Wanniski (1978, p. 40) offers a definition of economics that seems fairly adequate: "Economics is merely the study of why and how people produce, distribute and consume goods."

Folklore and popular thinking emphasize how difficult it is for economists to agree on conclusions on the nature of the economic process. One popular saying is that if all the economists were laid end to end they would not reach a conclusion. Like most popular views, this one is a combination of truth and falsehood. Economists do certainly disagree, but they also have an underlying stratum for agreement.

ELEMENTS OF ECONOMIC THEORY

The basis for this agreement is that practically all economists admit that their theories revolve around the relationship of supply and demand. If the supply of any goods or service goes up, the price tends to drop. Conversely, if the supply goes down, the price tends to rise. This, of course, assumes that demand is constant. If demand changes, then similar events follow. For example, if the price of strawberries suddenly increases from $1.00 to $2.00 a box, probably more farmers will bring strawberries to market; on the other hand, fewer customers will be lined up to buy. However, if the price of strawberries falls from $.35 to $.20, the number of buyers will be much greater, but the number of boxes brought to market by the farmers will eventually slacken. In this way, over a period of time, an equilibrium will be reached and strawberries will tend to move within a rather narrow price range that will be high enough to see that all the crop is sold. Many factors may disrupt this equilibrium — a drought reducing the supply or good weather producing a bumper crop. Similarly, the demand for strawberries might be increased by medical recommendations that people should eat a box a day to keep their complexions clear, or decreased by a shift in public preference from strawberries to some other type of fruit.

Now let us leave strawberries and return to a general consideration of supply and demand. If all economists agree that these are the important principles governing economic activity, why do they disagree so often on the effect of specific trends and policies?

Other Factors

The reason is that there are so many factors involved in the supply and demand relationship that it is difficult for any one or group of economists, even with the aid of computers, to evaluate all of them. The weather, a change in popular fads, an increase or decline in population, government policies, and a host of other factors all combine to influence the price of a particular commodity. If we move from the question of price to

45

a general forecast of whether the economy is going to be prosperous or depressed, the situation becomes even more complicated. It is difficult to foresee what the economy will do!

Market or Government — Which?

Since supply and demand are brought together by a price determined by buying and selling, we frequently refer to this as a "market" relationship. This market relationship finds its highest expression in capitalism. In a completely capitalist system, all economic relationships would be free to move directly in response to pressures from supply and demand factors. There would be no limit to how high or low prices, wages, or interest rates could rise or fall. No limit, that is, except the reluctance of the suppliers to produce what is demanded or of buyers to pay the price. In actual practice, no society is entirely a market type economy, neither has any society been able to escape the impact of the supply and demand equation. Capitalist societies do give a good deal of play to market factors, while socialist and communist societies try to limit them and to determine prices and wages by some type of governmental decision-making. Most of the argument over economic factors concerns the extent to which we can and should try to remove economic decisions from the market and place them, instead, in the hands of governmental planners.

LIBERALISM AND THE JUST PRICE

The Question of Just Price

Five hundred years ago, Church and state were both in general agreement that it was dangerous and/or immoral to leave prices and wages to the market and that a "just" price should be set by the proper authorities. Theoretically, this just price was one that would be fair to everyone concerned, both producers and buyers. Also, there would be a "just" wage that would give a suitable reward to all workers.

It is, of course, difficult to agree on what is an absolutely just basis. Some might say that each person involved should have an equal reward, but this has never been true — neither in the past nor present, not even in communist societies. Both the varying needs of people and the different amounts of power they may exercise in society make it practically impossible to pay everyone the same amount. Since equality did not seem to be feasible, in actual practice a just price meant what had been customary. People were used to what was customary, whereas anything that was new and disturbing would strike at least a part of the population as unjust.

However, a just price based on customary relationships was difficult to maintain when social change occurred. In the medieval period, social change was connected with the opening of trade routes that brought new materials to the market, and also with better techniques of labor and the introduction of machinery that tended to lower costs. These changes made it difficult to determine a just price. Should the price of food be maintained at its previous level if new agricultural machinery and transportation made it possible to produce it more cheaply? Should the price of cloth be maintained if new mills enabled manufacturers to produce it at lower cost? Both the business people who might increase their profits and the consumers who might buy more with their money opposed the restrictions that the just price policy imposed.

ADAM SMITH'S THEORY

About this time Adam Smith (1776), a man who classified himself as a "moral philosopher," looked at the situation and formulated a theory to meet it. Smith believed that the wealth of a nation was not determined by the amount of gold in its treasury as much as by the productive capacity of its citizens. This productive capacity would be maximized if people would use their abilities to earn the greatest possible reward. Thus, if farm prices were high, more people would turn to farming, production would increase, and the prosperity of both the people and the state would increase. Conversely, if farm prices were low, people would turn to more profitable pursuits.

Smith did not believe that it was necessary for any regulatory authority to make economic decisions for people. He believed that fluctuations of price, making activity either more or less profitable, would constitute a kind of "invisible hand" that would direct activities. Under these circumstances, specific direction by Church and state was not only unnecessary, but harmful. If some authority directed people to simply follow the market trends, then it was redundant. On the other hand, if it attempted to oppose market trends, then it would be forcing people into less rewarding types of activities and therefore be positively harmful.

Capitalism Once Thought of as Liberal

Smith's ideas gradually found acceptance by those who considered themselves "liberals" and helped to justify the overthrow of feudalism and the establishment of the capitalistic order. Now some may be surprised to see the term "liberal" equated with capitalism. A liberal was regarded as one who accepted change and wanted freedom for the individual. Capitalism was seen as a system that would bring rapid change and remove the individual from regulation; therefore, it was regarded as a "liberal" type of approach.

With the advent of capitalism, productivity greatly increased and the general standards of living in society improved. This was especially true in Western Europe and in North America. The rest of the world has remained, until recently, in the grip of a traditional feudalistic type of society and economic progress has been much less rapid.

Concomitants of Capitalism

Along with the rise of capitalism and the idea that government did not have the obligation to determine the details of all economic transactions, came the rise of political democracy. With political democracy came also the idea of voting by citizens and the formation of political parties to express competing views. The right to vote was at first confined to the wealthy (property owners), but was gradually extended to all adults. Supposedly, capitalism allowed people to follow their own economic interests, while political democracy both guaranteed individual rights and provided needed community services. This pattern of political democracy and capitalism was practically unquestioned for a long time and seemed to be gradually expanding over the world. In the last century, however, it has been questioned by the rise of two counter movements that we might label as communism and the welfare state. These two counter movements are by no means identical and we shall consider them separately.

KARL MARX AND COMMUNISM

Communism grew out of the writings of Karl Marx (1818-1883), particularly his three volume work, *Das Kapital*. Whereas Smith saw capitalism as a system that would lead to the maximum advance by all of society, Marx saw capitalism as a system designed to protect the interests of the owners of capital who would then be able to exploit the workers. Capitalism is a system in which those who have accumulated wealth can use it in the ways that seem most profitable to them. Money is a rough equivalent for capital and the term *capital* is used to indicate that money is needed to provide the equipment, buildings, factories, and other items needed for economic activities.

Marx Saw Violent Revolution as Inevitable

Marx not only felt that capitalism was a system controlled by business people who ground workers down to a subsistence level or lower, but also a fundamentally unstable system whose wild up-and-down swings would eventually prove intolerable.

Marx believed that economic concerns were the fundamental basis of society and determined everything else. Thus religion, politics, morality, and literature all reflect the influence of those who dominate the economy — in this case, the capitalists — and were designed to secure their continued dominance.

Eventually, however, alternating depressions and periods of prosperity would prove so unsettling, and the increasing misery of the workers so intolerable, that capitalism would come into question. Since the capitalists were relatively few in numbers, they would be overwhelmed by the aroused workers who would then set into operation a different system. Since capitalists controlled government, they probably would not agree to a peaceful overthrow and the rise of the workers would demand a violent revolution. This revolution might be disagreeable but would be justified by the great benefits it would bring in the long run.

Socialists Hope for Peaceful Change

This matter of violent revolution has probably been the main distinction between communists and socialists. Socialists accept much of Marx's analysis of the defects of capitalism and intend to replace the private ownership of the means of production with some kind of social (usually governmental) ownership and control. However, socialists are not sure that a violent revolution will be necessary and hope that success can be achieved through democratic means and electoral majorities. Also, they are not quite sure that all forms of capitalist activity are bad and, at least for a period of time, they may allow some private business to operate. Thus socialists are known as moderate and gradual reformers, although there is little basic distinction between their economic views and those of the communists.

Why Uncritical Christian Acceptance?

Many Christians have been attracted to the socialist or communist perspectives. This in spite of the fact that Marxians usually portray religion as a form of "false consciousness" whose function is to divert people from their real concerns by centering their attention on paradise in the next world — heaven.

While communist or socialist parties may attack Christianity, many Christians feel drawn to their ethical viewpoints. The Marxians speak of their concern for the poor and this coincides well with a similar concern expressed in the Bible. Further, communists denounce capitalists as selfish individuals and proclaim that they wish the good life for everyone and desire a regime of cooperation and service. Again the Bible frequently speaks of the shortcomings of the rich and says that people can serve God only by serving others.

The appeal of these ethical standards is so strong that some Christians follow Marxian leaders who have destroyed churches and whose weapons literally drip with the blood of Christian martyrs. This appeal has been particularly strong with young people impatient at what seems to them obvious injustice and tragic poverty. Communists are quick to denounce such situations, blaming capitalism and offering what seem to be concrete programs for their solution. While immediate prospects for the success of communist programs may be doubtful — indeed, the failure of communism to provide the basic material and social needs of their people is evident by the recent overthrow of their regimes in Eastern Europe. Despite their failure, some still believe that the trend of history is theirs. If the long-run struggle brings a triumph for communism that will literally usher in a new earth, then short-run considerations of expediency are not for the idealists, but only for the cowards.

The Results of Communist Action

But let us leave communist theory and look at the results of communist action. Communism has had its longest hold in the Soviet Union, although since World War II, it has been imposed on the states of eastern Europe and, more recently, on China and parts of Southeast Asia. In countries such as Viet Nam, it is comparatively new, and in Eastern Europe and China — despite Tiananmen Square — there seems to be a move away from communism to a freer type of economics. It is probably best to look at the record of communism where it has been in power longest, namely the Soviet Union.

Although many people felt that a communist state was completely unworkable, it has managed to function. The Soviet Union has seen a considerable amount of industrialization under the communist regime and it probably has a higher standard of living than was true in pre-communist days. Some authorities (Nutter, 1962; Faulkner, 1972), however, believe that the advance under communism is less than the progress that would have occurred if the improvements already underway before the communists seized power had been allowed to continue in a capitalistic society. Whether or not this is true, we must admit that communism can get things done. However, the cost seems to be tremendous and the results less impressive than progress in capitalistic countries.

Part of the cost has been the denial of political freedom: no free elections, no free political parties, no free operation of trade unions, and often a compulsory assignment to work. This was brought out most vividly when the communists decided to end individual farm ownership and move to collective farms. Many farmers resisted this since they had originally supported the revolution in order to own their own land. These dissident farmers were deported hundreds of miles from home and millions of them died — perhaps in terms of numbers, the greatest slaughter in the twentieth century (Dalrymple, 1965).

These sacrifices have not borne the fruit of outstanding success. Per capita income in the Soviet Union is less that a third of that in the United States and in western European countries (*World Almanac*, 1982, pp. 540, 542, 587). Industry has lagged considerably and agriculture even more. Prior to the communist revolution, Russia was an exporter of grain. It has never fed itself since the time of the communist takeover, and today exists only by importing food from the more bountiful farms of capitalist nations. Hopefully, the recent *perestroika* and *glasnost* movements of President Gorbachev are making a significant change in the Soviet Union.

CAPITALISM AND THE WELFARE STATE

In no country today is there a pure capitalist economy. This is because every country has made an effort to take some decisions out of the marketplace and use the power of the government to see that certain types of benefits are available to citizens of the country. Thus all of the noncommunist countries are known as "mixed economies," meaning that both the private market and governmental decision-making operate in the allocation of goods and services. In practice, this is true of countries with a strong socialist movement as well as those in which such a movement has not developed. This is because the socialists have usually despaired of securing a society operating completely on socialist lines, and have primarily confined their efforts to an expansion of welfare state functions. This trend has by no means been confined to socialist parties and, to some extent, every government today is operating a welfare state.

The welfare state has expanded to the point where many countries find that from one-third to more than one-half of their income is expended by government as contrasted to ten or fifteen percent some half-century ago.

Positive and Negative Impact

What is the impact of the welfare state on capitalist economies? For one thing, it has spread a "safety net" under business and workers in the economy so that times of depression will not produce unrelieved economic hardship. For another, it has provided medical care for needy citizens, the widowed and their children, and the aged. Also, it has led to an extension of a variety of services such as the provision of university and college education for an increasing proportion of people. All of this would be applauded by most of us.

There are some other effects, though, that are much more problematic, namely, confusion about means and ends. Simply stated, there is a possibility that we may be killing the goose that lays the golden egg.

Probably the greatest negative effect has been that increased taxation has meant that citizens have had less money to save and invest. Therefore, the amount of money being put into new capital to produce more goods has been steadily declining, in relative terms. The welfare state witnesses a continual appetite for more and more state services, regardless of economic conditions. The effect of this may be seen in two phenomena that characterize most countries in the world — inflation and the underground economy.

Inflation simply means that the price of goods and services goes up while the purchasing power of money declines. Thus most people have witnessed an expansion in their money incomes without a proportionate increase in what they can buy with that money. For instance, it took $300.00 in 1982 to purchase as much as $100.00 did in 1960. Inflation affects people differently. While some may have incomes that rise more than prices, others are severely hit. Probably the poor are the ones who suffer most, since the price of necessities usually increases more rapidly than that of luxury goods (Heilbronner and Thurow, 1981). In addition to the hardship it may impose on specific parts of the population, inflation makes any kind of economic planning difficult, and discourages thrift as well. Since money will be worth less tomorrow that it is today, it seems wiser to spend while prices are relatively low. Hence there is very little reward for thrift.

Why do we have inflation? Many factors contribute to it, and many causes have been suggested. The principal one is simply that governments are pressured both to increase expenditures as well as hold the line on taxes. It is appealing to vote for a humanitarian government, but it is by no means as popular to levy the taxes which make that kind of expenditure possible. Therefore, expenditures grow more than taxes. This results in government deficits that are met by an increase in the supply of money, by higher prices, uncertainty, and economic insecurity. It is questionable whether welfare benefits purchased by increased government appropriations may not actually lead to greater hardship by inflationary moves caused by such expenditures. Getting a proper balance between consumer expenditures and investment savings is by no means a simple matter, nor is it always easy to maintain government taxes and revenues. However, the failure to do this has resulted in inflation that has affected every country and is leading to a new reexamination of our welfare state policies (OCED *The Welfare State in Crisis,* 1981).

The Underground Economy

Much of the activity that goes on never shows up in business statistics and makes little or no contribution to tax revenues. This is the so-called "underground economy" present in all major industrialized countries today. This economy has gone underground to avoid government regulation and taxation. It has not only escaped taxation, but also any kind of regulation of working conditions, contracts with labor unions, or stipulation of wage payments. One notable form is seen in criminal activities, such as the illegal sale of drugs.

However, much underground activity at present consists of transactions that, if openly carried out, would be perfectly legal. Probably the simplest is the exchange of labor between two people. For instance, a plumber may fix plugged drains for a physician. He, in turn, may perform a tonsillectomy for the plumber without either of them accepting cash or reporting the income on their income tax return. Likewise, business people or workers may accept cash rather than checks, and thereby avoid paying taxes. In still other cases, entire factory enterprises may operate without the knowledge of the state, avoiding both taxation and social regulation. The amount of underground activity is hard to estimate, but it is obviously widespread in both capitalist and communist countries. Estimates are as high as 30 percent of the above-board or legitimate economic system.

Such underground activity obviously limits the expansion of the welfare state. If taxes or regulations simply drive activity into the underground market, welfare activities become ineffectual. Nor is the underground market necessarily limited to criminals. Legitimate business people may find that they are undercut by competitors whose lower costs result from tax avoidance. This leaves honest people with no choice but to either go out of business or use underground channels themselves. Thus the underground market is a threat to the entire economic structure (MacAvoy, 1982).

Latent Consequences of Government Regulation

Another aspect of the welfare state concerns unanticipated consequences of presumably benign government regulation. One example might be the minimum wage. This rule was made with the best of intentions, namely, the belief that no one should be expected to work for an amount too small to meet minimum needs. On this basis, a minimum wage was adopted by our government in 1935, and since then, it has been continually increased to keep up with inflation and rising standards of living.

However, it is questionable whether the minimum wage guarantees adequate compensation, or whether it simply prevents people from working. One economist has argued that the minimum wage has had a major negative impact on black teenagers and is responsible for their high rate of unemployment (Williams, 1981:27). Teenagers are obviously young and inexperienced and therefore may not be very productive. In addition, some have difficulties beyond a lack of work experience. Many are virtually illiterate and have not formed steady work habits, thus making them unreliable workers. One thing they could do is accept lower wages and thereby gain some skill and some contact with industry. However, because employers must pay the minimum wage they simply hire more qualified workers, leaving the less qualified completely outside of the industrial system.

THE MORALITY OF CAPITALISM RECONSIDERED

For many years, capitalism was long on practice and short on theory. Although Adam Smith was a moral philosopher and counted a society based on free markets to have moral claims, most who followed him have relied on an emphasis on practicality rather than morality. Thus, capitalism has been portrayed as a selfish, ruthless system concerned only with profit, while socialism has appeared as a benevolent society based on cooperation and regard for human welfare.

Gilder's Moral Argument

In recent years, this question has been reexamined, followed by a renewed appreciation of the viability of the capitalist society on moral as well as economic grounds. George Gilder (1981) has portrayed capitalists as essentially faithful to biblical precepts, since they are those who have to enlist the voluntary cooperation of other people. Therefore, they must make such cooperation attractive to people and must, to some extent, practice the Golden Rule. Since they do not have the power to coerce, it is only through voluntary relationships that business can carry on.

Also, capitalists have another aspect commonly associated with virtue: that is, they are willing to make present sacrifices for future gain or good. In other words, they are good people of faith. An investment represents an expense today and only a hypothetical profit tomorrow. It is because capitalists believe in the future and are willing to wait until their plans mature, that they are willing to engage in business enterprise.

Both present activities and planning for the future take place within a voluntary framework. Capitalists cannot persuade people to work unless they offer terms or work more attractive than those otherwise available. Likewise, they cannot sell goods unless the goods are at a price and quality that make them attractive to customers. Thus it is that Gilder perceives capitalism as fundamentally a society based on free association and therefore a moral society.

Novak's Defense of Capitalism

Another approach to the moral basis of capitalism is offered by Michael Novak (1977). He mentions three basic items in the creed of democratic capitalism. These are: (1) individual freedom and the methods of trial and error, (2) the innate selfishness and corruptibility of every human being, and (3) the virtue of a system of checks and balances.

Novak's first principle, individual freedom, simply means that basic economic decisions are to be made by the individual or groups of individuals rather than by the government. Under capitalism, individuals can save money, go into business as they desire, and move from one type of employment to another.

Both capitalists and governments in capitalist countries do engage in some planning. They try to project future markets and see that their equipment and sales force are in position to serve those possible markets. Governments will plan to provide infrastructures such as roads, harbors, and airports that facilitate transportation for business needs. However, the essential faith of capitalism is not in future planning, but in the ability of individuals to see opportunities that may evolve and to make decisions on this basis. When individuals are wrong, they may lose money, but they do not steer the entire country into disaster. Presumably a number of individuals will make the proper decisions, other people will imitate them, and progress will result.

The second point is a bit more complex and it relates to one's view of human nature. Here one sees the Marxist taking a view of the perfectibility of humanity. Humanity is essentially good but has been corrupted by imperfect institutions, in this case, the economic institutions of capitalism. When these imperfect capitalist institutions are removed, then a perfect human nature will flower. When this happens, individuals will no longer lie, cheat, steal, or take up arms against their neighbors. Under this classless society, one will think only of the good of total humanity. Current strife and greed as we know it in the world will disappear. Since a perfect society is the answer to troubles of human nature, we are justified in any kind of action that we think will lead to that perfect society. Instead of respecting human freedom, we will exile, imprison, or in extreme cases, execute those who do not appreciate the perfect world their communist masters are preparing. No sacrifice of present liberty is too great when it will bring us that complete and perfect freedom which is promised by the perfect communist society.

By contrast, the Christian believes that sin is a part of imperfect human nature. "If we say that we have no sin, we deceive ourselves and the truth is not in us" (1 John 1:8). Since sin is a part of basic human nature, it cannot be eradicated by changed social systems. It is something from which we can be saved only by the grace of God.

Thus, while Christians will construct the best type of social relations they can, they know that in any kind of social relations the evil tendencies of many may bring forth perversion and corruption. Consequently, Christians will not erect a system that requires complete virtue. Rather, Christians will see the need for a system in which the inherent defects and shortcomings of human nature may be countered and controlled. Christians are not surprised by the excesses and cruelties of Joseph Stalin because they are always aware that such demonic potential is a part of the nature of any person. Rather, Christians are surprised that any group of people would allow a system to develop in which one man could have such awful power for evil.

Novak makes a third point about checks and balances. Sometimes a rejoinder is made that capitalism is not really a matter of limited control, but a system in which a small group of men, without responsibility to the public, may get a monopoly of some kind of economic activity. Experience indicates this is a very unlikely outcome.

Not only do we have antitrust laws that attempt to restrict monopolies, but the very developments of economic activity work against such an outcome. For instance, the American automobile industry was frequently considered an example of oligopoly or shared monopoly, and General Motors in particular was thought to be so powerful that it could follow any kind of pricing policy it wanted. Yet competition is always a possibility. If it does not come from within the country it will come from some other part of the world. General Motors lost over a billion dollars in one working year and was forced to radically change its methods and procedures in order to remain a viable producer of automobiles.

This is an extreme example. Most businesses are less strong than General Motors and far more subject to the influence of changing markets, inventories, technologies, and the rise of new competition. Businesses do not serve the individual because those in business are virtuous; rather, whether they are virtuous or not, they serve because this is the only way they can make a profit. The greed or the stupidity of one business person is checked by competition from other people in business. Thus, the imperfect human beings who live in an imperfect world still find an escape from tyranny and an exercise in freedom.

Does Capitalism Generate Inequality?

Capitalism is constantly plagued by the complaint that it seems to generate inequality. By its very nature, foresight, diligence, work (yes, and sometimes luck!), some people are more successful and better rewarded than others. The question is asked, Is not this unchristian and undesirable? Should not a just society also be a society in which everyone stands in the same economic position? Perhaps the best answer from a Christian standpoint is found in the parable of the talents in which the master gave his servants an unequal amount of money, even as God gives men unequal talents, and commanded them to go forth and make a profitable investment. The servants who did so were praised; the one who was terrified and hid his talent in the ground was condemned (Matthew 25:14-30).

Socialism views economics as a zero-sum game. The essence of a zero-sum game is that there is only a fixed amount of goods available — what one person wins, another person loses. Capitalism is not a system of static egalitarianism, but of growing opportunity. The question is not so much, what do I have today, but, what kind of advance can I make tomorrow? Socialism offers a system of shared poverty — capitalism, a system of growing affluence. Which of the two has the truer understanding of the human condition? Which of the two has the greater moral justification?

Earn Well, Give Wisely

Does all this discussion mean that the pursuit of financial gain should be our only concern? Certainly financial gain is important. One of the advantages of capitalist society is that it does offer a criterion as to what kind of financial status is acceptable. That kind of criterion is indicated by the market. Our reward is not based on what we think is proper, but on how the rest of humanity evaluates our contributions. There is a lesson here for those who may be considering a life of religious service. Such a life is certainly not based on greed, but neither does it involve a dedication to penury. As the New Testament tells us, the laborer is worthy of his hire (Luke 10-:7), and those that preach the gospel should expect to live by the gospel (1 Corinthians 9:14).

But again one asks, Is it enough to urge people to look out for their own financial advantage? Is there not a case for a social welfare state and for private charity?

Of course, the answer to these questions is in the affirmative. People who are successful economically have a double obligation as stewards of the resources God has given them. On the one hand, they should conserve those resources and invest them so that, as in the parable of the talents, they may increase. On the other hand, they should use those resources to alleviate the needs of others less fortunate than themselves (Ephesians 4:28b), and to do things with other people that one cannot do alone. Thus it is that they will make contributions to church and charity.

Likewise, they will use their political influence to make the state an agency that helps to provide a better life for its citizens. A welfare state, however, does not stand by itself; it is not something sacred and beyond criticism. We should be sure that welfare programs actually promote well-being rather than the opposite. Welfare programs should not offer rewards for an irresponsible life or for lack of effort. Further, the demands of the welfare state should not be so great that people have no money to save and invest, for if this happens, the economic machinery on which we depend will begin to decay rather than expand. Certainly a vigorous private charity, a sincere religious devotion, and an effective welfare state are consistent with a capitalist view of economics. Historically, the development of philanthropy and capitalism have moved together.

DEVELOPING COUNTRIES AND CAPITALISM

Most nations in Asia, Africa, and South America have an income that is only one-third to one-tenth of that of the industrialized nations in North America and Europe, and still less than the wealthiest nations of all: the oil rich countries of the Middle East. The communist analysis of this difficulty is that foreign corporations, frequently referred to as "multinationals," have operated to keep such nations in poverty. It is charged that these multinationals buy up the raw materials of developing nations at a low price and sell them at a higher price in their home countries. Since the corporations cross national boundaries they cannot easily be controlled by any one country and therefore may run counter to national aspirations and desires.

The capitalist explanation of the difficulties of developing countries is that they do not have too much capitalism, but too little. Capitalist thinkers say people in these countries are not willing to undertake the risks of business activities, and also that the governments of these countries have placed too many hardships and roadblocks in the way of businesses. They point to government instability, high taxes, and lack of desirable infrastructure as major obstacles to progress. They say that the multinational corporations bring to developing countries capital, know-how, and linkage with world commerce. Further, they point out that the multinational corporations invest three-fourths of their funds in the already industrialized countries. Presumably, if this ratio could be switched, and a much greater percentage of the efforts of corporations devoted to developing nations, economic progress might be much greater (Novak, 1982).

The capitalist's remedy for underdevelopment is to expand the role of private enterprise and enable both domestic and foreign businessmen to have a greater degree of activity. They argue that the trouble with developing countries is not that some people are rich or that some foreigners are engaged in commerce; the trouble is that there is too little opportunity for wealth to be created and for incomes to increase. Rather than class warfare, they call for class cooperation and the creation of societies in which people would be free to invest their money now with the expectation of a return in the future.

THE TAX AND WAGE PROBLEM

In the scope of economics are included taxation, labor, and finance. The principle of supply and demand establishing a relationship applies to these as well as to the price of the goods. Arthur Laffer has brought our attention to the fact that the highest tax rate does not always produce the largest government income (Wanniski, 1978). In his famous Laffer curve, he has said that the tax rate can be so large that it lowers investment and stifles the incentive to work. Such a tax rate will yield less revenue than a smaller tax rate which will encourage economic activity and thereby bring a larger total return.

The same rule applies to the wages of labor. When Henry Ford started mass production for the Model T Ford, he offered a minimum wage of $5 a day, which before World War I was almost twice the going daily rate. He did this because such a wage was necessary in order to get intelligent and capable workers who would be consistent and regular in reporting for employment and in paying attention to their tasks.

People in business who offer a wage inadequate to attract quality labor will be penalized by ultimately having higher costs. On the other hand, a labor union that forces a wage level significantly above the market demand will find that it has priced itself out of the market. At best, it can draw its higher wages only by making it difficult for other people to get average wages. At worst, it will reduce the demand for products and therefore decrease the total number of workers employed in that occupation.

The effect of supply and demand also applies to finance. The government cannot meet its obligations simply by printing money rather than by raising taxes. If the amount of money is expanded while the amount of goods produced to be purchased remains the same, then the result is inflation, which means that a larger amount of money buys no more goods than a smaller amount did before.

CURRENT TRENDS

The decade of the eighties has seen a massive retreat from socialism and communism in eastern Europe, as well as in the Soviet Union and China. Developing countries which once blamed capitalism for their problems are now putting out a welcome mat to corporations. Governments are selling their industries and utilities to private companies and even the Soviet Union is favoring private markets. Before goods can be distributed they must be produced and capitalism stimulates production better than any system thus far developed. As Jerry Muller (1988) says, "Capitalism is now the name of the game!"

Study and Discussion
Questions

1. Explain the relation between the regulation of business and that of the underground economy.

2. What is the relation between the "welfare state" and inflation? Why is it hard to keep inflation down?

3. Is capitalism or Communism more compatible with Christian beliefs? Explain what Gilder means by business being forced to practice the Golden Rule and what Novak means by the "perfectibility of humanity."

4. Is it possible for business to serve society when business promoters are essentially selfish people seeking a profit?

5. Why have some Christians been attracted by Communism? Do the results of communist systems increase their attraction?

6. What is another name for what Adam Smith called the "invisible hand"? What are the good and bad features of the "welfare state"? Should the state enforce a just price?

7. Should Christian ministers live in poverty? What does the Bible say about this?

8. Socialism views economics as a zero-sum game. How does capitalism counter treat this view?

9. Many people in the developing nations are very poor. Is this because of capitalist exploitation? What other explanations might be offered?

10. Capitalism was once viewed as being liberal but, in the twentieth century, many considered liberal have been anticapitalist. How do you explain this? Would the people in the Soviet Union or Poland regard capitalism as liberal? Why or Why not?

References

Barrett, Richard E., and Martin King Whyte, "Dependency Theory and Taiwan," *American Journal of Sociology,* 87:1064-1089, March 1982.

Dalrymple, Dana J., "The Soviet Famine of 1932-34: Some Further References," *Soviet Studies,* XVI, 4 April, 1965, p. 498.

Faulkner, M. E., *The Industrialization of Russia 1919-1914,* MacMillan Company, New York, 1972.

Gilder, George, "Moral Sources of Capitalism," *Society* 18:24-27.

Heilbronner, Robert L., and Lester C. Thurow, *Five Economic Challenges,* Prentice Hall: Englewood Cliffs, New Jersey, 1981.

MacAvoy, Paul W., "The Underground: No Recess," *New York Times,* August 4, 1982, Sec. 4, p. 3.

Muller, Jerry Z., "Capitalism: The Wave of the Future," *Commentary,* 86:2126, December 1988.

Novak, Michael, "Why Latin America is Poor," *Atlantic,* March 1982, pp. 67-75. The *Atlantic* article is taken from his book, *The Spirit of Democratic Capitalism,* Simon & Schuster, New York, 1982.

"An Underpraised and Undervalued System," *Worldview,* August, 1977, pp. 9-12.

Nutter, G. Warrern, *Growth of Industrial Production in the Soviet Union,* Princeton University Press, Princeton, NJ, 1962.

Organization of Economic Cooperation and Development, *The Welfare State in Crisis,* Paris, 1981.

Smith, Adam, "An Inquiry into the Nature and Causes of the Wealth of Nations," The Modern Library: New York, 1937: orig. 1776.

Sweden Now, "Sex Isn't All It Should Be," *Sweden Now,* Vol. 15, No. 2, pp. 28-29, 1981.

Wanniski, Jude, *The Way the World Works: How Economics Fail and Succeed,* Basic Books, New York, 1978.

Williams, Walter E., "Employment and Transportation," in *The Fairmont Papers Black Alternative Conference,* Institute for Contemporary Studies, 1981, pp. 23-30.

CHAPTER 3
PARADIGMS OF DEVELOPMENT: INTRODUCTION

Ever since the inception of sociology in the mid-19th century, its theorists have wrestled with the problems of order and disorder that may be evidenced in the social world. Society appears to be two-faced: one face is orderly and integrated and the other is disintegrated and conflict-ridden. Few theorists have successfully merged the two perspectives, one stressing consensus and cooperation and the other emphasizing coercion and conflict.

Professor Jantzi's article provides a balanced presentation of the different theoretical paradigms that exist to account for the economic development and underdevelopment of nations. Some are rooted in structural functional theory that stresses order while others are based in conflict theory. Each paradigm offers solutions to the problems facing underdeveloped countries from a different vantage point.

The concern with historical developments and changes within society is as old as sociology. Its early theorists, including Ferdinand Tönnies and Emile Durkheim (whom we discussed briefly in the introduction to Ch. 1), were all centrally concerned about the new kind of society that had emerged in the so-called "modern era." These theorists sought to identify the nature of modern society, to explain its origins, and to explore the social consequences of its emergence. The explanations, however, were rooted in different and seemingly irreconcilable assumptions. The functionalist orientation of Emile Durkheim seemed far removed from the conflict perspective of Karl Marx.

During the 1940s, 1950s, and 1960s, structural functionalism, a perspective heavily indebted to Durkheim, dominated sociology in the U.S. It was structural functionalism, with its emphasis on consensus, integration, and equilibrium, that provided the theoretical underpinnings for modernization theory. By the late 1960s, structural functionalism as well as modernization theory came under heavy attack.

Modernization theorists described the development of modern society as a process of "differentiation." "Traditional" societies were simple and undifferentiated, containing a very limited number of social institutions. For example, in many pre-modern societies, the extended family is one of the most important social institutions, responsible for reproduction and socialization of new members, for serving as an economic unit, for being the center of religious activities, and performing other tasks that have been taken over by other institutions in modern societies. Modernization entailed the creation of more numerous and differentiated institutions (i.e., educational, religious, economic, political). Modernization theorists attempted to identify certain key social, cultural, economic and political changes that they felt were central to the emergence of modern societies in the West. This theorizing was then applied to programs to facilitate the movement of pre-modern societies into the modern phase. As Professor Jantzi notes, many church-sponsored programs were and still are rooted in theories of modernization and the inherent assumptions of structural functionalism.

As modernization theory and its parent, structural functionalism, came under increasing attack, there was a shift toward a theory of "growth with equity" during the 1970s. Growth with equity moved the blame for underdevelopment from the traditional structure of developing societies to the failure to integrate the majority of their populations into their economy. Large numbers of people were left without an economic role to play in the society, and this failure to integrate them into the work world denied them access to the benefits of development. Although there is a change in the identification of the problem, the source of the problem remains the same. The problem remains an internal one—a failure to change the value system of the structure of the developing country.

Growth with equity theory provides a modification of some functionalist assumptions inherent in modernization theory, but it is a relatively modest modification. Although the solutions to the problems facing developing nations are different, they do not represent a major paradigmatic shift. The problems identified are still internal to the developing nations and outside assistance (with either value change or structural change) by modern nations is advocated. At the base of both theories are untested assumptions about the cooperative and consensual nature of the persons providing and those receiving the assistance.

A major change in paradigms seemed to occur with what Professor Jantzi terms the "liberation-from-dependency" paradigm. Rather than blaming the victim (in this case, the underdeveloped nation) for its failure to develop the proper values or structures for modernization, this paradigm roots the problem in the international order. The "liberation-from-dependency" paradigm (also known as world systems theory) was developed by theorists who sought to replace structural functional theories with a revised and updated Marxist sociology. The theory's specific role was to provide an alternative to modernization theory's interpretation of social change in the modern era (See T. R. Shannon's *An Introduction to the World System Perspective*, 1989).

Professor Jantzi recognizes that there has been a shift from a model of integration to that of conflict in the "liberation-from-dependency" paradigm. He notes: "While the dominant view in the previous decades assumed common interests between the developed and underdeveloped countries, dependency theory and world systems theory found the respective countries to have clearly conflicting interests." The increasing gap between the rich and the poor could be accounted for by the exploitation of the peripheral countries (underdeveloped) by the core (developed countries).

The final paradigm, that of global interdependence, attempts to utilize insights from the other three paradigms, merging aspects of functionalism with that of conflict. The problems of underdeveloped nations require international cooperation, and it is in everyone's best interest to cooperate. Since the world system is made up of interdependent societies, economic and environmental problems know no boundaries. It implies if solutions are not found through consensus and cooperation, the price of inevitable conflict will follow.

Each of the paradigms discussed by Professor Jantzi has implications for the work of the Church in developing nations. Just as social scientists have not always been in agreement as to which paradigm is best, there is honest disagreement among Christians as to which paradigm to employ in Church-related activities. Classic Church missions have grown out of the modernization model that has fallen into disfavor among many contemporary social scientists. Professor Jantzi's analysis of the implications of the paradigm shift for missionary activities provides much food for discussion.

In further exploring appropriate Christian responses to the problems of developing nations, students might reflect on the biblical concept of the Church as the Body of Christ (1 Corinthians 12:12-26). We are, by analogy, all members of the family of God. As members of one family, we are our "brother's keeper" and we are obligated to help those who live under oppressive conditions (Genesis 4:9). We might ask, What is the responsibility of developed nations, especially in the light of the fact that Christ will judge all nations on the basis of their responses to those in need (Matthew 25:31-46)? The Bible clearly teaches that privilege carries with it concomitant responsibility. To renege on that obligation is to incur the judgment of God (Amos 3:2; Luke 12:48). How we give aid is a matter of choice; that we must help people of developing nations is not!

HELPING DEVELOPING NATIONS: SOCIO-POLITICAL PARADIGMS OF DEVELOPMENT
Vernon E. Jantzi

Development was a magic word for many years. It conjured up images of positive growth and good will. However, now it frequently carries negative connotations. For many it symbolizes societies with more means but less meaning, or economies producing more for a few and less for the many. The myriad meanings attached to "development" make it difficult to treat the topic with precision. Nevertheless, when one speaks of specific cases of hunger, lack of shelter, or illness, it is possible for people representing a wide variety of views on development to communicate with each other. For example, Ovidio Flores, a Honduran Church leader, recounts that when he once asked a "campesino" (peasant) what development was, the reply came back, "For me development is having corn and beans to eat" (Flores, 1983). While we may feel that development should be more than having enough food, everyone would agree that it would include, at least, "having corn and beans to eat."

Even though we may agree with the Honduran campesino or Goulet (1973, p. 128) that people "must have enough in order to be more," our theoretical visions of what constitutes underdevelopment and what causes it are constantly changing. Furthermore, they are often at variance with those of others. Over the years, there have been a succession of perspectives that have gained prominence.

Thomas Kuhn has constructed a model of how theoretical visions evolve; this model can be applied appropriately to the field of development (Kuhn, 1970). In his model, scientific paradigms always generate, along with evidence that confirms their validity, anomalies that they cannot explain. When the anomalies become too great or the contradictions too severe, a new paradigm emerges, viewing the same reality in a new light, interpreting it differently, and providing us with new understanding of the phenomenon and new ways to study it further (Evans and Stephens 1988).

DEVELOPMENT PARADIGMS: GUIDELINES FOR CHANGE

Holland and Henriot (1983) gave an excellent description and classification of the constantly competing dominant paradigms that have guided development activities during the past half century, summarizing them as economic, social, or political. Today an emerging perspective can be added to this list. The model of global interdependence is gaining acceptance as we enter the 21st century.

The respective prominence of the four models corresponds roughly with the four "development decades," a term first used by the United Nations in 1961 as a result of John F. Kennedy's proposal that the 1960s be labeled the "development decade." Like all theoretical models, the various development perspectives provide answers to a series of questions.

1. What is the problem that impedes development?

2. Where is the source of the problem located, internally or externally?

3. What is the general solution to the problem?

4. Where is the source of the solution located?

Modernization for Economic Growth, 1950s and '60s

Both rich and poor nations subscribed to the view that economic growth was stifled because traditional societies were unable to generate sufficient capital. This is the way we have thought about development for many years. It has been generally assumed that underdeveloped countries are poor because their people's traditional values, attitudes, and practices impede the accumulation of surplus. As a result, people lack capital which could be invested to produce new or more goods and services for the society. The solution, in this case, is "modernization" to provide people with a modern worldview that would motivate them to generate and invest capital, thus producing economic growth. The "modern personality" is characterized by a strong future orientation, confidence in the effectiveness of human action in the world, an openness to new ideas, and an individual-based perception of self as distinct from the extended family (Inkeles and Smith, 1974). These values and attitudes emerge as a result of contact with the West and/ or education in the natural and social sciences. Thus, the solution will arrive via transfer from the more developed countries.

At the close of the 18th century, modernization provided the underlying assumption for progressive Central American governments' invitation to Protestant missionary organizations to enter their countries (Nelson, 1984). Progressives wanted Protestants to start schools and other institutions in order to instill in the population modern values and the work ethic characteristic of the United States. Protestants, of course, willingly accepted the modernization challenge and established some of the finest elementary and high schools, hospitals, and nursing schools in the region during the first half of the 20th century (Jantzi, 1986).

The modernization paradigm, as summarized in the following chart, reached its zenith during the 1950s and '60s. In spite of certain difficulties during those decades, historically it was a period of almost unprecedented faith in the American system.

Modernization and Basic Questions about Underdevelopment

What is the problem? Traditionalism impedes the generation and investment of capital needed for economic growth.

Where is the source of the problem located? The problem is within the value system and practices of the developing country.

Economic growth did take place in poor societies but the benefits were experienced only by a small number of people within each country; this raised serious questions about the modernization model of development. Some critics doubted that it could even be called development, since "development" did not include a more equitable distribution of wealth, but only increased production.

Growth with Equity, 1970s

The development community's growing concern about how the benefits of economic growth were distributed focused attention on the marginal segments of the population in poor countries and the long-standing domestic structural arrangements that kept them at the economic margin. For example, a heavy reliance on capital-intensive export production greatly restricted the growth of most new employment possibilities for the marginal peoples.

In 1973 Robert McNamara, then president of the World Bank, called for development efforts to focus on the bottom 60 percent of the population. One way to do this was for developing countries to organize their physical territory by enlarging the transportation and communication networks. This would provide access for all in the population to society's goods and services. A developing country then would physically look more like a developed country as it structured itself to experience growth with equity (Mosher, 1969, E. A. L. Johnson, 1970).

Organizationally, Owens and Shaw (1974) articulated the need to regionalize and decentralize development programs in order to insure broad-based participation. In this way each region could design a development program that would identify their unique needs, plan appropriate programs, and work to implement them. Schumacher's (1973) "small-is-beautiful" philosophy was another basis for structuring development efforts to take marginal people into account. In the development literature of the period, "access" to the benefits of the society became a key concept. As summarized in the following chart, regionalization, decentralization, appropriate technology, and popular participation were all designed to provide such access. Growth was needed, but only growth with equity would solve the problem of social and economic marginality.

Growth-with-Equity and Basic Questions about Underdevelopment

Where is the source of the problem located? The problem lies within the value system and structures of the development country.

What is the general solution to the problem? Growth with equity is needed. This is achieved through modernization, but benefits of economic growth must be made available equitably to all via regionalization and decentralization. The use of appropriate technology and popular participation in planning and program implementation is necessary.

Where is the source of the solution located? Developed countries which emphasize equitable distribution provide the models for growth with equity. Organization technology is transferred from the developed countries.

The political aspects of development became more obvious during the decade as critics of the modernization paradigm called attention to the larger constraints at both the national and international levels that were hampering equitable development. In Latin America at least, a major impetus for this concern came from the 1968 Conference of Latin American Bishops in Medellin, Colombia. The Bishops called the Roman Catholic Church to give priority to the needs of the poor and criticized societal structures which perpetuated marginality poverty.

Liberation from Dependency, 1980s

The Second Development Decade serves in many ways as a transition from the modernization model to the politically revolutionary perspective of the late 1970s and early 1980s. At about the same time that McNamara was urging the World Bank to address the problem of marginality, another movement was growing, particularly in Latin America. This movement also identified the problems of underdevelopment, but stated they were derived form the nature of the international division of labor. Whereas the previous perspectives identified internal sources of the problem, the dependency perspective (as summarized in the following chart) saw it as an international problem growing out of the structures formed during the colonial era. Thus, even though underdeveloped countries were now politically "independent" their economies were still dependent on those of developed countries to which they had been linked as colonies. National enclave elites, as producers of primary products and consumers of manufactured, technological and cultural goods, usually provided these links (Camacho, 1978). Andre Gunder Frank (1966) referred to this phenomenon as the "development of underdevelopment."

Liberation-from-Dependency and Basic Questions
about Underdevelopment

What is the problem? Developing countries are dependent on developed countries. This leads to a distortion of national policies and the value system to the detriment of the national population.

Where is the source of the problem located? The problem lies in international economic and political structures and in enclave elites which subordinate the national economy to developed economies.

What is the general solution to the problem? The solution requires liberation from exploitative international and national structures. This involves reevaluation of national culture, development of a critical consciousness by people at all levels, popular/grassroots organizations to break the power of enclave elites, and the creation of a New International Economic Order.

Where is the source of the solution located? The solution is to be found in the developing country as people organize to restructure society. In addition, new international structures are needed, along with greater solidarity from the North.

While the dominant view in the previous decades assumed common interests between the developed and underdeveloped countries, dependency theory (Cardose and Faletto 1979) and world systems theory (Wallerstein, 1974) found the respective countries to have clearly conflicting interests. As the result of both changing arrangements experienced by underdeveloped countries, and the international monetary and tariff structures that gave rich countries the "unfair" advantage, any increased contact between core (developed) and periphery (underdeveloped) worked to the detriment of the periphery (Frank, 1966). This, then, explained the growing gap between rich and poor which occurred in spite of the economic growth poor countries had experienced during the first two development decades.

This model has been useful for countries such as Nicaragua where a popular revolution achieved a degree of independence. However, even in those contexts it became apparent that, in addition to breaking the structures of dependency, it is also vital to recognize and strengthen relationships that foster interdependence. The ecological and debt crises looming in Central America and other parts of the world produce consequences reaching far beyond geopolitical boundaries. Global cooperation is basic to long-term survival (Hedstrom, 1988).

Global Interdependence, 1990s

The global interdependence paradigm picks up strands of systems theory which highlight the interconnectedness of human welfare irrespective of national, cultural or ideological boundaries. As with the other paradigms, there have been people and organizations working at these issues for many years, but only recently has the perspective gained wide acceptance. USAID (the United States Agency for International Development) has targeted ecological and debt issues as major areas of its programs in Central America during the 1990s.

Problems of international debt and environmental deterioration are frequently linked to economic stagnation, especially in Central America. As economies fail, countries are forced to mortgage their future by borrowing heavily in order to maintain current levels of living. The natural environment is also exploited for short-term benefits. Standard reasoning posits that economic stagnation stems from an economic model that does not rely on an open and free market. International efforts to break down trade barriers of all types so that free trade can move economies into the production of goods and services are therefore important. Domestically emphasis could be placed on the revitalization of market forces and the privatization of public services and enterprises.

The same reasoning holds in the ecological arena. The special role of the different regions of the earth — tropical rain forests, polar ice caps, and the oceans — in sustaining life for all, forms the basis for such reasoning. Each country has an obligation to others to protect and enhance its unique ecological contribution to global welfare. We are inextricably bound together by the ecological web. If one country fails to act responsibly, we all suffer.

In the global interdependence model, the development solution to problems of debt and environmental deterioration is found at the international level. Nations meet to work out differences peacefully, putting aside ideological disagreements and short-term self-interest in the best interests of global welfare. This would require developed countries to address their ecologically destructive consumption patterns and trade practices in which harmful products such as banned pesticides and tobacco products are heavily marketed in poor countries. They would also need to be willing to bear part of the international debt burden.

CONSEQUENCES OF DEVELOPMENT PARADIGM CHANGE

Over the past half century different development paradigms have risen to prominence and then receded. As each became conventional wisdom of the time it shaped our activities and perceptions, affecting the type of programs implemented, the structure and mission of development organizations, and the shape of international political relations. Each model continues to exert its influence in some sectors.

Program Implications of Four Development Paradigms

A particular paradigm will appeal to, or fit, an organization on the basis of ideological or religious factors. Development organizations should regularly reflect on "why they do what they do," and "where they do what they do" in order to keep from blindly being led by a given paradigm. Let us consider three paradigms: modernization, growth with equity, and liberation from dependency.

Modernization for Economic Growth

This paradigm stressed the need to transfer human, cultural, and economic resources from the more developed world. Many international agencies were created or greatly strengthened in order to carry out this transfer. A clear division of labor exists between the governmental and nongovernmental international organizations. Since the national-level programs usually require infusion of large amounts of capital, multilateral or bilateral agencies like the World Bank, the United States Agency for International Development (USAID), or the Canadian International Development Agency (CIDA), tend to be most active in implementing development programs with national governments. For example, in Costa Rica and Nicaragua, these organizations sponsored the creation of new institutions like the national agricultural extension service and the Central American Management Institute (INCAE) which prepared the management teams for new companies to be formed in the region through the incentives offered by the Central American Common Market.

Regional programs are relatively unimportant for governments, as noted in the following chart. The churches are more active at this level. The Methodists in Costa Rica, for example, started work in rural areas in the 1950s and, among other things, established a rural center which served as a demonstration farm training center. This type of regional involvement represents a common strategy used by many Protestant organizations; it provides Protestant legitimacy within a predominantly Roman Catholic environment. It also is an attractive opportunity to establish a presence since the need was not being met by the government.

Modernization: Types of Organizations and Programs at Various Levels

---

International-level: International transfer agents: World Bank. USAID, Peace Corps, World Vision, Church World Service, Mennonite Central Committee, etc.

National-level: Infrastructure-type organizations and programs: agriculture extension, road systems, educational systems, energy systems, mass communication systems.

Regional-level: Infrastructure supplied largely by church in: demonstration farms and rural centers, hospitals, elementary and high schools, etc.

Local-level: Individual-oriented programs, in which foreign personnel play key implementing role in areas like: literacy, modern agricultural technology and practices, youth work, skill development for industry, basic health and social services delivery.

However, most church-sponsored development efforts take place on the community level and are frequently staffed and funded by foreign personnel and resources. Programs in literacy, health and agriculture focus on bringing "modern" technology and organization to bear on problems; church-sponsored development work intends to create in villages the attitudes necessary to receive and manage modern technology to allow them to move into the modernizing current taking place at the national level.

Growth with Equity

By the mid 1970s many development practitioners in Costa Rica and Nicaragua were demanding that poor people have better access to society's resources. In Nicaragua the government was not very interested in the issue of access, although it did respond to external pressure to redesign health and agricultural support systems to benefit more people. In both sectors, appropriate-technology practices and technology were used. The following chart shows that the same type of international organizations were important for transfer purposes. However, by the mid-seventies many added the consultant role to their programs. Planning skills were the new transfer element; this transfer was best done through *ad hoc* consulting relationships. The consultant/advisor role was one many local development practitioners suggested as most appropriate for foreign personnel.

Growth with Equity: Types of Organization and Progress

International-level: Transfer structures continue to be important, e.g., World Bank, USAID, etc. Consulting firms become increasingly important.

National-level: National planning ministries key to providing access through designing systems for regionalization and decentralization.

Regional-level: Creation of market towns; construction of road grid; regionalization of major public services; government often assumed basic services formerly provided by churches.

Local-level: Appropriate technology; paraprofessional programs in health, agriculture, etc.; creation of local planning structures to enhance popular participation.

During the 1970s countries identified economic and social marginality as a serious problem. Development plans were redesigned to provide wider access through setting up regional basic health, educational and agricultural support services. For example, Costa Rica created a planning ministry to give development this regional focus. In Nicaragua, the government was relatively unconcerned about issues of equity. However, in the Protestant sector a dynamic new organization, CEPAD (Protestant Committee for Relief and Development), was born as a result of the catastrophic 1972 earthquake in Managua, Nicaragua. A number of Catholic groups already working with both rural and urban marginalized sectors also joined. CEPAD's initial task was to deal with the damage caused by the earthquake, but it quickly moved into development programs and by the latter 1970s had created regional structures. This national coverage allowed CEPAD to become aware of, and make public, many atrocities committed by the Somoza government during its last years as it fought to remain in power. For some persons in the Protestant community, this activity created questions regarding the role of the Church in denouncing the political powers. For others, it seemed to be the only option open to Christians committed to working on behalf of the marginalized and oppressed.

As governments developed regional schemes, they displaced or took over church-sponsored institutions such as regional hospitals and high schools. These institutions often had been staffed by foreign personnel in key positions. In Costa Rica, the government activity eliminated the need for groups such as the Good Will Caravans. Where church-sponsored programs were not displaced they often took on regionalized patterns themselves. For example, in Nicaragua, CEPAD and PROVADENIC developed agricultural and health promoter systems that functioned from their regional offices.

At times, as in Nicaragua where many religious groups deeply mistrusted the revolutionary government, church denominations felt threatened by the government because public programs took over services traditionally provided by a specific church group in a given area. Most did not recognize this as a natural consequence of the particular development model adopted by the government.

Governmental expansion into the regional level enabled many church-related development programs to work with the "small-is-beautiful" model of technology. Once the regional infrastructure was emerging or in place, "appropriate technology" became a viable option. Paraprofessional (community promoter) programs in health, agriculture and education were created. In Nicaragua CEPAD and PROVADENIC trained, equipped and supervised local agricultural and health promoters from regional centers. Development professionals provided the minimal organizational input necessary to establish and nurture linkages with the regional center. This program "looked" more national because foreigners occupied fewer key positions. However, due to subtle or not-so-subtle pressures from external financing sources, a growing awareness of the lack of autonomy emerged. By the end of the 1970s this caused both governmental and private organizations to look seriously at the issue of dependency in relation to their own programs.

Liberation from Dependency

Governments or organizations committed to the principle of self-sufficiency frequently carry out programs similar to those illustrated in the previous model. As summarized in the following chart, regionalization and decentralization are important aspects of their development efforts. However, unlike the other paradigms, this perspective considers the source of the problem to be found at the international level. It posits that many development agencies function as part of the current international economic structure and thus perpetuate dependency. They are seen as part of the problem rather than providing the solution. In order to address underdevelopment, a new international economic order needs to be established that takes poor countries' economies and interests as the starting point, or at least, makes them of equal importance to those of the developed world.

Liberation from Dependency: Types of Organizations and Programs

---

International-level: Creation of a New International Economic Order focusing more on solidarity with poor countries and less on transfer of functions from the more developed world.

National-level: Regionalization and decentralization of governmental programs.

Regional-level: Creation of market towns; construction of road grid; formation of regional mass organizations.

Local-level: Work at creation of social consciousness; formation of locally-based mass organizations.

Often NGOs organizations will claim that they recognize the dependency issue and therefore are able to avoid being part of the problem. However, since their funding comes from the developed countries, they can expect to be pressured by groups within those societies who consider liberation projects to be detrimental. Organizations within developing countries, therefore, will be encouraged to structure their requests for funding according the current interests of the international agencies.

In Nicaragua, CEPAD has been able to work with all of its international cooperating organizations to form a consortium of funding agencies, of which CEPAD is presumably an equal partner. The consortium meets annually to study the needs identified by CEPAD and commit annual funding amounts to the general budget rather than to specific agency "pet" projects. This allows CEPAD to provide feedback to the international organizations as a full partner in the development process. More mutuality is thus introduced into the planning process than is often the case. The consortium arrangement has worked well in Nicaragua; it seems worth studying as a model for other countries.

During the 1980s Costa Rica and Nicaragua followed different development paradigms. Nicaragua opted for the liberation perspective and suffered international political consequences during the attempts to develop new national political structures. Costa Rica opted to continue using the growth-with-equity model and obtained considerable foreign economic assistance. In many respects the actual programs growing out of the two perspectives may be similar. The difference lies in the fact that the liberation model, especially in a revolutionary context like Nicaragua, develops new national institutions to serve groups which have newly achieved power, for example, organizations for women, small farmers, industrial workers, etc.

Regionalization is important in societies concerned with equity; it is essential in a revolutionary context in order to consolidate the Revolution. Regional organizations empower local communities by enabling them to join with other localities with similar concerns. However, the temptation is always present for the national government to subvert the process and convert it into a channel for government directives and a tool for control of communities and regional groups. During the 1980s, the Nicaraguan government constantly struggled with this issue in relation to the Sandinista Defense Committees and other popular organizations.

At the community level, in nonrevolutionary contexts as well as postrevolutionary societies, development workers oriented by the liberation framework may engage in what Paul Freire calls programs of *concientizacion*, the creation of a critical consciousness (Freire, 1969). In Latin America the Christian Base Communities within the Roman Catholic Church serve this function (Cook, 1985). In this approach, development workers are needed more for their solidarity than for their specialized knowledge or skills. However, when development workers identify with powerless groups in any society, they are often considered by the establishment to be subversives and labeled as communists, counter-revolutionaries, or something worse.

Organizational Dilemmas and Changing Development Paradigms

Most of our international development and mission agencies grew out of the modernization model with its heavy transfer emphasis, and continue to function within it; therefore, they suffer a common organizational problem. They must constantly convince contributors that the services of the organization are needed to bring about resource transfer to underdeveloped countries. At the same time staff personnel find it necessary to function within the structurally oriented paradigm. Internal friction and frustration for agency personnel is produced. Staff are "speaking out of the two sides of their mouth" in order to do what they feel is right at the field level, but at the same time must say things totally counter to what they now feel is needed for development in order to raise funds. This type of organizational dissonance affects governmental and non-governmental organizations alike. It is one of the difficult consequences of development paradigm change.

Reorienting International Political Relations

Changes in development paradigms reflect and mold altered understandings of international and domestic political relations. Until recently, competing East-West social, economic, and political interests constituted the core of conflict and tension in the world, particularly since World War II. This dynamic played itself out in development efforts as well. However, as our visions of underdevelopment and development changed, the nature of North-South interaction has assumed greater importance and we begin to question the legitimacy of the "natural" distribution of resources in society and the world. New configurations of allies and adversaries formed which now lie much more along a North-South pole than on an East-West axis. This awareness of North-South conflicting interests will become more evident as the West seems to be giving priority to changes occurring in the East.

As at the international level, our work in development programs within developing countries helps us realize that even though the poor countries have domestic problems they must address, a major aspect of underdevelopment lies outside their control. The interactions of North-South, or developed-developing country, international political and economic relations are overwhelming in their effects. Thus, the conflict about Nicaragua which opponents of the Revolution tried to portray exclusively in East-West terms, has clear elements of North-South issues as well. Former Nicaraguan planning minister, Xabier Gorostiaga (1987), warns that in the long-run, dependency on the North — whether it be East or West — will have detrimental effects on Nicaraguan and Central American development.

THE CHURCH AND DEVELOPMENT PARADIGM CHANGES

The Church's involvement in development efforts has raised interesting questions about the role and mission of the Church in the world. Just as perceived political realities have changed, so our theological visions have been modified and expanded. As we worked at world problems, we have gained a new understanding of the breadth, length, and depth of the Gospel. The Good News has become less unidimensional. The

Christian community is now searching for appropriate ways to express this new vision organizationally and institutionally.

Do Church Programs and Organizations Reflect the New Vision?

If we look at the assumptions which appear to undergird programs in our educational development institutions, the answer to this question may be inconclusive.

Educational institutions: church educational institutions by and large continue to perpetuate the idea of Northern, especially Western, superiority in all aspects of life. Even those programs that provide students with opportunity to experience other world cultures, unwittingly offer solutions from a Western perspective — be it the Gospel, a special skill, or applied scientific knowledge.

The development paradigm I would endorse as we begin the 21st century, suggests that educational institutions need to develop a sense of universal solidarity enabling us to rise above class and national interests. This is in line with our understanding of ultimate loyalty to Christ. Along with our professional skills, we need a truly global perspective (Goulet, 1973). We need a more serious commitment to learning from the poor countries of the South. All development workers should be prepared at our colleges and universities to be students in the broadest sense of that term. Although efforts are being made, it remains to be seen whether Church colleges and universities are willing or able to create structures which cooperate with host country institutions to provide students with a vision for development based on interdependence rather than unilateral transfers.

Development organizations: development agencies have been successful in recruiting persons to work in programs to alleviate poverty in developing countries. Generally these specialists are highly trained and committed to the people they serve. Agencies usually consider their work in developing countries as frontline activities in the struggle to overcome underdevelopment. I would suggest that this frequently blinds us to the possibility that a major portion of our effort needs to be carried out in the developed world. We need development agencies to provide institutional structures which will empower "returned" workers to create awareness of our own society's role in global underdevelopment, and to engage in constituency education or "reverse mission," as it is frequently called. Instead, we often designate returned workers to do public relations work and fund-raising, both of which reinforce false conceptions of the nature of underdevelopment.

The causes of underdevelopment are multiple. There are indeed internal problems to be addressed inside poor countries. However, we are less prepared to address systematically the international aspects of underdevelopment. Development organizations need to call us to look at our own lifestyle, our own understanding of citizenship, and our own recognition of the relationship of justice to authority and power. These are all topics with direct political implications (Yoder, 1972: Kraybill, 1976, 1978; Campolo, 1985; Sine, 1987). I challenge development agencies to devote as much human and economic resource to this task of education at home as are currently directed to problems in the developing countries away from home.

What Is the Nature of the Gospel?

Our understanding of the nature of the Gospel makes certain development perspectives more appealing than others. For example, the modernization perspective will appeal especially to those who view the Gospel as a means whereby individuals come to new life in Christ, since it stresses new values and the resulting change in one's worldview. Generally, development programs sponsored by church groups supporting this view will emphasize the transfer of technology, knowledge, cultural values, and goods. This may take the form of charity-type distribution efforts. Such Church programs rely heavily on foreign personnel directly implementing the project, and on high-pressured appeals for funds.

The growth-with-equity model appeals to groups who see the Gospel as calling us to individual conversion and a simple lifestyle that is reflected in Christian values of not being encumbered by this world's goods. Persons are appreciated for themselves rather than for their position or possessions. The understanding of the Gospel as portrayed in the writings of Sine (1987) and Campolo (1985) would be consistent with this perspective. Growth-with-equity development reflects an appreciation for the host culture and the attempt to adapt development input to the host context so that it is accessible to poor people. The emphasis is on equipping nationals to become self-sufficient. Foreign personnel and resources complement rather than control those of the host community. Financially, matching-fund arrangements are common. Foreign personnel serve as consultants or resource persons who enable local persons to carry out the program. In spite of all this, many local organizations formed under these conditions still will reflect neocolonial characteristics and experience conflict over who ultimately makes decisions and sets policy.

Liberation perspectives will appeal to those who see the Gospel primarily in terms of justice. While some persons holding this perspective do not stress the importance of personal conversion, most see conversion as a basic element supporting the call for a simple lifestyle (Sider 1977). Development programs which focus on justice work toward the creation of a new or radically restructured society in which the poor actually participate in decision-making with their interests seriously taken into account. The Church is called to be in the struggle with the poor and to engage in popular education to help people gain a new awareness of all the dimensions of the problem. To "accompany" the poor and to engage in "reverse mission" are important actions for those who see the Gospel through the justice lens. The Church is called to publicly recognize its sin of complicity in perpetuating unjust structures and to turn to a simplicity and solidarity with those in need.

The emerging global interdependence paradigm appeals to Christians who view the Gospel in terms of stewardship. This paradigm stresses the importance of proper care of the environment for the benefit of all. Although there is a certain kinship with mystical Eastern-type religious orientations frequently found among those who are concerned about ecological wholeness, spiritual conversion, simplicity of lifestyle, and justice are considered by Protestant and Roman Catholic groups as basic to good stewardship. This understanding of the Gospel transcends culture, citizenship, class, and denomination, and encourages development work which is in the long-term best interests of all. In order to accomplish this, global interdependence programs focus on the tendency of U. S. economy to externalize the costs of what we produce, and to emphasize the importance of global understanding so that we can work more creatively in caring for the highly interdependent natural and socioeconomic environment in which we live.

How Can We Institutionally Embody the New Vision?

We see institutional glimpses of the new vision, but the Christian community has trouble finding new ways to embody it. Some organizations have made the difficult changes and taken a liberation or global interdependence perspective. They have experienced conflict with traditional constituencies, resulting in loss of financial resources which then requires the scaling down of the organization. Interdenominational efforts, such as Wheaton '83, suggest the idea of "transformation" as a term to replace "development"" so that the transforming aspect of the Gospel is overtly included alongside the improvement of the standard of living. Evangelicals for Social Action is a group which attempts to bring together a wide spectrum of Christians to focus on the need for the Good News to include a call for personal conversion, simple lifestyle, justice, and global interdependence in environmental and economic issues.

The next several decades likely will see the Christian community — Roman Catholic and Protestant — coalesce around how we view the world and the role of the Church. Denominational groups will continue to be important but as they attempt to implement the Gospel described in Luke 4:18-19, some groups of Methodists, Catholics, Mennonites, Baptists, Presbyterians or Nazarenes may well find that they have more in common with kindred paradigm spirits in other denominations than they do with groups in their own. Preaching the Gospel to the poor, healing the brokenhearted, providing deliverance for the captives, sight to the blind and liberty to the oppressed also means working in our own society in order to make those things possible in the underdeveloped countries of the world.

Study and Discussion
Questions

1. What is the principal cause of underdevelopment according to the "Modernization for Economic Growth" perspective?

2. Why does the "Modernization for Economic Growth" development perspective appeal especially to many mission agencies?

3. What is the principal cause of underdevelopment according to the "Growth with Equity" perspective?

4. Guided by the "Growth with Equity" perspective, how did individual countries organize their national territory in order to provide greater access to services and resources to a greater number of their citizens?

5. What is the principal cause of underdevelopment according to the "Liberation from Dependency" perspective?

6. Why does the "Liberation from Dependency" perspective often view foreign mission and development agencies as an integral part of the problem of underdevelopment rather than a contribution to the long-term solution to it?

7. What is the principal cause of underdevelopment according to the "Global Interdependence " perspective?

8. What is there about the need to raise funds for development that often creates tension and frustration at the project implementation level in development programs?

9. On what basis might one assert that the changes in the Soviet Union and Eastern Europe will not really alter the nature of the problem of underdevelopment and the action necessary to overcome it?

10. Many colleges, universities, mission organizations, and development agencies sponsor short-term experiences in other cultures in order to prepare persons for future mission and development service. Why might these experiences be more harmful than good as a way to prepare persons to serve in a cross-cultural setting?

References

Camacho, Daniel. 1978. *La Dominacion Cultural en el Subdesarrolo*. San Jose, Costa Rica: Editorial Costa Rica.

Campolo, Anthony. 1985. *Partly Right*. Waco, TX: Word Books.

Cardoso, Fernando Henrique, and Enzo Faletto. 1979. *Dependency and Development in Latin America*. Berkeley: University of California Press.

Cook, Guillermo. 1985. *The Expectation of the Poor: Latin America Basic Ecclesial Communities in Protestant Perspective*. Maryknoll, N. Y.: Orbis Books.

Evans, Peter B., and John D Stephens. 1988. "Development and the World Economy." In *Handbook of Sociology*, ed. Neil J. Smelser. Newbury Park, CA: Sage Publications.

Flores, Ovidio. 1983. "What Is Development?" unpublished presentation given at the Mennonite Central Committee/Eastern Mennonite College "Transcultural Cultural Seminar," Harrisonburg, Virginia, June.

Frank, Andre Gunder. 1966. "The Development of Underdevelopment." *Monthly Review*, Vol. 18, No. 4, pp. 17-31, September.

Freire, Paulo. 1969. *La educacion como practica de la libertad*. Montevideo, Uruguay: Tierra Nueva.

Gorostiaga, Xabier. 1987. "Centroamerica 1987: hipotesis para un debate." in Edelberto Torres Rivas, et. al., Costa Rica: crisis y desafios. San Jose, Costa Rica: DEI

Goulet, Denis. 1973 *The Cruel Choice*. New York: Atheneum.

Hedstrom, Ingemar. 1988. *Sonos parte de un gran equilibrio: la crisis ecologica en Centroamerica*, 3rd ed. San Jose, Costa Rica: DEI

Holland, Joe, and Peter Henriot. 1983. *Social Analysis: Linking Faith and Justice*. Enlarged and revised edition. Maryknoll, NY: Orbis Books.

Inkeles, Alex, and David H. Smith. 1973. *Becoming Modern*. Cambridge, MA: Harvard University Press.

Jantzi, Vernon E. 1986. "Liberation Theology's Impact on Protestantism in Central America: The Case of Costa Rica and Nicaragua." Paper presented at the Annual Meeting of the Southeast Conference on Latin American Studies, Clemson, South

Carolina.

Johnson, E. A. L. 1970. *Organization of Space in Developing Countries*. Cambridge, MA: Harvard University Press.

Kraybill, Donald B. 1976. *Our Star-Spangled Faith*. Scottdale, PA: Herald Press.

_____. 1978. *The Upside-Down Kingdom*. Scottdale, PA: Herald Press.

Kuhn, Thomas. 1970. *The Structure of Scientific Revolutions*. Second edition, enlarged. Chicago: University of Chicago Press.

Mosher, Arthur T. 1969. *Creating a Progressive Rural Structure*. New York: The Agriculture Development Council, Inc.

Nelson, Wilton M. 1984. *The History of Protestantism in Central America*. Grand Rapids, MI: William B. Eerdmans Publishing Company.

Owens, Edgar, and Robert Shaw. 1974. *Development Reconsidered: Bridging the Gap Between Government and People*. Lexington, MA: Lexington Books.

Schumacher, E. F. 1973. *Small Is Beautiful*. New York: Harper and Row Publisher.

Sider, Ronald J. 1977. *Rich Christians in an Age of Hunger*: A Biblical Study. Downers Grove, IL: Inter-Varsity Press.

Sine, Tom. 1987. *Why Settle for More and Miss the Best?* Waco, TX: Word Books.

Wallerstein, Immanuel. 1974. *The Modern World-System I: Capitalist Agriculture and the Origins of the European World Economy*. New York: Academic Press.

Yoder, John Howard. 1972. *The Politics of Jesus*. Grand Rapids, MI: William B. Eerdmans Publishing Company.

CHAPTER 4
ENVIRONMENTAL CRISIS: INTRODUCTION

Professor Ferraro's presentation of hard facts and biblical admonitions will cause readers to give some serious thought to the environmental problems facing our country. His article implicitly challenges us to review our lifestyles to assess how we may be contributing to the environmental crisis. Hopefully it will even cause some to make changes that in some small way will lessen the damage done to the earth.

Ferraro's analysis of the ecosystem may be placed within a structural functionalist perspective. Functionalism assumes that the social world is a system made up of interdependent parts. Each of these parts have consequences for the maintenance of the system. Early functionalism tended to focus on the positive functions of each part, i.e., on the contribution the part made to the maintenance of the social system. More sophisticated function analysts never lost sight of *dysfunctions* or the consequences of action that tend to break down the system.

Most societal norms and practices have both positive and negative functions. For example, the so-called "baby-boomers," a cohort resulting from a high birth rate after World War II, have produced both positive and negative functions for our society. In many ways this cohort has been good for the economy. Its members required an increase in everything from baby products to schools when they were children and contributed to a growth in the housing industry as they started their own families. At the same time, however, one might raise questions about how this large cohort has negatively impacted our environment. Many members of this generation of largely two-income couples can afford to indulge in the very lifestyle that generates an over-supply of garbage that causes our landfills to overflow. In this illustration and many others it is possible to see how a social phenomenon can function positively for the economic system (at least in the shortrun) while simultaneously having dysfunctions for the ecosystem.

Professor Ferraro's article provides ample evidence of the dysfunctions of our economic system in its failure to be concerned with ecological issues. He asserts that it is the duty of every Christian to be concerned about the damage and destruction being done by Americans to God's creation. At the same time, some nonfunctionalists might contend that the article has not gone far enough. Two additional issues drawn from a conflict perspective could be used to supplement Ferraro's analysis: (1) an elaboration on the role of ideology in systems maintenance and change and (2) consideration of the effects of American environmental policies on the larger world community.

The ecosystem approach often fails to discuss adequately the ideological basis for actions taken in use and abuse of the environment. An ideology is a generalized belief statement which usually has a religious and/or philosophical base. It presumably prompts people to act in a certain manner. Christianity may be regarded as an ideology with a statement of belief on ecological issues. As Ferraro mentions in passing in his article, some writers have argued that Christianity has been a major contributing factor in ecological destruction (see for example, Jerry Rifkin: *Entrophy*, 1980, p. 235). All too often, God's command in Genesis (1:28) to "subdue" the earth and "have dominion over the fish of the sea and over the birds of the air" has been used to justify the exploitation of nature.

The older traditional theology that encouraged exploitation in the name of dominion fits well with a society that is in an "epoch of expansion" with its faith in unlimited growth and scientific technology (Jeremy Rifkin, *The Emerging Order*, 1979). As we enter an age during which we recognize the finite nature of our resources, the traditional interpretation of dominion has become obsolete.

Social activist Jeremy Rifkin, although himself not a Christian, suggests that it is evangelical Christianity's present growth (a "third great awakening") that "will help spark a profound change in the social and economic life of the nation" (*Entropy*, 1980, p. 234). This will come to pass, however, only if evangelicals accept the stewardship doctrine discussed by Professor Ferraro in this article as part of its theology. Christians must come to recognize that abusing the environment is actually a sin and an act of failing to obey God. We must acknowledge that interpretations of the Bible that have interpreted "dominion" as exploitation and abuse have reflected our culture rather than God's word to us. In a sense the failure of many Christians to take environmental issues seriously reflects how our faith can be shaped by our culture rather than our using biblical principles on creation to transform our world.

Another consideration that needs to be introduced into any discussion of ecological issues involves "global interdependence." In the last chapter, Professor Jantzi presented the global interdependence sociopolitical paradigm and noted how, from this perspective, ecology was more than a national concern. Air and water pollution, deforestation, the melting of polar caps, and the destruction of species have more than local implications, for we are a world community.

Unfortunately, this world community is very complex. Conflict theorists would say that the world system is controlled by the core or developed countries who exploit the periphery or the underdeveloped communities. As Professor Ferraro notes in passing, "Americans have been shielded from shortages." We have been protected in part through our exploitation of the resources of less developed nations. We have come to expect that we have the "right" to oil from the Middle East and cheaply made goods from China or Mexico. Furthermore, our ability to drain the resources of countries reduced to dependency by a world economic system has enabled us not to have to face up to the seriousness of the ecological disasters being heaped upon the earth.

All too often when companies are forced to comply with ecological regulations in this country, they are permitted to move their companies to other nations where they face no such controls. While this move may help to clean up the air in the United States, it increases the pollution of poor peripheral countries like Mexico. In accord with dependency theory and world systems theory, the land, air and water of peripheral countries is being exploited (along with the workers who are forced to work for subsistence wages) so that the core countries may maintain their inflated standards of living.

What should become more apparent as we continue our discussion of social problems is the interrelationship of the various components of the system. Not only are social institutions (family, religion, government, and industry) interfaced, but the social world is linked intimately with the physical world. Since humankind has a limited amount of freedom to either destroy or create, values (embodied in ideologies) are part of the system that guides social behavior. Even from a secular sociological perspective, Christian values are recognized as having helped to shape the social order. Cautious hope has been expressed for Christianity's ability to produce a new ideology that would take Americans away from a selfish and wasteful destruction of the environment. If this hope is to materialize, it will not come from an obsolete traditional theology but rather out of a fresh look at Scripture in light of our dwindling resources and in relationship to good stewardship.

As we reflect on the havoc wrought by our failure to act as responsible stewards of the resources God has entrusted to us, it might be well to reflect on Paul's caution: "Do not be deceived; God is not mocked, for whatever a man (woman, group, industry, or nation) sows, that shall he (she, they) reap" (Galatians 6:7). While the reference is explicit to our personal and social relations, certainly implicitly it refers to our use or abuse of the physical environment. As Ferraro emphasizes in this article, we are all part of God's ecosystem.

Therefore, we might well reflect on these questions: Does not God's command to "do justice" (Micah 6:8) and to "do good" to all humankind (Galatians 6:10) include responsible stewardship of our national resources? Does not Paul's admonition to "work out your own salvation with fear and trembling" (Philippians 2:12) imply that we must consider the global ecological consequences of our lavish lifestyle? These are but two questions the reader might ponder while reading Dr. Ferraro's article.

ENVIRONMENTAL ABUSE AND RESPONSIBILITY
Kenneth F. Ferraro

A handful of university students roll an "earthball" — a six feet in diameter replica of the earth — across the walkways of a large, midwestern public university to draw attention to the need to care for our planet. Is it the 1960s or the 1990s? While it could be either time period, this particular instance was observed in the latter decade. Abuse of the environment is not a new social problem. Rather, it is one with which most Americans are familiar. Because it is an issue which is familiar to most citizens, it oftentimes is relegated to lower priority in reports by a media and information network oriented to new "crises." Despite periodic infusions of effort to confront the environmental crisis, there is no ecological evidence to indicate that this problem has been solved. In fact, some scholars contend that we are headed for a global ecocatastrophe. The environment is and will continue to be a resurgent problem in the United States and other developed countries until we recognize that we are a part of a finite world.

In this chapter, we shall consider the extent of the environmental problem today and outline some of the causes of environmental degradation. Subsequently, we will discuss environmental responsibility from a Christian perspective and offer suggested solutions to the problem of environmental abuse.

THE NATURE OF THE PROBLEM

Assessing the extent of the problem of environmental degradation is dependent upon our understanding of the ecosystem. We live in a self-sustained community of animals, plants, and bacteria within an inorganic environment. Within the ecosystem everything is related to and dependent upon everything else in a very complex way. Thus, interfering with any of the relationships of the elements of the ecosystem may have latent consequences on other elements of the ecosystem, including the structure of human societies.

The Ecological Complex — POET
The dominant theoretical perspective for studying the environment has been the ecological approach. This perspective is based on the premise that understanding the real problems of society can best be approached as we study the ecosystem (Hawley, 1950; Duncan, 1961). From this viewpoint, the ecological complex of any ecosystem may be described as the relationships among population (P), organization (O), environment (E), and technology (T) — (POET). There is considerable interdependency among these elements of the ecological complex, so much that social change is tied to environmental modification (Beisner, 1990). But, unfortunately, in our quest for a better standard of living in modern societies, modification of the environment has had a number of deleterious effects. Though regarded as benign for so many years, environmental abuse must be confronted if we are to avoid an ecocatastrophe.

The ecological framework has been criticized on several grounds, especially because it often implies a finite universe. Commoner (1988) argues that the global ecosystem is not really a closed system — which can be understood by the spaceship analogy. He argues that the earth is not a closed, isolated system sustained by its own limited resources. Much higher powers — Commoner cites the sun and solar energy — play critical roles in influencing the earth. Thus, while being a "world person" is valuable, environmental responsibility entails universe or cosmological thinking.

Another theoretical perspective that has recently stimulated scholarly exchange has its roots in conflict sociology. Drawing from Karl Marx and Frederick Engels, it can be seen that just as capital enterprise can exploit labor, so can it exploit nature or the environment (Parsons, 1977). Humans impress their stamp on the environment in the process of economic development and cultural practice. Thus, economic colonialism and the global political economy are key concepts in understanding how various nations "imprint" the earth (Evans and Stephans, 1988). Whichever theoretical perspective is used, studying our environment shows clearly how nature has been exploited, usually in the name of progress.

United States — Worst Offender

While the problems of the environment are global in nature, the United States has played the major role in depleting the earth's resources and polluting the ecosystem. Though the United States comprises about six percent of the earth's population, it consumes more of the world's energy and natural resources than any other society. In addition, it contributes about one half of the industrial pollution of the world (Neubeck, 1986).

For years, Americans have been reared on the belief that there are unlimited environmental resources. Economic growth and progress have been highly prized, oftentimes based on the faulty premise that environmental abuse is just a part of the cost of social progress (Sagoff, 1988). It is important to recognize that we all play a role in the environmental problem and that the resolution of the problem will demand a concerted effort. The specific problems that must be addressed involve various types of pollution, land misuse, and resource depletion.

Air Pollution

This planet is designed in such a way that it has natural purifying systems. The air of the earth's atmosphere is being purified through a complex process involving wind, rain, and changes in temperature. However, the contamination of the air in the earth's atmosphere disrupts the recycling process that cleans the air that is so vital to life. Each year over 150 million tons of pollution are released into the earth's atmosphere by the United States alone. While these air pollutants come from various sources, the major culprits include industrial operations, electric power plants, and the internal combustion engines of automobiles and trucks (Neubeck, 1986).

There are many consequences of air pollution that are well documented with regard to their effect on human life. We have made some progress over the last 40 years in reducing particulates, lead, and carbon monoxide. Commoner (1988) notes that lead emissions decreased by 86% between 1975 and 1985, and we have seen a substantial reduction in the lead levels in the blood of Americans during this period. This is good news for our environment (Beisner, 1990). Unfortunately, while we have reduced emissions of lead and some other substances, we have not been nearly as successful with others known to create "acid rain" (U. S. Bureau of the Census, 1989). The two major acid-forming air pollutants are sulfur dioxide and nitrogen oxides (U. S. Committee on Energy and Commerce, HR, 1988). We know that air pollution increases the rates of lung cancer, cardiovascular diseases, colds, and coughing, and retards the recovery process of the body in dealing with other forms of illness (Neubeck, 1986). Obviously, the consequences of air pollution are more profound in some areas than others, with urban residents being the most likely afflicted. Even though living in New York City is like smoking 38 cigarettes a day (Rienow and Rienow, 1967), still many Americans are content to just accept the contamination of the air. Newscasters simply give us the pollution index, and environmental degradation is thus normalized — we grow accustomed to the idea that air pollution is to be tolerated.

Air pollution has led to the potential problem of global warming due to a "greenhouse effect" (McKibben, 1989). The earth's temperature has risen about one degree during the last century presumably because pollutants trap the sun's radiation in the atmosphere. The principal polluting gases which are identified with the "greenhouse effect" are carbon dioxide (50% of such gases), chlorofluorocarbons (20%), methane (15%), and nitrous oxides and chlorine compounds. Based upon past warming and current pollution levels some scientists believe the earth will warm by about 5 degrees centigrade by the year 2030 (Babington, 1990). Other studies dispute this, noting that many projections are predicted on land-based climate records which are not totally accurate. Still others cite evidence of global warming by studying Tibetan ice cores. Perhaps a 5-degree warming in 40 years is too high for our ecosystem but the consequences of even half of that warming could be catastrophic. During the one-degree warming in the last century, sea levels have risen about 5 inches. If polar ice melts from global warming, sea levels could rise anywhere from three to 25 feet (McKibben, 1989).

Water Pollution

Just as vital to life as the air we breathe is the water that we drink. The hydrologic cycle is a purifying process that cleanses our water. Nevertheless, we have come to tolerate water pollution on a massive scale. About 60% of the water problem is due to industrial waste resulting from the production of paper, steel, and organic chemicals, as well as the refining of oil. We average 10,000 reported polluting incidents in and around U. S. waters per year, about 93% of which involve oil (U.S. Bureau of Census, 1989). Consider the Exxon Corporation spill of 11 million gallons of crude oil in Prince William Sound during March 1989. That spill alone polluted hundreds of miles of Alaskan shoreline. Some ecologists feel the area has been irreparably damaged. The recent deliberate emissions of oil in the Persian Gulf greatly add to ecological imbalance.

The blatant pollution of water through municipal waste (sewage) generated in homes and commercial establishments also plays an important role in interfering with the cycle of life. A particularly troubling source of water pollution is the result of agricultural waste. Carson (1962) vividly portrayed the health and even mental health consequences of toxic substances such as pesticides used in farming and gardening. Equally detrimental is the widespread use of chemical fertilizers which, when washed into rivers and lakes, produce algae blooms. These blooms then consume huge amounts of oxygen, thus destroying much aquatic life. It is becoming increasingly apparent that there is a tremendous need for quality water while the supply is being rapidly diminished (Jones, Gallagher, and McFalls, 1988; McKibben, 1989).

Nuclear Radiation and Solid Wastes

One form of pollution of high public concern is nuclear radiation. Though ionizing radiation is emitted from a number of sources used in everyday life, such as color TV, microwave ovens, and X-rays, the peacetime production of electricity from nuclear power and the manufacture and deployment of nuclear weapons are generally considered the major concerns of nuclear radiation. Strontium 90 and other radioactive substances released into the atmosphere through nuclear explosions return to the earth in rain or drift down as fallout. They then lodge in the tissues and organisms, thereby giving way to various carcinogenic processes. At present, there are approximately 70 nuclear power plants in the United States, each having a life span of approximately 30 to 40 years. While we all profit from the production of electricity at such plants, it would be an understatement to say that little foresight has been used in determining what will be done with nuclear waste and even the plants when they become inoperable. Nuclear wastes are presently being stored in shallow underground tanks across the United States, but the lethal consequences of such materials continue for hundreds of years. The risk of "leaks" from the nuclear wastes is still being calculated.

While nuclear radiation is seen as a hazardous component of environmental degradation, the disposal of various solid wastes appears on the surface to be largely a cosmetic problem (Rosenbaum, 1973). Just consider the recent controversy over diapers. Since disposable diapers were invented in the 1960s, their use has grown so that now 80% of all American parents of infants claim disposables as their diaper of choice. Thus, disposable diapers comprise about 2% of all solid waste. Two-income families almost consider disposable diapers a "necessity" but the fact that one-third of our landfills are expected to be full within five years is spurring renewed examination of this modern convenience (Woutat, 1989).

Although we have seen considerable progress in recycling efforts, the average municipal resident still throws away about three pounds of net refuse each day (U.S. Bureau of the Census, 1989). While the disposal of solid waste represents a threat to the aesthetic quality of our environment, it also poses a number of problems that are not cosmetic in nature. For instance, if plastics are dumped, they do not decompose readily. If these and other materials are incinerated, air pollution is the result. Especially in the case of plastics, burning such materials releases lethal and/or carcinogenic gases into the environment.

The Threat to Human Life

What should be apparent while considering all these forms of pollution and others, such as noise pollution, is that we are not simply concerning ourselves with the destruction of the aesthetic order. Instead, it is readily apparent that pollution is a threat to the survival of the human species, as well as other organisms in the environment. While we are still uncertain of many of the long-term health consequences of various types of pollution, it is becoming apparent that the distribution of illness is linked to environmental conditions (Carson, 1962; Duncan, 1961; Edelstein, 1988; Epstein,

1976). Certain areas or regions are becoming associated with certain health risks, due to environmental abuse. The high incidence of cancer, birth defects, and respiratory and neurological problems at the Love Canal in New York is but one example of the atrocious results of environmental abuse. The plethora of hazardous chemical wastes and other pollutants in the United States and other modernized societies is a sad commentary on the human enterprise since the garden of Eden.

Exploiting and Despoiling Land and Resources

In addition to these various forms of pollution, many societies throughout the world have been exploiting and despoiling the land and its resources. The Western engineering mentality has manifested an attempt to control nature and bend it toward our desires, yet any ecosystem is a complex matrix of life processes and can, in the long run, be adversely affected by actions that may appear to be immediately beneficial. It is now known that the Sahara Desert was created partly by overgrazing and deforestation and that its boundaries continue to enlarge. Dams, canals, and man-made waterways also have the potential of upsetting the ecological balance so essential to life in the marshes and wetlands. Though it takes anywhere between three hundred to a thousand years to produce an inch of topsoil, American development has been stripping it from various areas at the rate of seven inches a year. We are only beginning to recognize the consequences of such actions, but the despoiling of the land continues (Edelstein, 1988).

There have always been shortages of essential commodities to human life, but Americans appear to have been largely shielded from such a reality for decades. The American public is learning once again to deal with shortages in energy and certain natural resources. The United States has been successful in so many ways and is able to boast the highest gross national product of the world. Yet, with such heralded growth, this six percent of the world's population consumes over half of the world's resources. The modern world is exhausting irreplaceable commodities at an alarming rate, and it is certain that there will be critical shortages of many minerals or other raw materials in the future (Jones et al., 1988).

Resources Are Finite

The United States and other nations are dependent on a few types of energy resources, particularily the fossil fuels; and the need of these sources of energy is constantly increasing (Humphrey and Buttel, 1982; Robertson, 1980). This dependence on fossil fuels places us in a precarious position for several reasons. First, the supplies of these fossil fuels are finite and steadily decreasing. Second, many of them must be purchased from other countries, several of which have particularly unstable governments. Third, the dependence on these fuels fosters environmental degradation. The burning of coal, oil or natural gas to generate electricity obviously pollutes the atmosphere. Also, obtaining large reserves of oil beneath the ocean floor poses special ecological problems. Obviously, any attempt to meet our energy needs with nuclear power rather than fossil fuel poses a number of different but equally serious environmental risks.

The consideration of the problems of resource depletion and pollution makes more vivid the complex set of interrelationships among the various elements of any ecosystem. To whom much is given much is expected, and America is certainly accountable for its degradation of God's creation. In attempting to solve any problem, it would be wise to get at the roots or causes of the problem. We shall now turn in detail to these issues.

CAUSES OF ENVIRONMENTAL ABUSE

The problem of environmental abuse may be analyzed within the framework of the ecological complex, encompassing the relationships among population, organization, environment, and technology. Let us consider how each one of the elements in the ecological complex is related to the modification of the environment.

Population

Following the work of Thomas Malthus, Paul Ehrlich (1968) has asserted that world population growth is the cause of the environmental crisis and several other social problems. If environmental deterioration is an inevitable outcome of overpopulation, then it seems relatively straightforward that if we limit or decrease the population, then the environmental crisis will subside. While there are benefits to be derived from limiting the population, it is foolish to think that a decrease in the rate of population growth will alone solve the environmental crisis. Beisner (1990) provides an excellent critique of the shortcomings of a "Malthusian" population growth thesis that polemically predicts disaster for the environment. On the contrary, most of the rape and contamination of the planet is the result of nations who do not have critical problems of overpopulation. One American child poses a greater ecological threat to the earth than dozens of children from less developed countries. Population growth adds to the environmental crisis, but as we shall see, there are other factors that must be addressed to effectively deal with this problem.

Technology

One of the strongest critics of Ehrlich's thesis that overpopulation causes environmental deterioration is Barry Commoner (1971, 1988). Commoner contends that the environmental problem is not a result of population but of several other factors, most salient of which is technology. As described earlier, many of the problems that we are now facing on the environmental front are the results of sophisticated technologies used in industry and for transportation. Indeed, with most technological advances there are latent consequences that are oftentimes dysfunctional to the ecosystem. For example, electroplating refers to the process of creating a protective metal finishing on a wide variety of consumer products, from refrigerators to paper clips, supersonic jets to hubcaps. We all profit from electroplating but the actual process of creating the protective finish requires large amounts of water for baths and rinses. In the U. S. alone, about one billion gallons of toxic waste metal water are dumped daily into public sewage treatment plants from electroplating. Thus, we all benefit from electroplating but it is having a much bigger detrimental effect on our water than most of the inventors, marketers, or consumers ever realized.

As a result of technological advances often yielding latent negative consequences to our environment, some public and even religious groups have developed a position of antitechnology. Yet, technology is not of itself evil, but technology consists of applications of science that may be either beneficial or destructive. As such, it might be helpful to have some mechanism of control over the applications of science rather than passively accepting the latest technological developments. At present, there are informal controls in the form of official agencies responsible for protecting the environment and interest groups that seek to promote a concern for the environment in the face of technological development. In the future, it may be helpful to develop more comprehensive standards for assessing the ecological impact of technological developments.

Organization

Economic organization and our social orientation to the environment are two primary dimensions of the concept of organization that have utility for understanding environmental abuse. In the United States our large gross national product means jobs and an increased standard of living for most citizens. Yet, it has been pointed out by Schnaiberg (1975) that the desire for economic growth often contradicts the desire for environmental quality. Figure 1 may be helpful to conceptualize the societal-environmental dialectic as described by Schnaiberg. Although economic expansion is almost assumed to be a sacred dogma in the western world, it is dependent upon environmental manipulation — extraction and abuse — in industrialized societies. Increased environmental manipulation often interferes with the natural ecosystem and produces a number of ecological problems. These ecological problems not only threaten human welfare, but also create threats to further economic expansion. Thus, it appears that we are faced with the dilemma of balancing ecological abuse and economic expansion.

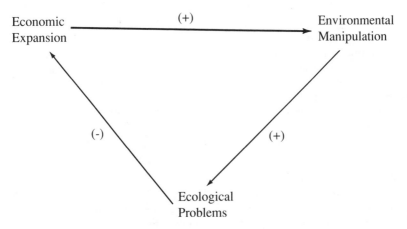

Figure 1. A model of Schnaiberg's Societal-Environmental Dialectic.

Commoner (1971) and Schnaiberg (1980) have both pointed out that the power of large corporations poses further threats for the environment. Specifically, the growth of monopoly sector firms, which are very technologically advanced and involved in resource-intensive production, has changed the nature of industry and marketing. These large firms that participate in oligopolistic markets attempt to cajole and manipulate consumers through advertising to continually consume more goods and services than they really need (Humphrey and Buttel, 1982). In addition, monopoly sector firms attempt to bias state policy toward the interest of large corporations to facilitate further economic expansion. As such, the decisions as to how much economic expansion should take place are held in the hands of a very small collection of individuals.

In our society, pollution, land misuse, and resource depletion are oftentimes identified as "costs" of a healthy economy. A relaxation of environmental standards during a time of economic recession is a hazardous policy for the environment. Thus, according to Schnaiberg (1975; 1980) and others, changes must be made in the economic organization of society if we are to avoid further ecological problems. While many large corporations try to focus attention upon litter and other such activities of consumers in creating environmental problems, Schnaiberg's work is most illuminating; he points out that the production institutions are the primary abusers of the environment (see also Domhoff, 1979, pp. 183,191).

In addition to our present economic organization, it is helpful to reflect on our social orientation to the environment to understand why abuse occurs. The biblical book of Genesis states that humankind, created in God's image, was given dominion over creation. While this has erroneously been taken as a sanction to dominate nature and exploit the environment, in reality it is a commission to be a steward of the earth. The fall of humankind not only resulted in an alienation from God and humanity, but it also alienated individuals from their environment (Genesis 3:17-19).

The values and attitudes so common to the American spirit of economic expansion are a manifestation of humanity's disrupted relationship to the environment. Material-ism, progress, and the exploitation of the environment typify the disrupted relationship between humanity and the environment. Jeremiah (2:7, 12-13) declares:

> And I brought you into a plentiful land to enjoy its fruits and its good things. But when you came in you defiled my land, and made my heritage an abomination . . . Be appalled, O heavens, at this, be shocked, be utterly desolate, says the Lord, for my people have committed two evils: they have forsaken me, the fountain of living waters, and hewed out cisterns for themselves, broken cisterns, that can hold no water.

In these passages, disobedience to God and the degradation of the environment are revealed as two evils. The land which God gave to Israel was polluted and abused. In addition the people turned from God, the fountain of "living waters" to "false gods," personified as "broken cisterns," which are not able to hold water. Though the population of the earth is much greater and our technology much more sophisticated for modifying the environment, humanity's orientation to the environment has changed very little.

While both population and technology are affecting the magnitude of ecological abuse in the world, the major cause of ecological disruption is humanity's alienation from the environment and desire for self-sufficiency and economic improvement. These forces permeate almost all of our lives but are also imbedded in the social structures that institutionalize the degradation of the environment. Although eliminating environmental degradation is a formidable task, it is one that demands our attention and response. Still the question remains, how can we help turn the tide toward environmental responsibility? To answer this question the next section discusses a framework for Christian action to help solve the problems of environmental abuse and offers some specific ways to bring about the healing of creation.

THE HEALING OF CREATION

> *For the creation waits with eager longing for the revealing of the children of God; for the creation was subjected to futility, not of its own will but by the will of the one who subjected it in hope that the creation itself will be set free from its bondage to decay and will obtain the freedom of the glory of the children of God. We know that the whole creation has been groaning in labor pains until now; and not only the creation, but we ourselves, who have the first fruits of the Spirit, groan inwardly while we wait for adoption, the redemption of our bodies* (Romans 8:19-23 NRSV).

In this portion of Scripture we get a picture of the travail that creation is now in, as well as the expectation of its redemption. At that future day when believers will be completely redeemed, so too will nature be ransomed from its present condition. Speaking of Christ, Paul also said, "For in him all the fullness of God was pleased to dwell, and through him to reconcile to himself all things, whether on earth or in heaven, making peace by the blood of his cross" (Colossians 1:19-20). Indeed, Christ's work of redemption extends not only to humanity, but to all things on earth and in the skies — the universe. Christians are to imitate Christ and participate in the healing of creation here and now (Schaeffer, 1970).

A Call For a New Orientation

The healing of creation begins with understanding and repentance. We must all recognize that we benefit from and participate in environmental abuse and be willing to turn to God for a more appropriate relationship to the environment. This new orientation to the environment is based upon several basic premises. First, we must recognize that "the earth is the Lord's and the fullness thereof, the world and those who dwell therein" (Psalm 24:1). Of all people, Christians should have a deep respect for the environment (Barnette, 1972).

Second, we should realize that the Bible does not teach any radical separation between the material and the spiritual (Granberg-Michaelson, 1981; Schaeffer, 1970). The schism between the material and the spiritual is characteristic of the modern mind set, particularly influenced by Plato. On the other hand, God relates to people and their land simultaneously (e.g., 2 Chronicles 7:14). Much of Christendom has been characterized by a lack of concern about environmental issues, and the Church remains relatively silent on environmental concerns. This is readily understandable given our preoccupation with personal matters, but God would also have us to be concerned about the land entrusted to us.

Third, our orientation to the environment should include our recognition of our dependence on it. It is interesting to note that in the creation account God made heaven and earth before humankind. Too often we assume that we can use the products of creation to bring about our desired goals. If the healing of creation is to come about, we must first recognize that we are dependent on our environment.

Finally, we must rediscover the meaning of the term *steward* (Barnette, 1972, Beisner, 1990). All too often the modern mind has interpreted the steward's role in terms of utilitarianism and management of the environment (Wilkinson, 1980). The biblical concept of stewardship does not involve mastery over nature, but a tending and serving of the earth (Genesis 2:1-25). This is also the tradition of some oriental cultures. We must be aware that God has created a world with natural purifying processes, and that our style of living should be congruent with these processes so that environmental restoration can become a reality.

Ecological Synthesis Preferred

A new orientation to the environment must, of necessity, foster a new orientation to economic organization (Rifkin, 1980). As discussed previously, continual economic expansion poses severe threats to the quality of the environment. Thus, some scholars have suggested that there must be limits to growth (Meadows et al., 1972). As pointed out by Allan Schnaiberg (1980), there are three basic positions reflecting the dialectic between economic-environmental relations. The first position, described as the economic synthesis, posits that there should be continued economic expansion without attempting to ameliorate environmental problems. The second position, which may represent a midpoint on the continuum, is planned security. From this position, business should continue as usual but with limited environmental protection. The environmental problems that are the most acute should bring about a regulation of activities. The final position, termed the ecological synthesis, entails major reforms to reduce environmental degradation through extensive controls over production, as well as the demands for goods and services. The ideal of the ecological synthesis is to create economic organization that is based on the use of renewable resources only.

In the United States, we have often followed the economic synthesis, but in recent times have approached planned scarcity. However, as Schnaiberg (1980) has pointed out, there is a propensity to return to the economic synthesis during times of economic recession. The economic synthesis cannot be sustained indefinitely, and to Christians, any support for the return to the economic synthesis is irresponsible. Recognizing our accountability to God, we must foster efforts toward the ecological synthesis, regardless of current political or economic conditions. Moreover, it needs to be noted that clean air and water laws also contribute to economic development. Jones et al. (1988) claim that clean air and water laws create 10 jobs for every one they have eliminated.

It should not be assumed that Western and democratic societies based on free enterprise are the only societies responsible for pollution. While the United States must assume substantial responsibility for the environment, it is becoming increasingly apparent that other societies have also abused the earth. Japan is another example of a major economic entity which has grossly polluted the environment. Many of the communist societies have also raped the environment to bolster their social progress. Numerous coal-burning electric plants in communist nations have yielded poor air quality and acid rain. The Soviet Union is facing major ecological problems because of gross water pollution and deforestation. Hale (1990, p. 17) asserts that *"Czechoslovakia is the most polluted country in Europe—perhaps in the world."* It appears that command economies have also fallen prey to the societal-environmental dialectic described by Schnaiberg.

Which Environmental Movement?

This movement toward the ecological synthesis necessitates a certain orientation toward participation in the environment movement in America. For simplicity, we may identify two major classes of participants in the environment based on the work of Schnaiberg (1980). The first category of participants includes the cosmetologists and the meliorists, and it primarily emphasizes consumer action in the solution of environmental problems. Concerns about problems of the environment, from this perspective, focus on the general patterns of consumer waste of resources and their disposal. In actuality, monopoly sector firms are favorably disposed to this category of environmentalism. As Marine (1969), has pointed out, many large firms have learned how to "rape" America and appease most of the pro-environmental public. For example, the "Keep America Beautiful" campaign was sponsored by the bottling and packaging industries to focus on littering as one of the chief problems of environmental abuse. It is gratifying to know that there is a growing consciousness of keeping America beautiful, and the control of litter is a laudable enterprise. However, if we expect to resolve the problems of environmental abuse through the alteration of consumer actions alone, we will fall short of our God-given call for the healing of the environment.

The second general category of participants in the environmental movement is comprised of the reformists and radicals. These individuals identify the main problems of environmental abuse as stemming from the nature of production and socioeconomic organization. In particular, reformists contend that production expansion produces ecological problems of all types: therefore, economic and political incentives need to be established to foster care of the environment (Schnaiberg, 1980). Thus, they seek governmental and legislative actions to affect the nature of production in the society. While some of the tenets of the radical position, such as the total restructuring of the capitalist industrial system, may be incongruent with some Christian perspectives, certainly Christians must be aware of, and willing to seek change in, the economic organization of our society. God calls on Christians to participate in the environmental movement at various levels. While environmental concern at any level is to be highly prized, we must recognize that both the production and consumption segments must be modified if any substantial healing is to occur. Thus, the specific ways in which we can help bring about the healing of creation are numerous and varied in scope.

ENVIRONMENTAL RESPONSIBILITY AND THE CALL TO ACTION

Repentance

The healing of creation can begin only with repentance. We must recognize that environmental abuse is a sin and seek forgiveness for our own personal actions which have violated God's commands. This brings about a new orientation toward the environment and economic organization. A change in attitudes and values must ensue as we reevaluate our own personal lifestyle and assume responsibility for our actions.

We must be more disciplined in our consumption and conservation of the earth's resources and recognize with the Apostle Paul that if we have food and clothing, we have the essentials of our earthly needs (1 Timothy 6:8). Besides altering our personal lifestyle, we must be willing to participate in collective action to preserve and heal God's creation. We are called to be stewards or caretakers of the earth. When we see ourselves or others abusing God's creation, we need to respond to our role as stewards. Above all, as Christians we should be vividly aware of our dependence on God for the solution of this or any problem (Wilkinson, 1980).

Prayer and Fasting

One of the most important steps for bringing about the healing of creation while recognizing our dependence on God is prayer and fasting. On numerous occasions God reveals himself as one who bestows grace on a righteous people. Believers should recognize that they have tremendous opportunities to alter the course of earthly affairs (e.g., Genesis 18:16-33; 2 Chronicles 7:14). Christians can participate in prayer and fasting to turn the tide of environmental abuse. As Prince (1973) describes, believers have access to powerful tools to change the course of history and bring deliverance and victory of God's reign on earth. Christians have the privilege of interceding before God to change the hearts of men and women to bring about the healing of creation. Prayerful reflection, personally and corporately, is an essential prerequisite for the thoughtful, healing action.

Recycling

Another way to aid environmental care is through recycling. Many types of objects which are discarded impose a serious problem in terms of solid waste disposal but can be readily used again and again. Recycling efforts have begun in the United States, with impressive gains in the recycling of paper, glass, and aluminum cans in the U.S. over the last 25 years (U.S. Bureau of the Census, 1989). We need to project an image that recyclers are good citizens and create recycling habits. We are also beginning to learn that recycling is cost-effective and profitable for our society. Education should encourage recycling to join the three R's in the classroom

Waste Reduction and Exchange

In addition to recycling resources, waste reduction and exchange will foster environmental health. Simplicity of lifestyle will aid the reduction of waste among consumers, and Christians should play an active role in the places of their employment to reduce waste. Though waste utilization has been a way of life in China for centuries, there are now a number of industries that are experimenting with waste exchange. Many industrial processes result in unwanted and oftentimes toxic substances. Yet, chemists are finding that these substances can be neutralized with other substances which frequently are the refuse of different industrial processes. Thus, two waste products can be neutralized if the proper combination of substances and conditions is established. In addition, further incentives should be given to programs which recycle waste products into energy or other needed resources. For example, sewage can be treated and utilized as fertilizer in agriculture. Procter and Gamble, Inc. have found that some disposable diapers can be mixed with other garbage to create a compost that can be used for landscaping or fertilizer. We have only begun to develop ways to exchange wastes and/ or recycle them, and such endeavors hold great promise in facilitating ecological care.

Collective Action

Participation in collective action to implement policies of environmental quality is certainly another way in which citizens can hasten respect for the environment. Such participation should lead to either explicit policy change by private industry or legislative control over production as well as consumption and disposal. Groups such as the National Wildlife Federation, Sierra Club, National Audubon Society, Wilderness Society, and Green Peace all work for environmental preservation, although they vary in their strategies for effecting change (Petulla, 1987). Christians should be willing to become actively involved in citizen organizations that seek to maintain and/or regain environmental quality but should gain an awareness of the organization's goals and strategies before joining their forces. Otherwise one may find that supporting one of these organizations means indirect support for some of the organization's goals and strategies of change which may be morally objectionable.

Though such grass roots organizations feel powerless against major corporations, their effects are, nevertheless, being felt in numerous ways on the environmental front. A recent example is how fast-food chains are now changing their packaging materials from plastic to paper products which are biodegradable or recyclable. It should further be recognized that there is nothing wrong with economic expansion if it is based upon operations that are not damaging to the environment. Industry that functions on renewable resources is most desired if we are to move in the direction of the ecological synthesis. Such industries should be given incentives for continued operation, while industries that are major polluters should be increasingly "taxed" for their offenses.

Church Involvement

In addition to participating in collective action in secular organizations, Christians should support and stimulate church activity to aid ecological quality. Many Christian denominations have already established an official position to promote the preservation and enhancement of the natural world (Brill, 1979; United Methodist Church, 1980). Christians should be aware of their Church's position on the environment and spur collective action to aid the healing of creation. There is no excuse for environmental irresponsibility in the church.

Technological Controls and Innovations

While technology is not the root cause of the environmental crisis, it does play a role in escalating the environmental problem Awareness of the effects of technological development is essential to the survival of the world and will aid the beneficial management of the ecological complex (Wilkinson, 1980). Along with the technological controls, incentives should be given for the development of new forms of energy to deal with the problems of resource depletion. God is calling scientists to get involved in the development of solar energy, ocean tidal power, and geothermal energy.

We need to make several changes in energy-related policies to avoid ecocatastrophe due to the "greenhouse effect." Greater use of natural gas will reduce several critical air pollutants. Coal must be burned more efficiently, perhaps through pressurized, fluidized bed boilers, and "stack gases" should be cleansed to cut emissions of sulfur dioxides and nitrogen oxides (U. S. Committee on Energy and Commerce, HR, 1988). More efficient residential use of energy and greater use of hydrogen fuels will also prolong and preserve the life of our environment (Winegar, 1989).

Education

Finally, educating the public remains one of the most monumental tasks essential to the healing of creation. We are all responsible for environmental degradation, and therefore, we must modify our lifestyles and the socioeconomic organization of our society. For all too long, pollution has been regarded as "beautiful" since it signaled economic expansion and further industrialization. Environmental quality had been regarded as a luxury by the public in the face of economic recession (Dunlap and Dillman, 1976). Though maintaining environmental quality is costly, environmental degradation is more costly. Air and water pollution alone cause over 20 billion dollars worth of damage annually to health, property, and agriculture in the United States (Julian, 1980). Medical researchers are discovering that we have poisoned our environment in a number of ways by noting its lethal consequences on the human race.

The public must recognize that the recycling of resources is profitable and that environmental concern creates jobs as well (Jones, et, al., 1988). Increasingly, we must recognize that we should not abuse natural resources, but utilize them in an equitable, nonabusive manner (Beisner, 1990; Wilkinson, 1980). Today, nature is groaning in travail to be released from its corruption. Jesus offers us an opportunity to participate in His redemptive work of the healing of the spiritual and the material world.

Study and Discussion
Questions

1. Why is there still an environmental crisis if the U. S. federal government created the Environmental Protection Agency in 1970?

2. Has America made progress in reducing air pollution during the last two decades? Describe the changes that have occurred.

3. From a sociological perspective, what are the major causes of environmental abuse?

4. Extend your answer to question 3 by incorporating your understanding of the Bible. Still try to think sociologically but use biblical principles to further guide your thinking.

5. Select the three portions of Scripture which you think best describe why we should be environmentally responsible. How often are these ideas discussed in your church? Why?

6. What is the societal-environment dialectic as described by Schnaiberg? Is this something that applies only to America or is it universal to all human societies? How do you know?

7. Some people argue that environmental abuse is simply the cost of progress: "If you want progress, jobs, and a strong national economy, you simply have to engage in using the earth." Do you agree? Why do you hold such a position?

8. Part a. Imagine that you have been asked to address a Sunday school class at your church on the subject of environmental responsibility. It is a class comprised of adults. What would you cover in 45 minutes?

   Part b. Repeat the above question, but this time assume you will be addressing 20 six- and seven-year-olds.

9. How would you describe the environmental movement in America today? Is it dominated by cosmetologists or reformists? How do you think the goals of these two constituencies should be represented in a federal policy on the environment?

10. Sit down and think about your home, car, lifestyle, and consumption patterns. What could you do to live your life with greater environmental responsibility? Perhaps some of the things you want to do, you cannot do yet because of the financial cost involved. If so, what can you do within the next five years to accomplish your goals? Once you have developed your plan, share it with a good friend or family member and explain why you think you should follow through on it.

References

Babington, Charles, "Greenhouse debate warming up." *Journal of NIH Research,* 2:39, 41-42, 1990.

Barnette, Henlee, H., *The Church and the Ecological Crisis.* Grand Rapids, MI: Eerdmans, 1972.

Beisner, E. Calvin, *Prospects for Growth: A Biblical View of Population, Resources, and the Future.* Westchester, IL: Crossway Books, 1990.

Brill, Earl H., *The Christian Moral Vision.* New York: Sebury, 1979.

Carson, Rachel, *Silent Spring.* Boston: Houghton Mifflin, 1962.

Commoner, Barry, *The Closing Circle.* New York: Alfred Knopf, 1971.

Commoner, Barry, "The environment." Pp. 121-169 in Peter Borrelli (ed.), *Crossroads: Environmental Priorities for the Future.* Washington, D. C.: Island Press, 1988.

Domhoff, C. William, *The Powers That Be: Process of Ruling Class Domination in America.* New York: Vintage Books, 1979.

Duncan, Otis D., "From social system to ecosystem." *Sociological Inquiry,* 31:140-49, 1961.

Dunlap, Riley E., and Donna A. Dillman, "Decline in public support for environmental protection: evidence from a 1970-1974 panel study." *Rural Sociology,* 41:382-390, 1976.

Edelstein, Michael R., *Contaminated Communities.* Boulder, CO: Westview Press, 1988.

Ehrlich, Paul R., *The Population Bomb.* New York: Ballantine, 1968.

Epstein, Samuel S., "The political and economic basis of cancer." *Technology Review,* 78:34-43, 1976.

Granberg-Michaelson, Wes, "At the dawn of the new creation." *Sojourners,* 10:12-16, 1981.

Hale, Ellen, "Clean capitalists, dirty communists." *Journal and Courier,* (Lafayette, IN): 13, 17, July 29, 1990.

Hawley, Amos H., *Human Ecology: A Theory of Community Structure.* New York: Ronald Press, 1950.

Humphrey, Craig R., and Frederick R. Buttel, *Environment, Energy, and Society.* Belmont, CA: Wadsworth, 1982.

Jones, Brian J., Bernard J. Gallagher III, and Joseph A. McFalls, Jr., *Social Problems: Issues, Opinions, and Solutions.* New York: McGraw-Hill, 1988.

Julian, Joseph, *Social Problems.* Third Edition. Englewood Cliffs, NJ: Prentice-Hall, 1980.

Marine, Gene, *America the Raped.* New York: Simon and Schuster, 1969.

McKibben, Bill, *The End of Nature.* New York: Random House, 1989.

Meadows, Donella H., Dennis L. Meadows, Jorgen Randers and William W. Behrens III, *The Limits to Growth.* New York: Universe, 1972.

Neubeck, Kenneth J., *Social Problems: A Critical Approach* (second edition) New York: McGraw-Hill, 1986.

Parsons, Howard L. (ed), *Marx and Engels on Ecology.* Westport, CT: Greenwood Press, 1977.

Petulla, Joseph M., *Environmental Protection in the United States.* San Francisco: San Francisco Study Center, 1987.

Prince, Derek, *Shaping History Through Prayer and Fasting.* Old Tappan, NJ: Revel, 1073.

Rifkin, Jeremy, *Entropy: A New World View.* New York: Viking, 1980.

Robertson, Ian, *Social Problems,* Second Edition. New York: Viking, 1980.

Rosenbaum, Walter A., *The Politics of Environmental Concern.* New York: Prager, 1973.

Sagoff, Mark, *The Economy of the Earth.* New York: Cambridge, 1988.

Schaeffer, Francis A., *Pollution and the Death of Man: The Christian View of Ecology.* Wheaton, IL: Tyndale, 1970.

Schnaiberg, Allan, *The Environment: From Surplus to Scarcity.* New York: Oxford University, 1980.

United Methodist Church (Board of Church and Society), *Social Principles of the United Methodist Church.* Washington, D. C.: United Methodist Church, 1980.

U. S. Bureau of the Census, *Statistical Abstracts of the United Sates: 1989* (109th edition). Washington, D. C.: U. S. Government Printing Office, 1989.

U. S. Committee on Energy and Commerce, House of Representatives, *Hearings: Acid Deposition Control Act of 1987.* Washington, D. C.: U. S. Government Printing Office, 1988.

Wilkinson, Loren (eds.) *Earthkeeping: Christian Stewardship of Natural Resources.* Grand Rapids, MI: Eerdmans, 1980.

Winegar, Karin, "Scorched Earth." *Star Tribune* (Minneapolis-St. Paul), 1E-4E, November 19, 1989.

Woutat, Donald, "Diapers to dirt." *Star Tribune* (Minneapolis-St. Paul), 1, 6, 8, November 19, 1989.

CHAPTER 5
UNEMPLOYMENT: INTRODUCTION

The problem of employment is one that has been central to sociology theory. Functionalists as early as Durkheim have seen it as an important basis for differentiation in society. Georg Simmel, an early theorist whose works have influenced functionalist thought as well as conflict theory, asserted that it was a person's "calling" or vocation that linked the individual to the social order. Work was basic to Karl Marx's understanding of person. It was through meaningful labor that men and women expressed their humanity. One of Marx's basic objections to capitalism is that it alienated or estranged workers from their labor.

Employment is perhaps the most important way individuals are given a place in the society. It links persons to the larger social order. Without a "job" to perform (whether it is paid or unpaid), persons tend to feel isolated and peripheral to the "real" world. College students, currently in training for their life's work, may be able to empathize partly with the important link that employment provides with the social world.

The employment sector, however, is part of a larger social system; and it is influenced by what goes on in other sectors. For example, in the last article Professor Ferraro discussed the problems caused by our use of fossil fuels to the ecosystem. Why hasn't the problem been corrected? One answer rests with the economic implications and their impact on employment. Forcing industry to clean up its act can lead companies to close rather than to comply, thus leaving people unemployed. Government, economic policies, the economic situation, and military activities are among the many other factors that affect employment rates. A revolt among taxpayers demonstrated by a refusal to vote for increased levies for education may impact not only the quality of education in that community but the employment rate for teachers. An upsurge or decrease in military spending would have its correlative effect on employment among the industries that rely on military spending. In other words, a change that is enacted in other parts of the system may have unintended consequences for the employment sector.

The interaction among parts, as Professor Lyon correctly observes, is not limited to changes within a society. His observations about a world recession and the effects of our Western policies on other countries demonstrate once again the importance of taking a world systems perspective when approaching most social problems. Given the interdependence of the different national economies, the measures we may use to alleviate unemployment problems in one society may increase the unemployment rates in other areas of the world.

The interdependence of nations in the world economy may be illustrated by protective tariffs and quotas used to keep out some goods manufactured in other countries. The United States may be trying to protect American jobs by restricting imports, but the cost to other countries may be high. This interdependence of nations raises a significant question for Christians: Who is my neighbor? Is one's neighbor only the textile worker in New England or the automotive worker in Detroit? Or is one's neighbor the worker in Bangladesh or the "wetback" from Mexico who illegally enters this country in search of work? In the parable of the Good Samaritan Jesus teaches us that as Christians we are to act "neighborly" and show mercy to those in need. Surely this applies to the international scene as well as to our own nation.

Professor Lyon's article also employs a sociological perspective that is derived from symbolic interaction theory. In sociology, the interaction perspective is concerned about the meaning that persons attach to their speech and activities. In line with this thought, Lyon correctly observes that we must distinguish between "work" (i.e. God-given activity) and "employment" (the fallen world's answer to work). Lyon further suggests that we redefine the "Protestant Work Ethic" as that which "restores work to its true meaning of a 'labour of love' before God." The implication of these different labels and the meanings that Christians may attach to them deserve even more consideration than Professor Lyon was able to give them here.

The section headed "Agenda for Action" makes an important point that we should not renege on our responsibility to ameliorate any of the social problems discussed in this book. As Christians we know that prayer does make a difference, not only in our personal lives but in our corporate lives. Sincere and heartfelt prayer for social concerns acts on our belief that God not only has a plan for the world but also has the power to intervene in both personal lives and in the social order. As Professor Lyon emphasizes, "We are repeatedly enjoined to pray — especially for those with power to influence the direction of society." As Christians we cannot focus so intently on the analysis of social problems that we neglect to engage in this powerful activity.

It is from a stance of prayer that we have the courage and power to pursue other priorities for action dealing with the employment issue. Through prayer and reflecting on biblical teachings, the Holy Spirit can give us attitudes of compassion toward the unemployed and can give us a new vision about work in our own lives. It is through prayer that we can be empowered to work for social justice, both for our local communities and in the larger world community.

The reader might question how prayer, a seemingly private devotional act, fits with sociology, the scientific study of social groups. Taking what is known as a symbolic interactionist approach that emphasizes the importance of subjective meaning attached to social phenomena allows us to consider the effects of prayer on human behavior. W. I. Thomas, an early symbolic interactionist, gave us the famous Thomas Theorem: "If men and women define situations as real, they are real in their consequences." Survey research by Poloma and Gallup (*Varieties of Prayer*, 1991) and Poloma and Pendleton (*Religiosity and Well Being*, 1991) clearly demonstrates that prayer can impact people's lives in such a way that, in turn, their action impacts the social order. For example, Poloma and Gallup found that prayer was related to religiously motivated political activism. Devout pray-ers were more likely to become involved in political causes than those who were less devout.

Professor Lyon rightly emphasizes God's compassion for those who are poor through no fault of their own. Not only did Jesus insist that we should do for others what we would have others to do for us if we were poor (Matthew 12:7), but the Apostle Paul insists that those of us who are strong — personally, as well as corporately — should help the less fortunate (Romans 15:1; Galatians 6:2). This concern for the poor, the unemployed, not only finds abundance of support in the great prophets, such as Amos, Hosea, and Micah, but actually goes back to the founding legislation of the ancient nation of Israel (Leviticus 19:9-10; 23:22; Deuteronomy 15:7-11; 24:10-22). The Christian student certainly cannot avoid wrestling with Professor Lyon's arguments which are rooted in Scripture. What changes would you make in our system and how?

As we conclude this first section of *A Christian Approach to Social Problems* it should be apparent that there is no single sociological perspective that can yield a complete picture of the socio-economic issues confronting society. The different perspectives discussed in Professor De Santo's introductory article are complementary and provide different emphases and descriptions of the various problems we have included in this section for discussion. The city, economics, sociopolitics, the environment, and work may all be approached through more than one sociological perspective. These differing approaches demonstrate the complexity of each issue and the difficulties in finding feasible solutions.

UNEMPLOYMENT
David Lyon

We live in an era of long-term global unemployment on an unprecedented scale. "Permanent unemployment" may be a better way to describe it. Many millions of people in the North of England and as many as a third of the potential working population of the South are affected. This spells for them not only miserable poverty and economic hardship, but also a debilitating sense of social worthlessness. The problems, which baffle the best social scientists, are also political dynamite. The importance of the issues should not be underestimated. If social and political concern is lacking over unemployment, then something is wrong with our very estimate of what it means to be human.

Social Problem or Trouble?

From a sociological perspective, unemployment becomes significant when it affects a large proportion of the working population. As C. Wright Mills pointed out, unemployment is only a "personal trouble" when only one person in a city of 100,000 does not have a job. It becomes a "public issue of social structure" when, say, fifteen million of fifty million employees are jobless. In this case "the very structure of opportunities has collapsed" (Mills, 19509, 1970, p. 15). So, he correctly observes, "Both the correct statement of the problem and the range of possible solutions require us to consider the economic and political institutions of the society, and not merely the personal situation and character of a scatter of individuals."

Why Not Christian Perspectives?

While a sociological perspective is required in order to understand unemployment, such perspectives do not appear in a vacuum. It is not mere detached academic interest that makes unemployment a "social problem." Human well-being is adversely affected, and it may be felt that injustice is present. In the growing mound of literature on unemployment, differing viewpoints are frequently related to either capitalist free-market economics or to more socialist-style analyses and policies. But how often is a Christian voice heard? If it is indeed a fundamentally *human* issue we are considering, then it is imperative that Christian perspectives be developed. Some of the debate in fact involves a discussion of matters historically linked with Protestantism, the work ethic, so Christian views ought to be articulated for that reason alone. A more basic reason, as we shall see, is that God is concerned about unemployment, both at the personal and the social structural level. Christian concern should grow out of neighbor-love, and be expressed in the effort to understand and to act in a demonstrable Christian fashion.

What follows is designed to raise awareness about unemployment, to hint at some biblical guidelines contributing to the development of a Christian perspective, and lastly, to suggest how an agenda for action might be constructed. Throughout, while the emphasis is on the *social* problems of unemployment, attention is also given to the *economic* and *political* dimensions, which are clearly inseparable from the social.

THE PROBLEMS

Unemployment is not simply going to go away. The fact that no easy solutions are available does not mean that solutions should not be sought. This applies both to the long- and to the short-term. For the first time since the interwar depression, unemployment has become a central fact of the social world, although as we shall see, the issues are somewhat different now. Millions of people, through no fault of their own, are jobless. They are searching for work that is unavailable. Technically, it is a problem of *flow* in and out of the job-market, to which we shall return below. For the majority, this means not only economic difficulty, but social stigma. To Christians, above all, this should call forth not only compassion for the sufferers, but also a challenging inquiry into the causes of inhumanity and apparent injustice.

Keynes — Full Employment

The historical situation may be read like this: like the United States, Britain was in an economic slump after the First World War, caused mainly by declining demand for the products of staple industries. Economist John Maynard Keynes urged the government to induce a recovery by increasing public spending, but to no avail. But America's President Roosevelt did just that, inaugurating his "New Deal" in 1933 and showing exactly what could be done to increase employment. In Britain, towards the end of the 1930s employment rose with re-armament (which, like the New Deal was a "state" initiative), further strengthening the Keynesian case. After the Second World War "full employment" became a standard platform of successive British governments, now persuaded by the Keynesian doctrine. This was an integral aspect of the famous "welfare state" Beveridge report of 1942. People were seen to have a "right to work," a sentiment that has fallen on hard times in recent years. Post-war economies were expanded, and purchasing power increased.

Thatcher/Reagan — Inflation

Here, however, was the rub. Within two decades inflation also rose to such a level that governments eventually stepped in to control that. The result? Under Thatcher in Britain, and Reagan in the United States of America, spending in the area of social welfare programs have been cut, and the big goal has come to be monetary stability. Like it or not, there is a direct connection between this and rising unemployment. Of course, no one wants inflation, but is it a greater evil than unemployment? This is a key question facing all of us. While it is true that the issues are extremely complex, and it would be foolish to blame all ills on "government," it is equally true that government plays a crucial role in deciding between these twin evils. Christians should be making economically informed efforts to swing governments in a more truly human direction.

Why High Unemployment?

Different diagnoses, as we have already seen, lead to different proposals as to how to cope with unemployment. But searching for causes of today's situation is a daunting task. The widest level on which the question can be answered is that we are in the middle of a world recession, in which falling demand has led to industrial contraction on a vast scale, and this to lay-offs. The recession was partly triggered by the skyrocketing oil prices in the early 1970s, but even that cannot explain all the features of world economic crisis! Other factors responsible for unemployment include the "microchip revolution" in which the electronic wizardry of information technology is displacing jobs. This includes jobs in the service sector, the very sector which could once be relied on to soak up lost jobs in manufacturing.

Recession Is World-Wide

The fact that it is a *world* recession, and not one simply affecting a few thousand advanced nations, means that, from a Christian perspective at least, the effects of our Western policies on others must be given careful consideration. Many manufacturing industries are being relocated in the South of the globe. If business enterprises in the North simply try to protect themselves, they may well be denying a market to their far poorer global neighbors, whose unemployment problems are considerably deeper than ours in the North. Already the falling prices of their raw materials along with the rising costs of their imports has led to enormous debt difficulties which only those with vision for *international justice* will ever be able to tackle.

All these factors and others have to be borne in mind by any who truly wish to understand and contribute to policy-directions relating to unemployment. No one knows whether there will be an economic recovery in the last years of the twentieth century. Even if there is, return to the high employment levels of the 1960s is far from likely in the North, while the situation in the South is even more difficult to predict.

THE MEANING OF UNEMPLOYMENT

Lest we fail to ground this discussion in human realities, let us consider who exactly *are* the unemployed? It is all very well to note that in the state in which I first wrote this — Michigan — the unemployment rate was over 14.4 percent. This was due largely to the crippled condition of the auto industry. In West Yorkshire, England, where I have my home, black unemployment has quadrupled over the last several years in our decaying industrial cities. But what do these statistics mean? Who is affected the most?

Unemployment Defined

For a start, note that "unemployment" refers to a *rate* of joblessness. Not only are many jobs opportunities drying up, but more and more people are chasing them. The unemployment registers, where we get our figures are filled with details of people without jobs — people who are fit, available, and looking for work. The unemployed are not therefore like a stagnant pool, but rather, like a bathtub with taps running, in which the drainage holes are becoming increasingly blocked. In Britain, 400,000 a month do finds jobs, and some vacancies do remain unfilled. But more people are taking longer to find employment.

Scapegoats? Blame the Victim!

Now we enter a controversial field. Why are those "drainage holes" so badly blocked? It is very common to look around for scapegoats, upon whom blame for unemployment may be pinned. Frequently, the unemployed are thought of as "scroungers." This does not usually refer to healthy, "frictional" unemployment, where people are merely in transit from one job to another, but to folk who claim benefits even though they have a part-time job, or, more likely, to those who are "unemployable" because they refuse jobs offered. Even here, we must distinguish between individuals who stay unemployed until something exactly like their previous job turns up and those who are willing to take any job and use it as a stepping-stone to the next. No one wishes to deny that there are fraudulent and lazy people around, who will jump at any opportunity to get something for nothing. But consider two other things. In the first place, what job would *you* be willing to take if you were laid off today? In the second place, the "scrounger" argument implies that much unemployment may be blamed on laziness. But responsible research in Britain (The Supplementary Benefits Commission) suggests only a small percentage of the unemployed are in this category at all.

The "why work?" syndrome, otherwise known as the "unemployment trap" affects government policy — government reports not withstanding. They say that benefits are too high, so potential workers have few incentives to work. But in fact, hundreds of thousands of individuals work for less than they would receive on benefits.

Other scapegoats may also be found, such as the inordinate demands of labor unions. But a cold look at the figures suggests two things. First, that the problems facing western and other economies are what economists call *structural* and *cyclical* unemployment. As mentioned earlier, things have been made no easier in the last decade by the oil crisis — which helped unemployment and inflation *simultaneously* to rise — and other factors such as the rapid development of foreign competition. Second, the vast majority of the unemployed are involuntarily out of work, and would prefer to have a job. Not only is unemployment hitting areas used to such troubles, it is spreading cancerously into traditional areas of stable, high employment, such as the Southeast of England, the Pacific Northwest, and most major urban industrial centers.

So who is most affected? Four groups in particular: (1) young people leaving school (who are the victims of a "last hired, first fired" policy), (2) long-term unemployed, predominantly male (well over a quarter of the unemployed in Britain have not had work for over a year, and many of them are unskilled), (3) blacks, especially in inner-urban areas, and (4) women who are often struggling to supplement an inadequate wage. All in all, it is a pretty bleak picture, and one which (in concert with other aspects of deprivation) makes news of inner-city riots and public demonstrations seem rather unsurprising.

The Tragic Human Costs

But if those groups are worst-hit, it is also true that everyone is worse-off. Less wealth is created, less taxes collected, poverty rises, and large sums are paid out in benefits. As suggested above, however, there are also human costs that cannot be measured in economic terms. There is the direct stigma associated with collecting benefits from a public agency, made worse when officialdom appears to agree with the popular view that the unemployed prefer to stay that way because they get more from the welfare state than they would from a job. But, more profoundly, employment carries with it a sense of social identity and participation in society that is lost when one is jobless. The unemployed are made to feel — just like they were in Victorian times when involuntary unemployment first became a publicly recognized part of the "system" of an industrial society — that they are moral failures, outcast from normal life. This also is a social evil — exacerbating others such as suicide, crime, illness, and divorce, that should not be tolerated. Certainly, this should not be tolerated by Christians!

A CHRISTIAN PERSPECTIVE

Having made oblique allusions to Christian perspective, it is now time to spell this out more clearly. Unfortunately, while as Christians we rightly begin our thinking considering biblical notions of work, this can distort our evaluation of the issues somewhat because it reduces the discussion to an individual level. Mass unemployment is a social-structural phenomenon, which calls for a just response on an economic and social level, as well as a personal level. So let us begin by seeing work in its God-given framework, and contrast that with today's situation. Only in this way can we begin to do justice to the complexities of mass unemployment, and respond in a fully biblical manner.

Human Worth in Biblical Perspective

Few will disagree that the Genesis account clearly establishes work as a central aspect of human life — not *the* center, but as part of what is typically human. Adam and Eve were granted the task of being caretakers of God's world, earthkeepers to steward the creation. Some Greeks, who denigrated work, and some Marxists, capitalists, and others who have elevated work above its proper importance are unbalanced from a biblical viewpoint. Work is simply one important dimension of being human.

> . . . a society in which families would enjoy a degree of economic independence based on an equitable share of the nations' wealth; in which a family could feel some social relevance and significance in its community; in which every family had the opportunity of hearing the message of divine redemption . . . and the freedom to respond to it (Wright, 1978).

It is important also to remember that work is one dimension among others, the other most closely related dimension being the family. The Old Testament ideal, which does not seem in any way to have been abrogated by the New, is well summarized by Wright:

> Our overriding social goal, then, should be for every family to have *enough,* and to have a social *place.* In the agrarian society of Old Testament times this meant the opportunity to work, to produce for the needs of one's family and others. The problem is that in our society having a job has come to be seen, not only as a means of finding social relevance, but of social *worth* in the community. The apostle Paul clearly linked working with a share in social resources and attacked laziness in these terms — if a person will not work, let him/her not eat (2 Thessalonians 3:10). However, Paul never suggested that persons without work *through no fault of their own* should be socially excluded, undervalued, or starved!

The Right to Work vs. Employment

In the modern world we have to distinguish among *work, jobs,* and *employment.* By work we mean specific tasks, and may include housework. By jobs we mean a place within a work organization, and by employment we mean time spent for pay.

Unremunerated jobs, such as the honorary secretary or the meals-on-wheels volunteer, and unpaid work, such as housework, are underrated in comparison with employment. And if, as we are suggesting, it is employment that really counts in contemporary society, then the questions of who has employment and who decides that, are extremely important. Work in the Western world today is not a matter of subsistence, toiling in the field to feed the family, or even of being part of a "nation of small shopkeepers." The fact is that the vast majority of people in modern societies, lacking the necessary capital to be self-employed, must depend on someone or some organization to employ them. Work is now rooted in the market mechanism. We must therefore seek a Christian way of applying biblical understandings of work to the modern situation, and this may involve an unpopular insistence that today's world has simply got it wrong.

The Bible makes plain not only that being in an unequal dependent relationship of employment is less than God's ideal, but it also warns against the likely inequities that arise in such situations. For example, James (5:16) mentions the cries of the unpaid laborers. The Old Testament principles of work required that all have access to the means of production. In those days it was primarily land. Labor on the family land was the norm, only to be abrogated in extreme circumstances. Thus, wage labor could form a sort of social insurance (Deuteronomy 24:15) until things improved or the "year of jubilee" came. Family security was the aim, although of course the interdependence of cooperative work was also present. But we have to translate the principles enshrined in Scripture into modern-day terms. Biblical writers never envisaged the chronic stagflation crises of advanced capitalist societies!

Protestant Ethic Critiqued

This is the reason why so much confusion arises over the so-called "Protestant Ethic," which many mistakenly believe to be biblical. Of course, it began life well enough, focused in the ideas of honest toil as a calling before God, done in loving obedience to God. But it was already a secularized version of this that came to underpin industrial capitalism. By over-emphasizing individual over against cooperative work, the Protestant Ethic drifted loose from its biblical moorings. We must take great care to distinguish, therefore, between a biblical understanding of work — the true ethic — and the ideology used to justify industrial work-discipline that has reduced people to "hands" and tied them, not to work-satisfaction, but to the clock.

This topic really needs a book-length treatment. In outline, however, the debate is as follows. Max Weber suggested in his justly famous book The *Protestant Ethic and the Spirit of Capitalism* that an aspect of the early development of capitalism was the impetus given to capital accumulation by Puritan Calvinism. The breakthrough, according to Weber, came with the Reformation teaching that men and women have a duty to glorify God in everyday life. Economic activity was not seen as mere necessity, but as being intrinsically worthwhile. At the same time, Puritans were discouraged from luxurious consumption of their wealth, and so plowed it back into their businesses as capital.

The problems associated with this thesis are both historical and Christian. Historical argument continues to this day about the adequacy of the Weber doctrine (see the excellent discussion in Marshall, 1982). But Christians also disagree about the Protestant Ethic idea. Some use Weber's work not only as if it supported the view that

Protestantism had a progressive impact in fostering capitalist development, but also as if it showed the Protestant Ethic to be an unambiguously good thing in the way it has itself developed. This flies in the face of Weber's own discussion in which he shows how the Puritans would have been horrified at the later capitalist use of their ideas. *The Protestant Ethic and the Spirit of Capitalism* is a classic sociological study of unintended consequence of practical responses to certain Christian doctrines. Proper biblical emphasis against wasting time at work, for example, when entwined with the capitalist ethos, became an unbiblical obsession and a tyrant (Banks, 1983).

Today another reformation-attitude is required to pry free biblical teaching from what is loosely referred to as the Protestant Ethic. Early treatment of the work theme, an essential background to unemployment, occurs in Genesis 1-3, when honest labor is seen as part of God's good intention for humanity. The Fall turns labor into toil, and is cursed, but the human importance of work is unrevoked. Work should ideally be meaningful and purposeful, involving cooperation with others. Stewardship cannot be separated from work (Luke 19:11-27, Joshua 13-19) which means that all people should have access to the means of production. Biblical teaching on work presupposes this. It further suggests that some control over production is also desirable alongside having an equitable share of the benefits of production. Motivation for work, then, is bound up with the organization of work. It is futile calling for a revised Protestant Ethic in situations where the Christian base is not only missing, but where aspects of the biblical requirements for work are systematically ignored by those organizing production (Hay, 1982).

To summarize thus far, Christians see work as a God-given, typically human activity, related to an adequate family life and to making a contribution to community well-being. Employment, in a context of little opportunity for true participation, is not the ideal context for work. Therefore, in a fallen world we must aim to minimize the dangers of such employment, including arbitrary unemployment, and attempt to stand for a truly Biblical Ethic that restores work to its true meaning of a "labor of love" before God.

Attitudes of Employed/to Unemployed

This makes the task of Christian employees a tricky one. They have to steer a course between an honest quest for justice before their employer (in the union or other official channel) *and* diligent, cheerful contentment with their lot (Ephesians 6:5-10 and Colossians 3:22-24). Having forsaken the latter aspect in our post-Christian society, many seem to use their discontentment as an excuse for disloyalty or laziness. The biblical call for justice among the power-holders is always matched by a call for patience among the powerless — an unpopular message for today's trendy left.

This also involves another crucially significant biblical principle, namely, God's concern for the weak, the poor, the helpless, and the vulnerable. The unemployed must, in the main, be seen as victims of a system in which they have no say, no clout. Thus, the thoroughly biblical emphasis on God's compassion and demand for justice for the weak and the poor. The psalmist said, "There is no one like you. You protect the weak from the strong and the poor from the oppressor" (3:10. TEV; see also Amos 5:24; Micah 6:8). This emphasis must enter the picture here, because in the modern world unemployment means more than "no work." It is something that happens to someone.

When it strikes, Christians have a duty to promote the welfare of the victims — "seek the peace and prosperity of the city. . . . Pray to the Lord for it, because if it prospers, you too will prosper. . . ." (Jeremiah 29:7 NEB). This also includes speaking to those in power, attempting to influence our societal direction towards social justice for the unemployed.

AGENDA FOR ACTION

Now that we have seen the massive scale of unemployment in the present, that will probably stretch into years ahead, and have tried to let biblical light shine on it, the time has come to suggest some priorities from a Christian perspective.

Prayer

Prayer is always a political priority in a biblical framework. (Needless to say, it is neglected in most books on social problems!) We are repeatedly enjoined to pray — especially for those with power to influence the direction of society (1 Timothy 2:1-2; Luke 18:1; Ephesians 6:18; Philippians 4:6). Why is this a priority? Because it indicates our utter dependence on a sovereign God. We cannot cope with our human lot on our own. Attempts to do so are simply counterproductive. Prayer also reminds us that as Christians we confess our dependence on God, a dependence which others have but do not confess. So we may not simply expect them to adopt a Christian outlook or practice. Thus we need to pray for strength to stand up for what we believe is right in God's eyes. In the context of unemployment, what we must stand for is ably summarized in this editorial from the *Monthly Record* of the Free Church of Scotland. Having pointed out that in human terms, unemployment is far more important that the Gross National Product or inflation, because its effects are not only economic, but moral, psychological, and spiritual, the writer goes on to say:

> Whatever therefore its other achievements, any government whose policies are leading to mass unemployment has failed. And if the unemployment is not merely accidental but a deliberate instrument of economic policy, then we must call into question not only the government's competence but its ethics as well.

Prayer is required if we are to have the courage to stand by convictions like this.

Attitudes

There are two main areas in which attitudes must develop in line with Scripture. The first is in relation to the unemployed. If our analysis is correct, most jobless people are such through no fault of their own. They are victims who cannot be blamed, and should certainly not be penalized for their plight. A Christian response to unemployment is not moralism about laziness — though in individual face-to-face situations in the Church we may wish to discourage any potential idleness among our unemployed. Rather, compassion and the quest for justice is called for. Let no Christians be found among those stereotyping the unemployed. Many do get demoralized and apathetic after the initial shock of lay-off, but many also enjoy the newfound release from industrial discipline and find new directions for their own initiative. Let us check before God and the facts, our image of an attitude to the unemployed.

The second area in which attitudinal change must come is with regard to the nature of work. Given the likelihood of unemployment remaining near its present level for some time, and in the knowledge that certain kinds of jobs have simply disappeared forever, it is imperative to gauge all jobs and employment in terms of biblical meaning of work as any occupation that has value in the eyes of God. There is, for example, no direct, necessary, or proportional relationship of reward to the person for services rendered, and therefore every encouragement should be given to those dependent upon government benefits to engage in voluntary community service or something similar. Within the Church, of course, steps should be taken to ensure that everyone has *enough,* especially those who are unemployed (2 Corinthians 8:13-15).

All this means that when Christians press for social justice, we should not merely argue for "full employment" or "job preservation," but imaginatively, for policies that lead to the creation of real jobs for the future. We should also struggle to get *work* seen as a necessary aspect of human life, which would mean for example making it easier for people to provide for their families, and to toil creatively, without necessarily being "employed" in the traditional sense. And Christians should be concerned, as we noted above, for justice at an international, global level.

Local Welfare

Of course, how this will be tackled depends on the neighborhood, the city, and the extent of unemployment. But it is imperative that we do consider what might be done both to ensure that families *do* have enough for a reasonable life, and that there *are* opportunities given for worthwhile work. The local church ought to be a model of how to cope with unemployment in both these aspects. At the same time, large local churches or parachurch associations may engage in wider projects expressing genuine biblical concern for the city. In Chicago's West Side, for instance, the Black Evangelical Association has plans for a factory employing unskilled blacks, making simple tractors for export to the Third World. In England, Christians in Bristol have set up a Christian Community Enterprise to help unemployed people and to make some contribution to the Third World.

Industry and Labor Unions

Again, this priority is one that will receive very different responses depending on local situations. However, this is an ideal moment for Christian witness both in positions of industrial influence, and in the unions. Those with opportunity to develop new initiatives for production should be encouraged to look out for ways of turning to "socially useful" production, and of providing meaningful employment wherever possible. If government money can be obtained to promote new, small firms, this should be used to create work. As far as union activity goes, Christians should encourage concern for the unemployed, who tend in some cases to be neglected as nonmembers as soon as they are laid-off. The flexibility and adaptability necessary to cope with today's rapid social-economic changes will be achieved only through imaginative initiatives including work-shaping and participation in decision-making. Schemes involving shorter working weeks, early retirement, part-time paid employment as a route to fuller employment may all be tested within specific circumstances. They are short-term measures, but ones in which ordinary workers may be able to have a say. Christian union members have a key role here.

Public Justice

However, when all is said and done about small-scale local initiatives at work-creation or family welfare, unemployment remains a political issue because it is rooted in the very structuring of society. The market mechanism is selective and impersonal. Every effort should be made to convince politicians not only of the seriousness of the situation in terms of human damage, but also of the need to rethink priorities in the light of new situations and to act for just solutions to the crisis. There's no going back to the boom — or the tired slogans — of the 1960s.

Most people in the West are not going hungry as they did in the 1930s, but let us never forget the unemployed and the underemployed of the Third World who are. However, they are rotting in enforced idleness, which may be little better than starving! There is hardship, economically, for families. Furthermore, active energetic people, made in God's image, are receiving neither encouragement nor the opportunity to realize an aspect of their humanity through work. This is an injustice that Christian people ought not tolerate — any more than God does.

Study and Discussion
Questions

1. Why do Christians hold different views of unemployment? Are they all equally biblical?

2. Why do we have to consider unemployment as a twentieth century problem, quite different from anything encountered in New Testament times? What difference does this make?

3. Some practical tasks:

    (a) What is the unemployment rate in your city or county?

    Why is it at this level?

    How does it compare with other areas?

    What is being done about it by the city, county, or area economical development committee and other leaders?

    Evaluate this response in terms of the size of the problem.

    (b) Is there a connection between unemployment and ethnicity and/or race in your town, city, or area? If there is a difference, what is it?

    Is there an *underclass* emerging, or is there one already there? (Cp. W. Wilson. *The Truly Disadvantaged.* Univ. of Chicago Press, 1988.)

    (c) What is the effect of unemployment on individuals and their families?

    Conduct a small qualitative survey among some unemployed people to see what the effects actually are.

References

Anthony, P. D., *The Ideology of Work*, London: Tavistock, 1977.

Banks, Robert, *The Tyranny of Time*, Canberra: Book House Australia, 1983.

Clarke, Roger, *Work in Crisis*, Edinburgh: Saint Andrew's Press, 1983.

Daniels, W. W., *The Nature of Current Unemployment*, 1983.

Green, Wendy, *The Christian and Unemployment*, Oxford: Mowbray, 1982.

Hawkins, Kevin, *Unemployment*, Harmondsworth: Penguin, 1979.

Hay, Donald, *A Christian Critique of Socialism*, Nottingham: Grove, 1982.

Marshall, Gordon, *In Search of the Spirit of Capitalism*, London: Hutchinson, 1982.

Marshall, Paul, et al., *Labour of Love: Essays on Work*, Toronto: Wedge, 1980.

Mills, C. Wright, *The Sociological Imagination*, New York: Oxford University Press, 1959.

Wright, Christopher, *What Does the Lord Require?* Nottingham: Shaftesbury Project, 1978.

PART II

ANOMIC INSTITUTIONS

CHAPTER 6
EDUCATION: INTRODUCTION

In refining Durkheim's concept of "anomie," contemporary theorist Robert Merton elaborated on the nature of the breakdown in social norms. According to Merton, "anomie" represents a disjunction between cultural goals and institutional means. In nonanomic situations, the institutional means are available to achieve the desired cultural goals. The most common disjuncture occurs when the cultural goals are accepted, desired and sought, but the appropriate institutional means are in some way thwarted.

On the societal level, public education was established in part to provide an equal opportunity for all to have access to social mobility in our society. In other words, "equal opportunity" may be seen as a cultural goal; public education was the institutional means to achieve that goal. "Work hard in school and you will achieve later in life" is an ethic that is assumed to be true by middle-class Americans.

As Professor Conklin demonstrates throughout her article, however, our credentialing and class-biased educational system calls this motto into question. The educational system has failed its vision to be a widespread mechanism for social mobility. This failure is particularly evident in considering the simple criterion of literacy to judge the efficacy of school performance. Although advances have been made against the problem of illiteracy over the past two centuries, there is considerable evidence that functional illiteracy (reading at a very low level) is still very much of a problem in the United States.

On a more micro level, there is another disjuncture between cultural goals and institutional means. Americans have been led to believe that education is a means to achieve the cultural goal of a "good life," As Professor Conklin points out, however, the relationship between education and income is not altogether clear. Although college graduates do enjoy higher status jobs than do high school graduates, the causal nature of the relationship has been called into question. Conklin's discussion of credentialism in our society and the manifest goals of schooling provide food for discussion of anomie on this level.

On an institutional level, each of the functions or goals of schooling listed by Conklin could be evaluated in terms of how effective the educational system is in helping people to achieve them. Conklin lists five goals, some of which are "manifest" (i.e. they are recognized and intended goals) while others are "latent" (i.e., they are not usually specified as a purpose of our educational system): instruction, socialization, custody and control, certification, and selection. Students might explore the specific means used by the educational system to facilitate each goal. They may consider further whether each of these goals is "functional" (i.e. they contribute to the maintenance of some social system) or "dysfunctional" (i.e. they work against some system).

Although the problems of education may be cast in a functionalist frame as we have done here, Conklin's analysis reflects more of a conflict orientation. Class privilege appears to be at work to maintain the social status quo through the educational system.

All too often training, which readily becomes obsolete, is the focus of the schooling enterprise — a focus that has the latent dysfunction of blocking upward mobility for the poor. An emphasis on education, which imparts the ability to think and write, would provide skills that have life-long utility. The stress on training over education is sometimes the product, Conklin asserts, of attempting to meet the short-run technical needs of industries.

Long-range problems for those with only technical skills when viewed in light of credentialism points to a perpetuation of the present class system. College graduation, a phenomenon that is highly correlated with social class, becomes a kind of screening device used for employment. Increasingly educational requirements are set by employers that do not necessarily reflect the skills needed to do a particular job. These requirements, however, are much less likely to be met by members of a lower social strata than those of higher ones.

Conklin's thought reflects the work of conflict theorist Randall Collins on credentialism. Collins has used a conflict perspective to explore how educational qualifications have been used as a resource in the struggle for power, wealth and prestige. He has noted that the educational elite share a given culture and use it as a criterion for employment in elite positions. The elite also try to instill a respect for its culture in the society as a whole.

The American educational system is (as are all other social institutions) part of the larger social system. Professor Conklin's article suggests ways in which it is interrelated to the economic system and the stratification system. There are other frequently noted problems in related social institutions that impact American education which are not discussed here. For example, a lack of family stability affects the performance of children in school both directly and indirectly. Single-parent households are more likely to suffer from poverty than are the children of two-parent families. The indirect effects of poverty can include a lack of proper nutrition which impedes learning, inadequate adult role models to demonstrate the benefits of education, parental inability to provide sufficient support for education, and (increasingly often) a drug-infested and violence-ridden milieu that never gives children a chance to be children.

Conklin takes an approach consistent with the theme of this text in dealing with the crisis or anomie facing the educational system. She challenges Christians to adopt a perspective different from the secular model that has made significant inroads into Christian thought. Using the work of Harry Blamires, whose central ideas are inspired by Scripture, Conklin challenges us to develop a "Christian mind." The Apostle Paul urges us to internalize "the mind of Christ" (Philippians 2:5-9 RSV), a mind committed to obedience and service to God. Paul also recognizes the conflict that we face in this world which constantly tries to get us to conform (Romans 12:2). But rather than conforming, he challenges us to bring our thinking into conformity to the mind of Christ (2 Corinthians 10:5).

This Christian mind dependent on revelation, however, is not to replace the secular mind that has been shaped by science and philosophy. Christ recognized the legitimate sphere of the secular when he commanded us to "render unto Caesar the things that are Caesar's" (Matthew 22:21). There must be a dialogue among the different ways of knowing, sorting out the truths of revelation, philosophy and science.

The Christian mind is needed for us not to lose sight of God. The Christian mind demands excellence, pursuing truth with all of our being. For the Christian this begins with the "fear" or reverence of God (Psalm 111:10). Jesus also commands us "to love the Lord our God with all of our heart, soul and mind" (Mark 12:29-31). Certainly this means that the Christian mind will be open to all the transformation that education (as opposed to training) can bring within us.

But as Christians we are challenged to respond as people of light and salt in this world. We are to be *in* the world, but not *of* it (John 17:11,15). There are at least three ways that we can be salt and light. First of all, we can work for equality of opportunity in schooling for all students. Scripture teaches us that God is impartial in His treatment of us, and we are commanded to imitate Him (Acts 10:34; Romans 2:11; James 2:1,9). There are two other possible responses, based on Merton's theory of *anomie*. The first Merton calls *innovation*. Innovation occurs when people reject the means (e.g. public education) and find a functional alternative to achieve the desired goal. Home schooling and Christian schools provide illustrations of such alternatives. A second response identified by Merton is more radical. People may reject both the means (e.g. public education) and the goal (the so-called "good life"), substituting other goals and other means in their place. Using Professor Conklin's article as a frame, we may ask ourselves to what extent we are required to reject both the secular goals that often entice us and the means that are offered by a thoroughly secularized educational system. As with other issues we are presenting for thought, there is no one answer.

PROBLEMS IN AMERICAN EDUCATION
Mary E. Conklin

Whether you watch the evening news, read *USA Today*, or pick up some periodical, you become aware of problems in the American educational system. More recently, complaints and concerns have centered on what is being taught and, especially, what is being learned or not learned in public schools. Afro-Americans, Hispanics and Native Americans press for special curricula, bilingual education, and especially designed programs to enable them to compete equitably in our society and also learn more about their own cultural heritage. Teachers are concerned about their personal safety in our inner-city schools, as well as that of their students. Other teacher concerns are growing class size and curricular changes. Parents want to have more influence in selecting what is being taught, and want to hold teachers more accountable for their performance. Within higher education there is debate about professional and technical curricula versus a retention of programs more reflective of a liberal arts orientation. Faculty, students, and college and university boards are polarized on the issue of "politically correct language" and a host of issues related to race and ethnicity, sexuality, and women's rights. Issues abound.

Prominent in all these discussions is the word *crisis*. The crisis in the educational system is that schools are not functioning as expected. There is frequently the assumption that schools are no longer as effective as they were twenty or thirty years ago. We fail to realize, however, that the "good old days" may be only a dream and not a reality. So we end up comparing the present to some mythical past, losing sight of persistent problems. We often falter in our attempt to compare results with stated aims. But who or what gets to define what the issues are and specify how the school should be operating? Schools involve teachers, students, parents, administrators, politicians, and the public who pays for the educational system. Should one, or all of these define what the problems are? Basic to any discussion of the problems in modern education is the question as to the place of education in our complex, technological society.

Sociology as a discipline seeks to be objective, value-free in its assessment. Thus, when the educational institution is being evaluated, the sociology of education can facilitate understanding. Sociologists who research education do not provide unequivocal answers to the problems, but they do specify the problems — and today's problems are different from those of a decade ago. In addition, they identify past, present and the emerging functions of the educational system, as well as manifest and latent functions. Sociologists seek to identify the major agents in the operation of the educational system, the organization of the school system, the formal and informal structure (as well as relationships), the effect schools have on students and the delineation of ideological positions that undergird various policies for funding programs.

To examine some of the problems associated with education from a sociological perspective, one needs to consider the basic societal orientation toward schools. Are schools seen as a *training* institution or as an institution of *education*? This is a fundamental question, for the answer determines what educational experiences are pursued, and helps to evaluate the effectiveness of contemporary public education in America.

Besides understanding the general societal orientation, we must identify the goals of education: What is it that we want schools to accomplish? The functions of education determine the *what* (content) and the *how* (method) of education. Thus the standard for evaluating schools emerges as we examine their functions. Finally, we can measure the effectiveness of schools by looking at their retention rate. How many students drop out of school? How many graduate and receive their diplomas? How do these rates vary over time? How do these rates relate to race, ethnicity and gender?

With this information as background, we will address three specific problems in education that have received a great deal of attention during the 1980s, and continue to do so today: (1) the issue of mediocrity in the schools, evidenced by declining literacy rates and performance on general competency exams; (2) credentialism — the increasing reliance on educational credentials to certify competence; and (3) the degree of inequality in education. These are problems that plague society in general, but are distinctly manifest in schools. We need to understand the relationship between the functions of the school and the problems it has. The concluding section considers these issues from a Christian perspective. The biblical injunction to be salt in the world indicates that Christians need to weigh what their response should be to these problems.

BACKGROUND ISSUES

Training or Education

As we consider the history of the American educational system, we find a recurring question: What is the basic function of the school? Some people think that the school should provide vocation preparation, while others believe the function of the school is not only to teach students the "3 R's" (reading, 'riting and 'rithmetic), but also to teach them to think critically and constructively.

The distinction that emerges is clear. Are the schools to *educate* or *train* (Hurn, 1985, p. 11)? The difference is not only relevant to secondary education, but also to post secondary education.

On the one hand, *training* emphasizes the acquisition of specific information conveyed by specially trained individuals in a designated setting, over a prescribed period of time. In this framework schooling is directly tied to vocation. Students are taught a designated body of knowledge, skills and values that will prepare them for future employment, and the emphasis is on memorization. *Education*, on the other hand, is designed to equip students with the ability to think critically, to be able to evaluate and analyze information from a variety of perspectives. Furthermore, education provides students with a diversity of perspectives that will enable them to interpret information in several ways. The focus is on how to *process* knowledge to draw inferences and engage in decision-making. Nyberg and Egan (1981, p. 2) refer to education as "critical discrimination" and the development of a historical perspective for the assessment of current events. Thus we find a difference in instructional emphases as we compare training and education — memorization and processing.

While training is an essential component of education, it by no means constitutes the whole. There is an important difference and this distinction has implications for the functions of schools, as well as for the development of curricula in schools and colleges. If the focus is on education the emphasis will be on course work that develops the ability to think and write, via disciplines in the humanities, social sciences, and natural sciences. If the focus is on training, programs in business and technology will be developed and proliferated, programs that are designed to teach specific skills. Therefore, the crucial question in the educational experience in the United States is this: do we develop programs and curricula in schools that recognize the value of education, or do we respond to the pressure of the labor market and emphasize vocational skills?

The difference between training and education is especially relevant to college education. If one is trained, what will be the short-term consequences? People often find it gratifying to work in jobs related to their majors — the short-term view. But Lynne Cheney, Chairman of the National Endowment for the Humanities, identifies the long-term view. She notes that many people change their occupations over a lifetime of involvement in the labor market; in fact, many completely change professions, e.g., ceramics engineer to psychologist. The fact that a substantial number of people in their thirties return to graduate school to complete a program significantly different from their undergraduate major bears witness to this shift. With the speed of technological advancement the specific jobs individuals train for today or the skills they acquire may not exist or be in demand five years from now. The development of *transferable* skills, along with the capacity to think, allows individuals to shift to new jobs with greater facility (Cheney, 1986, p. 7).

We next turn to consider the function of schools in our society.

Function of Schools

Schools have been an integral part of America since its founding. While provision for an educational system was not outlined in the Constitution, proposals did exist for a national school system. Even before the country existed as an independent nation, the colonies had a variety of schooling provisions. The years between 1812 and the Civil War saw the evolution of a free, public school system, including the advent of the high school (Pulliam, 1987, pp. 53, 65). During this period the principle of equality of all citizens (with the exception of Afro-Americans and native Americans) mandated an educational system that would provide mass education. In part, the massive influx of European immigrants who were Roman Catholic and/or spoke a "foreign" language during the early 1900s caused a great deal of concern among the predominant WASP (white, Angle-Saxon Protestant) citizenry: would the "American" culture and values be diluted and lost? The concern for equality, coupled with the desire to acculturate immigrants, prompted those who developed curricula to be certain that all were exposed to "American" culture — folkways, mores and values and a basic education that would equip them for success in their new homeland (Bowles and Gentis, 1976, pp. 20-24; Pulliam, 1987, p. 66).

Generally speaking, public schools are confronted with a twofold task, that of socialization and education. On the one hand, socialization includes education, but also the teaching of values and attitudes and, generally, prepares students to function as social beings. On the other hand, education involves the transfer of general information and knowledge that will enable students to enhance their gifts and abilities. When we think about what schools are to accomplish, our thoughts immediately turn to something akin to the "3 R's" that teach factual information that students are supposed to know. But we must go beyond this if we are to determine in a more substantive manner both the manifest (intended) and the latent (unintended) functions of education and the degree of fit between the functions and their outcomes.

Boocock (1980, pp. 6-7) draws on the work of Bill Spady to identify the five commonly agreed upon functions of school:

Instructional — Schools produce individuals equipped with the empirical knowledge and technological mastery needed for survival in the larger society.

Socialization — Schools transmit to individuals the attitudes, values, and interpersonal skills needed for the performance of adult roles.

Custody and Control — Children are legally obliged to attend school and schools are responsible for their care during specified periods of time.

Certification — Schools provide course credits, diplomas, and other credentials that are accepted by other institutions as evidence that some set of requirements or level of competence has been achieved.

Selection — Schools perform a sorting role that determines access to subsequent educational, occupational, and social positions and opportunities.

The above are some of the more common functions associated with schools by sociologists, although by no means is the list exhaustive (Hurn, 1985, p. 12). Let us now turn from a consideration of the functions of education to consider matters relative to attendance — successful completion, drop-out rates, etc.

Extent of Schooling

In America, spending time in school is an experience shared by virtually all. School buses roll the first day of class no matter whether one lives in Minnesota, Louisiana, Oregon or Connecticut. Statistics show just how universal schooling experience is. As indicated in Table 1, about 97.6% of the school-age population in the U. S. are in some form of schooling. The numbers have remained relatively constant for both whites and blacks across the last several decades.

TABLE 1
School Enrollment Rates
for 14- and 15-Year-Olds by Race

Years	All	White	Black
1970	98.1	98.2	97.6
1980	98.2	98.3	97.9
1985	98.1	98.1	97.9
1986	97.6	97.8	96.6

Source: *U. S. Statistical Abstract,* 1990, p. 128.

Approximately 74 percent of all Americans graduate from high school (see Table 2), but there is more variability in these percentages across time. The following percentages illustrate the fluctuations. Between 1960 and 1988 there was only a 4 percentage point difference, but this modest variation obscures changes that have occurred. The low high school completion rate in the 1960s sparked considerable concern and various reforms were instituted. Yet in a society where there is increased reliance on technology and rising educational requirements for employment, the fact that 25 percent of those who enroll in high school fail to graduate has negative consequences for employment opportunities. Overall drop-out rates have not changed since 1970, but there is a notable increase among minorities. In 1980, 16% of Afro-Americans and 29.5% of Hispanics had dropped out. By 1988, the drop-out rate for Afro-Americans had shrunk to 12.4%, but the rate among Hispanics remained unchanged (*U. S. Statistical Abstract*, 1990, p. 150).

TABLE 2
Percent of High School Graduates
and Drop-Outs for Selected Years

Years	Graduates	Drop-outs
1960	69.5	
1970	76.9	12.2
1980	71.4	12.0
1985	73.4	10.6
1987	73.0	
1988	73.9	10.9

Source: *U. S. Statistical Abstract*, 1990, pp. 150-151

Continuing with the educational statistics, 37 percent of those 25 years old and over have spent some time in college, while 20% of the population graduate from college (*U. S. Census, Statistical Abstract*, 1990, p. 128,

TABLE 3
Percent of High School Graduates Enrolled in College
or Completed one or more years of College
by Sex and Race and Hispanic Origin

				Male			Female		
	White	Black	Hispanic	W	B	H	W	B	H
1960	41.0	32.5	(NA)	47.1	33.5	(NA)	35.6	31.8	(NA)
1970	53.4	40.0	(NA)	60.8	41.2	(NA)	47.1	39.0	(NA)
1980	51.4	46.2	47.3	51.8	44.4	49.6	51.0	47.4	45.6
1985	55.3	43.8	46.7	55.5	43.5	44.9	55.2	43.9	48.0
1988	58.6	46.6	47.1	57.9	42.8	48.4	59.2	49.6	46.0

Source: *U. S. Statistical Abstract*, 1990, p. 151.

Looking at Table 3 we note that for the last two and a half decades there has been a steady increase in the numbers of whites attending college, while minorities showed a steady increase only until the 1980s, when there was a modest decline in the percentages. This decline corrected itself for minority women, but not for minority men. Among whites and Afro-Americans, a larger percentage of females than males attend college, but among Hispanics, more males attend college. Whites attend college in higher percentages than do Afro-Americans or Hispanics, but particularly among non-white males, a higher percentage of Hispanic males attend college than do Afro-American males, a pattern reversed among minority women.

The last stage for many individuals as they prepare for labor market participation rests on the completion of college. The number of college graduates has been increasing since 1940. If we just consider more recent high school graduates, in comparison with the percentage of those 25 years and over who are college graduates, we find that close to 28 percent are graduating from college with a four-year degree (*U. S. Census*, 1980, p. 101; *Statistical Abstract*, 1990, p. 164). This is significant because it is generally believed that a college degree is necessary for continued economic development. Additionally, both popular belief and public policy reflect the view that schooling not only is associated with, but causes economic success. Jencks, et al., in *Who Gets Ahead?* found that college graduates enjoy higher status jobs than do high school graduates, a relationship that is more pronounced for nonwhites than for whites (Jencks, et al., 1979, p. 162, 174). The relationship between education and earnings is not as clear-cut in the Jencks' (et al.,) analysis. As they note:

[W]e cannot be sure how the BA 'surplus' will affect returns to education in the future. Young BAs are now entering lower status occupations than in the past where earnings have not traditionally grown very fast as men got older. Thus, one might expect the earnings differential between college graduates and high school graduates ages 25 to 64 to keep falling as older college graduates retire and younger, more numerous cohorts of BAs compete for their jobs (Jencks, et al., 1979, p. 189).

TABLE 4
Percent of Persons 25 Years Old or Over
Who Were High School Graduates and College Graduates

Years	All	White	Black
1940	4.6	4.9	1.3
1950	6.2	6.6	2.1
1960	7.7	8.1	3.1
1970	11.0	11.3	4.5
1980	16.2	17.1	8.4

Source: *U. S. Census 1980, Characteristics of the Population, General Social and Economic Characteristics*, Vol. 1

With mixed views of whether training or education should be the goal of schooling, we have considered the basic functions associated with schools. These generally defined functions provide a standard by which to evaluate the activities of schools as discussed in the following sections. From the discussion on the extent of schooling, we know that millions of students are spending billions of hours in classrooms, but with what effect? Let us address ourselves to this question, as we consider three fundamental problems present in American schools: mediocrity, credentialism, and inequality.

MEDIOCRITY

> Our Nation is at risk . . . the educational foundations of our society are presently being eroded by a rising tide of mediocrity that threatens our very future as a nation and a people. What was unimaginable a generation ago has begun to occur; others are matching and surpassing our educational attainments (*National Commission on Excellence in Education*, 1983, p. 368).

These words opened *A Nation at Risk* (1983)), a report on the state of education in America. The introduction noted that "our society and its educational institutions seem to have lost sight of the basic purposes of schooling, and of the high expectations and disciplined effort needed to attain them" (*National Commission on Excellence in Education*, 1983, p. 368). To remedy this loss of purpose various recommendations were provided.

The exact expectations of schooling have fluctuated across time, but a constant concern over literacy has persisted. Literacy is basic to equality, facilitating the participation of all in government, an essential for democracy. Literacy has many different definitions, but Lawrence Cremin defines functional literacy as "the ability to read and write with sufficient skill to enable a person to engage in the full range of activities in which literacy was normally assumed in American society" (Cremin, 1988:656). Additionally, there is cultural literacy — the knowledge of the country's literature, history and grand traditions, and critical literacy — "the ability to think critically and creatively . . . [and] the abilities to analyze, synthesize, and evaluate what one hears and reads as well as the abilities to use data and knowledge" to make inferences, predict outcomes, and draw valid conclusions (Garcia, 1991, p. 92).

For decades, as Cremin points out, it was assumed that a prescribed number of years of formal schooling would guarantee literacy: "obviously" as more people were spending an increased amount of time in school, more people were learning to read and write. Cremin also states that although people are spending more time in school, the amount of time may not be enough to achieve the skill level required "to engage in the full-range of activities," since societal development did not remain static across the years. In the period between 1870 and 1980 the complexity of life has increased markedly, raising the level at which one must function. Thus, functional literacy at the minimum level required for participation in societal activities continues to increase, but so does the need to foster greater literacy.

Extensive and persistent controversy over the necessary level of literacy needed in the U. S. continues. How well have we achieved our goals? Jonathan Kozol is one educator who does not think we have achieved our literacy goals very well. Although we are spending about $4,509 per pupil per year (*Statistical Abstract*, 1990, p. 144), what is the return? Some place the rate of illiteracy at a third of the adult population; others place it between 10 and 13 percent of the adults 26 and older (Kozol, 1985). A MacNeil/

Lehrer News Hour telecast in 1986 reported that 10% of the population were functionally illiterate, and about 18% (47 million) could not read well (Ballantine, 1989, p. 36). The problem of illiteracy cannot be explained entirely by the high drop-out rate, since it is estimated that 15% of the recent graduates of urban high schools are reading at less than the sixth grade level (Kozol, 1985). While few would dispute that we have made progress in reducing illiteracy since the 1800s, we have by no means eradicated it.

Other researchers have tested students to measure their basic knowledge. While their results were not as devastating, they are still somewhat bleak. The International Evaluation of Education Achievement and the National Assessment of Educational Progress both seek to measure the knowledge and skills possessed by students at different ages. Cremin wrote "[Y]oung Americans did rather well in literature and in civics in comparison with their counterparts in other countries, less well in science and quite poorly in French and in mathematics." The results from advanced industrial nations were fairly similar (Cremin, 1988, pp. 661-662). He went on to note, "the most significant findings of the National assessment concerned the overall decline in the performance of American seventeen-year-olds in most subjects during the 1970s and early 1980s" (Cremin, 1988, p. 662; cf. Nyberg and Egan, 1981, p. 5).

To put the literacy debate in focus, one might compare literacy rates cross-nationally. Table 5 below gives us some idea of the literacy rate of other nations. Literacy rates are known to be highly inflated, so the values are at best only suggestive of the extent of literacy in a country. Since the literacy rate reported for the U. S. found in *The World Almanac* was 99%, one needs to assume that some license has been taken by other countries also.

TABLE 5
Selected Countries, Literacy Rates — 1980

Australia	100%
France	99%
Korea, Republic of	92-95%
Japan	99%
Mexico	83%
Yugoslavia	90%

Source: *World Almanac*, 1990

In regard to Japan, after consulting a variety of sources, there seems to be agreement that they have achieved 99% literacy.

Why the discrepancy between the U. S. and Japan, two advanced, industrialized countries, when Japan has a much more complicated written language based on ideographs? One answer is that American schools are failing to achieve one of the manifestly stated functions of education: to provide instruction to ensure that literacy is achieved. Outcome assessment is important, but it is equally important to understand why the schools are failing to achieve their objective. Nyberg and Egan write that the reason is political.

It is simply out of the question to base [literacy] tests on standards high enough to reflect a strong sense of competence or literacy [meaning: educated, instructed, learned to the point of fitness and adequacy] because about half of our high school students could not pass them. As it is, these students graduate anyway, and school officials thus avoid dangerous social and political consequences that would follow exorbitant school failure while they deck out statistically the ideal of equal educational opportunity for all. (Nyberg and Egan, 1981, p. 9)

Another answer as to why we are not achieving our instructional goals is that our methods of instruction are ineffective. Goodlad suggests that we are reaping what we have sown: antiquated, ineffective instruction. Administrators and policy makers have been aware for some time that all was not well at school; as a consequence various programs and strategies were implemented. Goodlad labels such attempts as simplistic remedies for the crisis facing American education. He notes that teacher training has not been overhauled, but "has remained mired in the past" (Olson, 1990, p. 8). In his review of institutions that prepare teachers, he discovered "teacher-education programs suffering from low status, a lack of clear missions, disjointed and poorly planned curricula and a mechanistic, uninspired view of teaching and learning" (Olson, 1990, p. 7).

In his article, "What you see is what you get — consistency, persistency and mediocrity in the classrooms," Sirotnik asserts that instruction in most classrooms for the last sixty years revolves around the age-old techniques of "didactics, practice, and little else" (Sirotnik, 1987, p. 231). Using the observational data collected by Goodlad, he found that immediate corrective feedback, the most touted pedagogical feature of classroom instruction, constituted just under 3 percent of instructional time elementary teachers spent interacting with students. At the secondary level, the estimate drops to less than 2 percent. Raywid, Tesconi, and Warren (1987, p. 331) suggest that "we must assign teachers more responsibility and concomitant authority," an idea echoed by the Public Education Information Network of St. Louis (MO) (1987). Raywid, et al., continue with the idea of accountability; schools ought to be accountable to their clients. Thus they acknowledge the need to improve the quality of instruction that is provided, as well as the need to restructure the organization of the educational system to involve parents and devise some way of making teachers accountable.

Goodlad believes it will take about a decade to improve instruction, and thereby reduce the rate of illiteracy. It would take that long to update and revitalize existing teaching-training programs (Olson, 1990, p. 9). Other researchers suggest the need to examine the structure of schooling (see Goodlad, 1987, and Raywid, et al., 1987).

Let us now move on from these problems to consider credentials, another function of the school.

CREDENTIALISM[1]

With mass education and the expansion of higher education, i. e., an increase in the number of institutions of higher learning, significantly more individuals are participating in some type of post-secondary educational program. This increase in the number of students is motivated by the perception that ". . . educational credentials have become the currency for employment" (Collins, 1979, p. 183). This assumes a relationship

---

[1]Much of the discussion on credentialism is drawn from an earlier work by the author.

between education and occupation. There is a positive correlation between the number of years of schooling and one's occupational status (Jencks, 1972). Collins (1979, p. 7) succinctly summarizes this empirical association:

> . . . the hierarchy of educational attainment is assumed to be a hierarchy of skills, and the hierarchy of jobs is assumed to be another such skill hierarchy. Hence education determines success, and all the more so as the modern economy allegedly shifts toward an increasing predominance of highly skilled positions.

But it is not only important to secure some post-secondary education; it is important to acquire a degree or diploma. Berg, in his book, *Education and Jobs: The Great Training Robbery* (1970), and Faia (1981) have found empirical support of the idea that degrees add value to an individual over and above the number of years of schooling completed.

One consequence of the involvement of more people in higher education at different levels has been the development of a crisis of credentials: "rapidly rising levels of educational qualifications are required for the same or similar jobs" (Hurn, 1985, p. 105). While we still do not totally understand why the relationship between education and jobs exists, educational research continues to find empirical support. Research suggests that it is the various intangibles, such as interpersonal skills or a sense of responsibility, that are gleaned from spending time in an academic setting.

It is generally recognized that not all colleges and programs are of equal academic rigor: requirements and competence in instruction vary greatly. As enrollment in colleges and universities has increased, there has been a proliferation of different types of credentials. Two responses were made to this plethora of credentials awarded. One response was the emerging need to evaluate academic experiences. We evaluate programs by the credentials they award: certificate, diploma or degree. Within each of these categories there is additional sorting and ranking that occurs, based on academic accreditation and the quality of the institution awarding the credential. Thus a degree from an Ivy League University, or one of the top-ranking state or private colleges or universities is more marketable than one from a nonprestigious college or university or community college.

What in essence has happened is that as competition for credentials increased, new levels of educational experience have been added, e. g., ranging from new programs at community colleges offering credentials (e.g., certificates, associate degrees) in every conceivable academic and vocational area, to those colleges and universities that offer continuing education programs in education and business at the master's level. As the educational ladder has been extended, access to higher status positions have become predicated on the possession of higher degrees. Once again the relationship between education attained and one's social class has become obvious. We have found that entrance to more prestigious positions is given to those with university degrees, and they are predominantly middle-class individuals. This relationship exists because social class position limits educational opportunity; i.e., there is the tendency for higher-class individuals to graduate from elite institutions, while working-class persons graduate from public community colleges and nonelite state universities. The consequence of the process of credentialing is that 1) the more commonly attained education is devalued.

The devaluation affects both its value in terms of the instruction allegedly received and the value of the credential in the labor market (Husen, 1987:133-134). 2) The other result is that public education, rather than providing a boost for those desiring upward social mobility, is perpetuating the status quo (Bastian, et. al., 1986, pp. 36-37).

The second response was that employers used educational credentials as screening devices for locating capable employees, as opposed to other internally devised selection processes, such as personality tests or other specially created inventories. Obviously employers want the best they can obtain for the salary and benefits they are offering. Additionally they want to select individuals as reliably as they can with the least amount of time loss and cost. Consequently, employers rely on credentials to evaluate applicants for positions.

Another reason employers use credentials to evaluate applicants is that technological developments require people with more preparation. The technocratic model postulates that education, or more appropriately, training, adds the skills and special abilities required by our advancing technology. In a still relevant critique, Collins (1979:193) says, ". . . it is apparent that the technical training rhetoric is a response to the crisis of the credential market rather than a substantively significant change in education content." Ivar Berg questioned whether the recipients of bachelor degrees actually possess superior qualifications in comparison with less-educated individuals.

Furthermore, Berg (1970, p. xiii) pointed out that the jobs in which many are located do not utilize the education these persons received. Writing several years later, O'Toole (1977, p. 126) identified the skills employers value in employees: "the capacity to engage in good human relations, problem-solving and analytical skills, the ability to cope with conflict, ambiguity, and complexity, a willingness to change, to be flexible and adaptable, and the ability to communicate, to lead, and to follow." An admirable list of traits, but none implies the need for special abilities associated with advancing technology nor suggests the need for advanced degrees. Finally, Collins found that the work situation, rather than formal training, was the site of learning (Collins, 1979, p. 193). More recently, Bastian, et al., (1986, p. 53) points out that "the impact of new technology creates an initial increase in skill requirements, followed by a sharp and enduring decrease as mechanization proceeds." In summary, the argument that technological advances require employees with higher levels of schooling, certified by the possession of ever increasing educational credentials, is not supported. The other problem that arises from this practice is that employees with credentials are often not challenged by their work, resulting in underemployment, i.e., working at a level below one's educational preparation.

However, we need to consider the consequences of this practice. With the surplus of four-year college graduates growing, the use of educational credentials for entry (not promotion) becomes the practice. Pincus (1980, pp. 344-345) wrote that

> . . . educational requirements set by employers do not necessarily reflect the skills needed to do a particular job. Educational requirements have been rising faster than the skill levels of available jobs as a result of the increasing level of schooling among the population.

Considering Pincus' remarks and the work of Collins, there are two conclusions we can draw: 1) employers have a preference for people with higher educational attainment, and 2) four-year degrees are becoming prerequisites not only for middle-level positions, but also for less prestigious entry-level ones.

Although the use of educational credentials may be an acceptable approach for employers, in actuality what occurs is a mismatch between educational requirements and the job skills required, with the education far outreaching the level of ability on the job. Perhaps more important is the long-term consequence occasioned by the relationship between college graduation and social class. There is a strong and positive relationship between social class and graduation which introduces the issue of social stratification that is inherent in credentialism. Thus jobs assigned on the basis of credentials serve to perpetuate the present social class system. The one positive outcome to occur with the credentials race is that fewer male students are completing college, as the guarantee for a payoff becomes more uncertain. Offsetting the decline in the number of males is the increased percentage of females who are attending college in an attempt to break out of the lower prestige jobs previously allocated to women (Collins, 1979, p. 194). It remains to be seen whether women will be able to convert this educational persistence into occupational advances.

So we have an escalation in credential requirements, with a slight substantive basis for it. The result is that people who possess the ability to perform a specific task, but do not have the credentials, are denied employment. This lack of access to employment is not spread uniformly across society, but discriminates against those in the lower socioeconomic groups.

INEQUALITY

Ever since the Supreme Court case of Brown vs. Board of Education in 1954, the problem of racial/ethnic discrimination and inequality in education has been a grave concern among educators and governmental leaders. When we discuss equality we must distinguish between two definitions: 1) in the 1960s, when we spoke of equality, our concern was equality of opportunity — equal access to quality schools. 2) beginning in the mid-1970s we defined equality in terms of performance and results. The first, equality of opportunity, is far easier to achieve, since compliance can be forced through legislation. It is much more difficult, however, to achieve equality of results; this can come only from accumulated effort of several years. A government mandate may initiate a program, but it will be several years before the results are in. In the 1990s the controversy over equality of opportunity and equality of results is continuing.

It is obvious to all that providing equal opportunity does not necessarily lead to equality of results. Equality in access does not guarantee equality in performance. In the schools of America, many believe that we have failed to provide even minimal levels of quality instruction to the lower class, the poor and minorities. They believe this is evident, since "50 to 89% of all inner-city students drop out of high school, and 28% of all students do not receive high school diplomas, and 13% of all seventeen-year-olds are functionally illiterate" (Bastian et al., 1986, p. 26).

This debate over the definition of equality has fueled at least two conflicting views with regard to schools: the meritocratic view and the conflict-oriented theory. Basically the meritocratic approach focuses on the ability of the individual student the school places the responsibility for success on the student. The meritocratic philosophy says that the rich and poor alike compete on equal footing in school; if we work hard, we will get ahead! Society is depicted as open; talent and effort rather than privilege and social origins . . . determine an individual's status (Hurn, 1985, p. 109).

Conflict theorists, however, believe that the advocates of meritocracy "blame the victim." They identify the problem as one inherent in our social structure, which rewards people unequally. They contend that for many years a college education has been perceived as a guarantee of upward social mobility. Yet the chance of experiencing upward mobility largely depends on our socioeconomic class origin. Our ascribed status, i.e., social class position at birth, determines the quality of education we receive, as well as the type of post-secondary education we will receive — either a two-year or community college, or four-year college or university. Also, our occupational status is directly related to the number of years of schooling completed. Consequently, lower- and working-class people who typically attend college less than four years have limited access to good-paying jobs; they are reserved for those who earn a four-year college degree. We find in social class origins, accordingly, a mechanism perpetuating social class differentiation and affecting the opportunity for social mobility.

For various reasons, the evidence supports the conflict theory. Hurn succinctly summarizes the research: "scholarly credentials and parents' social status have independent effects on occupation and earnings, which are more important than the effects of measured ability alone" (Hurn, 1985, p. 126). Jencks, in his landmark study, *Inequality,* says "[O]ur research has convinced us not only that cognitive inequality does not explain [in a statistical sense — amount of variance explained] economic inequality to any significant extent. . . . It simply means that variations in what children learn in school depend largely on variations in what they bring to school, not on variations in what schools offer them [students/teacher ratio, number of books in the library, etc.]" (Jencks, et al., 1972:53).

Variations brought to school — e.g., the quality of home life, parental concern for academic achievement, parental support and discipline — once again point to social class differences. Kohn (1972), Wright and Wright (1976) and others have demonstrated that socialization practices vary by social class. Clark's research on the relationship between family life and school achievement fleshes out the point Jencks made in reference to the variations that children bring to school. Clark provided ten case studies on low-income Afro-American families. He finds that the family socialization practices are significant in accounting for school success. Socialization practices with regard to explicit activities that nurture literacy, specific practices in social etiquette, and positive interactive communication help to explain the student's level of achievement in school (Clark, 1983, p. ix, xi). Reference to practices associated with socialization within the home acknowledges the operation of the "hidden curriculum" in schools — the need to meet the behavioral expectations of school personnel. Jackson (1968) points out that academic evaluation is closely related to the mastery of the "hidden curriculum" (e.g., staying in line, not making undue noise in the classroom, waiting your turn, etc.).

So it appears that the educational system does not allow all individuals to compete equally. As politicians and educators come to accept the assessment and indictment of schools as places in which an insufficient amount of training or teaching is taking place, especially among minorities and the poor, what possible solutions can be offered?

Several analysts see that equality and excellence operate in a contrary way; as excellence increases, equality decreases, and as equality increases mediocrity prevails. Why would this be the case? As we structure a schooling process in which a comparable number of Afro-Americans and whites achieve success, it is believed that standards have to be lowered or leveled (Adelson, 1985, p. 25). If we raise standards it is assumed that more working-class and lower-class children will fail to meet the standards. Is it inevitable that we have a system in which this trade-off occurs?

Critics would suggest that if both equality and excellence are promoted, we need an educational system that provides the conditions in which learning can occur and excellence can be attained (Bastian, et al., 1985, pp. 30-31). Some of the mechanisms involved in achieving both equality and excellence are suggested by Clark (1983). He provides insights that, if taken to heart, will enhance the educational competency of the family. As familial educational competence is raised, school success will increase. Additionally, Clark observes that if the role expectations and cognitive functioning in the classroom are compatible with that found in the home, effective instruction is likely. This approach puts the onus on the schools for greater awareness and sensitivity, rather than on students to alter their behavior according to the structure found in the classroom. Thus the educational system needs to be altered so that both these goals can be achieved.

CHRISTIAN PERSPECTIVE

It is relatively easy to identify problems in the educational institution, particularly as one reads contemporary publications. A more difficult question to answer is this: how should we think about mediocrity, credentialism and inequality as Christians? Does a Christian think about these problems differently from a non-Christian? Is there a proper Christian response to the problems outlined? I'd like to suggest a response somewhat removed from providing specifics, and outline a general approach to evaluating these issues.

One term that often creeps into religious discussions on education and its problems is secularism — an issue I've studiously tried to avoid. Here, however, as we consider how to think about the crisis in education, it is relevant. Blamires argues in his book, *The Christian Mind,* that secularism has made greater inroads than we commonly acknowledge. He wrote:

> [B]ut as a *thinking* being, the modern Christian has succumbed to secularization. He accepts religion — its morality, its worship, its spiritual culture, but he rejects the religious view of life, the view which sets all earthly issues within the context of the eternal, the view which relates all human problems — social, political, cultural — the doctrinal foundations of the Christian Faith, the view which sees all things here below in terms of God's supremacy and earth's transitoriness, in terms of Heaven and Hell. (Blamires, 1963, pp. 3-4).

Blamires is suggesting that secularism has not only invaded our practices but has influenced how we think. He describes us as dichotomous thinking people who tend to divide the world into religious and nonreligious. In the religious realm we consider such issues as morality and worship. Once we move to issues not defined as part of the religious realm, we are inclined to forsake religious ideals and evaluate nonreligious issues solely in terms of nonreligious criteria.

If we reject a religious view of life or fail to apply criteria, where applicable, to non-religious issues, Christians have, in effect, accepted the *secular perspective;* this means "a rejection of the supernatural — including all deities — and a faith that man alone, through modern science, can improve the world" (Herbert, 1987:55). Secularism, therefore, becomes an issue of concern since it has the ability to influence how we think. Nonetheless, the question remains, if we need to critically re-evaluate our thoughts and ideas, how does Blamires suggest we should see things?

He proposes that analysis of social phenomena should include a spiritual dimension, to see people as religious beings (Blamires, 1963:8). It is important to realize that Blamires is not arguing for the assumption of given views, but *how* or what methodology we should use, to examine issues. He observes that a Christian mind is "a mind trained, informed, [and] equipped to handle data of secular controversy within a framework of reference which is constructed of Christian presuppositions." We need Christian minds before we can have Christian thinking that leads to Christian action (Blamires, 1963, pp. 42-43). So step one is the cultivation of a Christian mind.

How do we go about acquiring a Christian mind? Blamires says that the Christian mind must be trained and informed, and with this preparation we can then process ideas. Blamires' thoughts seem to complement the ideas of Arthur Holmes (1975). Relating thinking to liberal education, Holmes maintained that liberal education is "an opportunity to become more fully a human person in the image of God, to see life whole rather than fragmented, to transcend the provincialism of our place in history, our geographic location or our job." Holmes applies this more specifically to Christian liberal arts and sees it as the acquisition of a liberal education in "the light of God's self-revelation" (Holmes, 1975). It becomes essential that, as we acquire information and look for answers, we not lose our bearings. Holmes observes that freedom of inquiry (or liberty) needs to exist, but to avoid drifting rudderlessly we must be committed to the Word of God (loyalty). But he insists that loyalty without liberty to think for ourselves is not education. We must remain connected to the Word of God as we look for answers. A Christian mind, then, requires that we work — that we think for ourselves carefully and rationally — to evaluate what occurs around us. By this, however, he means something more than attending Sunday school, and accepting a completed set of statements on "What We Believe." It may mean that within the Christian community there may occur spirited debate as to what is a Christian view. The Christian mind requires biblical knowledge as well as awareness of world events; it requires that *we think.*

The following questions illustrate the distinction that Blamires is positing. Does the present system of education really inform people in useful ways or is it a way of maintaining the status quo? Does the present education system improve our sensitivity to the Gospel, or tend to cause us to think that we are self-sufficient? Such questions are more reflective of a Christian mind. And the issues we raise could be extended to some length. It is important to mention here, however, that a Christian mind is not necessarily better than a secular mind. The secular mind uses the limits of earthly existence or criteria rooted in this world. Both are needed. But our tendency has been to emphasize the secular mind to the point that many Christian things are still contemplated from a secular viewpoint (Blamires, 1963, pp. 45-49).

It is important that we not lose our way as we wrestle in the world of ideas. We must constantly ask: what is our goal? Or, what is the purpose of life? Secular thinking abounds and has subtly invaded many areas. As Holmes has suggested above, and Walter echoes in his book, *Long Way from Home* (1979), we need to retain the eternal standard for evaluating ideas if we are to maintain our spiritual and intellectual bearings. Walter introduces the term "homelessness" in his discussion of how we evaluate events around us. Walter notes in society the increasing use of family, job, or other standards by which events are evaluated. When jobs are lost or friends die, the standard also is eliminated. With relative standards people experience homelessness. If our search for insight is to be fruitful we must not fall into homelessness.

Additionally, Blamires suggests that rigor in thinking is a prerequisite for the development of a Christian mind. Blamires writes:

> Men are less prepared than they were to stub their toes against unpalatable objective truth, to measure their littleness against high objective values, to discipline themselves for a test of strength in rigorous objective examination. This is because a secular tradition has now fully established itself which teaches that man's fulfillment and success lie, not in screwing himself up to the demands of a high vocation, but in molding all that he encounters in service to his needs (Blamires, 1963, p. 126).

Secularism once more has come to influence not only our methodology for living, but the goals we set for ourselves. As society has lost sight of God as the ultimate judge, our standards have suffered; we have lost sight of the pace car. To substitute for a lack of an unchanging standard, people set their own. Thus success has become manipulating what is around us to our advantage — the substitution for an eternal goal.

Besides the demise of the objective standard, Blamires alerts us to the need for excellence. Mastery is the target, mastery of both the secular ideas as well as the Christian or sacred ideas. Again we find Holmes addresses this point indirectly: "All of a young person's human potential must be as fully developed as possible, if the stewardship of his life is to honor God" (Holmes, 1975:29). The charge to develop one's human potential as fully as possible is a call to the whole-hearted pursuit of knowledge.

In response to the report, *Nation at Risk,* 1983, there has been a cry for reform: the search for excellence has become a central theme. As Timar and Kirp write, "given its nature, excellence cannot really be mandated; it is a condition to which we aspire." Thus students need to strive to be extremely good in all areas, and not be content to have average goals. The essential point here is that the goals be excellent regardless of our ability to attain them. Conventional practice suggests a relative standard rather than an absolute standard, but such a stance dilutes the conception of excellence. Furthermore, Timar and Kirp (1988, p. 39) define excellence in schooling as follows: "Aspirations to excellence are generally subtle and pervasive qualities: a love of learning, a sense of history, a command of analytical skills, an appreciation of humanistic values and life."

Is excellence a biblical principle? In the rabbinical code found in Leviticus, we find the principle of faultlessness for sacrifices — something that was to be offered to God. Animals were to be without blemish — a perfect specimen — no blindness, no broken limbs, no cuts or sores, and limbs of a proportioned size (Kiel-Delitzsch, 1949, pp. 435-436). In the New Testament Jesus articulates the principle, "Love the Lord your God with *all* your heart and with *all* your soul and *with all your mind* and with *all* your strength" (NIV, Mark 12:29). This does not suggest a dalliance with spiritual teachings, but an undivided pursuit — all your mind.

We are then challenged to seek the best, not only for the future, but also for the transformation that occurs in us. The focus needs to be expanded from what I can do with this training, to how will this change me. Part of our response needs to put this change in focus. As we reflect on the issue of training vs. education we need to see anew the benefits that accrue from an emphasis on being educated.

Exercising the approach Blamires advocates, we must consider the inequality that persists in our schools. A societal system that actively discriminates against segments of our society is clearly unchristian and contrary to the teaching of Scripture. The Pauline epistles endorse equality in the treatment of others — we are not to be respecters of persons. A system that perpetuates the ascendancy of the middle class needs to be changed. The Bible does not teach that we are all to be equal in social position. For example, while the parable of the Good Steward conveys the principle of stewardship of whatever resources we have (Matthew 25:14-30; Luke 12:41-48), rather than give negative sanctions to all for not pooling their talents and dividing them into equal shares, only the steward with the one talent was rebuked for his failure to use his talent. The educational system, originally devised to enable all to develop their respective talents, now restricts realization of one's potential; the educational system needs to be overhauled.

CONCLUSION

The problems of mediocrity, credentialism and inequality have been defined and explored with regard to American education. These are particularly important issues because of the negative short-term and long-term consequences to the individual students in schools. Also, there is a collective negative that accrues to society. These problems hurt us all. At points, reference was made to solutions. It is essential to remember that complex problems such as these cannot be remedied by simplistic strategies, as Goodlad said. The various constituencies of administrators, teachers, parents, and students must work together and not permit "turf" to determine outcomes. We need to think in our most creative mode.

As Christians we are faced by the particular need not to let our perception of these problems be swayed by societal definitions; mediocrity and equality must be seen clearly and remedied. Christians are not called just to consider the socially dominant factors, but to evaluate practices according to biblical standards, a standard that transcends the vagaries of societal dictates. Christians must be salt and light as we weigh the problems in education. We cannot compromise the standards of excellence we are called to, any more than we can participate in practices that perpetuate social inequalities.

Study and Discussion
Questions

1. Are education and training mutually exclusive? If not, why not? What are the relative merits of education over training?

2. Identify the enrollment patterns of whites, blacks, and Hispanics. Are the patterns the same for males as for females? What are the consequences of the enrollment patterns?

3. Schools are depicted as operating in a mediocre manner. What does this mean? What evidence is there of mediocre performance?

4. What events laid the foundation for the development of credentialism? Why did credentialism occur? Is credentialism still a concern?

5. What effect has credentialism had on the quality of educational preparation?

6. Why are fewer males attending college?

7. There is "talk" that school is the great leveler; everyone of the same ability is treated in an equal manner. How descriptive is this statement of the present state of American education?

8. Identify the two dominant theories found in the sociology of education to account for the variations in the amount of schooling received. Which theory appears to provide the most accurate description of schooling? What are the implications of this theory?

9. What is a Christian mind? Why is the formation of a Christian mind seen as a basic to Christian action?

10. What are the hallmarks of a Christian mind? Why is it important to develop a Christian mind? As we develop a Christian mind, do we forego a secular mind?

References

Adelson, Joseph. "Four surprises, or why the schools may not improve much." Pp. 17-18 in *Challenge to American Schools,* edited by John H. Bunzel. New York: Oxford University Press, 1985.

Ballantine, Jeanne H., *The Sociology of Education: a Systematic Analysis,* second edition. Englewood Cliffs, NJ: Prentice-Hall, Inc., 1989.

Bastian, Ann, Norm Fruchter, Marilyn Gittell, Colin Greer, and Kenneth Haskins, *Choosing Equality.* Philadelphia: Temple University Press, 1986.

Berg, Ivar, *Education and Jobs: The Great Training Robbery.* New York: Praeger Publishers, 1970.

Blamires, Harry, *The Christian Mind.* Ann Arbor: Servant Books, 1963.

Boocock, Sarane, *Sociology of Education: An Introduction,* second edition. Boston: Houghton Mifflin Company, 1980.

Bowles, Samuel, and Herbert Gintis, *Schooling in Capitalist Society.* New York: Basic Books, Inc., 1977.

Cheney, Lynne V., "Students of success." *Newsweek* 108 (September 1), 1986.

Clark, Reginald, *Family Life and School Achievement.* Chicago: The University of Chicago Press, 1983.

Collins, Randall, *The Credential Society.* New York: Academic Press, 1979.

Conklin, Mary E., *Postsecondary Educational Attainment and Occupational Outcomes: A Comparative Analysis.* Unpublished Ph.D. dissertation, The Johns Hopkins University, Baltimore, MD: 1983.

Cremin. Lawrence A., *American Education, The Metropolitan Experience, 1876-1980.* New York: Harper & Row, 1988.

Faia, Michael A., "Selection by certification: A neglected variable in stratification research." *American Journal of Sociology,* 86 (March):1093-1111, 1981.

Garcia, Ricardo L., *Teaching in a Pluralistic Society,* second edition. New York: Harper Collins Publishers, Inc., 1991.

Goodlad, John I., "A Study of schooling: Some implications for school improvement." Pp. 387-400 in *Justice, Ideology, and Education,* edited by Edward Stevens and George H. Wood. New York: Random House, Inc., 1987.

Herbert, Wray, "NO — Fundamentalism vs. humanism." Pp. 53 -60 in *Taking Sides: Clashing Views on Controversial Educational Issues,* fourth edition, edited by James W. Noll. Guilford, CT: Dushkin Publishing Group, Inc., 1987.

Holmes, Arthur F., *The Idea of a Christian College.* Grand Rapids: William B. Eerdmans Publishing Co., 1975.

Hurn, Christopher J., *The Limits and Possibilities of Schooling,* second edition. Newton, Massachusetts: Allyn and Bacon, Inc., 1985.

Jackson, Philip W., *Life in Classrooms.* New York: Holt, Rinehart and Winston, Inc., 1968.

Jencks, Christopher et al., *Inequality.* New York: Basic Books, Inc., 1972.

Jencks, Christopher et al., *Who Gets Ahead?* New York: Basic Books, Inc., 1979.

Keil, C. F., and F. Delitzsch, The Pentateuch, Vol. 1, *Biblical Commentary on the Old Testament.* Translated by James Martin, Vol. 1., Grand Rapids: Eerdmans Publishing Co., 1949.

Kohn, Melvin, *Class and Conformity: A Study in Values,* second edition. Chicago: University of Chicago Press, 1972.

National Commission on Excellence in Education, *A Nation at Risk.* Pp. 368-374 in *Justice, Ideology, and Education,* edited by Edward Stevens and George H. Wood. New York: Random House, Inc., 1983.

Nyberg, David, and Kieran Egan, *The Erosion of Education.* New York: Teachers College Press, Columbia University, 1981.

Public Education Information Network, "Education for a democratic future." Pp. 374-386 in *Justice, Ideology, and Education,* edited by Edward Stevens and George H. Wood. New York: Random House, Inc., 1987.

Olson, Lynn, "Teaching teachers to teach." *The Lamp,* 72 (No. 4):6-9, 1990.

O'Toole, James, *Work, Learning, and the American Future.* San Francisco: Jossey-Bass, Publishers, 1977.

Pincus, Fred L., "The false promises of community colleges: Class conflict and vocational education." *Harvard Educational Review,* 50 (No. 3):332-361, 1980.

Pulliam, John D., *History of Education in America,* fourth edition. Columbus, OH: Merrill Publishing Company, 1987.

Raywid, Mary Ann, Charles Tesconi and Donald Warren, "An environment for outstanding schools." Pp. 330-335 in *Justice, Ideology, and Education*, edited by Edward Stevens and George H. Wood. New York: Random House, Inc., 1987.

Sirotnik, Kenneth A., "What you see is what you get — consistency, persistency, and mediocrity in classrooms." Pp. 231-251 in *Justice, Ideology, and Education*, edited by Edward Stevens and George H. Wood. New York: Random House, Inc., 1987.

Timar, Thomas B., and David L. Kirp, *Managing Educational Excellence*. New York: The Falmer Press, 1988.

U. S. Department of Commerce, Bureau of the Census, *Characteristics of the Population — General Social and Economic Characteristics*, Vol. 1. Washington, D. C.: Government Printing Office, 1980.

U. S. Department of Commerce, Bureau of the Census, Statistical Abstract of the United States 1990. Washington, D. C.: Government Printing Office, 1989.

Walter, J. A., *A Long Way From Home*. London: Paternoster, 1979.

Wright, James D., and Sonia R. Wright, "Social class and parental values for children: A partial replication and extension of the Kohn thesis." *American Sociological Review*, 41 (June):527-537, 1976.

CHAPTER 7
RELIGION: INTRODUCTION

Our choice of a section heading for this part of the text, "anomie institutions," reflects the functionalist perspective that has been used extensively in these articles. Anomie is a sociological concept that describes a breakdown in norms or rules governing the social order. Its emphasis on problematic situations in society stands in contrast to the integration, harmony and order that is the focus of much sociological analysis.

Emile Durkheim, the founding father of sociology who introduced the concept of anomie into sociology, viewed religion as an important source of norms. He argued that norms guided human behavior and that they were a bulwark against the problems of anomie. Although he himself was an agnostic, asserting that the "old gods were dying or already dead," he did recognize the significant role that religion had played by providing these guiding norms.

Norms are a way of integrating people into social groups. Put another way, norms teach us the responsibilities we have to one another. Durkheim observed that agnostics for the most part lacked ties to a religious community. He also noted that Protestants, who favored individual conscience over communal responsibilities, had weaker ties with the religious body than did Catholics or Jews. When normative ties weaken, anomie increases. In his classic work on *Suicide*, Durkheim provided some evidence for his theory by observing statistical differences in suicide rates among Jews, Catholics, Protestants, and the unchurched. Those who had no religious identification were more likely than Jews, Catholics, or Protestant to commit suicide. Protestants had higher suicide rates than Catholics or Jews. Members of a religious body, particularly Jews and Catholics, were linked to an important social institution that gave them a greater sense of belonging.

In raising the question whether religion is "part of the problem or core of the solution," Professor Wallace is essentially asking whether the church itself has not become an "anomic institution." He mentions some of the founding fathers of the social sciences as well as contemporary writers who argue that religion has often worked against the order of the larger social system (as evidenced by the religiously motivated wars that continue to plague humanity). After discussing some of the negative functions of religion, in a Durkheim-like fashion, Wallace goes on to discuss its positive functions.

Wallace argues effectively that all societies have some kind of religion or substitutes for religion (communist ideology being a noteworthy example). If organized religion is prohibited, it appears that some kind of religious surrogate or "functional alternative" develops. Religion has been regarded by many structural functionalists as being vital for any society. In the modern world, religion helps to reduce anomie by fulfilling three basic functions: facilitating a sense of belonging, providing a meaning of life, and giving comfort in time of crisis.

Professor Wallace then departs from his implicit functional analysis to take a stance that would be unacceptable to most sociologists. His defense of Christianity, written as an apology that attempts to prove Christianity to be the true religion, goes beyond the subject matter of sociology. Although most Christian sociologists agree with his faith position, most would also assert that his line of thinking is not sociological but is rather theological.

To understand why Wallace's apology is not sociological, it might be helpful to discuss some of the different ways of knowing and where sociology fits into this scheme. Sociology claims to be a science, an approach to knowing that demands *empirical* evidence. The demand for empirical evidence differentiates sociology from two other important forms of knowledge, namely philosophy and religion. Philosophy relies on thought or reason to uncover the principles or rules that govern reality. Our Christian faith differs from both approaches to knowing in that it is based on divine revelation and our acceptance of this revelation on faith. Although we may employ reason (as did Professor Wallace) and although we may seek empirical evidence, it is the gift of faith that enables us to be ranked among Christian believers.

Professor Wallace's article has provided a functionalist base from which to examine religion. We can examine the functions religion is alleged to contribute to the modern social order. How well does religion provide belonging, meaning, and comfort that would help to shield its followers against anomie?

Data provided through Gallup polls and other surveys suggest that religion is positively functional for the individual. These surveys affirm the importance of religious beliefs and practices, and especially religious experience, as media through which God's comfort is extended. In a recent Gallup survey, for example, 65 percent of the respondents agreed or strongly agreed with the statement "What religion offers me most is comfort in times of trouble and sorrow." On the average, evangelical Christians (those who profess to have accepted Jesus as their personal Savior or to be "born-again") are more likely than nonevangelicals to find their religion to be a great source of comfort (see Margaret M. Poloma and George Gallup, Jr., *Varieties of Prayer*, Trinity Press International, 1991).

Survey data also support the existential function of religion. Although factors like income, health, and marital status tend to be more important than religion in determining satisfaction with life and happiness, religion is by far the best indicator of having a sense of meaning and purpose in life (see Margaret M. Poloma and Brian F. Pendleton, *Exploring Neglected Dimensions of Religion in Quality of Life Research*, The Edwin Mellen Press, 1991). Religious faith helps people to make sense out of their daily lives. It provides what theologians and some sociologists have termed a "theodicy" or a rationale for believing that God's divine purpose will be served in all that happens. The knowledge that "in all things God works for the good of those who love him" (Romans 8:28 NIV) provides assurance to believers.

How successful contemporary churches are in providing a sense of belonging is less than clear. Many Americans seem unwilling to make a commitment to any church community. The importance of individuality over community causes many modern Christians to play "musical church," changing denominations and congregations at whim. It leads others to abandon the institutional church altogether in favor of a more privatized faith.

On balance, religion appears to have positive functions on the individual level. Existing evidence suggests a strong faith does facilitate a sense of personal well-being. Proof that Christianity has functioned positively to improve our society and its composite institutions is far more difficult to produce. It is somewhat easier to conduct research on the micro level, demonstrating the effects of religious faith on individuals, than to prove that religion has a positive impact on the larger society.

The kingdom of God is *within* Christians, but is it also among believers? Does our Christian faith challenge believers to improve the social world in which we live or are we satisfied with its being an agent of personal comfort? The relevance of our faith for ushering in the kingdom of God is a matter that we should keep in the forefront as we examine other anomic institutions.

RELIGION: Christianity, Problem or Solution?

Richard C. Wallace*

Where is God in a world of crack-addicted babies, AIDS, serial murderers, starvation, racial hatred, pollution, and poverty?

RELIGION AS THE PROBLEM

Where does religion fit in the study of contemporary social problems? Can anyone believe that the Church has answers to problems as seemingly intractable as decaying American cities, cynicism permeating our society, continuous racial conflict, widespread drug abuse, or steadily rising suicide rates? Instead, doesn't the Church merely offer isolation and/or escape? Doesn't the Church either turn its back on widespread suffering or apply token "Band-Aids" to social ills? What solutions are provided by the isolated urban missions which offer Church members opportunity to do "something" about the hunger, poverty, and homeless, racial hatred, and drug abuse? Let us explore the justifications for either abandoning or embracing religion as a force helping to prevent and eliminate social problems.

First, let us look at the evidence, is religion a part of the problem? Some suggest that we ought to abandon traditional religion; then we could get on with the business of analyzing what has gone wrong with our social system and begin to work designing a better one. This perspective follows in the footsteps of one of the classic social theorists, August Comte. Comte believed that sociology would become the highest in the hierarchy of sciences (Coser, 1977, p. 9). Sociologists would replace priests and would institute a reign of harmony, justice, rectitude and equity (Coser, 1977, p. 13). Karl Marx held that religion was not only ignorance, but a major contributor to human suffering. Religious notions helped undergird oppression and served as a drug, a tranquilizing "opiate," moving attention away from the social problems at hand. Emile Durkheim, credited with conducting the first empirical sociological work, believed that all religions of the world did not involve contact with spirits or Gods as beings, but merely were symbolic representations of the social group itself. Durkheim would say that we conceive of a God and then project onto that God the role which, in reality, is filled by society itself. We portray God as ruler, omnipotent, omniscient, omnipresent, and eternal. Human society, not some God or gods, sets the norms. Society, in comparison to the strength, knowledge, and presence of mere individuals, rules as omnipotent, omniscient, and omnipresent. Society is also relatively "eternal" when compared to the lifespan of a human being. Durkheim, like many early and contemporary sociologists, viewed religion as mistaken in its teachings about reality, and even as a contributor to

*I especially thank Wendy Wallace for thoughtful suggestions and editorial comments.

social problems. We need not look far to find dismal and even reprehensible behavior in the name of religious causes. In the eighties Jim Bakker bilked millions of dollars from trusting older Americans who thought they were adequately preparing for their retirement. He and his assistants exaggerated the claims of security which his facilities could provide and squandered the money entrusted to them. All this came to public attention with the revelation that some of this money was paid to silence a former employee from whom Bakker had solicited sex. About the same time that Jimmy Swaggart, another public religious figure, was condemning Bakker's morality, Swaggart was himself soliciting a prostitute.

Not all religious abuses are so sensational; some involve much greater, though less recognized, harm. For example, sociologists note that organized religion and oppression often go hand in hand. Sociologists have documented a correlation between religiosity and bigotry. Some of the bloodiest wars in history have been "holy" ones. Indeed, religion-linked violence rages even in contemporary times. Consider Martin Marty's comment:

> Every year I write the *Britannica* and *World Book* yearbook stories on world religion. Look up the *World Book* one on religion for the last twenty years and every year there is Marty saying, "This is the year the Sikhs killed the Hindus, the Hindus killed the Muslims, and the Muslims killed the Buddhists, and the Jews and the Muslims are fighting, and in Northern Ireland, the Catholics and the Protestants are fighting," and some editor sends back the first draft and says, "Are you sure you want to file this under religion? It looks more like war!" That's what's happening around the world. People . . . don't become religious in order to kill other people. They come for opposite reasons, for solace, comfort and belonging to something. That's why you're religious. But when there is conflict, religion often heats it up (Marty, 1987).

Even if religion caused none of these problems, one might question how much good we can expect from such a seemingly feeble institution. Christianity includes the most adherents of all religions in the world, with a large majority of United States citizens professing their faith. A higher proportion of our citizens say they believe in God than virtually any nation on earth, yet only about half have attended a religious service in the past week and typically the service lasted one hour. The average person will spend 30 to 49 times this many hours at work or school, and 10 to 20 times more hours watching television. As a nation we spend more than triple the money we give to religious causes just paying the interest on the national debt. Most of the money given to religious organizations stays at the local level to pay for buildings and staff to serve the very people who gave the money. How can we expect such meager resources to affect social problems such as crime, poverty, drugs and suicide?

RELIGION AS THE SOLUTION

Has religion in general, and Christianity in particular, influenced the life of society? One way to discover how complicated things work is to start separating the parts and then see what happens. For example, take a spark plug out of a car and note the effect; leave the yeast out of bread dough and see what happens.

What would happen to society without religion? This is a difficult question to answer since even irreligious sociologists would concede that all societies exhibit some form of religion. Only in recent history have there been notable social attempts to proceed without religion. For much of this century, the Soviet Union has sought to follow Marx's plan for an improved society without religion. At the same time, however, early communist leaders such as Lenin were elevated to a virtual sacred status. Lenin's body lies enshrined and on display in an elaborate tomb and hundreds of Soviets have filed past it each day for decades, in a ceremony reminiscent of a religious service. Today, however, the Soviet Union has given up the effort to exterminate religion and is allowing churches to reopen.

Similarly, in China the Communist Party sought to eliminate traditional religious practices, but ultimately they enacted practices remarkably similar to earlier religious ones. For decades, they have carried and studied the little red book containing the teachings of Chairman Mao, in much the same way some Christians carry and study the Bible. It seems that a form of religious-like ritual and practice appears even in those societies actively suppressing organized religion.

The implementation of communism in China probably has cost more lives than all religious wars, even perhaps all wars in general. The documented killing of 25,000,000 for this cause exceeds Hitler's destruction of 6,000,000 Jews or the 12,000,000 lives estimated to have been lost in slave trading. Those who fault Christianity for "holy wars" can take little solace in the prospect of avoiding bloodshed by relying on secular utopian visions.

The fact that religion pervades all human societies shows the central importance of what it does for societies and individuals, and suggests that its function would need to be met by religious surrogates if organized religion were absent. Sociologist Andrew M. Greeley (1972) says that religion fulfills three basic human needs: 1) the need for belonging. 2) the need for meaning, and 3) the need for comfort. Religious beliefs and practices function as a social bond, holding society together. It gives people a sense of belonging and identity. Religion provides meaning in the form of answers to questions which go beyond the reach of mere empirical investigation. It provides a set of beliefs that answer ultimate questions, such as: What is the purpose of life? What is right and wrong? Where did the world "come from" and where it is ultimately headed? What happens to a person's consciousness or soul after death? By offering answers to these ultimate questions, religion helps to establish and maintain social order. A society that believes it is accountable to an omnipotent, omniscient God provides for its people reasons to follow norms that go beyond the authority mere humans enact and can reward or punish.

Religion also provides comfort to people in times of crises or death. It gives images of a better life after death. On the one hand religion promises the believing and faithful the hope of heaven. On the other hand, it warns the unbelieving and unrighteous that eventually they will appear before God in judgment.

SIFTING THE WHEAT FROM THE CHAFF

We have discussed how important religion in general is to all societies. But not all religions are equal, and not all are benign or based on truth. In this decade, for example, we find a small segment of the population worshiping Satan and gathering new recruits to Satanism. The media may exaggerate some aspects of Satanic cult activities, but from a Christian perspective such activities provide a contemporary example of a destructive religious movement.

How is it possible to determine the real from the counterfeit? Contemporary social science might suggest that we are ethnocentric (read "wrong") to evaluate another group by our standards. Social scientists may imply that the major religious faiths of the world are man-made, and the claims of God, gods, or spirits, are myth. These social scientists invite us to liberate ourselves from traditional understandings of reality and recognize that we have the ability to design a new and better social order ourselves. We should learn and respect all cultures and value systems. Few introductory sociology textbook authors entertain the possibility that those who believe in God may be in touch with the most significant Reality. Religious beliefs are discussed as if there are only differences in kind, not in worth.

The social vehicle suggested to carry us toward a better world is a more enlightened and involved government. Few social problems texts will suggest that an institution other than the state could introduce solutions for massive social problems.

We might accept this "enlightened" approach, discard old-fashioned, traditional myths, and turn to solving social problems through government intervention. For several years I followed this path, but I quickly learned that the "brave new world" of humanistic science is, in reality, quite barren. It offers few satisfying answers to the great questions of life. I found little consolation in being freed from my supposedly mistaken belief in God, and grew increasingly disillusioned with the prospect that government actions would be able to solve our deeply rooted social problems.

Let's turn to the question, "Which religion is 'true'?" It seems to me we have two options: we can regard Christianity as the Truth and all other religions as false, or we can find a common ground for diverse religious faiths. Many intelligent people have sought to reconcile the religions of the world. The Unitarian Universalist Church holds that there is truth in all the great religions of the world. Many find this belief satisfying and comforting. Instead of claiming that orthodox Christianity is the Truth, the good in all religions is recognized. This approach suggests that the search for God resembles several blind men examining an elephant. One touches the side and says, "This is a wall." Another examines a leg and says, "This is a tree." Still another feels the tail and says, "This is a rope." And finally the elephant sprays the blind man examining the trunk, and he says, "This is a hose." We know from our vantage point that all are experiencing the same elephant. According to this allegory, God is like the elephant, presenting very different realities in different times and places.

Surely God may have various features which seem as different as a trunk and a wall, but can we believe that all religions reflect the same reality? The closer we look the less common ground we find, and the most basic are the contradictions. Buddhism does not acknowledge the existence of a God. Hinduism believes in reincarnation, teaching that persons are physically reborn several times in their spiritual journey. Jews reject Jesus as the Messiah, and many Reformed Jews reject the idea of an afterlife. Christians do not recognize Islam's Mohammed as a prophet, and Muslims deny that Jesus rose from the dead.

While we might like to think we can take the best of each religion and build a better one, Jesus makes claims which are irreconcilable with those religions which fail to recognize Him as Divine and the only path to God. Either Jesus is the necessary way to God or He is not. Since no other religion teaches that He is the only way, we are compelled to decide whether Jesus is right or wrong. We cannot improve on truth by mixing it with falsehood. We must of necessity accept or reject Jesus Christ and His claim. Since a Christian is one who believes that Christ is Savior and Lord, and is committed to Him, alternate paths to God are not acceptable. If He is *the* Way, *the* Truth, and *the* Life (John 14:6), there can be no other (1 Timothy 2:5; Acts 4:12).

Even if we could find a compromise position on the significance of Jesus, we would fail on at least two other counts. *First*, in seeking to include all believers and their religions, we would have to include explicitly dark faiths and cults such as Satanism and black magic. If we decide to exclude religions which are obviously destructive, then we are no longer unifying all religions. *Second*, by what standard of truth would we measure religious claims? All religions and many atheistic philosophies make authoritative claims. Moses, Jesus, Mohammed, Confucius, Buddha, Marx, and Freud each offer values and "rules" to live by. Marx, for example, suggested that the rich and powerful exploit the masses, and that dissolving social stratification would lead to social and personal "salvation." Freud suggested that human misery arises when we deny anger and repress sexual urges. We are able to reach the "best of all possible worlds" only when we understand and deal with our unconscious motivation and resolve inner conflicts between our powerful drives and the requirement of civilization. Freud, Marx, and others describe a world and what it could be, but they do not answer the question of *why* it should be one way rather than another. Ultimately, these thinkers assume that the fundamental issue of what is right and what is wrong is a matter for human beings to rationally discern for themselves. When we disagree, for example, about whether one should burn the flag or abort a fetus, we first consult the laws and then ask the Supreme Court to allow or forbid the behavior. As a people we can redefine what is legally held to be right or wrong. As examples, we have recently "decriminalized" public drunkenness, state gambling, homosexual behavior, and abortion. At the same time we have criminalized certain types of pollution, marital rape, and ethnic or racial harassment. We could, *if* enough people agreed, legalize marijuana, cocaine, or even assault and homicide.

Although many see the legal code as a matter of public opinion, I do not believe that prevailing opinion defines what is morally right or wrong. But if the people do not decide what is moral and immoral, who does? If, in fact, we believe that God exists and reigns, and if we believe the Bible is our only infallible rule of faith and practice, the decision about whether abortion is right or wrong becomes *more than* a matter of humanly derived opinions of the Supreme Court or the American public.

The question still exists, however, why should we recognize one theistic moral claim over another? Those who say they know right from wrong because they know God through Jesus Christ may actually be:

1) following the real God.

2) following a misperception or misrepresentation of the real God.

3) following some other spirit which we assume to be the spirit of God. Throughout history, some people have served "gods" whose presence seem confirmed by works of magic or signs and wonders.

4) following a fictitious "god" which has no spiritual reality.

If Jesus is the only Son of God, and if He and the Father are one, then His moral authority rests not with human opinion or human reasoning. Jesus backed His claim of divinity by performing many miracles or wondrous signs, the most extraordinary of which was His resurrection from the dead, after having offered His body as a sacrifice for sin. No other figure in a major religion claimed to be the only Son of God; nor is any other religious tradition based on the claim of a resurrection. If Christ's claims are credible, they speak louder and clearer than any other faith claims.

Christ's claims *are* credible. Eyewitnesses of the events have written about them; those books make up part of the canon of the Bible. Throughout the history of the Church thousands have reported experiences with God. Many have been put to death rather than deny their belief in Jesus as the Son of God. Not only has this faith grown in its original setting, but belief in Jesus' claims has spread to every continent and most cultures of the world. Millions reared to believe other faiths have rejected them and accepted Jesus as their Lord and Savior. Christians, then, recognize a moral authority beyond themselves and other humans. This authority speaks clearly in Scripture and through the working of the Holy Spirit in their lives today.

BEARING FRUIT WITH JESUS

As a Christian I assert that social problems arise when people: 1) follow no religion, 2) follow religions that are dsyfunctional and do not make for "wholeness," or 3) fail to truly follow the teaching of our Lord Jesus Christ.

What social problems could yet arise and persist if all Christians faithfully followed Jesus? Christians need to recognize that we are often part of the problem. Too often we isolate ourselves and deny any responsibility for what is happening in our society. In considering social problems we need to realize the radical change and commitment with which Jesus has charged us. Perhaps the most neglected commandments are the two great commandments and the "Golden Rule." The first admonishes us to "Love the Lord your God with all your heart, and with all your soul, and with all your mind, and with all your strength." The second to "Love your neighbor as yourself" (Mark 12:29-31 NIV). The "Golden Rule" commands us to "Do to others as you would have them do to you" (Luke 6:31 NIV). The Christian and the Church are not to make people dependent by doing for them what they can do for themselves. But we are to care for the destitute, not only providing emergency relief, but also opportunities to be gainfully employed so that they can become independent and care for themselves (Galatians 6:2-5).

Christ unequivocally states that we cannot serve God and money, and the Apostle Paul reiterates this truth by saying, "the love of money is the root of all evil" (Matthew 6:24; 1 Timothy 6:10). He also cautions us against the sin of covetousness which he says is idolatry (Colossians 3:5). Living in an affluent nation such as the United States presents each of us with the temptation to make a god of material things. To all of us who do so, Jesus will say, as He did to the rich young ruler: "You still lack one thing. Sell everything you have and give to the poor, and you will have treasure in heaven. Then cone, follow me" (Luke 18:22 NIV). To those who have ignored the hungry and thirsty, the homeless, the sick, the naked, and those in prison Jesus will say: "Depart from me, you did not do for me. ... Then they will go away to eternal punishment, but the righteous to eternal life" (Matthew 25:41, 45-46 NIV).

Jesus charged us to love the victims of oppression, as well as the destitute, including even those who create problems for us. "Love your enemies, and pray for those who persecute you," He commanded (Matthew 5:44). Being a Christian not only means that God in Christ is our Savior, but also that He is our Lord. This means we have a greater sense of responsibility than those who do not profess to follow Christ. As Jesus said, "From everyone who has been given much, much will be demanded" (Luke 12:48 NIV).

HEARING THE CALL

How, specifically, should Christians approach social problems? No prescription for a particular social structure will insure that social problems will be eliminated. Furthermore, organized religion — even "Christianity" — is not the answer. Although the Christian Church has accomplished many noteworthy things, it also must admit to significant failures, and even atrocities. If organized or institutionalized Christianity is not *the* answer, what is?

Jesus the Christ is *the* answer! When people surrender their wills to Him, and seek His leading, He brings about marvelous works through them. In abiding with Jesus we can bear the greatest fruit. The roll call of outstanding "fruit-bearers" includes many notable in every sphere — home and foreign missions, politics, industry, and women and men of letters. Again, the greatest commandment is to love one another as Jesus loves us. Jesus wants to live with us, not only in our churches on Sundays, but in our homes, communities, workplaces, and especially in our hearts. When we seek to live with Jesus and love all others as He loves us, we can expect to make more progress toward solving the social problems which plague our society.

Study and Discussion
Questions

1. How does religion presently contribute to social problems?

2. Who are the major critics of Christianity now? What do they advocate in place of Christianity?

3. How is the Church addressing the three most pressing social problems of our time?

4. How true to the teachings of Christ is your local church regarding crack-addicted babies, AIDS, crime, hunger, bigotry, pollution and poverty?

5. What more could you be doing to relieve social problems?

References

Coser, Lewis A., *Masters of Sociological Thought: Ideas in Historical and Social Context,* 2nd ed. New York: Harcourt Brace Jovanovich, Inc., 1977.

Durkheim, Emile, *The Elementary Forms of Religious Life,* Translated by J. W. Swain. London: Allen & Urwin, 1915.

Greeley, Andrew M., *The Denominational Society.* Glenview, IL: Scott Foresman, 1972.

Marx, Karl, and Friedrich Engels, *(1843) Toward the Criticism of Hegel's Philoso phy of Rights,* Paris, trans. Glen Waas, quoted in Robert Freedman, *Marxist Social Thought.* New York: Harcourt Brace Jovanovich, Inc., 1968.

CHAPTER 8
PHYSICAL AND
MENTAL HEALTH: INTRODUCTION

The dominant approach to the sociological study of social problems tends to focus on the social structure. Both structural functionalism and conflict theory assume the reality of social groups and social institutions. Both theories are considered to be part of the "social facts" paradigm. This paradigm or model takes its basic assumption from Emile Durkheim's famous dictum to "treat social facts as things." The social system and its composite parts, including groups, institutions, social roles, and norms, are regarded as phenomena that are distinct from individual actors. According to this paradigm, "social facts" are the appropriate subject matter of sociology.

Both structural functionalism and conflict theory, however, have been criticized for a neglect of the human actor. It is claimed that men and women who occupy the social roles that make up societal institutions are often lost sight of. Another model known as the "social definition" paradigm combines the focus on social structure with that of individual interpretation of "social facts." The paradigm takes its name from W. I. Thomas's famous "definition of the situation": "If men and women define something as real, it is real in its consequences."

The labeling perspective discussed by De Santo in Chapter 1 fits into the social definition paradigm. This perspective is used by Professor Walker in defining health and illness. As he points out, disease, illness, and sickness are all convenient labels which identify particular behaviors. Illness in particular is a subjective feeling, a self-definition to denote pain, nausea, or anxiety. Sickness, on the other hand, implies a more collective definition by members of society and denotes a social status (rather than a biological condition as in disease or a social psychological condition as in illness).

Although Professor Walker employs both the social facts and the social definition paradigms in his article, his focus in suggesting a Christian response to health needs is largely within the social definition model. His discussion of physical and mental health does recognize the interface between the subjective (the mental) and the physical. He also recognizes that both are affected by the spiritual. In other words, spiritual health is intimately related to physical and mental health. It is holistic—the kind of total wellness of mind, body and spirit that we find reflected in Jesus' ministry.

Both spiritual and physical healings were an integral part of the life of Jesus, as well as the ministry of the early church. Theologian-psychologist Morton Kelsey points out that nearly one-fifth of the Gospels is devoted to accounts of miraculous healings by Jesus. The early Church, as described in the Book of Acts and in nonbiblical historical accounts, also reflects an openness to spiritual healing. It was only with the increased institutionalization of the Church and the development of an Aristotelian-based theology which dichotomized body and soul that miraculous healings became a rarity or a phenomenon not to be expected at all. All too often, body and soul were separated with medicine responsible for healing the body and religion responsible for curing the soul.

Recent surveys have shown that the belief and practice of spiritual healing is widespread (see Margaret M. Poloma, "A Comparison of Christian Science and

Mainline Christian Healing Ideologies and Practices" in the *Review of Religious Research*, June, 1991, p. 337-350). In one regional survey which gathered data from 560 randomly chosen respondents about their belief in spiritual healing, a clear majority (72%) said they believed that physical healing could occur as a result of prayer. Nearly a third of the respondents (32%) claimed to have personally received such a healing. Does spiritual healing have a place in any Christian discussion of mental and physical health? We believe it does.

Christians who believe in and employ healing ritual and prayer usually do so in conjunction with the use of modern medicine. Most Christians who claimed to experience a divine healing from a life-threatening condition made use of modern medicine. For example, the vast majority of those who reported being healed of some physical ailment as a result of prayer had visited their physician within the past year. Nearly three quarters of the sample (73%) agreed with the statement that "God usually heals through doctors." Most are reluctant to "blame the victim" when physical healing is not forthcoming, recognizing that God often uses our physical ailments for some greater spiritual good. It is noteworthy that James 5:13-16 may be interpreted as calling for the combination of medicine and prayer to combat illness. James recommends that those who are sick call for the elders to anoint them with oil (medicine) and to pray. (The reader may recall that in Luke 10:34, the good Samaritan poured oil on the traveler's wounds.)

Not all people, however, are equally likely to believe in, to pray for, and to report they have experienced diving healing. Margaret Poloma and Brian Pendleton (*Exploring Neglected Dimensions of Religion in Quality of Life Research*, The Edwin Mellen Press, 1991) found that older people, those with less income, and those with less education were more likely to respond affirmatively to questions about healing than those who were younger and more affluent. They also found that those who were suffering from some kind of health problems were also more likely to report having experienced a healing in the past than those who were in good health. What can be said about such findings from a sociological perspective?

Sociologists have attempted to explain the importance of religion to the elderly and the ill by invoking "deprivation theory." Deprivation theory claims that those who are "deprived" of the "good life" (good health, money, education, etc.) are more likely to be religious than those who are healthy and wealthy. Research tends to confirm this theory, namely that those who have less of what the world has to offer will turn to religious compensators for comfort. Poloma and Pendleton found this to be somewhat true, but they made another important observation in studying the results of their survey.

They divided their sample into two groups: those in poor health and those in good health. They then checked to see what impact prayer for healing had on the respondents' satisfaction with their health. They found that prayer for healing and other religiosity measures contributed to increased health satisfaction for those with poor health but not for those with good health. This finding fit well with Jesus' observation that the well do not need a physician (Luke 5:31). Those who had some physical limitations and who turned to the Divine Physician for healing were more satisfied with their health status and their general well-being than their counterparts who did not. Even if physical healing was not forthcoming, their faith seemed to make a difference in their subjective perceptions of well-being.

Deprivation theory and any such evidence that is used to support it can make some Christians uneasy. It makes our Christian faith in healing sound like a crutch. In light of Scripture, however, perhaps neither the theory nor the findings should surprise us. Jesus consistently reached to comfort and heal those who were suffering from physical disease as well as those tortured by mental illness. In the Gospels we find account after account of Jesus healing those He encountered.

Jesus reportedly also shared His healing power with His followers. In Luke's account of the sending forth the 72 disciples we hear Jesus say, "Heal the sick who are there and tell them, 'The kingdom of God is near you'" (Luke 10:9 NIV).

Accounts in the Book of Acts demonstrate that the practice of healing was very much part of the early Church. It was only with the increased institutionalization of the Church and increased reliance on rational theology that the practice of healing was forced to the fringes of Christianity. Research findings cited above, however, suggest that many Christians do believe in and practice spiritual healing and that such practices do make a difference in their lives.

Another biblical phenomenon related to health that most educated Christians are afraid to discuss is that of demon possession and oppression. Biblical accounts tell us of Jesus casting out demons and empowering His followers to do the same. Is it possible that demons have anything to do with some of the evil that destroys the minds and bodies of people in our contemporary society?

In his controversial book *People of the Lie* (Simon & Schuster, Inc., 1983) psychiatrist M. Scott Peck asks social scientists to explore the possibility that a personified evil force may be at the base of some sociopathological behaviors. Although he urges the reader to handle his book with care, the material he presents (including a chapter on exorcism) suggests that demons may be alive and well in modern society. Peck takes a cautious middle-of-the-road approach, avoiding the extreme of seeing a devil behind every bush but also challenging those who would use a medical model to explain all mental illness and all addictive behavior.

A holistic approach to health has gained much ground within the past decades. Often, however, it has been limited to studying and discussing the interface of physical health with mental health. Spiritual factors influencing health and well-being are only beginning to be included in this holistic model. A Christian approach should study the Scriptures, struggling to integrate a biblical spirituality (even aspects that seem controversial like healing and demonic forces) with what is known about physical and mental health.

PHYSICAL AND MENTAL HEALTH
J. Thomas Walker

The maintenance of health and the treatment of illness are basic functions in any society. A society must organize itself in such a way as to provide for and institutionalize the meeting of its health care needs. In this chapter we shall focus on the concepts of physical and mental health and how they have been institutionalized in American society. From this vantage point we will be able to assess the adequacy of health care in the United States and what this means for the committed Christian in American society. The chapter will be divided into four major sections: (1) defining health and illness, (2) the etiology of physical and mental health, (3) the institutionalization of American health care and (4) a Christian response to physical and mental health needs.

DEFINING HEALTH AND ILLNESS

Disease, Illness, Sickness
In order to understand the meaning of both good health and the lack of it, three concepts become important — disease, illness, and sickness. According to Twaddle and Hessler (1987, p. 125), these terms serve as convenient labels which identify particular behaviors. Disease involves an alteration in physiological functioning that results in a reduced capacity to function or a shortening of the normal life span. A disease is objectively measurable and exists whether or not it is recognized (Twaddle and Hessler, 1987, pp. 10, 39).

Unlike the objectivity of disease, illness involves subjective feelings on the part of persons who define themselves as unhealthy because they are experiencing pain, nausea, or anxiety. If these feelings are reported to others they may also be defined by them as being unhealthy. Illness is usually assumed to involve the presence of a disease, and often signals the need to seek medical care. But illness in not the same as disease, since one can be ill without a disease and be diseased without being ill (Twaddle and Hessler, 1987, pp. 88-89).

Sickness results when one is publicly defined as unhealthy, either by oneself or others, and is regarded as in need of treatment. In such instances the individual experiences a shift in social identity from one who was well but now is not. Sickness differs from disease (a sociobiological status) and illness (a sociopsychological status) in that it is a social status. One is socially labeled and treated as such. Sickness may be brought on by disease, an illness, or a societal reaction that defines the situation as "sickness." Although sickness is presumed to have a basis in a disease or illness, it can occur independently of either (Twaddle and Hessler, 1987, pp. 88-89).

The Medical Model
In modern medicine physicians treat diseases. In fact, they even specialize in

particular pathologies and limit their practices accordingly. They are trained to possess the scientific expertise necessary to identify and treat specific diseases in terms of their physical causes. This approach is known as the medical model, and explanation and treatment of illness in terms of disease.

The medical model is widely accepted both by the medical profession and laypersons as the most appropriate medical care in our society. When we injure ourselves or "catch a bug," we go to a physician who diagnoses, treats, and prescribes a remedy. Because the medical profession is closely aligned with new scientific and technological knowledge, we give the physician a great deal of authority over our bodies and even over our lives.

But the medical model with its emphasis on arresting the development of disease somewhat neglects the positive aspect of human functioning. An alternative perspective of modern medicine would give primacy to the means of keeping persons healthy; prevention prior to necessary treatment and care would be emphasized. This view transcends the medical model which focuses on the diseased state of patients and emphasizes instead the social world in which they live.

The Social Model

In contrast to the medical model, the social model of illness does just this. It explains illness on the basis of the social situations in which illness occurs. A better grasp of a positive conception of health is provided, along with preventive measures that can be taken to reduce illness. This model essentially stems from the perspective offered by Talcott Parsons who did seminal work in the sociological analysis of health and illness (Parsons, 1951, 1972, 1975). According to Parsons, health is more than the absence of disease. Rather it is a state of optimal functioning with regard to one's social roles. Illness is a disturbance in the capacity to carry out appropriate social roles, whatever the cause — physical, psychological, or social. Thus, to lose one's voice because of a cold might be of little consequence to a factory worker on a noisy assembly line. In fact, she/ he may simply choose to ignore the situation. But, given the same situation, telephone operators or professional singers would be likely to define themselves as sick and seek professional attention. In other cases one may not be able to carry out appropriate social roles, but yet be without disease in the medical sense. Such a person may come to be defined as sick in the psychiatric sense.

Mental Illness

Because mental illness can differ significantly from other illnesses, it deserves special attention. A major difficulty in discussing metal illness is that we know so little about it. While there have been many different systems of classification for mental disorders, none have been satisfactory. Nevertheless, there are three broad categories of mental disorders that constitute what is known as mental illness.[1] These are the

---

[1]Although the current professionally accepted source of psychiatric classification — the Third edition of the *American Psychiatric Association's Diagnostic and Statistical Manual* — recently reclassified the types of mental illness, we shall deal with the traditional classification of psychoses, the neuroses and psychosomatic disorders. This traditional classification is more appropriate for our purposes since epidemiological studies have also used this older classification.

psychoses, the neuroses and psychosomatic disorders.

The psychoses are the most severe and debilitating of all mental disorders. Psychotic persons are characterized by bizarre and unusual behavior, gross distortions of reality and a serious inability to function in the ordinary demands of everyday life. Delusions are typical and hallucinations may occur. Such individuals may be committed to mental hospitals because they threaten themselves or others, or because their behavior has simply become too intolerable to the community. Those with psychoses are much more likely than others with mental disorders to be institutionalized and, until recently, this placement was more or less permanent.

Neuroses are much less severe and debilitating than the psychoses. As compared to the psychoses, neurotic disorders lie closer to normal behavior. The neurotic person is in touch with reality but experiences high levels of anxiety. Anxiety is similar to fear but is either grossly disproportionate to the external threat or unrelated to such threat. The particular symptoms of neurosis vary with the way the individual has learned to cope with anxiety. Examples of neurotic disorders include obsessive-compulsive behavior, hypochondria, and various phobic and hysterical reactions.

The final major category of mental illness involves psychosomatic disorders. These disorders are without apparent organic causes, but result in physical illness. That is, psychosomatic disorders are impairments in the physiological functioning of an individual as a consequence of his/her emotional state. Examples of psychosomatic disorders include high blood pressure, ulcerative colitis, severe allergies and anorexia nervosa (a loss of appetite with possible physical deterioration).

A Definition of Health

Having looked at various conceptions of disease, illness and sickness as well as the major forms of mental illness, it is now possible to establish a meaningful definition of health. The World Health Organization uses this definition: "Health is a state of complete physical, mental, and social well-being and not merely the absence of disease or infirmity" (World Health Organization 1981, p. 1). This definition emphasizes the positive aspect of health in social as well as physical terns, recognizing that well-being must take into consideration the social and cultural environment in which individuals live. This definition will be used as a point of reference in looking at health care in the United States.

ETIOLOGY OF PHYSICAL AND MENTAL ILLNESS

Epidemiology

Epidemiology is a term frequently used by sociologists to denote the extent and distribution of illnesses within a population. By studying the epidemiology of an illness sociologists attempt to gain a better understanding of etiology or cause of the illness. These concepts were first used to understand contagion within the context of what can be called disease theory. By looking at who tended to contract what kind of disease under what particular conditions, researchers sought to understand the nature of the cause of a given illness. Epidemiologists do the same thing today in a more precise way, considering a greater variety of causal variables — biological, physical, social, and cultural.

National health statistics indicate a general improvement in our nation's health. In 1985 the death rate was 8.7 per 1,000 population, down from 9.5 for both 1960 and 1970 (*U. S. Bureau of the Census,* 1987, p. 73). People are living longer. The average life expectancy at birth in 1986 was 74.9 years, higher than it has ever been. However, on the average, females can expect to live 7.0 years longer than males, and whites can expect to live 4.0 years longer than black and other Americans (ibid, p. 70).

An Epidemiological Transition

The population of the United States has undergone a rather dramatic epidemiological transition since the turn of the century. The disease structure in this country has changed from communicable and infectious diseases to chronic illnesses. The three major causes of mortality (death) and morbidity (disease) in 1900 were pneumonia, tuberculosis and gastrointestinal diseases. These diseases were controlled through better sanitation, advancing science, and medical technology. By 1940 the three major causes of death had become heart disease, cancer and stroke. This change was accompanied by a national demographic transition in which both death rates and birth rates dropped. The result is an aging population with longer life expectancies and considerably more chronic health problems (Albrecht 1982, p. 365).

Lifestyle and Health

The three major causes of mortality and morbidity — heart disease, cancer and stroke — (*U. S. Bureau of the Census*, 1987:77) are largely a function of lifestyle rather than infectious contagion. As individuals have accepted the ideal image of the full, active American who is always on the go, and enjoying a life of abundance and leisure, American health has suffered. We are hypertensive, overweight, and ingest food containing high levels of cholesterol, salt and sugar. Our diets frequently consist of junk foods containing chemical preservatives, artificial sweeteners, and food coloring. Often our meals are not well balanced. Our foods are processed and, lacking in roughage, have been causally linked with digestive problems and cancer of the colon. Many of our "fast foods" are either broiled or fried and lack the nutrition that they would have if properly prepared. These factors all have a bearing on our nation's health and the incidence of chronic health problems — especially heart disease, diabetes, cancer, and nutritional or vitamin deficiency (Albrecht 1981, p. 370). Just because we are living longer does not mean that we are living any healthier, or that we enjoy a higher quality of life. Millions of Americans have significant work and lifestyle limitations due to the effects of such illnesses (*U. S. Bureau of the Census*, 1987, p. 108).

The Physical Environment and Health

We live in a polluted physical environment threatened by industrial and nuclear waste, and by the lack of clean air to breathe. Heavy quantities of carbon monoxide, sulfur oxides, hydrocarbons, and various particulate matter from industry and automobiles are thrown daily into the air that we breathe. Air pollution can pollute both land and waters through the falling of "acid rain." This invisible form of pollution has a pervasive effect on humans in both the food eaten and the environment in which we live. The earth's protective ozone layer is threatened by the use of fluorinated hydrocarbons with a resulting increase in skin cancer.

Social and Cultural Factors

Social and cultural factors also affect our health. As already indicated, females enjoy a considerably longer life expectancy than males. They also have lower mortality rates, which is partly explained by a marked number of accidents among men whose occupational and social roles expose them to physical danger. Males also experience greater occupational stress. Females are more biologically fit at birth than are males, but as adults tend to have higher morbidity, report illnesses more readily, and manifest a greater loss of productivity (Cockerham, 1989a, pp. 42-47).

Social class impacts on the chances one has for a healthy life so it is not surprising that low socioeconomic status correlates positively with illness. Those who are poor experience crowded living conditions, poor diet, low levels of income, and minimal education. The life chances and state of general health among the poor are significantly reduced in comparison with the larger population (Cockerham, 1989a:66).

The epidemiology of mental illness has also followed class lines. Numerous studies reveal that the lower the socioeconomic status the greater the likelihood for serious mental disorders (Faris and Dunham, 1938; Hollingshead and Redlich, 1958; Srole, et al., 1962; Dohrenwend, 1975, p. 370). Neuroses tend to be more prevalent among the upper classes, while psychoses are more likely among the lower classes.

Perhaps the most famous epidemiological study of mental illness was the Midtown Manhattan study first published by Leo Srole and associates in 1962. In this New York City survey of 1660 respondents, the results of judgments made by psychiatrists suggested that almost one-fourth of the representative population has serious psychiatric symptoms. Just as astonishing was the finding that only 18.5 percent were defined as without symptoms (Srole, et al., 1962, p. 138). While these figures do not reveal how many of the respondents were actually mentally ill, they do reveal the number which psychiatrists would diagnose as mentally ill. The implication is that mental illness is much more prevalent than one might expect, certainly greater than official hospital admission rates would suggest.

The Etiology of Mental Illness

The eitology of mental illness is considerably more difficult to discuss than that of physical illness. In the case of physical illness, we speak of objective symptomatologies and diseased states. But with mental illness we are concerned with evaluating human behavior. Subjectivity enters into what is presumed to be scientific diagnosis so that it is not unusual for two psychiatrists to diagnose the same patient quite differently.

Many different ideas and theories concerning the definition and cause of mental illness therefore exist. David Mechanic (1980, pp. 54-72) has conceptualized these into five major theories — hereditary, psychosocial development, learning, social stress, and societal reaction.[2]

The hereditary explanation finds mental illness developing from a genetic predisposition, while the psychosocial-development explanation stresses the influence of early childhood experiences, especially those in which the child has experienced significant rejection, hostility, or other emotional abuse. The learning approach views mental illness as persistent unadaptive anxiety responses learned in anxiety-generating situa-

---

[2]For a good discussion of the five major theories or explanation of mental illnesses, see Mechanic (1980, pp. 45-72) and Cockerham (1989b, pp. 69-108).

162

tions. The social stress explanation suggests that everyone has a breaking point and that mental disorders result when accumulated stress eventually overcomes the ability to cope. Finally, the societal reaction approach explains how an individual who is otherwise normal can become labeled as abnormal and encouraged to play out a deviant role which is then defined as a mental illness. Here a cause is attributed to social rather than medical factors.

Although significant truths are present in each of these explanations, our knowledge about the causes of mental illness is remarkably limited.

INSTITUTIONALIZATION OF AMERICAN HEALTH CARE

Dealing with medical problems involves more than going to a physician or hospital, getting cured, and then returning to one's everyday routine. The sick role is being played out; the individual is incapacitated and normal social roles are suspended.

The Sick Role — Advantages and Costs

The sick role, however, is not automatically accepted. Careful consideration of the advantages and disadvantages of the role is necessary before adopting the role. One, an obvious advantage is that one's particular situation can be medically managed so as to reduce the duration of illness. Second, significant personal attention and social support are rendered in a time of relative helplessness. In the case of a mental disorder, there may be less stigma attached to defining a situation medically rather than psychiatrically. Third, the sick role has special advantages of certifying financial need, gaining financial dispensations, or reducing various obligations.

Disadvantages exist as well. One is that taking on a sick role may require the disruption of a desired lifestyle. Another is that being sick costs money, and individuals might put off needed medical care in favor of other expenditures. Or, especially in the case of mental illness, being sick can entail an assigned stigma. In such instances the individuals must deal with the management of a spoiled identity or discredited self. Research by Phillips (1963, pp. 971-972) indicates that the community may increasingly reject those defined as seeking no help, or utilizing a clergyman, a physician, a psychiatrist or mental hospital. These findings suggest that a fear of the stigma associated with mental health assistance may cause some persons to avoid seeking help. Apparently, using a help source involves the reward of professional attention and also the cost of community rejection.

Although Phillips' research was limited to mental health care, there is little doubt that many people also avoid meeting their immediate general health needs. Fear of terminal illness, needed surgery, physician disapproval, community disapproval, or overburdening financial costs may be included in the reasons. This may also be true for the seeking of preventive health care.

Three Structures of Medical Care

Assuming that one has to seek medical care, three major types of structures become important — the medical profession, service delivery structures, and health care finance structures.

The Medical Profession: Physicians hold high professional status in our society.

They are intimately involved with the extremely important function of promoting health and saving lives. It is also true that since the mid-nineteenth century physicians have been developing scientific standards which set themselves apart from other health care practitioners, and have helped achieve their elite position in society.

Established in 1947, the American Medical Association (AMA) took up the cause of professionalizing medicine. Attempting to improve the quality of medical education the profession also standardized and monopolized medical knowledge and practice (Maykovich, 1980).

Today the AMA is organizationally powerful. It maintains professional control over medical practice and, as a consequence, physicians enjoy immunity from external judgment or evaluation. As a matter of fact, the power is so great that the AMA is able to define and have dominant authority over whatever can be thought of as illness, including mental illness.

Physicians in the United States are both geographically and professionally maldistributed. A shortage exists in rural areas and urban ghettos. As might be expected, physicians prefer to practice in areas of economic affluence. Consequently, the poor have less access to a physician and receive little professional medical attention except in acute situations. Due to increasing specialization, less than 13 percent of the nation's physicians are general practitioners (*U. S. Bureau of the Census,* 1987, p. 95); the rest are specialists. General personalized medical care is difficult to access regardless of social class.

Health Care Service Delivery Structures: Delivery structures include clinics, hospitals, nursing homes, and mental hospitals. These structures are called on to perform multiple functions in a rapidly changing society. In an increasingly specialized profession, the delivery structure — especially the hospital — have become complex bureaucracies. For patients this may mean fragmented and depersonalized care with no one professional relating to their total person. This is especially likely where interdepartmental communication among health care professionals is poor. Even when this is not the case, patients may view their physicians as more interested in the medical challenge that their illness represents than in their personal restoration to good health. The efficiency and/or profit interests of the institution may also be placed above the welfare of the patient. As a result, health care facilities are not considered very desirable places to be, unless one is seriously in need of crisis medical attention. Then they are the only places to be.

But if clinics and hospitals are not generally places to be, most mental hospitals are even worse. Erving Goffman has characterized the mental hospital as a type of "total institution." A total institution is a "place of residence and work where a large number of like-situated individuals, cut off from the wider society for an appreciable period of time, together lead an enclosed life, formally administered round of life" (Goffman, 1961, p. xiii). Mental hospitals are often geographically isolated, custodial rather than therapeutic in care, institutionally bureaucratic, and supervised by a psychiatrist. Personal independence and self-determination are sharply diminished and residents may be institutionally dependent (Goffman, 1961). The mental hospital serves primarily as a warehouse for those who are seriously and chronically mentally ill. By means of modern drugs or "chemotherapy," patients are managed rather than cured.

Over the past two decades, however, a strong trend toward the deinstitutionalization of the mentally ill has emerged. Policy thinking has changed from an emphasis on custodial or institutional care to community mental health care. With the Community Mental Health Centers Act of 1963, new community mental health centers were built which were intended to provide five mandated services: inpatient care, outpatient care, partial hospitalization, 24-hour emergency service, and community consultation and education. Additional services such as diagnosis and evaluation, rehabilitation and aftercare, public information, staff training, and research and planning were later included. These functions intended to promote both prevention and deinstitutionalization around the community or social model rather than a medical one. Unfortunately, the community mental health concept and its services were not well coordinated with mental hospitals. Deinstitutionalization was emphasized, but the needed community follow-up was lacking. Readmission to mental hospitals was common. Those who remained in the community often experienced a poor quality of life (Cockerham 1989a, p. 285). In some ways the community mental health concept created a built-in funding stream with which to carry out more or less conventional psychiatry. The medical model was retained, and consequently, the community mental health centers were not effective in attacking the social conditions that give rise to mental disorders (Cockerham, 1989a, p. 294).

Health Care Finance Structures: Health care is costly and is big business in the United States. For 1986 the amount spent per person in the United States in health care was a staggering $1,837, with the total national health expenditures for the same year being greater than 458 billion dollars. National health expenditures as a percentage of gross national product rose from 4.4 in 1950 to 5.2 in 1960, 7.4 in 1970, and 9.1 in 1980 and 10.9 in 1986 (*National Center for Health Statistics*, 1989, p. 150). This share of the gross national product indicates the increasing proportion of the nation's natural resources which are being allocated to health care. The situation is a matter of great concern both in terms of the rate of increase and the current absolute levels of health care spending.

Many reasons are suggested for the high cost of health care. One has been the monopolization of care by the medical profession, and the resultant shortage of physicians. In the past physicians have been able to charge their own fees in a market of limited competition. More recently, the tendency to specialize has meant higher doctor bills, since specialists charge higher fees and the patient usually must be seen by more than one physician. In addition, costly paramedical workers and administrators have been hired in hospitals and clinics, and expensive technology introduced.

The "medicalization" of society has also added to health care costs. The definition of sickness has become so expanded that physicians now maintain professional jurisdiction over physical, mental, and social conditions that were once not regarded as medical. Having gained a knowledge base in areas such as diet, child development, and drug and alcohol dependence, physicians began to treat such conditions as medical problems. Even excessive gambling and credit purchasing are being treated medically as addictions. The aura of knowledge and prestige associated with medicine has influenced many Americans to place great faith in medical progress and look toward physicians to cure almost everything. This heavy demand for health care services has also caused prices to rise.

Third party providers have been a major factor in increasing health care costs. Large private insurance plans (such as Blue Cross and Blue Shield) and government plans (such as Medicare and Medicaid) essentially guarantee payment for covered services. When the recipient of the service is not personally paying the bill, there is little incentive to keep costs down. Expensive tests and machinery are routinely used, increasing the related professional fees. Physicians, hospitals and nursing homes reap tremendous economic benefits from this financial arrangement; abuse is common.

Three major sources are available for the payment of health care services in the United States: private, out-of-pocket payment; private insurance; and government insurance. Private out-of-pocket payments accounted for 28.7 percent of personal health care costs in 1986, down from 65.5 percent in 1950. The decline in out-of-pocket payment reflects the significant increase in both private health insurance coverage and government coverage. Private health insurance now accounts for 30.4 percent; government coverage accounts for 39.6 percent (*National Center for Health Statistics*, 1989, p. 160).

While health care costs are expensive for everyone, they are especially burdensome to the working poor who are not likely to have either private or government health insurance. A far greater proportion of total family income is spent for health care services among low income families as compared to higher income families. Unfortunately, those least able to pay for health care costs must give up the greatest proportion of their incomes for it (*U. S. Bureau of the Census*, 1987, p. 91).

Health Care — Right or Privilege?

Traditionally health care has been thought of as a privilege in American society — a matter of individual responsibility. It has been viewed as a marketable commodity, the cost of which if desired, must be paid by the consumer.

However, the overemphasis of individual responsibility results in an attitude of "blaming the victim" toward those who possess the least power and resources to cope with the spiral in increasing health costs. The idea of individual responsibility must be balanced by recognition of the pain and suffering experienced in a social milieu over which individuals have little or no control (Conrad and Kern, 1981, p. 450). The institutional structures with which we presently deliver health care services were developed when medical practice was rather simple, carried out on a local scale, and less characterized by escalating costs than today. It might be argued that much of the health care plight of the poor could be laid at the door of the monopolistic American Medical Association, pharmaceutical companies, manufacturers of medical equipment and supplies, and other profiteers who constitute what might be called the American medical-industrial complex.

Most observers note that a serious crisis in the American health care system does exist and that something must be done to alleviate the burden of out-of-control costs. Adequate health care is increasingly viewed as a right rather than a privilege. This is exemplified by Congressional action which passed Medicare in 1965. At least for that 10 percent of the nation's population over age 65, medical care is now regarded as a human right. The ideology behind the Community Mental Health Centers Act of 1963 also interpreted mental health treatment to be a right, not a privilege. All segments of the population are to have access to mental health care regardless of the ability to pay.

National Health Insurance or HMOs

Some form of national health insurance is on its way. What seems to be most at issue is the question of the particular form that it will take. Generally, national health insurance is a broad term used to refer to legislative proposals by which the nation's entire population could be provided with health care services. The various proposals put forth plans for the government guarantee of payment. These plans could be placed on a continuum ranging from the most liberal to the most conservative. The continuum varies on three dimensions. First is that of coverage. Liberal plans cover more services, while the conservative plans cover only catastrophic major medical costs. Second is the degree of government control over the use of funds, physician distribution, and control over payments. Third is the source of funding. The more liberal plans are constructed on the basis of payment from general tax revenues. The more conservative plans rely on individual and employer payments (Denton, 1978, p. 303-305).

An alternative to national health insurance is the Health Maintenance Organization (HMOs). An HMO is a large prepaid group practice which provides all health services to a specific population. HMOs emphasize preventive medicine, since they derive the major source of their income from keeping their patients healthy and utilizing hospitalization less frequently. Emphasis is placed on services such as routine checkup, minor preventive surgery, and outpatient services. The objective is to keep costs down while providing sound, preventive health care. HMO physicians have a direct financial interest in keeping their patients well. Consequently, HMOs have greater cost control potential than the traditional fee for service medical practice which is geared toward dealing with fully developed health care problems. According to the Health Insurance Association of America, in 1988 the average monthly cost for individual coverage in a conventional plan was $98.00 and $209.00 for a family   For the staff-group HMO coverage it was $93.00 for an individual and $203.00 for a family (*Health Insurance Association of America*, 1989, p. 21). The HMO membership is the most advantageous since it guarantees preventive as well as therapeutic physician services, hospitalization, medical tests, and sometimes prescription drugs and other health needs at either little or no further cost.

Presently, HMOs provide health care for only a small segment of our nation's population, but the program looks appealing as a model for meeting national needs. In 1980 the number of persons enrolled in HMOs rose to 9.5 million, a threefold increase since 1970 and by 1987 the figure rose to almost 30 million (*National Center for Health and Statistics*, 1989, p. 173).

A CHRISTIAN RESPONSE TO HEALTH NEEDS

Christ the Healer

Since physical and mental health can easily be thought of as relating only to life on earth, some who are "other worldly" in their Christian emphasis might be tempted to neglect their importance to the Christian's life. However, it can be noted that a great deal of Christ's time and efforts while on earth were spent in healing the sick of mind and body. Unlike parts of the Old Testament where sickness and disease were seen as punishments inflicted by God, Christ's conception of illness was that it was not part of the divine order of things, but was rather a manifestation of the works of the devil. Sickness and disease represent constant reminders of humans falling away from God, into sin. Because Christ's mission on earth was to destroy the works of the devil and reunite us with God, it is not surprising that His earthly ministry involved healing those sick of body and soul. It is clear that Christ wants us to be whole and free from affliction. Even when some doubt was expressed by the leper that it might not be the will of Christ for healing to occur, Christ immediately put the question aside and healed the leper (Matthew 8:2-3; Mark 1:40-42; Luke 5:12-13).

Personal Christian Responses

Christ's teaching and the tenets of the Christian faith relate on two levels to the issues raised concerning physical and mental health. The personal or individual level deals with how the committed Christian should live. The social or institutional level deals with policy and forms of institutional change that need to occur if a Christian conception of social justice concerning health matters is to become a reality.

At the personal level Christianity teaches that the body is the temple of the Holy Spirit (1 Corinthian 6:19), and that we should be good stewards of the gifts of God (Matthew 25:14-39). Yet, we fail to take responsibility for many illnesses which we could control through knowledge and technology. The major illnesses of our day are primarily self-inflicted. The excessive use of alcohol, smoking, stressful lifestyles, junk food diets, overeating, lack of exercise, and the senseless pollution of the environment are all known contributing factors to afflictions such as heart disease, stroke and cancer. Since God has given us the means to deal with these illnesses, we are not being good stewards when we fail to act. Christ's command that we love and care for one another (Luke 10:29-37) also prompts the Christian to encourage wholesome health habits in others. This is especially so for parents who are entrusted with the responsibility of rearing their children in the way of the Lord (Ephesians 6:4).

Christ's life teaches us compassion for one another, an important factor in the promotion of positive mental health. Psychiatrists and psychologists have indicated repeatedly that the best preventive mental health is practiced by loving, caring individuals — husband or wife, relative, friend, or neighbor. Christ's meeting of the Samaritan woman at the well (John 4:4-43) illustrates the power of caring for another, even in the simple or routine everyday conversational setting. Seeing beyond the woman's presented mask, Christ discerns the spiritual and emotional conflict in her life. He then presents her with the opportunity to meet her innermost needs through faith.

The therapeutic power of love for others is difficult to overemphasize in matters of both physical and mental health. Many years ago in the preface to his *The Ways and Power of Love,* sociologist Pitirim Sorokin (1954, pp. vii-viii) said:

> Now more than ever I believe in the following truths, which are fully confirmed by our experimental studies: Hate begets hate, violence engenders violence, hypocrisy is answered by hypocrisy, war generates war, and love creates love.

> Unselfish love has enormous creative and therapeutic potentialities, far greater than most people think. Love is a life-giving force, necessary for physical, mental and moral health.

> Altruistic persons live longer than egotistic individuals. Children deprived of love tend to become vitally, morally, and socially defective.

Love is the most powerful antidote against criminal, morbid, and suicidal tendencies, against hate, fear and psychoneuroses. It is an indispensable condition for deep and lasting happiness.

In addition to Sorokin, others have noted the therapeutic effects of altruism. For example, Yalom (1985, p. 14) holds that altruistic acts are healing forces in motion. In group therapy, those who are demoralized with low self-esteem tend to respond positively when they are able to help one another. Their morbid self-absorption gives way to the refreshing esteem-boosting experience created by knowing that they are giving help and are important to others. According to Yalom, people need to feel they are needed (Yalom, 1985, p. 13).

But altruism is much more than a need to feel needed. It is the unselfish, creative, giving, caring, loving and doing for others which Christ lived and taught us to live (John 15:12). Its therapeutic value — physically, mentally, and spiritually — is undeniable. The conclusions by Sorokin and Yalom parallel Paul's exhortation to the Philippians that Christians should rejoice and let everyone see the unselfishness and consideration in all that they do (Philippians 4:4-7).

People may stigmatize or label others negatively because of perceived differences or limitations in the physical or mental functioning of the other. Stigmatization has a negative effect in the help-seeking process (Phillips 1963, p. 972); the stigmatized person is put at significant disadvantage in properly carrying out roles and expectations. Socially engendered stigma may constitute a stumbling block which keeps the labeled person from fully being what God intended (Matthew 18:6; Luke 17:1-2). Christians are cautioned about making such judgments (Matthew 5:21-26; 7:1-5).

In contrast, Christ's parable of the Good Samaritan taught charity and compassion toward our neighbors (Luke 10:29-37). Thus, the Christian is responsible to be personally sensitive to the needs of others and, if need be, help them seek the level of medical or psychiatric attention that the particular circumstances require.

While Jesus lived on earth He proclaimed God's dominion, taught a morality of love and forgiveness, and made willing persons whole and healthy. He persisted in healing in spite of those who opposed Him (Matthew 12:9-14; Mark 3:1-6; Luke 6:6-11). So, too, today's Christians must follow the example of Christ in promoting adequate health care for all of God's children. The great commandment — that we should love God with all our heart, soul, mind and strength, and that we should love our neighbor as ourselves (Mark 12:28-32) — directs us to a concern that people everywhere should be treated justly, regardless of their connection with our own personal lives. This commandment leads to the question: What can we do at the institutional level to promote an equitable and just health care delivery system for all?

Christian Response at the Institutional Level
We need to recognize that the private fee-for-service system, long argued for by professional medicine, is simply not meeting our nation's health care needs. Moreover, the fee-for-service system is often used to justify questionable, if not outright immoral, professional and business practices. While the American Medical Association was successful in raising the professional standards of medical practice, it also promoted the monopolistic practices that resulted in higher than necessary fees and a maldistribution

of practitioners. This system is as much a product of greed as need. Third party financing has failed to promote cost effectiveness and has been abused. Christians need to critically evaluate this system of overspending, increased costs and profiteering at the expense of those who are ill who possess the least financial resources. The health care system is in need of serious reform.

For millions of people the present health care delivery system does not deliver. And when it does, it functions in a setting of depersonalization with fragmented services. Unlike Christ's teaching and healing, it fails to address the needs of the whole person. Good health is all too often defined as the absence of the physical symptoms suggestive of illness. And as has been seen above, this neglects two very important points: (1) the complete well-being of the individual — mental and social as well as physical, and (2) illness prevention.

Wholistic Approach Needed

An exception to this can be seen in what has become the wholistic health movement in the United States. Among the first to present wholistic medicine was Granger Westberg, a Lutheran minister and hospital chaplain who recognized that clergy entered into patient relationships late in the course of a developed illness. This, Westberg thought, diminished their assistance. Westberg proposed early entry into a health problem so that the whole person could be treated — mind, body, and spirit. Today wholistic medicine emphasizes preventive education and health-screening programs, early intervention by other professionals in addition to physicians, and a team approach to remedial management which utilizes the patient, clergy, general practitioners, and medical specialists.

In the past, health care has been regarded as a privilege, and an economic commodity to be purchased if desired and if the resources were available. Powerful vested interests seek economic gain in the delivery of health care goods and services often at the expense of those who cannot keep up with the increasing costs. Christian concern requires us to search for a better system. We regard good health care as a human right, not something only for the privileged.

It is clear that a national health insurance is both needed and favored. What is not clear is the particular form that it will take. Because any form of national health insurance will create a heavy demand on health care services, a Christian perspective would suggest a program with high cost-control potential along with the guarantee of high quality service. A new system of payment is needed which might be based on a fixed fee for services over a given period of time, such as health maintenance organizations now offer. Prevention as well as cure must be emphasized. The program should provide adequate coverage and promote its responsible use by all concerned — purchasers and providers. The special relationship between physician and patient which is so important in the healing process needs to be broadened rather that diminished. Finally, national health insurance should be based on a social model rather than a strictly medical disease model. This would promote prevention and wholesome health — "a state of complete physical, mental and social well-being and not merely the absence of disease or infirmity" (*World Health Organization*, 1981, p. 1). A national health insurance could then squarely meet the need that it is intended to serve — the good health of all.

Study and Discussion
Questions

1. What are the strengths and weaknesses of the medical model of illness as contrasted with the strengths and weaknesses of the social model of illness?

2. How are physical and mental health related to spiritual health?

3. What can we do about our lifestyles that would improve our physical and mental health?

4. Why is it probably not accurate to assume that just because we are living longer we are also living healthier and enjoying a higher quality of life?

5. Just how serious is mental illness in our society and what can we do as Christians to reduce its debilitating effects?

6. What are the advantages and disadvantages of assuming a role of sickness in our society?

7. Describe the basic structure of the American health care system. How well does it meet the needs of the people who depend upon it?

8. If you were a special advisor to the President of the United States, what changes would you recommend in social policy regarding meeting our nation's physical and mental health needs?

9. Should health care in the United States be regarded as a right or a privilege? Why?

10. Describe, from a Christian perspective, the particular form that a sound national health insurance program might take.

References

Albrecht, Gary L., "Health Services." Pp. 364-387 in Marvin E. Olsen and Michael Micklin (eds.), *Handbook of Applied Sociology*. New York: Praeger Publishers, 1981.

American Psychiatric Association, *Diagnostic and Statistical Manual of Mental Disorders*, Third Edition (Revised), Washington, D.C., 1987.

Cockerham, William C., *Medical Sociology*. Englewood Cliffs, NJ: Prentice-Hall, 1989 (a). *Sociology of Mental Disorders*. Englewood Cliffs, NJ: Prentice-Hall, 1989 (b).

Conrad, Peter, and Rochelle Kern (eds.), *The Sociology of Health and Illness: Critical Perspectives*. New York: St. Martin's Press, 1981.

Dohrenwend, Bruce P., "The Epidemiology of Mental Disorders." Pp. 157-194 in David mechanic (ed.), *Handbook of Health, Health Care, and the Health Professions*. New York: The Free Press, 1983.
"Sociocultural and Social-Psychological Factors in the Genesis of Mental Disorders." *Journal of Health and Social Behavior* 16:365-392, 1975.

Dougherty, Charles, J., *American Health Care*. New York: Oxford University Press, 1988.

Dutton, Diana B., "Social Class, Health, and Illness." Pp. 23-46 in Phil Brown (ed.), *Perspectives in Medical Sociology*. Belmont, CA: Wadsworth Publishing Co., 1989.

Faris, Robert E. L., and H. Warren Dunham, *Mental Disorders in Urban Areas*. Chicago: University of Chicago Press, 1938.

Goffman, Erving, *Asylums: Essays on the Social Situation of Mental Patients and Other Inmates*. New York: Anchor Books, 1961. *Sigma: Notes on the Management of Spoiled Identity*. Englewood Cliffs, NJ: Prentice-Hall, Inc. 1963.

Health Insurance Association of America, *Source Book of Health Insurance Data, 1989*. Washington, D. C., 1989.

Hollingshead, August B., and Frederick C. Redlich, *Social Class and Mental Illness: A Community Study*. New York: John Wiley, 1958.

Maykovich, Minako K., *Medical Sociology*. Sherman Oaks, CA: Alfred Publishing company, 1980.

Mechanic, David, *Mental Health and Social Policy*. Englewood Cliffs, NJ: Prentice Hall, 1980.

Painful Choices. New Brunswick, NJ: Transaction Publishers, 1989.

National Center for Health Statistics, *Health, United States, 1989*. U. S. Department of Health and Human Services, Publication No. 90-1232, Public Health Service, Washington, D. C.: U. S. Government Printing Office, 1990.

Parsons, Talcott, *The Social System*. Glencoe, IL: The Free Press, 1951.
"Definitions of Health and Illness in the Light of American Values and Social Structure." Pp. 107-127 in E. Gartly Jaco (ed.), *Patients, Physicians and Illness*. New York. The Free Press, 1972.
"The Sick Role and the Role of the Physician Reconsidered." Milbank, *Memorial Fund Quarterly* 53:257-278, 1975.

Scheff, Thomas, "The Role of the Mentally Ill and the Dynamics of Mental Disorder: A Research Framework." *Sociometry* 26:436-453, 1963.
Being Mentally Ill: A Sociological Theory. Chicago: Aldine Publishing Company, 1984.

Schulberg, Herbert C., and Marie Killilea (eds.), *The Modern Practice of Community Mental Health*. San Francisco: Jossey-Bass, Inc., 1982.

Sorokin, Pitirim A., *The Ways and Power of Love*. Boston: Beacon Press, 1954.

Spitzer, Robert L., and Paul T. Wilson, "Nosology and the Official Psychiatric Nomenclature." Pp. 826-845 in Alfred M. Freeman, Harold I. Kaplan, and Benjamin J. Sadock (eds.), *Comprehensive Textbook of Psychiatry*, Vol. I. New York: McGraw-Hill, 1962.

Srole, Leo, T. S. Langner, S. T. Michael, M. K. Opler and T. A .C. Rennie, *Mental Health in the Metropolis: The Midtown Manhattan Study, Vol. I*. New York: McGraw-Hill, 1962.

Szasz, Thomas S., "The Myth of Mental Illness." *The American Psychologist* 15:113-118, 1960.
The Myth of Mental Illness: Foundations of a Theory of Personal Conduct. New York: Harper & Row, 1974.

Tubesing, Donald A., *Whole Person Health Care: An Idea in Evolution*. Hindsdale, IL:" Wholistic Health Centers, Inc. 1976,
Wholistic Health. New York: Human Science Press, 1979.

Twaddle, Andrew C., and Richard H. Hessler, *A Sociology of Health*. New York: Macmillan Publishing Co., 1987.

U. S. Bureau of the Census, *Statistical Abstract of the United States 1990* (110th ed.). Washington, D.C., 1990.

U. S. Department of Commerce, *Social Indicators III*. Washington, D. C., 1980.

Wolinsky, Fredric D., *The Sociology of Health*. Belmont, CA: Wadsworth Publishing Co., 1988.

World Health Organization, "Constitution of the World Health Organization." Pp. 1-18 in *World Health Organization,* Basic Documents (31st. ed.). Geneva: United Nations, 1981.

Yalom, Irvin D., *The Theory and Practice of Psychotherapy* (3rd edition). New York: Basic Books, 1985.

CHAPTER 9
AMERICAN HEALTH CARE: INTRODUCTION

In the introduction to the previous article on physical and mental health, our comments were framed largely by the social definition paradigm. Professor Mundy's article on the crisis facing the American health care system can best be approached through the use of the social facts paradigm. Both conflict theory and the structural-functional theory of *anomie* which we have used in introducing other articles may be used to appraise this anomic institution.

One aspect of the cultural goal for a "good life" is high quality medical care. It is a goal that many Americans take seriously. As Professor Mundy points out, no country in the world spends more on health care than does the United States. At the same time, however, there is no health statistic in which we lead the world. In fact, our infant mortality rate is higher than most other industrial nations. The means (spending of large sums of money) has not enabled the United States to reach the cultural goal. Clearly there are many facets of our health care system that are dysfunctional. The symptom of the problem is spelled out in the subheading of this article: "spending more and growing worse."

Structural functional theory, while acknowledging the problem of anomie, would tend to paint a more optimistic picture of our health care system than Professor Mundy has done. Its theorists would note the high cost of medical care but would emphasize the exceptional quality care that is available to those who can afford it. Granted that drug manufacturing companies seem to make exorbitant profits on their products and many doctors earn phenomenal salaries, the structural functionalist, pointing to the underlying principle of social exchange, would defend the basic system. Pharmaceutical companies must do expensive research to develop the new products, and the cost of research must be borne by those who require the product. If we want the best and the brightest to make the sacrifices to become physicians, then we must offer the reward of high salaries to entice them. Comparable arguments could be made for the high cost of hospital care, much of which goes into expensive high-tech medical equipment. If we want quality care, it is going to cost — and not everyone is going to be able to afford it.

Professor Mundy, guided by her Christian convictions, takes a conflict approach in discussing the situation. A conflict approach focuses on the powerful or the "haves" who tend to exploit the powerless or the "have nots." Mundy emphasizes the plight of the poor whose failure to receive adequate care contributes to our poor national health record. She observes how attempts to fix the current system with cost containment measures are especially hard on uninsured Afro-Americans and Hispanics. Mundy uses AIDS, a national health problem which is sure to grow worse, to discuss additional deficiencies in the system.

Professor Mundy recognizes and documents the problems, but she also points out Christian responsibilities. The bottom line is that there are many social inequities in our health care system, and these inequities are taking their toll on children, the homeless, minorities, and the elderly. The situation is aggravated by the growing number of Americans without any kind of medical coverage and the inadequate insurance of many who are privately insured. After painting a rather dismal portrait, Mundy challenges Christians to action by supporting much-needed changes in governmental policies affecting the distribution of health care.

We would like to suggest yet another line of thinking to challenge the reader. Can Christians be leaders in health care as some of their ancestors were? Ronald L. Numbers and Darrel W. Amundsen have edited an exceptional historical volume entitled *Caring and Curing: Health and Medicine in the Western Religious Traditions* (MacMillan Publishing Company: 1986) that helps to address the issue. This collection of articles was written specifically to discuss the interface of religion and health in traditions ranging from Judaism and early Christianity to the Reformed Protestant tradition, to contemporary established sects. Many of these traditions provide ideas for contemporary Christians responding to health care problems.

Many religious traditions possess a rich but often forgotten heritage of involvement in health care matters. Numbers and Amundsen note that both Jews and Christians have long stressed the importance of caring for the human body. In the previous introduction we briefly discussed the importance of healing in Jesus' ministry and in the early Church. The concern about illness and disease was rooted in the Jewish tradition in which Jesus was raised. Caring and curing has a fascinating history in the Judeo-Christian worldview, a history that can provide much food for thought.

For example, Elliot Dorff, author of the article on the Jewish tradition in *Caring and Curing* noted that "Jewish views on diet, hygiene, exercise, and protection of the body have distinctively religious roots . . . . God gave life to be enjoyed, but pleasure must yield to health as a value because health is necessary for one to function as the servant of God" (p. 13). The laws on diet and hygiene may not cure disease, but they did seem to have an important impact on its prevention. We might ask to what extent Christians have the responsibility to eat properly using the same rationale as the Jews have used for protecting our bodies. The Mormon tradition and the Adventist tradition are two contemporary examples of religions whose dietary laws are known to have important positive implications for health. Can we learn anything from these traditions?

An article on "The Roman Catholic Tradition Since 1545" by Marvin R. O'Connell provided examples of an institutional response to *Caring and Curing*. Various religious orders of men and women were founded to take care of the mentally and physically ill. Vincent de Paul (1580 - 1660) is credited with doing more "than any other individual to rationalize and institutionalize Catholicism's commitment to caring for the sick" (p. 135). De Paul founded various organizations to care for the physical needs of the sick, most noteworthy, the Sisters of Charity whose members serve in hospitals to this day. Although contemporary Catholic hospitals have been secularized (just as their Protestant counterparts have) and no longer differ from those operating under secular auspices, they do provide an historical example of a religious institutional response to a social need.

Christians need to think in terms not only of solutions to personal problems but to find creative solutions to public issues. Despite some of the controversy surrounding Oral Roberts University School of Medicine, Roberts did act on a vision to provide a creative institutional response to training health care deliverers. ORU went beyond the training provided by existing medical schools in combining prayer and the biblical practice of spiritual healing with conventional medicine. It had the vision of preparing young people to go out as medical missionaries to third world countries and to urban ghettos where medical care is unavailable. For a short while during the 1980s, the City of Faith promised to offer a Christian alternative to conventional medicine.

Although the City of Faith was forced to close its doors as the 1980s drew to a close, the vision of combining prayer with medicine may be found in other sectors. It is reflected in a number of hospital chaplaincy programs taking a holistic approach that includes prayer and healing. At ORU, the vision lives on in the Anna Vaughn School of Nursing and through the Christian counseling program at its School of Theology. Despite the failure of the City of Faith and ORU School of Medicine, the venture did provide an example of a creative Christian alternative to the current medical model.

Given the failure of the City of Faith and the secularization of most formerly religious hospitals, serious questions may be raised about the possibility of providing creative alternative Christian responses to the American health care system. Using the crises discussed by Professor Mundy, however, we would challenge students to be visionaries in thinking about unique Christian responses to these problems.

AMERICAN HEALTH CARE: SPENDING MORE AND GROWING WORSE

Karen Mundy

INTRODUCTION

One of the most memorable accounts of the Lord's compassion is found in the Gospels. The story is told of the woman with an issue of blood. This woman had spent all her money on physicians, only to become worse. In an act of desperate faith, she reached out to touch Christ and, in touching Him, her health was immediately restored.

The sick in America have reason to identify with the impoverishment of the woman who reached out to Christ. As individuals and as a society, we are spending more money than ever before on health care. Medical expenses are a major cause of bankruptcy for the working class and the middle class. Yet we are failing to provide decent care for large segments of the population. Health insurance has become uninsurance, unavailable to the people who need it most, including the sick, the poor, and, increasingly, America's children.

Erving Goffman uses the term "social desperadoes" to describe people who exist on the fringes of society, often marginal or unconventional, but always in need. The social desperadoes of Christ's time included lepers, Samaritans, tax collectors, and even a woman with an issue of blood. In the nineteenth century, America's "lepers" resided in tuberculosis wards. Today the lepers may be found in the AIDS wards, among damaged children, or perhaps in homeless shelters. The victims of the health care crisis inevitably include the social desperadoes of society, ranging from the very young to the very old. We are a society used to throwing away, or at least avoiding, unpleasant things and unpleasant people. And the sight of young people dying from AIDS, or of poor and small and runny-nosed children is something to avoid.

In social research, evaluation studies are used to assess the effectiveness of a program. A program's effectiveness is determined by its outcomes, not by rhetoric or vested interests. If the logic of evaluation research was applied to America's health care system, it would be considered an abysmal failure. Our society spends more money on health care than any other nation in the world. We are the only major industrialized nation without a comprehensive health care plan for its citizens. Our infant mortality rate is one of the highest among western democracies (Enthoven, 1989). Indeed, a baby born in Washington, D. C., has less chance of survival than a baby born in many Third World countries.

In 1989, the editors of *Health Care Financing Review* posed the question: "What can Europeans learn from Americans (about health care)?" Unfortunately for Americans, their answer to this question was, "not much." The editors did suggest that Europeans could learn from our mistakes. Enthoven, a professor of business at Stanford, even questioned the assumption that you could get the world's best health care in

America. After reviewing studies that pointed to the uneven quality of heart surgery in California, Enthoven wrote:

> Somewhere in America might be found the world's best medical care. But the merits of that claim will not be apparent to the families of hundreds of Californians who have died of inappropriate or equivocal open-heart operations in the low volume hospitals, especially if the widows are being hounded for payment because their deceased husbands did not have insurance (1989, p. 49).

The notoriety of American health care is indicated by a 1988 survey which found that 89 percent of Americans believed major changes were needed in American health care (Stimmel, 1990). According to 1989 national surveys comparing British, Canadian, and American public opinion, Americans are the most critical of their medical system. Only 10 percent of American respondents agreed with the statement, "On the whole, the health care system works pretty well." In comparison, 56 percent of Canadians and 27 percent of the British believed their health care system was effective (Enthoven, 1989).

The purpose of this article is to describe America's health crisis, a crisis which intimately involves issues of Christian mission and Christian service. It is my hope that this article will go beyond merely identifying the health care plight of our society to challenging Christians to make a difference in the lives of the sick. Like the Good Samaritan who was willing to claim a sick man — even a stranger — as his brother, we are called to become advocates for the social desperadoes of the American medical system.

SPENDING MORE BUT GROWING WORSE
THE HIGH COST OF AMERICAN HEALTH CARE

Soaring Health Care Costs

Currently, about $620 billion is spent on health care services in a $5 trillion economy (Ginsberg, 1990). During the twenty-year period from 1966 to 1986, health care costs escalated from $39 billion to 458 billion. The projected increase in health care costs in 1989 alone was $50 billion.

In 1977, health care expenses accounted for 7.5 percent of the gross national product (GNP). By 1987, health care costs had grown to 11.1 percent of America's GNP. In 1990, health care costs will go beyond 12 percent of the GNP (Stimmel, 1990; Enthovan, 1989). During the eleven-year period from 1976 to 1987, health care expenses exceeded inflation by almost 80 percent (Schneider, 1990).

In comparison to America's health care expenditures, most European countries are spending at the stable rate of 6 to 9 percent of their GNP. And European countries have universal health care coverage for their population (Enthoven, 1989). In contrast, America has 37 million uninsured Americans which includes 17.5 percent of the population under sixty-five.

Although the national health care system of Great Britain is often criticized, their health statistics are superior to ours for half the cost. We devote twice as much of our GNP to health care as Great Britain. Yet the life expectancies of the two countries are comparable and our infant death rate is considerably higher (Stimmel, 1990).

Medicaid and Medicare: The Price of Equivocal Success

Theoretically, the government provides health coverage for the poor and elderly in America. However, 3 out of 5 poor Americans are ineligible for Medicaid, a form of government subsidized medical care (Ginsberg, 1990). The percentage of the poor who are covered by Medicaid has significantly declined during the last fifteen years. In 1976, 65 percent of the poor received Medicaid. By 1986, only 38 percent of the poor were covered by Medicaid (Baldwin, 1989).

In addition to the poor, millions of employed Americans who have private insurance are underinsured, with little financial protection against catastrophic illness.

Among the poor who have Medicaid, only partial coverage is provided. Baldwin (1987) notes that the Committee on Care for the Indigent (American Hospital Association) now considers Medicaid a supplementary form of insurance. Many of the poor who fall through the gaps of coverage are America's children. Children and their single mothers constitute the largest proportion of the poor in America and are swelling the ranks of the homeless.

The government provides subsidized health care for Americans over the age of sixty-five in the form of the Medicare program. Unlike the patchwork coverage of poor Americans, the majority of older Americans benefit from this national program. Since the creation of Medicare in the 1960s, the mortality rate of the elderly has declined, with life expectancy at age 65 increasing by two and one-half years. Elderly Americans now visit the doctor as much as younger Americans, in contrast to the years before Medicare.

Medicare is costly. Like other sectors of health care, Medicare expenditures have increased dramatically. In 1982, the government spent $70 billion on Medicaid and Medicare. Five years later, in 1987, government funding reached $111 billion (Schneider, 1990). Part of this increase reflects the graying of the American population. More Americans are entering the eligibility group, a trend that will escalate as the baby boom cohorts reach retirement age. Today the fastest growing age group in America is comprised of those over eighty-five.

In an effort to contain Medicare costs, the federal government has enacted a system of reimbursement based on Diagnostic-Related Groups (DRGs). The government pays the health care institution and consulting physician an allocated amount of money, depending on the DRG classification. Types of medical care are assigned to one of 467 diagnostic categories.

DRGs have been effective in curtailing the upward spiral of medical costs. But there has been a price to pay in regard to the quality of care, especially in the case of complex illnesses. DRGs do not take into account the severity or complexity of an illness, the social circumstances of patients, nor the type of institution providing the care. For example, AIDS is an auto immune disease, with many manifestations. DRGs do not adequately cover the care needed in the treatment of AIDS. DRGS are also selective in the medical costs that are covered during an illness.

The DRG system addresses the issue of cost containment of medical care. But patients may suffer adverse consequences from this fixed payment system. When a patient's DRG benefits are exhausted, it is contrary to the financial interests of the hospital or nursing home to continue to provide care. The patient may be transferred to another institution or released prematurely in order to offset the financial losses of the health care provider. If the patient is readmitted, even for the same health problem, DRG reimbursement begins anew. Thus, health providers are tempted to use a revolving door strategy to guarantee DRG benefits. Such a disruption of care for the seriously ill or the chronically ill may have significant health consequences.

Although the revolving-door strategy of health care providers may ensure payment, it is associated with poor patient care. Ansell and Schiff (1987) note that hospital transfers to Cook County Hospital in Chicago increased from 1,295 in 1980 to 6,769 in 1983. The majority of transferred patients were uninsured blacks and Hispanics. Only 6 percent of the patients had agreed to the transfer. The mortality or death rate of transferred patients was twice the rate of those who were not moved. Ansell and Schiff assert that 250,000 emergency room patients are transferred each year solely for financial reasons (JAMA, 1987).

Stimmel writes:

> The potential for premature discharge in an attempt to maximize income has been recognized by the Department of Health and Human Services (HHS). HHS has given final approval for a statement to be forwarded to all hospitalized patients containing the process to be followed in contesting hospital-ordered discharge decisions. This not only will have the intended effect of informing patients of their rights but also will serve to condition consumers that, indeed, this system is not to be trusted (1990, p. 16).

In addition to the revolving-door strategy, another indirect result of DRGs is the elimination of hidden subsidies for the poor. Prior to DRGs, hospitals often added on costs to insured patients to compensate for their losses in treating indigent patients. Fixed-rate hospital payments have eliminated the subsidy for the poor. In response to this loss of hidden income, many hospitals have reduced their charity care.

Hospital Care: An Uncertain but Expensive Enterprise

Hospital costs account for about 40 percent of health care expenditures (Ginsberg, 1990). Public hospitals bear a disproportionate burden in caring for the poor, the homeless, and the uninsured. As health care expenses continue to climb, many public hospitals which serve poor neighborhoods are having to close their doors. Communities that need health services the most are least likely to have adequate medical facilities. In response to this problem, several states are developing "rescue" operations for public hospitals that are in financial crisis. These rescue operations provide additional state funding (Nemes, 1989).

The situation of public hospitals in Texas is an example of a system in a state of crisis. Texas hospitals provided $1 billion of uncompensated hospital care for each year during the period 1984-1987 (Baldwin, 1987). Public hospitals in states such as Texas must also serve large immigrant populations. Immigrant populations are likely to be disproportionately sick, poor, and uninsured.

The financial burden of hospitals serving poor communities is exacerbated by the increasing number of AIDS patients. Between 1985 and 1987, the AIDS caseload for public hospitals rose 101 percent, compared with a 34 percent rise in private hospitals (Pickney, 1988). By 1991, it is estimated that 400,000 persons will have been treated for AIDS (Solomon, 1989).

AIDS patients are more likely than other patients to be indigent and to require a high level of skilled care. Fifty-five percent of hospital costs for AIDS patients can be attributed to skilled nursing care (Taravella, 1989). Even as AIDS is increasing demands on hospitals, fear of AIDS is hindering hospital recruitment efforts. Taravella cites a survey of approximately 100 teaching institutions in the United States. Twenty percent of the hospitals reported that hospital employees had resigned because of fear and frustration pertaining to AIDS.

The consequences of AIDS is not confined to high risk urban areas. According to Gage, president of the National Association of Public Hospitals, AIDS is causing a "crowding-out phenomenon." AIDS patients are not only displacing other indigent patients, but they are also crowding out insured patients. Gage concludes, "AIDS is changing the nature and mission of some hospitals" (Pickney, 1988, p. 1).

The High Price of High-Tech

Advanced technology is a major factor that contributes to the high cost of health care. New technologies include sophisticated therapies to sustain life, ranging from the neonatal ward to the intensive care unit. The hospital is the center for high-tech utilization. Technological efforts to prolong life are especially associated with increased health care costs. For example, technology is an important part of the effort to preserve the life of premature babies. Hospital costs for premature infants typically exceed $100,000 per child. Premature babies are more likely to suffer brain and lung damage which will require additional medical care.

The decision to cut technology costs that prolong life is more than a medical decision. It is an ethical decision which determines who lives and who dies. For example, should physicians try to save all premature babies or limit their efforts to the babies that have a good prognosis? In an age of extraordinary medical costs, should society attempt to keep alive the very young and the very old? The question of who lives and who dies is especially salient in the case of obstetrical practice. Obstetricians who practice abortion must contend with the paradox of ending the lives of babies up to the age of six months, while struggling to preserve the lives of babies born at seven months.

Ginsberg (1990) makes some cautious projections about the future of high-tech spending. He anticipates the expenditures for high-tech medicine will continue to increase. Cost-control measures in the area of medical technology will probably not be effective. First, Americans expect state-of-the-art care and recognize the value of this care in medical diagnosis and treatment. Second, the demographics of American society preclude cost containment. As the ranks of the elderly increase, so will medical expenditures. The alternative to this cost increase is to ration medical care to the elderly. For example, one basis of rationing that has been suggested is to divide the elderly into categories of medical prognosis, with the most hopeless receiving only palliative treatment.

THE SOCIAL INEQUITIES OF HEALTH CARE

Suffer the Little Children and Forbid Them Not

The Lord stressed the value and worth of children in numerous biblical passages. Yet in regard to medical care, our society continues to "forbid" some children access to even the most basic health care. The state of American's children is a national scandal. The overall decline in children's health, as well as a decline in health services for poor children, has been well documented (Starfield and Budetti, 1985; Hughes, 1989).

Wise, in an editorial for the *New England Journal of Medicine*, deplores the "deterioration in the social well-being of children in America and the tattered commitment to the provision of medical care to all children in need" (1989, p. 1210). According to Wise, health insurance coverage for out-patient pediatric services has actually decreased. One in five American children are uninsured. The immunization rates among children declined during the 1980s, leaving children vulnerable to preventable childhood diseases. For example, 23 percent of all two-year-olds and 43 percent of nonwhite two-year-olds were not completely immunized against polio in 1985 (Wise, 1989).

Studies of the regional differences in the hospital rates of children point to significant variations in the health of children. Pockets of poverty continue to produce children in desperate need of health services. In some communities, hospitals have become a place of last resort for pediatric care, increasing the cost of health care. This is especially true in the case of AIDS. Gage writes:

> We have a class of children concentrated in several hospitals in the Northeast living their entire lives in an acute care hospital. They're born there, usually to a drug-addicted parent, and will die there and be buried in the hospitals. . . . The combination of AIDS and crack phenomena are presenting serious problems to urban hospitals (Pickney, 1988, p. 8).

One of the most distressing features of the AIDS population in the United States is the rising incidence of women and children with AIDS. In Central and East Africa, where AIDS is often transmitted heterosexually, the incidence of AIDS among women and children has always been significant. Some reports estimate that 10 percent of the female population in Central and East Africa carry the AIDS virus (Ryder, et al., 1989). The greatest increase of AIDS among women and children in the United States is found in inner-city areas. For example, 2 percent of the female population of an urban hospital in New York tested positive for AIDS (Scott, et al., 1989).

According to epidemiologists, 30 to 50 percent of children born to women with AIDS will develop the immune deficiency. Maternal transmission may occur in utero, during birth, or through breast-feeding (Rogers, et al., 1989). As of January 30, 1989, there were 1,393 reported cases of pediatric AIDS in the United States. Approximately 77 percent (n=1,080) of the children had acquired AIDS through maternal transmission. The remaining children contracted AIDS through blood transfusions (12.6 percent) or receiving blood due to a diagnosis of hemophilia (6 percent). In 3.9 percent of the pediatric AIDS cases, the cause of exposure was undetermined (Ruff, 1990).

A study conducted at Jackson Memorial Hospital in Miami, Florida, presented a bleak picture of the lives of 146 AIDS babies who received the disease from their mothers. Sixty-nine percent of the mothers had acquired AIDS through sexual contact, with another 30 percent receiving AIDS from intravenous drug use. The median age of developing AIDS symptoms for seropositive infants was eight months. After diagnosis, the median time of survival was three years and two months. The death rate of AIDS children was highest during the first year of life, with a 17 percent mortality rate by the age one. Fifty percent of the original 146 children had died by the age of 3 years (Scott, et al., 1989). The continuing high death rate of the remaining children suggests there will be no survivors. The absence of a plateau or leveling off of the death rate indicates the possibility of a 100 percent mortality rate.

Variations in the hospitalization rates of children are an indicator of the availability of alternative methods of health care. Perrin, et al., (1989). compared the rates of hospitalization of children in three communities: Rochester, New Haven, and Boston. Rochester, the most affluent community, had considerable lower hospital admission rates for children than either New Haven or Boston. Wise suggests that patterns of high hospitalization reflect health care systems that provide inadequate primary care. When poor children are hospitalized due to lack of good primary care, their illnesses are more devastating. In Boston, children have high rates of hospitalization for illness. This pattern of high use may indicate that there are few alternatives to hospitalization. In contrast, the low rate of hospitalization in Rochester points to an effective system of preventive care and an integrated network of neighborhood clinics.

Being poor in an expensive urban area such as Boston will have a more adverse effect on the well-being of children than being poor in less expensive communities. Housing costs are 70 percent higher in Boston than in Rochester (Wise, 1989). The increased cost of living exhausts the resources of poor families. Thus, the urban poor are left with poor living conditions that make them sick and with much less money to deal with these sicknesses.

No Place to Lay Their Heads: Health Care and the Homeless

The homeless population in American society has grown considerably during the last two decades, reflecting a rise in the incidence of poverty. A conservative estimate of the homeless is 500,000 (Wright, 1989). This figures does not include the marginally homeless consisting of those who have the potential to become homeless.

Poverty is the main cause of homelessness. But other factors also account for the rising incidence of homelessness. For example, there is a shortage of decent, affordable housing for lower-income groups. The release of the mentally ill into the community and problems with alcohol and drug abuse among the homeless contribute to the growing problem in our society.

Single mothers and their children are increasingly found among the homeless, reflecting their marginal economic status. As a group, single mothers and children constitute the largest proportion of federal relief recipients. In a 1958 study of the homeless in Chicago, 3 percent of the homeless were women. Today, 25 percent of the homeless in Chicago are women. And they are young women with children.

There has been a decline in the number of elderly among the homeless. In the 1950s and 1960s, most of the homeless were white males in their fifties. Today, the average age of the homeless is middle thirties, with minority groups over-represented. One-third of the homeless are veterans (Wright, 1989).

Physical and mental illnesses afflict the homeless population disproportionately. Researchers estimate the prevalence of serious mental disorder among the homeless to range from 20 to 50 percent. One-tenth of the homeless have a physical impairment that makes them incapable of employment. The high rate of disease and illness among the homeless is both a cause and a result of their circumstances. Inadequate nutrition, lowered resistance to infectious disease, poor living conditions, mental disorders, substance abuse, trauma, and inadequate or nonexistent medical care all contribute to the poor health of homeless people.

A Johns Hopkins University study on the health of Baltimore's homeless population confirms this profile. Unlike many previous studies, the Hopkins' sample included both the homeless who were receiving medical care and those who were not part of a clinic population. Approximately 56 percent of the homeless population were male and 66 percent were nonwhite. Age differences among the men and women were apparent. Men were, on the average, 7 years older than women. Unfortunately, the Hopkins researchers failed to report on the number of children among the homeless population. The youthfulness of the female group, however, does suggest the presence of small children among the homeless.

The Hopkins study indicates a high level of isolation among the homeless. Few subjects were currently married. Three-fifths of the subjects of both sexes had never married. This is in contrast to a 90 percent marriage rate in the overall society. Only one-fourth of the men and half of the women remained in contact with family members.

The physicians participating in the Johns Hopkins study evaluated the health problems of the homeless. An average of 8.3 health problems were found in men and 9.2 health problems in women. The men in missions and the women in shelters fared more poorly than the homeless who were incarcerated in jails. Eighty-five percent of the men and 67 percent of the women reported a history of substance abuse, most often alcohol. Both sexes were heavy smokers, an explanation for the high incidence of respiratory disorders. Two-thirds of both sexes had experienced some type of trauma, with one-third of the women reporting rape. Two-thirds of the women had gynecologic disorders. Dental problems, cardiovascular problems, and psychiatric disorders were also common (Breakley, 1989).

Although the homeless are an unusually sick population, less than half the men and only 30 percent of the women in the Hopkins study had a regular source of health care. Few of the subjects who reported substance abuse received help for their problem. Apart from the ethics of failing to provide health care for a highly disabled population, any effort to return the homeless to functioning roles in society would require treatment of their health needs.

Minorities and Health Care

A minority group consists of persons who are denied the resources and advantages of the dominant group in a society. In American society, blacks and Hispanics are considered members of minority groups and are over-represented among the poor. The disadvantaged position of minority groups is apparent in regard to health status and health care. For example, the life expectancy for whites is six years longer than blacks. The infant mortality rate of blacks is twice as high as that of whites (Council, 1990).

Although the black population has more illness than the white population, blacks are less likely to receive adequate health care. This is documented in a report by the Council on Ethical and Judicial Affairs of the American Medical Association (AMA). According to the Council, blacks with serious health problems do not receive as much life-saving intervention as white. Citing a 1989 study, the authors note that black men with significant heart impairment were half as likely as an equivalent group of white men to have angiography. And black men had only one-third the rate of bypass surgery as white men.

A pattern of differential treatment for blacks, in comparison to whites, has been found in studies of end-stage renal disease, cesarean delivery, and pneumonia. In these studies, being white is associated with more aggressive treatment or specialized care. Variations in treatment persist according to race even when controlling for social class (Council, 1990).

Growing Old in American Society: The Health Care of the Aged

Among developed nations, the United States ranks low in its treatment of older citizens. In fact, we are inhospitable to our elderly. Yet we are an aging society. In 1980, 11.3 percent of the population was sixty-five or older, constituting 25.5 million persons. By the year 2020, these numbers are expected to double to 51.4 million. The U. S. Census Bureau predicts that, in 2020, the average life expectancy will be 82.0 for women and 74.2 years for men (Schneider, 1990).

The greatest population increase among older Americans will be in the category of the "oldest old," age eighty-five or over. About two million people are in oldest old category, with a projected three-fold increase of this population by 2020 (Wallace, 1989).

The overall number of dependents in American society, consisting of children under eighteen and the aged, has actually diminished since the 1960s. This decline can be attributed to a decreasing number of children, even as the number of dependent elderly increases. Dependent children draw on family resources, in contrast to dependent elderly who often require government support. Thus, the number of dependents who are relying on the government for support, namely the elderly, is growing.

Medical expenditures for people sixty-five and older are three times higher than for the rest of the population. Thirty-six percent of health care costs can be attributed to the 12 percent of population sixty-five and over (Waldo, 1989).

Confidence in the federal government to fund medical care is misplaced. Federal health programs give only partial remuneration for medical care and often have great gaps of coverage. For example, Medicare, the program for the cohort sixty-five and over, pays approximately half of the recipient's medical bills. In 1984, the average out-of-pocket expenses for recipients was $1,059. Nor did out-of-pocket expenses include medical insurance premiums.

Studies of federal health expenditures indicate that the major reason for rising health costs has been increasing hospital and physician charges. Cost analyses may fail to reveal, however, that it is the "aging of the aged," or people eighty-five and older, who experience the most dramatic need for medical services. For people eighty-five and older, a large amount of their health care expenses are for nursing home and home health care. The elderly are the primary consumers of nursing home care, accounting for 90 percent of nursing home expenditures in 1987.

The majority of people who are sixty-five and over are not in nursing homes. Only 3 percent of men and 6 percent of women sixty-five and older reside in nursing homes. In the cohort of 65-74 years, 1 percent of men and women live in nursing homes. But among the group aged eighty-five and older, rates of nursing home use increase significantly. Fifteen percent of the men aged 85 and older and 25 percent of the women will enter a nursing home. A similar pattern is found for home health care, with increasing age resulting in a greater need for home health services (Schneider, 1990).

For men and women eighty-five and over, nursing home and home health care costs present a serious problem. During the period 1977-1987, nursing homes expenditures rose from $13.0 billion to $40.6 billion. The aged or their families had to pay 58 percent of the cost of nursing home care. Medicaid subsidized 36 percent of the cost, with Medicare paying a mere 2 percent (Waldo, 1989).

To receive government assistance for long-term care such as nursing homes or home health care, many of the elderly will spend themselves into poverty. By giving up their savings, homes and the other resources earned over a lifetime, the elderly will qualify for a program that is inadequate at best. Caretakers, usually aging wives, may find themselves financially devastated by the medical expenses of their spouse. Thus, poverty continued to have a feminine face in a country where being female often means being poor.

Older Americans are more likely to suffer from chronic disorders. Almost sixty percent of the eighty-five and over population have conditions which limit their daily activities. Yet our health care system is based on treating acute illnesses. Chronic conditions often require outpatient care and environmental modifications. Federal health programs provide little funding for palliative care and environmental changes.

There is a danger that the elderly and the poor will become scapegoats in the efforts to contain health care spending. Today, pressures from the DRG system of reimbursement have encouraged hospitals to release the sick back into the community. But government programs to serve the sick and the elderly in the community are woefully inadequate. Increasingly, the health programs of the elderly are seen within the context of a medical model which treats the individual, but ignores the factors that contribute to general well-being and quality of life. These factors include the living conditions of the elderly, decent food, social support, and social services oriented to the needs of an aging population.

AMERICA'S MEDICAL INSURANCE: THE NEW UNINSURANCE

A recent issue of *Hippocrates,* a health magazine, referred to medical insurance as the "new uninsurance." This phrase aptly describes the insurance situation in our society. The United States population is 240 million, of which 37 million are totally without health insurance. Since 1980, the number of uninsured Americans has increased by 25 percent (Stimmel, 1990). In four southern states, 20 percent of the population is uninsured (Baldwin, 1987).

Two-thirds of the uninsured are employed. Most of them are the working poor. And poor people are three times more likely to be without any insurance. The working poor have the highest illness rate of all employed groups. They are penalized for their labors by our society's failure to address their basic health needs. The solution for the working poor with medical bills is to quit working. This allows them to become eligible for public health care of dubious quality.

Almost half of the uninsured are children and young adults. There is no room for complacency in regard to medical provisions for these two groups. In their report on the health status of children, Starfield and Budetti (1985) note that the death rate for young adults, age 15 through 24, began to rise in the late 1960s. In fact, young adults are the only age group in American society with an increase in death rates. The consequences of having such a large group of children and young adults uninsured are significant. Prenatal and preschool health care is likely to be sacrificed, compromising the health of young mothers and their children. For example, poor mothers without prenatal care are at greater risk of having babies with low birth weight. Infants with low birth weight are more prone to serious illnesses and to die from these illnesses.

Americans who have private insurance are not untouched by the dramatic changes taking place in health care. Traditionally, most Americans have paid for their medical expenses through private health insurance. Conventional fee-for-service insurance is based on the consumer or the consumer's employer paying insurance premiums to cover medical care. This arrangement may be associated with high medical costs since there is little incentive for the consumer to limit use (DiCarlo, 1989).

The almost exponential rise in health care costs has led to alterations in private health care coverage for many Americans. Privately insured consumers are finding more restrictions in their policies, limiting the physicians and hospitals they use. And policyholders are incurring additional expenses in the form of insurance copayments and deductibles. Copayment provisions require the policyholder to pay a portion of his or her medical expenses. For example, a common form of copayment stipulates that the insured person pay 20% of the cost of medical care, after meeting the insurance deductible.

From 1977-1987, the cost-of-living in the United States increased 82.4 percent, with an annual average increase of 6.2 percent per year. Medical insurance premiums rose 171.9 percent over this same period, yielding an average annual increase of 10.5 percent per year. Although medical expenses increased 120.8 percent during 1977-1987 (8.3 percent per year), the rate of increase was not nearly so great as that of health insurance (DiCarlo, 1989). Medical insurance premiums escalated at a rate almost double the cost-of-living and one-third the rate of medical expenses even as this coverage was becoming more restrictive.

Two medical insurance trends clearly emerge from the 1980s. First, the number of Americans without any kind of medical coverage is growing each year and their risk of poverty significantly increases with any major medical expense. For the middle class, medical expenses continue to be a major cause of bankruptcy. Second, privately insured Americans are paying more for diminished coverage. And they will continue to pay more for less coverage if the current spiral in medical costs continues.

A CALL TO CHRISTIAN SOCIAL ACTION

The health care crisis is a social problem that has enormous consequences for our society. These consequences can be seen in the faces of sick inner-city children or among the poor in overcrowded emergency wards. The consequences of American health care are more formally evident in our health statistics, statistics which should be an embarrassment to any industrialized society.

Christians are often silent on health care issues. Perhaps the silence of Christians reflects the familiar discrepancy between values and actions. We may believe we are our brother's keeper, without allowing our beliefs to intrude on our behavior. But it is too easy merely to believe the right things. Christ calls us to put our beliefs into action, entering the world of the hungry, the homeless, and the sick.

188

Social problems is often a dismal area of study to students. The problems are so overwhelming and deeply ingrained in society that the situation seems hopeless. But as Christians, our hope is premised on a transforming Christ, not in circumstances. I recall a song entitled, "Whose Report Are You Going to Believe?" Christians believe the report of the risen, healing Christ, a Christ who healed all manner of sickness and deeply cared about the powerless. This Christ saw sickness and disease as enemies and has the capacity to heal groups and nations.

Our challenge is to follow the healing Christ, transforming ourselves and society in the process. Once we accept the reality of the healing Christ, we must consider the possibility of the healing of individuals, as well as social systems.

The basic mission of all Christians is to tell the Good News of Christ. But the Gospel is also told in the way we live our lives. There are specific things Christians can do to bring hope and justice to the lives of the sick. The following recommendations are presented in the context of joining Christian beliefs to Christian social action.

I recommend that Christians seek a fundamental transformation of our health care system. An effective national health program will have provisions for catastrophic illness, maternal and infant care, prevention of illness, and nursing home and home health care. I further recommend that Christians vote for and support government representatives who demonstrate a concern for the health needs of all people.

On a community level, medical facilities should be held accountable for their decisions regarding health care and delivery. Christians can make a difference in local health care through their personal actions. For example, Christians may choose to boycott doctors and hospitals that deny health care to the poor.

The Christian community is recognizing the importance of higher education in shaping values and actions. Unfortunately, there is a dearth of Christian graduate programs in the health care professions. I recommend the support of Christian colleges which are committed to the training of men and women in the health professions. In these colleges, service to the sick would be taught as a worthy calling.

Finally, on an individual level, I would like to encourage Christians to pray for the healing of the sick, petitioning the God who "calls things that are not as though they were" (Romans 4:17, NIV).

Not all Christians will agree with these recommendations. Nevertheless, it is time for Christians to seek justice in health care and to demonstrate compassion for the social desperadoes of American society.

Christians live out their lives in a world with serious problems. Yet Christians are never without hope. The Apostle Paul recognized the promise of hope in Christ. He writes, "We are hard pressed on every side, but not crushed; perplexed, but not in despair; persecuted, but not abandoned; struck down, but not destroyed" (2 Corinthians 4:8-10, NIV). It is time we showed a sick and dying world the hope of Jesus Christ. When we care for the invisible people in our society, the ones who are very small in size or perhaps small in status, then we mirror the love of Christ. It does not take too great a leap of faith to see Christ joining us for the journey into the strongholds of sickness and disease, even as He did long ago.

In the biblical account of the Good Samaritan, we are challenged to see the wounded as our brothers and sisters. Perhaps we are not able to go and tend the wounds of others in the third-world countries. But what about the babies dying in our own towns? Where are the Christians in the nursing homes and in the AIDS wards? Who cares for the wounded and the damaged, if not Christians?

It is time to return to the beginning of the article where the woman with the issue of blood was presented. She touched Christ and was made whole. It is still possible to touch Christ and to be made whole. Indeed, Christ can make whole a society that is filled with sickness and despair if He has a people who are called by His name.

Study and Discussion
Questions

1. American society is spending more than ever before on health care, yet European societies show better health care statistics. What factors contribute to America's poor performance in health care statistics?

2. Describe Medicare and Medicaid programs. How effective are these programs in taking care of the health needs of target populations?

3. What are DRGs? How have DRGs affected the health care of Americans?

4. The economic position of many public hospitals is precarious. What factors contribute to the economic instability of public hospitals?

5. The AIDS epidemic is having a serious impact on our medical system. Discuss the consequences of AIDS in regard to health care and delivery.

6. An important component in the diagnosis and treatment of illness is the use of sophisticated medical technology. What are the consequences of high-tech medicine?

7. According to the author, health services for poor children have actually declined in the last decade. Discuss the consequences of this society's "tattered commitment" to provide medical care to needy children.

8. What is the new "uninsurance"? Describe the state of health insurance in American society.

9. What are specific things that Christians, as individuals and collectives, can do to address the health needs of disadvantaged groups?

10. Compare the ministry of Christ to the sick with the ministry of the Church today to those who are sick.

References

Ansell, D. A., and Schiff, R. L., "Patient Dumping: Status, Implication, and Policy Record. *JAMA* 257:1500-1502, 1957.

Baldwin, Mark F., "Who Will Pay Indigents' Bills?" *Modern Healthcare* 17:2, 1987.

Breakey, William R., and Alan J. Romonoski, "Health and Mental Health Problems of Homeless Men and Women in Baltimore." *JAMA* 262:10, 1098.

Council on Ethical and Judicial Affairs. "Black-White Disparities in Health Care." *JAMA* 263:17, 1990.

Curran, James W., et al., "Epidemic of HIV Infection and AIDS in the U. S." *Science* 239:6610-616, 1988

DiCarlo, Steven, and Jon Gabel, "Conventional Insurance: A Decade Later." *Health Care Financing Review* 11:1, 1989.

Enthoven, Alain C., "What Europeans Learn for Americans?" *Health Care Financing Review*, 11:1, 1989

Ginzberg, Eli, "High-Tech Medicine and Rising Health Care Costs." *JAMA* 263:13, 1090.

Hughes, D., K. Johnson, S. Rosenbaum and J. Liu, "The Health of America's Children." Washington, D. C.: *Children's Defense Fund*, 1989: 62-64.

Levey, Samuel, and James Hill, "National Health Insurance—The Triumph of Equivocation." *The New England Journal of Medicine,* 320:18, 1989.

Nemes, Judith, "Several States Developing Programs to Help Financially Troubled Hospitals." *Modern Healthcare*, June 1989.

Pickney, Deborah S., "Knowledge about HIV Increasing, But AIDS Care Remains Elusive." *American Medical News* July, 1988.

Rogers, Martha F., et al., "Polymerase Chain Reaction and HIV Infection in Infants." *New England Journal of Medicine,* 320:1649-1654, June 22, 1989.

Ruff, A., "Pediatric AIDS." Lecture: Johns Hopkins University. Epidemiology of AIDS course. June, 1990.

Ryder, Robert, et al., "Perinated Transmission of HIV Infection in Zaire." *New England Journal of Medicine,* 320:1637-1642, June 22, 1989.

Schneider, Edward L., and Jack M. Guralnik, "The Aging of America: Impact on Health Care Cost." *JAMA* 263:17, 1990.

Scott, Gwendolyn B., "Survival in Children with Perinatally Acquired Human Immunadeficiency Virus Type I Infection." *New England Journal of Medicine.* 321:1791-1796, December 28, 1989.

Starfield, Barbara, and Peter P. Budetti, "Child Health Status and Risk Factors." *Health Care News* 19:6, 1985.

Stimmel, Barry, "The Study and Practice of Medicine in the Twenty-first Century: As for Whom the Bell Tolls." *The Mount Sinai Journal of Medicine* 57:1, 1990.

Taravella, Steve, "Impact of AIDS in Hospitals Chronicled." *Modern Healthcare*, 19:23, 1989.

Terris, Milton, "Lessons from Canada's Health Programs." *Technology Review*, Feb/Mar 1990.

Waldo, Daniel R., Sally T. Sonnefield, David R. McKusick, and Ross J. Arnett III, "Health Care Financing Trends." *Healthcare Financing Review*, 10:4, 1989.

Wallace, Steven P., and Carrol L. Estes, "Health Policy for the Elderly." *Society*, October 1989.

Wise, Paul H., and Leon Eisenburg, "What do Regional Variations in the Rates of Hospitalization Really Mean?" *The New England Journal of Medicine*, 320:18, 1989.

Wright, James D., "Address Unknown: Homelessness in Contemporary America." *Society*, Sept-Oct, 1989.

CHAPTER 10
FORMAL ORGANIZATION: INTRODUCTION

The process of increasing social differentiation is one that has been of great interest throughout the history of sociology. All of the early masters of sociological thought were concerned with how society moved from relative homogeneity to the heterogeneity that characterizes the modern world. Formal organization is an important aspect of this development toward modernity. Hillery's thought-provoking article on the city, the lead article for the first section of this reader, provides a foundation for Professor Ingram's discussion of formal organization as a social problem.

That there is increased differentiation and specialization of tasks in the modern world was a focus for the works of several of sociology's founding fathers, including Herbert Spencer, Emile Durkheim, and Max Weber. Later theorists, including Talcott Parsons, a sociologist whose works have been important in shaping modern social theory, built on the early discussions of the masters. These writings tend to bear the mark of a structural functional perspective in describing the modern social world in terms of a whole made up of interconnected parts. Change in the parts (and thus in the whole system) is often explained using an evolutionary framework.

Talcott Parsons, for example, advanced an evolutionary theory to account for the movement of societies from primitive to modern. For Parsons there are four main processes of structural change: differentiation, adaptive upgrading, inclusion and value generalization. *Differentiation* bears a strong resemblance to Durkheim's increasing division of labor in modern society, a process that includes the emergence of formal organizations. *Adaptive upgrading* delineates the process by which the emerging organizations are seen as doing the job better than previous methods. The example given by Parsons is the ability of modern factories to produce a greater variety of goods more economically than could peasant households. The problem of integrating the results of the changes in social structure into the larger society is resolved by *inclusion*. The new development is legitimated or given a stamp of approval through the establishment of *value generalizations*.

Professor Ingram's discussion, although it does not use Parsons' terminology, allows us to see how formal organizations emerge. They do seem to represent an improvement over earlier organizational modes (adaptive upgrading), and they do fit together into the larger society (inclusion). Despite the problems noted in the article, formal organizations have been legitimated—even by Ingram who says that he regards "bureaucracy and the corporation as among the most important social inventions of all time" and "modern society could not survive their removal." Although our cultural values have taught us that this organizational form is "new and improved," there are problems within the system; and these problems are the focus of Ingram's article. His discussion departs from structural functionalism's emphasis on the positive features of formal organization to assume a conflict-based critical perspective that takes a hard look at the effects of corporations and bureaucracies.

Ingram challenges both individual Christians and churches with the observations he makes about formal organization. He notes how these "greedy institutions" can cause personal fragmentation, having particularly negative effects on the family and personal relations. Within these organizations, even "good and moral" persons may act in questionable ways that they would avoid in their private lives. Ingram urges churches to fulfill their obligation to teach people about the evil in some corporate activities.

Churches themselves can fall victim to the problems of formal organizations. Many local churches have moved away from an earlier family-like association to take on the shape (and the dysfunctions) of formal organizations. Although there are obvious advantages to superchurches, they can (although they need not) suffer from having an organizational structure that is more akin to a well-oiled machine than to being the living body of Christ. The importance of each individual, particularly marginal members, may be lost in building campaigns, recruitment of new members, and developing countless specialized programs.

Problems of formal organization, as Ingram notes, may be even more apparent at the denominational level of Church government. Margaret Poloma's work *The Assemblies of God at the Crossroads* (University of Tennessee Press, 1989) discusses at length some of the problems found in a denomination that is a relative newcomer to the American religious mosaic. Following the lead from a theory of Abraham Maslow, Poloma analyzes the relationship between religious experiences and institutional development. According to Maslow, religious prophets and founders of the great religions of the world have had what he terms "peak experiences." Abraham, Moses, Jesus, and Paul, for example, all had intense experiences with God that guided their ministries. The organization that developed around their legacies, however, often seems devoid of religious experience. Maslow argues that organized religion can often amount to "nonpeakers" telling other "nonpeakers" about peak religious experiences. The Judeo-Christian tradition knows the stories of the encounters the various prophets have had with God but often fails to help people to have their own direct encounters. In fact, Maslow contends that religious organizations often become the archenemies of religious experience.

The Assemblies of God is a Pentecostal denomination that traces its origins to a revival in the early 20th century. Its founders believed they were experiencing a fresh outpouring of the Holy Spirit, complete with speaking in tongues, spiritual healing, miracles and prophecies. In accord with Maslow's thesis, men and women (mostly members of fundamentalist churches) who were having these experiences found themselves being asked to leave these churches whose leaders felt this outpouring was the work of the devil. In 1916 many who had experienced this Pentecostal revival joined together to form the Assemblies of God.

As the years have gone by, the charisma of the earlier times has become much more routine within the Assemblies of God. This denomination is learning what other denominations have learned before them: whatever else they may be, religious experiences are dangerous to religious institutions. Prophets can upset organizations (as Jesus did to the Judaism of his day); priests (and ministers) are less likely to cause problems to the institutional order. The Assemblies of God is much less open to the "signs and wonders" that the Scriptures tell us should accompany the proclaiming of the Gospel than it once was. Although many of its leaders are concerned about this development, there is little evidence that this concern has stemmed the erosion of charisma.

Poloma suggests that there are three possible courses when charisma encounters formal organization. First, charisma can try to resist all organizational attempts. Many Pentecostals took this route before the founding of the Assemblies of God in 1916, and rejected attempts to organize, to develop a creed, or to ordain ministers. They quickly learned a basic principle of sociology, namely that charisma cannot be maintained indefinitely without some form of organization. Christianity would not be here today if Peter and Paul had not been used to institutionalize the legacy of Jesus.

A more common outcome is the one suggested by Maslow, namely for the organization to quench charisma. Religious historians have traced this process in the early Church, noting that many experimental aspects of the early Church were completely lost after Constantine made Christianity the religion of his Roman Empire. A similar process can be found in the history of different denominations. For example, John Wesley's early Methodism included intense religious experiences as one of its components, providing a balance between "head" and "heart" that, for the most part, has been lost in modern Methodism. The same process is underway in the Assemblies of God.

Poloma suggests a third alternative, namely, in light of this sociological understanding we have of the inherent tension between charisma and formal organization, to accept the tension. Despite the misuse of the gifts in the early Corinthian church, Paul did not forbid their use. He did not rule out prophetic messages, but rather instructed the people to "test prophecy" and to "hold fast to that which is good." Similarly the modern Church should learn to live with the ambiguities and tensions that religious experiences inevitably will bring to a church.

Perhaps the observation Poloma made in relating charisma to religious organization can provide some seeds for thought as to how to humanize secular formal organizations. Formal organizations have proved to be very functional for society, but, as Ingram has pointed out, there is also the dysfunctional side of the corporate and bureaucratic organizational forms.

FORMAL ORGANIZATION AS A SOCIAL PROBLEM

Larry C. Ingram

One of the hallmarks of modern social life is the extent to which it is affected by formal organizations. Some believe that more organizations than people exist in our society. Such a claim is plausible when one takes into account the number of memberships held by any particular individual.

Each of these organizations makes some sort of demand upon people. These demands are for time, energy, money, loyalty, and/or thought. An organization's power can be inferred by both the quality and the quantity of members' responses to these demands. Since many organizations receive huge investments of one or more of the factors described above, we do well to mark the enormous power held by them (Vander Zanden, 1988, pp. 408-415).

This power manifested through formal organizations and used by their agents warrants the discussion of formal organization as a social problem (Shepard, 1984, pp. 477 ff.). The following discussion will identify (1) typical patterns found in formal organizations, (2) problems associated with these patterns, and (3) ways of addressing these problems. It is with respect to the latter (addressing the problems) that a Christian response is considered.

WHAT IS "FORMAL ORGANIZATION"?

According to Richard Daft (1986, p. 9), formal organizations are those which incorporate people into well-bounded structures specifically designed to accomplish a particular purpose. It will be helpful to analyze this definition in some detail.

The first element in formal organization is that of *incorporating people*; organizations literally use people to create a body or structure.

However, the "total self" or the "whole individual" is not brought into the organization, but only the *person*. The word "person" comes from the Latin "persona," which means *mask*. The term is taken from the theater where the mask was placed in front of the face to give dramatic emphasis to the part being played. Hence, the person (mask) was a way of screening off the individual traits of the actor so that the focus of attention could be strictly limited to the acted role.

This is a rather apt description of the way people are incorporated into organizations. They are brought in to play roles, with the emphasis placed upon those traits which are relevant to the organizational role. The residual complexity of the self is either ignored or treated as problematic from the point of view of the organization. For example, family obligations which may require time off from work represent the residual self manifesting itself from behind the mask. The organization experiences this as problematic and a difficulty since the organizational mask is unable to control the self.

A second element of organizations is their *boundedness*. Organizations have both physical and social limits which can be identified. We are able to determine where the organization is (its physical location) and who are its members (social size and composition). A difference exists between formal and informal organizations, illustrated by the certainty with which one can reply to the questions, "Where does the Baptist Church meet?" and "How many members does it have?" as opposed to, "Where do your friends get together?" and "How many friends do you have, anyway?" Certainty of boundaries helps to establish a basis for control. Members are expected to be loyal and subject to organizational discipline while nonmembers are not.

The third element of formal organizations is that they are specifically designed and *planned* rather than haphazardly developed. Stated differently, the structure of the organization is rationalized, so that a given activity is specified to occur at a particular time and place. What organizational participants are supposed to be doing is coordinated and routinized so that the efficiency of the organization is increased.

Finally, the preplanned activity is directed toward the achievement of *particular purposes* or *goals*. Organizations typically do not try to do everything but, rather, limit their concerns to a specified slice of social life. For example, to make profits, to deliver services, to provide entertainment, to educate persons, to protect property, to repair equipment, to promote health or for any of a thousand other reasons. This limited focus is one of the reasons organizations incorporate members as persons rather than selves.

In American society (and increasingly throughout the world), the first purpose (profit-making) is often combined with one or two others, but seldom does one organization try to do everything.

CORPORATE AND BUREAUCRATIC MODELS: THE UNDERLYING PRINCIPLES OF MODERN ORGANIZATIONS

By definition, modern organizations are collective enterprises. Even though many people are involved in the pursuit of varied purposes, modern organizations do not manifest enormous structural diversity. What impresses the observer is the remarkable similarity in structure among organizations pursuing different goals. Much of this similarity is due to the influence of two organizational models: the corporation and the bureaucracy. These two designs are among the most important social inventions of the modern era, and they have proven to be highly compatible with one another.

Corporation

The corporate enterprise is a joint-stock company (Shepard, 1984, pp. 477; Mott, 1965 pp. 148-149; Turner, 1972 pp. 42 ff). Instead of an individual entrepreneur (or perhaps a partnership) assuming the risk of developing a company personally owned and controlled, the corporation represents a pooling of capital from a large group of investors who then own shares in the company according to the amount of their investment. Through election of a board of directors by these owners, control is shifted from the owners to the directors. The directors then hire managers and subsequently pass a significant amount of operational control on to them.

A number of advantages can be identified with this process. First, the joint-ownership means that the risk of failure is distributed among many rather than between one or two persons, thus minimizing the loss any one individual may experience. The loss to any given individual is called limited liability, meaning that an investor is responsible to the corporation only to the extent of his/her investment (Lenski, 1987, p. 326). If a person purchases a block of stock for $10,000, that amount may be lost, but no more than that. The other assets of the individual are considered personal assets, and creditors may not take them to pay off corporate debts. Second, by separating ownership from control, managers can be selected from a pool of professionals familiar with that particular activity. The mistakes that develop from inexperience are therefore less likely to occur (Turner, 1972, p. 43; Shepard, 1984, p. 477). Investors need to be familiar with the business operations before purchasing shares of stock, making possible expansion of available capital. In addition, investors may divide their resources to invest in a variety of enterprises, increasing the likelihood that at least some of them will be profitable (Turner, 1972, pp. 42-43; Shepard, 1984, p. 477).

Although the corporate form is best illustrated by the business organization, it would be a mistake to ignore its influence on nonprofit organizations such as charitable enterprises, professional associations, universities, and even (less often) churches. All of these are typically characterized by a pooling of resources, a governing board representative of the larger body of member/investors, and a managerial staff in charge of daily operations. These nonprofit organizations and their supporters are thus able to benefit from the advantages of the corporation. For example, the contributions and investments of an individual may be given and divided among a variety of agencies, knowing that the work of each group is being conducted under professional supervisors and is overseen by a collection of directors. Obviously, having a board of directors does not guarantee the absence of mismanagement. It does, however, make mismanagement less likely to occur without eventual exposure.

Because enormous amounts of time, energy, and capital are invested in the creation and maintenance of a corporation, it becomes a unit of exceptional power. Corporate decisions to open or close a plant may mean that a given community undergoes transformation in either economic expansion or economic depression. This in turn affects the ability of the community to educate its young people or upgrade its water, sewer, garbage disposal, police and fire protection. The direction taken by these community services makes the areas more or less attractive to other businesses. Consequently, large corporations are able to gain significant concessions from government agencies and their own workers through negotiations over relocation (Bluestone and Harrison, 1982; Ford, 1988).

The overwhelming impact of the large corporation occasionally becomes visible to the general public through dramatic events. Several years ago the federal government offered Chrysler Corporation a loan of up to $1.5 billion to prevent the economic collapse of the corporation. What made the Chrysler case so dramatic was not just the amount of the loan, but the willingness of government to become heavily interested in private business. Mills' (1959) claim of collusion between the top layers of business and government was made much more believable, with far-reaching effects for many people.

Paralleling the problem of power is the problem of accountability. Since risk is spread broadly, and since managers operate with others' capital, ventures may be undertaken which exceed that which investors identify as acceptable levels of risk. In the event that the actions are costly, it is often difficult to assess responsibility and to know whom to hold accountable (Vander Zanden, 1988, pp. 410-411; Jackall, 1988, pp. 85 ff). A particularly instructive example is the difficulty of accessing responsibility for the failure throughout the nation within the saving and loan industry (Behar, 1990, p. 60; Gorman, 1990, pp. 58-59).

It may also be difficult to assign appropriate penalties for costly actions (Tobias, 1989). The actions taken by corporate officers are corporate actions. They are undertaken as if the collective body were a single actor. The corporation is a legal "person" but not a human body. This raises serious questions about the meaning and appropriateness of fines or restrictions on organizational transactions or advertising. It is not clear that the ritual degradation associated with personal guilt in legal proceedings can be applied to corporate actors (Garfinkel, 1956).

Part of the problem stems from the splitting of the self, to which we have already alluded. Actions undertaken as persons in roles may not be the same as selves operating out of their individual morality codes. The role played by the corporate officer is defined by the needs of the corporation, not by personal interest or personal social benefits. A striking discussion of this role-playing activity is offered by Patrick Wright (1979) in his biography of John DeLorean. DeLorean and others allegedly fought a losing battle on the board of General Motors over the decision to begin production of the Corvair. The car was known to have engineering problems, but the directors believed the market was ready for its appearance, so they voted to move ahead. DeLorean argued that these were good moral men charged with making General Motors a profitable corporation. Using this perspective they put a car of questionable quality on the highway. In Wright's book, this chapter is entitled, "How Moral Men Make Immoral Decisions."

One of the executives in Jackall's (1988, p. 6) study states the matter pointedly:

> What is right in the corporation is not what is right in a man's house or in his church. What is right in the corporation is what the guy above you wants *from you.* That's what morality is in the corporation.

Bureaucracy

Although often combined with the corporate form, bureaucracy has no necessary relation to the corporation and is just as likely to appear without it. For this reason, bureaucracy is probably the more pervasive form. Bureaucracy offers a design whereby the activity in an organization may be rationalized (Weber, 1922), made more efficient, and thereby achieve its goals. Bureaucratic principles seek to provide structure at minimal cost in terms of time and energy (and ultimately money). To accomplish this, emphasis is placed upon the rational processes of *specialization, routinizations,* and *coordination.*

Specialization defines work roles to allow the worker to develop expertise in a narrowly defined area. The logic of efficiency is represented since the person who does the same few things again and again becomes more skilled than one who must do many different things. A worker responsible only for typing can become an expert typist without having to worry about filing or running errands. In the same way, an auto assembly line worker can achieve maximum speed and minimize error if he is responsible only for installing generators rather than assembling the entire circuitry of the car.

It is important to note that the process of specialization is, from the worker's point of view, one of deskilling. That is, each worker learns only a small part of a complex task. She or he is deprived of both the satisfaction in producing a product (since he/she only participates in a small part of the process), and the power of negotiation that goes with the possession of broad knowledge and skill (Perrow 1036, p. 19). The narrow range of tasks increases speed and reduces error, and also requires minimal training time for new personnel.

Specialized tasks are made routine by developing an explicit set of procedures to explain what the worker must do. *Routinization* constitutes the second emphasis of a bureaucracy. The organization elaborates job descriptions and policies into a manual of formal rules governing the everyday activities of the bureaucracy. In theory at least, the behavior of each worker becomes predictable because it has been routinized. Each worker who assumes a particular position is expected to perform the same set of activities in essentially the same way. Bureaucratic routinization effectively limits individual variation (Merton, 1975; Weber, 1922). Put differently, the aspects of self behind the mask are ignored — the self is reduced to the "person."

The application of rules and procedures contains a description that is an integral part of a bureaucracy. Rules are applied without favoritism, so that job appointments and promotions ideally follow merit criteria rather than personal subjectivity (Weber, 1922). Here the logic of efficiency is that the best qualified person should get the job to ensure the highest level of performance. Demotions, discipline, and firing similarly should follow patterns of routinized, disinterested fairness.

The third major emphasis in bureaucracy is *coordination*. Because of specialization, a continuing need exists for the integration of work activities. The large number of narrowly defined roles requires supervision, planning, and coordination. The bureaucratic model places those jobs which are directly related to one another into departments or bureaus (from whence bureaucracy gets its name), and assigns the task of managing the bureau to a supervisor. Since the bureau is responsible for only one part of the overall work of organization, there is a need to have coordinators among the bureaus to integrate the tasks. If necessary, the coordinators may have supervisors, extending the structure of bureaucracy through a number of layers. This principle of hierarchical coordinating authority tends to shape the bureaucracy into a pyramid (Weber, 1922; Merton, 1957). Obviously, each additional layer increases the complexity of the organization. In order to avoid confusion, the increasingly complex structure then requires the continued rationalization of specifying procedures and relationships through formal policies. The logic of efficiency also requires that the number of persons who can be effectively supervised by one other person, (called the span of control), must be determined within each department. This often results in subunits with further increased complexity (Peter, 1986).

The creation of bureaus or departments may lead to intra-organizational competition and conflict. Claims for departmental loyalty may supersede interest in the success of the organization as a whole (Merton, 1957; Meyer, 1975; Perrow, 1986). Departments may seek a disproportionate share of organizational resources, frequently at the expense of other departments. Departmentalization therefore may lead to cross-cutting pressures along two dimensions of the organization: first, there is competing loyalty between the goals of any given department and the goals of the total organization; and second, there is competition for resources among and between departments. These cross-cutting pressures produce organizational conflict.

PERSISTENT PROBLEMS EMERGING FROM CORPORATE AND BUREAUCRATIZED STRUCTURES

While a fairly long list of problems has been associated with organizations that are structured by corporate and bureaucratic principles, our purposes here will be served by limiting our focus. The two problems of complexity and control are endemic to these organizations.

A disclaimer should be offered at this point in the discussion. Since the focus is upon the formal organization as a social problem, positive features of organizations will not be examined, and so this discussion is one-sided. Should there be any doubt about my appreciation for the positive features of organizational life, let me say unequivocally that I regard bureaucracy and the corporation as among the most important social inventions of all time. Modern society could not survive their removal (Lenski, 1978, p. 326). But the benefits of such organizations do not come without cost, and that is what this paper is about. Having said this, let us now consider the problems inherent in organizational life.

Complexity

Modern organizations are incredibly complex, in general become more complex as they grow larger (Durkheim, 1933; Mott, 1965) and survive longer (Quinn and Cameron, 1983; Daft, 1986, p. 184). Additional social sources of complexity are found in the separation of ownership and management, the development of specialization, and departmentalization. When the interest, rhythms, and goals of multiple units need to be matched and achieve integration, the resulting list of rules governing the organizations is necessarily large. Interaction between levels or units of the organization becomes correspondingly difficult. The highly differentiated nature of the organization presents obstacles to insiders as well as outsiders.

For the organizational outsider, the difficulty of locating the proper official to handle the business at hand is a consistent problem. Organizational functionaries are prepared by specialization to involve themselves only in a limited number of transactions. Confronted with a customer or client whose need falls outside their sphere of competence, such functionaries often decline to offer assistance (Merton, 1957). Occasionally this occurs because the official does not want to help, but more frequently it is the case that the employee does not know where the need can be met, only that it cannot be met in that department. The customer or client not only fails to receive service, but is further disillusioned by the apparent insensitivity or ignorance of the organization's staff.

A slight variation of this kind of difficulty occurs when officials take for granted that outsiders understand the nature of the organization. A favorite illustration came from a student of mine. Responding to a newspaper advertisement by a company offering summer jobs to college students, the student went to the company headquarters. Unfortunately, the advertisement carried only the name of the firm and did not say where the application should be filed. The student decided, quite reasonably, that the personnel office would be the place.

The receptionist in the personnel office did not question the statement that the student was responding to a newspaper advertisement seeking applicants. An application blank (rather lengthy) was handed out with the request to complete the form, and then wait until the personnel manager was available. After approximately one-half hour, the student was ushered into the manager's office. Following the usual amenities, the student was asked about the kind of work interests of the applicant. When the manager learned the application was for student work the response was, "You're in the wrong office. We hire student workers as part of our public relations program. You need to go down the hall to the Public Relations Office." So much for the first hour.

Nevertheless, being an obedient sort this student went to the Public Relations Office. There a second receptionist gave out a second application form — the short form for summer workers. Another wait, and then the introduction to a smiling public relations director. A repetition of amenities, following standard procedures for interviewing job candidates as outlined in the policy manual. "Now, tell me," came the question, "what kind of work would you like to do?"

Without hesitation the student indicated work to keep physically trim, perhaps in the firm's warehouse. Whereupon the public relations director's face lost its smile, and the voice said, "You're in the wrong office. We hire warehouse workers directly through the warehouse. You must go down to the warehouse and interview there."

In the report, my student did not go to the warehouse, but simply left. The report added, only half-facetiously, "I decided that if it was that difficult to find the place to be hired, I would never be able to locate the place to be paid."

Complexity may also appear in the form of paperwork. In Weber's (1922) seminal discussion of the bureaucratic model, he listed the keeping of written records as a key feature of bureaucracy. In many of our modern organizations, no action can be initiated without first completing one or more written forms. Applications for jobs, requests for court appearances, filing for welfare services, registration for schools, petitions for loans, and any number of other activities require the processing of numerous written forms which may effectively discourage those most in need of such services from seeking them, especially when the initial records are followed by additional paper work requests.

Complex paperwork may be illustrated by procedures surrounding the use of a credit card. In order to obtain such a card, the person usually must file an application. This is mailed to the company and processed, a term which designates as a minimum an investigation of credit rating and employment, duly recorded in writing (and probably stored in a computer). If the applicant is accepted, the card is issued (mailed) to the person along with a set of instructions as to its use, the liability of the user, and procedures for billing and disputing a charge. In many instances the card will be mailed from an address different from the one to which the application was sent.

Actual purchase involves signing a bill imprinted with the card. Copies are made in triplicate and distributed to the card holder, the business where the purchase is made, and the company which issued the card. The card holder is advised to file such purchase record until it can be checked against the charges sent by the issuing company, and if necessary, maintained for tax purposes.

Monthly billings are likely to come from a still different address, and if a dispute occurs the correspondence is to be addressed to an entirely different location. It is in fact possible that none of these offices are located in the same state. Should correspondence be sent to the wrong location, delays of weeks or months may occur, with interest on unpaid bills accumulating (although such interest is not applicable if the card holder wins the claim).

Whatever efficiency is gained by the organization through the specialization implied in this discussion is invisible to the customer or clients. The complex interactions are confusing and often discouraging. The system is experienced by the customer as coercive because the user must conform to its complicated paperwork to avoid penalty.

Control

This last statement brings us to the second problematic aspect of corporate bureaucracy — the issue of control. Already we have noted the ability of corporations to influence the communities around them through providing jobs and paying taxes. We have also shown that much of the individuals' discretion in decision-making is removed by routinized activity. Poloma (1989) has recently related how this process is adversely affecting the "prophetic initiative" within the Assembly of God denomination. She argues that rule-consciousness is becoming more evident in denominational meetings and threatens to undermine those who offer fresh ideas, in some cases forcing them to minister without official support. The tendency toward centralized decision-making has been identified by some as a contributing factor in the lengthy controversy still separating factions in the Southern Baptist Convention (Hefley, 1986). That religious organizations are struggling with these issues may be taken as evidence of how deeply pervasive and entrenched such problems are in our society.

Perrow (1986) places the issue of control squarely in the center of his study of organizations. He maintains that organizations are best regarded as tools for shaping the world as one wishes it to be shaped, and that it is simply naive to ignore the ways in which organizations are manipulated by their leaders to achieve their own personal ends.

A prime example may be the case where a company is allowed to decline in performance so that its best personnel can be removed, its liquid assets (such as cash) appropriated, and the firm sold for a loss to generate tax credits. What is seen as incompetence may reflect what some leaders wanted all along (Perrow, 1986, pp. 11-13). While such action may be profitable for the sellers, numerous jobs may be at risk as new owners seek to revitalize the company. Workers' individual economic fortunes are often determined by corporate boards utilizing other people's money.

Although organizations bring in only a segment of the self, there is a strong tendency at all levels of management to enlarge that segment so that the organization becomes the center of meaning and controls the rhythm of life for the worker (Whyte, 1956; Jackall, 1988). Workers then embrace their jobs completely and manifest no role distance (Goffman, 1961, pp. 106-110). Family obligations and community service are either disrupted or redefined to conform to organizational expectations. Church commitment becomes extrinsically motivated, so that attendance at worship is a matter of corporate visibility and service on the church board means another line on one's resume.

It is not only the work organization that may become the center of activity. Voluntary associations (including churches) which operate more or less exclusively on the basis of moral appeals are often guilty of absorbing so much attention from members that participation in organizational activities becomes a test of loyalty. Whether it is the corporation which moves its executives from plant to plant or a church that requires undivided loyalty to its program, one is confronting a "greedy institution" (Coser, 1974), an organization which seeks control of the conditions of life from some or all of its members. One must recognize that although the majority of organizations are greedy to some extent, there are major differences in the degree to which this is true.

Addressing the Problems: Christians and Their Organizations

I do not pretend to know the answers to many of the dilemmas presented by organizational life. Nevertheless, I believe that Christian faith should respond to human problems, and thus I want to make an attempt to indicate ways in which Christian commitment may have an impact upon the life of organizations.

First is the responsibility of the Church. Although it is not completely accurate (Moberg, 1972; Edge, 1977), the charge that evangelical churches do not address issues of social responsibility contains enough truth to warrant repentance in most local churches. Christians must stop acting as if God does not care about corporate decisions and bureaucratic controls which diminish the quality of human life. Surely there is moral failure when a bank targets specific neighborhoods for exclusion from loans. Surely it is a sin when a college can operate a highly profitable sports program but graduate less than one of three who have received athletic scholarships. Surely our Lord is angry when a grocery story in a low income area increases prices on necessary food items during the first few days of the month — the period immediately following receipt of pension and welfare checks. These organizational sins are at least as destructive of the good life as are personal sins.

What action can the Church take? The Church must inform its members about immoral and illegal organizational activity in the same way that it disseminates knowledge about pornography or drug abuse or illicit sex or abortion. It is the Church's responsibility to help members understand the nature of organizational life and how complexity and control affect the quality of the human experience. One of the most significant lessons the Church should have learned from the civil rights movement is the importance of helping its members monitor their social environment. And having monitored that environment, the Church must raise a prophetic voice to point to injustice, and work to introduce needed reforms (Micah 6:8; James 1:22-24).

At the local level, the development of large super-churches with highly specialized staff assignments may mean that families are never together in church. Family members are distributed into the specialized activity areas. Some persons may not understand the differentiated ministries and may be lost in the shuffle or even ignored because their needs are "not my area." As programs are elaborated, numerous scheduling conflicts over the use of facilities occur and give rise to turf struggles that may alienate persons from the church. Staff recommendation for budget priorities may have more to do with career enhancement than with ministry (see O'Dea 1961; Blizzard, 1956). In short, it is easy for the Church to become a group of believers who operate a formal organization rather than a community of disciples learning, teaching, and practicing Christian faith under the leadership of those with a special call to invest their lives in redemptive work (Ephesians 4:11-24). I do not think that the Church can do without an organizational structure, but this should not simply duplicate the culture of a secular corporation. Paul's admonition, "do not be conformed to this world" (Romans 12:2), must apply to our collective as well as our individual lifestyles.

When Christians participate in organizations other than the Church, they can bring into these settings a commitment to love their neighbors as themselves. Christian love is much more than the unbiased application of bureaucratic rules. It is to enter into the lives of others in a way that is creative, redemptive and outgoing. Such a stance precludes treating others only according to the organizational masks that they wear. Love requires that one go beyond the mask and become involved with the total selves of one's co-workers.

This cannot mean ignoring duty or allowing production to fall off while one deals with a continuing series of coworker's personal crises. This would not only reduce organizational effectiveness, but also might place one's own job and, therefore, the security of one's family in jeopardy.

However, the Christian can insist that members of the organization are of more value than maximizing profits (Luke 122:6-7, 15-21; Matthew 6:19 ff). Christians can demand that organizational decision-making consider the impact of policy on the lives of individuals and the community. Wherever one has the opportunity, one can seek reduction in complexity or release from control, or at least try to help others cope better. Encouragement, kindness, and patience are under-utilized values in organizational relationships, and Christians can alleviate much anxiety by practicing these values.

Finally, Christians can bring a sense of stewardship to the organization. The twin problems of complexity and control often combine with self-interest to generate a type of underlife in the organization (Goffman, 1966; Ingram, 1986). Individuals then find ways to subvert organizational demands and gain clandestine rewards. Jackall (1988) described the management practice of reducing maintenance spending to a bare minimum in an attempt to make one's units look more profitable and enhance one's chances of promotion. This action is obviously costly to the overall organization, as well as being potentially damaging to coworkers.

Self-centered, status-seeking attitudes are no more acceptable in work settings than they are within families or churches. To take a job is to commit oneself to do quality work. By remaining firmly attentive to the tasks at hand, the Christian can offer a visual example of one who treats life with reverence and life's obligations as service to God, not men (Ephesians 6:6-7; Galatians 6:7-9).

Study and Discussion
Questions

1. Distinguish between the concepts of self and person. What does the Bible teach about such a distinction?

2. In your own words, explain the concept of the corporation.

3. Identify some advantages of the corporate form of organization over the business concern started by a single individual.

4. Why is it difficult to control corporations?

5. What is the underlying assumption in bureaucratic organization? Explain.

6. How is the bureaucracy structured to achieve efficiency?

7. Explain the notion of complexity in formal organizations.

8. From your own experience, give one or two examples of dealing with complexity in organizations.

9. Discuss: "What is seen as incompetence may reflect what some leaders wanted all along."

10. Suppose you became the head of a large corporation. What are some ways that you might express your Christian faith in managing the organization?

11. Imagine that you are the pastor of a church. Would you preach on the kinds of problems identified here? Why or why not? What would you say?

References

Behar, Richard, "Catch Us If You Can." *Time*, Vol. 135, No. 13, 60, 1990.

Blizzard, Samuel, "The Minister's Dilemma," *Christian Century*. 73:508-510, 1956.

Bluestone, Barry, and Bennett Harrison, *The Deindustrialization of America: Plant Closings, Community Abandonment, and the Dismantling of Basic Industry*. New York: Basic Books, 1982.

Coser, Lewis A., *Greedy Institutions: Patterns of Undivided Commitment*. New York: The Free Press, 1974.

Daft, Richard, *Organization Theory and Design*, 2nd edition. St. Paul, MN: West Publishing House, 1986.

DiMaggio, Paul J., and Walter W. Powell, "The Iron Cage Revisited: Institutional Isomorphism and Collective Rationality in Organizational Fields." *American Sociological Review*, 48:147-160, 1983.

Drucker, Peter F., *The Concept of the Corporation*. New York: Mentor Books, 1964.

Durkheim, Emile, *The Division of Labor in Society*. New York: The Free Press, 1933.

Edge, Findley B., "The Evangelical Concern for Social Justice." *Religious Education*, 74:481-489.

Ford, Ramona L., *Work, Organization, and Power*. Boston: Allyn and Bacon, Inc., 1988.

Garfinkel, Harold, "Conditions of Successful Degradation Ceremonies." *American Journal of Sociology*, 61 (March):420-424, 1956.

Goffman, Erving, *Encounters*. Indianapolis, Indiana: Bobbs-Merrill Co., 1961.

Goffman, Erving, *Asylums*. Garden City, NY: Doubleday, 1961.

Goldner, Fred H., R. Richard Ritti, and Thomas P. Ference, "The Production of Cynical Knowledge in Organizations." *American Sociological Review*, 42 (August):539-551, 1977.

Gorman, Christine, "This Is a Rescue." *Time*, Vol. 135, No. 11, 58-59, 1990.

Greenwald, John, "Boom, Boom, Kaboom!" *Time*, Vol. 134, No. 17, 66-67, 1989.

Hefley, James C., *The Truth in Crisis*. Dallas, TX: Criterion Publications, 1986.

Ingram, Larry C., "In the Crawlspace of the Organization." *Human Relations*, 39:467-487, 1986.

Jackall, Robert, *Moral Mazes: The World of Corporate Managers*. New York: Oxford University Press, 1988.

Kamens, David H., "Legitimating Myths and Educational Organization: The Relationship Between Organizational Ideology and Formal Structure." *American Sociological Review*, 42:208-219, 1977.

Katz, Fred E., "Explaining Informal Work Groups in Complex Organizations: The Care for Autonomy in Structure." *Administrative Science Quarterly*, 10:204-223, 1965.

Lenski, Gerhard, and Jean Lenski, *Human Societies*, 3rd edition. New York: McGraw-Hill Book Co., 1978.

Merton, Robert K., "Bureaucratic Structure and Personality." *Social Theory and Social Structure*. New York: The Free Press, 1957.

Meyer, Marshall W., "Organizational Domains." *American Sociological Review*, 40:(October):500-615, 1975.

Mills, C. Wright, *The Power Elite*. New York: Oxford University Press, 1959.

Moberg, David, *The Great Reversal: Evangelicalism and Social Concern*. Philadelphia: Lippincott, 1972.

O'Dea, Thomas, "Five Dilemmas in the Institutionalization of Religion." *Journal for the Scientific Study of Religion*, 1:31-41, 1961.

Perrow, Charles, *Complex Organizations: A Critical Essay*. New York: Random House, 1986.

Peter, Laurence J., *The Peter Pyramid*. New York: William Morrow and Company, 1986.

Poloma, Margaret, *The Assemblies of God at the Crossroads*. Knoxville: The University of Tennessee Press, 1988.

Quinn, Robert E., and Kim Cameron, "Organizational Life Cycles and Shifting Criteria of Effectiveness," *Management Science*, 29:33-51, 1983.

Roy, Donald, "Quota Restriction and Goldbricking in a Machine Shop. *American*

Journal of Sociology, 57:427-442, 1952.

Shepard, Jon A., *Sociology*, 2nd edition. St. Paul, MN: West Publishing Co., 1984.

Tobias, Andrew, "Too Much Firepower to Fit the Crime?" *Time*, Vol. 134, No. 21, 74, 1989.

Turner, Jonathan E., *Patterns of Social Organization*. New York: McGraw-Hill Book Co., 1972.

Vander Zanden, James W., *The Social Experience*. New York: Random House, 1988.

Weber, Max, "Bureaucracy," pp. 196-244, in Hans Gerth and C. Wright Mills, *From Max Weber*. New York: Oxford University Press, (1958), 1922.

Whyte, William H., *The Organization Man*. New York: Simon and Schuster, 1956.

Wright, J. Patrick, *On a Clear Day You Can See General Motors*. New York: Avon Books, 1979.

Zald, Meyer N., *Organizational Change: The Political Economy of the YMCA*. Chicago: The University of Chicago Press, 1970.

CHAPTER 11
NUCLEAR MILITARISM: INTRODUCTION

As we have already noted in earlier introductions, the concept of system is a central one in sociology. Although Professor Kraybill does not explicitly employ it, conceptualizing the world as a set of interdependent parts does make an excellent framework from which to evaluate the information presented on nuclear militarism.

Systems are of different sizes, with component parts that may be living or nonliving. An individual person may be conceptualized as a system for medical or psychological purposes. Groups, social institutions, and societies are all conceptualized as systems by sociologists. At one end of the spectrum is microsociology, the study of human interaction in small groups, which may designate as few as two persons (a dyad). Macrosociology, on the other hand, focuses on larger social systems, with some theorists going as far as to say the entire world is a single system. Thus the parts of a social system may be individuals in interaction or it may be nation states. It is also possible to consider how social systems interact with nonhuman systems. (For example, in Ferraro's discussion of environmental concerns, social systems are interfaced with the ecosystem of nature.)

In the modern world the smaller social systems, including family, education, religion, and local government, are being more and more influenced by larger systems. In fact, the isolation of nation states appears to be an impossibility as we prepare to move into the 21st century. Modern technology, especially changes in communication and transportation, has made it impossible for even a nation to be an island unto itself.

As we noted in the introduction to Professor Jantzi's article on paradigms of development, some social scientists have begun to talk in terms of the entire world being a system subject to common influences. (The seemingly omnipresent Coca Cola may be regarded as a kind of symbol of this world system.) World systems theorists argue that there is in the last analysis but one system of theoretical importance — and that system is worldwide. This concept has been developed by Immanuel Wallerstein who observes that the capitalist economy is in fact a world economy that has its origins in the fifteenth century and has continued to expand its global dominance.

There are two points that may be helpful to note in using the world system perspective for analyzing the problem of nuclear militarism. The first is the decline in importance and power of isolated nation states. This discussion has been developed by Theda Skocpol who differs from Wallerstein in stressing political (rather than economic) factors as basic to world system analysis. Second, unlike a functionalist approach which depicts a system as basically one of consensus, harmony and cooperation, world system theorists emphasize a unity based on a variety of factors in inherent tension.

The fact that there may be a world system (rather than autonomous national systems) that affects both economic and political action is directly relevant to the issue of nuclear militarism. It is neither specifically an American nor a Soviet social problem, but rather a worldwide concern. It is one, as Kraybill demonstrates, that is closely intertwined with other subsystems, particularly politics and economics. Given the complexity and scope of the issue, nuclear militarism may appear to be beyond any hope of solution.

As Christians, however, we must remember that God is sovereign and has given us weapons that the world does not understand. The weapons that we have are not "carnal," or merely human ones (2 Corinthians 10:3-6)—particularly the power of prayer and fasting. Jesus instructed us to pray always and not to despair (Luke 18:1), and Paul assured us that the Holy Spirit intercedes for us, assisting us in our communication and intercession with God (Romans 8:26-28). Therefore, we should not underestimate their power and despair in this situation, but rather we should study the problem and attempt to stem humankind's destructive and suicidal tendencies.

Certainly the omnipotent God, the sovereign ruler of the universe, is concerned about all humanity. This is the emphatic message of the prophet Jonah. God wishes that all individuals come to repentance and live in fellowship with each other, as well as with God (Jonah 4:11). As Christians we believe that God's power is greater than all the diabolical forces of evil (2 Kings 6:8-23). Therefore, we must pray that God would turn the world's leaders from trusting in nuclear might, to trusting the living God (Isaiah 31:1-3). This means that instead of concentrating on the weapons of destruction, leaders of the nations must learn to "do justice, love mercy, and walk humbly with God" (Micah 6:8).

NUCLEAR MILITARISM
*Donald B. Kraybill**

The threat of nuclear war is a unique social problem in our modern era. In the words of the famous physicist Einstein, "Everything has changed since the first atom bomb was exploded except the way we think." Nuclear war, on the one hand, is simply an extension of conventional war and could be analyzed as the component part of national and international militarism. On the other hand, the characteristics of nuclear war are so uniquely different from conventional war that we make a gross error by assuming that nuclear war is just another type of war. Due to space constraints and the special features of nuclear war this chapter will focus strictly on nuclear militarism.

The Nuclear Arsenal

Our nuclear age is a precarious one with some 50,000 nuclear warheads scattered around the globe with the combined explosive power of over a million Hiroshima bombs (Sivard, 1982, p. 10). The atomic bombs dropped by American bombers on Hiroshima and Nagasaki were "peewees" by today's standards. One megaton bomb carries the equivalent power of one million tons of dynamite (TNT). How can we visualize a million tons of dynamite? It would fill the box cars of a freight train 300 miles long and would take six hours to pass at full speed (*Boston Study Group*, 1979, p. 63)! Another way to grasp the destructive power of a single megaton bomb is to visualize 100,000 dump trucks, each filled with ten tons of dynamite. The string of dump trucks would stretch nearly 379 miles, from Washington, D. C., to Columbus, Ohio.

Nuclear bombs in today's arsenal range from 40 kilotons (40,000 tons of TNT) to 20 megatons (20 million tons of TNT). The recent U. S. trend is to make smaller warheads of about 350 kilotons (350,000 tons of TNT). Counting only strategic (long distance) warheads, the U. S. and the USSR have about 13,000 megatons of nuclear firepower. A single MX missile will carry 10 nuclear bombs which can be aimed at separate targets (cities or military installations) and together they deliver 3.3 million tons to TNT — the equivalent of about 223 Hiroshima explosions. One Trident submarine (14-25 are to be deployed over the next ten years) can carry 408 nuclear bombs which can be exploded over 480 separate targets. Such a submarine carries about 19.2 million tons of TNT (over 1200 Hiroshimas) and could destroy 408 different cities. In the early 1980s the United States could destroy every Soviet city 40 times over, and Soviet fire power could bounce the rubble of American cities 25 times after the first attack. Military analysts estimate that with only five percent of their nuclear arsenals either of the super powers could effectively destroy the other.

CHANGES THAT MAKE WAR

During the 1980s the fragile balance of nuclear terror was shaken by several new

---

*Edited and briefly revised by Daniel Yutzy, Professor of Sociology, Taylor University.

developments. Both sides were developing a new generation of even more lethal and powerful weapons in addition to what was already deployed. The Unites States list was long; 100 MX missiles, 15-25 Trident submarines, 100 B-1 bombers, 4,000-5,000 cruise missiles, the neutron bomb, a stealth bomber, chemical weapons, laser weapons, and new conventional arms of all sorts. The Soviets were also developing new weapon systems. The history of the arms race, in a brief word, is that the United States, with one or two exceptions, had led the race with new technological advances. But the Soviets have usually caught up three to five years later. In the early 1980s most military experts agreed that the two superpowers were about equal in strategic strength when all of the relevant areas of comparison were considered.

Another change rocking the uneasy stability of the past is the technological advances that improve the accuracy of modern bombs, In the 1960s and '70s the weapons were so inaccurate that both sides could only threaten to blow up each other's cities in retaliation if the other side attacked first. The accuracy of the newer bombs is astonishing. After traveling some 6,000 miles between continents they can be dropped to within 300-600 feet of their target. With such accuracy both sides are developing the capability of destroying the other side's missiles or bombers in a first strike. This strategy of targeting the other side's weapons, known as "counterforce," is extremely dangerous. For in a time of international tension, if each side "thinks" the other side might strike first, then each is tempted to hit first because of the great advantage of destroying the opponents' weapons before they can be used. The shift toward counterforce, made possible by technological changes, has increased plans to "limit" nuclear wars to certain battlefields and to fight "prolonged" nuclear wars. All of this has made nuclear war thinkable and acceptable in the modern mind.

As the instruments of nuclear war become more numerous and electronically controlled, the possibility of nuclear weapons exploding by technical malfunction, error, accident, and terrorist attack also increases. There have been numerous false alerts, computer malfunctions, and human errors that have occurred in recent years. Some scientists are warning that our national security is increasingly weakened as we depend more and more on sophisticated electronic systems.

Beyond the potential of accidental nuclear war or sabotage is the growing threat posed by the proliferation of nuclear weapons around the world. In the early 1980s, six nations possessed nuclear weapons. In a 1982 publication Dun (1982) estimated that ten more countries would have the capacity to build nuclear weapons by the mid 1980s and that another ten could have the bomb by the early 1990s. Not all of the countries that could build a nuclear bomb necessarily will, but it is clear that the spread of the bomb is impossible to halt. It is one thing to have two giants controlling nuclear weapons with a gentleman's agreement not to use them, but it is quite a different and more precarious world when 20 countries have the arms to literally blow each other up.

Finally, the superpowers seem unable to arrest the growth and spread of nuclear weapons, in spite of arms negotiations and treaties. Even with the 1972 SALT I (Strategic Arms Limitation Talks) treaty, strategic (long distance) nuclear warheads alone in the United States and the USSR respectively, grew from 4,000 to 9,000 and from 1,600 to 7,000 between 1970 and 1980. The SALT II treaty was not ratified by the United States Senate and if START (Strategic Arms Reduction Talks) negotiations do not result in significant reductions, the number of strategic nuclear bombs will likely jump from the present 18,000 to nearly 30,000 by the late 1980s. In 1982, even as the nuclear freeze movement was growing and START negotiations between the superpowers began, the United States announced plans to build 17,000 new nuclear bombs over the next decade both for replacement and for new weapons. One of the ironies of the nuclear age is that attempts to limit and control weapons only produce more of them, since both sides aggressively build up their arsenals before negotiations so that they can "bargain from a position of strength."

All of these recent trends make the ominous threat of nuclear war by accident or design an increasing social problem. The *Bulletin of the Atomic Scientists* (1981) estimates that we are four minutes before midnight. As defence analyst Richard Garwin said, the chances of nuclear war are 50/50 unless serious arms control measures are enacted. George Kistiakowsky, the eighty-year-old Harvard chemist who worked on the first atomic bomb for the United States, believes nuclear war is very likely before the end of the century *if* the arms race is not stopped. In a recent interview, he said, "I am so old I probably won't see it, but most of you will probably be involved in a nuclear war" (Kistiakowsky, 1981, p. 24). Admiral Hyman Rickover retired as "father of the United States nuclear Navy" in 1982. In a Senate testimony that same year, when asked about the probability of nuclear war, he said, "I think we will probably destroy ourselves." These sages, seasoned with experiences, confirm the growing risk of nuclear war as a serious social problem.

THE EFFECTS OF NUCLEAR WEAPONS

The consequences of the nuclear threat include the probable destruction resulting from a nuclear attack, as well as effects that already impinge on our social system even if an attack never occurs. In an attempt to summarize briefly the major consequences of this social problem we will consider four effects of the nuclear threat: (1) immediate physical and human destruction, (2) long-term consequences, (3) present economic costs, and (4) social-psychological effects.

Immediate Destruction

The physical and human destruction flowing from a nuclear explosion is enormous and difficult to grasp. A one-megaton bomb sends a sizzling heat flash out across a wide land area frying people alive and setting off thousands of fires. In the center of the mile-wide fireball the heat is 27 million degrees, similar to the sun itself (Glasstone and Dolan, 1977)! In the immediate area of the explosion people and other objects containing moisture are vaporized by the enormous heat. Concrete explodes; stone and steel melt. Five miles away from ground zero clothing worn by unprotected persons ignites spontaneously and seven miles out newspapers lying outside houses ignite. Thirty miles away, persons looking at the explosion would receive retinal burns and even 50 miles away the fireball would feel much hotter than the noonday sun. A single one-megaton bomb would leave at least 10,000 severe burn victims who would need specialized medical treatment. In the United States as a whole, we have merely 2,000 special burn beds, and in the state of Pennsylvania only 60. In short, all the special burn facilities in the United States could not begin to cope with the burn injuries resulting from a single one-megaton explosion, let alone thousands of other serious injuries.

The bomb also produces a violent explosion with raging winds varying from 500-700 miles per hour at the center. The vicious winds and air pressure changes literally flatten everything 2.5 miles out in all directions from the explosion. Even 5 miles out most residences are destroyed. Ten miles away from ground zero plaster is cracked, structural joints twisted, glass cracked, shingles blown off roofs. Gigantic piles of rubble would fill the roads making transportation impossible. The bomb also gives off a powerful electromagnetic pulse which burns out electrical circuits shutting down electrical service and cutting off electronic communication.

A single one-megaton bomb exploding in the air would spread damage over 217,000 acres, with 30,000 acres severely burned or totally damaged. The human casualties would run high. The same bomb exploding over Detroit would leave 783,000 dead and 954,000 injured. Two 20 megaton bombs exploding over New York City would kill 9,583,000 persons and leave 3,654,000 injured (ACDA, 1979). That's right — two bombs would wipe out 9.5 million people in an instant! Estimates of the national death toll from a nuclear attack vary depending on whether a "counterforce" or "general" nuclear attack is assumed. A counterforce attack would be aimed at weapons facilities, whereas a general attack would involve industrial areas as well as energy supplies. A range of estimates of national casualties (not counting injuries) follows (OTA, 1979, pp. 63-108):

Estimates of Deaths in Millions			
	World War II	Counterforce Nuclear Attack	General
USSR	20.0	4 to 28	42 to 100
U.S.	4	2 to 20	20 to 165

Physicians argue that medical treatment would be nonexistent after a major nuclear confrontation. The only appropriate medical response according to them is prevention. Some doctors have said that even helping to develop civil defense plans in advance is an immoral act since it gives the false impression that it will provide protection and security which, according to the doctors, is an illusion.

Long -Term Consequences

Beyond the immediate devastation produced by a nuclear attack are numerous long-term effects that are highly unpredictable. The United States Office of Technological Assessment (1979:3), after studying the effects of several nuclear attack scenarios, concluded that "the effects which cannot be calculated in advance are just as serious as those which can be calculated." In other words the ugly effects of the blast, fire, and nuclear radiation which we can predict are only half the story! The other half of the story, the long-term, unexpected and unpredictable effects will be just as serious in their consequences as the predictable results.

There are several types of unpredictable long-term consequences. Sand-like radioactive fall, sucked up into the atmosphere by the explosions, would drop back on the earth over several weeks in unpredictable patterns as winds blow it several hundred miles away from the attack sites. Even 90 miles from ground zero the fallout would be 900 rems — twice the lethal dosage. Exposure to immediate nuclear radiation near the explosion, as well as to deadly radioactive fallout, will increase cancer rates around the world and raise the rate of natural mutations. Unborn children exposed to the radiation and fallout will suffer significantly higher rates of retardation and physical deformities.

Beyond the long-term human suffering, scientists believe that simultaneous nuclear explosions will "thin out" the ozone layer that protects us from the ultraviolet rays of the sun. Some estimate that 40-70 percent of the ozone layer will be destroyed by exploding only 10 percent of the superpowers' nuclear arsenal. A 20 percent depletion of ozone would severely scorch vegetation and burn the eyes and skin of humans and animals. The extent of ozone depletion after a nuclear war is an uncertainty that is debated in the scientific community. Another unpredictable result is possibly climatic, resulting from ozone depletion that could raise temperatures enough to prevent grain production in the present breadbasket regions of the world.

Moreover, insects and animals are vulnerable to death from radiation at differential rates. Cockroaches and other insects, for example, can withstand doses of radiation 100 times stronger than humans while birds are more vulnerable than humans. Thus, exposure to immediate radiation and radioactive fallout will disrupt and disturb the natural balance in the order of nature. Will insect populations grow rapidly if their natural predators, birds, are killed off at higher rates? Will such imbalances create secondary problems such as increased insect damage to crops? There are countless unknowns involving the explosion of many nuclear weapons that make the threat of nuclear war a big experiment indeed! It is the kind of experiment that we may only have one chance to run since the fate of the earth itself is at stake.

Beyond the human suffering and long-term ecological devastation is the question of whether the economy, industrial production, and social organization could ever fully recover to prewar levels. Conditions after a nuclear holocaust would welcome anarchy, authoritarian rule, public health epidemics, and unbelievable social chaos (Katz, 1982). Communication, transportation, manufacturing, and health care would be nonexistent or severely disrupted in major attack areas. It is debatable whether the present rate of industrial production and standard of living could ever be attained again after a major nuclear attack. Based on considerable research on Hiroshima survivors we know that the long-term psychological trauma is also quite severe.

One must note, however, that the recent dismantling of the Berlin wall followed by radical political and economic changes in eastern Europe have diminished the threat of an all-out nuclear exchange between the United States and the Soviet Union. Early '90s arms control agreements hold out the prospect for the first real reduction of nuclear weapons since Hiroshima and Nagasaki. But the massive weapons are still in place and the likelihood of nuclear terrorism has not diminished. The fearsome specter of Iraqi scud missiles potentially carrying chemical and nuclear warheads faced Israel, Saudi Arabia and the allied forces during Operation Desert Storm in 1991. Despite the accuracy of the U. S. Patriot antimissile weapons and persistent air attacks, some scuds got through. The prospect of a localized nuclear exchange in the Near East remains.

ECONOMIC COSTS

Concern over nuclear war frequently focuses on the ugly devastation after an attack and neglects the impact of the bomb on our society today. The massive commitment to militarism by the U. S. and the USSR denied citizens in both countries access to basic goods and health services in the '70s and '80s. The USSR spends 5 to 6 percent of its GNP for the military. However, the actual dollar amount is about the same in both countries since the United States' GNP is twice as large as that of the Soviets'. Nearly 50 percent of the annual United States federal budget is spent for the military, when the costs of past wars are taken into account.

In the five-year period of 1982-87 the United States planned to spend between 1.5 and 2.2 trillion dollars in military expenditures. This averages out to about $7,300 for every American over the five-year period. For each American household of four, using the most conservative figures, this would be equivalent to nearly $30,000 over the five-year period. The Unites States government planned to spend $34 million per hour, or $816 million per day, on the military over this five-year period. The 1983 military budget of 260 billion dollars would fill 260,000 cars, each with a million dollars, and they would stretch — bumper to bumper — some 600 miles, from Chicago to Washington, D. C. In 1982, when a war was not being fought, the United States government made massive cuts in all areas of federal spending — health, education, elderly, housing, and environment — except military spending. In the strategic areas, budget increases of 7 to 9 percent above inflation were planned over several years. As a direct result of the sharp reduction in federally funded social services the number of homeless or "street people" — mentally ill, alcoholics and drug addicts, unemployed single-parent families and the poor — in our major cities has increased.

Not only has the shifting of federal monies from social services to military priorities reduced the amount available for needed social services but such military spending also increases inflation, stagnates the economy, and increases unemployment. According to MIT economist Lester Thurow (1981), high levels of military spending will wreck the economy. Inflation is exacerbated by military production, since tanks and missiles cannot be worn or eaten. The production of nuclear arms requires capital, as well as human and natural resources to make products that are never sold in the marketplace. Employees of military contractors and military personnel receive wages that they use to purchase goods. Thus the normal balance between the demand and supply of goods is disrupted since more demand is chasing fewer goods. This can produce higher prices and more inflation for all of us.

Extensive military production chokes the industrial output of a country because raw materials, technicians, factories, and capital — which normally would be used to manufacture consumer products — are instead gobbled up by a military production to make products that no one can buy. A recent study of 13 major industrialized countries found that those spending the least on military costs experienced faster growth, greater investment, and higher productivity (DeGrasse and Gold, 1981). Military spending is also one source of the growing red ink in Uncle Sam's budget. Inflation dropped during the 1980s, accompanied by massive deficits.

A final economic effect that touches us today is the loss of jobs created by military spending. Contrary to popular opinion military spending does not increase the number of jobs, since it increasingly relies on sophisticated technology. Military production provides fewer jobs for each billion invested whereas industries such as education, construction, health care, and retail trade provide more jobs because they are more labor intensive. Anderson (1982) has shown that 9,000 to 10,000 jobs are lost for each billion dollar increase in military spending. Although only about 15 percent of the military budget is devoted to nuclear armaments, it is quite clear that the massive burden of military spending by the United States government is already touching the lives of its citizens, and some of them are literally dying now, even though a bomb has never been exploded. The same applies to the international scene where over a billion and a half dollars is allocated each day for military spending.

THE PSYCHOLOGICAL BURDEN

Beyond the economic burden imposed by high levels of military spending, the nuclear threat today also touches us in a more subtle but possibly more devastating fashion. According to psychiatrist Robert Lifton (1982) the psychological burden of living in the nuclear age is enormous — since we live under the shadow of human annihilation and extinction. The threat of nuclear war erodes the hope on which our personal collective lives rest. What does it mean to "yank the rug of hope" out from under an entire society? Children complain that the threat of nuclear war is unfair because they may not get a chance to live out their lives. Young parents hesitate to raise children in a world where the chances of a major nuclear war are 50/50. College students studying the futile attempts of nations to control nuclear arms are disillusioned with life and plead for just "one word of hope." In a psychological study of the effects of nuclear war on children John Mack (1981) says, "children are aware of the threat and live in fear of it." "Why," youth asks, "should we work hard to make good grades in school if the world is going to blow up?"

The threat of "the bomb" has injected a gnawing fear into the nervous system of our society. The erosion of hope strangles the meaning of life itself and accelerates the ethic of instant gratification. Is it any wonder that everyone wants an instant "high" from sex, alcohol, drugs, and leisure? Could it be that the subconscious threat of the bomb's terror produced the enormous American interest in death and dying that emerged in the decade of the 1970s? There is no way of knowing how the threat of nuclear war will affect the soul of our society in the long run. Like terminal cancer, it eats away at the gift of hope. We cannot see it and we cannot feel it, but it is there — quietly nibbling away at our collective soul. This squandering of hope, this smothering of the spirit of life is the one place, more than any other, where the nuclear arms race stands in sharp juxtaposition to the Christian faith — faith that nurtures hope.

The military policy of the United States is rooted in deterrence — the idea that threatening to use nuclear weapons in massive retaliation or in revenge against selected military targets is the best way to prevent an opponent from attacking you in the first place. This creates an ethical dilemma where threatening to do massive evil by using nuclear weapons might serve us for the good by preventing nuclear war and where doing good by gradual nuclear disarmament might trigger a horrendous evil, nuclear war. At least this is the moral dilemma that deterrence strategists pose since nuclear threats are believed to deter nuclear war. Does the hope that they deter nuclear war morally justify threats to use them? Thus we threaten the massive murder of millions in order to save the world. Is it morally tolerable to hold millions of citizens on both sides hostage to terror?

The Moral Dilemma

According to deterrence theorists the purpose of nuclear weapons is to prevent other nuclear weapons from being used. Nuclear weapons cannot be used as defensive weapons in the traditional sense because there is no defense against nuclear weapons. They can be used only offensively, for revenge or to scare adversaries. Nuclear weapons can be used for defense only in the sense that the threat to use them might prevent their use in the first place. Is there a moral distinction between threatening to use an instrument of war and actually using it? In terms of Christian ethics, is it permissible to threaten to use something that is immoral to actually use? And what if one's bluff is called and the choice is utter national embarrassment or the destruction of millions? The fundamental moral question of the nuclear age is whether or not Christians and the Church can support government policies based on nuclear deterrence.

The Christian Church has never welcomed war. However, over the centuries the Church has supported the involvement of governments and individual Christians in war when the war was considered morally "just." Nuclear war, however, explodes the traditional criteria of the just war formulation. Nuclear war would happen quickly, leaving no time to consider whether or not it was "just." Moral reflection in a nuclear age can occur only before an attack is underway. It is impossible to argue that more good than evil would result from a nuclear holocaust. It is difficult to protect innocent civilians in a nuclear attack because of the enormous blast, indiscriminate targeting, and unpredictable patterns of drifting, deadly fallout. Finally, a nuclear attack can never be a "defensive" attack. It will either be a first strike or a massive retaliation and cannot defend or protect a territory in the traditional sense.

An additional aspect of this moral dilemma is that nuclear weapons erase the historical social functions of warfare. Traditionally warfare served some useful social functions in spite of its destruction, e.g., acquisition of new territory, population expansion, access to ports, and valuable natural resources. The horrendous holocaust produced by nuclear weapons renders these traditional social functions of war meaningless. Hence the dilemma, these instruments of unimaginable terror make nuclear warfare obsolete and thus may prevent its occurrence.

A Critique of Deterrence

It is obvious that a nuclear war could never be morally justified by Christian ethics. But what about nuclear threats? The Church is being asked today to offer its religious blessing on policies of nuclear deterrence. Is not moral *toleration* of nuclear weapons tantamount to approving their use? Consider the following critique of nuclear deterrence from a Christian perspective (Geyer, 1982).

First of all, the Christian tradition links attitudes, intentions, and motives together in an inseparable moral chain. (Hating a brother is the same as murder.) A biblical perspective does not allow us to divorce preparations to fight a nuclear war from the actual war itself. An act like nuclear war would merely reveal the massive hatred that is already present in our collective hearts.

Second, deterrence theorists stress the risks involved in nuclear disarmament. No one, however, really knows what the consequences will be either way, with nuclear disarmament or with deterrence policies. There are risks involved in both directions. One can argue that the risks of nuclear war with a deterrence policy are just as high, if not substantially higher, than they would be with gradual steps of nuclear disarmament.

Third, deterrence is basically a "scare" policy. Nuclear threats increase an enemy's anxiety and provoke adversaries to produce more violent weapons which decrease the real national security of both parties. Since the primary purpose of nuclear weapons, according to this theory, is to frighten opponents, then you can *never* have enough nuclear arms. It is precisely the policy of deterrence that has stimulated and fueled the arms race over the past three decades.

Fourth, deterrence is based on the construction and manipulation of fear, as well as on threats of massive revenge. Neither of these aspects can be reconciled with basic Christian values of love, compassion, and the stewardship of human and natural resources.

Fifth, deterrence cultivates salvation by threat. If we believe that nuclear threats actually do save us, we are led to think that deterrence "works" and therefore, we pay little attention to serious disarmament efforts. Moreover, it is impossible to demonstrate empirically that deterrence "works." There are many factors that may have enabled our safe passage through the nuclear channel over the past forty-five years. But it is impossible to "prove" that nuclear deterrence was the sole, or even a contributing cause.

Sixth, the most dangerous assumption behind deterrence is that nuclear weapons will never be used. Is the chance of nuclear war greater if we threaten to use them, or if we declare we will never use them first? If nuclear weapons are morally tolerable, there is no way to guarantee that they will not be exploded either by accident, sabotage, or deliberate intent. To morally bless the construction and possession of nuclear weapons legitimates their existence and increases the likelihood that they will be exploded over human populations — again either by error, sabotage or the failure of deterrence.

The moral question of the nuclear age facing individual Christians, as well as the Church as a collective body, is simply this: can we support government policies that involve constructing, possessing, and threatening to use nuclear bombs when the explosion of a small number of these weapons would:

— kill millions of people,
— permanently injure millions of others,
— destroy thousands of acres of property and natural resources,
— contaminate the world's atmosphere and environment with deadly radioactive fallout,
— produce genetic mutations in future generations,
— severely disrupt the balance of nature,
— torture millions psychologically with fear and anxiety,
— threaten the social and industrial collapse of entire societies,
— raise cancer, retardation, and disease rates,
— cause unprecedented social, psychological, and physical suffering, and
— produce unpredictable long-term havoc just as serious as the expected consequences.

Can the Church be a partner in pursuing such risky national policies? Is there anything that is worth such enormous risks? Dare Christians allow God's good creation to be placed under such an ominous threat?

THE ROLE OF THE CHURCH

The Church in Europe and America is waking up to the nuclear threat and beginning to shoulder its moral responsibility by calling for the abolition of nuclear weapons, much as it earlier called for abolition of slavery in the United States. In summary, I offer a few observations on the role of the Church in a nuclear age.

First of all, the Church needs to clarify the sharp distinction between the biblical understanding of the sources of peace and those accepted by the nation states. In the historical context of Christian faith, peace comes through weakness, i. e., forgiveness, love, compassion, and negotiation — even with enemies. In the modern political arena peace is said to come through strength: military threats, larger arsenals, increased destructive capacity, and threats of massive revenge designed to induce fear.

Second, a key mission of the Church is truth-telling that debunks and shreds the mythologies surrounding nuclear war that are perpetuated by government propaganda and popular folklore to solidify public opinion in support of militarism. There are no winners in nuclear war. Being "superior" is meaningless when both sides can already destroy each other many times. Nuclear weapons cannot be used in defense — only in a first strike or in revenge. Larger nuclear arsenals reduce true national security. Enduring peace will never come from military threats of violence. Our real enemy is the bomb, not the Soviets, China or any other nation state. These and other truths of the nuclear age must be articulated clearly and persistently by the Church even though they run directly counter to popularly held myths of war that belong to an earlier era.

Fourth, the Church needs to reiterate the biblical witness that worship of the state and blind nationalism can subvert true allegiance to the kingdom of God. Christian believers need to be reminded that their ultimate worship and security resides with God and that the very nature of Christian faith is prostituted when the nation is not critically judged by Christian values. Nation states will always seek absolute sovereignty and expect their citizens to fall into dutiful subjection. The Church must work to desacralize the nation — calling it back to its proper role and reminding it that its purpose is to serve citizens, not to demand their lives on a burning nuclear altar. The role of government in the biblical sense, is to protect the good and punish the bad. Foreign policies that edge nations closer and closer to nuclear destruction can hardly serve the good of citizens. The Church in restraining the power of government will be seen as a threat not unlike the threat of Jesus to the principalities and powers of the Roman government.

Fifth, the Church must emphasize the international dimensions of the Christian Gospel. In the face of a truly international holocaust that threatens life in east and west, in socialism and capitalism, in free and in totalitarian societies, there is *one* world body that links humanity together across political and ideological barriers. The Christian Church is the one fellowship around the globe that should rise above national, ethnic, and political ties in its common confession that Jesus is Lord.

The dream for the future grows out of this international fellowship, a dream of Christian brothers and sisters standing up in east and west with the candle of peace in their hands. The future is in our hands. The issue is here and the time is now for the Body of Christ to join hands in a worldwide peace witness. This is the moment for the Church to be the Church, to proclaim the Good News that God is no respecter of person or nation, to say that in Jesus Christ there is no east or west, and to confess that Jesus Christ is the Prince of Peace. The Church is God's gift for such a time as this. This could be the Church's glorious hour. But a dream is only a dream until we act.

Perhaps we should all support this affirmation:

WE DECLARE WE ARE AT PEACE WITH ALL PEOPLE OF GOODWILL
We need no leader to define for us an enemy. Nor to tell us that we need security for and defense against. Instead we affirm that our earth's security rests not in armaments, but
   . . . in the justice of adequate housing and food,
     in the justice of meaningful education and work,
     in the justice of an economic order that gives everyone access to our earth's
       abundance,
     in the justice of human relationships nourished by cooperation.

We affirm people over property, community over privatism, respect for others
   regardless of sex, race, or class,
We choose struggle rather than indifference,
We choose to be friends of the earth and of one another rather than exploiters,
We choose to be citizens rather than subjects,
We choose to be peacemakers rather than peacekeepers,
We choose a nuclear-free future . . .
Before us today are set life and death;
We choose life, that we and our children may live.

International Conference of Disarmament,
June 1982

References

Anderson, Marion, *The Empty Pork Barrel*. Lansing, Michigan: Employment Research Associates, 1982.

Boston Study Group, *The Price of Defense: A New Strategy for Military Spending*. New York: New York Times Books, 1979.

DeGrasse, Robert, Jr., and David Gold, "Military Spending's Damage to the Economy." *New York Times*, December 30, 1981.

Dunn, Lewis A., *Controlling the Bomb: Nuclear Proliferation in the 1980's*. New Haven, Connecticut: Yale University Press, 1982.

Garwin, Richard, *Address to the American Association for the Advancement of Science*. Toronto: Unpublished Presentation, 1981.

Geyer, Alan F., *The Idea of Disarmament!* Elgin, IL: The Brethren Press, 1982.

Glasstone, Samuel, and Philip Dolan, *The Effects of Nuclear Weapons*, 3rd ed. Washington, D. C.: U.S. Department of Defense, 1977.

Katz, Arthur M., *Life After Nuclear War: The Economic and Social Impacts of Nuclear Attacks on the United States*. Cambridge, MA: Ballinger Publishing Company, 1982.

Kistiakowsky, George, "George Kistiakowsky: Champion of Arms Control." *Chemistry and Engineering News*, February 2, 1981:24, 1981.

Lifton, Robert Jay, and Richard Falk, *Indefensible Weapons*. New York: Basic Books, 1982.

Mack, John E., "Psychosocial Trauma" in *The Final Epidemic*. Ruth Adams and Susan Cullen, eds. Chicago: Educational Foundation for Nuclear Science, 1981.

Office of Technological Assessment (OTA), *The Effects of Nuclear War*. Washington, D. C.: U. S. Government Printing Office, 1979.

Sivard, Ruth Leger, *World Military and Social Expenditures 1982*. Leesburg, VA: World Priorities Inc., 1982.

Thurow, Lester, "How to Wreck the Economy." *The New York Review*, May 14, 1981.

U. S. Arms Control and Disarmament Agency (ACDA), "U. S. Urban Population Vulnerability." Washington, D. C.: ACDA, 1979.

CHAPTER 12
CRIME AND JUSTICE: INTRODUCTION

Classical sociologist Emile Durkheim believed that the move toward modern society was characterized by a transition from punitive sanctions to restitutive ones. This already has occurred in many violations against property and accidental injury to persons. For example, automobile insurance is designed to protect the person who accidentally causes injury or damage to another while making restitution (as much as possible) to the person wronged by the accident. In areas of civil concerns, restitution rather than punishment appears to be more acceptable.

In criminal matters, however, this drift is less apparent. Society's pendulum can swing between punitive and restitutive measures as evidenced by the return of the death sentence as an appropriate punishment for some crimes. Popular attitudes in supporting punitive, restitutive, or no punishment often mirror the ascendancy of a particular theoretical approach to the problem. Underlying these different approaches are conflicting assumptions about persons and their accountability for their actions.

Gray identifies and discusses five theories of crime which could be reduced further to three models or paradigms: social behavior, social fact, and social definition. The *social behavior* paradigm emphasizes biological and psychosocial factors in explaining human action. This model tends to view crime and criminal through a medical perspective. Proponents draw an analogy between illness and criminal behavior. Just as illness and disease are not voluntarily chosen, so too persons do not choose to perform criminal acts. The use of the "insanity plea" in some well-publicized murder cases provides one illustration of its use in a court of law. Professor Gray's discussion of biological theory provides a theoretical example of the social behavior paradigm.

Anomie and critical theory may be placed in a *social fact* paradigm. In other words, the position of persons within a social structure (whether it be the social fact of race, social class, or sex) is important in accounting for differences in crime rates. While the social behavior model emphasizes a lack of free will due to individualistic factors, the social fact model allows for determinism stemming from collective sources. Both anomie and critical theories consider the institutional and cultural origins of crime, nonetheless, with different assumptions about the alleged role of capitalism. Although not as deterministic as social behaviorism, in its extreme form social factism leaves little room for free will.

Ordinarily it is the social definition paradigm, of which labeling theory is one example, that best allows for voluntary action and human accountability. When applied to crime, however, labeling theory appears to be more deterministic than voluntaristic. The voluntary action is performed by those who do the labeling, while those who are labeled are victims of this larger social process. The emphasis in labeling theory is on "how law enforcement agents define and react to criminal behavior." Whether espousing a "social disadvantage thesis" or the "deviance amplification thesis," labelists still depict a determined image of person.

Christian sociology assumes a voluntaristic image of person that holds criminals accountable for their crimes. At the same time, justice must always be tempered with forgiveness and mercy. It is not only the criminal who has sinned; we have all sinned and fallen short of the glory of God. Moreover, as Gray notes, the Scriptures refer to the corporate responsibility of institutions that become corrupt and exploitative. The Christian sociologist insists that both society and the individual are responsible for the high incidence of delinquency and crime in society.

Recognizing the role of the collectivity in promoting criminal behavior is a sociological perspective, but one that can challenge Christians. Some sociological theories can stir an examination of our collective conscience. This is particularly true of labeling theory which raises the question whether the labeling process is a just one. Those who have bilked the saving and loan association out of billions of dollars are not considered criminals, for example, but an unemployed woman who defrauds the welfare system may be sent to jail. Our labeling system is one that is often class biased.

Gray suggests some ways "to lay the foundation for a long-term attack on the root causes of crime." One is to implement the Durkheimean observation that modern society was moving toward a more restitutive (rather than punitive) system of justice. Clearly the punitive system with its antiquated prison system is not working. Gray makes some important observations for altering correctional priorities and limiting the scope of punishment that need to be heeded. His discussion challenges the Christian community to seek to redeem the deviant, to be willing to forgive the penitent, and to assist in the reintegration of the released inmate.

Gray and other Christian sociologists see a possible solution to the high crime and recidivist rate in society's moving toward "restitution" and de-emphasizing repressive, punitive sanctions. His observation challenges Christians. While there are numerous volunteer religious groups who befriend inmates in prison, few attempt to work to assist the reintegration of the inmates once they are back on the street. One notable Christian group that seeks to use restitution as a means of treatment and redemption is Prison Fellowship founded by Chuck Colson. Colson, once a special assistant to President Richard Nixon, served seven months in prison as a result of Watergate-related offenses. His spiritual conversion and firsthand experience with America's penal system eventually led him to establish Prison Fellowship. One part of this program entails select prisoners being furloughed to help persons who have been victimized by crime. Time will tell whether these kinds of programs will facilitate a rethinking of theories of crime and appropriate measures to deal with it.

CRIME AND JUSTICE
Don Gray

If you had visited Philadelphia's famous Museum of Art about a year ago, you might have met a parking lot "attendant" named Eugene Harris. Harris would have charged you a typical fee of $3-$5 to park in the lot next to the Museum. The police were taking a dim view of Harris' activities, since this lot is one of the last free parking places in Philadelphia. Harris, a street person who slept in a nearby train station, believed he was merely exercising an entrepreneurial right that has made America great. He provided his "customers" with ticket stubs and employed an "assistant" when things got busy. He even learned how to create additional parking rows so as to fit the maximum number of cars into the lot. In his view, he was providing a needed public service and had a right to be reimbursed.

Police were frustrated in their efforts to shut Harris down, since complainants were not appearing to testify in court. Museum officials contended the problem could be solved simply by putting up a large sign announcing that parking is free. Only recently has this suggestion finally been implemented through the appropriate bureaucratic channels of city government. Time will tell whether Harris can continue to convince his more dubious customers to pay up merely by telling them that "nothing is free in Philadelphia" (Pothier, 1989).

The Debate Over Criminal Justice

This humorous fraud suggests a lack of consensus in our attitude toward criminal offenders. From the last half of the nineteenth century until recently, the goal of rehabilitation dominated criminal justice planning. Persons who violated society's laws had to be "resocialized." Therapy, job training, and education were offered to offenders to enable them to become productive, law-abiding members of the community.

Over the years, the rehabilitative ideal has increasingly come under attack from various quarters. Some have felt that the concept of rehabilitation is based upon faulty, even dehumanizing assumptions about human nature (Lewis, 1954). Others argue more pragmatically that it simply has not worked (Martinson, 1974). Still others claim that it results in overly lenient and inconsistent penalties which fail to deter would-be offenders (Wilson, 1983) and ignores the problem of "just desserts" (Von Hirsch, 1985).

Rehabilitation has also had its defenders, many of whom contend either that it does work when adequately implemented (Gendreau and Ross, 1987) or that it has been tried under coercive conditions inconsistent with the rehabilitative model (Marshall, 1981, pp. 30-31). Finally many critics have claimed that the real problem is not the individual criminal but an unjust system that punishes offenders while ignoring the social institutions that have shaped them (Ryan, 1971; Quinney, 1977; Reiman, 1984).

Two Crucial Questions

Obviously, this brief chapter cannot resolve the many issues raised by these conflicting claims. However, two crucial questions would seem to underlie contemporary debates about criminal justice. The first concerns the *causes of crime and delinquency.* Our ability to implement a social policy that will effectively control crime depends in part on understanding why crime occurs in our society. A growing consensus exists among corrections professionals that our present policies are ineffective at best, counterproductive at worst. At the same time, there is a deep cynicism regarding innovative proposals. If there is a way out of this dilemma, it would appear to lie in basing future policy on empirically supported theory.

The second question concerns the *implications of a Christian value perspective for criminal justice.* While criminological theory addresses pragmatic issues related to effectiveness, it cannot provide final answers to questions concerned with the meaning and ends of justice. Such issues must be addressed through perspectives that include value orientations. I am becoming increasingly convinced of the audacious premise that our criminal justice institutions can become more effective only if they function in a manner that is consistent with Judeo-Christian values.

THEORIES OF CRIME

Individualistic Explanations

A diverse set of explanations are united by the fact that they view crime as being somehow located "under the skin" of the offender. *Biological theory* attributes criminal behavior to hereditary or instinctual factors. While many of these theories have been discredited, they periodically reappear in altered form. Authors such as Lorenz (1966) and Wilson (1975) have argued that violent behavior has become instinctual in the human species through evolutionary processes or selection. Aggressive members are more likely to mate; therefore, their genes are passed on to the next generation. The obvious problem with this theory is that it does not explain the vast differences in rates of violence from one society to another. Sheldon (1949) has attempted to account for individual differences by hypothesizing a relation between an athletic physique, and an aggressive personality and delinquency among young males. Sheldon's detractors argue persuasively that these findings can be better explained by the tendency of delinquent gangs to select athletically inclined youth for membership.

Psychological explanations of crime have traditionally been dominated by psychoanalytic theories inspired by Freud. This perspective sees crime originating from a variety of personality maladjustments. It has been questioned because it fails to demonstrate that criminals are, on the whole, any more psychologically disturbed than noncriminals. This perspective has also lost much of its appeal in the correctional community because the therapeutic programs it espouses are usually too lengthy and expensive to be practical in a correctional setting.

A less individualistic psychological perspective that had become increasingly popular, due to its fairly immediate results, is B. F. Skinner's (1976) *reinforcement theory.* Behavior patterns are assumed to develop and persevere through a system of rewards and punishments. The theory has proved effective in highly restricted settings where the reward contingencies can be controlled. It has yet to prove itself in noninstitutional settings where a wide range of personal choice is possible. Critics contend that the theory does not account for complex, creative patterns of behavior (e.g.

language) that are not subject to gradual shaping through reinforcement. Many also fear that its full implementation ultimately requires a totalitarian society which controls all rewards and punishments.

Sociologists have been critical of individualistic theories for ignoring features of the broader social environment that encourage criminal lifestyles. Despite devastating criticisms, these theories have a broad ideological appeal because they locate the causes of crime primarily within the individual. This makes it easier for those of us who are not (officially) offenders to be absolved of responsibility for crime and to support simplistic "get tough" policies. Some also feel these theories absolve offenders as well. If my criminality results from an inherent trait over which I have no control, how can I be held responsible?

Sociological Explanations

Anomie Theory: Robert Merton (1938) proposed *anomie theory* as a challenge to individualistic theories. Merton contends that a society may encourage deviance by setting high goals for all its members without providing adequate means for some to achieve these goals. American society especially encourages property-related crime by the importance it places upon economic success without, at the same time, ensuring economic opportunity for all. Small wonder, then, that some economically disadvantaged persons turn to crime as an alternative way of achieving the American dream.

Merton's theory has important implications for criminal justice policy, not the least of which is the futility of attempting to control crime in America through harsh penalties alone. If the sale of illicit drugs, for example, is an alternative way to achieve a major social goal (i. e. financial success), can we expect that giving the death penalty to drug dealers will effectively deter drug trafficking? It should also be noted that our courts tend to be harsh on "street crime" (burglary, robbery, car theft), but relatively lenient on "white collar" crime (embezzlement, price fixing, etc.). Could one reason be that we admire ambition (provided it is respectable) more than we do honesty and integrity? A "great cloud of witnesses," including such diverse public figures as Spiro Agnew, Ivan Boesky and Pete Rose, speak quite eloquently to this issue.

Cultural Transmission Theory: E. H. Sutherland (1947) proposed *cultural transmission* theory both as a reaction to individualistic theories and as a way to account for a broader spectrum of criminal behavior, including corporate and white-collar crimes. Sutherland maintains that criminal behavior is learned as people absorb cultural definitions (norms, values, attitudes, knowledge) that are favorable to crime, particularly from those with whom they identify strongly.

Cultural transmission theorists see prisons as "schools for crime" because they segregate offenders in a situation where they identify strongly with one another due to their common plight (Carter, MeGee and Nelson, 1975, pp. 1-14). This makes prison culture a very effective system for instilling attitudes which support crime, especially with novice criminals who for the first time find themselves associating almost exclusively with other criminals. While this problem is widely recognized, few creative alternatives besides probation have received serious attention from our judges and lawmakers.

Labeling Theory: For over 25 years, anomie and cultural transmission theories were the dominant sociological perspectives on crime and delinquency. In the 1960s several new perspectives emerged. Of these, *labeling theory* has received much attention from both advocates and critics. Labeling theorists claim their perspective is unique because of its focus on why some persons are labeled criminal in contrast to the concern of other theories with criminal acts (Becker, 1963, p. 10). They would explain labeling by the *social disadvantage thesis.* Crime is more prevalent among the socially and economically disadvantaged not so much because these persons commit more crimes, but because they are less able to defend themselves against a criminal label. To support this thesis, labeling theorists observe that death row is almost the exclusive province of the poor — not because the affluent never commit murder but because the latter can afford adequate legal defence while the former cannot.

Labeling theorists also advance a second major proposition known as the *deviance amplification thesis.* Society tends to react to crime in a manner that perpetuates it, both by providing prisons as schools for crime and by rejecting ex-convicts when they attempt to return to society. Often unable to find a job or establish conventional friendships, ex-convicts have few survival options but to return to the criminal world. Labeling such persons deviant through the application of criminal sanctions is therefore to be avoided whenever possible (Schur, 1973). While this is not a necessary implication of labeling theory, the caution against penalties that leave a person permanently stigmatized deserves serious attention.

Critical Theory: Critical theory redirects the labeling analysts' critique from the criminal justice system to the larger society. Crime is viewed in Marxian terms as a response to economic injustice; legal statutes are presumed to reflect the interests of a corporate elite. For example, laws which promote corporate interests will be strictly enforced, while laws which threaten those interests (against pollution, price fixing, etc.) will be rendered ineffective. High rates of street crime may serve elite interests because they allow the ills of society to be blamed on the poor, who are seen as perpetrators of crime. This deflects public attention from exploitive economic relations that are characteristic of capitalist societies (Reiman, 1984) as well as from various types of "white-collar" deviance engaged in by elites (Thio, 1988, p. 98).

Critical theory proposes that modern industrial societies stand doubly condemned. First, they both allow and encourage economic exploitation of the poor; second, they blame the poor, the victims of this exploitation, for the ills of the social order. However, some critical theorists suggest there are limits to this victim-blaming strategy. As economic exploitation increases, the basic commitment of the more exploited classes to this order will be seriously weakened. Eventually, significant segments of these classes will engage in revolutionary activity aimed at the destruction of class rule (Balkan, Berger and Schmidt, 1980, pp. 53-54).

Social Control: The critics of critical theory claim that it is more an ideological attack upon capitalism than an empirical theory of crime (Gibbons, 1979, p. 187). *Social control theory* proposes that crime results from the failure of social institutions to forge strong bonds between the individual and society. When social bonds and controls are weak, persons are more likely to develop deviant strategies to achieve their ends simply because such strategies are more efficient. Hirschi (1969) identifies *four* major dimensions of the social bond as: (1) attachment to significant others, (2) commitment to pursue the rewards of conventional institutions, (3) involvement in conventional activities, and (4) belief in the moral validity of social rules.

Control theory provides a number of new insights, two of which deserve mention here. First, the wise society will make full use of multiple mechanisms of bonding and control, most of which are under the auspices of institutions other than those directly concerned with criminal justice. It is not sufficient merely to modify education or economics alone, without reference to relationships with family, political and religious institutions.

Second, control perspectives are compatible with an image of humans as morally responsible agents who are restrained to varying degrees but not determined by their social environments. This heretofore much disparaged assumption is gaining renewed respectability among criminologists (Van Den Haag, 1985; Wilson and Herrnstein, 1985; Cornish and Clarke, 1987). It is important for this discussion because it implies, among other things, that punishment can be just. Other theories discussed above tend at best to be ambivalent on this point.

In summary, sociological theories of crime imply *two* major criticisms of contemporary criminal justice. *First*, criminal justice institutions are ineffective because they treat offenders in ways that encourage further criminal behavior. The initial observations of cultural transmission theory concerning the effects of imprisonment are expanded by other perspectives to include the manner in which society treats the ex-convict and various discriminatory law enforcement practices. Social control theory raises serious questions about the extent to which modern society uses its potential to discourage crime. A growing consensus exists that the apparent failures of criminal justice institutions actually reflect more extensive kinds of social disorganization, some of which encompasses society as a whole.

The *second* major criticism contends that the very process of meting out justice is fundamentally unjust. A hint of injustice can be detected in Merton's contention that the goal-means distinction in American society covertly encourages certain forms of criminal activity. Labeling theory more explicitly claims that society continues to punish offenders long after they have officially paid their debts to society. Critical theory charges that an exploitive economic system severely punishes its underclass, whether they commit crimes or not. The failure to take these criticisms seriously underlies most of the shortcomings of criminal justice policies in America today.

While sociological theories generate some important insights that are consistent with a Christian perspective, they also tend to share some significant shortcomings. One notable example is the implicit assumption that people are by nature morally good or at least neutral. This leads to the conclusion that the problem of crime can be solved solely by appropriate changes in social structures. The issue then becomes, what kinds of changes and how much? While a Christian perspective is amenable to structural change, especially when it serves the interests of justice, its assumption of human sinfulness causes it to be more modest in its estimate of what such change can accomplish.

A CHRISTIAN APPROACH TO CRIME AND JUSTICE

Modern societies have been graveyards for innovations in criminal justice. Reforms that were heralded as humanitarian by one generation have been condemned by succeeding generations as cruel and unusual punishment. Programs for deterring crime and rehabilitating offenders have typically delivered far less than they have promised

(Ohlin, 1985). The history of criminal justice reform should serve to caution those who would propose panaceas for the crime problem. However, sociological theory suggests that one of the prime reasons why criminal justice reform fails is that it is seldom bold enough in its proposals. This is consistent with the biblical viewpoint that true reform involves drastic alterations in social institutions (1 Corinthians 5:6-7).

The discussion below will attempt to explore some ways in which a community can lay the groundwork for a long-term attack on the root causes of crime. The insights of sociological theory and the twin issues of effectiveness and justice will be highlighted, especially as they are viewed through the lens of a Christian value perspective.

Altering Correctional Priorities

Relatively neglected in the debate over the aims of punishment are the victims of crime. Colson and Benson (1980) conclude that victims are doubly exploited first by the criminal offender and second by the additional tax burden required to finance the expensive programs which the proponents of these models advocate. A creative alternative to imprisonment (the central feature of both rehabilitative and retributive programs) could be the widespread application of the concept of *restitution*. Under restitution, the offender is required to compensate the victim or the victim's family in order to restore equilibrium and peace to the community.

Restitution has a number of potential benefits, not the least of which is that the cost of crime is charged primarily to the offender. It is consistent with the rehabilitative ideal in that it allows the offender to identify with the loss suffered by the victim because the offender suffers a similar loss through providing compensation. This latter loss is also consistent with the aim of retribution, since it is (presumably) proportional to that suffered by the victim. When restitution replaces imprisonment, the offender is not exposed to a prison subculture and family ties remain intact. Moreover, a victim who is compensated is less likely to resist social policies designed to reintegrate the offender into the community or to resent monies spent to assist in the reintegration. Theoretically speaking, restitution is a viable alternative to imprisonment for most nonviolent offenders in that it has the potential to be both effective and just.

Restitution is being promoted vigorously by Christian organizations such as Prison Fellowship (started by Chuck Colson) and the Mennonite Church. Restitution programs now operate in every state and have reported a measure of success with juveniles and first-time misdemeanor offenders (Territo, Halsted and Bromley, 1989, pp. 548-552). Sheldon (1982, p. 417) concludes they have been much less effective with serious and persistent property offenders who have few job skills and thus lack the means to reimburse their victims. It appears, then, that before restitution can be successfully put into practice on a large scale with serious offenders, some fundamental changes must occur in our existing economic and educational institutions. Other correctional innova-tions that depend upon economic opportunity structures, such as "work release," experience a similar limitation (Jeffery and Woolpert, 1974).

Innovations that would reduce the social isolation of convicted offenders by integrating them into conventional groups (Cressey, 1955) experience opposition from a variety of interests. Communities often oppose the establishment of halfway houses in their neighborhoods (Krajick, 1980a). Labor unions and business associations have been known to fear competition from prison industries (Schaller, 1985, p. 308).

232

Corrections personnel (often under public pressure) resist experimental programs in prisons when these programs require a reduction in prison security (Wynne, 1985).

Reform is extremely difficult as long as public attitudes towards offenders are dominated by fear, suspicion, hatred, and narrow self-interest. These attitudes have made social isolation, rather than rehabilitation, the truly operative purpose of criminal justice in the twentieth century.

The Christian community can do much to alter public attitudes and create a social climate conducive to reform. However, we must first re-examine our own priorities and realistically assess the sacrifices that might be entailed (Luke 14:26-33). Are we willing to be like our Lord, who gave His life to reconcile sinners? Are we willing to take the risks (unduly minimized by some well-meaning advocates of reform) involved in efforts to give criminal offenders the opportunity to be reintegrated into society? Once we are committed to the interests of offenders as well as to our own (Philippians 2:4), it is possible to support reform in a variety of ways. Not the least of these involves raising our voices in favor of promising correctional innovations in the Christian community, where such innovations have traditionally been regarded with suspicion.

Limiting the Scope of Punishment

Scholars tell us that we misunderstand the biblical concept of "an eye for an eye" when we interpret it as a demand for stern retaliatory justice. The principle was intended primarily as a means for placing appropriate limits on punishment in an age when small offenses often resulted in a blood feud. Labeling theorists suggest that one of the principal problems of punishment in modern society is our failure to limit its scope. Though in theory their "debt to society" is paid when the sentence is completed, criminal offenders tend to suffer a more or less permanent rejection by society.

One dimension of this rejection has been demonstrated by Schwartz and Skolnick (1964), who distributed several versions of a resume at random on behalf of a fictitious applicant to unskilled hotel work. These versions differed only in their description of the applicant's criminal record. Among those employers who received the resume where no criminal record was mentioned, 36 percent expressed an interest in the applicant, while only 4 percent of those employers for whom the resume reported an assault conviction expressed a similar interest. On the other hand, a related study by the same authors found that doctors sued for malpractice suffer little, if any, permanent harm to their practices. These studies suggest that the stigma associated with "street crime" may be especially difficult for the working-class person to overcome.

The New Testament attitude towards the offender is one of discipline to be followed by forgiveness and restoration for the penitent (Luke 17:3-4; 2 Corinthians 2:5-10; Galatians 6:1). Paul was as concerned about what the failure to forgive would do to the character and witness of the Christian community as he was about the effects this failure would have on the offender (2 Corinthians 2:11). Labeling analysts are similarly concerned that the long-term effects of stigmatization can result in the creation of a permanent class of career criminals.

Christians can do many things to help offenders avoid permanent stigmatization and re-establish themselves as law-abiding citizens. Christian organizations such as Prison Fellowship, Yokefellows and the Mennonite Church have developed a diverse set of ministries to criminal offenders both before and after their release from prison. These include discipleship seminars, transportation and temporary housing for family members who visit prisoners, help in securing jobs and job training, and small fellowship groups where ex-offenders can obtain encouragement and help in readjusting to community life. Similar opportunities to help juveniles are available through such organizations as Teen Challenge, Big Brothers and Big Sisters.

Persons who become involved in these ministries will be following in the footsteps of John Augustus, a lay person credited with starting the probation system (Carter, McGee and Nelson, 1975, pp. 169-179). Augustus was able to convince judges to place persons convicted for drunkenness in his custody for a temporary trial period. During this time, he would try to help his "clients" in a variety of ways. Impressed with the results, the judges were often willing to levy fines rather than impose jail sentences on the offenders.

Though probation is the most common sentence given today by American criminal courts, the probation system has been highly criticized in recent years. Heavy caseloads, limited resources and court requirements that probationers be heavily monitored have hindered the ability of probation officers to establish effective helping relationships with most of their clients (Krajick, 1980 b). Without such relationships the rehabilitative goals of probation are much more difficult to achieve. Hopefully, Christian ministries to criminal offenders can provide a model for reform.

Balanced Law Enforcement

Discrepancies in judicial sentencing contribute greatly to the resentment many convicted felons feel towards society. Prison inmates with similar conviction records compare notes and discover unjustifiable differences in the lengths of their prison terms. Many prisoners also view their sentences as unjust because they perceive that others who have committed similar or worse crimes remain unpunished because of systematic judicial discrimination and corruption (Lizotte, 1978). These perceptions support critical theory, which views legislative and law enforcement practices to be favorable to the powerful and unfavorable to the poor.

Observations that support this viewpoint are legion, whether on the part of prisoners, journalists or social science researchers. A few examples are the following:

1. Those who commit "street crimes" such as burglary, robbery and auto theft are often given prison sentences; those who commit "white collar" crimes such as embezzlement, price fixing, and fraudulent advertising are seldom sentenced to prison (Cressey, 1953; Green, 1990, pp. 18-19).

2. In many states the laws against prostitution apply only to the prostitute, not her (or, nowadays, his) customers. Where the law applies to both parties, it is usually enforced only on the prostitute (Glaser, 1978, pp. 355-356).

3. Laws against corporate crimes, such as pollution and the dumping of hazardous wastes, are often ambiguous, weak and inadequately enforced (Simon and Eitzen, 1982, p. 124).

4. Many professional criminals and high-level figures in organized crime escape

prosecution and conviction in part because of collusion of corrupt politicians and law enforcement officials (Abadinsky, 1990, pp. 400-406).

Recent legislation to reduce sentencing disparities has promoted "flat sentencing" — minimum required sentences for certain crimes, the elimination of parole, and the reduction of judicial discretion in sentencing (Robin, 1987, pp. 318-322). While these efforts may reduce sentencing disparities, they do not address the problems of police and judicial corruption.

Christians have tended to be relatively unconcerned about these issues. By contrast, the Hebrew prophets denounced the leaders of ancient Israel because of officials who took bribes and judges who distorted justice, thereby ignoring the rights of the weaker members of society (Sider, 1980, pp. 174-187). At least some of the alienation experienced by prisoners — alienation that weakens their bonds to society — might be eliminated if we were to follow the scriptural injunction to have one standard of justice for all (Leviticus 24:22).

Those who sense a calling to this task can support local citizens' crime commissions and other "watchdog" organizations that seek to uncover discrepancies between ideals and practice in criminal justice, as well as promote legislation aimed at making the correctional system more equitable and effective. While these efforts may not result in an immediately detectable reduction in the crime rate, the long-range impact on society promises to be a beneficial one (Proverbs 29:4).

Sociocultural Change

If there is any common thread running through sociological theories of crime, it is that high crime rates are a direct result of our "American way of life." Various applications of the theories discussed above to youth crime reflect this view (Toby, 1970; Sykes, 1980; Bennett, 1987). One factor often cited is the importance our society places upon material affluence as a symbol of success and a source of self-esteem. For most youth, affluence comes through access to career opportunities and depends heavily upon educational attainments. Those who fail to meet the standards of our educational institutions often feel they are being unjustly deprived. This sense of "relative deprivation" creates acute resentment, reduces respect for legitimate authority (which tends to be weak to begin with in America), and increases the willingness of youth to use illegitimate means to achieve their goals.

This orientation toward using deviant means might be controlled in a social setting where informal social controls are strong. However, the growing instability of the traditional family and the anonymity of the urban neighborhoods in which most of us live severely weaken the effectiveness of these controls. Peer groups, from which youth take a wide variety of behavioral cues, are typically least supportive of conventional rules. Formal agents of control — police, courts, schools — are ineffective substitutes that in most instances fail to inspire either respect or fear. These and other features of American society foster a high youth crime rate that tends to carry over into young adult circles as well.

Until recently, most American criminologists thought that the "criminogenic" features just mentioned were endemic in all modern industrial democracies. However, Japan has a substantially lower crime rate than the United States, even though it is more urbanized, has more lenient sentencing practices and perpetuates remnants of its violent samurai tradition. Compared to officially recorded crime in Japan, in 1984 the United States had a homicide rate 10 times the Japanese rate, a rape rate 22 times as high and a robbery rate 114 times as high (Kalish, 1988, p. 3)! The enviable low rates in Japanese society have been attributed to its strong system of informal controls and the high respect its citizens have for traditional forms of authority (Bayley, 1976; Wilson and Herrnstein, 1985, pp. 452-457). The Japanese have stronger ties with their local communities and are less mobile, both socially and geographically, than their American counterparts. They tend to live in one neighborhood, work for one company and maintain the same network of friends for all or most of their adult lives. The Japanese divorce rate is about one-fourth that of the United States.

Peer groups are important in Japanese life, but they are much more integrated into the overall life of the community and supportive of conventional rules. The Japanese are highly attached to particular groups and are dependent upon them for their emotional security. They cannot easily change their group allegiances as Americans so frequently do. As a result, the Japanese are much less "individualistic" than Americans. Individual aspirations are subordinated to the continued integrity and well-being of the group. Moral departures not only stigmatize the individual, but bring shame upon the group as well. For this reason, the Japanese are not bashful about giving moral lectures to their peers and holding them responsible for conducting themselves appropriately.

In brief, these and other features of Japanese society give it a cohesive quality that is lacking in the United States and, for that matter, in other western societies. One beneficial outcome is a low crime rate.

Most Americans, Christians included, would probably find Japanese society overly confining. But this again raises the question of where our priorities really lie. Most serious analysts of crime in American have concluded that high rates of crime and delinquency are the price we must pay for the kind of society we have chosen to build. They have become pessimistic about the prospects for reducing the crime rate because there is little evidence that the dominant powers are willing to effect the necessary changes in either institutional structures (economic, educational, political) or the basic value orientations that dominate the public sphere.

Christians can collectively work towards long-term change first of all by re-examining their own priorities. Have we fallen into the materialistic trap of defining the quality of our lives by the abundance of our possessions (Luke 12:15)? We can reaffirm the message of the cross with its call to servanthood and its admonition to orient one's life to transcendental values. We can commit ourselves corporately to heed the call to discipleship and put the interests of others above our own.

Local churches can put this commitment into practice by supporting various efforts to rehabilitate delinquents, drug addicts and other offenders by altering the extreme materialistic values that generate crime. Programs that include this emphasis have already met with a measure of success (Stephenson and Scarpitti, 1969; Empey and Lubeck, 1971; Yablonsky, 1989). Again, Christian organizations such as Prison Fellowship are willing to provide both opportunities and practical assistance. Churches can also support various crime prevention efforts, including neighborhood watch groups and programs for youth (e.g., athletic leagues). Finally, they can increase their efforts to strengthen the family through various types of family-oriented seminars but most important of all, by becoming a genuinely supportive fellowship that reaches out to all segments of the community.

On a broader societal level, the Church can lend its support to serious and realistic efforts to alter the criminogenic features of American society. However, this requires a careful analysis of the various proposals for crime control.

PROPOSALS FOR CRIME CONTROL — A BRIEF CRITIQUE

Proposed solutions to the crime problem tend to fall into one of several types. In this writer's view, proponents of each type generate their proposals more out of an ideology that incorporates a broader social agenda than out of a realistic analysis of the facts of crime.

Liberally oriented analysts feel that the answer to the crime problem lies primarily in expanding economic opportunities for the underprivileged. While this strategy has merit for its own sake and may even have some ameliorative effect, it also appears to have severe limitations. For one thing, our impending ecological crisis suggests that the continually expanding affluence we have enjoyed is reaching its limits. Like it or not, our natural resources are finite and we will soon have to accommodate to this hard fact by scaling down our overall levels of consumption. Any increased affluence for the poor segments of society will require more frugal lifestyles on the part of the more affluent segments. Unless basic values change, attempts to distribute opportunities more equitably in America will encounter stiff resistance.

Moreover, even if we are able to expand economic opportunities for the underprivileged, there is no guarantee that this will result in less overall crime. In all probability, any reduction in street crime that occurs will be more than compensated for by an increase in white-collar crime. Given the American success ethos, moderately expanded opportunities will result in greatly increased expectations. We will then take advantage of the criminal dimensions of these opportunities almost as readily as we do the legitimate aspects.

Radical approaches to crime control are more sensitive to problems generated by the American success ethos. They propose to address these problems by more drastic alterations of the economic system that directly reduce discrepancies in wealth and income. They assume that as economic inequalities are lessened, the degree of deprivation experienced by individuals in society will be greatly reduced. One beneficial result among many will be a lower crime rate. The general interests of justice might be well served by some basic alterations in America's socioeconomic structures. However, the difficulties involved become apparent when it is realized that any such changes would be strongly opposed by dominant economic interests.

Moreover, the link between socioeconomic change *per se* and a reduction in the crime rate is tenuous. Societies that have introduced radical economic change, such as the Soviet Union, have still found it necessary to repress crime and have used heavy-handed totalitarian measures to do so. Recent news stories coming out of the Soviet Union also suggest that as it moves to incorporate some "free-market" elements in its economy, it is encountering a growing crime problem. The rapidity with which this problem has emerged raises a serious question as to how much a socialist economy has impacted the basic values of Soviet society in the first place. In any event, the roots of crime would seem to extend beyond the socioeconomic system.

The conservative approach seeks to control crime by strengthening traditional institutions such as the family and improving the effectiveness of law enforcement efforts. In America, the latter is more emphasized, usually through proposals for more severe penalties for street crime and less emphasis upon the constitutional rights of suspected offenders. These proposals enjoy widespread support, especially when there is strong public perception that crime is "out of control."

There are apparently some instances where increased law enforcement efforts serve to inhibit crime. Stricter penalties for drunken driving is a case in point. That this is not always the case can be illustrated by our much publicized "war on drugs." Massive arrests of drug dealers seem to have little, if any, effect upon the volume of illicit drug sales. This is not surprising when most drug addicts aspire to be dealers and many third-world countries are willing suppliers (Inciardi, 1986, pp. 163-198). Given the lucrative profits involved, it is doubtful that stricter law enforcement alone will have a substantial impact upon drug use until the powers delegated to law enforcement agents approach a level that is typical of totalitarian societies. We will then have generated a whole new set of problems that will make our drug problem seem relatively minor.

Conservative approaches have appealed to many Christians because they have been perceived to be consistent with a Christian perspective. Crime is believed to be a reflection of the individual criminal's sinful nature. Therefore, efforts to ameliorate the crime problem by changing social conditions, including most efforts to provide opportunities for offenders to be reintegrated into the community, are seen as futile. Harsh punitive measures are advocated in part because they are seen as the proper response of human government to lawlessness (1 Peter 2:14), in part because they are believed to deter the behavioral expressions of human sinfulness.

In this writer's view, there are at least two basic problems with this perspective, despite the fact that it contains a strong measure of truth. *First*, an appropriate biblical balance between discipline of offenders and their restoration to fellowship is lacking. Societies that fail to provide social mechanisms for reintegrating offenders run the risk of leaving them without hope, thereby fostering the development of a permanent criminal subculture. Perhaps this is one reason why Paul cautions the Corinthians to forgive a punished offender for the sake of the community, as well as that of the individual (2 Corinthians 2:6-11).

Second, while sin is a major reason for crime, it is not merely the offender's sin which leads that person into a life of crime. Those who promote the social conditions in which crime seems to flourish — exploitive economic arrangements, cultural standards that exalt success above honesty, secular worldviews that define the meaning of life in terms of material acquisitions, power and the like — must share the blame. It would appear to be just as important to correct these conditions in order to deter crime as it is to correct the defender.

In summary, while each of the major proposals for crime control has merit from a Christian perspective, each also has severe limitations. Given the growing trend in secular society to emphasize punishment, the best opportunities Christians have to ameliorate the problem of crime lie in the direction of establishing a truly biblical community that accepts and gives hope to the outcasts of society. This was the focal point of the earthly ministry of Jesus (Luke 4:16-19). A significant part of this ministry involves confronting the dominant powers with the basic reasons for their ineffectiveness in dealing with the crime problem (among others) and providing a model for a more just society.

What hope is there that such an idealistic proposal can enjoy even the slightest measure of success? Certainly very little if we rely either on our own persuasive powers or upon human goodness and reasonableness. Rather, our hope lies in the triumph of our Lord over the forces that govern our age (Colossians 2:15). Christians can take comfort in the fact that the cross — a criminal's fate — constitutes a program for human redemption that is both effective and just (Romans 11:33-34; 1 Corinthians 1:18-25). These qualities elude the best human programs in a complex world. Most important of all, the ultimate purpose is not to punish or condemn, but to forgive, reconcile and restore in order to bring into being a social order in which oppression, poverty, injustice and all the other evils related to crime will cease (Luke 1:49-55; Hebrews 12:5-11). While we look forward to the day in which this promise is fulfilled, we must become instruments through whom a partial fulfillment can become a present reality.

Study and Discussion
Questions

1. Why do you feel "experts" in criminal justice have such divergent opinions concerning how criminal offenders should be handled?

2. Is it important to understand why people commit various crimes in order to develop effective policies for dealing with crime? Why or why not?

3. Do you agree with the author's evaluation of individualistic theories of crime? Why or why not?

4. Which of the sociological theories of crime discussed above do you find most persuasive and why?

5. Are sociological theories of crime consistent with the concept of individual responsibility? With a biblical view of human nature?

6. Do you feel that restitution is a viable alternative to imprisonment in modern society? If so, for which kinds of crimes? What social changes would be required in order to make restitution more practical in American society?

7. What can be done to make criminal sentencing more equitable? What beneficial effects might result?

8. Do you agree with the author's view concerning the way our legal system handles white-collar and corporate crimes? Should these crimes be more or less severely punished, and why?

9. Why do you think the crime rate in America is so much higher than in Japan? What could be done to lower the former?

10. What kinds of innovations in corrections do you feel would make our correctional system more effective, and why? What contributions can the Christian community make to the correctional process?

11. Do you agree with the author's views on the conservative approach to crime control? Why or why not?

12. Do you feel that, on the whole, America is a just society? Why or why not?

References

Abadinsky, Howard, *Organized Crime* (3rd ed.). Chicago: Nelson-Hall, 1990

Balkan, Sheila, Ronald J. Berger and Janet Schmidt, *Crime and Deviance in America: A Critical Approach.* Belmont, CA: Wadsworth, 1980.

Bayley, David, "Learning about crime — the Japanese experiment." *The Public Interest* 44 (Summer):55-68, 1976.

Bennett Georgette, *Crimewarps: The Future of Crime in America.* Garden City, NY: Anchor Books, 1987.

Becker, Howard S., *Outsiders: Studies in the Sociology of Deviance.* New York: Free Press, 1963.

Carter, Robert, M., Richard A. McGee and E. Kim Nelson, *Corrections in America.* Philadelphia: Lippincott, 1975.

Colson, Charles W., and Daniel H. Benson, "Restitution as an alternative to imprisonment," *Detroit College of Law Review 1980* (Summer): 523-98, 1980.

Cornish, Derek, and Ronald V. Clarke, "Understanding crime displacement: an application of rational choice theory." *Criminology* 25 (November):933-47, 1987.

Cressey, Donald R., *Other People's Money.* Glencoe, IL: Free Press, 1953.

Cressey, Donald R., "Changing criminals: the application of the theory of differential association." *American Journal of Sociology* 61, (September):116-20, 1955.

Empey, LaMar T., and Steven G. Lubeck, *The Silverlake Experiment.* Chicago: Aldine, 1971.

Gendreau, Paul and Robert R. Ross, "Revivification of rehabilitation: evidence from the 1980s." *Justice Quarterly,* 4:349-407, 1987.

Gibbons, Don C., *The Criminological Enterprise.* Englewood Cliffs, N.J: Prentice-Hall, 1979.

Glaser, Daniel, *Crime in Our Changing Society.* New York: Holt, Rinehart, and Winston, 1978.

Green, Gary S., *Occupational Crime.* Chicago: Nelson-Hall, 1990.

Hirschi, Travis, *Causes of Delinquency.* Berkeley and Los Angeles: University of California, 1969.

Inciardi, James A. *The War on Drugs: Heroin, Cocaine, Crime, and Public Policy.* Palo Alto, CA: Mayfield, 1986.

Jeffery, Robert, and Stephen Woolpert, "Work furlough as an alternative to incarceration: an assessment of its effects on recidivism and social cost." *The Journal of Criminal Law and Criminology* 65 (September):405-15, 1974.

Kalish, Carol B., *International Crime Rates.* Bureau of Justice Statistics Special Report. Washington, D. C.: Government Printing Office, May, 1988.

Krajick, Kevin, "Not on my block." *Corrections Magazine* 6 (October):15-27, 1980.

Krajick, Kevin, "Probation: the original community program." *Corrections Magazine* 6 (December):7-12, 1980.

Lewis, C. S., "The humanitarian theory of punishment." *Res Judicatae* 6 (June):224-29, 1954.

Lizotte, A. L., "Extra-legal factors in Chicago's criminal courts: testing the conflict model of criminal justice." *Social Problems* 25 (June):564-80, 1978.

Lorenz, Konrad, *On Aggression.* New York: Harcourt, Brace, & World, 1966.

Marshall, Ineke Haen, "Correctional treatment processes: rehabilitation reconsidered." Pp. 14-46 in R. Roberg and V. Webb (eds.), *Critical Issues in Corrections: Problems, Trends and Prospects.* St. Paul, MN: West, 1981.

Martinson, Robert, "What works? — Questions and answers about prison reform." *The Public Interest* 35 (Spring):22-54, 1974.

Merton, Robert K., "Social structure and anomie." *American Sociological Review* 3 (October):672-682, 1938.

Ohlin, Lloyd, "Correctional strategies in conflict." Pp. 475-482 in R. M. Carter, D. Glaser and L. T. Wilkins, *Correctional Institutions* (3rd ed.). New York: Harper and Row, 1985.

Pothier, Dick, "Lot 'attendant' turns his scam into a windfall." *The Philadelphia Inquirer* (September 3):1A, 1989.

Quinney Richard C., *Class, State and Crime: On the Theory and Practice of Criminal Justice.* New York: David McKay, 1977.

Reiman, Jeffrey H., *The Rich Get Richer and the Poor Get Prison: Ideology, Class and Criminal Justice.* New York: Wiley, 1984.

Robin, Gerald D., *Introduction to the Criminal Justice System* (3rd ed.). New York: Harper and Row, 1987.

Ryan, William, *Blaming the Victim*. New York: Pantheon, 1971.

Schaller, Jack, "Work and imprisonment: an overview of the changing role of prison labor in American prisons." Pp. 397-315 in R, M. Carter, D. Glaser and L. T. Wilkins (eds), *Correctional Institutions* (3rd ed.). New York: Harper and Row, 1985.

Schur, Edwin M., *Radical Nonintervention: Rethinking the Delinquency Problem*. Englewood Cliffs, NJ: Prentice-Hall, 1973.

Schwartz, Richard E., and Jerome H. Skolnick, "Two studies of legal stigma." Pp. 103-117 in Howard S. Becker (ed.), *The Other Side: Perspectives on Deviance*. New York: Free Press, 1964.

Shelden, Randall G., *Criminal Justice in America*. Boston: Little, Brown, 1982.

Sheldon, William H., *Varieties of Delinquent Youth: An Introduction to Correctional Psychiatry*. New York: Harper & Row, 1949.

Sider, Ronald J. (ed.), *Cry Justice: The Bible Speaks on Hunger and Poverty*. Downer's Grove, IL: InterVarsity, 1980.

Simon, David R., and D. Stanley Eitzen, *Elite Deviance*. Boston: Allyn and Bacon, 1982.

Skinner, B. F., *About Behaviorism*. New York: Random, 1976.

Stephenson, Richard M., and Frank R. Scarpitti, "Essexfields: a non-residential experiment in group centered rehabilitation of delinquents." *American Journal of Correction*, 31:12-18, 1969.

Sutherland, Edwin H., *Principles of Criminology* (4th ed.). Philadelphia: Lippincott, 1947.

Sykes, Gresham, *The Future of Crime*. Rockville, MD: National Institute of Mental Health, 1980.

Territo, Leonard, James Halsted and Max Bromley, *Crime and Justice in America: A Human Perspective* (2nd ed.). St Paul: West, 1989.

Thio, Alex, *Deviant Behavior* (3rd ed.). New York: Harper and Row, 1988.

Toby, Jackson, "The prospects for reducing delinquency rates in industrial society."

Pp. 454-58 in H. Voss (ed.), *Society, Delinquency and Delinquent Behavior*. Boston: Little, Brown, 1970.

Van Den Haag, Ernest, "The neoclassical theory of crime control." Pp. 177-96 in Robert Meier, *Theoretical Methods in Criminology*. Beverly Hills, CA: Sage,. 1985.

Von Hirsch, Andrew, *Doing Justice: The Choice of Punishments*. Boston: North eastern University Press, 1985.

Wilson, Edward O., *Sociobiology*. Cambridge, MA: Harvard University Press, 1975.

Wilson, James Q., *Thinking About Crime* (rev. ed.). New York: Basic Books, 1983.

Wilson, James Q., and Richard J. Herrnstein, *Crime and Human Nature*. New York: Simon and Schuster, 1985.

Wynne, John M., Jr., "Prison Employee Unionism." Pp. 399-402 in R. M. Carter, D. Glaser and L. T.. Wilkins (eds.), *Correctional Institutions* (3rd ed.). New York: Harper and Row, 1985.

Yablonsky, Lewis, *The Therapeutic Community: A Successful Approach for Treating Substance Abusers*. New York: Gardner Press, 1989.

PART III

THE FAMILY AND RELATED ISSUES

CHAPTER 13
THE FAMILY: INTRODUCTION

If space had permitted, the issues discussed in Part III involving the family could have been included in our previous section on anomic institutions. Changes in sexual norms, family violence, problems of adolescents and the aged, and gender inequalities have all had an impact on the family and, in turn, on the larger social structure. The structural functional perspective enables us to describe how these problems have affected the family and how they are related to changes in the larger social structure.

Herbert Spencer, a British sociologist, and Emile Durkheim, a French sociologist, are usually regarded as the two theorists who laid the foundations for contemporary structural functionalist thought. Both noted how, as societies grew in size, they became more differentiated: that is, they have more and more parts. Essentially, Spencer, Durkheim, and others who contributed to early functionalist theory built on an analogy similar to the one used by the Apostle Paul in describing the church as the body of Christ. The parts must all be knitted together, each performing a specialized task for the good of the whole. Because of their interdependence, a change in one part affects all other parts.

In earliest society, scholars contend, the extended family was the most elementary social institution. Its members included the immediate family as well as what to us would seem very distant relatives. The family performed all social tasks of the day, including procreation, socialization of new members, and religious functions. As time went on, the military system developed to protect people from outside aggression (or to be the aggressors in its search for bounty and lands) and a religious system (often intertwined with the military) emerged, taking some control away from the extended family system. The process of differentiation had begun.

With differentiation the family experienced what William Ogburn has termed a "loss of function." The development of a military system, often led by a king, marked the beginning of the erosion of the family's economic autonomy. Taxes had to be paid and military service rendered to the ruling monarch. The emergence of religion as a separate institution had similar consequences. The family had little control in the struggles for power that developed between the political and religious systems.

As we consider the family in present day, a myriad of institutions exist to perform functions that were once the right and the responsibility of the family. The erosion of functions that began with the emergence of government and religion at the dawn of history continues. The family's responsibility to socialize its members has been taken over largely by the educational system. The family has lost its right to settle disputes to the court system, and its right to punish wrongdoers to the police and justice system. The family no longer is the center of economic production, being reduced largely to the relatively powerless role of being a consumer. Today technology has made surrogate mothering possible, thereby even calling reproductive function of the family into question. It is a much weakened family system that often finds it difficult to control its youth, or to take adequate care of its aged members.

While some social scientists have lamented the family's so-called "loss of function," others have interpreted the process of differentiation somewhat differently. Although they too have noted the changes in the larger society that have impacted the family, these scholars have stressed what they call a "shift" in family functions. Just as institutions tend to specialize in tasks, so too, the family has its specialization. Its primary function, these writers claim, is an affective one — that of providing emotional support in a world that is increasingly devoid of affectivity.

Jack Balswick and Judy Balswick begin their article by acknowledging the role functional analysis plays in defining and describing social problems. Their article, however, takes a somewhat different tack. Rather than describing what sociologists and anthropologists would term the "real culture" (as we have done briefly here), Balswick and Balswick present the "ideal culture" based on scriptural teachings. They intend their article to be a background piece to prepare students to better formulate a Christian response to the family-related issues discussed in the chapters that follow theirs.

It is important to remember that an "ideal culture," by definition, does not exist. Sometimes Christians look at scriptural norms and believe they were present in the family of yesterday. Many historians, however, have noted that the "good old days" were filled with serious problems, many even worse than today's. Women and children, for example, were considered to be the property of the husband and could be subject to his whims, with little or no protection from the law. Family violence and incestuous relations, if known to outsiders, were tolerated. There is historical evidence that the high infant mortality rate in medieval Europe may be due in part to parental neglect of very small children. It is important, as at least one family scholar has noted, that we not create a "family of western nostalgia."

Balswick and Balswick's article presents an "ideal culture," that is, a biblically prescribed system intended by God to reflect how He relates to human beings in Scripture and to dictate how we should relate to each other. Their four-phased biblical view of social relationships is described as covenant, grace, empowering and intimacy. This *ideal* model stands in stark contrast to the real social system based on "*contract* rather than covenant, *law* rather than grace, *possessive power* rather than empowering, and *personal distance* rather than intimacy."

Although the contemporary nuclear family is a good functional fit for a culture that emphasizes "feeling good," self-actualization, and individual rights, it seems to stand at odds with God's ideal. There is little in our egocentric culture that emphasizes commitment, responsibility and the common good. God's model of covenant relation, wherein God loves us when we are unfaithful as well as faithful, has been replaced with a contractual relationship, even in marriage. The result, for both Christians and non-Christians, has been a soaring divorce rate, battle-scarred children, and a failure to honor aging parents — among a host of other difficulties.

We would like to suggest, as do Balswick and Balswick, that the difficulties facing the modern nuclear family require a radical solution — one that goes beyond what even most Christians have been willing to consider. The nuclear family, some have suggested, is suffering from an emotional overload. It cannot meet the expectations that most have of it, namely to be the sole satisfier of affective needs. Christians do have another model that goes beyond any glorification of existing family forms. In fact, Jesus' own statements did little to reinforce the traditional Hebrew family (see Mark 3:31-34; Matthew 10:35-38; 12:46-50). Although Jesus did not intend to destroy the family, He provided a radical departure from the clannishness of the ancient extended family, and the even more selfish nuclear one of today.

It may be that we, as His followers, are all called to leave "home or brothers or sisters or mother or father or children or fields" in order "to receive a hundred times as much in this present age" (Mark 10:29-30). In other words, we may be called as Christians to surrender our culturally determined idea of appropriate family forms in order to become part of the family of God. We as Christians may be able to provide another model for family as we bind together in various types of Christian communities and churches that are family in deed, as well as in name. Some Christians are already involved in such attempts. These Christian communities range from the communal Hutterites, whose quaint ways are an anomaly to the urbanite, to the Christian intentional communities that attempt to create kinship ties based on a common commitment to Christ among nuclear family units. Regardless of the particular form that is utilized, Christians must reconsider the call to be part of the family of God and translate this call into action that will support the fragile nuclear family unit.

THE FAMILY: A BIBLICAL PERSPECTIVE ON RELATIONS AND STRUCTURES

Jack O. Balswick and Judith K. Balswick

In a previous chapter De Santo defines a social problem as anything that is dysfunctional to social systems. He further explains however, that Christians must go beyond this functional definition of social problems and base their understanding of social problems upon the "principles set forth in Holy Scripture" (De Santo, p. 3). The purpose of this chapter is to present biblically prescribed ideals of social relationships and social structures. With an understanding of these scriptural ideals, the reader should be in a better position to understand the Christian perspective taken in regard to each of the social problems analyzed in the following chapters.

BIBLICALLY PRESCRIBED IDEAL SOCIAL RELATIONSHIPS

There may be different ways to gain an understanding of biblically prescribed ideals of social relationships with humankind. When we draw upon biblical examples of God's relationship with the created ones and argue that this provides a model or paradigm of how human beings are supposed to relate to each other, we do so analogically. That is to say, by examining how God relates to human beings in Scripture, we get a glimpse of how we are to interact with each other today.

We suggest that a biblical view of ideal social relationships can best be understood as developing through the four phases of covenant, grace, empowering, and intimacy. We further suggest that social relationships must be understood as dynamic and maturing, and if not, are stagnant and dying. An overview of this process model of social relationships is visually presented in Figure 1.

FIGURE 1 A BIBLICAL MODEL OF SOCIAL RELATIONSHIPS

DEGREE OF
COMMITMENT

INITIAL COVENANT
"TO LOVE AND
BE LOVED"

DEGREE OF   "TO KNOW AND   MATURE   "TO FORGIVE AND   DEGREE OF
INTIMACY   BE KNOWN"   COVENANT   BE FORGIVEN"   GRACE

"TO SERVE AND
BE SERVED"

DEGREE OF
EMPOWERING

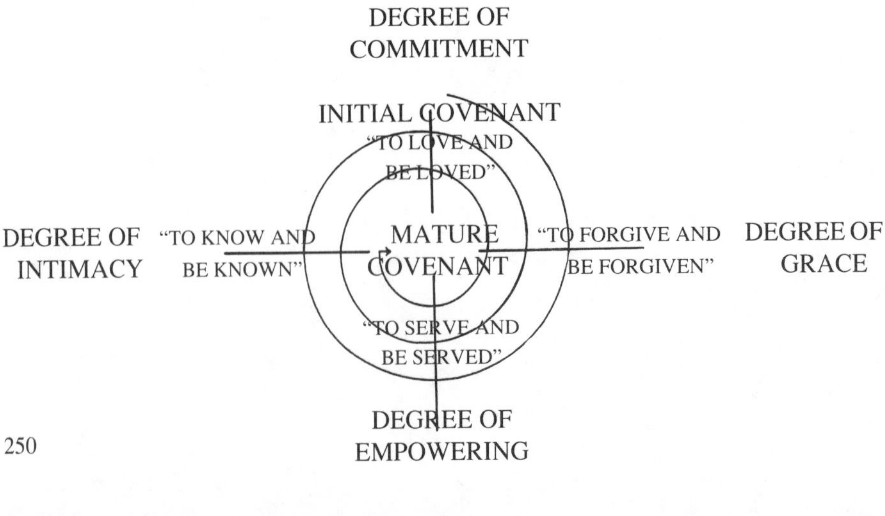

As suggested in Figure 1, the logical beginning point of any social relationship is that of a covenant commitment, which has unconditional love at its core. What develops out of the security provided by this covenant love, is grace. In this atmosphere of grace, persons have freedom to empower one another. Empowering leads to the possibility of mutual intimacy between persons. Mutual intimacy then leads back to a deeper, more mutual level of covenant commitment. This sequential process is represented in Figure 1 by a spiraling inward movement, an attempt to represent social relationships as potentially growing into even deeper levels of mutual commitment, grace, empowering and intimacy.

Growth in a relationship can be blocked at a point when one person in the relationship is unable or unwilling to reciprocate covenant love, grace, empowering, or intimacy. Since relationships are dynamic rather than static, we would argue that if a relationship does not move forward to deeper levels of commitment, grace, empowering, and intimacy, then it will stagnate and fixate on contract rather than covenant, law rather than grace, possessive power rather than empowering, and personal distance rather than intimacy. It should be noted that we are not proposing a closed system of interaction that leads to exclusivity, but rather an open system that promotes interaction beyond itself and that reaches out to others in the human community.

Covenant: The Commitment of Social Relationships

Covenant has a rich heritage in biblical theology. The biblical view of covenant leads to social relationships that are characterized as unconditional commitment. As the biblical meaning of covenant has eroded in modern society, however, social relationships have correspondingly come to be characterized as contractual commitment.

Covenant love was modeled by God throughout the Old Testament in relationships with various biblical characters. The first mention of a covenant is found in Genesis 6:18, where God promised Noah, "I will establish my covenant with you, and you will enter the ark." God instructed Noah and his family as to what they must do to save themselves, and they responded accordingly with their actions. In Genesis 17:7 God makes a covenant with Abram and Sarah, "I will establish my covenant as an everlasting covenant between me and you and your descendants after you for the generations to come, to be your God and the God of your descendants after you." Their participation in the covenant is required. God said, "As for you, you must keep my covenant, you and your descendants after you for the generations to come." (Gen. 17:9, NIV).

There are several things to glean from these accounts of God establishing a covenant with these people. First, we see that God established a covenant without needing assent from the recipients. It wasn't a matter of their agreement to the covenant or even their desire for it. The establishment of the covenant was based entirely on God's initiative and not a contractual offer founded upon the recipients keeping their end of the bargain. Second, God desired and even commanded a response from the recipients. Does this make the covenant conditional in that it would have been cancelled if there had been no response? We believe not, in light of the reference to an "everlasting covenant" in Genesis 9:16. Third, receiving the blessings of the covenant was conditional upon response to God's commands. Deuteronomy 11:26-28, states "Behold, I set before you this day a blessing and a curse: the blessing, if you obey the commandments of the Lord your God, . . ., and the curse, if you do not obey the commandments of the Lord your

God, ..." Fourth, God's covenant extended beyond Noah and Abraham to include not only their immediate families, but future generations. This seems to supply further evidence of the unconditional nature of the covenant. Whereas the blessings of the covenant were conditional, the giving of the covenant was unconditional.

Perhaps the best way to reflect upon God's covenant love is to utilize the biblical depiction of God as parent. The Old Testament picture of God is of one who continually forgives the wayward children of Israel, offering them restoration and renewal. The New Testament message (Hebrews) indicates the new covenant in Christ as an expression of God's unconditional love for us. The story of the prodigal son is a prime example of love that restores brokenness by demanding that the wayward son be given the honor of sonship.

There is an important reciprocal nature of covenant love in which God desires a response to the unilateral commitment. A mature covenant relationship is bilateral. This should be true for our relationships with others as well.

When emphasizing the relational aspects of covenant, Allen (1984, p. 32) summarizes that it is a relationship that "(1) comes about through interactions of entrusting and accepting entrustment among willing, personal beings; (2) as a result, the parties belong to the same moral community and have responsibility to and for one another as beings who matter; and (3) their responsibility in the relationship endures over time."

When covenants are a basis for social relationship, they can be of two types. The inclusive covenant is to be the basis of relationships between the whole of humanity, with God and with one another. All peoples of the world are created by God; we are all brothers and sisters. It is to the inclusive covenant that we appeal when we call for proper Christian response to global social problems such as poverty, world hunger, environmental destruction, and nuclear armament. In addition, however, there are special covenants, which are relationships of "entrusting and accepting entrustment between two or more parties that arise out of some special historical transaction between the members and not only from their participation in the inclusive covenant" (Allen 1984, p. 41). Examples of relationships based upon special covenant include marriage, parent/child, friends and neighbors in which we commit ourselves to mutually care for one another.

We are suggesting that God's love is to be the basic standard of human morality. Allen (1984, p. 77), in summarizing, says that to have covenant love is:

1. always to see self and others as essentially belonging together in community.

2. to affirm the worth of each covenant member, to regard each as someone who matters individually, irreplaceably, and equally.

3. to include every category of person in the covenant community and, therefore, in those we affirm for their own sakes.

4. to seek to meet the needs, both ultimate and proximate, of each person.

5. to be faithful in our commitment to others, both in our ultimate commitment to all members of God's inclusive covenant and in our special covenants with this or that person.

6. to seek reconciliation wherever alienation exists.

These are lofty ideals for human beings who are fallen creatures and who live in a fallen and sinful world. Nevertheless, the ideal of covenant love is given by God as a standard in living out our lives in social community.

Grace: The Atmosphere for Social Relationships

The word "grace" connotes the idea of a relationship. From a human perspective, the unconditional love of God makes no sense except as an offer of grace. Grace can be understood in its biblical context only in terms of God calling us to share in a gracious *relationship*. The Hebrew word, *chen*, traditionally translated grace, is translated as *favor* or *unmerited favor*. The Incarnation is the supreme act of God's grace to humankind. Christ came in human form to reconcile the world to God. Receiving the love and forgiveness provided in the death and resurrection of Christ offers us the possibility of human love and forgiveness from one another. We can forgive others as we have been forgiven, and love them with the unconditional love which we have received from God. Where there is an atmosphere of grace in a relationship, there will be a willing need and ability to forgive and be forgiven.

Social relationships were designed by God to be lived out in an atmosphere of grace and not law. Relationships which are based upon contract help to create an atmosphere of law, while relationships grounded in covenant engender an atmosphere of grace and freedom. The meaning and joy of being a Christian would be deadened if we conceived of our relationship with God in terms of law instead of grace, and the same is true with regard to human relations. At both the individual and corporate levels, law leads to bondage while grace encourages freedom and acceptance.

This is not to say that there is no place for law in human relationships. We need to note that when the Apostle Paul writes that "Christ ends the law and brings righteousness for everyone who has faith" (Romans 10:4), he does not mean to say that there is something wrong with the law, for the law points the way to live according to God's intention. The only problem is that since no human being ever fulfills all of God's law, one can never be made "whole" or be saved by the law. Therefore, Christ is the "end of the law" in the sense that He is the perfect fulfillment of the law. Because of Christ's perfection and righteousness, our righteousness is not dependent upon keeping the law. but upon our faith in Christ.

Although the covenant of grace rules out law, persons will accept rules or law in the form of patterns, order, and responsibility in relationships. In reality, much of the daily routine of life must be lived according to agreed upon rules, especially in large social organizations. McLean (1984:24) has insightfully observed that:

> In the covenantal root metaphor, law and covenant belong together. The dyadic relationship necessarily involves creating specific forms, rules, and laws to guide community and personal relationships. The need for law, pattern, and form is mandatory, but the particular shape of law needs to be understood as relative to the actualization of dialogical-dialectical relationships, the creation of whole persons-in-community. The issue becomes which forms, which laws, which patterns are appropriate to the maintenance of humanity?

Empowering: The Action Needed for Mature Social Relationships

Power is the ability to influence another person. Social science research reveals that the most common way in which people use power in social relationships is to control others (Szinozacz, p. 1987). In fact, most social science models of power assume that in using power, persons are not attempting to increase the power of the person(s) they are trying to influence. Instead, they are using power to assure the maintenance of a more powerful position in the next social interaction.

Empowering is a biblical model for the use of power which is completely contrary to the common usage of power in society at large. Empowering can be defined as the attempt to establish power in, not over, another person. Empowering is not merely yielding to the wishes of another person, nor does it necessarily involve giving up one's own power to someone else. Rather, empowering is the active, intentional process of enabling the acquisition of power in another person. The person who is empowered has gained power because of the encouraging behavior of the other.

The primary idea in empowering is that someone believes in you and wants you to reach your potential. This happens when that person recognizes and acknowledges strengths and potentials within you and then builds you up through encouragement and the development of these qualities. It is the affirmation of the other's ability to learn and become all they can become. It requires that the empowerer be willing to stand back and allow a person to learn by doing and making mistakes. It is not keeping one dependent on you but rather respecting the person as he/she tries, and then stand by or alongside that one with support. It is important that the empowerer respect the uniqueness of the empowered ones and value their unique ways of reaching competency. The empowerer is not to be controlling by enforcing a certain way of doing and being. The empowering event is a reciprocal process in which empowering takes place between people in mutually enhancing ways. We learn from one another and appreciate what we give and gain in that interpersonal exchange.

If covenant love is the commitment, and grace is the underlying atmosphere of acceptance, then empowering is the *action* of God in people's lives. The celebrated message of Jesus was that He has come to empower — "I am come that they may have life and have it to the full" (John 10:10, NIV). The Apostle John puts it this way: "But to all who received him, who believed in his name, he gave power to become children of God; who were born, not of blood nor of the will of the flesh nor of the will of man, but of God" (John 1:12). Anderson (1985) says that the power "of blood" would be power in the natural order, and "the will of the flesh" would refer to tradition, duty, honor, obedience and all that is a part of conventional power. In this verse, it is clear that power is given by God and not by either physical or conventional means.

The power given by Jesus is power of the personal order — power which is mediated to the powerless. In our sinful and powerless condition, God gives us the power to become children of God. This is the supreme example of human empowering. Jesus redefined the understanding of power in His teaching and by His action in relating to others as a servant. Jesus rejected the use of power to control others, and instead, affirmed the use of power to serve others, to lift up the fallen, to make the poor self-sufficient, to forgive the guilty, to encourage responsibility and maturity in the weak, and to give power to the powerless.

Power tends to reside in the hands of the person who possesses the most resources. Because of this, there is a temptation to believe that power is a commodity which is in limited supply. This view of "limited supply" has contributed to many of the social problems in contemporary society. It leads to a self-centered perspective, where each individual and social group in society tries to "maximize their returns" on their "investment" in the social exchange process. In the collective level there is the tendency for more powerful nations to keep poorer nations dependent upon them. In the frailness of our human insecurity we are tempted to keep others dependent upon us, and in doing so find a counterfeit security in having power over them.

The good news for Christians is that "according to Scripture, especially the New Testament, the power of God is available to human beings in unlimited amounts" (Bartchy, 1984, p. 13). Bartchy suggests that unlimited power is seen in such passages as Ephesians 4:13, where the "fruit of the Spirit" (love, joy, peace, patience, kindness, goodness, fidelity, gentleness, and self-control) is offered to all Christians. This very character of God is available in unlimited supply because God's resources are inexhaustible!

Covenant love in action can free people from dependency. It is the loving and empowering action seen in Jesus Christ that Christians need to emulate the most. On the community and societal level, as well as the personal one, Christians are called to live according to these extraordinary social patterns. Even though Christians are sinners saved by grace, God challenges us to live in relationships that follow the empowering principle. As we have been empowered by the Holy Spirit, we are called to empower others. We must recognize our own sinfulness and proneness to fail; however, we need to be optimistic in light of the grace and power available to live according to God's intended purposes. In considering a Christian response to the social problems presented in the chapters to follow, we suggest how an empowering model might effectively be implemented as covenant love in action.

Intimacy: The Knowing That Leads to Caring in Social Relationships

The ability of human beings to communicate with each other through elaborate languages makes it possible for us to know one another intimately. God is a personal God whom we can know intimately. Unlike the "gods" of the eastern religions, the God of Scripture wants to be *personally* related to us. In fact, we are encouraged to share our deepest thoughts and feelings with Him through prayer, since the Holy Spirit dwells within us.

Adam and Eve, in their perfect state stood naked before each other and before God without feeling shame (Genesis 2:25). It was only after the Fall that they tried to hide from God out of a feeling of nakedness and shame. Shame is a result of being deceptive, persons putting on masks and hiding from others, pretending to be something they are not. Where shame is present, intimacy is impossible.

Social relationships that are based on covenant and empowering are lived out in an atmosphere of grace, in which individuals communicate with each other in a caring and concerned manner. When one talks, the other listens because he wants to understand the deepest desires and longings of the other. They share themselves with one another and in that sharing come to know and understand themselves and others in deep ways. In this way, we emulate Jesus who selflessly took time to interact with children, to touch the pain of the leper, to allow Mary to wipe His feet with her hair. He walked among people, related to them where they were, and promoted their welfare by being submissive and loving in His relationships. The capacity of persons in social relationships to freely communicate feelings is contingent upon not fearing the other. The writer of the first epistle of John gives us insight into this notion when he says, "God is love. There is no fear in love, but perfect love casts out fear" (4:16, 18). God can express love with a perfect love that is unconditional. Covenant love as a basis of social relationships allows for intimacy without fear of rejection.

Jesus serves as a model of the type of communicative intimacy which persons in relationship should strive to have with each other. Recall that during His last days on earth Jesus asked Peter three times, "Do you love me?" Although there is no way to know with certainty the mind of Jesus during this encounter, we can be sure that He had a definite reason for posing the same question three times. It may be more than coincidental that Peter had earlier denied Him three times. Perhaps Jesus was giving Peter the opportunity to reaffirm the love which had been tacitly denied through his actions. Because our relations with others do often become strained, God desires that we communicate verbally our feelings with one another, and in so doing bring to maturity the covenantal nature of our relationship.

BIBLICALLY PRESCRIBED IDEAL SOCIAL STRUCTURES

The fabric of society consists of many interwoven layers of social structure. Most people can identify the major social units within which they live out their social lives, and which are the most important to them. The several layers of social structure in which our relationships are lived out can be conceptualized as forming increasingly inclusive concentric circles of people. Represented in Figure 2 are four different layers of social structure, along with the biblically prescribed ideal corresponding to each.

FIGURE 2   LEVELS OF SOCIAL STRUCTURE
AND BIBLICALLY PRESCRIBED IDEALS

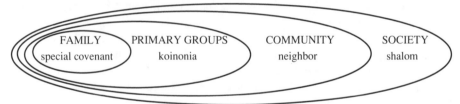

For most people the *family* is the central arena for living in social relationships. The biblically prescribed basis for social relationships in the family is a *special covenant*. Beyond the family, however, there exist *primary groups* in which persons find a sense of belongingness and personal identity. Although these primary groups can resemble family-type relationships, they are generally larger and more inclusive. The biblically prescribed ideal for primary groups is koinonia, that is, "fellowship" or sharing within a primary group. More inclusive than primary groups is the *community*, which consists of all those people who happen to reside in our neighborhood, town or city. These relationships between members of larger communities are often secondary and more impersonal. The biblically prescribed term for such relationships is *neighbor*.

Finally, at the most inclusive social structure level is *society*. Societies can represent the millions of people whose identity is shared by having common membership in the human race on planet earth. The biblically prescribed ideal for societies is *shalom*, or wholeness — the total well-being in the individual and the society. By discussing social relationships in light of what the Bible says about each of these four levels of social interrelatedness, we will be in a better position to understand the theological dimensions of the social-structural cause of societal problems.

Special Covenant: Social Relationships in Family

The basic unit in society, both sociologically and theologically, is the family. Sociologically, the family is the basic unit of society into which individuals are born, find their identity, and are socialized. The foundation for the family is the marital dyad. We believe God intends for marriage to be based on a mature, reciprocal, covenantal relationship between a man and a woman. Genesis 2:24 reads, "a man leaves his father and mother and is united to his wife and the two become one flesh." The marital relationship is the model that the Apostle Paul referred to when describing the bond between Christ (the bridegroom) and the church (the bride).

The family is meant to provide an intimate environment where persons can be themselves, without fear of rejection. It is to be a place where openness prevails because members have experienced unconditional love, acceptance, forgiveness and empowerment. This leads to a depth of mutual knowing and reciprocal caring.

Theologically, all that we have said about covenant, grace, empowering, and intimacy as the bases of ideal social relationships is supremely applicable to family relationships. In brief, we suggest that: (1) family life is to be based in a mature covenant commitment (unconditional and bilateral); (2) family life is to be established and maintained within an atmosphere of grace that embraces acceptance and forgiveness; (3) the resources of family members are to be used to empower rather than to control one another; and (4) intimacy is based on a knowing that leads to caring, understanding, communication, and communion with others. These four elements of Christian family relationships are a continual process: intimacy can lead to deeper covenant love, commitment fortifies the atmosphere of freely offered grace; this climate of acceptance and forgiveness encourages serving and empowering others; and the resultant sense of esteem leads to the ability to be intimate without fear. The end product of this process is a deep level of communication and knowing.

Living in covenant love is a dynamic process. God has designed family relationships to grow to a maturity which is analogous to that of individual believers who attain the full measure of perfection found in Christ (Eph. 4:13). The maturing of relationships eventually enables family members to reach out to persons beyond the boundaries of the family. Many of our contemporary social problems are at least partially attributable to the modern-day loss of a biblically based perspective regarding family relationships.

Koinonia: Social Relationships in Primary Groups

Most people in most societies are members of, and find a sense of identity and social support from, primary groups that exist beyond the family itself. Examples of such groups are churches, clubs, fellowships, sports and recreation and other common interest groups. Sociologically, a primary group serves as a mediating structure between the isolated, private world of the family and faceless remote societal structures. However, an increasing number of people in modern society have been unable to locate such supportive primary groups. Accompanying a decline in primary group relationships has been the loss of effective social control. As a result we have become vulnerable to our own moral laxity and to strangers around us, and an impersonal social environment has arisen, causing many persons to feel as if they belong to a "lonely crowd" (Reisman, 1956).

Some social scientists believe that networking has become the modern substitute for primary groups, and that it now serves as a mediating structure. Friendship networks, occupational networks, and religious networks can provide virtually all of an individual's social needs. However, because these networks are individualized and always subject to change, they lack the security, loyalty, commitment and sense of belonging which is found in the primary group.

Responses to the disintegration of primary relationships are varied. At one extreme, there are trends toward a type of extreme individualism which disowns significant dependence on, or commitment to, anyone else. At the other extreme people are experimenting with various forms of intentional primary groups that focus around some common value as economic sharing, family life, or religious devotion. In between are still others who search for a sense of community in such institutional contexts as the church or suburban housing developments. It is interesting that these communities often receive names like "Homewood," "Pleasantdale," or "Community Heights," designations that imply commonalty and identity.

We live in a mass society in which primary group identity and relationships are desperately sought after, yet prove to be exceedingly difficult to achieve. Moreover, the breakdown of such groups is one of the root causes of such social problems as juvenile delinquency, adult crime, racial discrimination, alienation, substance abuse, poverty and neglect of the elderly. The key to understanding God's ideal with regard to social relationships within a primary group context is found in the New Testament concept of *koinonia*. This term is used in the Bible to refer to a group in which persons are united in identity and purpose by way of a voluntary sharing of all their possessions. During New Testament times, people associated themselves with two main types of groups: *politeia*, or civic life, and *oikonomia*, or family life. Koinonia came to represent a new type of group situated between the inclusive, impersonal state and the exclusive, blood-based community of the household (Banks, 1980).

One of the metaphors which the Apostle Paul used to describe the church is that of the family. Christians are to see themselves as being members of a divine family, brothers and sisters in Christ. In 2 Corinthians 6:18 Paul quotes from the Old Testament, "... I will accept you, says the Lord, the Ruler of all being, I will be a father to you, and you shall be my sons and daughters." In Ephesians Paul states that "we are no longer strangers, but fellow citizens with the saints and members of the household of God" (2:19).

Nevertheless, the Bible rejects any notion of the family being an exclusive, self-contained group. In fact, there is much in the teaching of Jesus to suggest that one's loyalty is misplaced if it ultimately resides in the family. Thus Jesus speaks of "leaving," "dividing," "disuniting," and even "hating" one's family for the sake of God's kingdom. Of course, this is not an attempt to undermine family life, but a way of dramatizing the point that a Christian's loyalty must transcend ordinary family bonds and reside ultimately in the church, the family of God, as the primary group. In short, the church or community — the primary group which is practicing koinonia — will exude the

258

characteristics of family life.

The teaching seems to suggest that strong family relationships are not to be ends in themselves, but paradigms of how we are to care for each other in our primary groups. Jesus' attitude towards the inclusiveness of the family is clearly shown in Mark 3:31-35. While speaking to a crowd, He is informed that His mother and brothers have arrived. His reply is, "'Who is my mother? Who are my brothers?' Then looking around at those who were sitting in the circle about him Jesus said, 'Here are my mother and brothers. Whoever does the will of God is my brother, my sister, my mother.' " The common membership which we have in the Body of Christ binds all believers to Christ and to one another. These relationships are to be based upon covenant, grace empowerment, intimacy and koinonia. The concept of koinonia provides us with a model of the church as a primary group community. In his book entitled *Paul's Idea of Community*, Robert Banks (1980) argues that since the first Christian churches met in the homes of believers, the size of any fellowship was limited to twenty or thirty persons. Moreover, he suggests that both the nature and size of these churches reflected Paul's idea for Christian fellowship.

Recent social science research has found that people are typically able to maintain intimate relationships with a maximum of twenty-five to thirty persons. Those attempting to develop a network of intimate friends larger than this find that they lack the time, capacity, and energy to keep each friendship growing and vital (Pattison, 1984).

The decline of primary groups in modern society has more to do with the nature of contemporary mass society — with its forces of impersonalization, urbanization, industrialization, rationalization, dehumanization, bureaucratization, and secularization — than it does with the absence of Christianity. In the face of these societal changes, Christian churches that practice koinonia can demonstrate how persons are able to relate in primary groups as God intended. Sociologically, a primary group other than a Christian fellowship might function as a koinonia-type group. However, for this to be effective the primary group will have to share common beliefs, values, ideals and goals. Such groups of koinonia can be a model for how human beings may live meaningful lives in harmony with themselves, others and their Creator.

Neighbor: Social Relationships in the Community

Whereas the social relationships of family and primary groups are based upon special covenant commitment, this is not necessarily the case for relationships between people who live in the same community, whether it be a small town or large city. The relationships between persons living in the same community tend to be secondary rather than primary. A secondary relationship is one that temporarily focuses in the fulfillment of some immediate goal such as purchasing groceries or buying clothes. Is there a biblical basis for how persons are to relate in communities that are based on secondary relationships?

We believe the parable of the Good Samaritan gives a basis for the concept of neighbor as a normative model for all secondary community-based social relationships. Luke (10:25-37 NIV) records this parable as follows:

> On one occasion an expert in the law stood up to test Jesus. "Teacher," he asked, "what must I do to inherit eternal life?"

"What is written in the Law?" he replied. "How do you read it?"

He answered:"'Love the Lord your God with all your heart and with all your soul and with all your strength and with all your mind'; and, 'Love your neighbor as yourself.'"

"You have answered correctly," Jesus replied. "Do this and you will live."

But he wanted to justify himself, so he asked Jesus, "And who is my neighbor?"

In reply Jesus said: "A man was going down from Jerusalem to Jericho, when he fell into the hands of robbers. They stripped him of his clothes, beat him and went away, leaving him half dead. A priest happened to be going down the same road, and when he saw the man, he passed by on the other side. So too, a Levite, when he came to the place and saw him, passed by on the other side. But a Samaritan, as he traveled, came where the man was; and when he saw him, he took pity on him. He went to him and bandaged his wounds, pouring on oil and wine. Then he put the man on his own donkey, took him to an inn and took care of him. The next day he took out two silver coins and gave them to the innkeeper. 'Look after him,' he said, 'and when I return, I will reimburse you for any extra expense you may have.'

"Which of these three do you think was a neighbor to the man who fell into the hands of robbers?"

The expert in the law replied, "The one who had mercy on him."

Jesus told him, "Go and do likewise."

It would have been more simple for Jesus to make a distinction between those who are neighbors and those who are not. Instead, He makes the startling assertion that every individual is a potential neighbor. That is to say, neighbor-type relationships are created only when one person comes to the aid of another. Moreover, each of us is capable of both being a neighbor and having a neighbor. Thus, when I meet the needs of another, I am being a neighbor to that person. But when someone else serves me, then I have a neighbor.

The parable of the Good Samaritan is also a vivid illustration of Jesus' command to "love your neighbor as yourself" (Matthew 19:19). In our own lives, this commandment may be observed in such actions as to not change the television channel picturing the starving people of Africa, or taking notice of an account of racial or gender injustice that is described in one's newspaper, or by not neglecting the needs of the homeless. We must be willing to look and see before we will be urged to act, and then come to the aid of others as God would have us do.

When the call to be a neighbor is from God and not simply from a desire to be needed, the resultant action is an empowering one. In this regard, Frazier (1986, p. 268) comments that "a distinction must be made between the kind of aid that takes over and the kind that enables the recipient to continue the task. To take up the cause of another is not to give aid in the first sense. It is not to judge the other incompetent or weak or inadequate, and to set one's own self up as the superior deliverer of the needs. Rather it is to discern that point at which the other must be enabled to carry on a task, and to give that aid regardless of its seeming insignificance or lack of permanent value."

There is no promise that being a neighbor will result in having the other as a neighbor. Regardless of whether or not neighborliness is reciprocated, God calls us to selflessly serve those in need. As we attempt to give a Christian response to social problems, we will stress the need for social structural change on the community level that will render our secondary relationships more consistent with the biblical model of neighbor.

Shalom: Social Structure in Society

The fourth concentric circle in Figure 2 represents the many different larger layers of social structure which exist in all societies. These include the faceless impersonal social structures of the economic, educational, political and religious institutions. The social structures in each of these social institutions contain patterns of positions (status) and social relationships (roles) that are reinforced by an integrated set of norms. The end result is that much of contemporary social life can be lived out in impersonal, hierarchical, rationally based bureaucracies.

Important determinants of social status include factors of race, ethnicity, gender, social class, occupation, religion, age, level of education, residential area, and verbal ability. These factors, which find their justification in elaborate ideological systems, are legitimately employed only in certain contexts. For instance, an individual's level of learning is an appropriate yardstick for determining his or her status within the field of education. Because of her breadth of knowledge, a teacher should be accorded more honor than her students. Suppose, instead, that race or gender were used as the major criterion in determining an individual's status in education. One result of institutional racism or sexism is an implicit denial of internal grievance procedures for those discriminated against. In approaching social problems from the vantage point of the Christian faith, we stand on the firm foundation of biblical truth, and it will be from this basis that we evaluate the injustice of using social factors in determining societal position.

The Old Testament concept of *shalom* is a theologically appropriate one to describe the type of society in which institutions would function best. The term *shalom*, which is used 250 times in the Hebrew Scriptures, is usually translated as "peace." Peace in western cultures connotes the absence of conflict. However, in Scripture and Hebrew culture *shalom* is not seen as the mere absence of conflict but rather that which promotes human welfare in both material and spiritual ways. It denoted a culture characterized by justice and righteousness. For shalom to exist there must be justice and righteousness in the ethical structures of society; there must be a fairness in the way human beings relate to each other at each social structure level. Such a situation is poignantly described in the following passage from Isaiah:

> The wolf shall dwell with the lamb, and the leopard shall lie down with the kid, and a little child shall lead them. The cow and the bear shall feed; their young shall lie down together; and the lion shall eat straw like the ox. The suckling child shall play over the hole of the asp, and the weaned child shall put his hand on the adder's den (11:6-8).

Shalom carried with it a holistic connotation of societal well-being. It is "the human being dwelling at peace in all his or her relationships: with God, with self, with fellows, with nature" (Wolterstorff, 1983, p. 69). When any one of these relationships is out of focus, disrupted, at tension, or hurting, then *shalom* is not present.

Peace and justice find their common expression in the concept of *shalom*. While shalom is lacking, social problems inevitably arise. Social problems are often symptomatic of deeper spiritual and sociocultural injustices and inconsistencies.

Shalom is present only when special structures have been changed so that they empower rather than make persons excessively dependent or vulnerable. For example, chronic unemployment and oppression resulting in poverty must be eradicated before shalom is even approximated. Restoring *shalom* means eradicating the conditions which contribute to poverty. One way of eliminating poverty is to provide the poor with food, clothing, and shelter. Whereas this may be a good beginning, if the underlying oppressive conditions which cause poverty are not dealt with, then *shalom* is not present. It is essential that we provide possibilities for persons to help themselves by offering a means for them to reach their goals. In sum, a society characterized by *shalom* will not treat its people unjustly or in a paternalistic fashion.

A nation whose foreign policies are biblically informed will also be trying to implement *shalom* in international relationships. In a world economy where people in some countries are living in riches while people in other countries are living in relative poverty, *shalom* is not present. A biblically informed foreign policy in a rich country such as the United States will seek to foster economic development in a poor country. This may mean the affluent country will have to pay more for such commodities as coffee, bananas, sugar and raw materials in order to diminish the economic dependency of the poor country.

Conclusion

We have suggested that the biblically prescribed ideals for social relationships at the *family*, *primary group*, *community* and *society* structural levels are *special covenant*, *koinonia*, *neighbor*, and *shalom*, respectively. In conclusion we suggest two guiding principles: (1) God calls persons to give their priority commitments to the most exclusive social group of which they are a member; and (2) commitment to this exclusive group is to be the basis for developing inclusive rather than exclusive group commitments. Thus, a person's first priority of commitment is to his/her family, followed by commitment to the primary group, to the community, and finally to society. Families which are characterized by covenant love will reach out to *include* members of their primary groups as "brothers" and "sisters." Primary groups that are experiencing koinonia will openly include "neighbors" from the community as new primary group members. Community members who are willing to *be* a neighbor to others and to *let* others be a neighbor to them are creating the type of community that will be characterized by *shalom*. A Christian perspective in social problems is based on such biblically ideal social structures.

Study and Discussion
Questions

1. What are the potential pitfalls in attempting to give "biblically prescribed ideal" social relationships and social structures? Do you find this task to be necessary? Possible? Potentially dangerous?

2. How realistic is it for a Christian to attempt to apply the concepts of covenant, grace, empowering, and intimacy in all social relationships? Within which types of social relationships are these concepts most likely to be applicable?

3. Contrast *covenant* and *contract* as a basis for social relationships, giving examples from real life for each.

4. Is there any place for law in a relationship which is being lived out in an atmosphere of grace?

5. For which of the social problems discussed in this book can you think of examples of programs which have resulted in empowering? Examples of programs which have perpetuated dependence? Distinguish between empowering and enabling.

6. List your various primary groups in the order in which you would characterize them as exemplifying koinonia.

7. What are the protective social structures which might prevent you from hearing God's call to be a neighbor to others?

8. Give an example of a family, primary group, community and society which comes closest to exemplifying the biblical concepts of *social covenant*, *koinonia*, *neighbor*, and *shalom* respectively. For which of these do you find it the hardest to think of an example? Why?

9. Do you think it is theologically correct to think of sin as residing in social structures? Can social structures be thought of as evil?

10. Should our priority in attempting to ameliorate social problems always be on changing social structures? Are there some social problems which are best combatted by first converting the individual to the Christian faith?

References

Allen, J., *Love and Conflict: a Covenantal Model of Christian Ethic.* Nashville: Abingdon Press, 1984.

Anderson, R., "The Gospel of the Family." Unpublished manuscript. Fuller Theological Seminary, 1985.

Banks, R., *Paul's Idea of Community.* Grand Rapids: Eerdmans, 1980.

Bartchy, S., Issues of power and a theological of the family. Paper presented at seminar, Consultation on a Theology of the Family. Seminar, Fuller Theological Seminary, 1984.

Frazier, E., *B arth and an Evangelical Feminist Theology.* Unpublished dissertation: Vanderbilt University, 1986.

McLean, S., The language of covenant and a theology of the family. Paper presented at seminar, Consultation on a Theology of the Family, Fuller Theological Seminary, 1984

Pattison, M., The church and the healing of families, in "Consultation on a Theology of the Family." Seminar, Fuller Theological Seminary, 1984.

Riesman, D., *The Lonely Crowd.* New Haven, CT: Yale University Press, 1956.

Szinozacz, M., Family power relations and processes, in M. Sussman and S. Steinmetz (eds.). *Handbook of Marriage and the Family.* New York: Plenum Press, 1987.

Wolterstorff, N. , *Until Justice and Peace Embrace.* Grand Rapids: Eerdmans, 1983.

This chapter is based upon revisions of parts of chapter 1, "A Theological Basis for Family Relationships," in *The Family: A Christian Perspective on the Contemporary Home*, Jack Balswick and Judy Balswick, Grand Rapids: Baker Books, 1989, and chapter 3, "Christianity and Social Problems," in *Social Problems: A Christian Understanding and Response*, Jack Balswick and Kenneth Morland, Grand Rapids: Baker Books, 1990.

CHAPTER 14
VARIANT SEXUALITY: INTRODUCTION

Perhaps little has caused as much controversy within the Christian community as changes in sexual mores. While the mainline denominations fight proposals to depart from biblical norms on nonmarital sex, conservative religious groups have tended to make "sexual immorality" *the* sin of the day. Some spokespersons for mainline churches have openly challenged the importance of maintaining biblical norms regulating sexual behavior. Conservative Christians, on the other hand, have overlooked other sinful behavior (for example, not caring for the poor) in their zeal for preaching sexual morality.

As Professor Goold points out, the norms guiding sexual behavior are not universal, but rather vary from society to society. These norms, as do other norms, tend to differ among cultures and to change within cultures. American attitudes toward birth control provide one illustration. Early in the 20th century Margaret Sanger, who coined the term "birth control," launched a campaign to bring information about contraceptives to the public. She did this after visiting the deathbed of a young woman who died in 1909 while undergoing an illegal abortion. Sanger's campaign frequently was met with hostility and even arrest. When Sanger organized a conference on the topic of birth control in New York City in 1921, she was arrested and jailed.

Public attitudes and laws prohibiting the use of contraceptives changed gradually. In 1965, the last of the prohibitions against birth control fell as the U.S. Supreme Court finally struck down laws in Connecticut and Massachusetts. Undoubtedly good Christians were on both sides of the controversy, just as today Christians may not be in complete agreement about some of the issues raised by Professor Goold. Sociological and historical observations about differences and changes in sexual norms can help us to be more tolerant of different opinions as we continue to search the Scriptures and to pray for guidance regarding these issues.

It is important to remember, as Goold has emphasized, that the first law of Scripture is that of love — love of God and love of neighbor. That law must govern all that we do, including our sexual activities. It is not always easy, however, to determine whether or not we are acting out of love of God and neighbor. The angel of darkness can come disguised as an angel of light as we attempt to convince ourselves that our behavior is acceptable in God's eyes. Taking note of sociological data can be an aid in the process of discernment, especially when these "empirical facts" are reviewed through a functionalist perspective.

The functionalist perspective, with its attendant concepts of positive functions and dysfunctions, can provide a launching pad for considering variant sexuality as a social problem. There are personal, relational, and social costs or dysfunctions for permissive sexuality, including premarital sex, adultery, and homosexuality. The dramatic rise in teenage girls giving birth outside of marriage, for example, is accompanied by a host of medical and financial problems, all being the direct result of a general acceptance of teenage sex. The increase in venereal disease rates, and especially the spread of AIDS, provides another example of a dysfunction related to a violation of the biblical mandate of limiting our sexual encounters to marriage. Professor Goold provides other illustrations of the dysfunctional consequences of our sexually permissive society.

The dysfunctional aspects of variant sexual practices, we feel, represent less God's wrath visited upon sinners than the inevitable natural consequences of permissive sexuality. Biblical proscriptions were intended so that humankind might avoid the natural repercussions of illicit sexual behavior. Failing to heed these commands breeds a host of problems, which from a Christian perspective can be resolved only by obedience to God's law.

Human sexuality should not be viewed apart from the whole person and interpersonal relationships. We have been created needing committed and loving relationships — a need that is frustrated in illicit sexual encounters. In light of the negative functions of permissiveness on individuals, relationships, and larger society, Jesus' command to love one another would militate against modern sexual permissiveness, even if other biblical and more specific mandates on sexual behavior did not exist.

VARIANT SEXUALITY
Thelma E. Goold

INTRODUCTION

Definitions of sexuality and sexual practice vary widely from one culture to the next. Typically when social problems texts discuss sexuality, they examine deviant or variant sexuality as departures from the norms of a culture. Sexuality as a noun only came into use in the eighteenth century, but as an entity it is as old as creation. Foundations for our sexuality are given in the first chapters of Genesis, before the Fall. "So God created man in his own image, male and female He created them and said to them, be fruitful and multiply. . . . Therefore a man leaves his father and mother and cleaves to his wife and they become one flesh. And the man and his wife were both naked and they were not ashamed" (1:27-28; 2:24-25).

Sexuality — maleness and femaleness — are the creative handiwork of God and rooted in His very nature. Sexuality has been created by Him. Adam and Eve were not ashamed of their nakedness — an image of how we are to be in spirit before Him. God knows us as we are. We are not to deny our sexuality, but celebrate it. We are not, however, to worship our sexuality as American society suggests. Rather, we are to worship the God who has created us as sexual beings. In Scripture, the words, "to know," refer to both sexual intercourse and knowledge of God. This is why sexual intercourse in prohibited contexts and relationships is injurious, not just for the individual but ultimately for society. Both the individual and the society bear the consequences for misusing any of God's precious gifts.

We use the term "sexuality" to refer not only to reproduction and the pursuit of sexual pleasure but also to refer to our need for love and personal fulfillment. Sexuality is a part of who we are as total persons. The term incorporates the psychological, biological, behavioral, cultural, and spiritual. "Right or wrong, we see a sexual element in nearly all human activity, regardless of how nonsexual the activity might be" (Jones, Shainberg, and Byer, 1985, p. 5).

Typically, each society defines what it believes to be normal for that particular society. Over a period of time, however, what people consider "normal" changes and some behaviors that were considered deviant become acceptable to groups within that society. Sexual norms, therefore, become whatever the society defines them to be. Herbert Blumer (1969, p. 78) identified interaction as being shaped by the ways in which people interpret or define each other's actions. In addition, he says, "Human society is to be seen as consisting of their actions." Other theorists argue that society is comprised not only of actions but also the meaning behind those actions.

Phenomenological sociology relies on a "reflexive ability to penetrate to the core, or essence, of one's experience as it takes form, in consciousness" (Douglas. et al., 1980, p. 130). Albert Schutz (1967) stated that the meaning of behavior derives from its intentions. In examining sexual behavior, one must look not only at the behavior but also at the intentionality behind it. Schutz limited the application of the term "action" to behavior carried out according to some preconceived plan. We understand action as when we comprehend the goal it was intended to accomplish (Schutz, 1967, p. 61). The difficulty in studying sexual behavior, even reflexively, is that often the motivations of a person are not clear to him or her. It is possible for habits to become behavior without meaning. Nonetheless, we can repeat a behavior for so long that we forget its meaning, unless we reflect on our reasons for that behavior. There is a whole body of literature now about sexual addiction. It would seem that sexual addiction would be behavior without meaning — behavior that has lost sight of God's plan for sex.

From a Christian perspective, sexuality is both relational and sometimes procreative. The union of two is symbolic of the transcendent relationship between Christ and His church. To consciously or unconsciously separate it from its symbolic meaning is to commodify it. But sex is much more than just relational or procreative. Its meaning is found in the very nature of God. Sexuality, even as defined by the society, can be congruent with the laws of God and conscience — definitions that would promote laws of love and justice in a hurting world.

The way a society defines sexuality has consequences in that society, as those definitions are acted out in the society in the sexual behavior of its people. Reflecting on both definitions and behaviors gives a sense of how the members of society view themselves as sexual persons. When the definitions become distorted and people digress from God's revealed laws, problems inevitably result.

Rather than to focus on certain aberrant practices in society at any given point in time, (i. e., sadism, exhibitionism, fetishism, transvestism), which is the usual approach in social problems texts, I have chosen to focus on the larger social issues related to sexuality which are often problematic in our society. The issues to be examined are premarital and extramarital coitus, homosexuality, sexually transmitted diseases and child sexual abuse.

A BIBLICAL PERSPECTIVE

To use the terms variant or deviant sexuality implies a departure from what is considered to be "normal." Specifics on some aspects of sexuality such as masturbation are not discussed in Scripture, but there are certain principles that, when followed, make it possible for persons to enjoy lives that are fulfilling and honor their Creator.

The first law of Scripture is the law of love: "Thou shalt love the Lord thy God... and thy neighbor as thyself." When God created us male and female, He said it was "very good" (Genesis 1:26-27,31). Sexuality was a gift not only for procreation but also for relationship and recreation (Genesis 1:28; Song of Solomon 2:3; 8:3; 6:1-10; 7:1-9). Paul speaks of the husband and wife meeting each other's sexual needs (1 Corinthians 7:3ff). Sexual needs are to be met in the context of marriage, since Scripture teaches that premarital and extramarital sex are immoral. Such nonmarital sex not only separates us from God, but also constitutes a sin against our own bodies (1 Corinthians 6:12-17; 1 Thessalonians 4:17). The negative command of Exodus 20:14, "You shall not commit adultery," implies the positive side of the commandment, "You shall meet your sexual needs in marriage." Fornication and adultery (sex outside of marriage) are forbidden in several verses (1 Corinthians 6:18; Galatians 5:19; Ephesians 5:3, etc.). The reasons for these proscriptions is not that God wants to keep us from a good thing but because sex is such a wonderful gift He wants us to enjoy it in the context of the best possible environment. And that is in the committed marriage relationship.

Sexual relationships portrayed in the Bible are frequently connected with our relationship to a holy and loving heavenly Father. "Flee from sexual immorality. All other sins a man commits are outside his body, but he who sins sexually sins against his own body. Do you not know that your body is a temple of the Holy Spirit, who is in you, whom you have received from God? You are not your own; you were bought with a price" (1 Corinthians 6:18-20 NIV). Sex outside of marriage is deceitful. It violates the marriage vows and is a sin against one's partner as well as one's self. Genesis 2:25 says that Adam and Eve were naked and were not ashamed. To be naked with another person implies perfect trust and honesty. This symbolizes how we are to be in relationship to God — nothing hidden or concealed. Nudity is not meant to be shared with other than the marriage partner. Honesty requires that there be no shared secrets outside of marriage.

PREMARITAL AND EXTRAMARITAL SEXUALITY

Today's society requires longer periods of social adolescence and a longer time for school and vocational training. This period is about twice as long as it was a hundred years ago (Lauer and Lauer, 1991). A longer adolescence means a longer time for dating and a longer period before couples will marry. Since three-fourths of teen-age marriages fail, if couples wait to marry until a later age, they should have a chance of having a successful marriage. Prolonged adolescence has resulted in many teenagers not waiting until marriage to have sex. This promiscuity is due in part to the media that portrays sexual gratification as a means of achieving instant popularity and pleasure. Youth today are having sexual intercourse at earlier ages. One study showed that 69 percent of unmarried urban females have experienced vaginal coitus by age 19 (49 percent by age 17, and 38 percent by age 16). Male percentages reported usually run higher than female figures (Jones, Shainberg and Byer, 1985).

In early adolescence teens often accept the standards of parents, but as they grow older they may take on the more permissive behavior of peers and the permissive behavior portrayed in the media. Teens are less likely to become sexually active if their family relationships are close, accepting, and loving. Girls who get along well with their fathers are less likely to become sexually involved than those who do not have good relationships with their fathers.

In a study of students from 20 high schools, about one-third of those ages 15-17 had experienced sexual intercourse. There was a strong relationship between teens' attitudes about having sexual intercourse before marriage and reported intercourse experience. Two-thirds of virgin teenagers indicated that having sex before marriage is always or usually wrong (66.9%). Only 16 percent of the nonvirgin teens gave one of these two responses. Twice as many nonvirgin teens (58.6%) as virgins (29.5%) said that having sex before marriage is neither right nor wrong. There was a strong relationship in this study between sexual attitudes and sexual behavior. Religion was not the strongest influence on sexual behavior (Miller and Olson, 1988).

Teens who are sexually active are not consistent in their use of contraceptives. Their use of birth control often starts 6-12 months *after* the beginning of sexual activity and this use is often inconsistent and sporadic. Furthermore, most programs advocating contraceptive use have been oriented almost exclusively at females (Beck and Davies, 1987). The most effective programs seem to have emphasized communication, problem-solving skills, and voluntary involvement of the significant other, especially when the adolescent is allowed to maintain responsibility for his or her own behavior (Beck and Davies, 1987). More than one million teens get pregnant each year and 270,000 of these babies are born to unmarried teens. The cost to taxpayers is about 16 billion dollars. Each day 33,000 Americans will contract a sexually transmitted disease (Lowry and Towles, 1989; Lord, 1986; and Haviman and Lehtinen, 1990).

Abortion is frequently used as a birth control method by teen and adult women alike. In 1973 the Supreme Court ruled that states cannot place restrictions on a woman's right to an abortion during the first three months of pregnancy. Second trimester abortions can be regulated in certain medical aspects, and in the third trimester, states can impose medical restrictions because the fetus is viable at that point in the pregnancy. A predominant number of men and women still view abortion as legal or almost always legal (81%). However, as many as 33 percent sometimes question their position on abortion and wonder if it is all right (Abortion, *Gallup Report*, 1989). More than 30 percent of all pregnancies in the U. S. are not terminated by legally induced abortions as reported by the National Center for Health Statistics (1981) in (Jones, et al., 1985).

Various studies have shown that rates of premarital intercourse have increased significantly. In a study done over a ten-year period on a small university campus, the mean age of first intercourse decreased by 1.0 year for men and 1.2 years for women. The percentage of freshmen who were nonvirgins doubled for men and more than doubled for females. The numbers of coital partners also increased over this period. It seems that permissiveness with affection is an emerging norm in colleges and universities. In addition an increasing number of youth ascribe to the philosophy of "friendly sex" (Earle and Perricone, 1986; Grecas and Libby, 1976; and Robinson and Jedlicka, 1982).

But despite this growing permissiveness some researchers find among college age young people a new double standard has arisen. Characteristically, these persons have greater expectations for others than for themselves. The findings of Robinson and Jedlick (1982) show that there has been an increase in the number of women and men who say that premarital coitus for both males and females is immoral and sinful. Since 1975 there seems to have been a general tendency toward a return to the older attitudes, those which existed prior to the so-called sexual revolution. While attitudes are reported to have returned to the more traditional, behaviors continue to be very permissive.

SEXUAL VIOLENCE

Not only has there been an increase in sexual permissiveness among teens and college-age students, but there also has been a significant increase in the amount of violence, and sexual violence — including date rape — among teens and young adults. Kanin, in Heilbrun and Loftus (1986, p. 320), defines sexual aggression as a "forceful attempt by the male for sexual intimacy despite the female's obvious reaction to this behavior as offensive and disagreeable." Explanations for date rape include: 1) socialization of the male towards success, power and aggression, fostering efforts to obtain sexual goals, despite the partner's protests; 2) sexual scripts prescribing that men should seek sexual intercourse and women should avoid or resist; and 3) the influence of peer pressure on men to attain sexual goals (loc. cit.).

O'Keefe, Brockopp and Chew (1986, p. 465) identified violence among teen dating couples as one of the hidden social issues of the 1980s. In their survey of 256 Sacramento, California, high school students, they found that 35.1 percent had experienced some kind of abuse in their dating experiences. While "date rape" as a term was coined in the '80s, rape has been a serious social problem for a very long time. Date rape occurs when a sexual relationship is forced upon an unwilling partner during a date. Except for spousal rape, date rapes are the least reported of all rapes. Rape authorities, such as Brownmiller (1975), believe if women were to report date rape and if authorities would view it as a serious offense, the incidence of this act would be sharply reduced. Reporting and prosecuting rapists is very important, since 85 percent of them go on to repeat rape and commit other crimes (Jones, et al., 1985).

Numerous authors have defined rape as a crime of aggression, of violence, stating that it has little to do with sex or sexual feeling (Groth and Gary, 1981; McCary and McCary, 1984; Brownmiller, 1975; and Palmer, 1988). However, Palmer (1988) examines the rationale that states that rape is not sexually motivated and reasons that many of these statements are not logical or true. For example, although any woman and girl, regardless of appearance or age can be raped, most rape victims are between the ages of eighteen and twenty-five. Less than five percent of rape victims are over the age of fifty. "Vulnerability must be combined with attractiveness in order to account for the age distribution of rape victims" (Palmer, 1988, p. 525). Rape is certainly a crime of violence but the sexual element is there and must be accounted for. Smithyman (1978) found that 84 percent of the rapists studied cited sexual motivation "solely or in part" as the cause of their acts (quoted in Palmer, 1988, p. 518).

Society characterizes sexuality as romantic, involving foreplay, negotiation, etc., but in the case of date rape, violent action can follow denial or refusal on the part of the victim. Research shows that offenders are under the influence of drugs or alcohol as much as 50 percent of the time and rape is one of the fastest growing crimes of violence in America (Groth, 1984; McCary, 1984). Unfortunately, it is also the one crime where the victim must sometimes defend being a victim.

COHABITATION/MARITAL FIDELITY

In 1970, there were about a half million unmarried cohabiting couples. It is estimated that in the 1990s the number of cohabiting couples could reach as high as 3.5 million. Of all the couples who married in the first half of the '80s, 44 percent had been cohabiting couples. If is noteworthy that cohabiting does not seem to increase marital happiness nor does it decrease divorce rates. A Bentler and Newcomb study (1978) found that the divorce rate was just as high for cohabiters after four years of marriage as couples who had not been cohabiters. De Maris and Leslie (1984) found that couples who had lived together before marriage seemed no more satisfied with their marriages and if anything, less satisfied (in Haveman and Lehtinen, 1990).

Americans have traditionally placed a high value on marital fidelity. A Roper poll (1985) asked individuals to pick out items essential to a good marriage. Sexual fidelity was termed very important by 77 percent of men and 83 percent of women. A 1980s poll found that among couples married for ten years or more, 30 percent of the husbands and 22 percent of the wives had actually engaged in extramarital activity (Haveman and Lehtinen, 1990, p. 130). Apparently there is an inconsistency between what people say and what they actually practice.

Issues related to infidelity can apply both to married people and to unmarried couples who are emotionally committed. Affairs outside of one's relationship among unmarried couples has not been widely studied but the emotional trauma is as great for those couples as for married couples.

Statistics on infidelity are not highly reliable but the high divorce rate is indicative of its prevalence. Infidelity is often symptomatic of personal and/or marital problems. A high percentage of marriages do not survive affairs. With increasing numbers of women in the workforce and increasing time, mobility, money, and effective contraception, opportunities for affairs have never been greater. People have many reasons for extramarital affairs: sexual need or novelty, a need to feel loved, to prove they are attractive or macho, to get revenge, and mid-life crisis, are but a few.

Divorce rates in the U. S. have more than doubled since the 1950s and the current divorce rate is over half the marriage rate. Divorce is highest in the 20 to 24 age range and declines thereafter. Two important contributing factors to the high divorce rate are the liberalization of the divorce laws and the increased expectations for marital and sexual fulfillment (Jones, et al., 1985). Because of the pain involved for everyone, especially the children, professional marriage counseling should be considered before any final decision is made to divorce. Every year over a million children under the age of eighteen suffer because of family break-ups (Jones, et al., 1985).

God's miracle in Genesis parallels Jesus' first miracle at the wedding of Cana. Genesis (2:22) says that God "brought the woman to the man. . . ." Genesis (2:24-25) says that "a man shall leave his father and mother and cleave to his wife." The Song of Solomon (6:1-10; 7:1-9) exalts fidelity between married lovers, describing in vivid, poetic detail the relationship of married lovers. Techniques in sexual arousal between husband and wife are implied (2:3; 8:3). "The feelings, attitudes, imaginations, dreams, the spiritual and sexual joys . . . of married lovers are beautifully described" (Peterson, 1971, p. 390).

The above relationship is one which can best happen in the home where two people are committed to Jesus Christ, to His Gospel and to His purposes in their individual lives and in their marriage. The Ephesians (ch. 5) model emphasizes family and other relationships that are built on being filled with the Holy Spirit, mutually submissive, willing to be self-sacrificial, and are building each other up in the faith. The emphasis is on living as children of light and on finding out what pleases the Lord.

HOMOSEXUALITY

Homosexuality as a practice is as old as recorded history. How a society defines various aspects of sexuality and responds to its definitions is the result of social learning and perceptions. Kinsey and coworkers devised a seven-point continuum as a way of explaining homosexuality and heterosexuality. This continuum ranges from 0, exclusively heterosexual, to 6, exclusively homosexual. Thus, 3 would be a bisexual person. The person's classification on this scale refers to the degree of sexual responsiveness to persons of the same sex (McCary and McCary, 1984; and Jones, et al., 1985).

Greenberg (1988) has examined homosexuality and its social construction in a massive work that studies homosexuality and its social culture and history in various societies. Greenberg has identified four types of homosexuality:

> . . . transgenerational (in which the partners are of different ages), transgenderal (one of the partners relinquishes the gender or sexual identity associated with his or her anatomical sex and lays claim to the gender associated with the opposite sex), egalitarian (the partners are socially similar), and finally, nonegalitarian (the partners are from different economic strata in the society) (pp. 25-92).

The recently published study by Klassen, Williams, and Levitt (1989, p. 21), done under the Auspices of the Kinsey Institute, describes in some detail the public view of Americans regarding norms of sexual conduct in a number of areas. A majority of respondents favored laws against prostitution (62%), homosexuality (59%), and extramarital sex (52%). Kinsey researchers found that 60 percent of males and 33 percent of females have engaged in at least one overt act of homosexual play by age fifteen. Thirty-seven percent of the males and 13 percent of females engaged at least once in some form of homosexual activity to the point of orgasm (McCary and McCary, 1984).

"Homosexual relationships challenge the emotional and moral basis for the way our culture deals with sexuality" (Klassen, et al., 1989, p. 22). Attitudes toward homosexuality are strongly held by most Americans who fear and disapprove of homosexuality. In the 1989 Kinsey Report, 37 percent of respondents believed they could recognize homosexuals by how they looked and 56 percent said that homosexuals fear the opposite sex. Almost 60 percent agreed that homosexuals have very strong sex drives. Forty percent agreed with the proposition that there is an element of homosexuality in everyone (Klassen, et al., 1989).

McConaghy (1987) in a replicative study found that over 40 percent of both males and females were occasionally aware of homosexual feeling and supported the Kinsey data of 1938 and 1963 that homosexuality and heterosexuality are polar extremes on a continuum. These studies were completed with medical students and so are not entirely representative of the larger population.

The attitudes of Americans toward homosexual behavior remain highly negative. The 1989 Kinsey Institute Report showed that 86.3 percent of respondents felt that homosexuality between two persons who have no special affections for each other was always or almost always wrong. Seventy-nine percent believed that homosexual behavior between two persons who love each other is always or almost always wrong (Klassen, et al., 1989, p. 18). These responses were from data gathered during the 1970s, the so-called peak of the sexual revolution.

A Gallup poll reported that support for legalization of homosexual relations had declined from 45 percent in 1982 to 33 percent in 1986. This decrease in support for legalization of homosexual relations over a four-year period is probably due to the growing fear generated by the AIDS epidemic (*Gallup Report*, November, 1986).

Bell (in Klassen, et al., 1989, p. 165), stated that "homosexuality impinges on such questions as what it means to be male or female, what can be considered sexual pathology, what the purposes of human sexuality are, and so forth. Thus, homosexual relationships challenge the moral and emotional basis for the way our culture deals with sexuality." Homosexuals are often feared in the society as being sick, effeminate, dangerous and unnatural. In spite of these beliefs, most homosexuals appear and act like anyone else. These unreasoned and repulsed reactions to homosexuality are referred to as *homophobia*.

There are a variety of viewpoints about the causes of homosexuality, just as there are numerous fears surrounding it. About 43 percent of the Kinsey sample believed that young people become homosexuals because of the example and influence of older homosexuals. Nearly 40 percent agreed that people become homosexuals because of the family environment in which they were raised. Sixty-two percent believed that homosexuality is a sickness that could be cured, in at least half of all those who practice it. And 40 percent believed that 100 percent of the cases could be cured (Klassen, et al., 1989).

Theories about the causes of homosexuality are often more confusing than clarifying. The origins of homosexuality can be biological, cultural, psychological or a combination of these factors. Penner and Penner (1986) have identified three "critical periods" in which homosexuality might develop. These are: 1) birth to age two, when clear messages about being a boy or a girl are received by the child; 2) preschool years, ages 3-6, when same sex role models seem to be especially important. "It seems obvious that one reason why there are more male homosexuals than female, is that boys have more opportunity to model women, than girls have to model men" (p. 97); and 3) early adolescence, when the child is beginning to move away from parents toward attachment to peers. It is not unusual, at this age, for children to experiment sexually with same sex peers. During these years a boy may be approached by an older male and if his identification with male role models is weak, may respond to this person (Penner and Penner, 1986, pp. 97-99). While the Penners' "critical stage" theory is not statistically proven, their experience and those of others show that there is some validity to these ideas. We were created to be sexual persons, and so early sexual experiences are crucial in the kinds of bonding and orientation that take place during these critical stages.

"It is rare to discover one's sexual preference by accident. But traumatic molestation experiences of a homosexual nature usually leave a child confused about sexual identity" (Penner and Penner, 1986, p. 97). If molested, children often feel overwhelmed by guilt. If the experience was very traumatic, the child may have actually blocked it from consciousness. "We must do all we can to teach our children the reality that they are in charge of their own bodies, and neither a stranger or a relative should touch or violate them in any way which leaves them uncomfortable" (Penner and Penner, 1986, p. 99).

In addition, it is important to remember that people with a same sex preference need care, love and respect. The stereotypical portraits are invalid. Homosexuals are in all socioeconomic classes and may be found in all occupations. They get lonely, have pain and feelings just as others do. Christians should be the first to offer love and compassion.

A BIBLICAL ETHIC

In an increasingly secularized society a biblical ethic on any sexual issue is likely to be resisted, including the issue of homosexuality. Christians as well as non-Christians are divided on this issue.

Sex is a delightful gift intended not only for reproduction but for enjoyment (Proverbs 5:18-19). The Song of Solomon expresses in poetic language the mutual enjoyment a man and woman may find in each other. Not only does Scripture not speak approvingly about homosexuality, but nowhere does the Scripture mention finding sexual fulfillment with a person of the same sex. Apparently it was never a part of God's divine plan for us to use our gift of sexuality in a homosexual manner. It is possible for people to develop inappropriate gender identities and to bond in inappropriate relationships, but it is important to remember that in every situation God's grace and mercy are available to all.

Leviticus 18:22 and 20:13 identify several proscriptions about sexual behavior. The Hebrews were not to have sex with a neighbor's wife, with an animal, nor were they to "lie with a man as one lies with a woman; this is detestable."

The strongest sanctions are leveled against incest and homosexuality in Leviticus 20: 10-22: "If a man sleeps with his daughter-in-law, both must be put to death. If a man lies with a man. . . they must be put to death. . . ." These immoral behaviors would separate the Hebrews from their Holy God. They were not to live according to the customs of their pagan neighbors who lived in and around their land. All forms of sexual immorality — extramarital sex, incest, homosexuality, and bestiality — were forbidden. While these passages forbid certain sexual behaviors, they do not say that persons are "bad" for having feeling of attractions for a person of the same sex. They do, however, state that one is not to act on the basis of those feelings. Such behaviors are not permitted because they are contrary to the nature of God himself and His created order.

The sin of Sodom was described by D. S. Bailey (1954) as a "great and unnamed sin." Other scholars say his position is unsupportable. Genesis 19:4-9, 22-25 quote the men of the city who said to the master of the house, "bring them out to us, that we may know them." To "know" someone in this passage refers to intercourse just as it does in Genesis 4:1 and other places in Scripture (Oswalt in Keysor, 1979, p. 73).

Romans 1:25-27 contains the most specific references to homosexuality. Homosexuality is listed as one of several perversions which happen when people turn their backs on God and do not give thanks to God or glorify Him. This is part of Paul's larger discussion of original sin. People sin, engage in immoral behavior, because they are sinners. In S*crewtape Letters*, (1959), C. S. Lewis states that Satan has never created anything positively evil. He can only take what his Enemy [God] has created good and pervert it. The greater the power for good, the more power it can have for evil. Sexuality is a very powerful good in life when properly used within God's guidelines, but it can also be a powerful evil.

John says we can be "overcomers" through "Him who overcame" (1 John 5:4-6). We are influenced by culture, socialization, and at times heredity, but by His grace we do not have to act on those inclinations.

PORNOGRAPHY AND THE MEDIA

"Be careful how you think; your life is shaped by your thoughts," "What he(she) thinks is what he (she) really is" (Proverbs 4:23; 23:7b, TEV). In 1970, the Commission on Obscenity and Pornography presented considerable evidence that exposure to sexually explicit stimuli produced no adverse, antisocial effects on people. Recently, however, a number of researchers have begun to question the findings of the commission. Garcia (1985) did a study to test the relationship between exposure to different types of sexual material and attitudes toward women in several areas. Garcia found that the more exposure the subjects had to coercive sexual materials, the more sexist and exploitive were men's behavior and attitudes toward women. The study also showed that exposure to violent sexual stimuli correlated positively with pro-rape attitudes. The correlations were small in these results but some effects were indicated.

Winick (1985), in a study of "hard core" pornography, examined 430 magazines for sale at an adult bookstore in New York City. Since the 1960s there has been a continuing increase in the number of sexually explicit magazines and in the audiences for them. The study yielded 22 categories of content including the following: women in various degrees of undress (27.8%); male-female activity simulating intercourse (15.5%); actual male-female intercourse (8.4%); bondage and discipline (4.9%); oral genital activity, (2.9%); other categories included pictures of female body-parts, lesbians, young women, interracial homosexual interaction, fetishism, and group sex (pp. 207-208).

Findings by Malamuth and Donnerstein (1982) found that exposure to violent sexual materials "(a) is related to self-reported proclivity towards rape, (b) stimulates new rape fantasies, and (c) leads people to perceive rape victims as experiencing less trauma" (in Garcia, 1985, p. 379).

Cowan, et al. (1988) reviewed a random sample of 45 widely available x-rated video cassettes. More than half of the explicitly sexual scenes were coded as predominantly concerned with domination or exploitation. Most were directed toward women, and physical violence occurred frequently. The growth of the video-cassette rental industry and the popularity of x-rated films, coupled with the messages these films convey, is cause for great concern (p. 299).

In 1986, the attorney general's Commission on Pornography recommended a crackdown on pornography. Eroticized violence and themes of degradation have emerged as potentially the most harmful types of sexually explicit material. Several researchers have shown that male exposure to eroticized violence affects attitudes toward rapists and rape victims and acceptance of rape myths, producing an increase in aggressiveness toward female targets (Cowan, et al., 1988). It has also been demonstrated that violence, more than sexual explicitness, has the most significant effect on attitudes and behavior. Most of this material presents women as subservient to dominant males. "The effects of exposure to the fusion of sexuality, violence, and degrading images of women on attitudes about female sexuality is particularly relevant" in understanding why violence toward women is on the increase (p. 309).

Television has had a significant influence on sexual beliefs and practices as well. "In 1986, a full-page newspaper advertisement for Planned Parent Federation of America carried a headline, 'they did it 9,000 times on television last year'" (Lowry and Towles, 1989, p. 76). Television has become a major source of sexual learning for children and teenagers. Lowry and Towles replicated a 1979 study of sexual behavior on the soaps and found a substantial increase in sex between unmarried persons and a norm of promiscuous sex with few accompanying consequences (p. 76). In the 1987 study, there were 285 sexual acts involving unmarried partners and 12 involving husbands and wives, a ration of 23.7 to 1. This ratio would be 31 to one if aggressive sexual contact, prostitution, and other exploitive behaviors had been included. In this study there was no discussion about how to prevent pregnancy or sexually transmitted diseases. If the sample were projected for the year, 20,124 sexual behaviors would have occurred on the soaps, yet people rarely get pregnant or get STDs in "the soaps." "Safe sex," when mentioned, is usually treated as a joke (Lowry and Towels, 1989, p. 77).

The role of pornography in rape and child molestation has been reviewed and studied on a number of fronts. The concern of Marshall, et al.'s, study was the stimuli depicting the most serious sex crimes, (e.g., a male forcing a female to have sex or sex between adults and children). Goldstein, et al.'s (1971) studies indicated that sexual offenders had had considerable exposure to pornographic stimuli during adolescence (cited by Marshall, 1988, p. 284).

The 1970 Commission on Pornography and Obscenity found that most Americans are first exposed to explicit materials during adolescence. More that 50 percent of boys are exposed to explicit sex material by age 15; 50 percent of girls within the next year or two. By age 18, 80 percent of boys and 70 percent of girls have read descriptions of coitus and have seen pictures of it. The real culprit, however, is in the material that portrays violence, and in particular, violent sex. Studies have shown that exposure to violence on television increases children's level of violent behavior in real life (Jones, et al., 1985). Studies also show that children who are already having trouble handling their sexual-aggressive feelings are the most likely to imitate violence portrayed by the media.

CHILD SEXUAL ABUSE — CRIMES AGAINST CHILDREN

Perhaps one of the most difficult social issues to arise out of the misuse of sexuality is the sexual abuse of children. The effects of this abuse are far-reaching and long-lasting, as the child becomes the adult. The sexual abuse of children, pedophilia, is a serious legal offense, and almost all those arrested are males. Eighty-five to 90 percent of pedophilia involves someone known to the child — a relative, neighbor, or acquaintance. While the average age at conviction is 35, about 25 percent of these offenders are over 45. The molestation often happens for years before the offender is reported and arrested. Seventy to 80 percent of the offenders have been married at some time in their lives. Those who commit homosexual acts against children are usually relatives or acquaintances. Sometimes contacts are made through youth organizations. Those who sexually exploit children usually have been inadequately socialized and have poor interpersonal skills. They prefer the company of young boys because they do not feel comfortable around adults (Khatadourian and Lunde, 1975, pp. 341-343).

While it was once believed that incest was rare, we now know it is quite prevalent, not only amongst lower socio-economic groups but also among those in the upper social strata. It is one sexual offense that is universally condemned. Twenty percent of all female children and 9 percent of all male children are victims of sexual abuse (Jones, et al., 1985, p. 590). Incest involves any kind of sexual contact with relatives. It is more common between fathers and daughters than mothers and sons. Other offenders could be siblings, grandparents, aunts, uncles, and sometimes cousins. Children, especially girls, are at considerable risk of sexual abuse at the hands of parents and caretakers.

Children grow up in a world centered on adult beliefs and values. Abused children who tell their parents about the abuse often find that the adults refuse to believe them.

Several retrospective surveys of college-age females have identified a 20 to 30 percent rate of child sexual victimization. Strangers were involved in only 25 percent or less of the experiences. About half of the molesters were relatives, 22 percent resided within the child's home, and about 6 percent were fathers or stepfathers. These figures were drawn from a study of college students. High risk subjects would show even higher rates (Sgroi in Summit, 1987, pp. 175-176). "College girls in Finkelhor's sample, who were stepdaughters, experienced even higher odds of victimization: 50 percent. Surveys of foster children, runaways, drug addicts, and prostitutes show an incestuous background in the sixty to seventy percent range" (Summit, 1987, p. 176). Toufexis, in a recent issue of *Time* (September 24, 1990), relates that seven Roman Catholic clergy were charged in the mid-'80s with sexually abusing young boys in Louisiana. A more recent issue of *Time* (August 19, 1991), says, "Dozens upon dozens of priests have been accused of sexually abusing underage boys."

The misconceptions about sexual abuse of children are several:

1. Abusive parents are disadvantaged. (External stressors are prevalent in high risk families but internal stressors are similar for rich and poor.)

2. Abusive parents are basically criminal or psychotic. (The majority of abusive parents are normal intellectually and psychologically.)

3. Child abuse is rare. ("It is estimated that there are as many as 336,200 sexual offenses committed against children each year in this country" [Jones, p. 590]).

4. The abusive father is the victim of a provocative child. (This is a rationalization on the part of the father. Adult motivation can never be assigned to the child, [Jones, et al., 1985, pp. 590 ff]).

It is now known that stepfathers are far more often the molesters of their stepchildren (Jones, et al., 1985; Erickson, 1988). In one random sample survey of 930 adult women, 38% reported having experienced some form of unwanted sexual experience before age 14. Forty percent of these cases occurred within the family (Erickson, 1988). The legal requirements surrounding any form of child abuse are particularly important to understand. Most states now have laws that require anyone who suspects that a child has been abused or molested to report that suspicion to the proper authorities.

Childhood sexual abuse must be dealt with because of the traumatic effects it has during childhood, as well as on the abused child as an adult. Childhood victims suffer into adulthood with a variety of psychosocial problems. They may have difficulty forming interpersonal relationships, become asexual, and be rejecting of their own bodies. Furthermore, they may engage in self-hating, self-mutilating behavior and may become obese or develop other addictions. Personality disorders, distorted self-image, and occasionally even multiple personalities are reported among child abuse victims. Nightmares and attempted suicides are frequent. According to Williams and Fuller (in Strean, 1988, p. 465), 88 percent of sexually abused adults had repressed the memory for as long as 10 years (in Strean, 1988, p. 465). Not only are memories blocked, but if they do remember most children do not tell. Sadly, most children believe they are somehow to blame. Childhood sexual abuse is often intergenerational. As many as thirty percent of individuals who were sexually abused as children repeat the cycle with their own children (Strean, 1988, p. 465).

Several steps can be taken to help the child of sexual abuse or molestation.

1. Allow children to talk about how they feel. Let them talk about their hurt and angry feelings. Help the children understand that it is the offenders who are sick, not them, and that the offenders need treatment and need to be kept from hurting anyone else.

2. Reassure children of your protection. Sometimes they have been threatened. If at all possible, the offender should be removed from the home, not the children.

3. Help to reduce the children's feelings of guilt. The children need to know they are not bad or guilty and that it was not their fault even if the offender may have told them that it was.

4. Provide professional help. Parents and children will both need help in dealing with incidents and feelings about sexual abuse. The parents' reaction is very important to the process of the children's healing. If a parent is the offender, then outside help is definitely needed.

SEXUALLY TRANSMITTED DISEASES

Sexually transmitted diseases (STDs) are epidemic in our society. The misuse of sexuality in multiple and inappropriate sexual relationships has resulted in the spread of a variety of STDs throughout the population. Surveys reveal that people are widely aware of the risk of STDs but this does not seem to have changed their behavior very much.

The U. S. Public Health Service has kept records of the incidence of STDs for over forty diseases. In recent years, the combined number of cases of syphilis and gonorrhea has exceeded the combined total for all other diseases. There are an estimated 1 million new cases of gonorrhea each year but only about 1 in 4 is actually reported. Over 33,000 cases of primary and secondary syphilis are reported each year. It is important to understand that to be sexually active with anyone other than a sexually faithful spouse is to risk a sexually transmitted disease.

Birth control pills may have contributed to the STD epidemic because they have largely eliminated fear of pregnancy as a reason not to have sex. Sexual activity is begun at earlier ages with greater numbers of partners and, therefore, the risk of contracting an STD is greater than it has ever been. Gonorrhea and syphilis do not attack the sexual organs only. If left untreated, these diseases progress in any or all parts of the body including, heart, brain, and other vital organs. STDs can be transmitted to the fetus during pregnancy with often fatal or debilitating results to the newborn (Jones, et al., 1985, pp. 531-536).

Genital herpes, for which there is no known cure, is another STD, which afflicts over 20 million Americans. Another half million new cases are contracted each year. Women with genital herpes are at high risk to give birth to brain-damaged babies and to develop cervical cancer later in life (Jones, et al., 1975, pp. 531-536).

Vaginitis, Candida Albicans, trichimonis vaginalis, cystitis, chlamydia trachomatis, pubic lice (crabs), genital warts, and scabies are all sexually transmitted diseases. Chlamydia is a particularly damaging STD since the symptoms are often silent and many cases go untreated. Chlamydia has become one of the most common STDs. One study found that 22 percent of sexually active females are infected. Untreated chlamydia usually results in sterility and if the mother has the disease when pregnant, the baby is often born blind (Jones, et al., 1985, pp. 537-542).

Because homosexuals often have a variety of partners, some reporting hundreds of partners, they are particularly vulnerable to STDs. Specific sexual practices such as oral and anal sex contribute to the spread of diseases, including Hepatitis B and Acquired Immune Deficiency Syndrome (AIDS). AIDS is a particular concern for homosexual males but AIDS is also spread by IV drug use, contaminated blood used for transfusions, mother-to-fetus infections and heterosexual intercourse. AIDS is not the disease entity in itself; the human immunodeficiency virus (HIV) reduces the immune system's resistance to disease. The person then succumbs to one of the opportunistic diseases such Pneumocystis Carinii Pneumonia or Kaposi's Sarcoma (a kind of cancer). Unless sexually active persons, homosexual or otherwise, take proper precautions, they are at high risk for any sexually transmitted disease. Syphilis and gonorrhea also facilitate the spread of the AIDS virus (Cowley and Hagar in *Newsweek*, June 25, 1990).

There are serious physical effects of contracting an STD or AIDS, but the emotional and psychological effects can also be devastating. Acquiring any STD is a reminder that one or the other or both of the sexual partners has had sex with at least one other person. It really is true, that when a person has sexual intercourse, both partners bring into the experience all the other people with whom they have ever had sexual intercourse.

Because of the AIDS scare homosexual men are more likely to have changed their sexual behaviors and more are practicing "safe sex." Unfortunately, heterosexuals, for the most part, have not changed their sexual behaviors and are at increased risk for AIDS and other STDs. One recent study (Aral, et al., 1988) states that gonorrhea rates are higher among teens than any other age group. Clearly, families, schools, and churches must do much more to educate teens about the risks of sexual activity before and outside of marriage.

A CHRISTIAN RESPONSE

Any response to the issue of variant sexuality must come out of a sense of love and grace taught in Scripture. It is of necessity a difficult thing to contemplate the consequences of sexual sin, for they are very real and painful. There is a "sowing-reaping" principle (Galatians 6:7; Romans 6:23 RSV) in Scripture as well as the principles of love and grace. Important reminders are that God will never leave us or forsake us (Joshua 1:5; Hebrews 13:5), and His love is constant (Lamentations 3:22-23). God is rich in mercy, and His love will sustain us in dealing with the consequences (Ephesians 2:4; Psalms 55:22).

The first consequence is the lack of trust that develops as the result of non-commitment. D. H. Small states that there is no reversing the "shared secret." Once two people have had sex together, they can no longer behave as though they have not done so. Psychological and spiritual harm are inevitable. The following should be a guide that dating and engaged couples consider in their relationship. Rather than ask, "How far can we go?" better to ask: "Why do I want to go that far?" and, "How do my partner and I want to come to our marriage? What are the ways in our relationship that we can bring glory to God?"

The second consequence is the effects of extramarital relationships on spouses, children and extended family members. The breaking of trust is difficult to completely restore. Even if the marriage does not break up, there are often long-term effects. Each year over 1 million children are involved when families break up. They respond with distress, anger, loneliness, sadness, fear and guilt (Jones, et al., 1985; Lauer and Lauer, 1991).

The third consequence of sexual sin is that it puts distance between us and God when we break His laws. Remember, "we do not break God's laws, we break ourselves on them." God does not leave us but when we sin, our own guilt and loss of self-esteem may cause us to believe that we are worth less in His sight. The only way to remove this feeling of estrangement is to repent and ask God's forgiveness, as well as that of our spouse and children.

The fourth consequence is the social and economic costs to the individual and society. If a marriage breaks up, the wife is left with little financial support. She may be driven to seek public assistance to support her children, and in some cases, may end up homeless. Although there are many cohabiting couples, society is still not really comfortable or accepting of these arrangements and they often experience rejection. Much of society is becoming increasingly hostile toward homosexuals. Unwanted pregnancies among marrieds or unmarrieds have serious social and economic fallout. Finally as mentioned previously, consequences for STDs in society have been devastating physically, emotionally, socially, financially, and spiritually.

For the individual and society to be restored to sexual wholeness, several principles are important. Issues related to sexuality must be examined in the light of the Bible, which offers some general principles by which we are to live. Where sexuality is concerned, there is no such thing as "free love." There is nothing "fair" about an "affair." When we violate God's laws, there are always consequences, but, by "sowing in the field of the spirit, [we] will get a harvest of eternal life" (Galatians 6:7, *The Jerusalem Bible*).

A Christian ethic emphasizes social justice as defined by a loving heavenly Father. For example, it is never right to use another person to serve our own purposes, sexual or otherwise. When we serve others, we serve Christ. Christians must be open to admitting that child sexual abuse and sexual violence can go on in Christian or non-Christian homes and be willing to speak out against it and become advocates for the hurting and abused. To modify the admonitions in Matthew 25:31-46:

I was raped and you stood by me,
I was battered and you sheltered me,
I was abused and you intervened (quoted in Pellauer, et al., xxiii).

The primary emphasis of the Christian's life is not to fulfill self but to bring glory to God. "In all you do, in word or in deed, do to the glory of God" (Colossians 3:17).

Romans 12:1-2, "I beseech you therefore, [brothers and sisters], by the mercies of God that you present your bodies a living sacrifice, holy, acceptable unto God, which is your reasonable service. And be not conformed to this world: but be transformed by the renewing of your mind that you may prove what is that good, and acceptable, and perfect will of God."

Study and Discussion
Questions

1. Develop your own personal philosophy of sexuality. How do you see yourself as a sexual person? Are there any areas of your life that require healing grace for sexual hurt and damage?

2. Do you agree or disagree that premarital sex is not God's ideal for Christian couples? Why or why not?

3. Reflect on the kind of sex education you had as a junior high or high school student. If you were to develop a sex education program for junior high or high school, what would you want to include? Explain your reasons for your choices.

4. How did your parents communicate about sexuality? How satisfied were you with that communication? What will you do differently in your own family of procreation?

5. In today's world, how realistic is the expectation of marrying once and having it last for a lifetime? What is/was your expectation for yourself?

6. Twenty or thirty percent of today's college students have experienced sexual abuse or molestation as children. If you are one of these persons, how has it affected your life? If the offender was not a parent, do your parents know? How is healing happening for you?

7. What should the Church be doing to help victims of abuse? What steps can be taken to educate Christians and support abuse victims and their families?

8. At what age did you become aware that there are various sexual orientations? What are the factors in establishing your own sexual orientation?

9. How do you think Christians should relate to the issue of homosexuality and to homosexuals? How do you relate to them?

10. What have you done about the social problem of pornography? What are the ways pornography is damaging children and adolescents?

11. Why is rape the most underreported crime in America? How can victims of rape be helped and healed? How should the rapist be treated?

12. Most young people now know about STDs. Why do you think this knowledge is not a larger deterrent to sexual coitus outside marriage?

13. What should a Christian's reaction be to the AIDS problem? If a friend of yours got AIDS, how would you react to him or her, regardless of how they got the virus?

References

Abortion. *The Gallup Report.* February (Rep. #281):16-23, 1989.

Aral, S. O., J. E. Schaffer, W. Mosher, W. Cates, Jr., "Gonorrhea Rates: What Denominator is Most Appropriate." *American Journal of Public Health,* 78:702-3, 1988.

Beck, G. J. and D.K. Davies, "Teen Contraception: A Review of Perspectives on Compliance." *Archives of Sexual Behavior,* 16(4): 337-36, 1985.

Blumer H., *Symbolic Interactionism: Perspective and Method.* Englewood Cliffs, NJ: Prentice-Hall, Inc., 1969.

Boyajian, J. A. , "Standing by Victims of Sexual Violence: Pastoral Issues." In J.A. Pellauer, B. Chester, and J. A. Boyajian, *Sexual Assault and Abuse: A Handbook for Clergy and Religious Professionals.* San Francisco: Harper and Row, Publishers, 1987.

Brownmiller, S., *Against our Will: Men against Women and Rape.* New York: Simon and Schuster, 1975.

Christopher, F. S., "An Initial Investigation into a Continuum of Premarital Sexual Pressure." *The Journal of Sex Research.* 25(2): 255-266, 1988.

Cowan, G., C. Lee, D. Levy, & D. Snyder, "Dominance and Inequality in x-Rated Videocassettes." *Psychology of Women Quarterly,* 12:288-311, 1988.

Cowley, G., and M. Hager, "AIDS: the Next Ten Years." *Newsweek* (June 25):20-27, 1990.

Earle, J. R., and P.J. Perricone, "Premarital Sexuality: a Ten-year Study on Attitudes and Behavior on a small University Campus. *The Journal of Sex Research,* 22(3):304-310, 1986.

Erickson, W. D., N. H. Walbek, and R.K. Seely, "Behavior Patterns of Child Molesters." *Archives of Sexual Behavior,* 17(1): 77-86, 1988.

Garcia, L. T. , "Exposure to Pornography and Attitudes about Women and Rape: a Correctional Study." *The Journal of Sex Research,* 20:378-385, 1988.

Grecas, V., and R. Libby, "Sexual Behavior as Symbolic Interaction. *The Journal of Sex Research.* 12:33-49, 1976.

Greenberg, D. F., *The Construction of Homosexuality.* Chicago, Il.: University of Chicago Press, 1988.

Groth, A. N., and T.S. Gary, "Marital Rape." *Medical Aspects of Human Sexuality.* (March):122-131, 1981.

Haveman, E. and M. Lehtinen, *Marriages and Families: New Problems, New Opportunities.* (2nd Ed.) Englewood Cliffs, NJ: Prentice Hall, 1990.

Heilbrun, A. B., and M.P. Loftus, "The Role of Sadism and Peer Pressure in the Sexual Aggression of the Male College Student." *The Journal of Sex Research,* 22(3): 320-332, 1986.

"Homosexuality." *The Gallup Report.* 254(Nov.): 24-2, 1986.
Jerusalem Bible, The. Garden City, N. Y.: Doubleday & Co., 1966.

Jones, K. L., L.W. Shainberg, and C.O. Byer, *Dimensions of Human Sexuality.* Dubuque, Ia.: Wm. C. Brown, Pub., 1985

Katchadourian, H. A. and D.T. Lunde, *Fundamentals of Human Sexuality.* (2nd Ed.) New York: Holt, Rinehart, and Winston, 1975.

Klassen, A. D., C.J. Williams, and E.E. Levitt, *Sex and Morality in the U. S.: An Empirical Enquiry under the Auspices of the Kinsey Institute.* Middleton, CT: Wesleyan University Press, 1989.

Lauer, A. H., and J. C. Lauer, *The Quest for Intimacy.* Dubuque, Ia: Wm. C. Brown, Publishers, 1991.

Lewis, C. S. , *Screwtape Letters.* New York: MacMillan, 1959.

Lord, L. J. , "Sex with Care." *U. S. News and World Report,* (June 26-28): 53-77, 1986.

Lowry, D. T. and D.E. Towles, "Soap Opera Portrayals of Sex, Contraception, and Sexually Transmitted Diseases." *Journal of Communication,* 39(2): 76-83, 1989.

McCary, S. P. and J. L. McCary, *Human Sexuality.* Belmont, CA: Wadsworth Publ. Co., 1984.

McConaghy, N., "Heterosexuality? Homosexuality: Dichotomy or Continuum." *Archives of Sexual Behavior.* 16(5): 411-424, 1987.

Marshall, W. L., "The Use of Sexually Explicit Stimuli by Rapists, Child Molesters, and Nonoffenders. *The Journal of Sex Research,* 25(2): 267-287, 1988.

O'Keefe, N. K., K. Brockopp, and E. Chew, "Teen Dating Violence." *Social Work,* (Nov.-Dec.): 465-468, 1986.

Oswalt, J. N., "The Old Testament and Homosexuality." In Keysor, C. W., Ed. *What You Should Know about Homosexuality*. Grand Rapids, MI: Zondervan Publishing House. pp. 81-116, 1979.

Palmer, C. T., "Twelve Reasons Why Rape is not Sexually Motivated: A Skeptical Examination." *The Journal of Sex Research*, 25(4): 512-530, 1988.

Pellauer, M. D., B. Chester, and J. Boyajian, *Sexual Assault and Abuse: A Handbook for Clergy and Religious Professions*. San Francisco: Harper and Row, Pub., 1987.

Penner, C. and J. Penner, *A Gift for All Ages*. Waco, TX: Word, Inc., 1986.

Petersen, J. A. *The Marriage Affair*. Wheaton, IL: Tyndale House, 1971.

Petersen, J. A. , *The Myth of the Greener Grass*. Wheaton, IL: Tyndale House, 1986.

Robinson, I. E., and D. Jedlicka, "Change in Sexual Attitude of College Students from 1965-1980: A Research Note." *Journal of Marriage and Family*, (Feb.): 237-240, 1982.

Schutz, A. L., *The Phenomenology of the Social World*. Evanston, IL: Northwestern University Press, 1967.

Smithyman, S. D., "The Undetected Rapist." Ph.D. Dissertation. 1978. In Palmer, C. T. , "Twelve Reasons Why Sex is not Sexually Motivated: A Skeptical Examination." *The Journal of Research*, 25(4): 512-530, 1988.

Strean, H. S., "Effects of Childhood Sexual Abuse and the Psychosocial Functioning of Adults." *Social Work* (Sept.-Oct.): 465-467, 1988.

Stulberg, I., and M. Smith, "Psychosocial Impact of the AIDS Epidemic on the lives of Gay Men." *Social Work*, (May-June): 277-281, 1988.

Summit, R. , "Beyond Belief, the Reluctant Discovery of Incest." 1987. In Kirkpatrick, M., Ed. *Women's Sexual Experience: Explorations of the Dark Continent*. New York: Plenum Press, 1982.

Toufexis, A., "What to do When Priests Stray." *Time* (September 24): 79, 1990.

Winick, C., "A Content Analysis of Sexually Explicit Magazines Sold in an Adult Bookstore." *The Journal of Sex Research*. 21(2): 206-210, 1985.

CHAPTER 15
FAMILY VIOLENCE: INTRODUCTION

Professor O'Malley's article on family violence provides an excellent example of employing a variety of sociological perspectives when analyzing social problems. Her discussion includes the use of a wide range of theories that represent the social behavior, the social definition, as well as the social facts paradigms. What we can see from her analysis is that competing theories are not "true" or "false," but rather can compliment one another to reveal the complexity of a social problem.

The early explanations for family violence may be placed in the social behavior paradigm. These efforts were directed toward discovering personality traits and disorders that "caused" people to abuse family members, including mental illness and psychopathologies, as well as drug abuse. Theories that focused on the individual level, whether on biological or psychological causes of behavior, are able to explain only a small part of family violence.

Explanations from the social definition paradigm supplement those of the social behavior paradigm. The symbolic interactionist perspeetive, a more general theory that encompasses social learning and exchange theories, describes interaction that tends to impact family violence. The nature and quality of family members' interaction with one another, including child-rearing practices and marital relationships, tends to contribute to child, spouse, and elder abuse.

It is the social fact paradigm, however, that has dominated sociological analysis with its emphasis on the social milieu in which social action occurs. As O'Malley notes, two factors are especially important from this perspective in discussing a social-situational model: culture and structure. For a sociologist, culture includes the entire way of life of a society, all the physical objects created by its members as well as the nonmaterial abstract human creations. Nonmaterial culture, consisting of language, ideas, beliefs, values, rules, customs, skills, family patterns and myths, is particularly important in understanding family violence.

Sociologically speaking, the scriptures of any religion (including Christianity) are part of the nonmaterial culture. Common interpretation of them helps to influence the norms and practices of a society. As O'Malley points out, the Bible has been used to defend the use of corporal punishment in socializing children and to support male patriarchy. Both norms have contributed to a milieu in which violence may erupt in families.

Physical punishment, consisting either of spanking or hitting a child, depriving him of something desired, threats, or an angry tone of voice, is a common method of discipline. Many researchers have argued that punishment is not a particularly effective method of child socialization. Furthermore, it has been found to have negative consequences in that "violence tends to beget violence." When punished, any creature's first reaction (whether it be a human being or an animal) is usually to try to fight back. If that is impossible because of the opponent's superior strength, then the creature will try to run away. If necessary, the creature will finally comply, but dully and unenthusiastically. The general sociological assessment of the use of physical punishment is that it is a relatively cheap form of social control but that it is also relatively ineffective when compared with other psychological methods. Nevertheless, physical punishment is fairly popular in our society, with some Christians saying that God has blessed it. What Christians should be asking themselves is how well it fits in with Christ's command to love one another.

The Bible has also been used to support the patriarchal family, one in which authority and power is vested in the husband-father. This has been the dominant family type throughout human history, although the concept is a relative one. The degree of male authority varies considerably in different cultures and in different time periods. Religious writings have tended to mandate a patriarchal system. The Indian *Laws of Manu* (100 A.D.), for example, decreed: "In childhood a female must be subject to her father, in youth to her husband, when her lord is dead, to her sons; a woman must never be independent." The Koran (630 A.D.) stipulates: "Men have authority over women because Allah has made the one superior to the other, and because they spend their wealth to maintain them. Good women are obedient." Christianity is not unique in its historical support of patriarchy.

O'Malley challenges us to review biblical teachings against the cultural background of patriarchy. The patriarchal system has directly and indirectly affected the problem of violence against women by emphasizing the inferior and subordinate position of women. The cultural norms, whether they be of Hindu, Islamic, or Christian origin, have had a role to play in the perpetuation of violence against women. Some of these cultural norms have been enacted into legislation that permitted degrees of spouse and child abuse. Sir William Blackstone's *Commentaries on the Laws of England*, 1765, are illustrative:

> By marriage, the husband and wife are one person in law; that is, the very being or legal existence of the woman is suspended during the marriage, or at least is incorporated and consolidated into that of the husband; under whose wing, protection, and cover, she performs everything . . . Upon this principle, of a union of person in husband and wife, depend almost all the legal rights, duties, and disabilities that either of them acquire by the marriage . . . .

Although the ideal culture would be one in which the husband loved his wife as he loved himself (and did not abuse her), the patriarchal system set the stage for some domestic violence.

The culture may be seen as a base for the social structure. The family system, the legal system, and the religious system all embodied the patriarchal cultural norms. Although patriarchy has weakened considerably this century, male dominance does exist in residual forms. O'Malley and others contend that an ideology that furthers patriarchy, machismo, and male dominance is prone to violence.

Clearly, changes that would impact the degree of family violence in our society need to address the individual, interpersonal, and societal levels of analysis that are represented by the three major sociological paradigms. O'Malley makes us aware of the complexity of the issue through her insightful analysis — and also the complexity in any proposed solutions. Education, legislation, creation of shelters, and police response are all secular institutional responses to the problem of family violence in which Christians may be involved. Perhaps one of the greatest contributions that the Church as an institution can make toward dealing with the problem is to rethink some of the scriptures (as O'Malley has done) that tended to inadvertently foster family violence.

FAMILY VIOLENCE
Angeline J. O'Malley

Family violence is not a pleasant topic for study and discussion. When confronted with the facts and statistics, we are forced to acknowledge that violence is a reality of life for many families. Moreover, violence is a part of family life for many Christian families — even pastor/lay-leader families. Not only does violence occur in Christian homes, but it often goes unchallenged by the Church. In fact, the Church at times has contributed to mistreatment of women and children through complacency, insensitivity, and unbalanced teaching on male-female roles (Alsdurf & Alsdurf, 1989).

The acknowledgement of violence within the family disturbs our comfort zone. We like to think of family members as warm, loving encouragers and protectors. However, studies of physical violence within families reveal that the average citizen is more likely to be assaulted in his or her home by a family member than on the streets of the most dangerous city in the United States (Straus, Gelles, & Steinmetz, 1980).

Due to the private nature of North American families, it is difficult to obtain information on the amount of violence in families. However, the data that we do have indicate that it is not a rare phenomenon and that it is found in every kind of family. Furthermore, it can reach extreme levels. Family fights are cited as one of the most frequent reasons for police calls. Various studies indicate that family members comprise the largest single category of murder victims and that one-third of all murders involve relatives.

Prevalence of Violence

In one of the most extensive studies of child and spouse abuse, more than 2,000 American couples were interviewed (Gelles and Straus, 1979; Straus, Gelles, & Steinmetz, 1980). The researchers measured violent acts, not just abuse (which implies a destructive outcome of a violent act). It was found that within this representative sample of the nation, 16 percent of the couples admitted that they had engaged in at least one violent act against a spouse during the preceding year. Straus, Gelles, and Steinmetz (1980) concluded that at least 1.8 million women and 2.0 million men are abused each year by their spouses.

Results from this same study showed that 58 percent of the couples had used some form of violence toward children during the preceding year; 71 percent reported that they had done so at some time in past years (Gelles & Straus, 1979). The behavior reported by parents ranged from very mild to severe forms of biting, beating, and threatening with a weapon. Approximately 3 percent of the children had been kicked, bitten, or punched by their parents during the preceding year; and 8 percent had been similarly treated at other times. Four percent of the children were beaten at least one time while growing up, and 3 percent had been assaulted with a gun or knife. Considering the fact that these data are based on parental reports, we can speculate that the actual numbers are probably much higher.

Dating relationships, generally thought of in terms of romance, are also marked by violent behavior. More than 60 percent of the single people in one sample reported that they had been abused or abusive, or that they had engaged in aggressive behavior during courtship (Laner & Thompson, 1982). Nearly 12 percent of a sample of 644 high school students said that they had been involved in abusive behavior in a heterosexual relationship (Henton, et al., 1983). The abusive behavior included pushing, grabbing, shoving, slapping, kicking, biting, and hitting with the fist.

According to Gelles (1985), nearly a fifth of all families in the United States experience some form of family violence. Straus (1990) reports that three children, three wives, and two husbands are killed every day by their family members. Whatever the actual number of cases of abuse in families, those reported are sufficiently high to justify the assertion by Gelles and Straus (1979) that next to the police and the military, the family is the most violent social group in American society.

HISTORY OF FAMILY VIOLENCE

With the increased public awareness of domestic violence, it is commonly thought that a rapid increase in recent years in the amount and level of family violence has occurred. However, historical evidence suggests that the family has always been one of society's more violent institutions. Even so, domestic violence has not always been perceived as a problem. Violence against women and children has not in the past been viewed as improper or deviant. History of wife beating in Western society can be traced back to antiquity, in which the patriarchal family system was dominant. The husband, as the ruler and head, was expected to obtain obedience and to maintain control of his wife and children. In British common law, the "rule of thumb" allowed a husband to beat his wife but with a rod no thicker than his thumb nail to spare her permanent physical injury. As recently as the late nineteenth century in Great Britain and the United States, it was considered a husband's marital responsibility to control and chastise his wife through the use of physical force.

Until the twentieth century, children were regarded as property, subject to the whims of the family and society. Infanticide was practiced from early times through the Middle Ages. Infants could be put to death for several reasons: if they cried too much, if the family was already too large, or if the infants were sickly, deformed or had some perceived imperfection. Girls, twins, and children of unmarried women were especially vulnerable to infanticide (Robin, 1983). The biblical account of Abraham's intention to sacrifice his son Isaac to God illustrates the practice of offering babies to appease gods. In ancient Rome, a father could sell, abandon, or kill his child and still remain within the norms of society. Throughout history, children have been neglected, abandoned, and exploited.

Severe physical punishment of children was justified by the belief that it was a necessary part of discipline. Even today, the Bible verse, "He who spares the rod, hates his son" (Proverbs 13:24) is often quoted to justify beatings. While much of the physical and mental abuse experienced by children today is behind closed doors, it is not uncommon to see a child being hit or verbally abused in a public place.

Recognition of Family Violence as a Social Issue

As we have seen, the occurrence of family violence is not a new phenomenon. What is unprecedented is the recognition of such violence as a social problem. In the past, family violence was regarded as an isolated problem in disturbed families. Until 1970, *The Journal of Marriage and the Family* did not contain any reference to family violence. In contrast, the July 1987 issue contained a concentrated cluster of articles dealing with violence between family members. Furthermore, it is quite common to find at least one, and maybe several, articles dealing with domestic violence in any given issue of this journal.

The change in public attitude toward family violence did not happen overnight. In the United States, the roots of change can be traced to New York City where concern about the maltreatment of children led to the founding of the Society for the Prevention of Cruelty to Children in 1871. Other cities followed the example of New York City, and dedicated individuals began a concerted effort to make the public aware of the plight of many of the city's children. Even so, it was not until the early 1960s that Henry Kempe introduced the term "battered child syndrome." In 1961 Kempe conducted a symposium at the American Academy of Pediatrics that stimulated interest in the problem of child abuse.

Two major social forces were responsible for bringing family violence to the attention of the public. The children's rights movement of the 1960s focused attention on abused and neglected children, while the women's movement of the 1970s heightened public awareness of the problem of battered wives. In the late 1970s, attention was directed to the sexual abuse of children. As recently as the mid-1980s, abuse of elderly parents began to receive attention. It is now recognized that family violence is a social problem and that it is widespread and complex. Research has demonstrated that family violence transcends ethnic group divisions and social classes and occurs, to some degree, in almost all segments of society.

The consequences of domestic violence are well known. Spouse abuse exacts a high physical, psychological, and social price. Abuse may result in physical injuries requiring medical attention or hospitalization. Some abuse ends in death. Wife abuse is frequently cited as grounds for divorce, and is correlated with child abuse and child behavior problems. Victims of child abuse may suffer physical injury, neurological and intellectual impairment, developmental deficits, mental health problems, and behavioral problems. Domestic violence is a social issue that cannot be ignored!

Studying Family Violence

Two major challenges face those who study and investigate patterns of family violence. First, the issue is a sensitive one. Taboos prevail against discussing such a personal subject with either friends or strangers, making it difficult to gain access to the victims of violence and to establish rapport with them. In addition, the private nature of the family makes it difficult to use traditional research strategies to measure the extent and patterns of domestic violence. Questions also exist concerning the reliability and validity of data which have been obtained from self-report measures.

The second challenge is a conceptual one. Broad and varied definitions of abuse make it difficult to compare research findings of different investigators. Variations in definition also make it difficult to separate out of the data particular categories or levels of violence. For example, the National Survey of Family Violence (Gelles & Straus, 1979) defined violence as an act carried out with the intention or perceived intention of physically hurting another person. The physical hurt may be a slap or it may be murder; the definition does not make the distinction.

Three questions are typically addressed in a study of violence between intimates: 1) How widespread is such violence? 2) Who is at risk? 3) What causes people to be violent? The first question has been addressed at the beginning of this chapter. The remainder of the chapter will deal with the second and third questions, and also address implications for response by the Christian community.

CHILD ABUSE

Child abuse research, since it had the longest history, offers the largest body of findings. Child abuse is broadly defined and includes behaviors beyond the use of physical force: malnourishment, failure to care for and protect a child, sexual assault, failure to clothe a child, and psychological abuse (Lincoln & Straus, 1975). Increasingly, attention is being focused upon the devastating and long-term effects of emotional maltreatment — the continual belittling and degrading of children by parents and other caretakers.

Emotional abuse can be as harmful to children as physical abuse. Children who have suffered emotional maltreatment tend to feel unloved, rejected, unwanted, inferior, inadequate, and unrelated to any social unit. The effects of emotional abuse also include impaired self-esteem, emotional instability, unresponsiveness, and negativity. Maltreatment usually does not occur in one form, or in isolation from other types of abuse. Because the physical forms of abuse have received more attention and have a more extensive research base, this section will focus on physical and sexual abuse.

Physical Abuse

The term "child abuse" is intended to draw attention to those acts which deviate from appropriate standards of behavior for caretakers. It must be remembered that such standards carry over time, across cultures, and between social strata.

According to the above definition, child abuse would not include spankings that are moderate, noninjurious, appropriate to the age of the child as well as to the misdemeanor, and administered within the context of love and discipline — not administered out of parental anger. However, it is essential to note that spanking is the least effective form of discipline and more appropriate ways to instruct a child usually exist.

Statistics on child abuse are generally reliable, but estimates suggest that from 400,000 to 1.5 million children are vulnerable to physical injury. The harm from physical abuse can be severe. A 1983 study reported in the October 25 edition of the *San Diego Tribune* noted that two or three New York City children under the age of 6 were dying each week as a result of parental abuse or chronic neglect (Lauer, 1986).

Researchers have been successful in identifying who is at risk for physical child abuse partly because it is possible to obtain access to information from caseloads of child protection agencies. Children who have been physically or sexually abused are those who come to the attention of protective services.

Studies do not confirm the once-popular stereotype of child abusers as disturbed individuals. Rather, abusers are found to be parents caught in highly stressful and non-supportive circumstances. The high risk factor of stressful environments has been well documented. Low-income parents, teenage parents, parents without partners, and parents with unwanted children have all been demonstrated to have higher rates of abuse (Smith, 1984).

Parents are more likely to be abusive when caring for a child who has special needs such as illness, congenital defect, or hyperactivity; these needs demand intensive and extensive care. In addition to the physical and emotional fatigue which results from providing special care, the parents may find themselves socially isolated. Studies have shown that being cut off from family, neighborhood, or institutional supports generates a significant stress-related risk factor (Garbarino, 1976).

Child abusers have also been found to have ineffective and conflict-prone styles of parenting. They have unrealistic expectations of children, are overly reactive in their dealings with children, and have difficulty rewarding children for good behavior (Wolfe, 1985). Those who abuse children are more likely to have been subjected to harsh and abusive treatment as children (Straus, et al., 1980). This does not mean, however, that abused children are destined to be child abusers as adults. Many abused children grow up to be nonabusive parents.

Sexual Abuse

By comparison, much less is known about the risk factor underlying child sexual abuse. However, it is clear that the factors are different from those identified for physical abuse. For example, poverty and economic stress have both been shown to increase the risk for sexual abuse as they do for physical abuse (Finkelhor & Baron, 1986).

The terms "child sexual assault" and "child molestation" refer to the exploitation of a child for the sexual gratification of an adult. Such sexual abuse includes a wide range of activities — from incestuous behavior in the home to child prostitution and the use of children in the production of pornographic materials. Due to the nature of the problem, it is difficult to estimate the scope of the problem. A conservative estimate is that by 18 years of age, 19% of girls and 9% of boys are sexually abused (Finkelhor, 1984). Those at greatest risk are females and pre-adolescents between the ages of 10 and 12 (Finkelhor, 1984). Since most offenders are related to or known by their victims, child molestation most frequently occurs in the child's home (Geiser, 1979).

Retrospective studies of adults who were victims of sexual abuse as children have the significance of several family conditions. Daughters appear to be at greater risk for sexual abuse when their natural father is gone from the home, especially if they are living with stepfathers. Not only are the daughters at a greater risk than average from stepfathers, they are also at a higher than average risk from friends of the stepparent or friends of the natural parents. Daughters of single mothers who are actively dating and bringing home men friends, seem also to be at increased risk (Finkelhor, 1984).

Children seem more vulnerable to sexual abuse when the mother-child relationship is difficult due to the mother's illness, becoming incapacitated or emotionally unavailable. If the parent's marriage is characterized by conflict, this also has been found to put children at risk (Finkelhor & Baron, 1986). It is not entirely clear why these are risk factors. Perhaps family situations contribute to parental emotional deprivation and poor supervision of the children, both of which may be related to higher vulnerability.

It is recognized, with great sadness, that children and adolescents who have physical or mental disabilities are more likely to be sexually assaulted or abused than are youth without disabilities. The higher incidence of sexual abuse among this population has been attributed to social naivete, low self-esteem, and dependence on caregivers (Moglia, 1986). A study of blind females found that over 50% of girls who were blind from birth reported one or more forced sexual experiences (Welbourne, Lifscitz, Selvin & Green, 1983).

SPOUSE ABUSE

Wife Abuse
A rapid accumulation of new studies in the 1980s has led to the firm conclusion that there is little that distinguishes the battered wife from other women. Earlier notions that battered women held traditional attitudes regarding sex roles, suffered from low self-esteem, or manifested certain personality traits have not been substantiated by recent research. Instead, characteristics of the husband appear to be the best predictors of wife abuse (Finkelhor, Hotaling, & Yllo, 1988).

The composite of battering men, revealed by numerous research studies, is of individuals with extensive patterns of maladjustment and antisocial behavior. According to Hotaling and Sugarman (1986), batterers are more likely to have low educational attainment, low income and low occupational status. They are more likely to have low self-esteem, low levels of assertiveness and little sense of personal efficacy. Their history is likely to include sexual aggressiveness; violence toward others, including their children; and in some studies, police records. One of the most consistently replicated findings is that batterers, as children and adolescents, witnessed violence and abuse in their families of origin. Again, we must be careful not to conclude that witnessing violence at home destines one to be an abuser. There are many individuals who witnessed abuse at home as children who have grown up to treat their wives with great respect. But these are not the people seen by mental health professionals and social agencies — from whom we draw our data.

Most physical abuse and violence toward wives does not take the form of beating; it takes the form of throwing things, shoving, pushing, grabbing, slapping, or hitting. There is considerable evidence that a relationship exists between external stress and wife abuse. Incidents of violence tend to be more common at selected times such as during a wife's pregnancy, or following the husband's drinking. Other stress factors associated with wife abuse include unemployment of the husband, jealousy, and problems with children. These findings are consistent with general stress that suggests family violence occurs when an individual is under stress and lacks personal resources and coping strategies.

Existing research data is heavily concentrated in the areas of child abuse and wife abuse. The husband may also be a victim of spouse abuse.

Husband Abuse
Historically, it has been considered socially acceptable for wives to slap their husbands. Surveys show that wives often exceed their husbands in the use of physical violence during marital conflict. Although husband-wife relationships are primarily

male dominant, the use of physical violence has been found to be one of the few areas of marriage that approach equality between spouses (Straus, 1980). However, the effects of this violence are far from equal; Straus found that husbands usually cast the last and most damaging blows.

The high rate of violence by women can be explained by: 1) retaliatory violence; 2) implicit cultural norms that make the marriage license also a hitting license; 3) childhood training in the use of violence within the family; and 4) the high degree of frustration involved in marriages when the wife is relatively powerless in comparison with the husband (Straus, 1980).

Mutual Abuse

Mutual abuse is more common than either husband or wife abuse alone. Whereas husbands in a mutually abusive situation tend to view their marriage relationship as mutually violent, wives view their husbands as the violent one (Browning and Dutton, 1986). Both spouses report more violence for their partner than they are willing to acknowledge for themselves. Furthermore, spouses are more likely to report their own victimization rather that their own use of violence.

The effect of family structure in child abuse has already been discussed. It is evident from data on stepfamilies and remarriages that spousal abuse is also related to the social structure of the family. Findings show that spouse abuse is more likely in stepfamilies and families in which one or both spouses have been divorced, remarried, and reconstituted than in never-divorced intact families (Kalmuss and Sletzer, 1986). Explanations have centered on previously learned behaviors, the recurring selection of spouses who dominate or can be dominated, and higher levels of stress in remarried families. In any case, we can expect abuse to continue in reconstituted families unless there is third party intervention.

Spouse Abuse and its Effect on Children

Marital violence not only affects the husband and wife but also extends to those who witness the abuse — specifically their children. Children who witness the abuse of a parent may be at risk for behavioral and emotional difficulties, including psychosomatic disorders and aggression. In an exploratory study, students who witnessed parental violence were significantly more anxious than students from families with satisfactory relationships. Female students, in addition, showed elevated levels of depression and aggression (Forsstrom-Cohen & Rosenbaum, 1985). These findings are consistent with the "learned helplessness" model of wife abuse. When children see mothers in helpless situations, children get the message that women are helpless to control their own lives. This promotes depression in females — the ones most likely to identify with the victim-mother. In contrast, men who witness parental violence avoid depression because they are likely to identify with the aggressor-father. However, because they identify with the aggressor, these males are more likely as adults to abuse their wives.

ELDER AND SIBLING ABUSE

Elder Abuse

Elder abuse, with its short research history, has few national estimates. The figure quoted most frequently is that about 4% of the elderly are subjected to physical or mental abuse or both (Eastman, 1984). The elderly parent, abused most frequently and taken advantage of by sons and daughters, has become the stereotype of elder abuse. Our perceptions have centered around aging parents, particularly the mother.

Contrary to popular belief, the typical abused adult, rather than being a dependent, is more likely to be an older person supporting a dependent child of a physically or mentally disabled spouse (Pillemer, 1985). Older spouses are as likely as adult children to be guilty of abuse. Men are as likely to be victims as are women. The mistreatment may range from passive to active neglect to verbal and physical abuse.

No single factor has been identified as the cause of elder abuse. As with child abuse, explanations of elder abuse focus on learned patterns of violence, unresolved family conflict, the stress of caregiving, lack of family supports and pathology (mental illness, alcoholism, and drug abuse). The salient finding for intergenerational abuse and neglect is that violence occurs primarily within the context of shared family residence (Pillemer & Finkelhor, 1988).

Among the middle-agers, commonly referred to as the "sandwich generation," parental care combined with family stressors may deplete the family member's coping resources. Middle age is frequently a time of heavy occupational and financial demands, one in which there may be children and teenagers still at home. The middle generation may also be supporting young adult children who have not yet left the nest or young adults who have returned home after a divorce, job loss or other difficulty. Plus the young adult may return with spouse and children! As the baby boomers age and our population grows older, abuse of the elderly will demand increasing attention and concern.

Sibling Abuse

Sibling abuse receives the least amount of recognition and attention. It is the most frequent and also the most accepted form of violence with families today. Results of the Straus and Gelles research revealed that 40 percent of the children involved in the study had hit a brother or sister with an object during the preceding year, and 82 percent had engaged in some other form of violence against a sibling. This kind of behavior between siblings is not only tolerated, it is accepted as a normal outgrowth of sibling rivalry and jealousy. The conflict usually revolves around the distribution of resources (money, toys, and parental attention) or the family division of labor — otherwise known as chores. Identical acts between parents and child or husband and wife are in contrast grounds for criminal charges and social service intervention.

SOCIOLOGICAL EXPLANATIONS FOR FAMILY VIOLENCE

Early investigations placed the explanation for interpersonal violence within the psychology of the individual in the form of psychopathologies, mental illness, and alcohol or drug abuse. Efforts were directed toward discovering personality traits and disorders that "caused" people to abuse family members. Research indicates that less than 10 percent of family violence is attributable solely to psychological factors (Steele, 1978).

Current research suggests that a diverse and complex set of factors contribute to abuse within families. Any explanation of family violence requires a consideration of social factors, as well as psychological ones. Specific family environments, child-rearing practices, marital relationships, social attitudes, and social institutions affect the amount and level of violence between intimates.

Characteristics of family life which potentially can create a warm, supportive, and intimate environment also have the potential for making the family a violence-prone setting for its members and their interrelationships. Gelles and Straus (1979) have identified the following characteristics which contribute to making the family a violence-prone setting: the intense time spent interacting with one another; the wide range of activities and interests of family members; the intensity of involvement in impinging activities of multiple members wanting different things at the same time; the right to influence and attempt to change the behavior of others; the sexual age and differences which make the family an arena of cross-cultural conflict; the assignment of roles based on ascription rather than in interest and competence; the privacy and insulation of the family from both social control and assistance with conflict; the difficulty in terminating long-term marriage commitments and the impossibility of terminating birth relationships; the high levels of stress brought on by continual family changes associated with births, jobs, and aging; and the social norms which provide parents with the right to use physical violence.

Social-situational Model

A social-situational model of family violence is based upon the assumption that abuse and violence can be explained by two major factors: 1) external structural stress; and 2) cultural norms which sanction force and violence in the home. Considerable evidence suggests that there is a relationship between external stress and family violence. While family members recognize that they are expected to be loving and caring toward one another, some families do not have the psychological, social, or economic resources to meet these expectations. Structural stresses such as unemploy-ment, divorce, remarriage, limited educational resources, and illness may prevent individuals from meeting the expectations of society, friends, neighbors, family and even themselves.

Findings from cross-cultural research suggest that group norms and values often encourage or condone abusive behavior. The scripture, "Spare the rod, spoil the child" (Proverbs 13:24), seems to give social approval for the use of physical punishment in the United States. Yet, research across cultures shows that there is a relationship between the incidence of child abuse and wife abuse and the use of physical punishment with children. Incidence of abuse is either low or nonexistent in those cultures which do not practice or condone the physical punishment of children.

Drawing from general stress theory, family violence is likely to occur when family members are under stress and lack personal resources and coping strategies. Inability to meet expectations due to lack of resources, combined with cultural approval for violence may lead family members to adopt violence and abuse as a means of coping with structural stress.

Social Learning Theory

The underlying assumption of social learning theory is that children learn behavior that is modeled by significant persons in their lives. From this perspective, a reasonable explanation for violence is that it is learned at home. As noted earlier in the chapter, the family is the place where people are most likely to experience violence. The family is also where children first learn to cope with stress and frustration. Not only may individuals learn behavioral patterns of violence within their families, they may also learn social and moral justifications for their behavior: "I am doing this for your own good."

Social learning theory has gained widespread acceptance because it makes intuitive sense and because we have observed behavioral patterns of abusers and victims that have been passed down from one generation to the next. At the same time, there are many who escape the cycle of abuse. Less publicized is the fact that many victims of family violence do not grow up to become perpetrators or victims of abuse. Rather, they make personal commitments never to inflict such anguish on other people.

Patriarchy and Wife Abuse

At the macrosocial level, Russell and Rebecca Dobash (1979) provide a context-specific explanation for spouse abuse. The Dobashes assert that wife abuse must be examined against the background of a society that is patriarchal. They argue that economic, religious, and legal institutions have affected the status of women throughout history and therefore have directly or indirectly helped to create the problem of violence against women. The institutions emphasized the inferior and subordinate position of women and supported male domination and power. The Dobashes (1979) assert that the problem of wive abuse lies in the continuing struggle against this domination. The Dobashes' theory is helpful for explaining how society, itself, can be one source of violent behavior.

Social Exchange Theory

Gelles and Cornell (1985) have proposed the use of social exchange theory to integrate the central elements of the various theories. One of the major assumptions of the exchange theory is that human interaction and choice are guided by the seeking of rewards and the avoidance of punishment and costs. From this perspective, family members would be expected to use violence only when the real or perceived costs of being violent did not outweigh the rewards.

The rewards and costs of violence operate at personal, familial, community, and societal levels. Potential significant costs of violence include retaliation by the victim, arrest, imprisonment, loss of status, or family dissolution. Thus, police intervention, criminal charges, imprisonment, loss of status, and loss of income are forms of social control that have the potential to raise the costs and lower the rewards of violent behavior. Social control is only one facet of the possible responses to family violence. Research during the last two decades recognizes abuse as a dysfunction that requires prevention and treatment rather than punishment.

PREVENTION AND TREATMENT

The dynamics of family life are complex; sources of family violence are not fully understood; and family specialists do not know exactly how to eliminate or decrease the problem. Research does show that family violence is rooted in the fundamental problems of the family such as early parenthood, poverty, male dominance, and physical punishment (Strays, 1990). In addition, there is consensus about who is at risk and what types of families are likely to experience domestic violence. This information can form the basis for prevention programs aimed at reducing the amount of family violence by targeting vulnerable groups.

Family Life Education

Aggression has been linked with cultural values and patterns. Common denominators of family violence appear to be social stress and isolation. Violence is frequently the result of a lack of social supports in times of personal and family stress. Besides the observable and measurable support problems, there is also an amount of intense conflict or alienation within some families that cannot be measured. It is reasonable to assume that supportive problems occur in most families some of the time, and they may occur in a few families most of the time. It is essential, therefore, that family life education programs are made accessible to those populations most vulnerable to violence and abuse. Ideally family life education programs should be accessible to all families, so that members can learn ways to reduce and manage stress. In addition, such programs often become supports for individuals and couples dealing with similar issues.

Family life education can be offered in churches, schools, and community centers. Television, newspapers, and magazines are effective tools for disseminating information. Within family life education groups, couples learn to relate to each other as equals and to negotiate differences, reducing violence and divorce. Individuals have the opportunity to learn and practice problem-solving and communication skills in a "safe" setting. Couples are encouraged to develop support networks and to seek out appropriate professional help.

Family life education programs help families develop realistic expectations for marriage and family life. Adults learn how individuals and families change over the life span. This information can provide a knowledge base for awareness of personal needs as well as those of spouses, children, and other family members. Adults with an understanding of human development are more likely to hold realistic expectations for themselves, their mates and their children.

Workshops help parents learn effective discipline strategies and how childish behavior can be managed without using violence. Divorce recovery workshops and family life education for stepfamilies reduce potential abuse by helping individuals recognize and deal with issues and stresses related to changes in family structure. Workshops targeting the sandwich generation heighten awareness of support services available for aging family members.

Family life education is crucial for all members of the family, including children and teenagers. Learning about patterns of human development contributes to self-understanding and awareness of needs of siblings, parents, and grandparents. All family members benefit by learning to communicate and care for one another, to solve problems and to manage personal and familial stress.

Shelters

Shelters are a vital community resource for physically abused wives, providing needed respite from the abuser, a time and place to think clearly, consider alternatives, and to make decisions concerning the future of the relationship. Over 700 shelters in the United States provide room, board, and support services to battered wives. The effects of a shelter stay seem to vary according to the individual. For women who are able to take control of their lives, a shelter stay reduces the likelihood of new violence. For others, shelters have no impact; they may even trigger retaliation by the abuser.

Police Response

Police response with a follow-up arrest is another community resource that appears to be effective in spouse abuse incidents. Research shows that, during a two-year period in one California county, arrests deterred new wife-battery incidents. Reduction in wife-battery was greatest and especially effective for batterers whom police would ordinarily be inclined to arrest (Berk & Newton, 1985). Minneapolis experiments compared the effectiveness of three options: arresting the abuser, providing arbitration for the couple, and separating the couple. The study found that arresting the abuser resulted in a significant reduction in the amount of further reported abuse (Sherman & Berk, 1984). As a result of studies like these, police departments around the nation are beginning to adopt mandatory arrest policies in cases of wife abuse.

In Lexington, Kentucky, government and mental health agencies are redefining how their county should deal with spouse abuse. Their efforts include an arrest-minded Domestic Violence Unit at the police department, a pro-prosecution stance at the county attorney's office and a therapy program that teaches spouse abusers how to break the recurring pattern of violent behavior. If an abuser pleads guilty, he is given a choice: he can face fines, probation, and possible imprisonment; or he can enroll in the Domestic Violence Diversion Project.

The project is a 16-week program designed to teach abusers how to deal with their anger in nonviolent ways. If the abuser successfully completes the course, charges are dropped. The course covers such topics as anger management, communication, stress reduction, conflict reduction, and the role of drugs and alcohol in spouse abuse. Simultaneously, there are therapy groups for the women. The women are taught that abuse is a lethal way to communicate, placing physical safety at risk, and how to disengage from the batterer.

Legislation

Child Abuse and Treatment Act Legislation has been passed to protect the rights of children. All states and territories have protective statutes that assume basic child protective rights. Spouse abuse is beginning to be addressed by the legislative systems. Marital rape, a relative common form of sexual abuse experienced by wives, has been recognized as a crime in 44 states. Family professionals are calling for national policies on equality between men and women at home and in the workplace.

Courts must affirm protection for children and spouses. Why is it acceptable to hit a child, brother or spouse? The same behavior toward an employee, coworker, or a salesperson is not tolerated. Furthermore, in these cases it is considered criminal behavior. It is essential that resources be allocated for treatment programs for those who have been abused as well as for abusers. Ultimately, policies aimed at prevention are the only effective long-term answer. Community programs, activities and projects aimed at preventing abuse of children and other family members need our strong and committed support.

A CHRISTIAN PERSPECTIVE

Biblical Teachings

Family violence is sin. It is contrary to God's plan for the family and for human relationships. God's plan for His people is peace and love. Misunderstanding of biblical teachings on the authority of the husband and submission of the wife, as well as the Christian community's historical teaching that marriages should be kept in tact at all cost, have contributed to the problem of family violence. The emphasis has incorrectly been placed on wives submitting to their husbands, instead of on mutual submission. Couples need to understand that wifely submission is a result of trust in Christ not in the role of wife. All believers are expected to submit to other believers out of reverence for Christ (Ephesians 5:21).

The gender-role stereotype of the husband as a strong, dominant, aggressive leader is a cultural one; it is not supported in Scripture. The Bible affirms the husband as leader of the family; but society's notion of the naturally aggressive and authoritarian male is false. The biblical style of leadership is servant-leader. The supreme example of leadership is Jesus Christ who came to serve (Mark 10:42) and who gave himself up a fragrant offering and sacrifice (Ephesians 5:2).

Common Christian interpretations of suffering have reinforced the belief that pain and suffering are the result of personal sin. This interpretation has fed the guilt of abused wives and children, strengthening their perception that somehow the abuse is their fault and that they deserve it. Whereas personal sin generally does result in suffering, it cannot be reasoned that all suffering is due to the sufferer's sin. (The experience of Job illustrates that suffering is sometimes the result of other than personal sin. In his case, it was the result of an other-worldly confrontation between good and evil.)

Furthermore, because the Bible reveals suffering as a model of Christian devotion — part of a divine plan to reveal the glory of God and to promote Christian maturity — abused wives are encouraged by some clergy to stay in an abusive marriage out of faithfulness to God, serving as a model to their husbands and to the world of Christian devotion. 1 Peter 2:12 is offered as scriptural support for this stance. However, "the longer the abused woman stays in her situation, the more her partner's and her own respect for herself erodes. Children in such situations initially support their mother, but after prolonged exposure to the violence and her failure to do anything about it, they become disillusioned with her and often begin to side with the abusive father" (Suttor & Green, 1985, p. 15). If the abused woman is a Christian, she brings about the reverse of Peter's intended effect (1 Peter 2:12); and the world begins to question and eventually to reject the woman for her lack of appropriate action.

How do we reconcile the belief that Scripture does not require a woman to make herself and her children vulnerable to repeated abuse with scriptural teaching on the commitment to marriage? It may be necessary for some couples to separate for a period of time. Separation does not indicate a lack of commitment. Rather, because of commitment to one another and to the institution of marriage, a time of separation can be used constructively to rebuild a relationship. It can be a holy time of repentance, healing and growth. Separation can be viewed as an opportunity to learn new patterns of relating to one another and new ways of coping with stress and conflict.

An abusive act is never an isolated event; it increases the probability of additional acts of abuse. The various forms of abuse discussed in this chapter are related to one another and have common roots. They are part of a system which impacts everyone. Abuse is everyone's problem including the Church's. Christians may either feed the cycle of abuse or help to break it. It is vital that we take personal and communal responsibility for challenging and reducing the present level of violence within families.

Personal Response

God's people help prevent abuse by reporting suspected cases of child abuse and by supporting legislation that sends the message to the community that abuse is wrong. Violence-provoking external stress can be alleviated by reducing poverty, inequality, unemployment, and by working for adequate housing, food, medical care, and educational opportunities. Christians who support legislation that allocates resources for services to families play a significant role in the reduction of domestic abuse and violence.

The ultimate solution to the problem of family violence is not with police action, courts, or governments. It is the transforming power of the love of Jesus Christ expressed through His people and His Church.

His people can show compassion for the abused and the abuser. Most abusive people are confused, stressed out, and undisciplined. They need understanding, information, services, and treatment; they need a friend, the love of God, and the transforming power of the Holy Spirit. God's people can provide that needed friendship; we can share God's love; and we can link the abused and the abusive to information, services, and opportunities for treatment.

Families at risk for violence and abuse have unrealistic expectations of themselves and others. Dysfunctional patterns of dealing with frustration and stress have developed. From a Christian perspective, new perceptions of self and others, self-control, growth, and behavioral changes come through new life in Jesus and the power of His Holy Spirit within the context of a supportive Christian community. The Body of Christ is The Community with the resources — specifically, The Source — of forgiveness, reconciliation, healing, and love.

The Church's Response

There are churches in every community seeking ways to reach out to those in need. Church members look for mission fields across the world, while the needy sit in their midst and live within the shadows of their steeples and crosses. The Church is the one institution in the community where we find individuals of all ages and families at all stages of the life cycle. It is the one institution most likely to have contact with families over the lifespan. Consequently, family life education and family ministry programs in local churches are excellent avenues for dealing with family concerns from the cradle — or conception — to the grave. Because of the Church's involvement with families during times of crisis and transition, it is able to offer intentional, consistent, and continuous ministry — as opposed to hit-or-miss, cafeteria-style efforts.

Churches are beginning to offer awareness, intervention, and treatment programs.

302

Some programs are being offered directly by the Church. Others are cosponsored with community agencies and local schools. It is reasonable to assume that only a percentage of victims will be identified; and an even smaller percentage of that group will receive treatment services. Consequently, it is important to emphasize programs and ministries that focus on prevention. Preventive efforts have the potential of reaching large numbers of individuals and short-circuiting abuse before it occurs.

The cycle of family violence can be broken through education of today's parents and also of their children who will be the parents of tomorrow. Premarital counseling, marriage enrichment, parent education, divorce recovery, stepfamily education, financial management seminars, and stress management workshops help family members develop realistic expectations for self and others and strengthen communication and coping skills. Much of the needed education can be included within existing structures of the Church such as Sunday school, vacation Bible schools, workshop services, youth groups, retreats, and special activities and events. Within a circle of Christian fellowship and discipleship, persons experience God's love, gain new insights and skills, and develop a healthy balanced view of self.

In spite of various preventive efforts, there will always be family members who attack one another. Abusers and the abused need someone to listen, to care, and to lead the way to recovery. Professionals are required by law to report child abuse cases. Those guilty of abuse therefore cannot call a doctor, therapist, or social service agency without fear of being reported and having their children removed from the home. In the case of adult abuse, there is fear that the abused spouse will be encouraged to abandon the abuser, criminal charges will be filed, and community reputations will be tarnished. The Church can respond to this need by providing shelter and counseling for the abused, establishing support groups for the abusive and abuser, and staffing crisis hotlines. Some churches sponsor Parents Anonymous chapters for those at risk of child abuse, train lay counselors to work with victims of abuse, and provide relief for exhausted and stressed parents through drop-in nurseries, mother's day out, and other forms of volunteer respite care. Intercessory prayer groups undergird the various family ministries.

A single congregation cannot possibly provide all the needed resources and ministries. At the denominational and community level, churches need to cooperate with one another with community agencies to serve those who are suffering or at risk of family violence. Churches can pool resources, cooperate at the point of programming, and together collect funds and recruit volunteers for community agencies that serve families. A cooperative spirit as we serve those in need is a prime example of discipleship. "If you have love one for another, then everyone will know that you are my disciples" (John 13:35, GNB).

Study and Discussion
Questions

1. Define violent behavior. Be specific. Is violence ever justified in families? Under what conditions? Explain your answers.

2. Describe characteristics of family life which make the home a violence-prone setting for family members.

3. Identify and explain the major factors associated with violence against children.

4. ˙ What are the characteristics associated with marital violence? Why do many women stay with their husbands in spite of repeated abuse?

5. How is family structure related to child and spouse abuse?

6. How has the Church contributed to mistreatment of women and children?

7. As Christians, what is our personal responsibility for challenging and reducing violence in society? What are some specific ways that we can carry out this responsibility?

8. Discuss the role of the Church in the prevention and treatment of abuse within families.

9. What is your church presently doing to meet the needs of families within the congregation? Families within the community? What needs are currently not being met within your church? Community?

10. What additional ministries, programs, services, could your church initiate to meet needs?

References

Alsdurf, J., and P. Alsdurf, *Battered into Submission: The tragedy of wife abuse in the Christian home.* Downers Grove, IL: InterVarsity Press, 1989.

Berk, R. A., and P. J. Newton, "Does arrest really deter wife battery? An effort to replicate the finding of the Minneapolis Spouse Abuse Experiment." *American Sociological Review*, 50, 253-262, 1985.

Browning, J., and D. Dutton, "Assessment of wife assault with the Conflict Tactics Scale: Using couple data to quantify the differential reporting effect." *Journal of Marriage and the Family*, 48, 376-379, 1986.

Dobash R. E. and R. Dobash,*Violence Against Wives.* NY: Free Press, 1979.

Eastman, P., Elders under siege. *Psychology Today.* January, p. 30, 1984.

Finkelhor, D. , *A Sourcebook on Child Sexual Abuse.* Beverly Hills, CA: Sage, 1986.

Finkelhor, D., *Child Sexual Abuse: New Theory and Research.* NY: Free Press, 1984.

Finkelhor, D., and L. Baron, "Risk factors for child sexual abuse." *Journal of Interpersonal Violence*, 1. (19), 43-71, 1986.

Forsstrom-Cohen, B., and A. Rosenbaum, "The effects of parental marital violence on young adults: An exploratory investigation." *Journal of Marriage and the Family*, 47, 467-472, 1985.

Garbarino, J. A., and G. Gilliam, *Understanding Abusive Families.* Lexington, MA. D. C. Heath & Co., 1983.

Geiser, R., *Hidden Victims: Sexual Abuse of Children.* Boston: Beacon Press, 1979.

Gelles, R. J., "Family Violence." In R. Turner (Ed.). *Annual Review of Sociology*, II. 347-367. Palo Alto, CA: Annual Reviews Inc., 1985.

Gelles, R. J. and C. P. Cornell, *Intimate Violence in Families.* Beverly Hills, CA: Sage, 1985.

Gelles, R. J., and M. A. Straus, "Determinants of violence in the family: Toward a theoretical integration." In W. R. burr et al. (Eds.), *Contemporary Theories about the Family.* vol. 1, (pp. 549-581). New York: Free Press, 1979.

Henton, J., R. Cate, J. Koval, S. Lloyd, and S. Christopher, "Romance and violence in dating relationships." *Journal of Family Issues*, 4. 467-482, 1983.

Hotaling, G., and D. Sugarman, "An analysis of risk markers in husband to wife violence: The current state of knowledge." *Violence and Victims*, 1 (2), 101-124, 1986.

Kalmuss, D., and J. Seltzer, "Continuity of marital behavior in remarriage: The case of spouse abuse." *Journal of Marriage and the Family*. 48. 113-120, 1986.

Laner, M. and J. Thompson, "Abuse and aggression in courting couples." *Deviant Behavior: An Interdisciplinary Journal*. 3. 229-244, 1982.

Lauer, R. H., *Social Problems and the Quality of Life*. Dubuque, IA: Wm. C. Brown Publishers, 1986.

Lincoln, A. J., and M. A. Straus, *Crime and the family*. Springfield, IL: Charles C. Thomas Publisher, 1985.

Moglia, R., "Sexual abuse and disability." *SIECUS Reports*. 14(4), 9-10, 1986.

Pillemer, K., "The dangers of dependency: New findings on domestic violence against the elderly." *Social Problems*, 33. 146-158, 1985.

Pillemer, K. and D. Finkelhor, "The prevalence of elder abuse: A random sample survey." *The Gerontologist*. 28. 51-57, 1988.

Robin, M., "Historical introduction: Sheltering arms: The roots of child protection. " In E. H. Newberger (ed.), *Child abuse* (pp.1-41). Boston: Little, Brown, 1983.

Sherman. L. W. and R. A. Berk, "The specific deterrent effects of arrest for domestic assault." *American Sociological Review*, 49. 361-272, 1984.

Smith, S. L. "Significant research findings in the etiology of child abuse." *Social Casework*. 65. (6), 337-346, 1984.

Straus, M. A. "A sociological perspective on the causes of family violence." In M. R. Green (ed.), *Violence and the Family* (pp. 7-31). Boulder, CO: Westview Press, 1980.

Straus. M. A. "Family Violence." In D. H. Olson & M. K. Hanson (Eds.) *2001: Preparing Families for the Future*. (pp. 26-27). Minneapolis, MN: Bolger Publications/Creative Printing, 1990.

Straus, M. A., R. J. Gelles, and S. K. Steinmetz, *Behind Closed Doors:*

Violence in the American Family. Garden City, NY: Anchor Press, 1980.

Suttor C., and H. Green, *A Christian Response to Domestic Violence: A Reconciliation Model for Social Workers.* St. Davids, PA: North American Association of Christians in Social Work, 1985.

Welbourne, A., S. Lifschitz, H. Selvin, and R. Green, "A comparison of the sexual learning experiences of visually impaired and sighted women. " *Journal of Visual Impairment and Blindness*, 77. 256-259, 1983.

Wolfe, D. A. "Child-abusive parents: An empirical review and analysis." *Psychological Bulletin*, 97. (3), 462-482, 1985.

CHAPTER 16
GENDER INEQUALITY: INTRODUCTION

In both secular and religious writings, perhaps no single topic in family issues has received more attention than the changing roles of men and women. The debate continues to rage over what is determined by nature and what is learned through nurture. The social behavior paradigm, for example, would emphasize the preeminence of biology over social learning. The social definition paradigm, on the other hand, would place its emphasis on the process by which meanings have been socially created and differ from culture to culture. The social fact paradigm, like social definition theories, favors nurturing or social learning over biological interpretations in explaining gender differences.

The nature-nurture debate has a parallel concern in the writings of Christians who seek to determine what is revealed by God and what is an artifact of a particular culture. For example, did God ordain that women were to be controlled first by their fathers and then by their husbands or is patriarchy a product of particular time and culture? Christians are far from agreement about the specifics of appropriate gender roles, with writings ranging from traditional patriarchal tracts to the call for equality from Christian feminists.

Sociology of knowledge, a branch of sociology, concerns itself with how we know what we know. Most sociologists would note that the Scriptures themselves have been produced in a particular cultural milieu. Although most readers of this book accept the Bible as the Word of God, they likewise realize that there was a specific cultural milieu through which the revelation of God was transmitted. The Holy Spirit has used human instruments to convey God's truths, and these human instruments lived in a patriarchal culture. Many of the writings bear this patriarchal bent, with Jesus' teachings being a noteworthy exception. In spite of its patriarchal human origins, however, the Holy Spirit has given us a word that is often patriarchal (if we adhere to the letter of the law), but is remarkably equalitarian in spirit. This equality is perhaps best summed up in Paul's statement: *"In Christ there is neither male nor female"* (Galatians 3:28).

Until recently, western culture has been overwhelmingly patriarchal. From a sociology of knowledge perspective, this patriarchy has influenced philosophy, art, science — in short, all knowledge systems, including religion. Patriarchal values still influence the Church where theologians, priests, and preachers alike often interpret the Bible from the perspective of a male viewpoint. For example, many gloss over biblical passages that reveal feminine traits of the Godhead, while emphasizing the masculine ones. Similarly, female characters such as Mary, the mother of Jesus, Deborah, Esther, or Mary Magdalene, are rarely preached about with the same admiration as Nehemiah, Jeremiah, Peter or Paul. Patriarchal values often blind believers to feminine values found in the Scriptures.

Secular feminists have alerted the larger world to the sexism inherent in our culture. Christian feminists have attempted, with much less success, to do the same in the Church. Unfortunately the male bias runs deep and many Christians are reluctant to even consider the possibility that a cultural bias has influenced their reading of the Bible.

Recent research findings reported by Kathryn Feltey and Margaret Poloma ("From Sex Differences to Gender Role Beliefs," *Sex Roles*, August, 1991) suggest that the sexism found in many churches may be detrimental to attracting persons who subscribe to equalitarian gender roles. Feltey and Poloma used survey data collected from 584 randomly selected respondents to determine the impact that gender ideology has on religiosity. Their gender role ideology index contained five items: (1) "women should take care of running their homes and leave running the country to men," (2) "it is much better for everyone if the man is the main provider and the woman takes care of the home and family," (3) "it is more important for a wife to help her husband's career than to have one herself," (4) "when men and women are in the same organization, women should let men take the lead and try not to take over," and (5) "most men are better suited emotionally for politics than are most women."

Feltey and Poloma found that both men and women who took a more traditional stance on gender ideology scored much lower on five of the six criteria used to measure religiosity than those who took a more modern position. Those who were more traditional in their attitudes toward gender roles were more likely to adhere to orthodox Christian beliefs, to pray and to attend church more frequently, to have experiences of God during prayer, and to report that religion was very important to them. The only measure of religiosity not impacted by the gender ideology scale was divine intimacy. Neither a traditional nor a modern attitude toward women's roles seemed to affect the closeness of a respondent's relationship to God. What their findings do suggest, however, is that while subscribing to a modern gender ideology does not seem to influence one's personal relationship with God, it does affect men's and women's involvement in institutional religion. The traditionalism in many churches may be keeping away those with a more equalitarian ideology.

Professor Lindblade's thought-provoking article provides a challenge to Christians to rethink traditional attitudes. She suggests that gender inequality is at the base of all stratification, and that it is the place to begin to diminish inequality in relationships between men and women. Her biblically based and sociologically informed presentation serves as a good transition between Part III on the family and Part IV on inequalities.

GENDER INEQUALITY:
A SOURCE FOR SOCIAL STRATIFICATION

Zondra Lindblade

Social stratification: the systemic, unequal distribution in society of valued objects, opportunities, and life chances. This system is like a layered cake — the top layer gets the frosting, and the bottom layer bears the weight. For many, the "American Dream" means getting a greater individual share of the frosting. Personal "success" is defined as achieving a higher position and is symbolized by material goods and elite services — cars, fine houses, cruises to the Bahamas and season tickets to the symphony. Social esteem is also associated with success. Admired persons (we know they are admired because these are the ones we select to be the elders in our churches, the presidents of community organizations, and the chapel speakers in our colleges) are those who have fulfilled the obligation of striving for high status, and who have won over the competition. Upward social mobility is seen as a goal of a college education — the satisfaction of parents' hopes and a sign of God's blessing.

But the "dream" is zero-sum game — only a few win the frosting, many bear the weight, and some scramble for the leftover crumbs. Whether we are looking at experiences of the elderly, women, the poor and/or ethnic minorities we find the situation at the bottom layers repeated — demeaning environments, often inhumane and unloving treatment from the "frosting" group and subtle injury to human dignity and self-respect. *Do we care as long as we are moving toward the frosting?*

But it is also possible that the winners are really losers. The ones who get the frosting come to think of themselves more highly than they ought to think. Their activity often is focused on the symbols of accomplishment — prestige, recognition, money — rather than the substance of achievement itself (Abrahamson, et al., 1976). As Christians run toward the frosting, our momentary rejection of servanthood and even integrity may become permanent. The culture has "squeezed us into its mold," and we center most of our activities on protecting favored positions in society or on getting closer to the frosting.

Most sociologists refer to this system of frosting, cake, crumbs, and resulting alienation by using technical-sounding phrases such as "social class system," or "system of inequality," or "stratification system." These conceptualizations hide the stark, ugly realities of injustice that are generic to any kind of status hierarchy. Christians, along with others, use complex rationalizations to support social inequality. "Blaming the victim" is a favorite — unequal treatment is deserved because the group has gotten old, has unacceptable skin color, is defined as lazy, and/or was created to be helper, not

---

A version of the material in this chapter has been previously published in Leming, Michael, et al. *The Sociological Perspective*: A Value-Committed Introduction. Grand Rapids, MI, Zondervan Publishing House: 1989.

leader. Or we dislike the inequality, but shrug and recognize that "this is a sinful world," and will remain so until Christ returns. Eschatology helps to take care of any momentary sense of responsibility for the losers. Some of us even rationalize that injustice can be used by God to bring the group to faith in Him, that social position will change when the group is reconciled to God, or that God will help persons adjust to their degrading social positions.

We need to examine the sociological descriptions of systemic inequality and its destructive effects. We also need to expose our carefully packaged rationalizations and see them for what they are. They are not truth; they are lies. Perhaps a chapter on stratification in a sociology text begins the process. However, the continual and growing presence of systemic inequality suggests that studying about inequality has not done the job — for many have read chapters on stratification in the past and have continued their lifestyle unchanged. We do not yet understand the injustice, nor do we act. Looking at *three* contemporary examples of social inequality may deepen our understanding and move us to action.

FIRST, THE EXAMPLE OF POVERTY: "LOOSE MORALITY"

Recent media attention has focused on the "underclass" in the United States. This group is made up of those living in poverty from one generation to the next. They are quasipermanent recipients of social welfare who live out the attitudes of the "culture of poverty" — lack of goal striving, apathy, hopelessness, and perception of external barriers to getting ahead (Lewis, 1966). Sometimes a loose sexual morality is associated with the welfare dependence of this group. Let's examine the evidence related to loose morality, and investigate how the social inequalities of American society may contribute to the situation.

It is true that pregnancies among unmarried teenagers have increased to epidemic proportions in the underclass (NCHS, 1984). Health care indicators show a cycle of related physical miseries — malnourished teen-age mothers producing low birth-weight and/or physically handicapped infants who have diminished life chances, diets with insufficient protein for the child's healthy brain development, deprivation in parenting skills and lack of positive coping mechanisms for mothers raising children alone. These miseries seem to be the result of individual and immoral choice. However, in what ways could the inequities of the system shape these choices?

As we look more closely, we find young women with little education, no opportunities, and few career goals trying to gain self-esteem and identity by bearing children. Traditionally, women have found this role to be one of deep meaning; even as a choice of last resort, being a mother is being someone. Children also provide hope for the future. Read what one welfare mother says about the meaning of her children in her life:

> To me, having a baby inside me is the only time I'm really alive. I know I can make something, do something, no matter what color my skin is, and what names people call me. When the baby gets born I see him, and he's full of life, or she is, and I think to myself that it doesn't make any difference what happens later, at least now we've got a chance, or the baby does. You can see the little one grow and get larger and start doing things, and you feel there must be some hope, some chance that things will get better; because there it is, right before you, a real, live, growing baby . . . at least he's *some* sign. If we

didn't have that, what would be the difference from death? (Coles in Vander Zanden, 1986).

But why no marriage? One of the effects of social inequality is to diminish the number of underclass males who fit the "suitable mate" pattern — most are unemployable with little hope of access to formal education. Since a post-industrial society uses education as an avenue by which jobs are filled, schooling could provide a way out of the underclass. But if men and women are functionally illiterate (cannot read or write at the fourth grade level) little possibility exists for anything other than repeating the generational cycle of welfare.

Why hasn't public education taught the necessary skills to members of the underclass? Housing patterns provide one answer; schools are supported by property taxes, and the underclass is concentrated in low-income areas. Neither the local government nor the state has incentives to upgrade the quality of education for those who can least afford it, and who are not likely to become politically influential. Neither has the middle-class (not even those who are religiously motivated) generally been willing to sacrifice time, money, or effort to address the difficult task of education for the poor. After all, we might have to live in their communities in order to teach effectively. We might have to sacrifice expenditures for our children in order to pay for upgrading education in the slums. We might slow down our social mobility if we try to increase theirs.

In the underclass, then, lack of functional literacy is a characteristic of potential marriage partners; such men are not very good risks as husbands, fathers and providers. The actual number of "good" marriage partners is also limited. Some underclass males are already in prison, some are drug or alcohol addicts, some have committed suicide and some are dead as a result of street violence.

Perhaps sexual immorality explains less about teenage unmarried pregnancies in the underclass than does the social stratification system and its inequities.

SECOND, THE EXAMPLE OF WORLD SYSTEMS: DEPENDENCY/WAR

We live in a shrinking world. Geographically distant events affect the United States and our personal hopes and dreams. Japan increases/decreases the number of automobile imports coming into this country, and we wonder what will happen in Detroit. Iraq invades Kuwait, and young American soldiers in camouflage uniforms find themselves pitching tents in an Arabian desert. Isolation is no longer a viable choice. Even those nations which have attempted closed borders — the Soviet Union, China, Nepal — discover their survival requires economic, political and social interaction with other countries. Unfortunately, the interaction is structured by a global stratification system. Wallerstein (1979), Chirot (1986), and others have written extensively about a three-tiered world system. The "core" societies have industrialized, with resulting economic and political advantage. Japan, West Germany, and the United States would be examples of this powerful group, sometimes referred to as "MDC" (more developed countries). The "peripheral" or Third World societies are the underdeveloped nations or ones with few natural resources. El Salvador, Afghanistan, Mexico, and the Philippines are some examples. These are labeled "LDC" (less developed countries). Between these two are the "semi-peripheral" countries with developing industry, but still dependent for their economic health on the activities of the core nations. Italy, Spain, and Austria are examples.

Tension and conflict are characteristic of this global stratification system. Both world wars, the continuing military-guerrilla outbreaks, and the violence in the Middle East represent extreme measures which the core, peripheral, and semi-peripheral nations take to protect and/or better their economic and political positions. Twentieth-century nations do not seem to recognize that characteristics of national moral fortitude, generosity, concern about global human rights, and a high quality of social and spiritual life also could bring respect, power, and authority. Mahatma Gandhi suggested these were the qualities India needed for achieving independence from England and for developing into a strong, influential nation (see Erikson, 1969). Perhaps the nations believe moral values will be automatically nourished when economic and political positions are strong.

In trying to explain global inequality, some would again "blame the victim." A nation is backward and traditional — still kinship-based with little interest in high-level technology or efficient organizational structures. The people are lazy, event-oriented, nonambitious or illiterate. If only the LDCs would become more like the developed world, the global inequities would diminish. But the core nations are so far ahead in their control of the world market and in applications of sophisticated technology, that it seems unrealistic to hope the Third World will ever taste the frosting.

Exploitation may be one reason for the core nations being ahead of the others. Many of today's less developed countries were colonies of Europe (and especially of England) in the last century. The colony provided the raw materials for the successful industrializing of Europe, but little capital was returned for the colony's own development. Although some historians suggest there were benefits for the colony in this arrangement, it seems clear that the system exaggerated the gap between the rich and poor by rewarding the landowning elite at the expense of the general population and the economic development of the colony.

Today many of these countries, not independent, are experiencing "neocolonialism" — the domination of their economies by multinational corporations and outside investors. Multinationals often discourage indigenous manufacturing, choosing instead to sell to the LDC the manufactured products of the core (Barnet and Muller, 1977). The LDC attempts to export crops such as coffee, sugar, and tea, hoping that these will bring in capital to fund industrialization. Instead, the small group of landowning elite again benefit, while all others remain poor. At the same time, communication networks beam by satellite the TV panoramas of "Dallas," "Dynasty," and other extravagances of the core. The Third World desire for material goods adds to the internal restlessness and destabilizes those countries barely surviving on the crumbs.

What does it mean for a Christian from the United States to recognize the stratification system of the world's winners and losers? We shrink from the enormity of the problem, especially when we understand its self-perpetuating nature. We remind ourselves that we really cannot do much. But we forget that God is more powerful than the global system and that He is the one calling us to do justice.

THIRD, THE EXAMPLE OF GENDER: BIOLOGY/CREATION ORDER

Societies differ in the type and amount of social inequality that exists. The simplest and most common systems are based on age and sex. All human societies — present and past — are stratified on at least these two characteristics. Let's examine inequities based on the sex of the person.

Although some would suggest that women in prehistory were the dominant leaders (E. Davis, 1972; Stone, 1978), most evidence indicates that patriarchies have been the cultural norm (Rosaldo and Lamphere, 1974). Patriarchy is a system in which males have the primary decision-making power. Control over other members and over dispersal of valued objects in the society belongs to the males. Opportunities for valued life chances come first to them.

Anthropological explanations for patriarchy focus on biology and environment (Harris, 1977; Chodorow, 1978). Female reproductive cycles of menstruation, pregnancy, childbearing and the nursing of infants require a "close to home" lifestyle for women. Because of the emotional and physical bonding of the mother and infant, women are "instinctive" mothers. Males, however, are not "natural" fathers. Society must carefully teach, reinforce and reward fathering behaviors (Mead, 1975). Part of the male reward is higher status, power — more frosting. Male duties include protection, providing for the family and controlling whatever surplus he has gathered. The surplus is an important feature of one analysis of gender inequality, since it encouraged individual ownership of property (Engels, 1942). If the property can be increased and protected it can be used for barter and for power to control others. Females usually do not control the property or have access to the power that it creates. High status and dominance, therefore, belong to males.

This explanation is not adequate. Why would private property become the source of higher status? Since both property and children are vital to the survival of any group, why should both not be equally valued and equally rewarded? Similar questions are asked today: Why are the "masculine" characteristics of logic, assertiveness and dominance valued and rewarded while the "feminine" qualities of intuition, long suffering and submission not rewarded but taken for granted? *Why is the male point of view regarded as the human point of view* (Gilligan, 1982)?

Some writers use the biblical record to explain male dominance (Elliot, 1976; Clark, 1980; Bloesch, 1982). They suggest that God assigned both function and position for women and men. He planned gender roles to be complementary and hierarchic. Males are strong, decisive, dominant and external in their activities because God made them that way. Females are a weaker creation: nurturant, subordinate and meant to function inside the home.

However, viewing gender as complementary is not a distinctive drawn from the biblical record. Dualism has been prominent in human philosophy. For example, an all-encompassing dualistic world view expressed as "yin" and "yang" structured activities and human relationships in traditional China.

When the "creation order" is used to validate male dominance — Adam was formed first, and then woman — the chronology described in Genesis 2 presents difficulties. What do we do with the animals when we accept patriarchy based on this order of creation? Most of us do not think that males get the tip frosting, animals the frosting in the middle, and women bear the weight. The chronological perspective also suggests that Adam bears God's image and the woman bears Adam's image. She should be subordinate to the man, who is subordinate to God. First Corinthians (11:3, 8-9) often is used to support this idea: "But I want you to understand that Christ is the head of every man, and the man is the head of a woman, and God is the head of Christ . . . For man does not originate from woman, but woman from man; for indeed man is not created for the woman's sake, but the woman for the man's sake" (NASB).

Reading on in the passage, however, we find the Bible careful to complete the picture of who comes from whom, *and "all things originate from God"* (1 Corinthians 11:11-12). God has made the "hierarchy" into a circle.

It is not by accident that in the Gospels Jesus Christ chose to use Genesis 1 in His discussion about marriage (Mark 10:6-9). This creation account raises different questions for anyone supporting gender hierarchy from the scriptural account. The order here is one of ascending complexity and achievement. If chronology is a necessity and sufficient explanation, then woman is the crowning achievement and should be given the highest status (Bilezikian, 1985). Using the creation order — whether from Genesis 1 or 2 — as support for gender stratification raises more questions than it answers.

Poverty, global stratification and gender hierarchy exist everywhere and are stubborn in their persistence — advantageous for some and devastating for others. *Why do these systems of inequality exist? Is stratification a "law" of human behavior? What might be appropriate Christian responses to the various answers given to that question?*

WHY DOES STRATIFICATION EXIST?

Stratification Is the Result of Individual Differences

Stratification persists because it is a result of basic individual differences. Achievement is determined by genetic abilities (Wilson, 1978). Every person has a natural difference in talent that no amount of social manipulation can change. Rewards for these differing abilities gradually develop lopsided social systems of inequality. Aristotle said: "It is thus clear that there are by nature free men and slaves, and that servitude is agreeable and just for the latter . . . Equally, the relation of the male to the female is by nature such that one is superior and the other is dominated" (in Kerbo, 1983).

Because He is the Creator, giver of individual abilities, and ruler over all things, God ordains some to have the frosting and others to bear the weight or get the crumbs. This argument indicates that the appropriate response to structured inequality is acceptance.

A Christian Response

Who can argue against the reality of individual differences? And who would dispute the need to divide up jobs to be done, matching ability to job? A Christian response accepts both of these to be real, but sees the ranking of them in any kind of hierarchy to be a social construction. Arbitrary measures of worth are assigned, usually by those in power and along lines of their own self-interest. In addition, the ranking of human abilities suggests that God created some characteristics noble and others disreputable. Scripture warns about such thinking: "The eye cannot say to the hand, 'I have no need of you,' or again the head to the feet, 'I have no need of you.' On the contrary, it is much truer that the members of the body which seem to be weaker are necessary . . . on these we bestow more abundant honor" (1 Corinthians 12:21-23, NASB).

Individual differences do not presume or require ranking. Accepting stratification because it reflects individual differences is rejected.

Social Order Requires Stratification

Systems of inequality are necessary for smooth, efficient functioning of society. Many jobs in society are not pleasant and some require rigorous and long preparation. Qualified persons are difficult to find. The stratification system offers the incentives of prestige, power, and money to attract competent persons and leaders (Davis and Moore, 1945).

This perspective also recognizes that people at the top may exploit their positions, further exaggerating the inequalities which natural talent conceived. Exploitation is unfortunate, but does not disprove the fact that a stratification system remains the most efficient way to attract and reward gifted persons for taking on the priority tasks of the group. It is built on our understanding of human nature, varied abilities, and factors of motivation.

This second perspective suggests that the appropriate response to social stratification is appreciative acceptance, with restraint put on excessive exploitation.

A Christian Response

The necessity argument is based on society's growing demand for leadership and the assumption of a dwindling supply. Perhaps much more is occurring. *First*, an "efficient" society is seen here as an end — value in itself — rather than as a means toward human goals. *Second*, it is not clear that the level of an important task is intrinsic to its ranking. Some people have unpleasant, dirty but important jobs and do not receive high status. Garbage collectors are one example. Also, some tasks require extensive training, but receive only moderate prestige and money. Pharmacy might be an example. *Third*, if the importance or the task is not intrinsic, then who decides which jobs are essential? *Fourth*, the supply has not dwindled; rather, qualified persons are denied leadership opportunities because of race, sex or religion.

The stratification system also tends to crystallize the top roles and then draw only from this pool. Consider the medical profession. The doctor may be selected for a church leadership position because "physician" is a prestigious and highly regarded profession rather than because the person is wholeheartedly following God and willing to assume a servant role. Others in the church who are not doctors or lawyers or successful business persons may possess valuable and needed spiritual gifts but are not chosen.

For the Christian, leadership is servanthood. Jesus put it this way: "Whoever wishes to be great among you shall be your servant" (Matthew 20:26, NASB). Servanthood fits best in a system where leadership is flexible rather than hierarchic. The "needs" of the social order cannot be used to justify stratification.

The Power Elite Wants to Dominate

Stratification is a result of power and the domination of many by the few. Such a system does not reflect individual differences, not is it necessary for society to function. In fact, stratification limits the discovery and use of human abilities present in the group. Many never have opportunity to contribute, even though they may have great gifts.

316

Qualified persons are scarce, not because no one wants the job, but because those in power keep others out. Favored positions are protected by restricting recruitment, training, and access to opportunity. This represents an exercise of power, not nature or necessity (Dahrendorf, 1968).

A rationale supporting social inequality as natural, morally right and good for all is created and communicated by those at the top. These persons also control the institutions of the social system — education, politics, economics, the law and family life. Since both the rationale and the system are embedded in each person's world view, any challenge must be directed first against the deceptive rationale and then against the system itself. Because the powerful will not easily give up their advantages, the appropriate response to stratification is revolution.

A Christian Response

Both the Old and New Testaments warn us about the deceptions of powerful people and express God's special care for the oppressed. We recognize that power can corrupt. Marx suggests revolution as the appropriate response — smash the offending systems and something beautiful will grow out of the ashes. But revolution doesn't work that way; it merely recycles the oppressed and the oppressor. The oppressed-turned-ruler will "lord it over" others when the opportunity comes.

The Christian rejects revolution as an appropriate response to structured inequality.

Stratification Is a Result of Sin and Rebellion

Structured inequality is present everywhere and persistent not because it is built on individual differences created by God, nor because it is functional and necessary for social order, nor merely because some are powerful and exploit others. *Hierarchy exists because women and men rebel against God, as Adam and the woman did at the beginning of human history.* Stratification was not a part of God's original plan. The mandate containing instructions to "be fruitful and multiply," to "fill the earth and subdue it," to "have dominion . . . over every living thing" was given by God equally to both created persons (Genesis 1:28).

But the woman and the man disobeyed God. The first and most destructive effect of their sin was separation from God, and then from each other. What happened next is relevant to our discussion of hierarchy and injustice. The sweeping mandate given to the woman and Adam changed; their roles radically diminished in scope and function. The woman's activities now focus on *childbearing*. She receives the "be fruitful and multiply" aspect of God's original commandment. Adam names the woman "Eve" because she is the mother of all the living (Genesis 2:23). Adam's activities diminish to that of worker. He received the "subdue the earth" part of the mandate. Thorns and thistles plague him; sweat and toil are his constant companions. Not only have the activities of the man and woman narrowed, their relationship to each other has become asymmetrical. Adam will "lord it over" Eve — dominance and hierarchy are now part of their experience — as they are of ours today.

Since Adam and Eve, every one of us has sinned and is separated from God and from one another. Why, then, should we be surprised to discover hierarchy and dichotomized roles present everywhere and persistent? But they are *not* natural; they are *not* necessary. They are the results of human rebellion against God. But they are so culturally familiar that we must be reminded they are sin.

The appropriate response to social stratification is not acceptance or control or revolution, but repentance and reconciliation.

A CHRISTIAN RESPONSE TO GENDER INEQUALITY

Let's assume this fourth answer is correct. Stratification is not a "law" of human behavior; it is the result of evil. Can it be changed on earth? Many groups — the Marxists, Jim Jones' group, the Oneida Community — have tried to abolish stratification. None succeeded. Oppression was recycled, or leaders turned tyrants, or ends were used to justify immoral means.

Erich Fromm (in Kerbo, 1983) and others have noted that social change cannot occur unless people have undergone *moral change*. Christians know that believing in Jesus Christ begins such moral change. We start to see ourselves and others with new eyes. But the moral change isn't automatic or instantaneous. We can choose to open our eyes wide or to stay blind, to work for the kingdom or to be squeezed into our culture's mold.

Suppose Christians caught a glimpse of human partnership as it was before sin. Suppose Christ's work on the Cross was understood to reconcile the twisted horizontal relationship among humans as well as the broken vertical relationship between humans and God? Suppose working for the kingdom of God meant social action against all expressions of hierarchy in the human group? Where would you begin?

Perhaps we might start where the problem first began. Restore mutuality between the woman and man. Allow the reconciling love of God to make the difference. *Judge the hierarchy for what it is — a manifest of our sinful nature to "lord it over" others.* Refuse to make hierarchy sacred or absolute. Few contemporary issues are more volatile than gender inequality. Maybe there is a good reason. The serpent wants us to continue to "enjoy" the fruits of rebellion, and will work hard to frustrate attempts toward reconciliation. As we read the human story in Genesis, we find the "lording it over" activities begin with the male and female, quickly spread to Cain, and then are generalized to all nations. Even Israel fell to the lowest level of global stratification, becoming a slave nation. The fundamental gender hierarchy provided the model for other patterns of domination.

Gender Mutuality Restored in Christ

But do redemption and reconciliation in Christ really speak to these issues? Does God intend male dominance to diminish as a result of belief in Christ? If He does, the New Testament should indicate changes in relative position and activities of women and men. *Five* pieces of evidence from the New Testament may whet your appetite for further biblical study.

1. *Education for women.* Contrary to the expectations and in spite of the disapproval of His disciples, Jesus taught women in ways that violated cultural norms. He assumed that women do have personal experiences with the Son of God (John 4). In the disagreement between Mary and Martha, Jesus took Mary's side. The culture did not encourage education for women; Jesus affirmed the fact that spiritual study was for women as well as for men (Luke 10:38-42).

2. *Baptism.* The Old Testament sign of Israel's covenant relationship with Jehovah was male circumcision. In the New Testament the sign of belief is baptism. Wonderfully, the Acts 8:12 account of baptism specifically mentions that women joined men in publicly proclaiming their relationship with God.

3. *Priesthood of all believers.* In the Old Testament, priests who handled the sacred things and mediated between the people and God had to be males from the tribe of Levi. The change in the New Testament is startling. Old Testament rituals necessary to approach God are no longer required; immediate access into His presence is possible for every believer. Women now do not have to go through a male to approach God, or to know His will for their lives. The Book of Hebrews describes the new priesthood of *all* believers. Women and men are priests — both can intercede for others, both can know His will directly, both are called to be His ministers.

4. *Spiritual gifts.* Now the work of God is to be carried out by those assigned spiritual gifts rather than those with religious roles assigned by birth and tribe and gender. The Bible does not divide the gifts by sex — with men being given those of administration, preaching and teaching, and women given hospitality and helps. Rather, the Holy Spirit gives the gifts to whomever He wills (Romans 12; 1 Corinthians 12), and each of us is responsible to nurture and use our gift in loving service for Him.

5. *In Christ, no hierarchy.* Galatians 3:23-28 focuses on three hierarchic relationships of New Testament cultures: Jew-Gentile, slave-free, and male-female. The context of these verses initiates the end of social hierarchies for those "in Christ."

For the Christian, then, structured inequality — whether "vindicated" by individual differences, supposed societal need, power, or even scriptural proof-texts — *cannot be justified.* Christ's redemptive work reconciles us not only to God, but also to one another. Gender mutuality, not hierarchy, powerfully models His kingdom. Mutual respect, responsibility and opportunities for leadership for both men and women need to be developed at all levels in the Church, at the workplace, in the family, and in governing structures. We need to socially construct our human worlds so they are characterized by *structured equality* rather than structured inequality.

Perhaps you would choose, instead, to first diminish stratification among the poor or between the races. But do not overlook the fact that the initial result of rebellion against God was *gender* inequality. Modeling mutuality in this relationship includes all our life experiences — it is daily, and deeply personal. As the style of life together in the kingdom of God, male-female mutuality has potential to affect the inequities in all other relationships: race, poverty, occupation and among the nations of the world. Without the modeling of gender mutuality, stratification will persist, along with the inadequate justification sustaining it.

Study and Discussion
Questions

1. If back issues of your college newspaper are available, randomly select several of the earliest issues, several issues from fifteen years ago, and several issues from the current school year.

   Read through the issues one era at a time, and jot down student activities which are mentioned. Make special note of those activities which appear to confer high status or symbolize student "success." Use these observations and construct a social stratification system of each era.

2. Most societies have tried to revise or destroy systems of inequality. Why do you think no society has been successful?

3. Assume you wish to diminish structured inequality in the United States. Would gender hierarchy be the place to begin? Explain your thinking.

4. Is there a stratification system among the students at your college? If so, what is the basis for the ranking? Assume you would wish to change the system — where might you begin? Explain.

5. Could you be a biblical Christian and perpetuate a caste system? Give your reasons.

6. Assume that some academic disciplines and majors are more respected than others at your college. What are the most frequent explanations given for the ranking? In what ways would scriptural teachings about the body of Christ critique the ranking?

7. Discuss whether or not you consider the effects of the Fall as described in Genesis 3 to be connected to structured inequality in society today.

8. Do a word study using Bible, concordances, Bible dictionary and other helps. Select from the following words or phrases:
   WOMAN
   PRIEST
   SUBMISSION
   SPIRITUAL GIFTS

   Compare your findings from the Old Testament with findings from the New Testament. Summarize the similarities and contrasts.

References

Abrahamson, Mark, Ephriam H. Mizruchi, and Carlton A. Hornung, *Stratification and Mobility*. New York: Macmillan Publishing Company, 1976.

Barnet, Richard J., and R. E. Muller, *Global Reach: The Power of the Multinational Corporation*. New York: Simon and Schuster, 1977.

Bilezikian, Gilbert, *Beyond Sex Roles*. Grand Rapids, MI: Baker Book House, 1985.

Bloesch, Donald, *Is the Bible Sexist?* New York: Cornerstone, 1982.

Chirot, Daniel, *Social Change in the Modern Era*. New York: Harcourt, Brace & Javanovich, 1986.

Chodorow, Nancy, *The Reproduction of Mothering*. Berkeley, CA: University of California Press, 1987.

Clark, Stephen B., *Man and Woman in Christ*. Ann Arbor, MI: Servant, 1980.

Coles, Robert, *Children in Crisis*. Boston: Little. Brown & Company, 1964.

Dahrendorf, Ralf, *Essays on the Theory of Society*. Palo Alto, CA: Stanford University Press, 1968.

Davis, Kingsley, and Wilbert E. Moore, "Some Principles of Stratification." *American Sociological Review*, Volume 10:242-249, 1945.

Davis, Elizabeth Gould, *The First Sex*. New York: Penguin Books, 1972.

Elliot, Elisabeth, *Let Me Be a Woman*. Wheaton, IL: Tyndale House, 1976.

Engels, Friedrich, *The Origin of the Family, Private Property, and the State*. New York: International Publishing Company, 1942.

Erikson, Erik, *Gandhi's Truth: On the Origins of Militant Non-Violence*. New York: W. W. Norton and Company, 1969.

Gilligan, Carol, *In a Different Voice*. Cambridge, MA: Harvard University Press, 1982.

Harris, Marvin, "Why Men Dominate Women." *New York Times Magazine*, November 13, 1977.

Kerbo, Harold R., *Social Stratification and Inequality*. New York: McGraw-Hill Book Company, 1983.

Lewis, Oscar, "The Culture of Poverty." *Scientific American*, Volume 215,
    p. 19-25, 1966.

Mead, Margaret, *Male and Female: A Study of the Sexes in a Changing
World*, New York: William Morrow & Company, 1975.

NCHS, *Advance Report of Final Natality Statistics*. Washington, D. C.:
National Center for Health Statistics, 1974.

Rosaldo, Michelle Zimbalist, and Louise Lamphere, ed., *Women, Culture, and
Society*. Stanford, CA: Stanford University Press, 1984.

Stone, Merlin, *When God Was a Woman*. New York: Harcourt Brace, 1978.

Wallerstein, Immanuel, *The Capitalist World Economy*. Cambridge: Cambridge
University Press, 1979.

Wilson, Edward, O., On Human Nature. Cambridge, MA: Harvard University
Press, 1978.

CHAPTER 17
ADOLESCENCE AND YOUTH: INTRODUCTION

Adolescence and youth is an invention of modernity. One way to demonstrate this is to study some early paintings in a local art gallery. If an observer were to analyze the faces in these paintings, he or she would observe that the children looked very much like adults. Until about the 18th century, most artists depicted even very tiny children simply as miniature grown-ups. Young persons in their teens, having already taken their positions in the larger society, would be indistinguishable from other people significantly older than they. Adolescence simply did not exist.

Sociologists ask how this development of adolescence came about. One answer is found in the process of differentiation that is the basis for functionalist analysis. As changes took place in society that made it economically infeasible for young people to marry and begin families during their early teenage years, there also developed an extended period of dependence beyond childhood. As Professor Peters notes, these changes in the social structure of western society include "urbanization, modernization, changing patterns within the family, aspiration of the young and increasing individualism" — all of which contributed to forming the subculture we call adolescence.

Subcultures in themselves are further evidence of the social differentiation process. A very simple society would have one culture in which nearly all members tended to participate. These societies, in the words of Ferdinand Tönnies, "were united in spite of all dividing factors." There was little diversity to serve as bases for the development of subcultures.

Adolescence may be regarded as one of many subcultures within modern western society. A *subculture* is a group that shares in the overall culture of the society but also has its own distinctive values, norms, and lifestyle. Ordinarily when we think of a subculture, we are most likely to imagine a particular ethnic or religious group who shares norms, customs, and perhaps even a distinct language that is different from the dominant culture. In their search for self-identity and autonomy, young people have created an *adolescent or youth subculture* that distinguishes its members from the larger society. This differentiation is particularly pronounced in the areas of leisure activity, music, sports, and dress, which are used by adolescents to separate themselves from their parents' world.

Being a member of a subculture may have positive or negative implications for the person and for the larger society. One of the positive functions of being marginally situated (i.e., being on the brink of the adolescent subculture and the adult-dominated larger culture) is that it enables a person to take a fresh look at the overall culture. Not yet fully enmeshed in the adult world, young people are in a position to take a fresh look at their culture and its values. At times, out of this new view of an old world, young leaders emerge who effectively challenge the existing social order. For example, students participated in efforts to break down racial segregation in the south during the 1950s and 1960s, and led protests against the Vietnam War in the late 1960s and early 1970s. Although student-led protests of any national consequence appear to be an anachronism in the United States, many students have become involved in more localized efforts to change their society, including Habitat for Humanity, Covenant House, Teen Challenge, and Skinner Associates.

Being marginal to the larger society, however, can have negative consequences. Some of the problems associated with adolescence, discussed by Professor Peters, demonstrate the failure to integrate young people into the larger social order. Differentiation, according to functionalist thought, must be accompanied by integration of this newly emergent social phenomenon. The social problems related to adolescence discussed by Professor Peters point to the fact that such integration is often weak. The high suicide rate for adolescents discussed in the article, for example, is one indication of a lack of integration. As Emile Durkheim discussed in his classic work on suicide over a hundred years ago, persons who are less integrated into the social order are the most likely to commit suicide. Adolescents are not well integrated into the larger society through marriage, parenthood, employment, or other such positions that facilitate a sense of belonging. Delinquency, substance abuse, and premarital sex may be other signs of the alienation of youth from the larger culture. Young people may engage in such activities in an attempt to belong more fully to a subgroup in which these problematic behaviors are accepted.

Since adolescence is a modern invention, the Bible is able to provide few direct guidelines for addressing adolescence as a social problem. Insights can be gleaned from the Scriptures, however, that may help Christians to deal with the problems associated with adolescence and youth. For example, parents should be mindful of Ephesians' (6:4) admonition to parents not to provoke their children, just as children must be obedient to the command to honor their parents.

Other less direct commands relevant to adolescence also may be gleaned from a biblical perspective. Since all Christians (including adolescents and youth) are called to be functioning members of the body of Christ, churches must make sure that their young people are not alienated or estranged from the world in which they live. Churches are in an excellent position to create organizations that blend aspects of the adult culture with certain facets of the adolescent subculture. Many churches are already performing that task fairly well in providing a place where many of its young people can feel a sense of integration and belonging.

Adolescence is a time of transition from the world of childhood into the world of accepting adult responsibilities. Many young people are often ready to take on more responsibility than they are permitted to assume. Churches and Christian colleges should try not only to serve young people, but also provide opportunities for them to serve others. In ministering to the needs of others, the transition to adulthood may be eased as young people feel a greater sense of belonging through their involvement in an adult world.

The so-called "generation gap" appears to be very much with us, suggesting a tension between the youth subculture and the dominant culture of the adult world that is not likely to disappear. What we wish to suggest is that this tension may be life-giving and creative. Youth and adolescents are in a dependent state during which they are learning to take their positions in the larger social world. Adults, however, can learn much from the fresh vision and idealism that often comes from God-centered young people. May adolescents and youth take heart in the words of Paul to Timothy as they seek to act on their idealism: "Don't let anyone look down on you because you are young, but set an example for the believers in speech, in life, in love, in faith and in purity" (1 Timothy 4:12 NIV).

ADOLESCENCE AND YOUTH
John F. Peters

While childhood and adulthood have been readily identifiable stages of human development throughout history, youth is an invention of modern civilization. This in-between stage has emerged because of significant changes in the structure of western society, such as urbanization, modernization, changing patterns within the family, aspirations of the young, and increasing individualism. The phenomenon of youth as a political and ideological subculture were most pronounced during the sixties when many young people became disillusioned with the practices and goals of American society. In recent years a small proportion of youth echo similar sentiments with regard to civil rights, foreign relations, pollution and ecology. Youth today are more readily distinguishable as a subculture because of their distinctive music, fashions, and leisure activities. In general these distinctions are not subversive but complement the consumer interests of the larger society.

Youth and Adolescence Defined

The term *youth* is not easily defined. The stage begins between 12 and 15, depending upon when parents or adults start to relinquish control, and when teenagers assert forms of independence. One may be youth-like in a particular social environment (with one's peers or in school) but child-like in another (in the home).

The end of youth is even more difficult to pinpoint. Maturity is defined in many ways, with an age range between 18 and 29. Youthful facial features or small physical frame are appearance markers which inhibit the assignment of maturity. Living at home or being financially dependent upon parents also reinforces association with a nonadult stage. Behaviors which effectively designate one as an adult are: at least six months of consistent full-time employment, independent living, a college degree, a career, marriage, and bearing a child. Legal definitions for full adult rights and privileges vary by state and by activity; one must be 16 to obtain a driver's license, age 18 to write your own excuse slip in high school, age 18 to vote and legally drink, or age 21 to sign your own bank loan. Minimum age requirements are also legally established by states as to when a person may abort, marry, or have an operation in a hospital without the consent of a parent. There is some debate whether a teenage female needs parental permission to use contraceptives, or if pregnant, an abortion. Paradoxically there is no comparable social concern over a teenage male's use of contraceptive devices, if he is sexually active.

The Latin origin of the word "adolescence" means to "grow into maturity." In contemporary society, adolescence refers to a status with uncertain and diffuse guidelines, and which yields equally uncertain behavior. Terms such as teeny-boppers, kids, teenagers, juveniles, early adolescence, and late adolescence differentiate this group even further. The peculiar nature of adolescence first becomes a concern to parents when children disobey parents' wishes or experiment with values (especially sexual) inconsistent with those of the parents. School authorities show concern about classroom disorder, rowdiness or vandalism. Public annoyance grows with video arcade life, street gangs, sexuality, violations of motor vehicle use, and most poignantly, alcoholism and drugs. Is it fair to say that adolescents and youth are most identifiable as either a stage or subculture because of their deviance? If normative behavior is defined by the older generation, this premise is true. However, there are other characteristics to youth subculture. Most youth do not have parenting responsibilities. Their productive function is generally marginal and their consumer participation is restricted to relatively few items. Sizable public funds are spent on education to prepare them for adult functioning in society. Churches spend a growing proportion of their energy and budget in religious education, youth-centered social activities, mission-focused experiences, and on graduate and seminary institutions. Youth's participation in the workplace and on the national scene is recognized by babysitting, fast food employment service, sports, military service, and many other temporary and sporadic activities which are essential to the functioning of a society.

ACHIEVING SELF- IDENTITY

Generation Gap

The concept of *generation gap* is often used to explain the differences between youth and older generations. The term implies distinctiveness in values, taste, style, attitudes and behavior based upon generation membership. The generation gap concept frequently posits adolescents and youth against parents, commonly held norms, values, and accepted patterns of authority and institutions such as the school system. This is a conflict position. Others depict youth as passive, narcissistic, irresponsible, and superficial. The younger generation must be revitalized if we wish to avoid the demise of our culture. However, the older generation might do well to recognize that they have been the socializing agents in the creation of youth's attitudes and behaviors. From the adolescents' perspective the older generation might be described as traditional, bound by the status quo, old authority structures, inflexible, security conscious, and insensitive to social injustices.

The concept of generation gap in modern, dynamic society amidst rapid change, seems most appropriate. Innovation and technological change permeate all sectors of life. Secularism substitutes for the sacred. Personal gratification has replaced community consciousness. Consumerism is rampant. There is a desire for instant fulfillment rather than delayed gratification. The mass marketing media has little regard for the traditional values of chastity, fidelity, or asceticism, and uses gloss, titillation, sexism and superficiality to achieve its goal. However, such social upheaval is not necessarily along generation lines. It is characteristic of a pluralistic society.

The concept of generation gap has been exaggerated, as are the over-simplified social disruptions described in the paragraph above. Though social change is more evident in recent decades compared to earlier times, no national rebellion based upon generational differences has taken place. Western societies are marked by a remarkable degree of continuity while allowing for the most part, ordered change. Youth may evidence some temporary deviance, but 10 to 15 years later the vast majority demonstrate attitudes and behaviors that are not too different from that of their parents. At the same time the idea of youth subcultures is a significant area of social and academic investigation (Brake, 1985).

Self Identity

A teenager's *self-dentity* is likely the most common problem experienced by this age group. *Self-identity* is one's own private version of the set of traits and personal characteristics that best describe him or her (Hopkins, 1983, p. 69). It includes one's sexuality, sex-role orientation, drives, abilities and beliefs. Self-identity continues to be a volatile and fertile development issue through adolescence. Though some view late adolescence as a crisis of identity experience, Erikson (1968) sees it as a necessary turning point, where the autonomous self is addressed and a private version of one's traits and characteristics define a self set apart from all others.

Erikson (1968) identifies the adolescent stage as one of achieving identity versus identity diffusion. Erikson sees this phase as a normative crisis, one of psychosocial moratorium — standing back and analyzing the self before assuming an adult role.

One's self-identity is strongly affected by reference groups, since norms and values are acquired from one's reference group. A person may have multiple and conflicting reference groups with contradictory values. Peers may encourage immediate gratification, hanging out, and contemporary fashion in dress, while parents advocate delayed gratification (get good marks by studying now), work, and wearing of more conventional clothing. Shifting of reference groups may occur during the adolescent years, particularly when families relocate when one changes schools, or when the family form changes (from single to dual parents, one of whom is a stepparent).

Autonomy

Adolescents seek autonomy in *three* distinct areas. With *emotional autonomy*, the adolescent begins to relax ties with family and to build bonds of love, support and confidence in others. With *behavioral autonomy* one acquires skills and courage unique to oneself. *Ideational autonomy* is found in struggling with basic ideas and values. This contributes to the establishment of one's own convictions (Sebald, 1984, p. 133). These three areas of autonomy initially affect family relationships, but have implications for other spheres such as school, peers, and employers. Mannheim (1944) reminds us that this process of independence need not be seen as a social problem because the individual must move from parental dependency to independence in order to become a full functioning adult in our society. Parents play an important role in their adolescent's independence. The best environment is moderate parental control which is neither too lax nor too stringent. The development of autonomy may be referred to as individuation, which is also enhanced when both parents agree on control measures.

It is readily recognized that peers have an important influence upon adolescents. The dramatic shift in social orientation from family to peers begins at about the 5th grade and becomes significant after the 7th grade (Bowerman & Kinch, 1959; Floyd & South, 1972). Peers are influential in matters of leisure activity, music, sports, and dress, but studies show that parents have the stronger influence on career choices and educational goals. Peers are also influential in such socially deviant behavior as smoking, drinking, and drug use.

PARENTS AND YOUTH

Whether from a broad social, Church, or parental perspective, youth are seen as a social problem in parent-youth relations. Where these problems exist, Christians view them as acute and fundamental because of both Old and New Testament teachings regarding parent and child roles (Deuteronomy 5:16, 18-21; Ephesians 6:1-3). Some parents expect absolute obedience from their adolescent children.

Though most children may not explicitly obey their parents in all family matters through the preteen years, there is often a sense that one or both parents are omnipotent (and even possibly omniscient). This view changes in early adolescence. In the modern era, adolescence provides a unique experience in parent-child relationships. The adolescent may behave in an independent manner for the sake of self-assurance or experience because the act is one's own. In some cases the behavior is done intentionally in opposition to parents!

Youth's development of a healthy autonomy from parents is somewhat dependent upon the type of parental authority. One finds minimal adolescent autonomy with *autocratic* parents who tell the adolescent what to do. Maximum adolescent autonomy is found in the home of the *permissive* parents. In such a household, adolescents experience almost total freedom, a situation which does not allow for wholesome growth in autonomy. Both of these types of parenting will most likely experience rebellious adolescents (Balswick & Macrides, 1975; Kandel & Lesser, 1972). In the *democratic* household, problems and issues are discussed. Decisions are made cooperatively and in a atmosphere of respect. Adolescents increase their autonomy with experience and maturity. Members in democratic families experience more support with one another and value the sentiments and wishes of each other. Adolescent rebellion is least likely to occur in the democratic household.

Parents influence adolescents in a wide array of areas. French and Raven (1959) have classified *five* sources of social influence or power that have been appropriately applied to parent-adolescent relations (McDonald, 1977, 1980). With *referent* power the adolescent turns to parents for guidance. Referent power is nurtured by the adolescent liking the parent. Parental referent power is commonly found in an adolescent's educational pursuits as well as behavior in heterosexual relationships. In general adolescents with strong referent orientation toward parents will be most susceptible to parental influence compared to the adolescent with weaker referent orientations.

The development of spirituality is strongly enhanced when teens see parents as referents in spiritual matters. However, many Christian homes do not have this type of relationship and their youth look elsewhere for spiritual referent power. Some persons say that the degree of intimate emotional bond between parent and child makes it impossible to objectively address all matters of the family relationship. An amiable youth director or older empathetic friends in the Church may provide additional spiritual referents. Often adolescents who attend a church's youth group are spared some societal dysfunctional activities. Along with sensitive, caring youth leadership, churches must have programs which are oriented to youth activities: sports, service, possibly some travel, humor, and discussion on contemporary youth issues. Such programs require a specific commitment on the part of the entire church body (Martinson, 1988).

Expert power is based upon the belief that the parent possesses useful knowledge.

Formal education contributes much to expert power, but is not the only source. The adolescent who is keenly interested in cars or in culinary activity might find the parent's expertise in mechanics or cooking of great value. Adolescents may also appreciate the understanding of parents in relationship formation and continuance. Adolescents may have superior knowledge in some areas of computers, fashion, sports, and possibly scientific discoveries. The adolescent's superior knowledge may sometimes be seen as a threat by the parent, but in the democratic family such knowledge can serve to enhance family relationships.

With *legitimate* power the adolescent sees the parent as having the right of control. This power can be seen as authority and is somewhat circumscribed by cultural norms. In North America legitimate authority is interpreted variously by social class, race, ethnicity, and religious orientation. East Asian families often have a stronger sense of legitimate power than do Anglo-Saxons. The biblical commandment of "Honor your parents" endorses legitimate power, though its practice must be clothed in patience, respect and love. Some parents use this commandment as license, and are harsh, inconsiderate and selfish. The result is that children are provoked, a dysfunctional situation the Apostle Paul urges one to avoid (Ephesians 6:4). This view of the absolute authority of parents over children is also found in nonevangelical Christian families. Many teenagers balk at parental legitimate power and soften their contempt only as they enter their early twenties.

French and Raven also recognize *reward* and *coercive* power. The influenced person, in this case the youth, perceives the parent to have the right to dispense rewards (no curfew, use of the family car), or to administer punishment (being grounded).

The Judeo-Christian tradition has endorsed parental authority through childhood, adolescence and to some degree the adult years. Our guide to biblical living comes to us from the context of a pastoral people, and at best, the very beginning of the development of the nation-state. Modernity has catapulted societies into a very different social structure. There has been a dramatic decline in the socialization role of the family and Church in providing values, morality, and responsible social attitudes. Schools educate youth for the nation-state. The media inculcate a norm of self-gratification and strongly endorse the goals of the marketplace. Peer influence encourages nonfamilial bonding. Has this new direction come because counterforces were too strong for the family? Or did it come by default, an inadequate functioning family?

These extra-familial influences have affected the family system. Children are exposed to a wide range of values, some of which are secular, individualistic, and contrary to the earlier socialization of their parents. Parents often do not socialize or even recommend that their children take a career similar to theirs. Research shows that family relations are the worst through the adolescent years (Rollin & Feldman, 1970). Many parents are concerned, worried, always hoping for the best. But even middle class families who have some control over their children's social environment (i. e. choice of residence or school) are not immune from negative influences on their adolescent's social environment merely by sending their children to Christian elementary and secondary schools. Christian parents must decide whether this is justifiable, or whether they might be avoiding parental and community responsibility.

The changing family role requires considerable family adaptation. Though socialization was often seen as unidirectional, it is now bidirectional. Parents socialize children, but the reverse it also true. Socialization is reciprocal. In a university sample it was found that parents were strongly influenced by their children in sports, personal care (clothing, physical appearance), leisure activities, politics and religion (in that order) (Peters, 1985). Parents were affected in both knowledge of the specific item and to a lesser degree, in changing their own behavior regarding tolerance of youth, sexuality, minority peoples, and the handicapped (in that order). Caring and sensitive parents will listen to the cares and concerns of the adolescent, even if they seem irrational, ill-founded and foreign to the parent's experience.

Ambert's (1990) research based on family autobiographical material of university youth found that children of immigrant families play a key role in facilitating the necessary adaptation of parents to the North American way of life. These youth not only face the unique problem of being drawn into the youth culture of the new society, but they also encounter restraint and resistance from their parents. Youth in large nonimmigrant families reported limited individual attention from parents, that "they did not count." Firstborn described themselves as experiments, in that younger siblings were treated with greater tolerance and flexibility. A few sensed that they had been a strain on their parents' marriage or remarriage, particularly through their early teen years. "I made their first years together very difficult," and, "I did not give him (stepfather) a chance," were two comments made.

Patriarchy

Today's youth find themselves in the midst of monumental change toward gender equality. The influences of feminism and changing gender roles challenge traditional biblical thinking and effect Christian behavior. Many young Christians seek fairness and justice, while Christian practice in the past has typically been patriarchal, specifically showing the subordination of women. The private domain of the home is a place where other traditional gender roles are evident in curfew observance, teenagers' permission to use the family car, and in doing in- and outdoor chores (Peters, 1991). Some Christian female youth in particular, question the Church and Christianity, especially when they see leadership roles securely held by males. The alternatives for these young women are not attractive: leave the church, transfer membership to a nonpatriarchal church, seek to reform their present church, or remain subordinate. The young Christian feminist may also face difficulties in finding a compatible marriage partner. Christian men who are gender-equal in mind and in practice are few in number.

SPECIFIC AREAS OF CONCERN

Suicide

Suicide ranks third in the death of adolescents. Rates have escalated dramatically over the past two decades, particularly for females. The actual rate of suicide for males aged 15-24, however, is still about four times that of females. The suicide rate varies among college students, with Harvard and Yale showing a higher rate. North American Indians have an unusually high rate of suicide. Actual suicide rates are considered conservative due to the disguised means of reporting some deaths (automobile accidents) and due to the social stigma of suicide.

Deaths are always painful for families and friends. There are at least *three* reasons why child and adolescent suicide is viewed as death at its worst. In the *first* place death is seen as premature. Many hopes are shattered. *Second*, we have an enormous emotional investment, pride, pleasure, and a sense of immortality in our children. In this sense a child's death robs us of a large part of ourselves. *Third*, a child's suicide is devastating because of the parental sense of responsibility toward children. The child's psychological and physical well-being are considered the parents' responsibility (Sudak, Ford & Rushford, 1984, pp. xvii-xviii).

Though some patterns in suicidal behavior are known, there is yet much to be learned. Suicide among children and youth is often unplanned and impulsive, symbolizing a desperate wish for help. There is no pattern by day of week, day of month, or holiday for violent deaths of youths, as is found among other age cohorts. Estimates of the ratio of suicide attempts to fatalities vary: from 120:1 in children to 5:1 in adults (Corder, et al., 1974). Successful youth suicides are more often found among males because they use violent means, while females use passive and less dangerous means.

Though some societies view suicide as an honor or human right, North Americans view this means of death as negative, alarming, and a social problem. Our suicide rates are about half that of Finland, Austria, or Denmark. The causes for suicide are multiple and complex (Grueling & DeBlassie, 1980). Psychological causes focus upon depression, stress, neuroses/psychoses, guilt/anger, and immature personality development. Though suicide is not hereditary, family dysfunction is a contributing factor to suicide, particularly among children (Teicher, 1973, p. 133). Conditions in the modern urban milieu may also contribute to low self-esteem, anomie, isolation, and the lack of social cohesion — all factors which influence the possibility of suicide.

Sexuality

Adolescence is the period in which a person goes through greater psychological change than at any other period of life. One such change is that of sexuality: awareness of body parts, erotic feeling and expression, masturbation, the association of feeling with sexuality, and possibly sexual intercourse. Adolescents may satisfy their curiosity by reading "forbidden, dirty" books, telling off-color jokes, and using sex slang. The Peplau, et al., (1977) study shows that these behaviors indicate the need for love, intimacy, and acceptance from another person.

The sexual drives and urges of youth today are no different than that of other generations. However, the fact that sexually explicit stimuli are omnipresent with few clearly defined guidelines for their control or expression creates a new context for sexuality. Many youth today are either sexually uninformed or ill-informed. They find themselves in a society with pluralistic sexual values pervaded by an individualistic ethic. Most Christian youth know that liberal sexual standards are unacceptable to their Christian parents.

Many Christian parents view contemporary sexual practices in the U. S. as a social problem. The Bible teaches the sanctity of sex and love. Marriage is a permanent sacred bond between two heterosexual partners. Christians believe that violations of this standard will reap damaging results to the individual, the family, and the nation. For these reasons young people are to be disciplined, cautious, and respect one another.

By and large our society has accepted a liberal sex standard. In fact, often high school counselors give advice on types of contraception use but not on abstinence as an option.

American youth are assumed to be sexually active. It follows then that educators and legislators are concerned about "responsible sex," interpreted as the avoidance of pregnancies. Unwanted or early pregnancy usually yields multiple problems: incomplete education, limited occupational skills, lack of parenting skills, single parenthood, expenditures the parent(s) are unable to meet, and social welfare dependency. Our society recognizes the problem as *threefold*: cost in assistance and further training, the limited occupational opportunities of many of these young parents and the cycle of dependency from one generation to the next. Christians would add a further concern in that often single pregnant women choose a therapeutic abortion. (In 1985, 75% of all abortions in the U. S. were for single women.)

Substance Abuse

This section addresses *three* debilitating health problems that confront youth: *drug abuse*, *smoking* and *excessive drinking*. (See the earlier chapter on *Substance Abuse* for a more extensive treatment.)

a. *Drug Abuse*

Some consider drug abuse to be the greatest youth health problem. Drugs may be grouped into specific categories: narcotics, stimulants, depressants, hallucinogens, marijuana, and inhalants (Rice, 1987, p. 303-322). Alcohol and nicotine are also drugs. The availability, cost, effect and purpose of drug use varies. For example, the consequences of morphine and heroin use are severe. They are extremely physically addictive, and both drugs are expensive. Reports of cure for the person addicted to heroin are rare. Marijuana (ganja, hashish, hashish oil) impairs the memory and concentration, alters time and space sense, impairs vision, and retards reaction time. Driving under the influence of marijuana, which is an intoxicant, is hazardous. Research suggests that heavy marijuana use may impair future reproductive capabilities.

Inhalants are much more readily available, and used more often by younger teens. The inhalants include nail polish remover, plastic glue, gasoline, antifreeze, cleaning fluids, and paint thinner, all of which are sniffed to give an intoxicating effect. The memory, intellectual functions and judgments of users are impaired, accompanied by blurring of vision, slurred speech, headaches, dullness, dizziness, staggering, and drowsiness. Accidental deaths occur during the intoxicated state, such as falling from heights or placing a plastic bag over one's head. Use of inhalants is a serious drug problem.

The National Commission on Marijuana and Drug Abuse has identified five patterns of drug use (*Drug Use in America*, 1973). *Experimental use* of one or more drugs is short-term use, usually for reasons of curiosity or a new feeling experience. Such individuals consider themselves in control of their lives. Social-recreational use occurs among friends who seek a shared experience. The frequency and intensity vary, but these users also consider themselves in control of their behavior.

Circumstantial-situational users desire to achieve a known and anticipated effect; stimulant use to stay awake or taking a sedative to relieve tension in order to sleep. Drug dependency is a danger here. For the intensified drug user daily use relieves a persistent problem or stressful situation. Many such users continue with conventional social and economic activity, depending on frequency and intensity of use. The compulsive drug user has a high frequency of use over a long duration and is both psychologically and physiologically dependent. These users include the street "junkie," the opiate-dependent physician, and the barbiturate-dependent housewife.

A nationwide survey of high school students indicates that alcohol use (92.6%), cigarette smoking (70%) and marijuana use (55%) are the most frequently abused drugs (Bell and Battjes, 1985). Other nonprescribed drugs used by high school students are inhalants (19%), cocaine (16%), hallucinogens, sedatives and tranquilizers (about 13 % each). Through the early '80s most drug use by senior high schoolers declined, but the use of stimulants, cocaine, heroin and inhalants showed some increase (Bell & Battjes, 1985).

Peers are a strong influence in the use of drugs, since teenagers spend much time out of earshot and sight of parents. Drug abusers tend to come from families with negative adolescent-parent relationships. They are more likely to have parents who drink excessively, or to come from broken homes. Research among marijuana users shows that a large proportion come from families in which children are permitted to do whatever they want, where parents are exerting extreme control, or where a hostile, negative relationship exists between son and father.

b. *Smoking*

Smoking is not identified as a major social problem. Because of its direct relation to cancer and other maladies such as heart disease, will smoking be seen as a social problem before the turn of the century? By age 30 about one-half the population in the U. S. are smokers. About half of all youths who smoke began before age 12. Adolescents begin smoking because of the effectiveness of advertising, imitation of parents, pressure from peers, and need for self-esteem. They continue to smoke to relieve tension, because of habit and addiction, for sociability and pleasure and to satisfy the need for oral activity (Rice, 1987, p. 324-325).

Though there is a slight increase in current female adolescent smoking, overall tobacco use has declined in North America. (The tobacco industry now successfully markets its products in third world countries.) Several factors have contributed to this decline: the discovery that secondary smoke is harmful to the nonsmoker's health, greater public awareness of the cancerous effects of tobacco use, desire for physical fitness, existence of restricted areas for smoking and possibly the high cost of cigarettes.

c. *Excessive Drinking of Alcoholic Beverages*

Social drinking is culturally accepted within our society, even among many Christians. However, excessive use of alcohol is a specific social concern. Students identify drinking as the "most serious social problem at my school" (Solorzano, 1984). Alcohol is closely linked to crime, to automobile accidents, homicides (59% are alcohol related), child abuse and family violence. Unwanted pregnancies have frequently occurred while intoxicated. Alcohol abuse during pregnancy causes over 200,000 premature deaths a year (*U. S. Dept of HEW*, 1980), and the discovery of fetal alcohol syndrome has increased concern about the use of alcohol during pregnancy.

Youth begin to drink long before reaching the legal age to do so. Sometimes alcohol use begins at home under parental supervision, generally on special occasions. In later adolescence, drinking takes place outside the home with the peer group and away from adults.

Research shows that 65% of all youth between ages 12 and 17 and 95% of all youth between 18 and 25 have used alcohol (*U. S. Bureau of Census*, 1985). Of those 18-25 years of age, 68% say they are current users of alcohol. About 6% of all male and 4% of all female seniors in high school drink at least 20 days out of any month (Johnston, O'Malley & Bachman, 1985, p. 55).

Some states have raised the legal drinking age from 18 (during War years) to 20 or 21. The high automobile accident rate among 18- and 19-year-olds, and evidence that those under age were having easy access to alcohol precipitated these changes.

Alcohol is often abused on many North American college campuses where youth exercise "freedom" from the restraint of parents and community. The freshman orientation "pubcrawl," where bus loads of students frequent a number of pubs or bars in one evening is an example of such abuse. It is not uncommon for college students to spend more money on alcohol and beer than on food. Students who are heavy drinkers show the following characteristics: lower academic grades; greater use of drugs such as laxatives and tranquilizers; poorer general health; more oversleeping, missing of classes and cheating (Moos, et al., 1976).

Delinquency

For those adults who automatically see youth as rebellious, delinquent behavior is almost expected and somewhat accepted. "Sowing wild oats," a type of social or legal deviance, can take many forms. Delinquency is defined as failure or neglect to do what duty or law requires. Delinquent acts range from driving without a license (72%), skipping school (75%), fist fighting (87%), to sending in a false fire alarm (10%) (Self-reported statistics by grade 11 and 12 males, Kratcoski & Kratcoski, 1985).

Criminal charges can be readily differentiated by sex and age (Table 1). About 82% of all charges are made against males (with prostitution and runaways being primarily female). A bias may exist in charges being initiated and executed which exempt more females than males. Juveniles are disproportionately represented in burglary, motor vehicle theft and arson, while the 18-24 age cohort are more strongly represented in murder, robbery, and liquor law violations. Curfews and runaways pertain only to those under age 18, by definition of law.

Table 1

U. S. Males Arrested, by Charge, in Percent, Under age 25, 1986

Charges	Under 18	Age 18-24	Under 25
"Serious" Crimes			
Murder and non-negligent			
Manslaughter	9.5	34.3	43.8
Forcible Rape	15.7	29.2	44.9
Robbery	22.6	38.1	60.7
Aggravated Assault	12.8	28.3	41.1
Burglary	35.2	34.2	69.4
Larceny-theft	30.9	27.6	58.5

335

Motor Vehicle Theft	39.9	33.3	73.2
Arson	40.5	22.3	62.8
"Nonserious" Crime			
Vandalism	41.3	29.3	69.6
Weapons Carrying	15.5	33.6	42.6
Driving with Intoxication	1.4	27.1	28.5
Liquor Laws	26.2	51.0	77.2
Drunkenness	2.9	23.5	26.4
Disorderly Conduct	14.8	35.3	50.1
Curfew, Loitering	100.0	—	—
Runaways	100.0	—	—

Charges in each of these items was at least 86% for males in the U. S. population with the exception of the last 4 items which were 91%, 81%, 75% and 43% respectively.

Source: U. S. Federal Bureau of Investigation, Crime in the United States, 1988.

The juvenile court system was first introduced in Illinois in 1899. Philanthropists, intellectual feminists, penologists, and social scientists dramatized the vulnerability of children and the undesirability of placing juveniles with adult offenders; by 1925 all but two states had juvenile courts and institutions (Mirande, 1975, p. 191). Reformers argued that juveniles were incapable of criminal intent unless they understood the consequences of their actions. Courts were given great latitude in handling juvenile cases. Rehabilitation rather that punishment was the focus.

Over the last decade the juvenile court has come under considerable attack. Basic human rights such as the right to counsel, the right to cross-examine witnesses, and the right to timely notice of charges have sometimes been violated. The courts operate with a class bias. Lower-class adolescents are more likely labeled delinquent or incorrigible, are more likely to be perceived as hard-core delinquents, and receive harsher treatment. Juveniles may be defined as delinquent for reasons other than violations of the criminal code: being truant, incorrigible, habitually using foul language, growing up in idleness, and smoking (Cohen, 1970, p. 368). Some observers feel the juvenile courts are too lenient. They maintain that juveniles commit serious crimes, are treated leniently by the courts, and therefore, are not deterred from further criminal behavior.

The lack of school success as shown in poor grades, lack of adjustment and classroom misconduct is associated with delinquency. Affluence and hedonistic values and life-styles contribute to delinquency. The whirl of activity arising out of the relatively easy access to cars, alcohol, drugs and pocket money include delinquent associated activities: parties, rock concerts, driving around and hanging out. Peer group involvement is a contributing factor, as poignantly evident in gang behavior. Neighborhood and community factors affect delinquency; a rapid cultural change and societal unrest increase delinquency rates. Many values are questioned. Immigrants who were previously considered exemplary in abiding by the law, such as East Asians, now have their own gangs in the large cities.

Over the past two decades a number of Christian service agencies such as Teen Challenge, Teen Haven, Skinner Associates, Calvary Ministries, Covenant House, and World Impact have developed outreach ministries to troubled youth. The social problems of youth may be addressed in various ways, and may be preventive as well as problem-solving in focus. The Christian can act responsibly by working to change legislation on the federal, state and county level. The believer in the Church community can become involved by encouraging youth participation. Individuals can show friendship and kindness by spending time with youth. Parents face continual challenges of being a role model, listener, financial provider, emotional presence and stabilizer. Dialogue, openness, confidence, trust and some degree of risk are all characteristics of the relationship between youth and adult.

Suggested Further Reading

Books:
Bibby, R., and D. C. Posterski. *The Emerging Generation.* Toronto: Irwin, 1985.

Campolo, Anthony. *Growing Up in America.* Grand Rapids, Mich.: Zondervan Publishing House. 1989.

Martinson, Roland D. *Effective Youth Ministry.* Minneapolis: Augsberg Publishing House. 1988.

Posterski, Donald C. *Friendship: A Window on Ministry to Youth.* Scarborough, Ont.: Project Teen Canada. 1985.

Study and Discussion
Questions

1. Comment on the ambiguity of the adolescent period.

2. Defend or critique the "generation gap" concept in our society today.

3. Why is self-identity so important in the adolescent/youth period?

4. Discuss parent-adolescent relations. How can parents facilitate adolescence through the troubling years?

5. How can the Church community facilitate adolescents and youth?

6. Explain why you feel the period of adolescence was easier or more difficult for your parents.

7. Discuss how Scripture seems to acknowledge an adolescent stage, and how Scripture assists adolescents and youth in and through this stage.

8. Discuss the effect gender-equal norms will likely have upon female adolescent/youth delinquency in the coming years.

9. Where is society reacting too strongly to adolescent deviance? Where could society react more strongly to adolescent deviance?

10. Discuss the various ways the Church and Christians are actually ministering to youth. Can you identify areas where needs still exist?

References

Ambert, Anne-Marie, *Children's Effect Upon Parents*, unpublished manuscript, 1990.

Balswick, J. O., and C. Macrides, "Parental stimulus for adolescent rebellion," *Adolescence*, 10, 253-266, 1975.

Bell, C. S., and R. Battjes, *Prevention Research: Deterring Drug Abuse among Children and Adolescents.* NIDA Research Monograph 63, Rockville, MD: National Institute on Drug Abuse, 1985.

Bowerman, C. E., and J. W. Kinch, "Changes in family and peer orientation of children between fourth and tenth grades," *Social Forces*, 37, 206-211, 1959.

Brake, Michael, *Comparative Youth Culture*, Boston: Routledge & Kegan Paul, 1985.

Cohen, Bruce J., *Crime in America.* Itasca, IL.: Peacock, 1970.

Corder, B. F., W. Short, and R. F. Corder, "A Study of Social and Psychological Characteristics of Adolescent Suicide Attempters in an Urban Disadvantaged Area," *Adolescence*, 9:1-6, 1974.

Drug Use in America: Problem in Perspective. Second Report of the National Commission on Marijuana and Drug Use, March 1973. Washington, D. C.: U. S. Government Printing Office, 1974.

Erikson, Erik H., *Identity: Youth and Crisis.* New York: Norton, 1968.

Floyd, H. H., Jr., and D. R. South, "Dilemma of youth: The choice of parents or peers as a frame of reference for behavior," *Journal of Marriage and the Family*, 34:627-634, 1972.

French, J. R. P., Jr., and B. Raven. "The Bases of Social Power." In *"Studies in social power,"* D. Cartwright, (ed.). Ann Arbor, Mich.: Research Center for Group Dynamics, Institute for Social Research, University of Michigan, 1959.

Greuling, J. W., and R. R. DeBlassie, "Adolescent Suicide," *Adolescence* 59:589-601, 1980.

Hopkins, R. Roy, *Adolescence.* New York: Academic Press, 1983.

Johnston, L. D., P. M. O'Malley and J. C. Bachman, *Use of Licit and Illicit Drugs by America's High School Students,* 1975-1984. Rockville, MD: National Institute on Drug Abuse, p. 55, 1985.

Kandel, D. B., and G. S. Lessor, *Youth in two worlds: United States and Denmark.* San Francisco: Jossey-Bass, 1972.

Kratcoski, P. C., and Kratcoski, J. E., "Changing patterns in delinquent activities of boys and girls: A self-reported delinquency analysis," *Adolescence*, 10, 83-92, 1975.

Mannheim, Karl. *Diagnosis of Our Time.* New York: Oxford University Press, 1944.

Martinson, Roland D., *Effective Youth Ministry.* Minneapolis: Augsbrg Publishing House, 1988.

McDonald, G. W., "Parental Identification by the Adolescent: A Social Power Approach," *Journal of Marriage and the Family*, 39 (4):705-19, 1977.

McDonald, G. W., "Parental Power and Adolescents' Parental Identification: A Reexamination," *Journal of Marriage and the Family*, 42:289-96, 1980.

Mirande, Alfred M. *The Age of Crisis.* New York: Harper & Row, 1975.

Moos, R. H., B. S. Moss and J. A. Kulik, "College-student abstainers, moderate drinkers, and heavy drinkers: A comparative analysis," *Journal of Youth and Adolescence*, 5:349-360, 1976.

Peplau, L. A., Z. Rubin, and C. T. Hill, "Sexual intimacy in dating relationships," *Journal of Social Issues*, 33 (2) 86-109, 1977.

Peters, John F., "Gender Socialization of Adolescents in the Home," unpublished manuscript, 1991.

Peters, John F., "Adolescents as Socialization Agents to Parents," *Adolescence*, Vol. XX, (80):921-933, 1985.

Rice, F. Philip, *The Adolescent.* (5th ed.). Boston: Allyn & Bacon, 1987.

Rollins, Boyd C. and Harold Feldman, "Marital Satisfaction Over the Family Life Cycle," *Journal of Marriage and the Family*, 32:20-28, 1970.

Sebald, Hans. *Adolescence: A Social Psychological Analysis*, (3rd ed.). Englewood Cliffs, NJ: Prentice-Hall, 1984.

Solorzano, L., "Students Think Schools are Making the Grade," *U. S. News & World Report*, August 27:49-51, 1984.

Sudak, H. S., A. B. Ford, and N. B. Rushfath. *Suicide in the Young*. Boston: John Wright, 1984.

Teicher, J. D., "A Solution to the Chronic Problem of Living: Adolescent Attempted Suicide," *Current Issues in Adolescent Psychiatry*. J. C. Schoolar, (ed.). New York: Brunner/Mazel, 1973.

U. S. Bureau of the Census. Depart of Commerce. *Statistical Abstract of the United States.*, 1985. Washington, D. C.: U. S. Government Printing Office, 1985.

U. S. Department of Health and Human Services. Office of Human Development, *Status of Children, Youth, and Families*, 1979. DHHS Publication No. (OHDS) 80-30274, August 1980.

U. S. Federal Bureau of Investigation, *Crime in the United States*, 1988.

CHAPTER 18
AGING: INTRODUCTION

As is documented and discussed in Professor Allen's article, the United States is an aging society. With lower birth rates and increased longevity, the over-65 age group is increasing disproportionately in size. With this change in social structure comes a host of problems that must be addressed.

Professor Allen discusses the problem of aging within the framework he terms "value conflict," a framework that may be incorporated into the functionalist theory of *anomie*. There is a disjuncture between the cultural values which glorify productivity, beauty, health, and strength and the value of maintaining the dignity of older members of our society. In line with Robert Merton's theory of anomie, the institutional means are often not available for elders to achieve the "good life" proffered by our cultural values. Older adults are assumed to have little of value to give our rapidly changing world and consequently are denied access to the institutional means that would permit access to adequate health care, housing, and a position of dignity.

There is an interesting paradox that may be found in examining more closely the values that Professor Allen discusses in his article. There has been an historical emphasis, as he points out, "upon individual achievement and material success in our society [that] tends to emphasize independence, self-sufficiency and productivity as motivating factors which develop self-esteem and social worth." This value, reflecting what Max Weber had called the "Protestant ethic," has its origins in biblical interpretations offered by some of the descendants of the reformers of Christianity. According to some groups of Christians even today, material prosperity is a sign of God's favor.

The Protestant Ethic has been credited with playing an important role in the development of our capitalistic economic system, a system that has provided many of us with an exceptional standard of living. Our affluent society has afforded us with benefits that have enhanced the status of the individual while at the same time diminishing the importance of the collectivity. The western world has been blessed with an abundance of God's good gifts; and since the basic needs for food, clothing and shelter have been met for most Westerners, serious attention has been paid to implementing "individual rights." Somehow we seem less dependent on each other than we would be if we lived in a world of scarcity rather than of abundance.

In this process of emphasizing individual rights we have often downplayed issues involving social responsibility. For example, most of us would be totally dismayed at the practice of the elderly voluntarily taking their own lives so as not to use resources desperately needed by younger members of the society. Yet in poor subsistence level societies this practice does occur, a norm which puts the collectivity ahead of the individual. The collective need to survive as a people can take preeminence over the right of any individual to extraordinary care.

Although we do not advocate this practice of self-elimination of the infirm and weak elderly members of a society, we feel there is a principle that we need to consider. As wealthy as our society is, our resources are not boundless. (It might be good to review the chapters on health and health care in the previous section in conjunction with the discussion of health and aging.) Are we as Christians expected to support measures to keep people alive at any cost, as taught by the late Francis Schaeffer? Or should this individual right be balanced against collective needs? Is all euthanasia an evil that Christians must fight?

Some Christian medical ethicists would disagree with Schaeffer's position that euthanasia is always wrong. What they would argue is that we need not use "extraordinary" medical measures (including most forms of so-called "life support systems") to prolong life. We are not permitted to take our own lives or those of anyone else, but these theologians would say that God does not expect us to use artificial and mechanical means to prolong the natural process of dying.

Health issues, including the sensitive topic of euthanasia, is but one of the areas discussed by Professor Allen, in which the delicate balance between collective responsibilities and individual rights needs to be assessed. The Bible teaches us the worth of each individual (c.f. Matthew 10:29), yet at the same time urges us to follow Christ's example of selflessness (c.f. Philippians 2:1-8). This paradox is a difficult one to apply on an institutional level, yet it appears to have validity there just as it does in our individual lives.

These questions about how to respond to scarce resources, including the burden of paying for the costly programs to support our aging population, have often been addressed from a conflict (rather than a functionalist) perspective. Conflicting theorists are likely to point out that the elderly are forced out of the labor market because of a labor surplus in the modern world. Industrialized societies have a chronic problem of unemployment and underemployment, and it tends to deny the old the opportunity to compete for many jobs. (The old share this problem with the young: while compulsory schooling keeps the very young out of the work force, compulsory retirement ensures that the old give up their jobs.)

According to the conflict view, the middle-aged group has wrested the control of social resources from the aging group. Any improvement in the situation of the aged would have to come about through a change in the power relationships between the middle-aged and the elderly. Some analysts have contended that this shift of power is already taking place. As the proportion of the population that is old increases, the elderly are effectively challenging the structured inequality between themselves and the other age strata. If this redistribution of power is in fact occurring, the focus of the problem will not be the aged but rather class-based problems.

There is some indication that this redistribution of power is occurring, with wealthier older persons flexing their political muscle at the polls. The fate met by the Claude Pepper Commission's recommended catastrophic insurance program for the elderly, provides one example. This program was to have been funded by the elderly, with the government providing subsidies to help people below the poverty line. Wealthier older persons did not want to fund the health insurance of poorer older Americans, and the catastrophic health insurance program failed to receive the needed support for passage.

For the Christian there are no simple solutions to the problems of aging in a modern industrial society. Many of these problems identified by Professor Allen are intertwined with other social problems discussed in this text. We live in a world of limited resources and the just distribution of these resources demanded by God's command will always be a challenge to implement.

AGING AS A VALUE CONFLICT
Michael A. Allen

Social Values, Aging, and Social Problems

Is a social problem partially due to conflicting values between and within groups in a society? While certain values about what is desirable are common to virtually all groups in a society, many values vary from group to group. In any society there are both shared and diverse values among various groups. "In essence, any social condition becomes a social problem when there are 'value clashes' about the condition" (Lauer, 1989, p. 17). The value conflict approach to social problems assumes a power struggle over whose preferences or values will be expressed. Each of the contending groups strives to establish social conditions which support values which the group has designated as preferable.

The historical emphasis upon individual achievement and material success in our society tends to emphasize independence, self-sufficiency and productivity as motivating factors which develop self-esteem and social worth. Does aging pose a threat to any of these personal/social values? Individuals who value individualism, self-sufficiency, productive and material wealth/comfort, may believe these life preferences are threatened by their own aging, the aging of family members or the demographic aging of society in general. Growing older may threaten self-reliance, personal freedom and life satisfaction because of the reduction of economic resources or because their level of self-sufficiency is reduced. When older adult family members become increasingly dependent, the social costs in the form of additional taxes due to demand for services for the elderly, self-sufficiency and privacy of the nuclear family may also be threatened.

Many attitudes and values held by people in our society place a negative connotation on the older adult and the aging process. *Ageism* is the systematic discrimination against older adults and it is directed toward many differing groups. Ageism affects males and females, the physically fit, the ill, and people who are married, divorced, single, or widowed. Too often such a system of unequal treatment is based on a belief that older adults constitute a homogeneous group of individuals who are inferior, due to their existence in the latter stage of life. Losses in physical and mental skills, capabilities, and the ability of the older adult to contribute to society are often exaggerated, as Robert Butler, a former director of National Institute of Mental Health has stated:

> At best the living old are treated as though they were already half dead. . . . In America childhood is romanticized, youth is idolized, middle age does the work, wields the power and pays the bills, and old age . . . is a period of quiet despair, deprivation, desolation. . . . (1975).

This statement still has validity in the 1990s. Will the increasing number of people living longer in the United States now require a *value shift* to facilitate a more appreciative collaborative and positive disposition toward aging? Or will the current value system be reinforced and the growing number of older adults be summed up as an ever-increasing *burden*?

The population of older adults is projected to increase numerically and proportionately into the twenty-first century. One of the most dramatic and dynamic demographic changes in the United States has been the aging of our population. At the turn of the century, 4 percent of our population, numbering around 4 million, had reached their sixty-fifth birthday or more. Today, nearly 14 percent of the population has reached their sixty-fifth birthday or more, representing over thirty million men and women. The present older adult population of the United States is equivalent to the entire population of Canada. Each day, fifteen hundred additional persons reach their sixty-fifth birthday in the United States.

What are the demographic trends projected for the future? Between 1946 and 1964, the "baby boom" occurred, with 76,400,000 children born. Due to the proportionate size of the "baby boom generation" it continues to cause change and some stress on social values and structure/functions of social institutions in the United States. Schools were among the first to feel the impact of this large population cohort. Competition in employment, overburdened pension plans, social security, medical and social care are also current and long-range concerns. The critical years for our nation will be between 2010-2030. By 2030 there may well be over 50 million of retirement age, or nearly twice the number of persons over sixty-five that there are today. Certainly our secular society will have to adapt and change to meet the needs of the "greying of America." How might the role and function of the Church change? Not only do the elderly have needs the Church must minister to, but they need outlets for service within the Christian community that are not presently available.

PROBLEMS OF AGING

Labels, Social Attitudes, and Negative Self -Worth

Attitudes, social likes and dislikes are personal. They may develop out of individual preferences, but often they are logical extensions of societal beliefs and values. What are the social attitudes that people have in the United States toward the aging? Only 20 to 30 percent of the public twenty years ago was negatively disposed toward older adults, yet older adults were viewed as undesirable companions (McTavish, 1971). Harris and his associates found that a large majority of their respondents considered the twenties to the forties as the preferred age. Those who did select later stages of life tended to do so because, to them, later life represented a period of reduced responsibility, pressure and increased enjoyment. Poor health, disability and financial anxiety were the main reasons people did not choose the sixties or seventies as desirable ages (Harris, 1975). How are such attitudes formed? Certainly the mass media plays an ever-increasing role in shaping the attitudes help by the general public. Most Americans watch television more than three hours a day, with TV viewing serving as the leading pastime of preschool, middle age and older adults (Moss and Lawton, 1982).

In a study of Saturday morning cartoons, one research team found that 95 percent of the characteristics attributed to children in these programs were positive, compared to only 52 percent positive characteristics for both adults and older adults (Bishop and Krause, 1984). The research findings using thirteen daytime "soap operas" found 71 percent of the primary male characters concentrated in the 20 to 50 age range. Slightly under 10 percent were "older," a modest underrepresentation. The main women characters, however, were more age-concentrated, with 60 percent judged to be under 40. Only 7 percent were "older," a major underrepresentation. Only 3 of the 404 primary characters, .007 percent, were judged to be over age 70 (Elliott, 1984).

With this kind of underrepresentation, and the presence of negative social labels from mass media, associates and relatives, older adults feel their independence threatened and their vulnerability increased. In response, they may 1) emphasize the positive contributions they have made in the past, 2) ignore and deny negative societal attitudes toward them, 3) accept the diminished role expectations or 4) identify with new support systems as they take on the elderly role.

Almost 75 percent of the older adults live in urban areas which have social and medical support systems. About 74 percent of those sixty-five to seventy-four years of age live in homes they own; this is also the living arrangement for 69 percent of those seventy-five and older. About 80 percent of these elderly own their homes free of mortgage indebtedness. Long-time home ownership gives older adults a sense of independence and security, and is a positive factor in their experience of aging (Golant, 1984). Their homes provide them with a source of identity through a series of family events and lifelong memories (*New York Times*, 1986). Furthermore, 54 percent of those over sixty-five and 63 percent of those sixty-five to seventy-four years old are still living in homes with their spouses (U. S. Department of Commerce, 1989, p. 49).

Yet for many over age seventy-five, housing becomes an increasing problem due to loss of their spouse and/or their health. Only 8.5 percent of the population over age 75 live with their spouse in their home (U. S. Department of Commerce, 1989, p. 49); 40 percent of those over 75 live alone and have increasing difficulties maintaining their homes. These are driven to seek alternative living arrangements due to increasing utility rates, heating costs, taxes which exceed their fixed incomes, and difficulty making home repairs (Senate Committee on Aging, 1986). Despite financial pressures to leave the home, older adults resist moving from familiar surroundings because of the social and emotional ties they have with their home, church, and community. There is a reluctance to leave the familiar for the unfamiliar, for the *age-segregated* housing alternatives such as boarding homes, retirement communities and retirement centers.

The options of alternative housing have become less available even for those who would select them, due to the increasing demand and cost. Increasingly, those who live in planned retirement communities are financially elite, with average monthly charges ranging from $400 to $2,000 (Pogrebin, 1988). The nation's housing shortage has placed increasing pressure on the older adult lower middle and middle income home owner through *gentrification*. Gentrification refers to the upgrading of the social class composition and housing stock within a neighborhood (Eckert and Murray, 1984). The gentrification process unfortunately creates competition for housing between generations; the younger, upwardly mobile, more affluent upper middle class professional (Yuppies) search for homes in urban neighborhoods. They are willing to pay more for housing; prices are thus inflated, property taxes rise; and the older adult residents on fixed incomes are pushed out. Gentrification also increases the displacement of lower income older adult residents from low-cost daily/weekly rental hotels. Such single-resident-occupancy hotels are being destroyed and replaced with high-cost condominiums and apartment complexes for the younger affluent population (Shannon, 1989). At the same time older adults, especially from the lower and lower-middle classes are being pressured to sell their homes and to move out of apartments and hotels, the federal government is reducing expenditures allotted for low-cost public housing.

The combination of the loss of homes through gentrification and the reduction in the proportion of available housing increases the numbers of elderly entering the "new homeless" population.

Family Relationships

As society moved from agriculture to an urban/industrial economy in the late nineteenth and early twentieth century, a shift occurred in family structure, function and value system. The extended farm family emphasized interdependence, mutual reliance and intergenerational sharing of responsibilities, and served as a common social, psychological and spiritual support system. In an urban/industrial society the nuclear family offers the advantages of flexible socioeconomic relationships, independence, self-sufficiency and privacy. Today, however, with increased longevity, pressure is being placed on the middle age "sandwich generation" to accept the traditional role of child rearing and also that of caring for aging parents. In the United States 80 percent of those over sixty-five live with their adult children. Thus, the sandwich generation is faced with a conflict. On the one hand, they seek to gain self-respect through being independent, self-reliant and private about personal needs within the framework of the nuclear family; but, on the other hand, they are pressured into interdependent responsibilities across generations. The current and future needs of the intergenerational family call for mutual reliance. But this is being undermined by three family values: 1) the older generation does not want to be a "burden," and so refuses assistance from their children; 2) social gerontophobia, fear of aging, on the part of the children often makes them hesitate about current and future "what ifs" in life — these middle-aged children fear they may *stigmatize* their parents with an "old" label by discussing the wants and needs of growing older; 3) most care providers are wives and daughters who experience increasing role conflict due to the contrary demands of employment and the traditional female "caring" role (Deane, 1989).

Health

In the late nineteenth and early twentieth century, technological and medical advancements in antibiotics and inoculations helped control *infectious diseases*. Although early twentieth century medical emphasis on prevention and curative strategies for controlling infectious diseases enabled the youth to live longer, medical research has not controlled the chronic illnesses of the elderly. By definition, chronic illnesses are of long duration. The causes are often unknown, although certain social, psychological, behavioral and environmental conditions have been found to be associated with some chronic illnesses. The course of the illness is usually progressive and irreversible. Treatment includes control of symptoms, maintenance and rehabilitation. Modifying one's lifestyle through change in work patterns, environment, eating and drinking habits are ways of dealing with stress which may diminish the likelihood of contracting such illnesses. The chronic illnesses most associated with aging are heart disease, arthritis/rheumatism and cancer (National Center of Health Statistics, 1986). However, it is important to realize that chronic conditions do not always lead to limitations and

347

disabilities. Furthermore, disabilities which accompany aging are often not the result of the normal aging processes, but the result of pathological conditions that are preventable and treatable. The proportion of older people disabled by heart disease, arthritis/ rheumatism, and cancer can be expected to fall as our knowledge of these pathological conditions is expanded and cures are found.

Another serious problem older adults face is rapidly rising health costs which are increasing as larger numbers of older adults become disabled and require long-term care. Twenty-six percent of the disabled population over 65 suffers from heart conditions; 20 percent from arthritis/rheumatism; and 18 percent from cancer (National Center for Health Statistics, 1986). As the health of older adults worsens, their chances of needing more intensified long-term and institutional care increases. Although less that 5 percent of the older adult population is living in an institution on any given day, about 35 to 40 percent of older adults do spend some time in a nursing home before they die, primarily due to chronic health problems (Pogrebin, 1988). Who is going to care for the older adult? Who is going to pay for the long-term care health costs? Are the future younger generations going to be willing to pay higher taxes to provide for increased public health care, or would they rather pay lower taxes and assume greater personal responsibility for their care by utilizing family resources? Currently, the average middle class older adult couple expends their lifetime assets in approximately three years of nursing home care. It seems obvious, therefore, that public assistance is needed if proper health care is to be provided for the elderly.

The existing political debate over who is to assume responsibility for long-term care continues without resolution. In 1989 a catastrophe medical insurance program was approved, and became national policy. Older adults soon realized that only the population over age 65 would pay for the benefits rather than the cost being shared by the entire population. This resulted in the rescinding of the catastrophic insurance program. Currently, the Claude Pepper Commission is recommending a national long-term health care policy with two strategies: 1) nursing home care with older adults paying 20 percent for the first three months, with subsidies provided for those whose incomes are lower than twice the poverty level; 2) home and community-based care made available to the severely disabled (those needing help eating, bathing, toileting or dressing) and to those who have mental impairments. Beneficiaries would pay 20 percent of the cost of these services. The government would provide subsidies to help with incomes below the poverty level. There is, however, doubt that such a program will be approved; the increasing national debt, and the estimated $60 million annual cost of the Pepper Commission recommendation inhibit passage (Advocates Senior Alert Process, 1990). It should be noted that the growing insecurity and anxiety of the older adults as they age stem not from the fear of death, but rather from the loss of health and the long-term care that might result in gradual, but steady loss of lifelong savings and the fear of being placed on welfare.

Euthanasia and the Ethics of Aging

As the life span increases, ethical issues are being raised. Should we introduce artificial life support systems? Should we extend the life of the terminally ill with such "machines," or should we allow them to die with dignity? Should we honor living wills, and permit euthanasia? Does a person have the right to die? Does an older person have the right to live if this involves enormous expense to the public? Should the use of limited resources such as kidney dialysis and organ or heart transplants be prohibited if the patient is past a specific age?

The term *euthanasia* comes from a Greek word meaning "good death," and implies a death without pain. The proponents of euthanasia distinguish between *active* and *passive euthanasia. Passive euthanasia* is commonly defined as the practice of not introducing any life support or extraordinary medical measures (such as intravenous feeding, use of a respirator, or heart massage) when a person is diagnosed as terminally ill, or dying without hope of regaining health. Many of those who support passive euthanasia believe persons should have this moral and legal option if medical technology is prolonging the dying process rather than enhancing the living process. *Active euthanasia* is the practice of withdrawing life support systems which are already in place — commonly called "pulling the plug."

Recently there have been changes in the legal systems of 14 states and Washington, D. C., which allow individuals to instruct their families and medical personnel about their choice of medical procedures should their health fail or their condition become terminal. Such instructions are called *Living Wills* and must be prepared while the individual is mentally competent. The wills are notarized and copies given to family and medical staff. Living wills can be revised or revoked by the individual; they are not legally binding on representatives of the medical professions.

Conservative evangelical theologians, such as the late Francis Schaeffer, do not recognize the distinction between active and passive euthanasia (Schaeffer, 1979). Schaeffer refutes the right of Christians to participate in euthanasia on the basis that people are acting as God by deciding under what conditions they will die. Schaeffer feared euthanasia would become a future practice as one way to reduce suffering and/ or health care costs. Instead, it would diminish the dignity of life through wholesale murder of older members of the society.

A CHRISTIAN RESPONSE

"The King will reply, 'I tell you the truth, whatever you did for one of the least of these brothers of mine, you did for me'" (Matthew 25:40, NIV).

Relationships and Self-Worth

Relationships in our achievement-oriented society often seem to emphasize individualism, self-sufficiency, and privacy as a means of enhancing personal and material wealth. The function of social relationships is viewed as serving individual ends. Relationships are primarily instrumental with expressive relationships minimized. From a Christian perspective, however, emphasis needs to be placed on the values of community, cooperation, collaboration, and interdependence. Relationships function to develop self-worth based upon mutual respect for one another as children of God. Rather than the secular emphases on the independent/dependent dichotomous relationship, Christian thought emphasizes reciprocity and mutual interdependence in human interaction. Wives submit to their husbands (Ephesians 5:22), while the husbands are to love their wives as Christ loved the Church (Ephesians 6:1-2; Mark 6:13), while parents play their role with loving justice and without provoking their children to anger (Ephesians

6:4). Such value statements reinforcing reciprocal relationships also enhance the worth, dignity and self-esteem of older adults in intergenerational relationships.

Ageism

The Christian belief/value system of respect for the dignity and worth of every human being as a child of God, makes possible the transformation of ageism to a positive appreciation of aging (Psalm 84; Romans 12:2). Christians need to be visible and active with those who see older adult persons with dignity, who have potential to grow spiritually, socially and psychologically, even though they may have diminished physical capabilities (2 Corinthians 4:16). Specifically, how might Christians counter the secular society's negative impact on the aged? The Christian community might examine carefully their perceptions and expression of concern for the elderly. The use of prepositions such as "to" or "for," as an example, may be overemphasized. Directed ministry may foster a feeling of dependency on the part of aging members, and can easily slip into patronizing attitudes on the part of those giving such services.

Churches can keep senior citizens involved in ministries and services by emphasizing the prepositions "by" and "with." The Church then encourages the independence of older persons and affords them opportunity to use their abilities constructively, but without overemphasis on age-segregated activities.

Housing

Church groups have broadened housing alternatives for older adults through their varied nonprofit models. In Kansas, for example, five older adult widows living in separate large, older homes with escalating taxes and maintenance costs, have combined living arrangement in the most suitable home. Four widows have liquidated their assets and agreed to assist the fifth widow in remodeling the joint cooperative home and to share property taxes, monthly utility and grocery costs. They have agreed to share their skills in cooking, driving, house cleaning and business/tax financing, while at the same time recognizing that they will have reduced space and privacy. Such older adult cooperatives also facilitate intergenerational needs by releasing homes of the elderly to the younger married couples market.

Other housing options include the purchase of an older home, employment of Christian nurse and/or social worker, and the development of a boarding arrangement inhabited by several older members of the church. We also find in Christian college communities an increasing trend of "house-sharing" between older adult church members and Christian college students. College students may receive free or minimal cost housing in exchange for providing maintenance and personal services such as grocery shopping, cooking, grass/snow removal and transportation. Local churches have also purchased land near the church and developed older adult Christian communities with low-cost condominium and duplex housing. All these creative alternative housing efforts require interdependence/cooperation, trust and sometimes loss of personal privacy.

Health

Christian denominations are being challenged to engage in demographic research and planning to respond to health care needs as we approach the 21st century. Several denominations have already developed fine retirement communities and nursing homes. A tremendous need exists to continue development of alternative and institutional care facilities such as home health care, adult day care, retirement homes with lifetime care and nursing homes. Christian colleges should be developing curriculum to provide gerontology professionals such as geriatric nurses, social workers, psychologists, business administrators, activity directors and chaplains to ensure that a Christian health facility maintains a Christian atmosphere. Chaplains to housing and health facilities sponsored by Christians should not only serve denomination members and other Christians, but should also reach out into the larger secular community.

Family Relations

Much education needs to be done in the area of family relations. For example, there must be an increase in early childhood training and in later life retraining on the need for intergeneration relationships within the family. Emphasis must be placed on mutual reliance and interdependence, rather than on polar dependence and independence. Too often our culture breaks the nuclear family into satellite families, which are geographically mobile and isolated. Nuclear families become increasingly independent and estranged from each other, creating adjustment difficulties when older adults face an aging crisis. The present nuclear family structure, together with society's individualistic value system, does not facilitate interdependence, shared space or the kind of lifestyle suitable for the inclusion of older adults. There is a growing need for cross-generations to examine the reciprocal admonition of Scripture: "Honor one another above yourselves" (Romans 12:10, NIV) and "let us consider how we may spur one another on toward love and good deeds" (Hebrews 10:24, NIV). The two or more generations must make every effort to increase meaningful discussions about the "what if" circumstances in life.

Adult "children" need to listen for the needs of their parents and learn how to work with them to maintain their dignity and sense of self-worth. At the same time, elderly parents must perceive their adult "children" as mature and dependable individuals whom they can trust. Older adult parents must learn how to be vulnerable and receive from their children.

Successful Aging

Older adult Christians who develop a positive Christian lifestyle in the older adult years and keep themselves active in worship and service can consider themselves "successful." These same Christians will aspire to demonstrate the fruit of the Spirit — "love, joy, peace, patience, kindness, goodness, faithfulness, gentleness and self-control" (Galatians 5:22-23, NIV). The spiritual fruits plus the norms expressed in the beatitudes provide a counterculture value structure that offers solace and comfort for the Christian. While older adults may feel alienated from the "world" because of ageism, they will take heart from the words of Christ: "I have told you these things, so that in me you may have peace. In this world you will have trouble, But take heart! I have overcome the world" (John 16:33).

Study and Discussion
Questions

1. What "value clashes" imply a social problem in the aging process of United States society?

2. What is ageism? What is its impact on society and the individuals of our society?

3. Why is there increasing concern about the aging population of the 21st century?

4. What is the role of the mass media in creating attitudes toward aging? Get examples from television and radio commercials, newspaper ads, watching films, daily "soap" operas, and general television programming.

5. What housing problems do the older adult population face in our society? How does your local community or hometown provide housing services?

6. Would you rather pay higher taxes for the care of your parents by government programs, or pay lower taxes and care for your parents in your own future home?

7. Should there be a national health care program for older adults? How should it be financed? Only by older adults or the entire working population?

8. Does an older adult have the right to die? Can a Christian support the practice of passive euthanasia or active euthanasia? Why or why not?

9. How may a Christian belief system overcome negative self-worth and ageism?

10. How may the church provide social alternatives on issues of housing, health and family relations with older adults?

11. What is your definition of successful aging?

References

Advocates Senior Alert Process. *Update* 6 (3), Washington, D. C., A.S.A.P. Publication, 1990.

Atchley, Robert C. *Social Forces and Aging*. Belmont: Wadsworth, 1988.

Bishop, James M., and Daniel R. Krause. "Depictions of Aging and Old Age on Saturday Morning Television." *The Gerontologist*, 24:91-94, 1984.

Butler, Robert M., *Why Survive? Being Old in America*. New York: Harper & Row, 1975.

Cavanaugh, John C., *Adult Development and Aging*. Belmont: Wadsworth, 1990.

Cowgill, D. O., *Aging Around the World*. Belmont: Wadsworth, 1986.

Deane, Barbara, *Caring for Your Aging Parents: When Love Is Not Enough*. Colorado Springs: Navpress, 1989.

Eckert, J. K., and M. J. Murray, "Alternative Modes of Living for the Elderly: A Critical Review," pp. 95-128 in I. Altman, M. P. Lawton, and J. F. Wohlwill (eds.). *Elderly People and the Environment*. New York: Planum Press, 1984.

Elliott, Joyce, "Daytime Television Drama Portrayal of Older Adults." *The Gerontologist*, 24:628-33. 1984.

George, Linda K., and Lucille B. Bearon, *Quality of Life in Older Persons: Meaning and Measurement*. New York, Human Sciences Press, 1980.

Golant. S. M., *A Place to Grow Old*. New York: Columbia University Press, 1984.

Gray, Robert M., and David D. Moberg, *The Church and The Older Person*. Grand Rapids: Erdmans Publishing Company, 1977.

Harris, Lewis, and Associates, *The Myth and Reality of Aging in America*. Washington, D. C.: National Council on Aging.

Harbert, Anita, and Leon H. Ginsberg, *Human Services for Older Adults*: *Concepts and Skills*. Belmont: Wadsworth, 1979.

Jacob, Norma, *Growing Old: A View from Within*. Wallingford: Pendle Hill Publications, 1981.

Johnson, Eric C., *Older and Wiser: Wit, Wisdom and Spirited Advice from the Older Generation*. New York: Walker and Company, 1986.

Lauer, Robert H., *Social Problems and the Quality of Life*. (Fourth Edition) Dubuque: William C. Brown Publishers, 13-28, 1989.

U. S. Department of Commerce, Bureau of the Census, 1980-89. *Statistical Abstract of the United States*. Washington, D. C.: U. S. Government Printing Office, 1986.

U. S. Senate Subcommittee on Aging. *Aging America: Trends and Projections*. Washington, D. C.: U. S. Government Printing Office, 1986.

Wilson, Albert J. E., III, *Social Services for Older Persons*. Prospect Heights: Waveland Press, 1988.

PART IV

INEQUALITIES AND RELATED ISSUES

CHAPTER 19
RACE AND ETHNIC RELATIONS IN AMERICA: INTRODUCTION

Beginning with the framing of the Declaration of Independence through to newspaper headlines today, race and ethnic relations in the United States have been topics of concerned discussion and sometimes violent action. In 1944 Harper and Row Publishers distributed the classic two-volume work by Gunnar Myrdal, *An American Dilemma*. Myrdal, a Swedish sociologist and so a more neutral observer of the American scene, noted the growing disparity between statements reflecting our national ideal of human equality and the actual practice of unequal treatment in the United States based on race. Slavery's legacy of race problems — discrimination in housing, employment and education — still existed in various forms in 1944. Today this legacy continues and now includes other ethnic and racial groups in addition to African-Americans.

Is America a racist nation, or is she racially neutral? In his introduction, Professor Chasteen asks that we not accept anyone else's statement that American society is racist, but instead carefully consider the evidence for ourselves. As the relatively new theoretical perspective of *interpretive sociology* suggests, Chasteen wants us to examine the evidence, discover the meaning it has for us and to build, if we can, an alternative case. Professor Chasteen provides evidence of many ignoble aspects of American history, and brings us up-to-date regarding current race and ethnic relations. He discusses the experiences of Native-, African-, and Mexican-Americans, and concludes with suggestions for the role of the Church in hyphenated America.

In addition to the helpful and new information given about each of the three racial groups, the reader is encouraged to explore material about Native American tribes and legalized gambling (which seems on the surface to be an economic bonanza); their struggles to maintain fishing and hunting rights; and their continued efforts to set the historical records straight with regard to *Wounded Knee* and other white settler/Indian conflicts.

Social theorists have employed three major sociological perspectives to analyze race relations. *Structure-function theory* has explained racial conflict as resulting from inadequate socialization of the subordinate group. Some functionalists justify subordinate roles and their related minimal rewards by the argument of necessity — only those most committed to dominant values and possessing identification with the dominant group can effectively lead and be honored by the system. By definition, this perspective erects barriers to achievement by minority groups. Professor Chasteen notes socialization factors in his discussion of the inadequate functioning of Native Americans who have migrated to urban centers in the United States, and the differing values Mexican-Americans received through the socialization experiences of their culture. For the functionalist, values provide the organizing core of the social system; religion is often perceived as supplying those values. The author of this chapter reminds us of the many ways in which Christianity and religion have been used to justify, legitimate, and support the exploitation of Native Americans, and African-Americans. Christians are made aware of the distorted and twisted uses some have made of the biblical text and of Church tradition.

A second perspective, *symbolic-interaction theory*, explores the misunderstandings generated when communication symbols are exchanged between a dominant-resident group and the newcomer. Symbols are interpreted differently; misunderstandings become distortions which in turn become defined negative realities with respect to the newcomer. Chasteen points out the symbolic differences between the white settlers and Native American tribes with regard to ownership of land, and the contemporary legal symbols of law and individual rights which somehow permit continued disenfranchisement of the African-American. We are reminded of the pervasive and insensitive use of symbols such as "black" and "white" to reflect evil and good, and the powerful feelings of alienation which symbolic interaction can evoke. Professor Chasteen also suggests that we are moving toward tighter uniformity in our symbols. One example of this might be the "English Only" legislation being passed by increasing numbers of states.

Conflict theory is the third perspective employed in race relations analysis. Does society really benefit most when the status quo and the dominant group are maintained? Might this not be a convenient justification on the part of those in power to hold on to their prestige and position? Are the non-WASP groups unqualified to lead because they lack merit, or because they are denied opportunity by institutional racism and structural barriers? The conflict theorist would hold that those in control of the educational, economic, and political structures of society do not easily share that control. In fact, this perspective strongly suggests that moral and social force are necessary to bring about cooperative and constructive relations among competing groups.

For what reasons, however, would a pluralistic society seek to develop mutual respect and equal treatment among disparate groups? — for the sake of social harmony? — because this is crucial for long-term societal survival? — for the sake of abstract human conscience? Each of these reasons could be argued: Whose conscience? or what definition of "harmony?" We agree with Professor Chasteen that the powerful and enduring content of the Old and New Testament Scriptures forms the solid foundation needed to build a pluralistic, but nonracist society. The biblical message documents that God created each person in His own image, thereby making every individual of inestimable value. Each human is loved by Him, and so He calls believers to 'in honor prefer one another'; to 'bear one another's burdens'; and to 'love neighbors as ourselves.' In the concluding section of this chapter, Professor Chasteen offers suggestions for what a distinctive and constructive church role might be in 'hyphenated America.'

In addition to the networking and denominational activities the author suggests for the Church, you might wish to consider contributions which individuals and small groups can make toward the building of positive race and ethnic relations. Although not specifically directed toward issues of race, materials in the chapters on "unemployment," "Helping Developing Nations," "Problems in American Education," and "Poverty" relate to many of the difficulties faced by Native, African, and Mexican Americans and contain helpful suggestions for microlevel action.

RACE AND ETHNIC RELATIONS IN AMERICA
Ed R. Chasteen

"Let the facts speak for themselves." All of us have been told this so often that we have simply taken it for granted that we have been given good advice, some words of wisdom that will guard us against rushing too soon to judgment. What in fact we have been told is a bit of nonsense: facts don't speak; only people do.

Facts are meant to make a case, the way lumber is meant to build a house. Just as the carpenter cannot leave it to the lumber to build the house, so the sociologist cannot leave it to the facts to make a case. As the carpenter must know how to build a house before beginning to arrange the lumber, so the sociologist must know how to make a case before beginning to work with the facts.

The following discussion of race and ethnic relations in America uses facts to make the case that America is a racist nation, that its institutions treat nonwhites unfairly, that all Americans — white and nonwhite — pay a price for this racism. You may disagree. Good. Find different facts. Learn how to make a case. Give *your* voice to facts. Try to persuade others to agree with you. That's how communities and churches and countries are given direction and take action.

Here we go.

Oliver Wendell Holmes once observed that the axis of the earth protrudes through everyone's hometown. It does; otherwise pockets of people all over the planet would not feel bound to the place and to each other. Sociologists and anthropologists have given a name to Holmes' observation: *ethnocentrism*. Without a feeling of goodness and rightness in who we are and where we live, social life would be difficult. Nations, communities, families, athletic teams, armies, churches, clubs, schools — any group of people tend to be ethnocentric in the sense that belonging to their group ties them to each other and energizes their lives.

But ethnocentrism pushed too far is destructive. When people go beyond thinking that their way of life is good to thinking they are better than another group, trouble lies ahead. Feelings of superiority are soon translated into rationalizations of prejudice and discrimination. Unfair, unequal, and unjust treatment of other nationalities or races or religions come to be seen as appropriate responses to the flaws of inferior people.

With its creed of equality, justice, and democracy America has been considered a *melting pot* — a place where cultural differences disappear after a generation or two, leaving a homogeneous population, all speaking the same language, holding the same values, and all having the same rights. When such *assimilation* proved more difficult than anticipated, *pluralism* was advocated, allowing Americans to retain elements of their ethnic origin built around a core of basic values which all people in the country would hold. National policy has shifted between assimilation and pluralism throughout American history and will no doubt continue.

In this short chapter, space does not permit discussion of all the diverse nationalities, cultures, religions, and races drawn to America. We will examine the experience of

Native-Americans (Indians), African-Americans, and Mexican-Americans. We will also examine the role of the Church and Christian teachings in both the development of America's racial problems and in attempts to solve them.

NATIVE-AMERICANS

Observation: Native-Americans migrated to North America 25,000 years ago.

Observation: The first European came to North America 500 years ago.

Questions: Who discovered America?

Early Europeans wrote back from America telling their friends about the vast amount of "uninhabited" land. However, tens of thousands of Indians lived in America; the land was uninhabited only by European definition. Because Indians lived in harmony with the land, they made little change in the natural order and their presence went undetected. To the European, accustomed to mastering and exploiting the land, the wilderness of America did indeed seem unoccupied.

Indian and European notions of land ownership also differed. In the European tradition individuals held title to a certain piece of land and could do with it as they pleased, selling or giving it to their heirs as they chose. Land to the Indian was given as a trust by the gods to all people; individual ownership was blasphemy, an offense against the spirit world. Indians in their dealings with Europeans were tricked or forced into signing papers surrendering their lands, but they did so with the clear knowledge that lines upon a page could not affect their relationship to the land. To the European, however, the signed documents and exchange of some coinage were sufficient to secure physical control of the land. When the Native Americans did not comply with European "ownership" or treaties, the white settlers expelled tribe upon tribe from ancestral lands, burned and sacked whole villages, raped and murdered women and children, defamed Indian character and culture, introduced alcohol and created a helpless dependency which put the Indians "in their place."

A place of poverty, filth, and disease was developed. This place allowed neither the continuation of traditional Indian culture nor the adoption of European culture. This was a place apart from other Americas, a place no one else wanted because of the heat, the cold, the barren soil, the isolation. What was this place? *It was the Indian reservation.* Today, in addition, it is a place with no jobs, poor schools and little hope. A place where people die 25 years earlier than everyone else in the country. A place drowning in alcohol, awash in the blood of the young who die by their own hand rather than live without honor. The reservation is both the problem and solution for Indians: the problem because it isolates and restricts; the solution because it is the only place where what is left of Indian culture is kept alive.

Indians are the only *native* Americans. They are also the *invisible* Americans. Only in history books are the 250 distinct Native-American tribes which once ruled this land individually identified. By the single name "Indian" separate tribal identities have been summarily dismissed. The image of an American Indian is portrayed on late night TV and is someone who rides bareback upon a spotted pony, a feather headdress trailing down his back; one who lives in a buffalo-hide tepee, dances to the beat of tom-tom and mercilessly attacks the frontier fort scalping everyone inside. Undoubtedly, of all things Europeans have stripped from the Native-American, the loss that has had the most devastating effect is the *loss of identity* and *honor*.

The legacy of the once proud Native-American cultures does not serve the Indian well in the rough-and-tumble, give-and-take of American special interest politics. The stoical acceptance of life operates to deny Indians a voice in decisions that determine their status and activities in today's American system. Other racial and ethnic groups speak with a loud voice and demand attention. But to do battle in that fashion for Indians is a losing proposition, no matter what the outcome. If they raise their voice in a way that draws attention to their situation they are not being "Indian." Yet not to raise their voice is to continue the slide into the black bottomless hole occupied by society's discarded peoples.

The Native-American population in 1980 numbered about 1.36 million (Kitano, 1991, p. 173). This small number — less than one-half of one percent of all Americans — is divided several ways: by a U.S. government-dictated status as treaty or nontreaty Indians, by a designation as urban or reservation residents and by many different tribal loyalties. At one early point in the relationship between European and Indian the separate tribes were considered sovereign nations. The newly formed United States government signed peace treaties with these separate nations. The unusual terms required the tribe to surrender lands in return for a promise of rights to other specified land and to payments by the U.S. government "as long as the grass grows and the waters flow." These treaties remain in force to this day and obligate the United States to provide health and welfare programs and monies to the descendants of these tribes. The treaty obligations of our government to such tribes are as legally binding as the treaty obligations this country has with England, France, Russia, or any other country. But after a few years the United States ended its practice of treating Indian tribes as sovereign nations; this made it possible to take lands without the formality of signed treaties. The descendents of these nontreaty Indians today enjoy none of the rights guaranteed to treaty Indians (Kitano, 1991, pp. 165-66).

Until 1924 Indians were not citizens of the United States and were not protected by any of the laws that apply to other Americans. Though Indians today are citizens, they are still considered a unique responsibility of the federal government. State laws do not apply on Indian reservations. The reservations are federal territory in somewhat the same way as Washington, D.C. Though ownership of the reservation is said to rest with the tribes, and tribal councils have a voice in running the reservation, the real power over the reservation and all aspects of Indian life rests with the *Bureau of Indian Affairs* (BIA), a branch of the Department of the Interior in the federal government. On rare occasions, the director of the BIA has been Indian. Through most of its history, however, the BIA has been operated by non-Indians and its programs geared *more* to federal land management than to Indian welfare.

Indians have long sought to have the BIA moved from the Department of the Interior to the Department of Health, Education and Welfare. Indians believe that such a move would focus the work of the BIA on Indian needs rather than on those of the ranchers, loggers, miners, and oil men who now pressure the BIA to do things with the reservations which Indians oppose and from which they do not profit. Most non-Indian interests favor the termination of the federal status of Indians placing them under state authority along with all other citizens. Some Indians also favor this. But if this were done, it would then be possible to assign ownership of tracts of reservation land to individual Indians who could sell or work them as they wished. The result would be a disaster for Indians and a bonanza for Euramerican ranching, mining, timber, and oil interests. Euramericans would soon buy up the land, as has already happened on those few reservations allowed by the government to parcel out plots of reservation land to individual members of the tribe.

Tribal ownership of the reservation is the only safeguard against the disappearance of the last remaining Indian acres in this country. The realities of Indian life suggest that few individual Indians could say no if offered more money than they had ever imagined for a pitiful little piece of desert, swamp or mountainside. When advised to turn down such offers and stay on their land, more might be asked of them than is humanly possible. If I were Indian and received such an offer, I have no doubt what my answer would be. I would think of my children and the food and medicine the money would buy for them. I would think of my wife and her poor health. I would think of the city where I could rent a house and get a job. And I would say yes. I would leave my land in order to feed and clothe my family.

I would become an *urban Indian* as other thousands of my brothers and sisters have become. I would move to Minneapolis, Chicago, Kansas City, Wichita or Phoenix. I would look for work: having few job skills, I would take whatever marginal employment I could get. I would work at that job if I could stand the humiliation of being told I am stupid and slow. I would work indoors if I could stand not seeing the sun and feeling the wind. I would work until the little bit of money made would fail to feed my family or pay the rent; then my self-respect would not let me beg for help and alcohol would become my best friend. My family would not understand how things are done in the city; they would be too proud to ask strangers for help and the welfare system does not know how to respond. Urban Indians live between the cracks because Indians are technically the responsibility of the federal government. But the feds *won't* help if the Indian has left the reservation to live in the city.

Indian culture has been all but destroyed. Black Elk, the legendary medicine man of the Oglala Sioux described what had happened to his people. "But the *Wasichus* (white man) has put us in these square boxes. Our power is gone and we are dying, for the power is not in us any more. You can look at our boys and see how it is with us. When we were living by the power of the circle in the way we should, boys were men at twelve or thirteen years of age. But now it takes them very much longer to mature" (Neihardt, 1959, p. 166).

Indian culture is inseparable from the land territory which is the spiritual domain Indians inhabit, the place where humanity lives in harmony with nature. Here are no polluted skies or rivers, no gouging and reshaping the earth, no wildlife driven to extinction, no acquiring of goods beyond what a person can immediately use. Indian territory measured by the acre is all but gone. The spiritual domain has been overrun, its voice faintly heard above the babble of other claims.

Gresham's Law is usually applied in another context, but what it says may have relevance here. After a lifetime observing the monetary system, Gresham concluded that cheap money will always drive more precious currency out of circulation. Thus we have paper money rather than gold, and European rather than Indian land territory.

An Indian prayer is seldom heard in modern America. But let us conclude this section with a prayer by the Sioux children of the Red Cloud Indian School in Pine Ridge, South Dakota:

> O GREAT SPIRIT,
> whose voice I hear in the winds,
> And whose breath gives life to all the world,
> hear me! I am small and weak, I need your
> strength and wisdom.
> **Let me walk in beauty**, and make my eyes
> ever behold the red and purple sunset.
> **Make my hands** respect the things you have
> made and my ears sharp to hear your voice.
> **Make me wise** so that I may understand the
> things you have taught my people.
> **Let me learn** the lessons you have hidden
> in every leaf and rock.
> **I seek strength**, not to be greater than my
> brother, but to fight my greatest enemy — myself.
> **Make me always ready** to come to you with
> clean hands and straight eyes.
> **So when life fades**, as the fading sunset,
> my spirit may come to you
> without shame.

AFRICAN-AMERICANS

White Americans may grow tired of hearing of slavery, but that is the central historical event of the American experience. Slavery may have had some beneficent aspects as some white scholars have argued, but it is still the enslavement of one group of humans by other humans. To give even the appearance of justifying slavery exhibits barbaric insensitivity. Some tortures may not be as cruel as others, but that fact can in no way justify any torture at all.

The first blacks arrived as settlers in the American colonies in 1619, one year before the Pilgrims landed at Plymouth (Franklin, 1969, p. 71). There were 20 of them; they came as *indentured servants*, as did most of the white colonists. In exchange for their passage to the colonies, indentured servants agreed to work for a specified number of years, seven being fairly common. After that obligation had been worked off, the servant was free to make his or her own way in the new world. Almost from the beginning, the colonies suffered a labor shortage. The fairly small number of new arrivals from Europe and the high death rate that prevailed among them insured that the labor supply constantly fell below demand. Attempts were made in early colonial times to conscript Indians as laborers. However, they would soon disappear into the forest and leave the colonists short-handed. Being few in number and different in color, blacks were conspicuous members of colonial society. They were accustomed to hard work in their homeland, and European colonists quickly hit upon the idea of enticing more Africans to undertake passage to the colonies as indentured servants. There was little incentive, however, for blacks to migrate to a new country and live among foreign people. Those blacks who did come after 1640 found that they had no contracts of indenture as earlier servants had, and could not look forward to gaining their freedom after a specified time. Some, in fact, discovered that they had contracts stating they were servants for life.

By 1661 it was apparent that drastic measures were necessary if the labor demands of the colonies were to be satisfied. In that year Virginia became the first colony to legalize Negro slavery (Franklin, 1969, p. 72). Maryland followed suit in 1663. By the early 1700s, all the southern colonies had sanctioned slavery. How were these European colonists, many of whom had immigrated for religious reasons, able to justify the enslavement of other people? Their implicit reason for doing so was to meet the labor demands, but their earliest explicit justification offered for slavery was that Negro souls, otherwise damned, could be Christianized and saved. Initially slave-owners were concerned that slaves might be entitled to freedom if they became Christian. Officials of both colony and Church went to great lengths to assure owners that slaves could not be freed merely by becoming Christian. Instead, slave-masters were urged to cooperate with the Church in order to rid the slave of his African "heathenism" which erupted with disturbing frequency in revolts and bloody rebellion. A *Christian slave* would be more hard working and docile (Franklin, 1969, p. 86). By the mid 1700s slavery had spread to all the colonies. Some colonies were more moderate in the slave codes they enacted, but slavery as an institution flourished throughout colonial America.

In cultures of the past, a slave was one whose people had lost in battle, and slavery was a condition which the next battle might change. In early America, however, two things were different: the color of the slave, and the value system of the master. Europeans who came to North America in the 1600s came as settlers. Those who traveled to South America went principally as adventurers. Settlers travel in family groups; adventurers travel in bands of single men. Settlers plan to stay; adventurers move on. The relationships established by settlers and adventurers with the native people are quite different. As family units, settlers soon create barriers between themselves and native people in order to protect their women and children from what they define as an inferior culture and people. Adventurers just as quickly adapt themselves to the native culture, marrying the women, fathering children in and out of marriage, and working more or less as equals with the native men.

American settler-colonists soon came to look on the Indian as a savage. This belief was effective in keeping Indian and European apart. In the same way an elaborate system of racist beliefs was created by the colonists, the central doctrine of which held that blacks were actually less human than whites. The legacy of slavery casts a long shadow across the relations of modern-day Americans, black and white. Racism was conceived in early America as one way to rationalize slavery; though slavery is now dead, racism still lives.

The philosophical roots of American racism may be traced to precolonial Europe where white men had long written derogatorily about black-skinned men and women. They maintained that black skin was a curse of God, a mark of servitude, and the badge of sin. They said that blacks lacked restraint over sexual impulse, were defiant of authority, and that their fallen state was below that of Adam. Blackness was a mark of the devil, a symbol of greed and lust. It remained for the American colonists, however, to coordinate, systematize, and extend those racist motions into that full-blown system of beliefs which eventually supported the economic, political and social order undergirding American slavery.

The colonists first distinguished themselves from both Indians and Negroes by calling themselves "Christians," apparently an effort to put distance between themselves and the "heathen" Africans and Indians. Later in the 1600s, the colonists began to replace "Christian" with "English," perhaps indicating that some of the Africans and Indians were no longer "heathen" and the name "Christian" would no longer create the proper distance. As the number of non-English-speaking immigrants grew after 1700, the term "English" was slowly replaced by "white." Thus the distinction which was first religious, then national became — as it is today — racial.

Slavery officially ended in 1865, but the racism which supported it is alive and well across the length and breadth of America in the 1990s. Racism lives in virulent form in those religious groups which actively support the Ku Klux Klan and still believe that God has a special fondness for lighter skin. Racism lives in the political system where Martin Luther King, Jr., is a "black" leader but John F. Kennedy or George Bush is never called a "white" leader. Racism lives in industry where unions accept as members only those whose friends and relatives are already in, and exhibit little concern for the economic plight of nonwhite people. Racism lives in employment so long as the outstanding token African-American is conspicuously displayed by the white company but the bulk of black youth can find no jobs. Racism lives in "amateur" sports when colleges keep black athletes eligible by enrolling them in "mickey mouse" courses, use their athletic skills to fill sports stadiums, but seldom graduate those same athletes. Racism lives in professional sports when black superstars get few opportunities to make commercials, and when a black must be a starter to make the team. Racism lives when the players are black and those who run the organization are white.

Racism lives in the neighborhood when blacks cannot buy a house in a white area even though the law says discrimination is illegal. Racism lives in education when "forced busing" is manufactured as a divisive issue to mask white resistance to integrated housing. Racism lives in a society which tells blacks that they can get a better job when they get a better education; they can get a better education when they make enough money to live in a better neighborhood. All they need to make that money is a better job. Racism lives in a white psyche that does not question beige-colored bandaids labeled as "flesh-colored," or question that the only blacks around are cooks and janitors. Racism lives in the black soul that shrivels like a raisin in the sun and learns to hate — both self and society.

As bad as it is, racism is made worse by denying it exists; by both black and white assuming that the other really is what they seem. Racism is the legacy of slavery which causes both black and white to distort their view of self and each other. When a lighter skin is valued among blacks, blacks are racist. When whites speak of blackmail, the black sheep, black ball; when a white lie is more acceptable than a dirty black lie, whites are racist. When a black is punished more severely for a crime against a white than for one against a black, or when a black suspect is identified in the media by race and white is not, then racism is alive and well. When blacks must be conscious of their race in all the dealings of daily life and whites can safely ignore their racial designation, racism lives. When an interracial couple is ostracized by both blacks and whites, racism lives. When sexual relations between a white man and black woman are more acceptable to whites and between a black man and a white woman more acceptable to blacks, racism — and sexism — live. So long as it makes the slightest difference what is the color of their skin — so long as skin color has any more relevance than eye or hair color — just this long will racism live.

Slavery ended more than a century ago in this country. The chains and whips are gone. The white master and the black mammy are figures of the past. The law now says that white and black are equal and they should be treated with equal respect and justice. That is reason to rejoice. But if that day ever comes when the hearts and minds of all Americans — black and white — are rid of racism then we can know that the words of the old Negro spiritual have finally come true:

"Free at last, free at last; Thank God a'mighty, Free at last."

MEXICAN-AMERICANS

Attending school as a boy growing up in Texas in the 1950s, I was required to learn the history of the state. I learned that Texas joined the Union in 1845 after a small band of Texans had beaten the Mexican army. The most famous battle, in what Texans call their "war for independence," was the *Battle of the Alamo*. In this battle, a handful of brave Texans, including James Bowie, Davy Crockett and others of similar renown, held off thousands of Mexicans for days until they were finally overrun and brutally killed. "Remember the Alamo" became the rallying cry of the ragtag Texas army, enabling a resolute and resourceful General Sam Houston to defeat General Santa Anna. Finally, and against great odds, he was able to win Texas independence.

As a junior high student thirty years ago, I came away from the study of Texas history worshiping those heroes of the Alamo. I made a wooden bowie knife like the one I was told James Bowie had used in hand-to-hand combat with a number of unlucky Mexicans. I was awed by the bravery of the Texan captured in the Battle of Goliad who voluntarily gave up his life for a comrade. Their Mexican captors passed black, and white beans among them, and those who drew the black bean were shot. One Texas soldier whose name went unrecorded, but whose bravery lives forever in Texas history, traded his white bean to a friend who had drawn a black. He gave his life for his friend. It never occurred to me at the time that those Texans had been made bigger than life to me. I never questioned the image of Texans and Mexicans that was forming in my mind from the version of history I was taught. In the years since, much has changed for me. I moved from Texas; I began to read other accounts of history; I visited Mexico. I know now that what I was taught to call the "Texas War for Independence" was, from the Mexican perspective, an invasion by foreigners and a revolution of political extremists. Mexican soldiers were doing their duty, fighting bravely against revolutionaries who were continually and surreptitiously supplied with men and weapons by a hostile foreign power — the United States of America.

Many accounts of Mexican bravery are chronicled by those who wrote of the war from the Mexican point of view. In these accounts, the rebellious Texans fought unfairly, hiding in ambush and shooting those unprepared for battle. In the Mexican history book, the war was finally lost because the United States, though unofficially neutral, supported and supplied the rebellious Texans.

The entire southwestern United States up until about 100 years ago was part of Mexico. All the land from Texas to California was taken by force from Mexico. Several million Hispanic people still live in the American southwest. The fortunes of war have made them by nationality American, but culturally they are Mexican. Thousands of Mexican-Americans live in other parts of the United States. Chicago, St. Louis, Kansas City, Phoenix, and other cities scattered across the heartland of America contain sizeable Mexican-American communities. All of these communities are kept alive by people who find meaning in their traditional culture and values. However, they are also isolated from the larger culture by the unwillingness of the majority to let them participate fully and equally in national life.

In 1970 ninety percent of all Mexican-Americans lived in five western states: Texas, New Mexico, Arizona, Colorado, and California (Moore, 1976, p. 55). The two states of Texas and California contained more than 80 percent of the Mexican-Americans, Los Angeles is the fifth largest Spanish-speaking city in the world and San Antonio, where the Texans won the Battle of the Alamo in the 1840s today has the largest Mexican-American population in the state. The total size of the Mexican-American population in the United States in now estimated at nine million. This estimate is little more than an educated guess, however. The Census Bureau did not count Mexican-Americans until 1930. Since that time minority people have been undercounted by the census because they are difficult to find, they have learned to be less trusting when dealing with those who speak for the government, and they often do not speak English well. Whether or not the Census Bureau estimate of the Mexican-American population is accurate, it is certain that this group, when included with other Hispanic groups, is the fastest growing minority population in the country.

The typical Mexican-American family is larger than that of Anglos, Blacks, Puerto Ricans or Native-Americans. The median age of Mexican-Americans is nine years younger than the median age of the population as a whole. This means that public schools have a big job to do if Mexican-American youngsters are to receive the education they need in order to join mainstream America. Public education is failing to meet its obligation to Mexican-Americans. By any standard other than those of schools in underdeveloped countries, the output for Mexican-Americans is exceptionally poor. In the Southwest, Mexican-American adults have an average of three years less education than Anglos. Mexican-American adults in Texas have received on the average only 6.7 years of schooling.

About all anyone knows with this little schooling is how to read and write. He or she is not likely to get a job with any future or at more than minimum wage. It is no wonder then that in Texas, a Mexican-American male earns 40 percent less than an Anglo male; in Arizona and California, 25 percent less. Almost one-fourth of all Mexican-American families in 1970 fell below the poverty line defined by the United States government. In terms of occupation, 53 percent of Anglos are white-collar workers, compared to 22 percent of Mexican-Americans. On the other hand, 21 percent of Mexican-Americans are laborers while only 5 percent of Anglos make their living in this way (Moore 1976, pp. 60-66). The educational and employment opportunities of Mexican-Americans do not fit with the rhetoric of the United States on subjects of justice, fairness, and promises to reward those who try hard.

As is true for other American minorities, Mexican-Americans suffer an image problem: they all take daily *siestas*; they do things *manana*; they like bright colors, hot food, fast music; they talk funny. They are known as pepper-bellies, greasers, wetbacks, mescuns. They all love tacos and peppers. In the movies Mexican-Americans play bandits or side-kicks. From Pepito who was always apologizing to Judy Canova on radio in the 1940s to the Frito Bandito on television in the 1970s, Mexican-Americans have been pictured as bumbling or dangerous. That has changed somewhat in the last 15 years as Mexican-American individuals and organizations work to counter their negative image. A moving epic poem published in 1972 by Rodolfo (Corky) Gonzalez, called *Yo Say Joaquin* (I am Joaquin) looks back on Mexican history and the endurance of the people and celebrates the unconquerable appetite for freedom of the Chicano.

Chicano was a term formerly used to describe the poor, lower-class Mexican. In the 1960s Chicano became the adopted name of those restless young leaders who sought to elevate the status and image of the Mexican-American. Chicano is the term most often used today by the media and by Anglo society when referring to Mexican-Americans. This change in name indicates a change for the better in the image Anglos have of Mexican-Americans. In a society that spends billions for advertising and packaging, an improvement in image can open many doors. By calling themselves Chicanos, Mexican-Americans are also changing the image they hold of themselves. In his two books, Oscar Acosta sees Chicanos as good people pitted against a hypocritical system and so doomed to lose no matter how much they want to accept the values of the Anglo schools, the courts and the Church. As a successful criminal lawyer and a former Baptist missionary, Acosta has made good in Anglo society. What he says, therefore, should be taken seriously by that society. Acosta's first book, published in 1973, is the story of his life and he entitles it, *The Autobiography of a Brown Buffalo*. The book describes Acosta's childhood and his coming of age; it is the story of an outsider forced to fight for acceptance, only to realize the hypocrisy of that acceptance. Acosta's second book, *The Revolt of the Cockroach People*, continued his story in fictional form. Throughout the intense political activity of 1968-1970 in East Los Angeles, Acosta forms his definition of himself as a "brown buffalo" because he and his people are unwanted survivors of the West, doomed to be hunted to death like cockroaches and buffalo. Acosta sees Chicanos must be an active minority, fighting their disadvantaged position with the sophisticated institutional weapons of the Anglos: using the law, appealing to the courts and the Constitution, pushing for better schools, jobs and housing.

In 1965 Cesar Chavez organized the strike of Mexican farm workers in the Delano grape orchards of California. Also in 1965 Corky Gonzalez founded the *Crusade for Justice* in Denver. In 1966 Ries Tijerina and his supporters occupied the Kit Carson national forest in Mew Mexico to publicize their claims that these lands had been illegally taken from Mexican people when the United States seized the Southwest from Mexico. These three men and events have given symbolic birth to the Chicano Movement. Other individuals and organizations also began their work about this time. The first *La Raza* (The Cause) conference was held in 1967; La Raza was to become the rallying cry of the Chicano movement. The United Mexican-American Students (UMAS), the Mexican-American Youth Organization (MAYO) and the brown berets were also organized in 1967 (Moore, 1976, p. 9).

America *is* a nation of immigrants. Except for the Indians the ancestors of all of us came to this country no more than a few generations ago. We are a diverse people thrown together by the accidents of history and politics. A careful reading of the record of our years as a nation clearly shows the strength which comes from our diversity. That record also indicates that democracy is supported — not because individual Americans believe in justice and equality and therefore treat others as they wish to be treated — but because interest groups organize themselves and by threat and promise prevail in competition with other interest groups.

A threat to Mexican-Americans is the illegal Mexican alien. As many as one million a year crossed the Rio Grande during the late 1970s and early 1980s. They were trying to escape the dismal conditions in Mexico, which currently has one of the highest rates of population growth in the world, and also one of the highest unemployment rates. These illegal aliens — or undocumented workers as some choose to call them — fan out across the United States. Finding and deporting them is so difficult that in 1978 President Carter proposed granting amnesty to all Mexican aliens then in the country. Amnesty would allow them to stay and eventually to become citizens. This proposal drew a hail of criticism, yet in the 1980s under President Reagan such a bill was passed by Congress.

Black Americans generally oppose moves to legalize Mexican aliens. Not only would this action, in their opinion, greatly increase the size of the Mexican-American population (perhaps doubling the number), it would also attract other illegal aliens, and make the problem worse in the long run. Blacks and other minorities resent the fact that illegal aliens take jobs away from them because the aliens will work for less and cannot complain about working conditions, given their illegal status. Employers are attracted to the illegal aliens because they will do unattractive, dirty, low-paying work. Blacks, and even some Mexican-Americans, argue that if illegal aliens were not available, those jobs would go to them at higher wages and under better conditions.

Mexican officials show little inclination to stem the tide of illegal aliens. Minimal economic opportunity exists in Mexico; forcing Mexicans to stay and try to survive would also bring tremendous pressure for change in Mexican society. Desire for such change might stimulate violence within the country and against the government itself. The United States government knows this. If the border were sealed and the illegal alien flood restricted, Mexico might be engulfed by revolution with their democratic government overthrown and replaced by a dictatorship. The prospects of a totalitarian government bordering Texas and California is frightening; the United States government unofficially seems willing to tolerate illegal aliens as a defense against that possibility. More must be done to solve the illegal alien problem if Mexican-Americans are to escape the backlash of resentment from Anglo society, and from the majority of Mexican-Americans who are legally in this country.

America is stronger as a nation when individual ethnic groups are at maximum strength. The Chicano Movement, the Black Movement, the Native-American Movement and the smaller stirrings in ethnic communities across this nation are hopeful signs. The democratic system can work — if not equally well for everybody — at least with compassion and a recognition that it is not yet perfect. However, even though civil rights movements in all minority communities picked up momentum in the 1960s, they lost that momentum in the 1970s. It would be tragic if the political conservatism of the 1980s brings a halt in the 1990s to these needed improvements in the lives of minority Americans.

THE CHURCH IN HYPHENATED AMERICA

The forces of uniformity march lockstep through American society. A common architecture springs like dandelions across the national landscape, creating a visual symbol of the mass mind fashioned by the mass media. Fewer Americans speak other languages. Only 8 percent of all United States colleges and universities now require a foreign language for admission, as against 34 percent in 1966 and 85 percent in 1959. Only 15 percent of American high school students study a second language, and barely a handful of them pursue those studies for more than two years. Giant universities spew out human replacements for giant corporations, locking both into a process of institutional cloning which threatens to reduce national life to a sterile sameness of thought and action. The mass media assaults citizens with a common perspective on current events and a common definition of what makes "news." Against this deluge of homogeneity, millions of Americans erect ethnic barriers holding back the flood and cultivating little islands of humanity which otherwise would be inundated. Using their hyphenated status as a shield, these Americans do battle with the leveling agents of American society. The display of native dress, the use of native tongue, the aroma of native food — all furnish hyphenated Americans a status apart. No longer a part of the thundering herd, no longer dismissed as the silent majority, ethnic Americans achieve both community and identity through "hyphenation." Anonymous Americans struggle to revive their ancestral past; ancient traditions and faintly remembered myths are embraced as anchors against the numbing sea of sameness.

How is the Church to minister to these millions who are declaring their ethnic independence? To abandon them to do their own thing is to abandon the Great Commission. The Church will cease to be the Church if it does not teach and preach in all the ethnic communities of America. But the Church in ethnic America must do its work with a greater sensitivity than the Church has demonstrated in the past. Although the majority of ethnic institutions and values are not antagonistic to the Gospel, they are fragile and foreign. Without the nurturing which only the Church is likely to supply, they will not make it.

Cooperative evangelism has been attempted in ethnic communities with promising results. Luis Palau's 1980 Hispanic crusade in Los Angeles brought approximately 125 evangelical churches of different denominations together in "previously unknown cooperation" (*Christianity Today*: August 8, 1980, p. 38). Cooperative ministries can be a freeing experience for the Church. By requiring denominational cooperation, ethnic ministries can rid the Church of its overemphasis on competition between fellow Christians. Operating in areas outside our usual cultural understanding allows us to see with new eyes those features of our faith which come more from cultural assumptions than from biblical truth. Community and fellowship are central concerns of both the Church and ethnic communities. If for no other reason, the Church must act to protect and strengthen ethnicity in order to keep these values alive.

The Church has most successfully practiced its ethnic ministry in black America. The result today is a strong black Church able to powerfully address the spiritual and physical needs of black-Americans. The strength of the black Church is a reflection of the hardships out of which it has come. To hear the black preacher and the black choir, to realize that the Church is the strongest, most independent institution in the black community, to witness the effective and far-reaching work of the black Church in attacking problems of African-Americans is to rejoice, to know that the promise of the Church is not hollow.

If denominations would extend their cooperative efforts now evident in community clothes closets, food pantries, and ministerial alliances to include ethnic ministries, much could be accomplished both to advance the Church and retain the integrity of the community. Christians have demonstrated that churches can work together; they have opened their doors to newly arrived Christian immigrants and refugees who had no place of worship. By allowing them to use the Church building on Sunday afternoon or during the weekdays when the building is not in demand, the local Church has done two vital things. First, the Church makes it possible for the newly arrived to practice their faith, to draw together for strength and encouragement in the midst of a culture they do not understand. No greater witness to its compassion and concern could the Church give. Second, the Church establishes an outreach program into already existing ethnic communities. Once the new ethnics have made their initial adjustment to American culture, they are able to turn their attention to the established ethnic communities. These new ethnics can exert a Christian witness in ethnic communities which American Christian could never accomplish, and without damaging the culture.

We are one body in Christ; that we must never forget.

Study and Discussion
Questions

1. In what sense is ethnocentrism beneficial to social life? How can it become destructive? Give examples to support your answers (pp. 5, 6).

2. How is it possible to discover a place where people already live? In what sense did Europeans discover America? Explain the difference in definition of land ownership between Native-Americans and Europeans (p. 3).

3. How do Indians lose by demanding attention (p. 5)?

4. Explain the distinction between treaty and nontreaty; urban and reservation Indians (pp. 5-6).

5. What would be the likely outcome of terminating the federal status of Indians and assigning ownership of reservation lands to individual Indians (pp. 6-7)?

6. When and why did racism originate (p. 12)?

7. How did the first Europeans who came to North and South America differ? How has this difference affected present race relations (p. 11)?

8. What evidence does the chapter cite to support its charge that racism lives (pp. 13-14)?

9. Describe the Texas War for Independence first from the Texan's point of view and then the Mexican's (pp. 15-16).

10. How does the socioeconomic status of Mexican-Americans compare to that of the majority population (p. 17)?

11. Discuss the use of "Chicano" to describe Mexican-Americans. How has the term affected their image?

12. What is the relationship between Afro-Americans and Mexican-Americans (p. 21)?

13. What is the role of the Church in hyphenated America (pp. 22-25)?

Bibliography

I have listed below the books that have informed my perspective on American race relations. Several of them are biographies of Afro-American, Mexican-American, and Native-American leaders in the struggles of their people for freedom and justice. From reading these biographies, I have come to appreciate both the contribution these people made to the American character and the intractable problems they were forced to confront.

Acosta, Oscar Zeta, *The Autobiography of a Brown Buffalo*. San Francisco: Straight Arrow Books, 1972.

Acosta, Oscar, *The Revolt of the Cockroach People*. San Francisco: Straight Arrow Books, 1973.

Andrist, Ralph K., *The Long Death: The Last Days of the Plain Indians*. New York: Collier Books, 1964.

Armstrong, William H., *Warrior in Two Camps: Union General and Seneca Chief*. New York: Syracuse University Press, 1978.

Bahr, Howard M. et. al. (editors), *Native Americans Today: Sociological Perspectives*. New York: Harper & Row, 1972.

Cleaver, Eldridge, *Soul on Ice*. New York: Delta Books, 1964.

Davidson, Margaret, *I Have a Dream*. New York: Scholastic Inc., 1986.

Davis, Angela Y., *If They Come in the Morning*. California: National United Committee to Free Angela Davis, Inc., 1971.

Davis, Angela Y. ,*Women, Race, and Class*. New York: Random House, 1981.

Douglass, Frederick, *Narrative of the Life of Frederick Douglass, An American Slave*. Virginia: George Banta Co., 1982.

Du Bois, W. E. Burghardt, *The Souls of Black Folk*. Connecticut: Fawcett Publications, 1961.

Franklin, John Hope, *From Slavery to Freedom: A History of Negro Americans*. New York: Vintage Books, 1969.

Harding, Vincent, *There is a River: The Black Struggle for Freedom in America*. New York: Vintage Books, 1983.

Howard, Helen Addison, *Saga of Chief Joseph*. Lincoln: University of Nebraska Press, 1978.

Kelsay, Isabel Thompson, *Joseph Brant (1743-1807): Man of Two Worlds*. New York: Syracuse University Press, 1984.

King, Martin Luther, Jr., *Why We Can't Wait*. New York: Harper and Row, 1964.

Kitano, Harry, *Race Relations*. (4th ed.). New Jersey: Prentice-Hall.* 1991.

Levy, Jacques, *Cesar Chavaz*. New York: W. W. Norton and Co. Inc., 1975.

Linderman, Frank B., *Plenty-Coups: Chief of the Crows*. Lincoln/London: University of Nebraska Press, 1962.

Martin, Tony, *The Pan-African Connection: From Slavery to Garvey and Beyond*. Massachusetts: Schenkman Publishing Company, 1983.

McNeil, Genna Rae, *Groundwork: Charles Hamilton Houston and the Struggle for Civil Rights*. Philadelphia: University of Pennsylvania Press, 1983.

Moore, Joan, and Harry Pachon, *Hispanics in the United States*. New Jersey: Prentice-Hall, 1985.

Moore, Joan W., *Mexican-Americans*. New Jersey: Prentice-Hall.* 1976.

Neihardt, John G., *Black Elk Speaks*. New York: Pocket Books.* 1975.

Nieman, Donald G., *Promises to Keep*. New York: Oxford University Press, 1991.

Oates, Stephen B., *Let the Trumpet Sound. The Life of Martin Luther King, Jr.* New York: Plume Books, 1982.

Olsen, James C., *Red Cloud and the Sioux Problem*. Nebraska: University of Nebraska Press, 1965.

Raines, Howel, *My Soul is Rested: The Story of the Civil Rights Movement in the Deep South*. New York: Penguin Books, 1983.

Robinson, JoAnn Gibson, *The Montgomery Bus Boycott and the Woman Who Started It*. Knoxville: University of Tennessee Press, 1987.

Sandoz, Mari, *Crazy Horse: The Strange Man of the Oglalas*. Lincoln: University of Nebraska Press, 1971.

Scheer, Robert, *Eldridge Cleaver*. New York: Random House, 1968.

Staples, Robert, PhD., *The Urban Plantation: Racism and Colonialism in the Post Civil Rights Era*. Oakland: The Black Scholar Press, 1987.

Stedman, Raymond William, *Shadows of the Indian: Stereotypes in American Cultures*. Norman: University of Oklahoma Press, 1982.

Stowe, Harriet Beecher, *Uncle Tom's Cabin or Life Among the Lowly*. New York: Penguin Books, 1981.

Takaki, Ronald, *Iron Cages*. New York: Oxford University Press, 1990.

Taylor, M. W. , *Harriet Tubman: Anti-Slavery Activist*. New York/Philadelphia: Chelsea House Publishers, 1991.

Terzian, James, and Kathryn Cramer, *Mighty Hard Road: The Story of Cesar Chavaz*. New York: Doubleday & Company, 1970.

Vanderwerth, W. C., and William R. Carmack, *Indian Oratory: Famous Speeches by Noted Indian Chieftains*. Oklahoma: University of Oklahoma Press, Norman, 1971.

Wilkins, Roy, and Tom Matthews, *The Autobiography of Roy Wilkins: Standing Fast*. New York: Penguin Books, 1984.

Woodson, Carter G. , *The Mis-education of the Negro*. Washington, D.C.: The Associated Publishers, Inc., 1969.

*References cited in this chapter.

CHAPTER 20

SUBSTANCE ABUSE: INTRODUCTION

While Pablo Escobar of the Medellin Cartel of Colombia, S.A., has surrendered to Colombian police, his fierce rival, Gilberto Rodriguez Orejuela, of the Cali Drug Cartel, has moved into the dominant position in the drug trade. Blaine Shannon (*Time*, July 1, 1991), says, "The Cali combine produces 70% of the coke reaching the U.S. today, according to the DEA, and 90% of the drugs sold in Europe." The Cali cartel is also attempting to corner the drug market in Japan, and if the Cali cartel makes an alliance with the *yakuza* (Japan's organized-crime network), watch out."

When Gilberto Rodriguez Orejuela, of the Cali Drug cartel was asked, "Why do you think Americans consume so many drugs, especially cocaine?" he answered: "Because they live in a consumer society where every day means a struggle, where they have to work very hard in order to lead a decent life, and where everyone has to take care of himself without being able to count on anyone else, a friend or the next-door neighbor" (*Time*, July 1, 1991). This is certainly one psychological rationalization. It helps to explain the sense of alienation and fragmentation that pervade much of modern society, especially among the middle and upper classes. In complex societies such as ours that are undergoing rapid social and technological change, a state of *anomie* develops. *Traditional ways* are challenged and undergo change and they are replaced by new value systems, each competing for the allegiance of people. Individuals become confused in their search for meaning, often "buying" the beliefs and values that seem most expedient and satisfying. Whereas in traditional societies the family and clan form the basic unit, in modern societies the individual becomes the basic unit. Personal happiness becomes more important than the family, church or community. For a sizeable minority drugs, including alcohol and tobacco, provide a dysfunctional way of coping. We say dysfunctional because it may provide a way of coping in the short run, but in the long run their use proves destructive.

While drugs also provide an escape for some of the underclass and poor in our urban centers, they provide an opportunity to "get rich quick" through the sale of illegal drugs. As Robert Merton states in his *anomie* theory, the poor and minorities are often denied access to the *means* that would enable them to be successful in our society. In our society the *goal* (success) is measured in monetary terms. Those who accept the *goal*, monetary wealth, and feel they are denied access to legitimate means, innovate and use illegal means, the sale of drugs, to achieve success. Some, however, reject both the goals and the means, and *retreat* to drug abuse as a means of escaping the "rat race."

Professor Van Wicklin's chapter deals with one of the most serious social problems facing our nation. He says the drug business is so large that "if the international cocaine industry were a Fortune 500 corporation, it would rank in the top ten alongside such megaliths as Ford Motor Company and Gulf Oil."

The illegal drugs he discusses are: *Heroin*: over one-half million users and overall cost to the taxpayer is over 10 billion dollars. *Marijuana*: over 50 million have tried it, and over 10% of our population use it regularly. Children and youth use it a great deal, and it serves as a "gateway drug"—it leads to the use of harder drugs. *Cocaine*: it is probably the number one drug. It is illegal and is used by elites in sports, the professions, and the world of entertainment. Ten to 20 million use it. *Crack* and *ice*, smokable versions of cocaine, provide quick highs or fixes.

A tremendous toll is taken not only by illegal drugs, but by *alcohol* and *tobacco*. Van Wicklin estimates, conservatively, that 100 million Americans consume alcohol. (Others place it at 75%, or about 180 million.) The devastating effects of alcoholism include over 10 million alcoholics, over 31,000 deaths due to alcohol, excluding over 25,000 deaths annually due to drunken driving. This does not include those thousands of deaths and injuries due to the use of alcohol in relation to homicides, suicides, rapes, and crimes committed by both juveniles and adults.

It is estimated that there are over 50 million users of tobacco, smoke and smokeless types. A fair percentage of these are youth, females, especially among the underclasses, who can least afford it. We are all aware that cancer, cardiovascular diseases, and emphysema are highly correlated with tobacco usage.

But there are other legal drugs that are abused, namely, prescription drugs and over the counter (OTC) drugs. An alarming 1.5 million Americans are hospitalized each year because of the negative side effects of OTC drugs.

Using alcohol, Van Wicklin shows how subcultural values influence usage and legislation. The United States went from acceptance of strong liquor during the colonial period to Prohibition in 1920, a change brought about largely by the influence of the Women's Christian Temperance Union. This group was largely a WASP organization. Van Wicklin also points out how subcultures differ in their attitude towards usage of alcohol. He points out that Scripture does not demand abstinence, but it does warn against drunkenness.

Drug abuse is heavily concentrated in major urban centers, although it is also present in rural areas and small towns. In New York City 70% of the heroin abusers are Afro-Americans and Puerto Ricans—largely the poor. Women compose a large percentage of the abusers, the effect of which impairs their offspring. *Time* (May 13, 1991) estimates that 1 in 10 fetuses are damaged by crack. In metropolitan areas such as New York, Boston and Los Angeles, the percentage of crack babies is over 20%.

In his discussion of etiology (theories of causation) Van Wicklin includes biological, psychological and sociological theories. He cites Kathleen Merikangas, a genetic epidemiologist, who states that if both parents are alcoholics, their children have a 90% chance of becoming alcoholics if they drink. Psychological factors may also predispose one toward alcoholism, factors such as personality deficiency, boredom, curiosity, and a desire for excitement or adventure.

Social factors are highly correlated with drug abuse: peer pressure, the media (TV, movies), parental example, degree of bonding between parents and child, etc.

The sociological theories that Van Wicklin cites all offer some help in understanding drug abuse. The structural functionalist theory asserts that all institutions are interrelated; a change in one invariably affects the others. If the family, church, school, government or economy fail to meet needs, the individual is often adversely affected. For example, if family ties are weak, or the person feels rejected, he or she might turn to drugs to compensate for that particular lack. Adams and Gullotta (1983) report that "for young people, the move from alcohol to marijuana is associated with anti-Establishment feelings toward schools, church, and community." Van Wicklin says that members of dysfunctional families are especially vulnerable.

The conflict perspective sees the drug problem as one caused by a clash of values. The affluent members of society have their legal drug, alcohol, but they label marijuana and other drugs as illegal and their users as deviant to keep the less affluent in their place. Since the law, police and judiciary are all "controlled" by the upper classes, this discrimination and exploitation are not difficult to sustain.

A variety of efforts have been and are being employed to deter and eliminate drug abuse in America, from Nancy Reagan's "just say no," to the federal government's War on Drugs. The war is being fought on two fronts: *one* focusing on eliminating the *supply*, and the *other* on eliminating the *demand*. Van Wicklin is skeptical about the effectiveness of "scaring" users through information about the adverse effects of drug abuse. He says the human mind is more "rationalizing than rational." "According to cognitive dissonance theory, one will likely ignore information that is incompatible with habitual behaviors and attitudes."

To affect the demand, education components have been used in schools and in the media. Scare tactics, stricter punishment, and suggested alternatives are a few approaches.

One treatment program that has enjoyed measured success is Alcoholics Anonymous (AA). We believe its success stems from several components of the program which are consistent with Christian principles. 1) Individuals acknowledge their need for God ("as they understand God"). 2) Individuals accept responsibility for their own behavior. 3) They agree to work on their deficiencies. 4) They agree to seek reconciliation to others, and to make restitution to those they have wronged. 5) They acknowledge their need for others and for community. As an AA maxim states, "By the crowds they have been broken; by the crowds they shall be healed."

Finally, Professor Van Wicklin concludes with a mature Christian response to the problem when he states that there is no easy answer to a complex social problem such as drug abuse. He bases his thoughts on Arthur Holmes' (1983) concept of persons "as responsible relational beings in the context of God's creational design, human depravity and plan of redemption." Van Wicklin sees deliverance from addiction growing out of peoples' right relationship to nature (i.e., use what God has created for the purpose for which it was intended). Persons must relate responsibly to others and to society. When they are dysfunctional in their behavior society must avoid taking either of two extreme positions: one, that of totally blaming others for their problem; and two, that of solely blaming the individual. We are all frail, sinful people. What addicted persons need is the patience, empathy, forgiveness and love that God offers in the gospel. If we reflect these attributes we can be used of God to help people find healing.

SUBSTANCE ABUSE
John F. Van Wicklin

A Statement of the Problem

If you were asked to name the number one problem drug of today, what would your answer be? Would it be heroin? Heroin has been called the "hardest" drug for a variety of reasons. Five hundred thousand people in the United States use this powerfully addictive substance. The economic costs of law enforcement and treatment programs for heroin addiction exceed ten billion dollars annually. Furthermore, such an estimate does not take into account such factors as the erosion of civil liberties, diversion of power and money to organized crime, corruption of law enforcement officials, or the pain suffered by family members and friends of addicts (Kaplan, 1983).

Would it be marijuana? Currently, this is the most widely used illicit drug with an estimated 11 to 12 million current users nationwide and over 50 million who claim to have tried it at least once (Long, 1986). Children and youth are far more likely to use marijuana than heroin, and some consider it to be a "gateway" drug because its use generally precedes that of so-called harder drugs (Newcomb & Bentler, 1989). Yet, despite its highest rate of use among illicit drugs, marijuana may be less dangerous than legal drugs such as alcohol or tobacco, and there are many who call for decriminalization.

What about cocaine? Heroin has harmful effects but relatively few users. Marijuana has many users but milder effects. Cocaine makes a bid for number one by combining illegality, celebrity status, high use, and a variety of deleterious effects. Inciardi (1986) reports an estimated 10 to 20 million regular cocaine users in the U.S., with 5,000 each day using it for the first time. Although casual use appears to be declining, regular use and dependency are increasing. Cocaine is the largest single producer of illicit income, with Americans spending an estimated 60 billion a year on its use (Contreras, 1989, September 11). Indeed, if the international cocaine industry were a Fortune 500 corporation, it would rank in the top ten alongside such megaliths as Ford Motor Company and Gulf Oil (Long, 1986).

Smokable versions of cocaine (crack) and methamphetamine (ice) are making illegal stimulant use the most rapidly expanding drug problem by offering quicker highs at lower cost (Long, 1986). The former U.S. government drug czar, William Bennett, claims that crack cocaine is the most critical drug problem facing the nation today (Bennett's drug war, 1989, August 21). Crack is associated with a variety of personal and societal problems. For example, emergency room admissions linked to cocaine increased by 86% in one year (1988), and the number of crack cocaine arrests in New York City rose from zero to over 19,000 in just three years (Hour by hour, *Newsweek*, 1988, November 28).

So far our search for the number one drug problem has been confined to illicit drugs. Are we looking in the wrong place? Some would claim that the two most abusive drugs in terms of number of users and magnitude of consequences are alcohol and tobacco (Newcomb & Bentler, 1989). Julien (1988) estimates that of over 100 million drinking

Americans, ten million are problem drinkers, and over 31,000 deaths are directly attributed to alcohol each year. Furthermore, alcohol is considered to be a factor in 50% of fatal vehicular accidents, 70% of homicides and suicides, and 40% of rapes (Scarpitti & Anderson, 1989).

What about tobacco? Julien (1985) believes that cigarette smoking is the most widespread example of drug dependence in the country. With over 50 million smoking Americans, the amount of illness and death produced by tobacco may outweigh the accumulated effects of any drug. Because of its availability, experimental use with this drug has widespread prevalence during preadolescence. The mixed message of promoting the sale and distribution of this legal but harmful drug may undermine the credibility of programs aimed at restricting or preventing other forms of drug abuse. One example of inconsistency is the rather tolerant attitude toward cigarette smoking in many alcohol and drug treatment facilities.

Have we exhausted all candidates for number one? Retail pharmacists dispense about 1.5 billion prescribed drugs annually, six percent of which are psychotropic in nature—e.g. antianxiety, antidepressant, antipsychotic and sedative prescriptions (Graedon & Graedon, 1980). Demand is likely to increase now that pharmaceutical companies, in an attempt to increase their share of the $30 billion dollar U.S. market for prescription drugs, are bypassing the doctor to pitch media advertisements directly to consumers. The consumer already has in excess of 300,000 over-the-counter (OTC) drugs from which to choose including laxatives, antidiarrheal products, emetics and antiemetics, stimulants, sedatives, cough suppressants, antacids, analgesics, and weight control products—to name just a few categories. Negative effects resulting from prescribed and OTC drugs are sufficient to hospitalize over a million-and-a-half Americans each year.

Taken together one can make a case for drugs as a major social problem facing Americans today. Illegal drug trade alone has been labeled "the worst international crime crisis of the century" (Bennet's drug war, 1989, August 21, p. 18). A sociological view of the extensiveness of the drug problem can be seen in its impact on major institutions such as family, economics, politics, and education. Drug abuse is rattling the foundations of society by upsetting the proper function of its institutions.

Twenty-five percent of American families are troubled by problems stemming from alcohol abuse, and alcohol is considered to be a factor in over 60% of child abuse cases (Scarpitti & Anderson, 1989). One in ten newborns is exposed to drugs by a pregnant mother, and the alarming escalation of crack cocaine addiction among women of the underclass is seriously threatening an already tenuous family structure (Hour by hour, Newsweek, 1988, November 28).

The drug economy reaches into the "hundreds of billions" of dollars each year for research and development, marketing, consumption, drug abuse prevention and treatment, and law enforcement. International banking centers such as those in the Miami area, make vast sums of money in foreign investment of illegal drug money, and money laundering operations (Lermoux, 1985, February 18). Worthy social problems lack funding in part due to lost taxes not collected on illegal drug money, and the diversion of vast sums to fight the drug problem. Drugs affect the political process through powerful alcohol and tobacco lobbies, corruption of public officials, and the murder or intimidation of honest public officials. Governments of many Latin American countries are unable to protect their people or economy from the ravages of international drug trafficking. Indeed, uncontrolled violence and destruction in Colombia has earned that country the title "Lebanon of Latin America" (Contreras, 1989, September 11).

The early impact of drugs on education can be seen in the perceived need for teachers in a New York City Head Start program to instruct preschoolers about crack before they even begin the usual prereading program (Children of the Underclass, 1989, September 11). In general, chemical dependency at all grade levels compromises quality of education. Although prescribed drugs have enhanced learning receptivity for many, countless others have developmental disorders and deficiencies stemming from licit and illicit drug use.

Institutions do not exist in isolation—changes in one reverberate through others. Without too much difficulty one can identify ways in which family problems brought on by drug abuse have influenced political, educational, and economical changes. For example, how much litigation has been instigated and how many organizations have been started by spouses or parents whose families have been torn apart by alcoholism or drunk driving? How much more money would be available to provide low-interest loans to college students, or to fund shelters for homeless families if less money were needed to fight the escalating war on drugs?

ISSUES PERTAINING TO DRUG ABUSE

What constitutes drug abuse? To what extent is drug abuse a sickness, a sin, or just a label? Why are some drugs "licit" and others "illicit?" What makes drug abuse a social problem? Should efforts to reduce the drug problem focus more on curtailing supply or demand? Of the many intervention strategies—e.g. informational campaigns, scare tactics, punishment and deterrence, stricter law enforcement, more prisons, stepped-up customs searches and border patrols, involuntary drug testing, treatment programs, decriminalization—which are effective? Which are not?

Julien (1988, p. 265) defines drug abuse as "the use of any drug for reasons other than its assigned purposes." Abuse is a relative matter because the purpose assigned to a drug varies according to societal norms and attitudes. As Fort (1969, p. 229) observed (in one of the first comprehensive analyses of drug use), "one man's beverage is another man's drug; one country's drug is another country's medication; and one agency's subsidized crop is another bureau's focus of criminal law enforcement."

For some people abuse might mean anything nonmedical including recreational use of alcohol or caffeine. Abuse usually refers to excessive drug use or use which impairs one's functioning and is potentially harmful to oneself or others. Associated labels include problem use, addiction, and dependency. Addiction has been used to refer to a state of physical need, whereas dependency may only refer to a strong psychological need. However, increased knowledge has blurred this distinction to a point where many prefer to speak of varying degrees of dependency. One problem in defining abuse as dependency is that drugs like caffeine can be very habit-forming but produce relatively little harm for all the pleasure provided.

To view drug abuse as a social problem raises other issues. The standard approach to social problems sees them in human terms alone, arising through perceived violations of ever-changing norms and recognized as a problem by enough people to warrant collective, remedial action. As social norms change, social problems vary in their nature.

For example, Royce (1981) observes that views toward alcohol use have undergone several changes in the past three centuries. In colonial America even the Puritans drank, although drunkenness was disapproved. Beer was even served in conservative Protestant seminaries. Clark (1976) notes that among the early settlers, few tasks required icy sobriety, and generally speaking a "soft alcoholic cloud" helped to soften the harshness of pioneer living.

In the 18th century, Americans consumed less alcohol in the form of wine or beer and much more in the form of distilled spirits. Among the reasons for such change were increased taxes on wine imports, problems with local wine cultivation, and difficulties with transporting beer in bulk. This shift to hard liquor was one factor associated with an upswing in intemperate drinking and related social problems.

During the 19th century a number of local temperance movements arose, many of which pushed the issue from temperance to abstinence. For example, the Women's Christian Temperance Movement was really a movement for abstinence. This push for abstinence led to a national prohibition amendment in 1920. However, such an attempt to legislate against long-standing traditions resulted in widespread disregard for the particular law, and ultimately the amendment was repealed. Today, attitudes about alcohol range from abstinence to indulgence, depending in large part on one's sociocultural background.

Who Uses and Abuses Drugs?

Drug use varies according to such factors as gender, age, racial and ethnic background, social class, and demography. Men of all ages are more apt than women to abuse alcohol and most illegal drugs. Women more often than men use prescribed and OTC drugs—especially sleeping pills, tranquilizers, and analgesics. However, gender differences appear to be diminishing, possibly due to ongoing changes in gender roles (Leavitt, 1982; Scarpitti & Anderson, 1989).

Experimenting with or using cigarettes, alcohol, and at least one illicit drug (most likely marijuana or cocaine) is rather common among the adolescent population; whereas heroin use is relatively rare. At the other end of the age scale, the elderly represent 10% of the population; yet they account for over 25% of the use of prescribed drugs. Many of the elderly in institutionalized care are considered to be overmedicated (Barton & Hurst, 1966; Leavitt, 1982; Newcomb & Bentler, 1989).

Racial and ethnic identifications are related to drug use. For example, Native Americans have exceptionally high rates of alcoholism, whereas rates are rather low for Asian-Americans. Italians and Jews are more apt to drink in the home, whereas the Irish are more apt to drink outside the home. White college students are significantly more likely to use cocaine, marijuana, and hallucinogens than Blacks or Hispanics (Scarpitti & Anderson, 1989).

Drug use and abuse varies according to socioeconomic indicators as well. Social drinking is more a phenomena of the college-educated professional, whereas problem drinking reaches its highest levels among shift workers and the unemployed. Cocaine is a drug of choice for the affluent, who are estimated to comprise 70% of crack cocaine users. At the other end of the spectrum, 44% of the homeless are substance abusers, a statistic that undoubtedly represents a mixed bag of cause and effect, i.e. drug abuse as both a cause and consequence of the condition of homelessness (Leavitt, 1982; Newcomb & Bentler, 1989; Return of, 1990, January 15; Scarpitti & Anderson, 1989).

These variables interact as well. For example, although women tend not to abuse drugs as often as men, a surprisingly large percentage of heroin addicts (20 to 30%) are urban women of low income and education. Also, crack cocaine dependency is rather high among inner-city women of the underclass. Although blacks do not tend to use or abuse substances as often as whites, heroin addiction is exceptionally high for inner-city blacks and Hispanics. In New York City, 75% of heroin addicts are either black or Puerto Rican (Children of the Underclass, 1989, September 11; Scarpitti & Anderson, 1989).

There are also profiles of indicator variables for certain kinds of drug use. One recent magazine article identified the prototypical, affluent crack user as age 30 to 40, single or divorced, in a high pressure job, with little inner peace, and a history of moderate drug use and heavy drinking (Plague without, 1989, November 8). In a recent survey, those most likely to be heavy drinkers are urban dwellers in East or Pacific coast states, of low income and education, single, divorced or separated, and either Protestant, Catholic, or without religious affiliation (Scarpitti & Anderson, 1989).

MOTIVES FOR SUBSTANCE ABUSE

To seek a single reason for the misuse of drugs is futile. Problematic use is certainly the result of an interaction of biological, psychological, and sociocultural conditions.

Biological Factors

Drugs reduce biological drives. For example, alcohol may quench thirst, analgesic drugs may lessen pain, stimulants may eliminate drowsiness and provide additional energy, and narcotic drugs such as heroin may produce pleasure comparable to that of sexual orgasm. Still other drugs enhance or alter sensory experience, relieve symptoms of physical illness, and alleviate emotional distress. Also, an addiction may be accompanied by new physiological cravings as compelling as hunger or thirst.

Experimental and casual drug use appear to be tied to social factors, whereas abuses such as alcoholism may be partly genetic. One recent study by Kathleen Merikangas, a genetic epidemiologist, implicates heredity as a contributing factor in drug abuse. She reports that a child of two alcoholic parents has a 90% chance of abusing drugs if he or she ever starts using them at all (Adler, 1990, February). This suggests a possible constitutional or heredity factor, yet socialization could account for the correlation as well, in that parents pass on more than their genes to their offspring. Although it does appear that intensified use has ties to internal emotional and biological conditions, solid empirical evidence is still lacking.

Psychological Factors

Personal motives for drug use include curiosity, a spirit of adventure, research purposes, spiritual insights, and defiance of authority. Drugs may also be used to improve creativity, gain new insights, add meaning to life, remove inhibitions, facilitate communication, gain acceptance, and to escape or retreat from boredom, psychological pain, emotional distress, or personal pressures (Julien, 1988).

A common explanation of drug abuse states that there is some deficiency in the personality of the user. It is the sick, the less-than-whole, and not the well-adjusted person who becomes chemically dependent. Yet if this is so, one should be able to identify consistent personality differences between abusers and nonabusers. Despite a recently observed link between drug abuse and antisocial personality disorder (Adler, 1990, February), evidence of such differentiation is weak at best. One confounding element in such research is that drug abuse can create personal deficiencies which are then mistakenly identified as causes.

There are many unsubstantiated theories that relate substance abuse to such factors as oral fixation, insufficient mothering, latent homosexuality, or manifestations of a "death instinct." Such theories tend to overstate the role of the individual and give too little attention to sociocultural factors. Individuals may not fully understand why they drink or use drugs. As Durkheim (1950) suggests, the real reasons may lie outside of personal awareness and be irreducible to a psychological level of explanation.

Social Factors

The major determinants of initial drug use appear to be the agents of socialization in one's life — peers, parents, and various social surrogates such as music, television and movies. Of a wide range of social variables, Newcomb and Bentler (1989) consider peer influence (modeling of use, supplying drugs, encouraging use) to be the strongest and most consistent factor in a young person's decision to initiate drug use. Parental example is significant and not only with respect to the particular drug in question. For example, adolescents whose parents smoke and drink alcohol are more likely to use alcohol, marijuana, and other drugs (Fawzy, Coombs, & Gerber, 1983; Hundleby & Mercer, 1987). The degree of emotional closeness in the parent-adolescent relationship is a factor in drug use as well, perhaps because lack of closeness strengthens the level of peer influence (Blum & Richards, 1979; Lassey & Carolson, 1980).

Not only parents and peers but the media also has a profound influence on youth. It is commonly known that the average young person in America spends more time with the media of television, movies, and music than any other activity besides sleeping. The cumulative impact of the extensive social learning on attitudes and behavior is immense. Although empirical content analyzers of television programming report surprisingly little portrayal of illicit drug use, consumption of alcoholic beverages is conspicuously present in a variety of primetime shows (Greenberg, 1984). Social learning of drug use would include identification with movie and television heroes, musical lyrics, and what is observed and learned about personal drug habits of professional athletes, entertainers and other celebrities.

The impact of several decades of television even led to a "sentience" theory of drug use, first cited by Loken (1973). According to this theory, children brought up on a steady diet of television come to expect and even prefer stimulation without much activity. Getting "turned on" to a drug may be influenced by the passive stimulation of the media habit.

From the media, one receives a more direct appeal to use drugs. Alcohol, tobacco and pharmaceutical industries are "legal drug pushers" for whom increased consumption means higher profits. Advertisers use a variety of highly effective techniques to market their products. For example, alcohol is linked to sexual attractiveness, popularity, excellence, and a fulfilled life—strongly implying that the beverage is the essential ingredient. Advertisers seek to create new needs (e.g. embarrassing aging spots) in order to market new products. Eventually one expects to find a chemical cure for any and every departure from the American ideal.

Drug advertising is very one-sided in that warnings about associated dangers of drug use are far less salient than all of the touted benefits. Attempts to legislate for more responsible advertising may be frustrated by the government's vested interest in increased drug use. Although the collective costs of drug abuse for society are enormous, federal revenues from luxury taxes on alcohol and tobacco comprise one of the highest sources of government income. Far more income is generated by these taxes than is targeted for social problems connected with abuse (Scarpitti & Anderson, 1989).

Sociological Theories and Drug Abuse

A number of sociological theories have been developed in an attempt to explain why people use and abuse drugs. For example, a functionalist perspective would view drug use by members of the underclass as a means of escaping otherwise unbearable social conditions. A lower class youth may turn to drugs to escape the pressures and responsibilities of a middle class lifestyle (Geis, 1970; Newcomb, Maddahian, & Bentler, 1986).

The symbolic interactionist focuses attention on the consequences of labeling the drug user. Societal members "in good standing" may unconsciously seek to lessen their guilt about offering too little assistance to underprivileged members of society by labeling them as deviant. Once the negative label is assigned, it may be easier to see the labeled as deserving their condition. The negative stereotypes are also internalized by the "deviant," resulting in a vicious cycle of self-fulfilling prophecy. Another example of the interactionist perspective can be seen with Americans who label themselves as "rugged individualists" in the "land of opportunity." This may influence their style of drinking or drug use. As historian Clark (1967, p. 224) observed several decades ago, our drinking says to the world, "I bow to no king and to no priest...I do what I want...I deserve my indulgences and my life is my own." This seems just as valid an observation for the 1990s.

A conflict perspective gives attention to disagreements among groups within a society about the nature of the drug problem. That which is overlooked or condemned may largely reflect the values of the dominant class or culture. Members of counterculture may sense hypocrisy and resent the imposition of the prevailing culture's lifestyle. Ideological conflict is likely to manifest itself in disagreement over such matters as the legal status of particular drugs, what constitutes drug abuse, and how one reacts to an alleged abuser. Groups will also disagree in their view of the drug problem as a sign of societal breakdown or a necessary route to social reform.

By way of illustration, consider the contrasting perspectives of conservatives and libertarians regarding the legalization of drugs such as marijuana and cocaine. Over 70% of Americans oppose the legalization of marijuana, and virtually all oppose the legalization of cocaine. The use of illicit drugs is seen as posing a real danger to the fabric of society. When used by youth, drugs may undermine the socialization process. By contrast, libertarians advocate the repeal of laws prohibiting drug use because of the threats they pose to personal freedom and the right to privacy, the market they provide for organized crime, and the absence of standards for drug quality. Thus, conflicting perspectives may be seen as healthy correctives for negative ramifications of mainstream views (Bahr, 1989; Fine, 1985).

A social structural approach which examines the failure of institutions offers significant insight into the drug problem. Properly functioning institutions of family, education, politics, economics and religion provide for the needs of society members. When one after another of these institutions fail to meet the needs of individuals, drug abuse may be one of the unfortunate results. It is of interest to note how many of the variables which divide drug abusers from nonabusers pertain to the failure of an institution. For example, Newcomb and Bentler (1989) associate abusive drug use with low income, low education, disturbed families, heightened exposure to crime and criminal role models, and lack of religious commitment. Adams and Gullotta (1983) report that for young people, the move from alcohol to marijuana is associated with anti-Establishment feelings toward parents, school, church, and community. The move from marijuana into other illicit drugs occurs more often for those who feel alienated from their families and community.

A loss of connectedness with family members or friends is commonly associated with substance abuse. When parents are warm and supportive, adolescents are much less likely to use illicit drugs (Dembo, Grandon, LaVois, Schmeidler, & Burgos, 1986; Marcos, Bahr, & Johnson, 1986). Berkman and Syme (1979) calculated a social network index (based on the number and quality of one's social contacts) for nearly 7000 adults. Socially isolated individuals were more likely to engage in poor health habits such as smoking, drinking and overeating. In addition, they concluded that the lack of a social support system increases one's vulnerability to disease and death. Alcoholics Anonymous offers further testimony to the importance of social relationships in remediation from substance abuse. Although not affiliated with any particular religious group, their popular twelve steps include admitting to dependence upon a "higher power" and a need for social support in the recovery process.

The converse of social alienation can be seen in a social support system which effectively limits the extent of drug use. This type of social control can be seen in what Keller (1970) calls "the great Jewish drink mystery." Jews have the highest percentage of adult drinkers among major religious and ethnic groups (about 90 percent), yet Jews have one of the lowest rates of alcoholism (Aronow, 1980). Apparently Jewish culture encourages drinking at ceremonies or festive social occasions but strongly admonishes against drinking for personal, hedonistic reasons. However, if one is influenced by a community which strongly supports drinking or drug use, even to excess, then chemical dependency may be associated with one's extent of association with that community. The statement is significant because one may believe that drug abuse is only a product of social estrangement.

Allow one final comment about this plethora of correlational data and implied causality. There is the distinct possibility that one may become so caught up in searching for the causes of chemical dependency that one relieves the abuser of any sense of personal freedom and responsibility. We may consider that abuse to be inevitable or necessary when it is truly voluntary. Thus, while there are many factors which undoubtedly influence the nature and extent of drug use, one would do well to hold onto a measure of personal freedom or control.

INTERVENTION STRATEGIES FOR DRUG ABUSE

A presidential declaration of war on drugs, the appointment of a drug czar, and the allocation of billions of dollars annually to fight the drug problem are all reasonable steps—given that the escalating drug problem is threatening our very way of life. Most of the criticism of the presidential initiative is not with the idea of waging war, but with battle plans and priorities and with the fact that the battle is being waged with too little firepower.

In the face of an escalating war, the decriminalization movement has been losing ground. For example, the National Organization for the Reform of Marijuana Laws (NORML), a 6,000 member organization headquartered in Washington, D.C., has lost considerable support in the last ten to fifteen years. Yet, arguments for decriminalization are not without merit. For example, to legalize marijuana as a "controlled substance" in a manner similar to alcohol and tobacco would diminish some of the inconsistency or hypocrisy in the categorization of licit and illicit drugs. It would also allow for more quality control in product development. In addition, legalizing drugs might undercut the growth of organized crime, and allow for the diversion of money from law enforcement to strategies for prevention and treatment. Take, for example, the difference in treatment of heroin addicts between Britain and the United States (Judson, 1974; Kaplan, 1983). The British label addiction a disease and do not consider it, in and of itself, a crime. Heroin is clinically prescribed for the needy addict on a limited basis and in the context of helping one to recover. Britain's disease model has succeeded in reducing the numbers of addicts by getting them into treatment programs. The black market for heroin has diminished, and so have the number of arrests for nondrug crimes. Also, more rehabilitating heroin addicts have entered the work force, facilitating their reintegration into society.

Strategies for fighting the drug problem in America can be roughly divided into supply-focused and demand-focused efforts. Supply-focused strategies work on reducing the supply of drugs grown, processed, or manufactured in the United States or entering the country from Latin America, Asia, and the Middle East. Procedures include crop eradication (largely a failure), border patrols and customs searches, and undercover action by DEA officials. In addition, efforts have been made to cooperate with other countries in the arrest and extradition of drug traffickers, and the deployment of military forces. One very recent strategy involves restricting the sale by American chemical manufacturers of certain chemicals necessary for the processing of some illegal drugs.

Many would argue that the supply of drugs to the United States exists primarily in response to the great demand for them. If no one wanted to abuse chemical substances, the pumped up drug economy would deflate. Demand-focused strategies thus work at preventing, deterring, or treating the user. Prevention efforts include disseminating information to users or potential users about the dangers of drug use. One of the more well-known prevention strategies to emerge from the mid-eighties was "Just Say No," a national campaign to provide information about the harmful effects of drugs and to encourage young people to be willful resisters. Unfortunately, most empirical studies of such drug education programs have demonstrated that they have had little effect on drug use (Hanson, 1980).

Why would this be so? Certainly, knowledge is preferred to ignorance; however, knowledge alone is relatively ineffectual because the human mind appears to be more "rationalizing" than rational. According to cognitive dissonance theory, one will likely ignore information that is incompatible with human behaviors and attitudes. For example, smokers are more apt to deny evidence of health risks and to employ rationalizations than nonsmokers. Also, heavy smokers who *are* more aware of health risks, tend to label themselves as "moderate" smokers (Aronson, 1984; Kassarjian & Cohen, 1965; Tagliacozzo, 1979). Apparently it is easier to rationalize than to stop smoking, and such rationalizations undoubtedly apply to the use of other drugs as well.

Deterrent efforts are another significant part of a demand-focused strategy. The assumption is that individuals will avoid drug abuse out of fear. Fear of the harmful consequences of drug use undergirds the advertisement that compares one's brain on drugs to a fried egg, or the production of scary movies like "Reefer Madness." Involuntary drug testing, random searches of school lockers, dorm rooms, and suitcases, and use of lie detector tests all play on the fear of detection. Fear of punishment would underlie the drive for stiffer penalties and stricter enforcement of the law.

A more positive approach to prevention and deterrence not based on fear is the generation of alternatives to drug use (Julien, 1988). This approach begins with an exhaustive analysis of every possible motive for drug use. These would include physical, emotional, interpersonal, political, intellectual, philosophical, and spiritual motivations, just to name a few. One then enumerates alternative activities of a legal and wholesome nature that will address each motive. For example, alternatives to a sensory motive for using drugs would include sensory awareness training, sky diving, and experiencing the sensory beauty of nature through swimming, running, or mountaineering. Of course, some of these alternatives would not be as viable for those who are economically underprivileged. However, meaningful, low-cost alternatives to drug abuse could include exercise, some "risk" sports, social-political activism, meditation, and religious involvement (Schlaadt & Shannon, 1986).

Finally, there is the focus on treatment for the chemically dependent. Common medical strategies involve chemical treatments such as cocaine blocking substances, methadone treatment of heroin addicts, and deterrent drugs such as antabuse which cause unpleasant side effects when used with alcohol. There are both inpatient and outpatient clinics throughout this country that provide crisis intervention, detoxification, and counseling to cure drug abusers. Though such facilities are an essential part of any effective drug treatment strategy, Newcomb and Bentler (1989) warn that the use of these programs for the casual user of alcohol or marijuana may be more harmful than the "disease." For example, there is the danger of mislabeling the casual user and then placing him or her for treatment with "hard core" abusers. The observational learning that might result from negative role models could outweigh the intended benefits of treatment.

One of the most successful treatment programs for alcohol abuse has been Alcoholics Anonymous which emphasizes abstinence, a supportive community of recovering alcoholics, and admission of dependency on God and others to help with one's problem. Many other programs dealing with a wide variety of addictions have been modeled after this program. For example, Synanon is a live-in program for drug addicts based on principles derived from Alcoholics Anonymous. Synanon has had its share of difficulties; however, there are now hundreds of residential treatment centers in this country that credit their initial inspiration to Synanon and Alcoholics Anonymous (Jones-Witters & Witters, 1983).

Residential facilities are a popular treatment option at present. These therapeutic communities remove one completely from the drug environment and provide around-the-clock assistance to drug abusers from others who have undergone similar experiences to overcome their addiction. The group bond that eases the pain of withdrawal appears to support one AA maxim which states, "By the crowds they have been broken, by the crowds they shall be healed."

There are a number of helpful sources which summarize a wide variety of drug prevention and treatment strategies. For example, Eiseman, Wingard, and Huba (1984) provide a collection of helpful articles on drug education and prevention, and rehabilitation and treatment programs. Leavitt (1982) provides an excellent chapter on the prevention and treatment of drug abuse. Tobler (1986) provides an interesting review of over 143 drug prevention and education programs for adolescents. His meta-analysis offers five broad categories of prevention and treatment — affective enhancement, generation of alternatives to drug use, education or informational approaches, peer programs focusing on refusal and social life skills, and combinations of knowledge and affective approaches.

CHRISTIAN PERSPECTIVES

A truly Christian perspective on the social problems of substance abuse joins a broad view of God's special revelation with an understanding of what God has enabled people, regardless of religious affiliation, to uncover through inquiry, observation and controlled research. A recent journal article (Bridgman & McQueen, 1987) nicely demonstrates the imbalance that can arise in this area. Apparently some Christians are baffled by the success of AA programs because the highly emphasized dependency upon God is not mediated through Jesus Christ (thus, why would God listen, let alone intervene?). The authors explain that God also works through natural laws which anyone can discover and apply. The dynamics which underlie certain forms of psychological healing may not be different in kind from those of biological healing. Certainly, in the medical realm, few Christians today would give greater weight to a physician's faith commitment than to his or her medical credentials.

Arthur Holmes (1983) has developed a framework for viewing the nature of personhood from a Christian perspective, and he hopes that it will facilitate a proper understanding of human activities in many diverse areas. In essence, Holmes' perspective views persons as responsible, relational beings in the context of God's creational design, human depravity, and the plan of redemption. This biblically based approach to human nature provides a framework within which the social problem of drug abuse can be effectively studied.

On the one hand, as human beings, we are apt to feel good when we are living in accordance with our created nature. In other words, when one is properly related to God, the environment, and to other persons, and when one has a semblance of personal control, then one feels fundamentally "good." On the other hand, a loss of important relationships, a sense of helplessness, addiction, or being "out of control" creates the emotional distress which may lead to intensified drug use as an escape.

The remainder of this chapter will provide a few examples of how Holmes' theory may be used to develop a broad, Christian perspective on substance abuse. The following categories of "nature, interpersonal relations, and God" represent major delineations in his approach.

One's Responsible Relationship with Nature

One reads in Genesis (1:28-31) that God blessed woman and man in relationship to nature and called the whole relationship "very good." God created us with physical needs and desires, and He created natural elements to meet those needs. A rather conservative position is found in the words of Morey (1973, p. 16) who claims that "man's duty is to discover the right use of each created thing and to use it only for the purpose for which God has created it. We must look upon every plant, drink, and drug as having some function in created reality."

Assuming Morey is correct, one still struggles with discerning the correct uses of nature. Even our most benevolent attempts to use chemicals for the alleviation of human misery may lead to even bigger problems. For example, one need only think of the use of thalidomide in the early sixties. Designed to relieve the symptoms of morning sickness during the first trimester of pregnancy, the drug produced devastating birth defects in the resulting offspring. One could also question an excessive reliance on OTC or prescribed drugs for any and every affliction. The biblical admonition, "tribulation brings patience" seems to suggest that at least some of the time one ought to work through a difficulty rather than turn to some chemical that will give instant relief from suffering.

Although most Christians recognize the use of drugs for medicinal purposes, many question the use of any drug for recreation or entertainment. Such a view could lead to a puritanical association of all pleasure with sin—a vantage point from which it would be difficult to understand Jesus transforming water to wine in order to augment the enjoyment of guests at a wedding feast. Nevertheless, a problem remains for Christians to discover consistent principles for recreational drug use.

One's Responsible Relationship to Others and to Society

It has been said that our very identity is socially bestowed in that it is hard to think of a single aspect of self-image which does not derive much of its meaning from our relationship to other persons. If one's very identity is social in nature, it follows that drug attitudes and behaviors are heavily influenced by others.

As one examines the interpersonal dynamics of substance abuse, one would do well to avoid an extreme view which either completely denies or fully embraces human freedom. For example, a radically deterministic view may alleviate the abuser of any personal responsibility for chemical dependence and shift the blame through the use of such labels as "disease" or "aberrant conditioning." Similarly, deterministic intervention avoids reference to blame or punishment and focuses instead on rehabilitation or reconditioning. The "devil-in-a-bottle" theory is a good example of placing the blame for alcoholism on the drug itself. However, this view does not easily account for the casual user who remains in control of his or her drinking.

Another extreme perspective holds the individual entirely responsible for drug abuse. Some abstainers or casual drug users may lack sympathy for the chemically dependent and judge them harshly for not exercising control. Such a position may simply reveal one's ignorance of dysfunctional socialization which leaves its victim with a powerful need to anesthetize emotional discomfort. It may also reveal limited awareness of the extent to which a proper upbringing can produce an "immunizing" wholeness.

Thus, to rule out responsibility altogether may rob the abuser of the confidence needed to turn life around. To condemn the abuser insensitively for personal failure misses the mark in its arrogant disregard for one's own need of forgiveness by God, and in the Christian mandate to love others.

One's Responsible Relationship to God

Standard social problems textbooks view life in human terms alone. In order for a social problem to exist, a significant number of people must identify it as such. This relativity is understandable if human interaction constitutes the sole basis for defining a problem. However, Christians add a theistic perspective. Humans are not free to fashion a morality based on majority rule or the perceptions of the ruling party. They must take into account their dependence upon and accountability to God, as well as their responsibility to society.

Do Christian perspectives negate relativity completely? According to several Christian social scientists there is room for some flexibility (Lyon, 1983; Mayers, 1974; Perkins, 1987). One can affirm biblical authority and still uphold the truth of socioculture relativity. This is possible primarily because most biblical principles allow for considerable latitude of cultural expression. If a biblical principle is not violated, then the value or worth of an activity may be evaluated in the context of cultural norms. Take for example the biblical principle of moderation or temperance. In light of this principle, one cannot condemn controlled use of alcoholic beverages as sin. Rather, the appropriateness or inappropriateness of moderate drinking appears to be a matter of cultural relativity.

Are there any situations in which cultural relativity would be negated by biblical authority? Again, take the matter of drunkenness in relation to the biblical principle of moderation. If members of a particular ethnic group tolerate or encourage drunkenness, this cannot be viewed as appropriate simply because the majority of people think of it that way. To the Christian, a social problem of drunkenness exists even if the entire community accepts the condition.

William F. Buckley (1981, September 26) makes an important distinction between denominational and universal issues. Denominational issues (e.g. vows of celibacy, eating kosher foods, etc.) must be set apart from universal issues such as the sanctity of human life. The former should be confined to one's local community, whereas the latter are common concerns of humanity whether they originate from within religious circles or not. Thus, the matter of complete abstinence from alcohol appears to be more denominational in scope and should not be allowed to clutter the busy agendas of congress or the courts. However, if some forms of excessive drug use are truly destructive of human potential and social order, then these are matters for Christians to pursue beyond the confines of the church. The zealous efforts of religious groups for national prohibition appear in retrospect to have been an improper extension of rather provincial standards. However, religious activism over the problems of alcoholism and drunk driving seem well placed given the universal concern about family upheaval and the tragic waste of human life.

As a Christian, one's major objective is not the pursuit of self-interest, but the well-being of all people and the glory of God. Perhaps a good general principle, short of complete abstinence from drug use, would be to consider the personal results of drug-related activities in light of the works of the Spirit of God and the works of the flesh. The work of the Spirit is to produce such qualities as love, joy, peace, patience, kindness, goodness, faithfulness, and self-control (Galatians 5:22). Are various forms of drug use relevant to the development and maintenance of such qualities? Are various forms of drug use in any way associated with the works of the flesh such as fornication, uncleanness, enmity, strife, jealousy, wrath, and envying (Ephesians 5:19-20)? We are to love God with all our heart, mind, soul, and strength (Mark 12:30). Does drug use open one's heart to God, clear one's mind, increase one's strength? Or does the use of a given drug harden one's heart (or unpredictably stop it from beating), cloud one's thinking, or dull one's reactions?

There is no simple answer that will hold for all forms of drug use. One may consume a moderate amount of a fine wine in a manner which facilitates the enjoyment of a pleasant social experience such as an evening meal or a wedding celebration. One may remain clear-headed and deeply appreciative of the variety of God's wonderful created order. On the other hand, a hallucinogenic trip may lead one to think of oneself as God. A drunken stupor that clouds one's mind, taxes one's liver, lessens self-control, and disrupts one's family life appears to be anything but a proper state for any human being, let alone a Christian.

Finally, if drug abuse is indeed a major social problem, then one question should be added to those raised at the beginning of this chapter. Might I not find an opportunity to serve God and humanity in some alcohol or drug-related ministry, counseling, or treatment program?

Study and Discussion
Questions

1. What would you name as the number one drug problem in America today? Support your answer.

2. What do you consider to be the most important changes in the area of substance abuse in the past ten years?

3. Describe the relationship that exists between the drug problem and major institutions such as economics, politics, education, and the family.

4. How does drug use relate to such factors as gender, age, racial/ethnic background, and social class?

5. How would you construct a biological, psychological, and sociological environment that would have the *highest* likelihood of leading one into substance abuse? What kind of environment would have the *lowest* probability of leading to substance abuse?

6. What is the "sentience" theory of drug use? Describe the variety of ways in which the media relates to the use and abuse of substances.

7. Using a major sociological theory (functionalism, symbolic interactionism, conflict theory, social structural theory), describe important aspects of the drug problem.

8. Explain the basic difference between "supply-focused" and "demand-focused" strategies for dealing with the drug problem. Give examples of each of these strategies.

9. Why are informational campaigns relatively ineffectual in dealing with the drug problem?

10. Review the section of this chapter that deals with a Christian perspective on drugs. Identify an element within this section with which you agree or disagree, and indicate why you feel the way you do.

References

Adams, G. R., and T. Gulotta, *Adolescent Life Experiences*. Monterey, CA: Brooks/Cole, 1983.

Adler, T., "Drug abuse linked with antisocial disorder." *APA Monitor*, p. 12, February 1990.

Aronow, L., *Alcoholism, alcohol abuse, and related problems: Opportunities for research.* Institute of Medicine, National Academy of Sciences. Washington, D.C.: National Academy Press, 1980.

Aronson, E., *The social animal.* (4th Ed.). New York: Freeman, 1984.

Bahr, S. J., *Family interaction.* New York: Macmillan, 1989.

Barton, R., and L. Hurst, Unnecessary use of tranquilizers in elderly patients. *British Journal of Psychiatry*, 112, 989-990, 1966.

Bennett's Drug War, "Bennett's Drug War." *Newsweek*, pp. 16-19, 1989, August 21.

Berkman, L. F., and S. L. Syme, "Social networks, host resistance, and mortality: A nine-year follow-up study of Alameda County residents." *American Journal of Epidemiology*, 109, 186-204, 1979.

Blum, R., and L. Richards, "Youthful drug use." In R. L. Dupont, A. Goldstein, and J. O'Donnell (eds.), *Handbook on Drug Abuse* (pp. 257-269). Washington, D.C.: National Institute on Drug Abuse. Department of Health, Education, and Welfare, 1979.

Bridgman, L. P., and W.M. McQueen, Jr. "The success of alcoholics anonymous: Locus of control and God's general revelation." *Journal of Psychology and Theology*, 15 (2), 124-131, 1987.

Buckley, W. F., Jr. (Ed.), "Goldwater is wrong on religion and politics." *New York Times,* 1981, September 26.

"Children of the Underclass.", *Newsweek*, pp. 16-23, 1989, September 11.

Clark, N. H., *Deliver Us from Evil: An Interpretation of American Prohibition.* New York: Norton, 1976.

Contreras, J., "Anarchy in Colombia." Newsweek, pp. 30-32, 1989, September 11.

Dembo, R., G. Grandon, L. LaVois, J. Schmeidler, and W. Burgos, " Parents and drugs revisited: Some further evidence in support of social learning theory." *Criminology*, 24(1), 85-104, 1986.

Durkheim, E., *The Rules of the Sociological Method*. Chicago: Free Press, 1950.

Eiseman, S., J. A. Wingard, and G. J. Huba, (Eds.), *Drug Abuse: Foundation for a Psychosocial Approach*. Farmingdale, NY: Baywood, 1984.

Fawzy, F. I., R.H. Coombs, and G. Gerber, "Generational continuity in the use of substances: The impact of parental substance use on adolescent substance use". *Addictive Behaviors*, 8, 109-114, 1983.

Fine, G., *Talking Sociology*. Boston: Allyn & Bacon, 1985.

Fort, J., "A world view of drugs." In R. Blum (Ed.), *Society and drugs: Social and Cultural Observations* (pp. 229-243). San Francisco, CA: Jossey-Bass, 1969.

Geis, G., "Hypes, hippies, and hypocrites." *Youth and Society*, 1(4), 365-379, 1970.

Graedon, J., and T. Graedon, *The People's Pharmacy*. New York: Avon Books, 1980.

Greenberg, B. S., "Smoking, drugging, and drinking in top rated TV series." In S. Eisman, J. A. Wingard, & G. J. Huba (Eds.), *Drug abuse: Foundation for a Psychosocial Approach* (pp. 198-204). Farmingdale, NY: Baywood, 1984.

Hanson, D. J., "Drug education: Does it work?" In F. R. Scarpitti, & S. K. Datesman (Eds.), *Drugs and the Youth Culture* (pp. 251-282). Beverly Hills, CA: Sage, 1980.

Holmes, A., *Contours of a World View*. Grand Rapids, MI: Eerdmans, 1983.

"Hour by hour crack." *Newsweek*. pp. 64-75, 1988, November 28.

Hundleby, J. D., and G. W. Mercer, "Family and friends as social environments and their relationship to young adolescents' use of alcohol, tobacco, and marijuana." *Journal of Marriage and the Family*, 49, 151-164, 1987.

Inciardi, J. A.,*The War on Drugs*. Palo Alto, CA: Mayfield, 1986.

Jones-Witters, P., and W. Witters, *Drugs & society: A Biological Perspective*. Monterey, CA: Wadsworth, 1983.

Judson, H. F., *Heroin Addiction in Britain: What Americans Can Learn from the English Experience*. New York and London: Harcourt Brace Jovanovich, 1974.

Julien, R. M., *A Primer of Drug Action* (4th ed.). New York: Freeman, 1985.

Julien, R. M., *A Primer of Drug Action* (5th ed.). New York: Freeman, 1988.

Kaplan, J., *The Hardest Drug: Heroin and Public Policy*. Chicago: The University of Chicago Press, 1983.

Kassarjian, H., and J. Cohen, "Cognitive dissonance and consumer behavior." *California Management Review*, 8, 55-64, 1965.

Keller, M., "The great Jewish Drink Mystery." *British Journal of Addiction*, 64, 287, 1970.

Lassey, M. L., and J. E. Carolson, "Drinking among rural youth: The dynamics of parental and peer influence." *International Journal of the Addictions*, 15(1), 61-75, 1980.

Leavitt, F., *Drugs and Behavior* (2nd ed.). New York: Wiley, 1982.

Lermoux, P., "The Miami connection." *The Nation*, pp. 186-198, 1985, February 18.

Loken, J. O., *Student Alienation and Dissent*. Scarborough, Ontario: Prentice-Hall, 1973.

Long, R. E., *Drugs and American Society*. New York: The H. W. Wilson Company, 1986.

Lyon, D., *Sociology and the Human Image*. Downers Grove; IL: Inter-Varsity Press, 1983.

Marcos, A. C., S. J. Bahr, and R. E. Johnson, "Test of a bonding/association theory of adolescent drug use." *Social Forces*, 65(1), 135-161, 1986.

Mayers, M., *Christianity Confronts Culture*. Grand Rapids, MI: Zondervan, 1974.

Morey, R. A. *The Bible and Drug Abuse*. Nutley, NJ: Presbyterian and Reformed Publishing House, 1973.

Newcomb, M. D., and P. M. Bentler, "Substance use and abuse among children and teenagers." *American Psychologist*, 44(2), 242-248, 1989.

Newcomb, M. D., E. A. Maddahian, and P. M. Bentler, "Risk factors for drug use among adolescents: Concurrent and longitudinal analysis." *American Journal of Public Health*, 76, 525-531, 1986.

Schlaadt, R. G., and P. T. Shannon, *Drugs of Choice* (2nd ed.). Englewood Cliffs, NJ: Prentice-Hal, 1986.

Tagliacozzo, L, "Smoker's self-categorization and the reduction of cognitive dissonance." *Addictive Behaviors*, 4, 393-399, 1979.

Tobler, N. S., "Meta-analysis of 143 adolescent drug prevention programs." *Journal of Drug Issues*, 16, 537-568, 1986.

CHAPTER 21
POVERTY: INTRODUCTION

Professor Burton carefully presents the statistical and comparative experience of poverty in the United States. The data are sobering and poignant. From 1970 to 1990 the numbers of Americans who are poor have increased sharply with American children making up one of the largest percentages. Our children are more likely to be living in poverty than the children of eight other major industrial countries of the world. Homelessness is becoming epidemic in the United States and increasingly involves families with young children. Further, having a regular job is no guarantee that the individual or family will escape the experience of poverty; growing numbers of the working poor are teetering on the brink of economic disaster. Rural and small town poverty exists and is growing. Professor Burton reminds us to be responsible Christians and citizens and to know what is happening with thousands of Americans, and to recognize the call of God to respond to their need.

Sociological theories dealing with stratification both describe the situation of the poor and attempt to explain why some are poor and others not. Inherent in the explanations are suggestions for intervention on behalf of the needy. Early explanations of poverty used structural-functional theory, and applied the perspective primarily at the *micro*-level of social experience. The indigent individual was thought to be without economic resources because of personal failure or individual handicap. The poor person was disabled, or lazy, or untaught. The appropriate level for action against poverty was at the micro or individual level and involved rehabilitation; increased motivation, self-esteem and personal responsibility; or education.

Professor Burton also places poverty within a functional paradigm, but adds to the micro-level several *macro*-level factors associated with low economic status in the United States. Such factors include failure of the educational structure, lack of delivery of needed health care, and the disintegration of the American family. The author also notes that technology has brought about a restructuring of economic institutions away from heavy manufacturing economy toward the service industries. In the transition, many Americans have become unemployed or underemployed. In a time of pervasive structural and economic change and until equilibrium of the system can again be established, theorists from both the micro- and macro-level perspectives predict continuing social disorganization, such as increased crime, homelessness and individual alienation from the political process.

Other theoretical perspectives have also been used to describe and explain poverty. The conflict theorist would add to Professor Burton's functional analysis the factors of economic exploitation and oppression. This theoretical view focuses on ways in which the powerful take advantage of those less powerful. Conflict theory would note the Ivan Boeskys who defraud large and small investors, the grocery stores in low income communities which charge higher prices for basic foodstuffs than do stores in middle and upper-middle class neighborhoods, and the corporations which fraudulently use pension funds set aside for retired workers. For the conflict theorist, reducing the numbers of the poor involves addressing issues of power abuse, and exploitation.

Several chapters in this book also touch on poverty issues; a more complete understanding of the various social theories and the interaction between macro- and micro-level variables can be developed by reviewing the discussions in the "Economics" and "Social Stratification" chapters.

We agree with Professor Burton that God unmistakenly calls His Church to respond with care for the poor. From the Old through the New Testament examples and commandments are given and then repeated, instructing believers not to neglect our neighbors in need. Many of us respond with deepening feelings of helplessness; what can one person do to change the conditions of the poor? In addition to reminding us of God's special concern for the needy, Professor Burton addresses this sense of helplessness. He provides practical suggestions of personal and organizational ways to support, sustain, and accompany those who are living in poverty.

An article written by Richard Lee, "Poverty in Chicago," follows Professor Burton's chapter and offers a powerful and personal window illustrating for us the diversity and humanness of the poor. We are given opportunity to share his world of the urban street, and to see additional practical responses to God's call to love and to serve those who are in need around us.

POVERTY

C. Emory Burton

INTRODUCTION

While walking the streets of Philadelphia one day, Loretta Schwartz-Nobel found an 84-year-old woman, Martha Roca, in an abandoned house. Loretta went out and bought food for her. Down a narrow alley she found Julia sitting in a doorway on a torn green plastic chair; she had gone from 150 pounds to 90. She was wearing one of her two dresses. She had no teeth, and her toes peeked through straw slippers. Roaches were crawling on the linoleum. When asked, "Do you get much food?" she replied, "No." Once she had fallen; once someone grabbed her bag, robbing her of most of what little she had in it. Starting an investigation, Schwartz-Noble found that there were tens of thousands of other people in Philadelphia desperate for food. They are America's hidden poor (Schwartz-Noble, 1981).

What Loretta saw changed her picture of America. In the alleys of south Philadelphia she found old people living in one- and two-room shacks, sometimes without heat, water, gas or food. Visiting the hovels and back alleys of other American cities, she discovered that there were thousands in the same poverty-stricken condition. Even in the nation's capital the plight of the poor was shockingly evident. Some were living on cheap, mostly starch diets. Loretta met the mother of five living in a single room. When the mother was asked what the children ate, she replied, "Rice. They never complain as long as I cook enough rice to fill them up" (Schwartz-Noble, 1981, pp. 20-21).

THE INCIDENCE OF POVERTY TODAY

Despite a long economic recovery, poverty remains a serious problem in the United States. Burghardt and Fabricant (1987) speak of "the most abject poverty witnessed in this country since the Great Depression." Poverty actually increased in the early 1980s, and declined slightly in the latter half of the decade; the rate (about 14 percent) now remains higher than any year since the 1970s (Greenstein, 1989).

About 32.5 million Americans — nearly one out of seven — live below the poverty line (Eitzen, 1989). That is eight million more than in 1978, a year with nearly identical unemployment rate. Not only may poverty be found among inner-city dwellers, but poverty rates have remained high for nearly all types of Americans. From 1978 to 1988 the white poverty rate rose by 20 percent, and poverty in nonmetropolitan areas went up from 13.5 percent to 16.9 percent (Greenstein, 1989).

Two studies corroborate the view that poverty remains a major problem for many Americans, particularly black, Hispanic, Native American and Appalachian families. In a report by the Urban Institute among eight Western Industrial democracies, the United States had the highest percentage of children living in poverty (*Christianity Today*, Dec. 9, 1988). The Harvard-based Physicians Task Force on Hunger in America (1985) argues that hunger and malnutrition are more widespread than they have been since the 1970s.

At the end of 1987, the gap between rich and poor families was the widest in 40 years, according to the Bureau of the Census. The wealthiest 40 percent of American families received 67.8 percent of the national family income, and the poorest 40 percent received 15.4 percent (Howell, 1988).

There is little doubt that still more Americans are going hungry as the nation sags into what some economists are already calling a major recession. *The New York Times* reported that at least 44 states have indicated increases in food stamp and welfare enrollments (*Barre-Montpelier Times-Argus*, Aug. 21, 1990). The depletion of a federal emergency food assistance program has sent local food providers scrambling. Churches, food pantries, and local agencies experience steadily increasing requests for food products. Programs that were intended to provide temporary relief have become permanent.

POVERTY DEFINED

The official line of poverty is set by the Office of Management and Budget. The Bureau of the Census is the major supplier of statistical information on the poor. The present standard definition for poverty is based on purchasing patterns of 1955, when the average family spent 33 percent of its income on food. Each welfare program has its own rules for determining poverty status and eligibility, and each state sets its own "standards of need" for eligibility.

No universally accepted definition of poverty exists. Eitzen (1989) defines the poor as those who, because of a lack of resources, are denied adequate health, diet, clothing, and shelter. Some would add that the following attributes characterize the poor: a low level of self-esteem, a restricted view of personal effectiveness, and a sense of separation from the society (Beeghley, 1983).

While there is some controversy about the extent of poverty in this country, most sociologists believe official estimates are low. Further, a large category of people considered "near poor" could fall into the ranks of the poor with just the slightest misfortune (Beeghley, 1983).

SOME CATEGORIES OF THE POOR

Children

Possibly the most directly affected and the most vulnerable to poverty are children. Too many are living in poverty, doomed to a combination of neglect, abuse, failure in school, chemical addiction, run-ins with the law, and even premature death (*Minneapolis Star and Tribune*, July 25, 1990).

Over 21 percent of the children under 15, and 23 percent of those under five, are poor (Eitzen, 1989). That is at least one in every five children; in 1970, it was one out of six. The poverty rate for children under 18 dropped from 27 percent in 1959 to a low of 13.8 percent in 1969 and then back up to its present level of 21 percent today. While almost 50 percent of black children under six live in poverty, 39 percent of Hispanic children also experience low income conditions (Spates and Macionis, 1987). Many of these children live in female-headed households. Every week 211 children in the United States die from poor maternal health care and infection.

There are children in this country who have never seen a ball, a rattle, a bell or a mirror. Sticks and rocks are the only toys. Rags and old clothing serve as blankets. Some stay home from school because of lack of shoes and clothing. Most poor children never go to a dentist. Senator Daniel Patrick Moynihan (1989) stated that by the turn of the century about half of all American children "will have lived some parts of their lives in poverty."

Women

In all age categories, American women are more likely to be poor than American men. This fact is so striking that the phrase "feminization of poverty" is now commonly used by sociologists. Female heads of household comprise the largest category of the poor. The number of female-headed families with income below the poverty line was 1.9 million in 1959; by 1983, this number had doubled, and is even higher today. "In 1986 about 28 percent of households headed by white women were poor, but over 50 percent of households headed by black and Hispanic women were poor" (Macionis, 1989, p. 334).

Benefits available in Aid to Families With Dependent Children, the nation's primary government support for single heads of households, have been significantly reduced in real terms in the past decade (Dunn, 1984; Joe and Rogers, 1985). The 1988 legislation requiring welfare mothers to work in order to receive benefits is highly controversial. Many believe that these requirements are unjustified, unless the shortage of good-paying jobs, lack of availability of child care and health insurance, and the worsening housing crisis are addressed (Kemper, 1988; Conover, 1989).

Low income working parents are disproportionately hard hit by child-care expenses; poor families spend 25 percent of their income on child care and the near-poor spend 16 percent, according to a Census Bureau study (*Boston Globe*, Aug 15, 1990).

The Elderly

Largely because of expanded government programs, the percentage of the elderly in poverty has declined, so that today it is no higher than that of the population as a whole. However, there are still a substantial number of poor or near-poor among the elderly (Eitzen, 1989). While a few programs exist to assist the elderly in finding work, lack of employment and age discrimination are special problems for them. Widows are especially vulnerable.

According to the Census Bureau and nonprofit social agencies, about two million of the elderly poor in America are living alone, and a disproportionate number of them are women, blacks, and Hispanics. There are also 1.6 million elderly living alone who are classified as "near poor," whose income is slightly above the $5,393 poverty level defined for an individual. It is estimated that only 50 percent of those eligible for supplemental security income receive it (*Dallas Morning News*, Aug. 20, 1990). The elderly suffer most from rising housing and utilities costs. Many older people are forced to choose between eating and paying the rent or the electricity (Burghardt and Fabricant, 1987). Many elderly experience poverty for the first time upon retirement. Older blacks are especially vulnerable.

Minorities

Black family income has been decreasing in the 1980s. According to the Center for Budget and Policy Priorities, the income gap between black and white families in America is widening (*Christianity Today*, December 9, 1988). A typical black family made 56.1 percent of the typical white family's income (Howell, 1988). When overall assets such as property, investments and other wealth are taken into consideration, the relative condition of blacks is even worse (Oliver and Shapiro, 1990).

While in absolute numbers most poor people are white, the proportion of those in poverty remains three times higher for blacks than for whites. Poverty among blacks outside the South has soared. While the poverty rate of Hispanics is lower than that of blacks, it is well over twice that of the white population as a whole (Eitzen, 1989). Language and cultural barriers prevent many Hispanics from seeking help.

Native Americans are another minority group experiencing dire poverty. Because they have been isolated on reservations, job opportunities for most are virtually non-existent. Poor sanitation, discrimination against Indians who have moved to cities and cutbacks in federal programs have all adversely affected the American Indian's opportunities for a fair share of the "good life" (Harrington, 1984; Rogers et al., 1988).

Rural Poverty

The difficulties of American farmers in the 1980s have been well chronicled (Rogers et al., 1988; Harrington, 1984). Declining land values, overinvestment, inflation, bad weather and a drop in farm prices have all led to severe economic trouble for thousands of farmers. Farmers in Iowa and other states are in the ironic position of accepting government food stamps.

Trouble on the farm also means trouble in the small towns of America. Relative isolation, lack of job opportunities and lack of community services reflect problems in such communities. In addition, low-paying jobs, lack of affordable child care and high health insurance costs form a closely woven net that continues to trap rural families (*Milwaukee Journal*, 1990).

The famous documentary, "Harvest of Shame" presented by journalist Edward R. Murrow in 1960 introduced the plight of the migrant worker. Local churches and ecumenical organizations have spoken out against the exploitation, low pay, bad housing and difficult working conditions of the migrant worker. The problems encountered by migrants have a special effect on the children, who lack a community and educational base because of the frequent moves (Rogers et al., 1988; Harrington, 1984).

One of the denominations addressing the plight of the migrant workers is The United Methodist Church, which adopted the following resolution:

> Calling for special attention is the situation of farm workers in the United States. Traditionally they have been among the most poorly paid, housed, educated, and poorly served by health, welfare, and other social agencies. They have been systematically excluded from all, or nearly all, the benefits of social legislation (United Methodist Church, 1984).

The Appalachian area in the eastern United States has had a long history of poverty. Even today, as many as five million people in this essentially rural area are poor. Most of the younger, more talented people have left the area, since farming in the southern

Appalachian region holds little promise of being able to sustain the farm residents at an adequate income level. Lack of transportation and medical care are additional concerns (Rogers et al., 1988; Auletta, 1982).

A recent account reports that today Appalachia is as much a symbol of the nation's failures as it was 30 years ago. Coal is the primary industry, but the continued mechanization of mines has put 80,000 people out of work in the last decade. While federal spending has made a huge difference, parts of the region, especially in eastern Kentucky, remain desperately poor (*Boston Globe*, August 19, 1990).

Urban Areas

Residents of the central city — who are often members of minority groups — are at least twice as likely to experience poverty as suburban dwellers. Large cities are suffering for several reasons: industry has moved out, housing has deteriorated, schools are less adequate, the percentage of broken and single-parent families is high, and there is a large criminal and drug subculture (Spates and Macionis, 1987).

As central cities were losing their low-skill employment base in manufacturing, they simultaneously came to house a growing number of poor minorities, and so created a serious employment "mismatch." Furthermore, urban minorities are geographically isolated from high-paying jobs because manufacturing plants have moved to the suburbs and beyond. Minorities are also socially isolated from high paying jobs in the central city by a lack of education (Massey and Eggers, 1990).

In addition, urban areas are the locale for a particularly acute current social problem — the homeless. Burt and Cohen (1989) state, "Homelessness is at base a function of poverty." The media have made Americans aware of the destitution and suffering of thousands of persons sleeping on grates, in cardboard boxes, or on benches under blankets of newspapers. Few contemporary social problems rival homelessness in the amount of public attention received during the 1980s (Burghardt and Fabricant, 1987).

Best estimates on the number of homeless in the United States are 500,000 to 600,000 (Burt and Cohen, 1989). Some fear that the ranks of street people may swell to several million by the end of the century (Spring, 1988).

Deep cuts in federal housing subsidies and insufficient checks on high cost private development over the past decade have dramatically increased the numbers of homeless. Federal funding to low-income housing has been cut from over $35 billion to $7 billion (Smith, 1989). The demand for homeless shelter jumped by 21 percent in one year (1986-1987), and has steadily increased. Nearly one-fourth of the nationwide demand for shelter goes unmet (*Christianity Today*, February 5, 1988). Beth Spring (1989) claims that "today's homeless bear little resemblance to the stereotypical skid-row bum. Instead, they are beginning to look a lot like our next-door neighbors." Widespread reports show a marked increase in the number of families and younger people among the homeless. Some are abused teenagers pushed out of broken homes; rescue missions find fewer hitchhikers, vagrants and transients, but more "hometown" people. One survey found that single men make up 49 percent of the homeless; families with children, 33 percent; single women, 14 percent; and unaccompanied youths, about 4 percent (Spring, 1989).

Stephen Burger, who runs a mission in Seattle, says, "We are seeing more and more people who are close to the line economically .... Even people living out in the suburbs are often only one or two paychecks away from disaster" (quoted in Spring, 1989).

Controversy exists about the extent of mental illness among the homeless. One study found 16 percent of the homeless to be mentally ill (Snow et al., 1987), while other studies estimate the mentally ill to comprise 33 percent of the homeless. The government policy of deinstitutionalization of mental hospitals in the 1960s contributed greatly to this problem. Erosion of stable family life also may be an important, but often unrecognized, part of the problem (Christensen, 1990).

Many homeless lack sophisticated work skills. The transition from smokestack industries to service and high-tech jobs has left thousands of laborers unemployed. Multifamily low-rent units have been torn down or converted to luxury condominiums with no alternate low-cost housing being provided. Rent allowances covered by welfare were frozen for ten years at their 1975 levels, while rent costs everywhere steadily increased. Federal funds for building or rehabilitating low-income housing dropped from $32 billion to $9 billion nationwide. In 1970, two affordable units were available for every one poor renter household. By 1983, only one affordable unit was available for every two poor renter households. The problem continues to escalate. The number of government subsidized housing units has slowed to a virtual trickle (Greenstein, 1989).

It is almost impossible to locate an affordable unit for a family that can pay only $150 a month. Many persons live on disability checks of $468 a month in cities such as New York and San Francisco where the average monthly rent for a small apartment is well over $500 (Smith, 1989). In 1985, 63 percent of poor renter households paid half or more of their income for rent (Burt and Cohen, 1989).

Community development corporations, tenant cooperatives, churches, labor unions and others are capable of playing a major role in providing decent, affordable housing, if they receive the necessary capital, technical assistance and support (*Christianity and Crisis*, April 18, 1988).

Katie R. Smith (1989) says:

> Charitable efforts from individuals and groups, while important, will not wrench up the roots of homelessness and substitute for government-provided infrastructures. The people who make up the "points of light" in our churches and communities also need the resources that government can provide in increasing the availability of affordable housing and support services.

SPECIAL PROBLEMS OF THE WORKING POOR

An important part of the picture is the increase in the number of people who work, but are still poor. The Center on Budget and Policy Priorities reports that more than two million people who work full-time year-round do not earn enough to escape poverty (Beeghley, 1983). More than 40 percent of all poor people over age 14 worked in 1987, and the number of working poor has increased by 50 percent since 1978 (Kemper, 1988).

Levitan and Shapiro (1987) dispel the basic American myth that work provides a route out of poverty. In 1985, two million adults worked full-time and yet their families were poor. Another seven million worked part-time or at seasonal jobs and were poor (quoted by Fernandez, 1989). Slightly more than half of the new jobs created since 1980 in this country were at full-time annual wages of less than $12,000 (Kemper, 1988).

Until the recent modest increases, the minimum wage would provide less than $7,000 a year; this amount is not sufficient for raising a family of three above the poverty level. Some seasonal workers make less than this, and a large number make only slightly more. Most Americans would agree that if a parent works full-time, year-round, his or her family should not have to live in poverty (Greenstein, 1989). Assuring this would be of only modest cost to the government.

SOME CORRELATES OF POVERTY

Sociologists identify a number of factors likely to be associated with poverty. If several of these are found in one family, the combination may ensure poverty status.

Inadequate Education

The level of educational achievement is a crucial determinant of a person's future income. Thousands of young people in overcrowded, poorly staffed inner city schools and some in isolated rural schools, have little motivation to complete high school. Many must work to help their families obtain the basic necessities to survive.

Poor children, especially from minority families, may feel discriminated against in the school system. The school experience often is a sequence of social failures and disappointments. The usefulness of such courses as literature, biology, civics and history is ambiguous at best. Little love for learning is acquired in homes that have no reason to value it, and where parents are not intellectually supportive (Eitzen, 1989). Poor children have inadequate diets, poor clothes and often live in homes that are overcrowded.

Those who are uneducated have much greater difficulty in learning about employment options. Even routine job-seeking activities may be difficult. The inability to speak English well, to understand employment application questions, to fill out detailed forms, or to grasp instructions, is a serious impediment to a job search.

School districts with a better tax base have superior facilities, better teachers and support programs. The lower the social class, the lower the percentage of students who plan to go to college and the greater the number of school discipline problems. Both of these factors affect the higher percentage of failures and school drop-out rates (Beeghley, 1983).

Illiteracy

Even those who have completed some high school may not be able to read at a sixth-grade level. The low level of literacy greatly hampers future educational, occupational and social adjustments. Jonathan Kozol estimates that 20 percent of American adults are functionally illiterate (quoted in Eitzen, 1989).

Poor Health

All studies show a correlation between income and health; the poor tend to have much worse overall physical and mental health then the nonpoor. Poverty and illness go together. Communicable diseases among children under five were two and one-half times higher in the slum area as in other parts of the city (Beeghley, 1983). High infant mortality, low life expectancy and malnutrition are associated with poverty.

The poor are vulnerable to acute, short-term diseases of all sorts as well as chronic, long-term ailments. The rate of visual impairment is twice as high among them. Preventive care such as routine medical examinations, immunizations, and proper nutrition are accessed infrequently (Physicians Task Force, 1985). Among the factors that block the poor from proper medical care are the high cost of medical services, the fact that the poor are much less likely to have insurance (at least one-third of the poor are not covered by Medicaid), and that the poor are less likely to define themselves as ill. A doctor or dental appointment can mean a full workday lost; the poor rarely have the luxury of paid sick leave (Champagne & Harpham, 1984).

There is a strong inverse relationship between income and psychological disorders of all kinds. Due to economic strain the prevalence of psychoses increases as measures of occupation, income, and education decrease (Eitzen, 1989).

Poor Housing

Dilapidated housing is one of the most evident correlates of poverty. In addition to those without a home, thousands of Americans live in shelter that is unfit or barely adequate for human habitation. Falling plaster, inadequate ventilation, overcrowded rooms, the presence of rats and other unhealthy conditions are common in inner-city areas and in some rural communities. Poor families may live in dwellings with no hot water, inadequate plumbing, no shower or tub and little furniture (Harrington, 1984).

Among the serious effects of home overcrowding are increased stress, poor development of a sense of identity, sexual conflict, family tensions and lack of adequate sleep. Some of these problems undoubtedly are related to poor work and school performance of the children living in such situations.

Poor Family Life

The family is the most important social institution for children to develop values, habits, discipline and life goals. It is enormously difficult to find an adequate substitute for an intact family (Eitzen, 1989).

Beeghley (1983) points out that many children are raised by parents who are still children themselves, and who lack both marriage and parenting skills. High divorce and desertion rates exist among poor families, in large part due to the conflicts and stress engendered by economic tension. The fact that many divorced males do not pay child support further compounds the plight of poor female-headed families.

The percentage of all babies born out of wedlock has more than doubled since 1970. Growing up in a poor, single-parent household increases the likelihood that a young woman from such a home will herself bear a child out of wedlock. She is also more likely to divorce if she does marry (Christensen, 1990).

Crime

Criminal behavior reflects the vulnerability and limited choices available to poor persons. The lower the social class, the higher the arrest rate; the lower the social class, the less able to post bail and the longer the time spent in jail prior to trial; the lower the social class, the higher the conviction rate and the longer the prison sentence (Beeghley, 1983; Eitzen, 1989).

Our country places great value on occupational and economic success, but for the poor there are limited legitimate means for achieving success. As Robert Merton states in his "social strain theory," vice and crime may appear to some of the poor as reasonable responses to the lack of legitimate opportunity (cited in Beeghley, 1983).

Needy persons are more likely to be victimized by street crimes than the nonpoor (Harrington, 1984). The lower a person's social class, the more the legal system works to his or her disadvantage. Because of a lack of knowledge and financial resource, the poor find it difficult to utilize the legal system to protect themselves.

Lack of Political Participation

The lower the social class, the lower the rate of political participation. The poor lack the economic, social and personal characteristics that normally stimulate participation. They do not belong to political or other voluntary organizations because membership takes transportation, literacy, decent clothing, child care, money for dues and freedom from fear (Beeghley, 1983). For these reasons, the poor often are unable to use the political structure to protest when their interests are harmed.

TOWARD AN EXPLANATION OF POVERTY

The view that poverty reflects immorality and that the poor are primarily responsible for their plight has been rejected by most social scientists. The large number of working poor also contradicts such a view. This does not mean that those individuals and families who are poor are merely victims of society and have no responsibility for their own situation. Most sociologists, however, emphasize that the plight of the poor is largely due to structural changes in society such as increased unemployment, low minimum wage, the move from manufacturing to a service economy and cuts in federal programs (Eitzen, 1989).

Technological change has displaced many workers and closed opportunities for new entrants, especially unskilled and semiskilled workers. In addition, the exporting of jobs through investments in plants overseas is an important factor. Millions of workers are not in unions, and wages are often so low that the working poor remain in poverty. Not only are jobs vanishing in production, but also on the farm. The mechanization of agriculture has displaced thousands of farm workers (Beeghley, 1983; Burghardt and Fabricant, 1987).

Oscar Lewis has advanced a view known as the "culture of poverty." He suggests that poverty is not simply the absence of money, but includes a distinctive way of life involving fatalism, inability to postpone gratification and other self-defeating traits that tend to perpetuate themselves (Eitzen, 1989). This view has evoked considerable controversy, but it does underscore the fact that poverty tends to be accompanied by a whole life-style that will take massive efforts to undo.

Consensus is growing among sociologists and policy makers that wages should be increased in order to move the working poor out of poverty. One way to accomplish this is to increase the "Earned Income Tax Credit," which would provide a wage supplement for the working poor geared to family size (Popkin, 1990). This policy has both conservative and liberal support.

Affordable health coverage and child care need to be made available for the working poor. Medicaid is not extended to most parents in working families (with the exception of pregnant women); neither are most of the children in these families covered by Medicaid (Greenstein, 1989). Improvement in this area would benefit inner-city and rural residents alike.

THE CHRISTIAN APPROACH

One of the central social concerns of the Bible is the plight and suffering of the poor. Interestingly enough, the Scriptures almost never place the poor in the center of the narrative; it is the nonpoor who are addressed. The Bible asks that the prosperous set right the condition of poor persons (Gittings, 1988).

Psalm 146 is one among many passages that tells of God's concern for the hungry and the oppressed. Indeed, care for the poor is central to the nature of God. God not only acts in history to liberate the poor, but He identifies with the weak and destitute. Proverbs 19:17 says, "He who is kind to the poor lends to the Lord."

Amos saw firsthand the terrible oppression of the poor. He saw the rich "trample the head of the poor into the dust of the earth"(2:7), and perceived that the lifestyle of the rich was built on the oppression of the poor (6:1-7). Noble (1990) believes that the primary cause of poverty in the Old Testament is oppression.

Many biblical texts assert that God lifts up the poor and disadvantaged. God aids the poor, but the rich He sends away empty. Sider (1978) suggests that God actively opposes the rich because they oppress the poor and neglect the needy. Schmidt (1989) claims that "Jesus clearly condemns the possession of wealth," and "every time Jesus offers an opinion about riches, it is negative." Jesus' advice to the rich young ruler (Luke 18:18-30) calls for him to abandon his possessions, and give them to the poor. Either God or wealth is one's master or "employer" (Matthew 6:24). In the parable of the Rich Man and Lazarus, the rich man was found guilty for neglecting the poor man at his gate (Luke 16:19-31).

Luke pictures the Good News as a message of salvation for the poor, sick, sorrowful, weak, lowly and outcast (4:18-19). The parable of the Good Samaritan (Luke 10: 25-37) and the parable of the Last Judgment (Matthew 25:31-46) are two of the better known sayings of Jesus on this subject. A living faith is the one that demonstrates compassion for those in need: "If a brother or sister is ill-clad and in lack of daily food, and one of you says to them, 'Go in peace, be warmed and filled,' without giving them the things needed for the body, what does it profit?" (James 2:15-16).

The Bible also points out that the giving of material things has spiritual implications (e.g., John 13:35; 1 John 3:17). Those who are rich in this world have a special obligation to invest in a heavenly reward by caring for the needs of others (Gruden, 1989). Paul's collection for the needy in Jerusalem is an example (Romans 15:25-27).

The Roman Catholic Church has been outspoken on this issue. In Latin America the Bishop's Conference in 1968 terminated the Church's traditional alliance with landowning and industrial elites, and the military. Looking upon a continent rife with injustice and oppression, the Bishops condemned the "institutional violence" of the ruling classes and called for land reform, income redistribution, and the creation of movements to empower the poor and bring about their political and spiritual liberation (Peerman, 1989).

The U.S. Catholic Conference pastoral letter on the American economy released in

1984, was a call to re-examine economic priorities in light of the Church's "preferential option for the poor." The document advocated a biblical view in which the economy serves people. It argued that the right to private property is not absolute but is limited by concern for the common good.

> The justice of a community is measured by its treatment of the powerless in society, most often described (in the Bible) as the widow, the orphan, the poor and the stranger in the land (1984).

The document states that economic justice must be measured not by what it does for the rich or the middle classes, but by what it does for the poor. It rejects the classic trickle-down theory which emphasizes the benefits of increased wealth without concern for how such wealth is distributed.

Drafters of the Roman Catholic document flatly deny that people receiving welfare benefits are persistently dependent on that source of income. It is not true that most are not working; nor is it true that the others could work if they wanted to. The document calls for national welfare standards and a rejection of "workfare schemes" (*Newsweek*, November 19, 1984).

While all agree that Christians should do more as individuals and through churches to help the poor, there is disagreement over the role government should play. Because of the structural elements of poverty, many Christians believe that both the public and private spheres need to be involved.

SOME CHRISTIAN EFFORTS

Perhaps the first things individual Christians can do is learn all they can about the biblical view of poverty, and about some of the things a sociological perspective can contribute. (Sources listed at the end of this chapter may be a starting place.) It is also important to find out about specific needs in our own church family and neighborhood. We need to be clearly aware of the problems which face individuals and families. What is the timetable before catastrophe strikes: how long until the house is lost, or a needed operation becomes impossible? Our means of helping should support the goal of assisting a person or family to make their own best decisions (Gittings, 1988). We must ask ourselves what resources are available to help persons in need. Sometimes the problem can be solved through the personal resources of the helper: a hundred dollars from the individual's bank account, or the suggestion of a lawyer's name from legal aid.

More frequently, the need goes beyond our personal resources, and we are sent back to the local church. Almost every congregation has a committee for outreach and emergency service. The pastor can often open up committee agendas rapidly (Gittings, 1988). If the church as a whole lacks the resources to meet the need, seek the pastor's help in making further approaches to possible funding sources, perhaps from the denomination or the community. Ecumenical bodies, service clubs in your area, the local health-care agencies and the United Way may be useful (Gittings, 1988).

Of course money is not always what is needed. Individuals may benefit from counseling, spiritual undergirding or a community of support. For example, Mary Noland of Adair, Iowa, is a farmer who is still in business but struggling to survive.

Nevertheless, she has found time to consider the condition of neighbors who are worse off than she. The first thing that Mary Noland did for her neighbors was to establish a farm women's support group. The group has grown to a circle of 15 to 20 women who meet weekly to talk through their concerns. Next Mrs. Noland started a couple's support group. Most recently, she has arranged for mental health professionals to visit her community in order to develop alternative work skills and income. The Presbytery of Des Moines, desiring to learn more about helping beleaguered farm families, has created an Emergency Aid Fund, administered through Mary Noland, which ensures that no one in the area goes hungry. Area offices of other denominations have similar stories to share (Gittings, 1988).

Churches in the farm belt have done much to assist farm families. In Nebraska the Farm Crisis Network, funded by a long list of Roman Catholic and Protestant bodies, is a state-wide organization that provides financial, emotional, legal, medical, housing and food services to impoverished families. One feature of the operation is the Farm Crisis Hotline, a counseling service that provides emergency services to families in need (Gittings, 1988).

Similar help is provided by such organizations as the Iowa Inter-Church Agency for Peace and Justice, the Kansas Interfaith Rural Committee, the Louisiana Interchurch Farm Crisis Coalition, the Minnesota Council of Churches, the National Catholic Rural Life Congress, the Federation of Southern Cooperatives/Land Assistance Fund, and many other groups (Gittings, 1988).

The San Francisco Network Ministries provides services to the elderly poor, the homeless, addicts and alcoholics, illiterates, people with AIDS living in poverty, prostitutes and people with various mental and physical disabilities struggling to live on meager benefit payments (Hope, 1989).

A Georgia church has a long tradition of opening its doors in times of need. Like many other churches, it has a shelter for the homeless. But someone thought about the feet of people who wander the street during the day looking for work. So this church has arranged for regular podiatric care in the shelter, a service whose necessity seems obvious once one has seen it in operation (Gittings, 1988).

The Christian Connection, involving a number of churches in Ontario, organizes discussion sessions at the Niagara Regional Detention Centre. With Church help, a contractor in Alabama has set in motion an employment program for released prisoners. A congregation near the large prison in Ossining, New York, has added an associate pastor to its staff for the sole purpose of working at the huge institution with inmates and their families. And in Brooklyn, the new Gethsemane Church is made up of former prisoners and their families, and those who have taken an interest in their lives (Gittings, 1988).

To be faithful to the biblical witness and to the tradition of the Church in ministering to the "least of these my brethren," both individual Christians and entire churches must respond to this urgent issue of poverty in the land.

Study and Discussion
Questions

1. Are there poor people in your community? Are they women, children, elderly, minorities, or some other category?

2. Do you know any working people who are poor or nearly so?

3. Are there specific problems in your community related to schooling or family life?

4. Do you think the poor are oppressed or exploited? In what way?

5. List some explanations of poverty that seem to make the most sense. Are these personal, structural, or both?

6. Using a concordance, look up several references to the poor in the Bible. What does it say about them?

7. What is the attitude of Scripture towards wealth? How does this differ from the attitude of our culture?

8. Does your denomination have a statement on poverty or economic issues? What does it say?

9. In helping the poor, do you think the emphasis should be on private or government programs? Why?

10. Does your church have a committee or program for reaching out to poor people? How might it be strengthened?

References

Auletta, Ken, *The Underclass*. New York: Vintage Books, 1982.

Barre-Montpelier (Vermont) *Times Argus*. August 21, 1990.

Beeghley, Leonard, *Living Poorly in America*. New York: Praeger Publishers, 1983.

Boston (Massachusetts) *Globe*, August 15, 1990.

Burghardt, Steve, and Michael Fabricant, *Living Under the Safety Net*. Newbury Park: Sage Publications, 1987.

Burt, Martha R., and Barbara E. Cohen, "Differences Among Homeless Single Women, Women With Children and Single Men." *Social Problems*, 36-5 (December): 508-524, 1989.

Christensen, Bryce J. , "On the Streets: Homeless in America." *The Family in America*, 4-6 (June): 1-8, 1990.

Champagne, Anthony, and Edward J. Harpham (eds.), *The Attack on the Welfare State*. Prospect Heights, IL: Waveland Press, 1984.

Christianity and Crisis, "Homelessness, Housing, and Hope." 48-6 (April 18): 123-124, 1988.

Christianity Today, February 5, 1988:48.

Christianity Today, December 9, 1988:56.

Conover, Patrick, "Welfare and Work: A Dispute." *The Christian Century*, 106-13 (April 19): 419, 1989.

Dallas Morning News, August 20, 1990.

Eitzen, D. Stanley, *1989 Social Problems*. Needham Heights, Massachusetts: Allyn and Bacon.

Gittings, James A., *Breach of Promise: Portraits of Poverty in North America*. New York: Friendship Press, 1988.

Greenwood, Elma L., *How Churches Fight Poverty: 60 Successful Local Projects*. New York: Friendship Press, 1967.

Greenstein, Robert, "Making Work Pay." *Christianity and Crisis*, 49-3 (March

6): 57, 1989.

Harrington, Michael, *The New American Poverty*. New York: Holt, Rinehart and Winston, 1984.

Howell, Leon,"The Poor Grow Poorer." *Christianity and Crisis*, 16-7 (November 7): 338, 1988.

Joe, Tom, and Cheryl Rogers, *By the Few for the Few: The Reagan Welfare Legacy*. Lexington, Massachusetts: Lexington Books, 1985.

Kelly, George A., *The Catholic Church and the American Poor*. New York: Alba House, 1976.

Kemper, Vicki, "Welfare Reform: Helping Whom?" *Sojourners*, 17-11 (December): 5-6, 1988.

Macionis, John J., *Sociology*. Englewood Cliffs, New Jersey: Prentice-Hall.

Minneapolis (Minnesota) *Star and Tribune*, July 25, 1990.

Newsweek, November 19, 1984.

Noble, Lowell, "Oppression: The Missing Concept." *Christian Sociological Society Newsletter*, 17-2 (February): 10-11, 1990.

Popkin, Susan J., "Welfare: Views From the Bottom." *Social Problems*, 37-1 (February): 64-79, 1990.

Rogers, Everett M., Rabel J. Burdge, Peter F. Korsching, and Joseph F. Donnermeyer, *Social Change in Rural Societies*, Third Edition. Englewood Cliffs, New Jersey: Prentice-Hall, 1988.

Schaller, Lyle, *The Church's War on Poverty*. Nashville: Abingdon Press, 1967.

Schmidt, Thomas, "The Hard Sayings of Jesus." *Christianity Today*, 33-8 (Mary 12): 28, 1989.

Schwartz-Nobel, Loretta, *Starving in the Shadow of Plenty*. New York: G. P. Putnam's Sons, 1981.

Sider, Ronald J., *Rich Christians in an Age of Hunger*. Downer's Grove, Illinois: Intervarsity Press, 1978.

Smith, Katie R., "Give the Homeless a Chance." *Christianity Today*, 33-10 (July 14): 8, 1989.

Snow, David A., Susan G. Baker, Leon Anderson, and Michael Martin, "The Myth of Pervasive Mental Illness Among the Homeless." *Social Problems*, 33 (June): 407-423, 1986.

Spates, James L., and John J. Macionis, *The Sociology of Cities*. Belmont, California: Wadsworth, 1987.

Spring, Beth, "Home, Sweet Home." *Christianity Today*, 33-7 (April 21): 15, 1989.

CHAPTER 22

POVERTY IN CHICAGO; A Practitioner's View

Richard B. Lee
Olive Branch Mission

New Kid on the Block

Chicago and poverty are new to me. I was happily reared in a Christian subculture by a family that lived in the suburbs. We were socialized in the church and worked in it at every opportunity. My peer group was my Sunday school friends; I went to a Christian college, worked at Christian camps during the summer and did occasional short-term missions projects. My first job was working with Christian college students at various Christian schools around the United States. Through life I had acquired contacts, skills, attitudes and a reputation that helped me succeed in my world. I believed my Christian faith was vital to my life, but had so many other supports that it was hard to know whether I was trusting in Christ or in my circumstances.

Then, with God's encouragement, I decided that my Christian life had to be put to a test. Would my faith suffice in an environment foreign to me? How would my relationship with Christ fare in a context where my skills did not matter, in a world where I did not know the rules, and the people around me did not care about me? Could I live life as a Christian in an environment where no one cared that I could play the guitar or that I had a master's degree? What if the color of my skin, my education and my standards of behavior were liabilities rather than assets? I wanted to go to a place where I was solely dependent on Christ; not Christ and my contacts, not Christ and my resume, not Christ and anything. Just Christ. I decided to go to the inner city, an environment I had avoided with little effort my whole life.

CHICAGO

I came to Chicago to prove to myself that a life built on Christ, and none other than Christ, could be lived and would be worth living. The first person I noticed on the Near West Side of Chicago was a woman standing on a street corner holding a man's jacket while he beat her. She did not resist. When he was done she returned his jacket to him and they walked off together. The scene confused, scared and angered me. Over time, I learned that she was one of the neighborhood prostitutes and the man was her "owner" or pimp. I had witnessed a routine re-establishing of their relationship.

Not Mr. Roger's Neighborhoods

Chicago is the third largest city in the United States; Three million people live within the city limits, and five million more live in the surrounding metropolitan area. It is much too big and diverse for anyone to identify with the whole. The common person identifies with the people and turf within a few blocks of home, one's neighborhood. It seems a more manageable chunk. Bridgeport, Canaryville, Back of the Yards, Pill Hill, Pilsen and Chinatown are a few of them, each with its peculiar ethnic makeup, socioeconomic status and problems. To some people, this is their "world." They live their whole life within a few blocks of home. Going to another neighborhood might feel as threatening or dangerous to them as going to a foreign country.

The Gold Coast and the Projects

Often neighborhoods that are right next to each other are very different. The Gold Coast along Chicago's near north lake shore is one of the most prosperous areas in the United States, with a per capita income of over $50,000. Most of the residents are white. The neighborhood immediately west of The Gold Coast is Cabrini Green, a low income housing project managed by the city. The vast majority of its residents are black. It is one of the poorest neighborhoods in the United States with an annual per capita income of about $3,000. The physical distance between these two neighborhoods is 2 blocks. The socioeconomic and cultural differences between them are immense.

Skid Row: Welcome to My Neighborhood

West Madison Street on the Near West Side of Chicago is a "skid row" district. For over a hundred years it has been a place of bars, brothels and rescue missions. On the Near West Side prostitutes have no time or money for a cheap motel room. Skid row brothels are dark alleys or the front seat of a car. Major drinking hangouts are cracked sidewalks, hidden doorways, or street-side gatherings of acquaintances willing to share a cheap bottle of wine or beer. It is the bottom rung on society's ladder. This is where I have lived and worked, and where I develop my perspectives on poverty. I work at a "mission."

There are all kinds of people in my neighborhood. Some of them are very smart and good-looking, while others are mentally limited and homely. Still others are smart, but worn out. Here we have young and old, and people from a variety of ethnic groups. Most of our guests are African Americans because our surrounding neighborhoods are mostly African American. Some work; some are retired; some have never held a paying job in their lives. Some are mentally ill. Some are addicted to drugs; some are gentle and kind. Some used to be wealthy, while others have received government aid for years — even generations. Some have tried hard to stand on their own, but consistently failed in their attempts and have given up all hope of ever succeeding. Others are fighting with all their might to get off the street. About the only thing they all hold in common is a gathering place, the Olive Branch, "A Ministering Community since 1876." They come to the mission to eat, meet their friends, get out of harsh weather or make a phone call. They may get their mail here or drop in to talk with a staff member about a problem or an opportunity to get ahead. They are the poor and homeless people of my neighborhood.

Subcultures Are Different

We tend to be uncomfortable with those we do not understand. We often judge them unfairly, and out of ignorance. Since we put distance between "us" and "them" this serves to perpetuate the stereotyping. My interaction with these people has kept me from assuming convenient stereotypes. I cannot feel sorry for all of them, or hate all of them, or call all of them lazy, or be afraid of them.

The urban poor are a distinct subculture. In fact, they constitute several distinct subcultures. Urban ministers or workers would do well to reckon with the diversity of subcultures in our urban areas, whether they be racial or ethnic or socioeconomic subcultures. "Foreign" missionaries and business men and women often take training in cross-cultural values of the people to whom they hope to minister. Those who skip these steps are markedly more frustrated and less effective as a result. The same is true of urban workers. Many people want to help the poor, but they do not take the time to learn about the subculture of the people they want to help. They assume that since they live in the United States they are just like us — that they want all things we want and, therefore, they respond to things just like any other "normal" person would.

When "normative" is defined as the experience of the majority, there is a different set of norms in my poor urban community. *The following behaviors and experiences are normative in my subculture in Chicago* (as well as in many of our urban poor areas in the United States): premarital sex, teen pregnancy, 14-year-old mothers, 30-year-old grandmothers and 45-year-old great-grandmothers, having no father at home, dealing with hard drugs and gangs, dropping out of high school, never having a bank account, going to jail, being on welfare or public assistance, buying food with food stamps and assuming that life will always be this way. Clearly this society has norms, values and perspectives on life that are different from those held by middle class Americans. While the family is not as stable as it used to be, we still think that the average American child will have two parents, earn a high school diploma and be able to read, and perhaps go on to college, or at least secure a decent job and be able to help support a family. The majority of people who read this chapter will probably not become drug addicts or go to jail. They will probably have good health insurance to meet their needs and live "to a ripe old age." The woman who stood on the street corner and let a man beat her and then walked off with him experienced none of the above. She grew up in a different subculture — a different "world"!

As a Christian, I have come to realize that "there, but for the grace of God, go I." People of the street are not all that different from you and me. I have served soup to a "skid row bum" who graduated from a "cream of the crop" Christian liberal arts college — my alma mater. Many of those poor who are on the streets now and who come through the mission are well educated and have owned homes and held prestigious positions. While some have never known prosperity, others have. There are many routes to poverty. One Christmas season a man in fine clothes, with a woman on his arm and full of Christmas cheer, pulled up in a taxi and plopped down several hundred dollars in cash to help the "homeless," then scooted on to his next Christmas party. Next season we met him in line joining several hundred others for a meal at the mission. He had lost it all. "We" are not better than "they." We may be numbered among them some day. Christ calls us to minister to the needs of the destitute, for in so doing we are ministering to Him (Matthew 25).

Faces of Poverty

"Nora" had been a prostitute for many years. It showed. Her body was devastated. She was quite pudgy, with many scars on her arms and head. Her mouth looked as if it had callouses or warts all around it. It was a venereal disease she had contracted through oral sex. Frequently she was bandaged, or stitched up from some blow she had received. Sometimes she wore big sunglasses to hide her swollen black eyes. Even in this condition she would be working out on the street to make some money for her pimp and herself. She had to work to live.

There are not only "Noras," there are many other faces of poverty in the city as well. Some are homeless families. Some are working poor, while others are on government assistance, both living in housing projects. Some are senior citizens on fixed incomes living in transient hotels. There are other persons who work daily but earn too little to support either themselves or their families. Still others are runaways. And finally, besides the alcoholics and drug addicts, there are the mentally ill who have been deinstitutionalized. Many of these are homeless, while others live in halfway houses or cheap, dilapidated rooming houses. Poverty affects each person differently.

Definitions of Poverty Vary

Not only are there many faces to poverty, but people differ in their definition of "poverty." While there are social dimensions to poverty, it is to a great extent an economic issue. Beyond that the consensus gets fuzzy. To some, poverty is not having enough money to buy what the average person or family has; to others, it is not being able to buy what is needed. To our government, it is any family of four with an income below about $13,000. But to others it is a state of mind.

Some describe poverty as the inability to produce. If one cannot put into this world as least as much as one takes from it, then he or she is poor. "Poverty" is a relative thing. There are always some who are richer or poorer than we, no matter where one is located on the socioeconomic ladder. For example, many immigrants in the United States see our urban poor as "rich" compared to the abject poverty they saw in their country of origin. After all, the "poor" in the United States have clothes, an apartment or house, and even a car!

Addressing poverty issues is a massive task. Some argue that only a small percentage of the population is desperately poor. Also, we should not feel too bad about it. Of the 3 million people living in Chicago, 15,000 to 40,000 are homeless. The number is hard to pin down because the definition of homelessness is even more debated than the definition of poverty. Moreover, a person with no permanent address is hard to account for. The 1990 census takers made a special effort to count our homeless population. It was a difficult job. Many advocates of the homeless believe the rate is twice as high as the largest count. We may never know.

In any event, we are our "brother's keeper," and Jesus reminds us that the good shepherd searched for the one lost sheep, and the woman scoured her home for the one lost coin that was precious to her. Ratios and percentages do not come into play. We have plenty of poor among us, and we are responsible for their welfare.

Homelessness

Many kinds of people are homeless. Children and youth constitute a large number of them. Many have run away from home or have been kicked out by their parents. The streets are a hard place to live. They get caught up in prostitution or pornography in their struggle to survive. Runaways encounter a lot more people who abuse, ignore, or judge them than people who want to help them. Most runaways do not start out street smart; they learn their survival skills through trial and error, and get very damaged in the process.

Another kind of homeless person is the adult who has, or had, a job and a place to go home to every night. For many of these, however, the income from the job did not keep up with the cost of living. Some of these live in poverty and have cheap housing, but become homeless when the apartment building they are living in is sold to a developer who makes it into a high-priced condominium. Does not society have an obligation to provide low income housing for its citizens?

When people who are working lose their home it becomes much more difficult to keep a job. They no longer have a place to store clothing, take baths, or rest after work. If they have a family, their problems are grossly compounded. A myriad of new and oppressive circumstances affect their capacity to hold a job. Then, unfortunately, there are others who have a job that pays well, but their money is syphoned off by an expensive addiction to alcohol or drugs. Their addiction robs some of the capacity to keep a job or a home.

Housing projects were created to be temporary housing, set up to help families save money to buy their own home. Now they house people who cannot afford decent housing at market rates. Families may live in them for several generations. Many of the people who eat at a day shelter, or mission on skid row, or sleep in an overnight shelter, are waiting to get into "the projects." The waiting list for some projects is several years long. Some will not even apply. Even this low cost housing is not available to them. They are, by anyone's estimation, living in poverty.

When I first came to Chicago I was naive in my understanding of "evil." I thought there were good people who make the world a better place in which to live, and there were bad people who make it a worse place. I was unaware of *systemic evil*. Systemic evil is an integral part of our laws, organizations, and standard procedures, and as a result the poor, the weak, the uninformed and the "innocent" are abused. It demands the most effort and sacrifice from those who are less able to give or to risk.

For example, in many neighborhoods poor people have been forced to move, and their inexpensive housing has been destroyed so that more expensive housing can be built. They are compelled to find other options and are given little or no help in relocating. Thus, "good" businessmen and women, with the aid of federal, state and local government, are able to maximize their profits at the expense of the poor. Of course the various governments get more taxes, while the poor "get moved!"

I understand why city encourages development. Low income housing is not "profitable." Not only do owners of cheap property not maximize their profits; government does not maximize its tax revenues. After all, the city does need tax revenue to run, to hire men and women for the police and fire departments and to plow snow from its streets in the winter, not to mention the multiplicity of educational, cultural and welfare programs. Tax revenue is good for the city. The more money a city has, the better it can take care of its poor — as well as its wealthy. Because the city needs revenue, certain areas of the city that are generating marginal tax revenue are targeted for redevelopment.

But it is difficult for a person with a small amount of money to relocate. Imagine owning a room full of basic marginal or "garage sale" furniture: a bed, a chair, a table, a dresser, a TV and a set of shelves. Imagine running out of money every few days, and having to go to a place that serves free meals to nourish yourself until the next check arrives. Now imagine having to locate another cheap room in a city where there are too few rooms available. If you can find one, imagine figuring out how to get your belongings to it. No truck, no friends with trucks, no money to rent a van or truck, no credit card to put up as a security deposit for the truck even if you had the money to rent it. Moving is a difficult and expensive proposition for a poor person. Now imagine the problems or complications if one is responsible for a family of five or more.

There really is not "room at the top" for everyone. All are not created equal. Our I.Q.s, our gifts and abilities vary greatly. There are people who cannot fend for themselves socially or economically. Try as they may, they will never make more than minimum wage, or slightly above. Unfortunately, too many believe it is solely the fault of the individual. It's their problem. Our nation's structure puts some energy into taking care of the poor among us. But we do not do an effective job of helping economically marginal families and individuals. Our motives may not be malicious, but we are very uninformed and selfish in our decision making. Rather than lifting the poor up, we keep them down. We encourage dependence on government aid. We offer inadequate public services. Hospitals are less receptive to those who are less able to pay. Police are the least helpful to those who suffer the most violence. Street cleaners are less attentive to poor neighborhoods. Banks are reluctant to locate or invest in poor neighborhoods, or to lend to people who are poor. Actually the practice of systematically refusing to invest in poor neighborhoods (called redlining) had become so prevalent that laws were written to make it illegal. But it is a difficult law to enforce.

Reversing Poverty

People who are poor have many strengths and capacities. They must have an exceptional amount of tolerance to be able to endure difficulties that would lead many to despair. Figuring out how to survive and to support children on a limited income frequently requires ingenuity and creativity. Living from check to check, having enough food one day and not nearly enough on the next demands flexibility. Standing in line, knocking on doors, trying to get the powers that be to provide the resources so desperately needed requires persistence. One can find many worthy qualities among people in poverty. Recognizing and cultivating these qualities is an important way of relating to our poor brothers and sisters.

In spite of these worthy character traits, poor people may not have the resources they need to meet their own needs. In spite of their strengths they may lack education, vision, functional lifestyle habits, hope, contacts, or opportunities. These are qualities and skills that come to us through the process of socialization within the family, as well as through the experience at school, church, and other community organizations. The poor are often deprived of many of these positive benefits because of circumstances of birth and because of exploitation. To reverse the cycle of poverty requires commitment from people who have the financial and moral resources to restructure society to make it more equitable.

But even when we do try to help individuals, we will not necessarily succeed. For example, the Olive Branch Mission tried more than once to set up "Nora" with an apartment in another section of town. We hoped she would break the hopeless cycle she was in and learn a new way of life. Each time she voluntarily abandoned the new circumstances and returned to the same neighborhood, and the same pimp, to do the same work. This was very confusing. Why would someone reject such an opportunity?

I think she came back because it was the life she knew. She was familiar with the territory, with the rules and with the limits of life on West Madison Street. What we offered was strange and threatening. It had no boundaries. She could not handle the new responsibilities or the new opportunities. She returned to what was "comfortable" for her.

THE OLIVE BRANCH: WHERE ARE WE HEADED?

Six years ago our mission served breakfast to 90 people. Today we serve about 200 at breakfast and 300 at supper. More people need our support services, as their marginal income is not enough to live on. The plight of the poor is compounded by the fact that during the past decade government resources to help the poor have been cut back dramatically. It seems as though even what little they had was taken away.

Some visitors to the Olive Branch express concern that we feed people without requiring evidence that they are trying to improve themselves. We are perceived as encouraging freeloading and laziness. Others perceive that we are "feeding the hungry and clothing the naked," as Jesus commanded us to do. People who are bottomed out also deserve society's care. Other organizations work with a different clientele and have different expectations. They believe people must prove they are needy, or prove that they are trying to improve their circumstances. These organizations will help people who are trying to help themselves. Still others address societal structures that make poor people poorer and discourage those who are trying to better themselves or their circumstances. Such organizations or individuals may lobby politicians to make new laws, or serve as watchdogs to make sure selfish people are not taking advantage of the poor. They may provide helpful services for the poor that they otherwise could not afford, such as legal services. The types of organizations in society that minister to the needy are quite diverse, but they all attempt to meet the physical, spiritual, social, political or educational needs of the poor. No one person or organization can do everything; neither can it work alone. Each organization is a piece of the picture, contributing to the whole. The ultimate goal of all helping organizations is to enable individuals to become self-reliant, responsible persons. At the Olive Branch we believe that Jesus Christ does it best. Christ alone is the answer to *all* of one's problems, but it takes time, prayer and much patience and support on our part as Christians if God is going to use us to help make people whole.

What can I change?

What if the difference between Nora's life and the life we desired for her is an illustration of the difference between my life and the life God wants for me? I am tempted to respond in the same way. When God reveals a better way of living I am often tempted to reject it because I like where I am. I know my boundaries and the way things work. I am afraid of what is unfamiliar and beyond my grasp. So I reject God's gifts and cling to what is familiar. May Nora's story teach me to sacrifice the "good" for the sake of the "best," God's best.

This is an increasingly urban world. Urban areas, with their size and density, magnify the best and worst society has to offer. It is a fascinating place to live. It is a place in which we can achieve humankind's best in art, theater, music, architecture, cross-cultural richness, museums, technology and more. But the city is also a place where poverty, pain, abuse, guile and deceit can seem overwhelming. Yet it is a wonderful (full of wonder) place to live.

The city is not for everyone, but the reader may believe that God is calling him or her to work, live and serve there. If that is the case, remember that we are called by Jesus to be salt and light in this world. Salt should be rubbed into its host to not only retard decay, but also to destroy decay and heal the body.

The Olive Branch has been in Chicago, ministering to the poor and needy for over 100 years. I challenge the readers to consider the city as a place where he or she might make a difference for Christ and the kingdom in whatever vocation God is calling.

Study and Discussion
Questions

1. Who are the poor?

2. How poor does one have to be to be considered poor? Why does it matter?

3. Why is it important to identify the poor?

4. How should my attitude towards a person differ because he or she is poor?

5. If there are not very many people living in poverty then it is not a serious problem. If there are a large number, then it is a problem worthy of my attention. Is this true?

6. How does God perceive the poor?

7. How do I perceive the poor?

8. What does God do on behalf of the poor?

9. What do I do on behalf of the poor?

10. What does Jesus have to say about the poor, especially in Matthew 25? If this were the only teaching of Christ, what does it say about the necessity for "good works?"

CHAPTER 23
POPULATION AND HUNGER: INTRODUCTION

As Dr. Wang points out in her chapter, "the world has shrunk in size," and we now live in what has been called a "global village." We can no longer live in isolation as nation states; our "backyards" are visible to all the world via satellite television. Supersonic jets, fax machines and the vast array of electronic mass communication equipment have made us all neighbors. Whether it is the plight of the starving people of Ethiopia, those devastated by typhoons in Bangladesh, or the hundreds of thousands made homeless by either volcanic eruptions in the Philippines or by earthquakes in Central and South America or Armenia, "you are there!" Indeed no nation is an island unto itself. Therefore, Dr. Wang is correct in saying that the problem of population size and world hunger is every nation's concern. As Professor De Santo suggests in the Introduction, the world is really "one body" and the nations are merely parts of it. When one part suffers, the other parts are all impacted.

The question naturally arises, What has brought on this crisis the world now faces vis-a-vis overpopulation and hunger? While the answer is complex, it is also simple. On the other hand, the developed nations (e.g., Europe, North America and parts of Central and South America, Japan, Singapore, Hong Kong, Korea and Taiwan) have modernized and improved their standard of living in every area of life — economics, technology, health and medicine, nutrition and education. This modernization has resulted in a relatively stable economy and population. While there are relatively poor people in all developed countries, for the most part absolute poverty is minimal, if not nonexistent.

On the other hand, the developing nations (e.g., much of Africa, parts of Central and South America, China and other Asian states) suffer from a population explosion and periodic food shortages. Conditions in the poorest of these nations is so critical that the United Nations estimates that literally thousands die daily of starvation, malnutrition and disease. It is also in the Third World that a population explosion is taking place, where it is estimated that three fourths of the world's population live.

The problem in Third World countries is compounded by the fact that urbanization is occurring at a rapid rate without the concomitant modernization that took place in the developed world. As a result, when people flock into cities in these countries there are few jobs, virtually no habitable housing — not to mention sanitation and all the other things we associate with modernity. Therefore, those who migrate to the burgeoning metropolitan areas cannot adequately care for themselves or their families, forcing them to look to the nonexistent welfare state to sustain them. Dr. Wang says that "by the year 2000 seventeen of the world's twenty largest cities will be in the Third World."

What is the responsibility of the United States and other developed nations to these Third World countries? More to the point, what is the responsibility of Christians and the Church?

According to the United Nations, "every human being has the right to adequate nutrition, shelter, basic health care, and education." By implication they are saying that the developed world has a moral responsibility to feed the hungry and help lift the standard of living of developing nations.

While both the Old and New Testaments teach that we are to feed the hungry and care for the needy, the question is, What is the best way to do this? Dr. Wang presents *five* perspectives on the interrelatedness of population growth and food. The *first* perspective is the classic Malthusian theory. He maintained that both positive (e.g., war, famine) and preventive (e.g. delayed marriage, abstaining from sex in marriage) checks help control population growth. His attitude towards the hungry was akin to that expressed by Herbert Spencer in his Social Darwinian view. In essence they say: "Don't feed the hungry. If they can't make it on their own, let nature take its course. Only the fittest should survive!"

The *second* perspective is that of the Technological Optimist. This view suggests that we have been in crisis situations in the past and through the scientific and technological advances we have made in modern societies we have been able to overcome our problems. Therefore they feel confident that we will be able to feed the hungry and control population growth without destroying the environment.

A *third*, the Environmental Crisis perspective, suggests that the earth is like a "lifeboat"; it can carry only so many people. If we overload it, it will sink and all will perish. Therefore it would be best not to feed the hungry in a nation in which they will not take measures to control population growth.

The Demographic Transition theory is the *fourth* perspective. It states that nations in the developed world have all successfully passed through three stages, from high death and birth rates to low and controlled death and birth rates. It is their hope that as Third World nations modernize, they will also reduce and control their population growth. This will occur if we help them modernize. The question is, Do we have the time?

The *fifth* and final one is called the Distributive Justice perspective. "The focus of this perspective is on production and distribution of basic needs such as food, rather than on increasing the Gross National Product or industrial development. Responsibility for hunger is placed on the global maldistribution of resources that leads to 'the rich getting richer and the poor getting children.'" Dr. Wang points out that "it is demand, not need that determines where the world's food and other resources go." The "trickle down" theory of economics has worked much less effectively in the Third World than the small success it has experienced in the United States. The core or developed nations have been using up a lion's share of the natural resources of the periphery or developing nations. Furthermore, those who have benefitted most in Third World countries are not the masses who live in poverty, but the elites who already live in luxury.

Which of these five perspectives do you feel are most consistent with Christian principles? Answer the three questions she asks: 1) "Is our world in a lifeboat situation?" 2) "Is population growth the greatest threat to worldwide ecological balance?" 3) "Will feeding hungry people cause their population to increase?" But before you read the chapter, give some attention to what Scripture has to say about the hungry and poor.

The Bible admonishes Christians to show compassion towards the hungry and poor. The Psalmist says of God, He "executes justice for the oppressed; and gives food to the hungry" (147:6). Moses instructed the Hebrews to leave grain in the fields for the poor to glean (Leviticus 19:9-10; Deuteronomy 24:21). Further, we are instructed to provide food not only for the alien (Jeremiah 7:5), but for our enemies (Proverbs 25:21). Especially noteworthy are the teachings of the literary prophets of the eight century B.C.

426

They proclaimed God's judgment against those who oppressed and exploited the poor. Although numerous references are cited below, the reader will profit from examining them because they demonstrate God's concern for the hungry, poor and needy, as well as God's wrath against those who oppress and exploit them. See Amos (2:7-8; 4:1-3; 5:11; 8:4); Isaiah (3:5; 10:2; 58:6,10); Jeremiah (2:34; 22:16); Ezekiel (16:49=50; 18:7; 12; 22:29).

But it is in the works and words of Jesus that God's compassion for the hungry and poor is overwhelmingly demonstrated. The unique message of the parable of the Good Samaritan is foundational (Luke 10:25-37). In this parable Jesus teaches that neither similarity of race nor religion is a prerequisite to receiving assistance. Need is the only criterion! Anyone in need should be helped. Jesus then gave the "teacher of the Law's" question a different turn. He had asked, "Who is my neighbor?" After he shared with him the parable, Jesus asked him, "Which one of these (priest, Levite, or Samaritan) do you think was neighbor to him who fell among thieves?" The obvious answer is "the Samaritan." Then Jesus commanded him, "Go thou and do likewise!"

When we think of Jesus and the hungry, our minds almost automatically turn to the experience when He fed 5000 (Mark 6:30-44). Then there are other relevant parables such as the parable of the Rich Man and Lazarus (Luke 16:19-31) and that of the Last Judgment (Sheep and Goats) (Matthew 25: 31-46). In the first He teaches that if we fail to share with the hungry and poor we will be excluded from the kingdom. In the second parable Christ says that entrance into the kingdom is limited to those who feed the hungry, clothe the naked, etc. Jesus also warns us about the insidious nature of materialism and covetousness. He said that "it is hard for a rich man to enter the kingdom of God" (Matthew 19:23). He told the "rich young ruler" who apparently made a god of his possessions that he had to choose between his "idol" (possessions) and "eternal life" (Matthew 19:16-30).

After you have read this chapter, ask yourself which of the five perspectives square with Christian principles? Think about what churches and parachurch groups are doing to feed the hungry. Ask yourself, What more could be done to solve the problems of overpopulation and hunger? Does feeding the hungry only magnify the problem? Why or why not?

POPULATION AND HUNGER
Bee-Lan C. Wang

WHAT IS THE PROBLEM?

Hunger is not new to the human condition. Those of us who live in the industrialized world sometimes forget this, but the need for food has been the main factor in humankind's struggle for survival throughout most of our history. What then is new about the situation in which we find ourselves today?

Two things have become evident in the last half of the twentieth century. First, the world has shrunk in size, and we are living now in what is in effect a global village. Countries and communities in widely separated parts of the globe have become interdependent ecologically, economically and politically. Second, human population growth and standards of living have reached unprecedented proportions. Consumption of resources in the rich world, as well as the million-and-a-half babies born each week, are straining the earth to its limits.

It took seventeen centuries for the world's population to grow from the estimated 250 million in the first century to one billion in the eighteenth century. It took less than two centuries to add the next billion. By World War II, the world population was about 2.5 billion. Since the end of the war, it has more than doubled, so that it is now 5.3 billion. At these rates of growth, it takes only about ten years to add another billion people!

Population control or family planning programs that started around 1960 and gained momentum through the next few decades have helped to lower the world population growth rate from its all-time high of 2.1 percent per year in the 1960s to 1.7 percent today. Even so, sometime near the middle of the twenty-first century, world population may double again, even with continuing the modest success of current programs to lower birth rates.

The high birth rates of this century have resulted in a population profile or pyramid with a very broad base. Half the world's population is less than thirty years old. This means that even if the younger generation bears fewer children per woman than their mothers did, birth rates (as a percentage of the total population) can still go up because there will be proportionately more women of childbearing age in the next few decades.

Does the continued existence of widespread hunger and malnutrition in the world today mean that the world is not producing enough food to feed the present population? Can we produce enough food for the future population which is still growing by about 80 million new mouths a year? The answer is yes if we take the world as a whole, but only a conditional yes if we consider by themselves those countries which are currently suffering from hunger. The United Nations estimates that by the year 2000, there will be at least sixty-five Third World countries that will not be able to feed themselves.

Worldwide, enough grain is produced to provide 3000 calories to every human being each day. But much grain is not used directly to feed human beings. Countries such as the United States which produce more grain than needed for human consumption, feed most of their grain to animals. People in these countries obtain their calories by eating much higher on the food chain. It is an unhealthy diet and a much more expensive one, but one that they can easily afford.

The countries that suffer from hunger either do not or can barely provide enough to feed their own people. Most of these countries are in Africa, but there are many outside that continent — Haiti and Bangladesh being the best known examples. These are also the countries with the highest population growth rates, close to 3 percent per year in some places. This means that their population will double in about 25 years.

Clearly, a complete mismatch exists between the distribution of resources and of people. While the poor countries are growing fastest and are hungrier each year, the rich countries are close to zero-population growth. As this situation continues, proportionally more and more of the world's population will be among the ranks of the poor and the hungry. The Third World (a politically based term), which came to be known as the "Two-thirds World" because it contained the majority of the world's people, now has three quarters of the world population. By the year 2020, the "South" (as the Third World is now sometimes called) will have about 85 percent of the world's population.

Population imbalance also occurs within the poor countries themselves, through rapid internal urbanization. While in 1980 the Third World had nine of the world's largest cities, by the year 2000 seventeen of the world's twenty largest cities will be in the Third World. Mexico City and Sao Paulo will head the list with populations of at least 20 million each! Urban population growth rates that are more than twice as fast as those of the country as a whole have already strained the infrastructures of such cities to breaking point. Traffic is snarled, running water and sewage disposal are totally inadequate or simply unavailable, and housing is in slums and shantytowns, if not under bridges and on sidewalks. In addition to malnutrition and hunger, disease and crime are endemic. High birth rates and rural poverty have combined to push populations toward this catastrophic and rapid urbanization, in spite of nonexisting employment, housing or schooling in the cities.

What is the Answer?

How can we begin to solve these problems of population growth and world hunger, and what part can or should the rich countries play? Should the United States, and the world as a whole plan to put increased food production at the top of our priorities, and at the same time distribute food more equally to areas of greatest need? The answer depends both on your social-scientific perspective and on your philosophical-moral premises.

In this chapter, attention is focused on what appears to be a vexing ethical dilemma faced by the United States and other industrial nations that are in a position to send aid to poor countries. On the one hand we find individuals and groups, such as the Environmental Fund (EF) (an organization of scientists and other prominent persons) warning of impending worldwide disaster as a result of uncontrolled population growth. The EF believes that sending food to hungry people is a prescription for disaster because:

> Each piece of land has a specific carrying capacity ... [and] there are definite limits to how many people a given unit of land can support. Food aid violates the carrying capacity principle by artificially allowing more people to live on the land than can live from it...the inescapable result of saving lives today will be an even greater number of lives lost tomorrow.

Therefore, the EF recommends a suspension of all U.S. food and technical assistance to any country which has a population growth rate above the world average unless that country adopts population control measures. The Environmental Fund bases its position on the contention that increased food available to starving people reduces the death rate without influencing the birth rate, thus accelerating population growth. This in turn will mean increased human misery (there will be more hungry people in the future), since agricultural production cannot keep pace with population growth.

On the other hand, the U.S. Congress passed the Right to Food Resolution in 1976 and established that U.S. foreign policy shall be guided by the principle that every human being has a right to adequate nutrition. The Right to Food Resolution implies that those in a position to extend food aid to starving people are morally obliged to do so, in direct opposition to the EF position.

It appears, therefore, that we are faced with two choices: either we allow people to die today through lack of help or we feed hungry people today and allow them to multiply, only to suffer and die tomorrow. The latter choice will result in massive starvation, since we will not be able to alleviate human hunger for the multiplied millions.

Whether these are indeed the alternatives we face is the issue of this chapter. If the EF's analysis of the world's population-food situation is correct, then the obvious conclusion is that biblical teachings in this area are ultimately foolish, and, indeed, immoral from the utilitarian point of view. The Bible clearly commands us to feed the hungry (for example, Deuteronomy 15:11; Matthew 25: 31-46; James 2: 15-17). Are we to obey if doing so will mean causing greater total human misery tomorrow, misery that cannot be met by the resources available? Before answering this question, let us examine more closely the premises of the EF's analysis. Is population growth really the basic cause of mass starvation and malnutrition today? Will feeding hungry people cause greater population growth? What is needed to bring population growth under control? The following section summarizes *five* perspectives on interrelationships between population growth and food. These perspectives are evaluated in the light of social science research findings and their philosophical assumptions and then examined from the perspective of biblical teaching.

THEORETICAL PERSPECTIVES ON POPULATION

Classical Malthusianism

Thomas Robert Malthus was an English economist whose controversial *Essay on The Principle of Population,* first published in 1798, underwent several editions throughout the nineteenth century. The basic principles of *Malthus' theory* are very simple: (1) food is essential for the existence of human persons; (2) "passion between the sexes" will continue to exist and to result in population growth; (3) population grows "geometrically" whereas, at best, food increases only arithmetically. The rising curve of population growth, together with the straight line increase of food supply, means that periodically population will overshoot the capacity of resources to support it. "Positive checks" will then operate to keep population down by increasing the death rate. These checks are *famines*, *disease*, and *wars*, the likelihood of which increases when there are inadequate resources for human needs and wants. Thus, the population growth curve fluctuates around the limits set by the available food supply, and, given human propensities to procreate faster than food can be produced, most of the world's population is poor most of the time.

In second and subsequent editions of his *Essay*, Malthus allowed that "preventive checks" might also operate to keep population growth down by reducing birth rates. These are essentially what he termed "moral restraint" through *late marriage, reduced frequency of sex relations within marriage, and no premarital or extramarital sex relations.* However, Malthus did not think the effect of "moral restraint" would be significant. Further, he did not approve of the practice of contraception.

The classical Mathusian theory of population implies that an increase in the food supply or income would result in either fewer people dying, or in more marrying earlier and having more children. In either case the result would be increased population growth, thereby nullifying the effects of the additional food or income. Malthus therefore looked with disfavor on welfare programs in England during his day and, if he were living today, he would probably think it equally unwise to send food to starving people overseas.

Technological Optimism

Malthus wrote his *Essay* at the time of a debate among English intellectuals regarding the perfectibility of man. Enlightenment philosophy, together with the impressive amount of economic and technological progress made by modern science at the time, led many thinkers to believe that human ability to meet resource needs was limitless. Indeed some believed that one day it might even be possible to grow "food for all in a flower pot." Many therefore rejected the idea that scarcity of food would serve as a check on population growth.

The long history of human population growth, as far as archaeological methods can determine, does contain evidence to support the optimists' position. Human population grows along an S-shaped curve, as does most biological population in a constant environment. Each species placed in a particular environment multiplies slowly at first and then at an accelerating rate in exponential fashion, until "environmental resistance" exerts negative pressure on the "biotic potential" for growth. The rate of growth slows to zero and the population growth curve flattens out at the top of the "S." The basic difference between humans and other creatures, however, is the human possession of culture, which includes a store of knowledge that is constantly being increased. Through improved technology, humans can change the environmental resistance to population growth and alter the carrying capacity of the land.

Thus, during the hunting and gathering era before agriculture was known, it is estimated that the human population grew very slowly, if at all. Human ability to provide food was limited, since considerable amount of energy was required to locate daily resources. The introduction of agriculture at about 8,000 B.C. brought revolutionary improvement in the energy output-input ratio of food-producing activities. Humans were able, for the first time, to control their food supply by harnessing the natural ability of plants to convert solar energy into food energy. Civilizations sprang up around the world as a result of the agriculture revolution. At the same time, the size of the human population expanded from about 5 million around 8,000 B.C. to 200-300 million at the time of Christ, and then to about 500 million by 1650, in typical S-shaped fashion.

Then the eighteenth century brought the industrial revolution to Western Europe. Through the application of modern scientific knowledge, it was possible to harness inanimate sources of energy, such as the fossil fuels, to supply human needs. Agricultural techniques and medical knowledge also greatly improved. These developments increased birth rates and dramatically decreased death rates, resulting in a population explosion in Europe that did not slow down until well into the twentieth century. As the effects of modern science spread, particularly medical science and new measures of public health and preventative medicine, other continents also began to trace a similar population growth curve. In addition, death rates in the Third World declined dramatically after the two World Wars, resulting in a population explosion in these countries. For the whole world, then, the new knowledge discovered during and since the Enlightenment has enabled human population to grow in numbers beyond previous limits.

The decades of the 1950s and 1960s, when the world's "population explosion" became evident, were also the decades of dramatic advances in the technology of food production. The "Green Revolution" resulting from the scientific breeding of new varieties of seeds was able to double and triple crop yields in many regions of the world. World grain production per capita increased by about 40 percent from 1950 to 1984. (We cannot assume, however, that the increase was enjoyed by the poorest peoples of the world; much of this improvement went to enhancing the sophisticated diets of the rich, as well as to feeding the growing populations around the world.)

Technological optimists believe that new scientific breakthroughs can increase worldwide food production even further without ecological damage. Solar energy is a virtually limitless resource that has barely begun to be tapped. Unorthodox methods of food production such as drip irrigation and aquatic cultivation are yet to be used on any significant scale. And there is always work continuing on newer varieties of plants and animals that grow faster and are more resistant to disease.

The Environmental Crisis Perspective

This perspective sounds a word of caution to those who look to technology to solve our problems. Since 1984, world grain production per capita has *decreased* by about 14 percent. This decreased production of the late 1980s has hit the poor the hardest. Effects of chemical fertilizer overuse, decreased productivity of irrigation, lowered ground water levels, and hot and dry summers followed by torrential rains and soil erosion have all combined to diminish the optimism engendered by the Green Revolution. Even the United States can no longer be counted on to produce more grain than it consumes each year.

Are we once again pushing against the limits of our environment? Do the present ecological crises of deforestation, the greenhouse effect, soil erosion and the desertification of previously cultivatable regions mean that we have reached the limits of the carrying capacity of the earth? Many observers believe that population growth in most parts of the world has increased beyond the carrying capacity of the land. Activities such as overgrazing (example, the Sahel), deforestation (examples, Ethiopia, India), and ill-conceived "development" projects (example, the Aswan Dam) may even have permanently reduced soil capacity to grow food.

Ecologists such as Garrett Hardin and Paul Ehrlich caution against attempts to grow more food by altering the environment through forest clearing or irrigation. In the long run altering the environment may interfere with the ecological balance and cause permanent damage. According to their view, such alteration exacerbates, rather than eliminates, the basic cause of hunger — too many people.

When a population exceeds the carrying capacity of its environment, the inevitable result is massive disaster. Malthus' "positive checks" of misery and vice, famines and diseases, come into full play and death rates rise dramatically. The population growth dynamics of some biological species such as annual plants and insects exhibit what will happen. Their populations increase at an accelerating pace until environmental conditions change (for example, seasonal climatic cycles), at which point a massive die-off occurs because the total population exceeds the carrying capacity. A graph of the population plotted against time in such a case yields a J-shaped curve. The extent and precipitousness of the die-off is proportioned to the degree to which the population had exceeded the carrying capacity.

The classic statement of this position is probably Garrett Hardin's "The Tragedy of the Commons" (1968), which has been reprinted many times. He begins with the premise that the problem of overpopulation has no technical solution. Rather, it is a question of values or morals. In a situation where pasture land is open to all (the "commons") and ownership of cattle is private, individuals acting in their own interests would tend to increase their herds as much as possible. They would do this because the cost of an additional cow (the grass eaten) is spread among everyone, while the gain goes in its entirety to the individual owner of the cow. However, when all the herdsmen do the same thing, the result is overgrazing and destruction of the pastures, bringing tragedy to all. Thus, "freedom in a commons brings ruin to all."

Our society, observes Hardin, is like a commons, given the philosophy of the welfare state which takes care of the basic needs of the poor. However, since freedom in a commons results in disaster for all involved, the welfare state means that freedom to breed must be curtailed. By this reasoning, therefore, the United Nations' Universal Declaration of Human Rights contradicts itself. If every man, woman, and child is entitled to food, health care, education, and so on, this implies that the state or the world has the responsibility of meeting these needs. It logically follows, then, that people cannot be entitled to have as many children as they want. Yet the Declaration implies that contraceptive information and devices should be made available primarily so families will not have more children than they want. Hardin believes this is a recipe for disaster.

Essentially the same moral issue is posed by another metaphor, that of the "lifeboat." If there is a lifeboat capable of carrying only fifty people, and there are already fifty on board, what should be done about the people outside the lifeboat? If they are brought aboard, all will die. This would be a greater tragedy than refusing to permit those outside of the lifeboat to come on board. Assuming that overpopulation is the basic cause of world hunger, this perspective calls for applying strict population controls rather than freely dispensing food and/or technical assistance to enable poor countries to increase their agricultural productivity. This is similar to the position of the Environmental Fund summarized earlier.

Demographic Transition Theory

The *demographic transition* is one of the most widely documented generalizations in social science. It has taken place in all of the industrialized countries, and apparently it is being repeated in some of the more advanced Third World countries such as South Korea, Taiwan, Singapore, and Costa Rica. It is a transition from high birth and high death rates, to low birth and low death rates. This takes place in three stages. The first stage is one in which high birth rates are matched by high death rates. This is characteristic of preindustrial societies. In the second stage, improved nutrition and health cause death rates to fall while birth rates remain high, resulting in high rates of natural growth in population size. In the third stage, birth rates fall, eventually reaching the low level of the death rate, resulting in zero population growth.

Europe experienced its phase of rapid population growth during the eighteenth and nineteenth centuries and entered the third stage of the transition (declining birth rates) almost a century ago. Europe has now completed the transition. In contrast, most Third World countries are still in the second phase of high growth rates, which they entered only about fifty years ago. While a few Third World countries have experienced significant reductions in their birth rates in the last twenty years, none has completed the transition. With a relatively young population and birth rates still significantly above the now low death rates, rapid population growth continues. However, demographic transition theorists such as Paul Demeny (1989) expect Third World countries to complete the downtrend in birth rates as they become more developed.

As a theory, demographic transition suffers from lack of an adequately detailed causal model. Just how and why did birth rates decline in Europe? Are the same forces operating in the Third World today?

Historical evidence indicates that the state of birth control technology was not as important in explaining the decline of European birth rates as the motivation that people had for holding down their family size. Effective birth control techniques such as the pill, sterilization, under-the-skin implants and injections became available only in the last few decades; yet preindustrial societies had controlled their population size in a variety of ways through the practice of celibacy, delayed marriage, abstinence, coitus interruptus, and even abortion and infanticide. Clearly, fertility rates are governed by cultural norms and social structural factors, and the role of technology is simply to make it easier for people to achieve the level of fertility desired in the culture.

The demographic transition in Europe was set into motion by structural transformations that happened as a result of the industrial revolution. First, beginning in the eighteenth century and accelerating in the nineteenth, population became increasingly urban until this century, when now the majority is urban. Fertility declines were not recorded till after 1900.

The second change correlated with the decline of birth rates in Europe was the growth of the middle class, and the spreading of middle-class lifestyles and values to these sectors of the population. The wage earner is the most common type of person in industrialized societies, and farming is almost entirely commercial. Under these circumstances, and especially since the abolition of child labor, children are no longer the economic assets they once were. Old-age security plans are another feature of modern societies, reducing the need for children to provide for elderly parents.

The third major change was the rise of public education and compulsory education laws. As children stay longer and longer in school, their economic productivity decreases to zero. They again become economic liabilities to their parents. In addition, the necessity of secondary and postsecondary education for those who aspire to modern occupations serves to increase the average age at marriage, thus postponing childbearing.

Most Third World countries have been undergoing similar changes, with some significant differences. First, as a result of the introduction of modern methods of public health and disease control, the reduction in death rates experienced by these countries is much more precipitous, resulting in the well-publicized population explosion of the twentieth century. This population explosion has therefore occurred ahead of economic modernization in the Third World. Third World urbanization is taking place not so much because of increasing economic opportunities in the cities, as was the case in Europe, but because of rural poverty and hunger.

Second, Third World countries are attempting to modernize their economies while they are in a position of international weakness, whereas Europe's industrialization occurred during its heyday of world conquest and colonization. Those countries which have successfully developed despite this disadvantage, such as Singapore, Taiwan and South Korea, have a burgeoning middle class and have had successful family planning programs. Many others, however, are still struggling to feed, clothe and house their people, and are much less able to provide education or jobs in the modern sector.

Proponents of the demographic transition approach to the problem of world population growth argue that simply pushing birth control is not enough. What is needed is greater socioeconomic development in the Third World. Industrialized countries should increase especially their educational and modern job creation aid to the Third World. Greater multinational investment in the Third World should also be encouraged.

Distributive Justice

The fifth perspective on the population-hunger issue emphasizes *distributive justice*. Adherents of this position agree with transition theorists that the socioeconomic development of poor countries is the only ultimate solution. However, they tend to disagree on how it should or can be done. The focus of this perspective is on the distribution of basic needs such as food, rather than on modernization or "Westernization." Responsibility for hunger is placed on the global maldistribution of resources and the fact that "the rich get richer and the poor get children."

The world's resources are without doubt unevenly distributed. For example, the United States comprises less than 5 percent of the world's population but consumes over one third of its total nonrenewable resources, such as oil and other minerals. The annual grain consumption per person in India is about 400 pounds, but it is close to 2000 pounds per American. In the U.S., most of the grain is consumed indirectly, by feeding it first to cattle and other livestock, which are then consumed by human beings. The feeding of grain to cattle reduces the amount of food calories and protein available for human consumption by a factor of ten. World trade figures show that the rich nations (North America, Europe and Japan) import more protein from the poor nations than vice versa. Much of the world tuna catch, for example, is consumed by American people and pets, and one third of the African peanut crop goes to Europe for livestock feed.

Such facts as these underscore the statement that demand, not need, determines where the world's food and other resources go. Demand as an economic concept means the amount of a given commodity the market will buy at a given price. Demand is generated by people with cash to spend. Need, on the other hand, is equally true of all human beings. Whether rich or poor, we each need protein in the amount of about .08 percent of our body weight. Most Americans could cut meat from their diet and still eat enough protein to meet this requirement. Clearly, world consumption patterns are guided by purchasing power, not basic human need. The demand versus need concept is expressed in another way by Lester R. Brown who considers growing affluence an equal, if not bigger, challenge to the earth's ecological limits than population growth (1974 a,b).

Proponents of the distributive justice position further argue that millions are hungry today, not because population has outrun the earth's capacity to produce food, but because of wasteful and excess consumption by people in rich countries. They argue that much of the world's best cropland is being used to grow nonessentials for the rich. Many tropical countries have given over their most fertile soils to the production of rubber, coffee, bananas, and sugar cane for export to the affluent countries. In return, the elites of the Third World countries import manufactured goods, automobiles, and luxury items for their own use, as well as oil and machines needed to run their fledgling industries.

Social scientists, such as dependency theorists, argue that trade in itself is not bad, but the patterns of trade between rich and poor countries have benefited the rich and exploited the powerless poor majority. As an example, the price of manufactured goods sold to the Third World has risen over the last decades much faster than the price of raw materials exported to the industrialized West. Much of the commercial agriculture in poor countries is controlled by multinational corporations whose chief interest is to reap as much profit as possible from the poor countries, rather than to make sure poor people earn enough to eat.

In brief, this position puts the blame for world hunger on an inequitable world economic system, not on population growth. While it cannot be denied that rapid population growth in poor countries aggravates the problem, supporters of distributive justice point out that birth rates will be brought down only when the poor are assured a decent level of nutrition, health, education, and security. This will make children unnecessary as economic insurance for their parents. A new world economic order of fair trade and increased aid along with Third World land reform is called for.

EVALUATION AND CONCLUSIONS

Why should we in comfortable rich countries of the West be concerned about world hunger? Don't we have enough to do to correct our trade imbalance with such countries as Japan, and to balance our national budgets? Will trying to spread our resources around do any good at all in terms of reducing world hunger, or will it in fact make the situation worse?

Humanists like Garrett Hardin believe that *"there is no Global Population Problem"* (1989, emphasis added). The United States should not only stop sending food aid overseas, but we should also close our doors to immigration from poor countries. Any help given to poor countries to ease their population-food problem will not reduce infant and total mortality rates but will make the problem worse. To return to the lifeboat metaphor, it will sink the boat only if we allow more people in it. According to this view, it is better that some die than that all die (e.g. Fletcher, 1976). And, says Hardin, "injustice is preferable to total ruin" (1972).

Biblical injunctions to share with the poor would indeed be folly in a situation where population has exceeded the carrying capacity, if it is true that well-fed people produce more babies than starving people. So, let us ask, and try to answer, these three questions:

(1) Is our world in a lifeboat situation? Has world consumption of food and other resources exceeded, or will it soon exceed, the carrying capacity?

(2) Is population growth the greatest threat to worldwide ecological balance?

(3) Will feeding hungry people cause their population growth to increase?

Note that carrying capacity is a changeable quantity, depending on the technology humans employ to gain a living from the environment. Methods such as slash-and-burn agriculture, logging and strip mining are extremely destructive of the environment, and reduce its ability to support life. Industrial pollution of the atmosphere and chemical pollution of our water resources also have the same effect, not to mention depletion of nonrenewable resources such as oil. So, the answer to the first question, Are we in a lifeboat situation? is, Yes, if we are not careful. But we already are developing technologies to use the earth in a less destructive way. We need to continue to teach and/ or force people to be ecologically responsible so that doomsday does not come in the form of a worldwide ecological disaster.

The answer to the second question, . . . Is population growth the greatest threat . . . ? is no. Although population growth is a problem which has to be addressed, the fragile earth is in danger primarily because of the wasteful levels of consumption and irresponsible methods of production of the rich countries. The economic systems of the world, be they capitalist or socialist, are based on ever increasing material production and consumption. "More is better" is a value assumption. Is it? The Bible warns of the dangers of materialism, and tells us not to live "by bread alone." Worldwide ecological disaster, if and when it comes, will result more from the consumption of the rich than from the reproduction of the poor.

The answer to the third question, Will feeding poor people cause their population growth to increase? is yes. In the short run population will increase because adults and children will stop dying from hunger and malnutrition. However, in the long run, growth does not need to occur. Well-fed people usually do not produce more babies than hungry people. Mothers have reduced fertility when fewer children die, for two reasons, biological and behavioral.

The biological fact is that breast-feeding is a fairly effective contraceptive. Therefore, when a baby that is being nursed by its mother dies, the mother's body ceases to produce milk and her ovaries resume the production of ova, so that she is again capable of becoming pregnant. The pursuit of private profits has led to social norms in many Third World countries which go against planning programs to lower birth rates. Infant formula was promoted so successfully in some Third World countries that breast-feeding became unpopular. Western baby food companies had turned to Third World markets when lowered birth rates in the West reduced demand for their products. It is ironic that we will market infant formula when there are profits to be made, but will refuse to send food to starving peoples for fear their numbers will increase.

In many poor countries, it is extremely important that at least one son lives to adulthood so that he can support his parents in their old age. Individual decision-making is necessary to lower fertility rates. Berg (1973) used computer simulation to show that under the then current age-specified mortality rates in India, a couple had to bear 6.3 children in order to have a 95 percent probability that one son will survive to the father's sixty-fifth birthday. The average number of births per family in India was then 6.5, confirming the finding in another study that "families continued to have children until they were reasonably certain that at least one boy would survive. Once they had this number they attempted to stop having more" (Taylor, 1973). Friscancho, et al., (1976) examined an urban area in Peru and discovered that the poorest mothers had a greater number of live births than their less poor counterparts, and that mothers with more deaths among their children had more live births.

Adults base their expectations on how many children will survive on what they observed to be true among their siblings and friends when they were children. Thus, improved nutrition and health measures that reduce child mortality will have the effect of reducing fertility rates over the long run. However, it is possible to shorten the time lag by making awareness of child survival a direct and conscious reason for accepting family planning (Taylor, 1973).

Human beings do not reproduce like prairie dogs (an animal whose population dynamics have been extensively studied). We possess the ability to anticipate future events and we make decisions based on these expectations. Poor peasants are behaving rationally, not stupidly, when they have large families under conditions of high child mortality. Study after study has shown that birth rates fall when conditions of life improve so that children are no longer as likely to die, when people feel secure about being provided for in old age, and when modern education and jobs are available, especially to women. Third World countries that have the most successful family planning programs are those which have managed to improve women's educational opportunities, to raise the socioeconomic level of the population and to promote the use of modern methods of contraception.

By and large, the countries that seem to be suffering from chronic famine do not have successful family planning programs. They are the ones that most need our help. This help should be given in three ways: (1) relief aid in the form of emergency supplies of food and health measures; (2) development aid to help the people learn to use more productive and/or less ecologically destructive methods of agriculture and to promote technologically appropriate economic development and education; and (3) money and more effective and safe contraceptive technology for family planning programs.

Is population growth a global problem? Of course it is. The earth is too small and our destinies too interrelated for the answer to be otherwise. But this is not to say that there is only one effective global solution to the problem. Population policies need to be decided by each country for itself. We can attempt to influence these policies, of course, through the use of reason, the sharing of information and research findings and the material help we can offer.

In the book of Genesis we read that God gave humans authority and responsibility over the rest of His creation. Aspects of the image of God in us — such as rationality and freewill — are to be exercised in the carrying out of this mandate. In direct disobedience to God, however, we have tried to be our own master and have sought after other gods. The god of materialism and a disrespect for God's created world have led to today's precarious, global ecological situation.

Throughout the Bible, God reveals His character as one of justice and love. God favors the kind of society where people are assured of a productive livelihood and just wages (Deuteronomy 15; Amos 2:6-8; 4:1; 5:11-12; James 5:1-8). God knew that human injustice would result in a situation where "the poor you will have with you always." Therefore, God instructed His people to reflect His character by being generous to the poor and needy (Deuteronomy 15:11 et al.).

The demographic transition and distributive justice positions come closest to reflecting both biblical truth and scientific evidence. Feeding the hungry and meeting other basic needs, including livelihood, security and education, are not foolish things to do, contrary to what some humanists and modern-day Malthusians would argue. While the position of the technological optimist gives credit to our God-given ingenuity, it runs the risk of putting ultimate faith in technology alone. Our technology can be used either as a tool to help eradicate hunger, or it can be used to pursue the false god of irresponsible and uncaring economic growth. How do you think it is being used today?

Study and Discussion
Questions

1. In most societies, women are the primary caregivers as well as the childbearers. How will fertility rates be affected as societal sex roles change? Identify the specific variables that you think will have the most effect (e.g. political power, education, jobs, values, or belief systems, et cetera), and say why.

2. Why do people want children? How do young married couples in this society decide when to start having babies? When do they decide to stop? How would your answers be different if you lived in Kenya or Brazil, or the People's Republic of China?

3. It has been estimated that about half of the trash produced in American communities is packaging. What does this say about the economic factors that affect the use of natural resources in this society? How difficult would it be to reduce this amount to 10 percent?

4. Find out what different kinds of things go out under the name of "foreign aid." What percentage of American foreign aid goes directly to the poorest people in receiving countries?

5. Food is often used as a political tool or even a military weapon. Has the West or the rich countries used food in this way? Which Third World countries are or have been using food as a weapon? When, if ever, is this justifiable?

6. Often, there is surplus agriculture production in the U.S. How can there be a "surplus" when many other countries do not have enough? Why does the U.S. often pay its farmers to hold excess acreage off of production instead of simply exporting the excess food and helping to reduce our trade imbalance that way?

7. Is it health consciousness or economics (price) that has led Americans to reduce their consumption of red meats in the last 10-15 years? Has this trend led to more food being available for aid to hungry countries? Why or why not?

8. "Freedom in a commons brings ruin to all." Is our world really like a commons? If it is not, why not? If it is, or if you think it ought to be, would you advocate the use of population controls such as mandatory sterilization or abortion, or a baby tax (instead of tax exemptions)?

9. Does the fact that a country does not produce enough food for its people necessarily mean that that country's population has exceeded its carrying capacity? Name some countries that you think have indeed exceeded their carrying capacity. What can be done to bring the carrying capacity and population back in balance again?

10. Most rich countries are approaching or are already at zero population growth. They have completed the demographic transition. Speculate on what major change or factor might cause the populations of these countries to start tracing another curve, or to make another kind of "transition."

References

Bauer, P.T., "Population Scares," *Commentary*, 84(5), pp. 39-42, November, 1987.

Demeny, Paul, "World Population Trends," *Current History*, 88(534), pp. 17-19,58-65, January, 1989.

Fletcher, Joseph, "Feeding the Hungry," in George R. Lucas, Jr. (ed.), *Lifeboat Ethics: the Moral Dilemmas of World Hunger*. New York: Harper and Row, 1976.

Frisancho, A. Roberto, Jane E. Klayman and Jorge Matos, "Symbiotic Relationships of Higher Fertility, High Childhood Mortality and Socioeconomic Status in an Urban Peruvian Population," *Human Biology*, 48, pp. 101-111, 1976.

Goldsmith, Edward, and Nicholas Hildyard, eds., *The Earth Report: The Essential Guide to Global Ecological Issues*. Los Angeles: Price Stern Sloan, 1988.

Hardin, Garrett, "There is No Global Population Problem," *The Humanist*, 49(4), pp. 11-13, 32, July/August 1989.

Exploring New Ethics for Survival: The Voyage of the Spaceship Beagle. Baltimore: Penguin, 1972.

"The tragedy of the Commons," *Science*, 162, pp. 1243 48, 1968.

Hartman, Betsy, *Reproductive Rights and Wrongs: the Global Politics of Population Control and Contraceptive Choice*. New York: Harper and Row, 1987.

Malthus, Thomas Robert, *An Essay on Population*. London: Dent (reprinted), 1958.

Miro, Carmen A. and Joseph E. Potter, *Population Policy: Research Priorities in the Developing World*. Report of the International Review Group of Social Science Research on Population and Development. New York: St. Martin's Press, 1980.

Schumacher, E. F., *Small is Beautiful*. New York: Harper and Row, 1973.

Taylor, Carl E., "Nutrition and Population," in Alan Berg (ed.), *Nutrition, National Development and Planning*. Cambridge: MIT Press, 1973.

CHAPTER 24

SOCIAL STRATIFICATION: INTRODUCTION

Sociology developed out of a secular, nontheistic view of the world, which, while enlightening in some ways, is blinding in others. As a science, sociology insists that empirical evidence, not religious faith, philosophy, or any other nonempirical source, should be the heart of writing and research. This emphasis on "empirical fact" may produce a narrow, one-dimensional view of the world if sociologists fail to do research in the area of religion. Topics such as agapic love, the power of prayer, "faith healing," devotional reading and financial giving were once neglected areas of sociological research. But now a growing number of sociologists have begun to do research in the field of religion, and they are demonstrating that religious beliefs do indeed impact both the values and the behavior of believers. While sociologists do not authenticate or validate the truth or falsity of a religion, they are able to measure the impact of religion and thereby give a more holistic or two-dimensional view of life. We are indebted to a host of sociologists, from Durkheim and Weber to contemporary ones such as Poloma, Moberg, Berger, Stark, Bellah, Wuthnow and Yankelovich — to name just a few — who are helping us arrive at a more realistic concept of modern lifestyles.

Christians who are "in the world" but hopefully not "of it," can help to overcome certain blindspots in sociology. Professor Smit attempts to do this in his discussion of stratification. He reviews the two most popular theories of social class and finds both of them wanting. There is a blind spot among many sociologists created by a disjuncture between their theories on social stratification that stress a selfish, egocentric person, and their personal optimistic liberal philosophy about humankind's basic goodness. Professor Smit uses the light of scriptural principles to scrutinize different theories of stratification.

In an objective fashion Dr. Smit sets forth four positions that Christians have espoused: (1) acceptance of the existing system of social stratification, (2) a demand for total equality, (3) decrease inequality by individual action, and (4) decrease inequality by social change. Using biblical mandates of "justice" and "stewardship," he challenges the reader to evaluate the four positions *vis-a-vis* social stratification and to decide which is most consistent with the two basic mandates.

The institutional church, as well as religious people, are stratified. The Bible does *not* advocate abolishing socioeconomic classes. Both in the Old and New Testaments the issue is not whether or not there should be strata; both accept them as a given. The issue is how the roles of those occupying various strata should act them out. All that we have is to be viewed, as Dr. Smit mentions, as a trust from God — our power, our wealth, and our gifts — and we are to use them in a way that glorifies God and serves our brothers and sisters:

> Beware lest you say in your heart, 'My power and the might of my hand have gotten me this wealth.' You shall remember the Lord your God, for it is he who gives you power to get wealth...(Deuteronomy 8:17-18a).

> We who are strong ought to bear with the failings of the weak, and not to please

ourselves; let each of us please his neighbor for his good, to edify him. For Christ pleased not himself...(Romans 12:1-3a)

Moreover it is required of stewards that they be found trustworthy. . . . What have you that you did not receive? If then you received it, why do you boast as if it were not a gift (1 Corinthians 4:2,7)?

So, whether you eat or drink, or whatever you do, do all to the glory of God (1 Corinthians 10:31).

Whether master or servant our Lord and the apostles remind us that we are being judged, and will be judged, on the basis of how we exercise our stewardship relative to the material wealth and the gifts God has entrusted to us (Matthew 25:31-46; Luke 12:13-21; 18:19-31; 2 Corinthians 5:10; Ephesians 6:5-9). We have a duty to act responsibly (Luke 16:7-10). The prophet Micah (6:8) makes God's expectations crystal clear: "He has showed you...what is good; and what does the Lord require of you, but *to do justice, love mercy*, and to *walk humbly* with your God." We who name the name of Christ must be a neighbor, ministering to the needs of others (Luke 10:25-37). Regardless of our status or station in life, our lifestyle must be that of a servant (John 13:1-17). Not only in Jesus' role as Teacher, but also in His role as our Lord, Jesus played the role of servant. Accepting the ascribed status we have, we are expected to honor God and love others (Matthew 5:43-48). We are to follow in Christ's steps (1 Peter 2:21). The norms of the world are not those of the kingdom of God, where leaders must serve (Mark 10:42-45). Those who would be first must be last (Mark 9:35), and those who desire life must die to self (John 12:24-26, Mark 8:35).

One of the latent consequences of stratification is obviously inequality, and inequality tends to generate negative attitudes and behaviors such as jealousy, envy and covetousness, as well as prejudice and discrimination. The problems of prejudice and discrimination have always plagued human society, and unfortunately the Christian church has always been guilty of these twin evils. One reason the religious establishment of Jesus' day did not appreciate His ministry was that He did *not* discriminate against people, whether they were rich or poor, or because they were of a particular racial or ethnic group. His opponents explicitly mentioned His impartiality, howbeit in a patronizing manner (Luke 20:21; Mark 12:14). Jesus was not impressed by a person's lineage or position (Matthew 3:8; John 3:1-3). Unfortunately, when the Christian church began, it perpetuated prejudicial and discriminatory ways of relating to people who were "different." James specifically mentions how the rich were shown favoritism (2:1-7), and Paul had to deal with selfish, arrogant "rich" Christians who discriminated against their poor fellow Christians (1 Corinthians 11). It would be pleasing to God if we could testify that divisions based on socioeconomic class, race, or ethnicity were nonexistent in the church today, but they are. The trite saying is true: "The eleven o'clock hour on Sunday morning is still the most segregated hour of the week!" Granted that many groups, for cultural and linguistic reasons meet in their own fellowship, much of the division is based on socioeconomic class, as well as racial/ethnic differences that we perpetuate out of pride. It is not only a "white" problem, for even within racial/ethnic groups the church is stratified.

When we read the words of Jesus' intercessory prayer, "Holy Father [I pray] that they may be one, even as we are one" (John 17:11), what does this mean? Do we take it at face value? Did He really mean that *all* Christians should fellowship within one church, regardless of socioeconomic class, race or ethnic background? Do Jesus' words in John 10:16, where He speaks about different *folds* within the one *flock*, provide an out to human nature's "weakness" or "sinfulness?"

As Professor Poloma put it: It is in the light of the paradoxical teachings of Jesus and the examples that He has set for us that Christians must analyze and judge the extent to which stratification is a social problem.

SOCIAL STRATIFICATION
William Smit

Give me neither poverty nor riches,
Grant me only my share of bread to eat.
Proverbs 30:8

The Bible and modern sociological literature have at least one thing in common —
they both have a great deal to say about social stratification. Of course one will not find
the term "social stratification" anywhere in the Bible, but one can find many references
to wealth and poverty, honor and disgrace, power and servitude. The term social
stratification is used today to encompass all the ways in which people are socially
unequal. It has been defined as the system for distributing that which is scarce. Every
society has such a system. All societies have at least some inequities, some "strata," built
right into their social structures. The Bible contains many references to systematic
inequality. There are over four hundred separate passages in the Bible on the subject of
poverty alone (Oostdyk, 1974). From the content of these as well as other passages, it
is clear that God cares about social stratification (Psalm 35:10; Job 5:15-16; Isaiah 61:1;
Luke 1:52-53, 15:2).

We, too, should care about social stratification. We should concern ourselves about
the system of inequality in our own society in which we all participate. In this concern
sociology may be of some help, since stratification is a major focus of sociological study.
Sociologists have learned that there is very little in a socioculture system that can be
described and analyzed adequately without reference to social stratification. It is a
pervasive influence in our lives, to the point of almost dictating our diet, clothing, type
of residence, manner of speech, friendships, leisure activities, and many of our values
and attitudes. Is this good or bad? Should we thank God for social stratification or is
it the "work of the devil?" Sociology cannot tell us, but it can at least make us aware of
how the system works and what our own place is in that system. Once we understand
the system, it is up to us, in the light of Scripture, to decide what needs changing and what
should be preserved in that system. Sociology can only tell us what is, *not* what ought
to be.

There is one point, however, at which sociology comes close to asserting something
about the goodness or evil of social stratification. This is when it goes beyond describing
and tries to explain why every society has a stratification system. Explanations for the
prevalence of social inequality are of two types, the one a conservative view and the other
a radical one. These two views can be traced back throughout written history (Lenski,
1966). In modern sociological thought these have taken the forms of functionalist theory
(the radical view). In this chapter, after a brief overview of these two types of
explanations for the universality of social stratification, we will discuss what seems to
be a major inadequacy in both of them and then we will look at some Christian views of
social inequality.

THE FUNCTIONAL VIEW OF STRATIFICATION

The best known statement of the functionalist position on stratification was presented by Kingsley Davis and Wilbert Moore in 1945 (Davis and Moore, 1945, pp. 242-249). It is their contention that, since all societies have a system of stratification, there must be some basic need, some function, that stratification fills. That function is "placing and motivating individuals in the social structure." They see stratification as a system of rewards given by society to people who fill positions that are both (1) functionally important and (2) require special talents or training, or involve undesirable work. "Social inequality is thus an unconsciously evolved device by which societies insure that the most important positions are conscientiously filled by the most qualified persons" (Davis and Moore, 1945, p. 243). Without unequal rewards some essential tasks would not be undertaken by anyone competent to do the job and society would disintegrate. If all positions were rewarded equally, why would anyone expend time and money preparing for a position obtainable with very little effort or expense? Why work at a dirty and dangerous job if a clean and safe one pays as well? If a person has a talent for leadership, why bother to try to use it as a mayor or governor if the rewards of such offices are no more than those of clerk-typist? Thus, social stratification is seen as an essential part of the general system of division of labor and mutual cooperation in each society. Functionalists believe most people understand and accept the need for social inequality. People may want to improve their own place in the system, but they accept the system.

THE CONFLICT VIEW OF STRATIFICATION

Conflict theorists argue that the key to inequality is power, that is, the ability to get one's way in the face of opposition. Society is divided into groups of people with similar interests. Some groups have an interest in keeping things the way they are and some groups would benefit from change. There is constant struggle between these interest groups for control of limited resources. The group with the greatest power wins out and, within certain limits necessary to keep the society functioning, sets up a stratification system to its own advantage. This system is maintained essentially by coercion. In Karl Marx's version of this, control of the means of economic production is the basis of all social stratification. In more modern sociological versions, it is often suggested that a person may belong to a variety of interest groups at the same time, not all of them related to or concerned about economic production (Dahrendorf, 1959: Chapter 5). This makes the conflict much more complicated than Marx suggested, but Marx is still seen as essentially correct in calling attention to the fact that inequality results from a constant competition for goods and privileges.

Conflict theorists believe that it is mostly the advantaged in a society who accept the existing system of stratification as fair and proper. The disadvantaged accept the system only when ignorant of their own self-interest. When those who are "getting the short end of the stick" realize their common position (develop "class consciousness" in Marx's terms) they will act in concert to try to improve their position. The action they take may be within the system, such as collective bargaining and demonstrations, or it may take a more extreme form, such as riot and revolution. Sometimes they do nothing overt, but this does not mean they are content with their lot. The dissatisfaction of the lower classes is one of the reasons that social stratification systems are always somewhat unstable and always changing. Conflict between interest groups is a normal part of every society. Some would add, however, that a time may come when a classless society develops, in which inequality, and consequently conflict, will be eliminated.

SELFISHNESS - THE COMMON THEME

While sociologists often discuss the differences between conflict and functional theories of stratification, we would like to point out one important similarity between them. (For other similarities see: Lenski, 1966; Kemper, 1976). To put it baldly, they both tell us, perhaps without always meaning to, that the reason for inequality is selfishness. This can be seen in the functionalist argument from its emphasis on motivation. Certain people, we are told, must be given special privileges if they are to be motivated to fill important positions. The suggestion that people might do what needs doing in society for other than selfish reasons is dismissed as naive and wishful thinking. The key to the conflict argument, on the other hand, is exploitation of the weak by the powerful. People with power use it for selfish ends. They may band together in a group (such as a social class), but only because it increases the power of each member. Those who are in an advantageous position do all they can to hold on to what they have and pass it on to their children. People fight, not to establish a just society, but to get as much as they can into their own hands.

The difference in the two positions is that the functionalist sees stratification as the way society channels selfishness for the public good, while the conflict theorist believes stratification enhances the individual's selfishness and, therefore, is better done away with or at least minimized. This is, of course, a very important difference, but note especially the similarity just pointed out — namely, that they both explain the universality of inequality as due to selfishness. This is very interesting because it is not at all what many people expect from sociologists. Sociologists are often portrayed as unrealistically optimistic about human nature and our capacity for altruistic behavior. For example, Reinhold Niebuhr (1932: XVI), a very influential American theologian, has written:

> The Sociologists, as a class, understand the modern social problem even less than the educators. They usually interpret social conflict as the result of a clash between different kinds of "behavior patterns," which can be eliminated if the contending parties will only allow the social scientist to furnish them with a new and more perfect pattern which will do justice to the needs of both parties. With the educators they regard ignorance rather than self-interest as the cause of conflict.

From what we have seen, this is not an accurate criticism of either functional or conflict theorists. Both not only acknowledge but actually stress people's tendency to act in their own self-interest. Why then do Niebuhr and others accuse sociologists of denying people's self-seeking nature? The answer to this question, we believe, lies in the difference between social theory and the personal philosophy of the social scientist. Although social scientists may personally be very optimistic about people's humanitarian nature and their willingness to help others, when involved in social theory construction they tend to conceive of people as controlled basically by self-interest. Langdon Gilkey (1966, pp. 93-94), describes this difference as follows:

> One of the queer things about the modern liberal academic culture is that the social scientist, when he considers man as the object of his study, accepts a "realistic" view. He assumes...that men are determined by social and economic forces which lure, compel, or elicit their self-interest, voting as their pocketbooks or their social position dictate.... When, however, the social scientist speaks of man's destiny, of the possibilities for man's life which his new knowledge can bring him, he looks to another side of man for his evidence. Here he expresses not what he has found out as an investigator, but what he hopes for and believes as a man.

As part of their personal philosophy, social theorists may believe and hope whatever they want to about people's goodness and their willingness to resolve differences in unselfish ways. But when they are developing social theory they are trying to explain the empirical world, and that world has taught them the most predictable thing about humans is that they will do what is to their own advantage. They behave in unselfish ways just often enough to confound our attempts to predict their behavior accurately, but every social scientist knows that a theory which assumes people's selfishness will fit the facts of life more accurately than one which assumes their unselfishness (Lenski, 1966, p. 30).

Can Christians agree that selfishness is enough to explain social stratification? We think not. Of course, we will not be surprised at a theory of stratification which assumes people are self-centered. After all, not one is without sin and the essence of sin is to place self-interest above all else — above the interests of others and above the will of God. Besides, the Bible tells us that riches are often gained by evil and dishonest means (Psalm 73:3-12; Isaiah 3:14-15; Ezekiel 22:25; James 5:1-6). Yet, without denying the importance of selfishness, it is important to see that there are also other reasons for social inequality. For one thing, Scripture tells us that some people are richer than others because of hard work (Proverbs 10:4) or obedience to God (Deuteronomy 28). Poverty may result from idleness (Proverbs 6:10,11), pleasure seeking (Proverbs 21:17), or as a punishment for transgression (Deuteronomy 28; Leviticus 26). Members of the Church of England (Wilson, 1971, p. 260) for many years sang a verse from their hymnal which declared:

> The rich man in his castle,
> The poor man at his gate,
> God made them, high and lowly,
> And order'd their estate.

This sounds rigid to the modern ear, suggesting a feudal system with little or no social mobility, but it does point to the biblical position that ultimately it is God who decides who will have honor and wealth and who will be poor and humble (1 Samuel 2:7). This should not be interpreted to mean that riches are always a sign of God's favor or poverty a sign of God's disfavor. As John Calvin (Graham, 1971, p. 67) said:

God distributes unequally the frail goods of this world in order to investigate the goodwill of men; he is examining man...If a man is liberal when he has means, seeking to do good to those in need of his help, this is good proof. If the other, being poor, takes patiently what it is pleasing to God to send him, not being solicitous of fraud nor other malice although he is suffering and his condition is hard — this is also a good and useful test.

Why is there stratification? God examining people, hard work, laziness, oppression, unequal abilities, ambition, and other factors are all relevant considerations. Certainly stratification cannot be explained entirely by the pursuit of self-interest, for there are many other reasons for it as well. From a sociological perspective, our major interest is in the social reasons for stratification. We have already mentioned the argument that society needs to motivate people to fill certain positions, but there are also more direct social structural reasons for inequality. That is to say, it is not just a matter of getting people to enter and stay in certain positions, but also involves giving them the means to carry out the tasks of those positions. There are positional requirements for inequality as well as motivational requirements. Perhaps this will become clearer if we consider briefly each of three major dimensions of social stratification — power, privilege, and esteem — and consider how each of these has social structural functions.

THE FUNCTION OF POWER

Power should not be seen merely as a reward that is given by society to a person who fills an important position. Power is often an essential part of a position itself. Without it a person could not do what is expected. Even some of the most severe critics of the functional perspective agree that power is necessary in some situations and, of course, functionalists realize power is sometimes essential to the functioning of position (Moore, 19, p. 16; Tumin, 1963, pp. 19-20).

In every social group there is some division of labor, some specialization of function, some differences in what is expected of each member. This is unavoidable for two reasons. First, people have been given different gifts. We are not all capable of doing all the things that need doing in society. Second, it is to our advantage to specialize, because it is difficult to conceive of any group getting along without some specialization. Specialization, in turn, demands coordination. There must be someone who has the responsibility to make sure everything that needs doing does, in fact, get done. To make sure, for example, that not everyone is so busy hunting that no one takes time to care for the children. This problem is partially solved by the development of cultural norms specifying that certain kinds of people are supposed to do certain things. Thus, the norms may demand that men hunt and women take care of the children. In hunting and gathering societies, in fact, the norms are just about adequate to handle the need for coordination. But not quite. Even in such societies there is some need for leadership. The norms can teach a general pattern, but there are some situations such as a hunt or a religious ceremony, where leadership is required. Some person or persons must have authority to tell other people what to do. Someone must be given power that others do not have. This happens even among people who feared personal authority and tried to do without it. Decisions were made by the entire community, meeting several times a week. But they soon found it very difficult to maintain this pattern. Someone had to be given authority, if only in minor matters (Spiro, 1956, p. 94).

All this suggests that, although we cannot say exactly how much, there is an unavoidable absolute minimum amount of power concentrated in the hands of one or a few members of any group. Since this is true for the family, for the kibbutz, and for small hunting and gathering communities of 40 to 50 people, how much more true in industrial society. We cannot exist today without a great deal of concentration of power in order to coordinate this complex social system. Parents must have power over their children, teachers over their pupils, the government over its citizens and employers over employees.

In addition to coordination, there is another reason for the concentration of power which may be seen as functional. That is the need to limit deviance. In a small group setting everyone may share equally in this function, but in larger groups it becomes necessary to assign some of it to special positions. To say that a function of authority is to control deviance suggests people do not always follow the rules willingly, that they must, at least sometimes, be coerced. Is this not the same as saying that selfishness is at the root of power differentials? Yes, but the point is quite different from the functional and conflict emphasis. As we say, they both explain stratification as primarily a result of selfishness. Here we are saying that a function of power is to limit selfishness. Without such a structured control of selfishness it is almost inevitable that a society will slide into anarchy.

In summary, coordination and control are two socially functional reasons for the concentration of power. People usually recognize this necessity and give such power legitimacy. People in positions of coordination or enforcement will be entirely ineffective without some power. Most people will conform and obey because they have internalized the norms that say they should, but there is always enough resistance to require some enforcement. Even those who want to do "what is right" are still sometimes in need of someone to tell them what needs doing. It is common to think of power as a characteristic of certain people, but here we are saying that functionally it is necessary to have certain positions to which power is attached, regardless of the particular people who fill those positions. Lord Acton may very well have been right when he said, "Power tends to corrupt, and absolute power corrupts absolutely," but we must give power to certain positions nevertheless. Consequently, it seems wrong to think of power as inherently evil or entirely the result of selfishness. Some power is functionally necessary. This is recognized in all societies by the designation of certain power as authority — the kind of power accepted by the norms as properly belonging to certain positions. For example, the police are recognized by almost everyone in our society as properly having the right to use force in many situations where ordinary citizens may not. We do not mean to imply that all authority, all legitimate power concentration, is functionally necessary. There is a tendency for authority to expand beyond the absolute minimum necessary to the position. So just because a person has authority to do something does not mean it is functionally necessary. Police might be given the authority to use certain weapons to treat people in ways which are not at all necessary to carry out their jobs. The fact that some, and perhaps even most, authority is not functionally necessary, should not blind us to the equally important fact that there is also some authority which is functionally necessary.

THE FUNCTION OF PRIVILEGE

A second major dimension of social stratification is the unequal distribution of privilege, by which we mean access to goods and services. There are two social functions of unequal privilege. One is meeting positional requirements. There are many positions that must have access to certain artifacts or facilities, what we might call "the tools of the trade." A farmer cannot be a farmer without land; a doctor requires the use of certain instruments; and a manufacturer will not be able to function without machinery. A second function of inequality in privilege is *meeting personal needs.* Children need schooling, the sick need care, the weak need protection. The supply of such needs will, necessarily, cause inequality in the expenditure of goods and services. Although the needs being met are individual, indirectly they are also social. A society will not function if basic needs of a significant number of its members are not being met. Since such needs differ from person to person, it follows that a certain amount of inequality in privilege is socially functional.

In most societies, of course, inequality in privilege goes far beyond the minimum demanded by social necessity. It cannot be demonstrated that such large differences serve any social structural requirement. Also, it should be noted that just because a position requires access to certain things, it does not follow that such things must belong to the person who occupies the position. In fact, very often they do not. Teachers do not, typically, own the classrooms they use. Bus drivers seldom own the buses they drive. There are communities in which most, if not all, positionally required goods are commonly owned. The person filling a position may use the "tools of the trade" but does not own them. A Hutterite farmer does not own the land he works; it is owned by the entire community. Even in this situation of communal ownership, however, there still is some inequality, because not everyone in the community is given equal access to the commonly owned property. For all practical purposes, there may be little difference between a system of private property and one of communal property when it comes to unequal access to things needed to carry out positional activities. Some inequality in privilege is clearly necessary to the functioning of society, but the need for private wealth is not demonstrable, since some communities seem to get along without it.

THE FUNCTION OF ESTEEM

It is obviously true that people are constantly evaluating each other. A variety of terms, such as esteem, respect, prestige, honor, and approval are used to refer to this process. Sometimes these terms are used almost interchangeably and the differences between them are not at all clear. We would like to follow a helpful distinction made by Davis and use *prestige* to mean the amount of favorable regard attached to a position in the social structure, and *esteem* to refer to the amount of favorable regard given to a certain person, based on performance in a position (Davis, 1942, p. 312). For example, in a well-known American prestige scale a Supreme Court Justice is consistently given the highest rating of all occupations listed. The position, Supreme Court Justice, clearly has high prestige. Yet a particular person serving as a Supreme Court Justice may be held in either high or low esteem, depending on performance in office.

This distinction between prestige and esteem is very important in discussion of social stratification. It seems clear that esteem differences can and often do help in the functioning of society. Esteem may be expressed in many ways, including prizes, awards, applause, or verbal expressions of appreciation and praise. If a fireman risks his life to save a small child, we all feel that somehow he should be honored. He is unlikely to receive any financial reward or increase in power, but his self-sacrificing behavior is an expression of values that we would like to reinforce. We want to hold him up to others as an example to follow. The one way open to us is through esteem: the "pat on the back," words of praise, and perhaps an "outstanding citizen" award. By praising those who do their work well and dispraising those who do not, we remind each other constantly of our common values and norms, without which no society can function well. We should remember, however, that, as Tumin points out, esteem is not a zero sum game (Tumin, 1955, p. 421). That is to say, if one person is given more, someone else does not necessarily get less. It is possible, and even common in some small groups such as the family, to have all members highly esteemed by other members. But just how much inequity in esteem is socially functional? Some, but precisely how much there should be, seems impossible to estimate.

Need we praise and honor certain positions more than others? That is to say, do we need a system of prestige as well as esteem? The functionalist says that we do. Moore (1963, p. 16) argues that the difference in prestige functions as "a sign of acceptance of the legitimacy" of other inequities (power and privilege), but fails to explain why this "sign" is necessary. If by virtue of two respective positions one has some power to control another's behavior, will society collapse if one does not call the other "Sir" while doing as told? Must one prove by some gesture or word (in addition to following orders) that he/she agrees that another has the right to tell him/her what to do? We think not. We can see the need for obedience, but not for deference. It is hard enough for most of us to take orders; it only makes it more onerous if we must, in addition, show deference to the person giving the orders. No doubt deferential behavior reinforces a subservient position, helping to keep one in the habit of doing as one is told, but it could be argued that power most needs the support of prestige precisely when there is the least agreement as to its legitimacy. In which kind of society is "bowing and scraping" most common, one in which power differences are minimal, or one in which the concentration of power is so great that even the most ardent functionalist would agree it is beyond social necessity and perhaps even dysfunctional? At any rate, it seems that the experiences of various communication groups, such as the Hutterites and kibbutzim, demonstrate that it is possible to have power differences without accompanying differences in prestige. The two are separable. Power differences are necessary, but prestige differences are not.

To summarize thus far, we have seen that the two major current sociological perspectives on social stratification, although differing in many important ways, are similar in implying that the major reason for inequality is the self-seeking nature of human beings. This may be true, but we should realize that there are also very important social structural reasons for inequality. Minimum amounts of differences in power, privilege, and esteem are structurally necessary to the adequate functioning of any society. Differences in prestige and privately owned wealth, on the other hand, although very common, do not seem to have a necessary social function, and may very well be entirely the result of self-centered motives stressed by both functionalists and conflicts theorists.

CHRISTIAN DISAGREEMENT ABOUT SOCIAL STRATIFICATION

With some notable exceptions (Niebuhr, 1932: Brunner, 1945), Christian writers have not addressed themselves to the question of how much social inequality is functional. Most Christian writers seem more interested, quite rightly, in what the Bible teaches and what Christian leaders of the past have had to say regarding stratification than in what sociological analysis can tell us about its functionality. Yet there is little agreement among Christians as to how much stratification is good and proper. Christians can be found propounding almost every conceivable position regarding stratification, often claiming that they clearly have the support of Scripture. By ignoring many subtle differences, we can categorize the various positions into four, as we discuss in the following pages.

Acceptance of the Existing System of Social Stratification

Those who accept the existing systems of social stratification are those who are most likely to have an almost completely functional view of inequality. They are likely to quote from Romans 13:1 about how all authority is given to God. The Bible also tells us to render honor to whom honor is due (Romans 13:7), and does it not say that there will always be poor people (Mark 14:7)? Of course, there are some poor people who deserve our help, and it is good for our own souls to give such help, but most are poor because of laziness or some other behavior involving disobedience to God. They get exactly what they deserve. Was it not the Apostle Paul who said "If anyone will not work, let him not eat?" Andrew Carnegie once said, "Those worthy of assistance, except in rare cases, seldom require assistance" (Morgan, 1963, p. 83). Bishop Lawrence of Massachusetts argued this position at the beginning of the 20th century. He said: "In the long run, it is only to the man of morality that wealth comes. We believe in the harmony of God's universe...Godliness is in league with riches" (Yinger, 1970, p. 358). From this perspective, wealth is concentrated in the hands of those who are most worthy and most likely to use it productively for the good of all. Riches are a sign of God's favor (Psalm 37:22-26; Proverbs 10:22; Ecclesiastes 5:19). It is true that the Bible speaks of equality among people, but this is seen as referring to the equal value of all souls in the eyes of God, not as a call for social equality. Those people agree wholeheartedly with the functionalist that without a good deal of inequality the motivation for hard work would be gone and social order would dissolve into chaos.

A Demand for Total Equality

At the opposite end of the spectrum (from those who accept the status quo) there have always been, since New Testament times, those who believe that Christ calls us to live in a society with as little inequality as possible. This is considered the ideal set forth in passages such as Acts 2:22-27, Acts 4:32-35, and James 2:1-9. We know that the church at Jerusalem had a community of goods. Later, one of the early church fathers, Gregory of Nyssa, wrote, "We are all of the same family; all of us are brothers. And among brothers it is best and most equal that all inherit equal positions" (Taylor, 1973, p. 19). These radical egalitarians argue that relationships between Christians should be based entirely on love. Decisions should be shared. No one person should have power over others. Inequality of wealth should be kept to the absolute minimum necessitated by differences in need. James tells us not to go along with common prestige rankings. Private property should be limited to small personal items or be done away with entirely. There must be a total transformation of society or, if that is not possible, Christians should separate themselves into their own equalitarian communities. The Hutterites of Canada and the United States are examples of people who live by those principles today.

Decrease Inequality by Individual Action

Most Christians today are probably in this position. They believe that some inequality is good and functional and some is bad and due entirely to selfishness. Because all of us sin, Christians as well as non-Christians, it is unrealistic to expect radical egalitarianism to become very popular. Nevertheless, it is the Christian's duty to act as unselfishly as possible and come to the aid of those in need. No one can tell us how to do that. We must each decide for ourselves. If we have become wealthy in a legal way, we can indeed see our wealth as a gift from God, but as John Calvin says in an earlier quotation, it is given us as a test. Will we use it selfishly, or to God's glory? Each of us must decide how the power, privilege, and prestige given us can best be used to God's glory. Scripture gives us some guidelines when it tells us that the poor have a right to share in our wealth (Deuteronomy 24:14-15). To keep what we do not need when someone else needs it is not our right; it is theft. Charity is incumbent on everyone with wealth when there are those without basic necessities (Luke 12:33, 14:13; Ephesians 4:28; James 1:27; I John 3:17). The Church should constantly call this to our attention, but since our property is our own — private property being ordained by God — we are each, individually, responsible to see that social stratification does not become extreme, that no one suffers poverty in the midst of plenty. Evil comes from within our hearts, so there is no point in trying to solve the problem of inequality with new laws or with revolution. What we need is a renewal of Christian values and a new dedication to helping the poor. As the French sociologist, Jacques Ellul (1976, p. 319) has said:

> We have to realize that no economic or political transformation will bring about any fundamental change at all. What will happen is simply that one problem will give way to another and one injustice to another. Variations of degree are possible for a time, but nothing decisive is accomplished. It is from within and by the mighty act of Jesus Christ that situations change.

Decrease Inequality by Social Changes

Some Christians are not satisfied with leaving the problem to the individual conscience. "Look where that kind of thinking has gotten us," they say. Rich Christians have too often told the poor that they should not be so materialistic; that they should concern themselves with their immortal soul and then they will have "pie in the sky when they die." They paternalistically offer "relief," while hanging on to their own superior positions tenaciously. The consequences have been a poverty class in rich countries and the exploitation of poorer countries by richer countries. It is true that complete equality is unrealistic, but we hardly need worry about that. It is true that individual action is necessary, but it is insufficient. At present we have a dominant class that runs things largely for its own benefit. Over 25% of the wealth in the United States is owned by 1% of people. There have been no significant changes in the pattern of income distribution since World War II. When Mrs. Horace Dodge died in 1970, it was reported that she left an estate of over $100 million. She had inherited $59 million from her husband in 1920 and put it into tax-free municipal bonds. During the intervening 50 years, we are told, while earning over $1 million a year in interest, she never had to pay any federal income tax (Taylor, 1973, p. 70). At the same time, many live in crowded, rotting tenements, with inadequate food and little opportunity for employment. We cannot hope to reduce such gross inequities by personal charity or even government welfare handouts. It is argued that the system which makes this all possible must be changed. It is naive not to recognize that government already has a very strong influence on the social stratification system. What is being suggested is not government interference in a presently free system, but a change in the way government already influences social inequality.

It is argued that each person has a right not only to basic subsistence needs, but also a functional position in society. Each person should have the opportunity to develop God-given talents and gifts. No one should be treated as a burden we would be happier doing without. The most individualistic view, which argues for "charity" and "welfare payments," makes the poor dependent and apathetic, if not openly hostile. It tells them they have nothing to offer us and robs them of a sense of worth. Besides, it has not worked. There are millions of people in North America who, in spite of all our "Christian charity," lack adequate food and clothing and cannot afford heat for their homes in winter. Some go so far as to say that if things do not improve, the downtrodden have the right to rise in revolt to establish a more equitable system. A variety of less radical suggestions have also been offered: a change in the inheritance system, a guarantee of a job for everyone who wants one, free higher education, a higher minimum wage, a good government housing program, a better tax system, and public ownership of all natural resources. The suggestions are varied, but the common theme in this fourth position is that a decent standard of living and an opportunity for full participation in society should become inalienable rights and the poor should no longer be dependent on the goodwill or guilty consciences of the rich. It is also argued that the individualistic approach fails to recognize the existence of social sin, that is, evil built right into the social system. Changing hearts is not considered enough; we must also change social systems if we are to solve social problems. Christianity has had an influence for social reform in many times and places in the past. It should continue to do so in the future. We must change the system, they say, to one that is more in keeping with biblical teachings, and that means greater social equality. We should, as Christians, follow the example of Christ and "set at liberty those who are oppressed" (Luke 4:18).

BIBLICAL PRINCIPLES

Which of these is the correct position? People usually are attracted to the one that is most in their own interest. The better off we are, the more we are apt to want to keep things as they are, and the worse off we are, the better radical equalitarianism sounds. This is true of Christians as well as non-Christians. If, however, we sincerely want to evaluate the four positions mentioned and can stand the discomfort this will probably cause, consider two fundamental biblical principles that are referred to constantly in Christian literature on social inequality. These are justice and stewardship.

Justice

Of course the question of whether the system is just is precisely what divides the conservatives and the radicals. No one is against justice; we simply cannot agree on how it is to be achieved. The principle of justice is often stated as "to each his due," but what is a person's "due"? Although the Bible does not give us a simple outline of a just social system, the repeated and passionate protests against injustice in both the Old and the New Testaments give us an indication of what a just society would look like. It is a society in which the poor are not treated as second class citizens, but are recognized to have legitimate claims to a share in all basic necessities of life. Also, as Henry Stob tells us, in a just society each member is acknowledged to be an image bearer to God and given the opportunity to fulfill his/her God-given potential. That does not mean total equality, because God has made each of us a unique creation with individual abilities and needs. Stob says, "Justice is served when each man is given both the freedom and the opportunity to attain to the level of personal achievement of which he is capable" (Stob, 1978, p. 133). Which of the four positions mentioned above is most likely to promote a just society?

Stewardship

The second biblical principle that should have a strong influence on our view of social stratification is that of stewardship. Unhappily, stewardship has come to be interpreted by many as a requirement that a certain proportion of one's income (usually 10%) be given to church and "charity." Once we meet the obligation, we can do whatever we want with the rest. This is not the biblical view. The Bible teaches that everything, including our very selves, belongs to God, as Creator. We are caretakers in God's world. There is no absolute human ownership of anything. Some have been entrusted with more than others. We are stewards not only of our wealth, but also of our power and prestige. Thus we are called to a life of constant and careful consideration of whether our system of social stratification is evidence of good stewardship. Which of the four positions above is most likely to help us to be good stewards of God's creation?

CONCLUSIONS

Power, privilege, and esteem are not evil in themselves. There can be no doubt that a certain amount of inequality in each of them is functionally necessary, and even when inequality goes beyond the functionally necessary we cannot automatically call it evil. Power can be seen as given by God as a means to control evil and to maintain social order. The danger is that the powerful often begin to use their power for selfish ends. The Gospel does not include or approve of a particular economic system. Scripture does not condemn wealth, but rather the common practice of the rich to forget their role as stewards of God and to begin to think of their riches as their own to dispose of as they see fit. Esteem and prestige differences tempt us to forget that it is only God who should be glorified. There is also the danger of treating the poor and powerless as somehow inferior human beings. The Bible tells us over and over that God is aware of this tendency and promises to come to the defense of the needy. The basic danger of social stratification, then, is that the inequalities in society which we cannot do without — the functional minimums of power, privilege and esteem — are used by people entrusted with them for their own selfish ends. It is this that creates an unjust system. We should constantly remind ourselves of the ultimate seat of all power, privilege, and esteem. The traditional ending of the Lord's Prayer states: "For Thine is the kingdom, the power, and the glory, forever and ever. Amen."

Study and Discussion
Questions

1. Explain the two views of social stratification discussed at the beginning of this paper (function and conflict). Which one do you consider more accurate? Why?

2. Distinguish between the four dimensions of stratification (power, privilege, esteem, and prestige) mentioned here. In what ways and to what extent are each of these functional to society? Give specific examples.

3. Distinguish between the four positions mentioned regarding the amount of stratification. Think about the people you know well. Which of these positions are they likely to prefer? Would some of them disagree? In what way is the position people take on this question related to their own place in the social stratification system?

4. Which of the four positions regarding how much social stratification should be permitted is closest to your own view? Why do you choose this position over the other three?

5. Why do you think there is no single agreed upon Christian position on stratification?

6. Is "rich Christian" an oxymoron? How about "powerful Christian?"

7. The Hutterites form communities in the U.S. and Canada in which there is very little personal property or personal decision-making. A person's first thoughts are for the good of the community, not personal desires. Would you be at home in such a community? Why or why not?

8. How do you explain the presence of so many poor people in rich countries like the U.S. and Canada? Could these countries eliminate poverty? How? What would it mean for the stratification system?

9. Explain the biblical principles of justice and stewardship. How do they apply to social stratification? In this regard, do we live in a just society where people practice stewardship?

10. How do you interpret the text from Proverbs with which this paper begins? In answering this question, it may help to read verse 9 also.

References

Brunner, Emil, *Justice and the Social Order*. New York: Harper and Brothers, 1945.

Dahrendorf, Ralf, *Class and Class Conflict in Industrial Societies*. Stanford University Press, 1959.

Davis, Kingsley, "A Conceptual Analysis of Stratification" *American Sociological Review*, Vol. 7:3, 1942.

Davis, Kingsley, and Wilbert Moore, "Some Principles of Stratification." *American Sociological Review*, Vol. 10:2 No. (April 1945): 242-249.

Ellul, Jacques, *The Ethics of Freedom*. Grand Rapids, MI: Eerdmans, 1976.

Gilkey, Langdon, *Shantung Compound*. New York: Harper and Row, 1966.

Graham, William, *The Constructive Revolutionary*. Richmond, VA: John Knox Press, 1971.

Kemper, Theodore, "Marxist and Functionalists Theories in the Study of Stratification: Common Elements that Lead to a Test," *Social Forces*. Vol. 54:3, pp 559-577.

Lenski, Gerhard, *Power and Privilege*. New York: McGraw-Hill, 1966.

Moore, Wilburt, "But Some are More Equal Than Others," *American Sociological Review*, Vol. 28:1, 1963.

Morgan, Bruce, *Christians, The Church and Property*. Philadelphia: Westminster Press, 1963.

Niebuhr, Reinhold, *Moral Man and Immoral Society*. New York: Charles Scribner's Sons, 1932.

Oostdyk, Harv, "Poorology," *The Other Side*. Nov.-Dec., 1974.

Spiro, Melford, *Kibbutz*. New York: Schocken Books, 1956.

Stob, Henry, *Ethical Reflections*. Grand Rapids, MI: Eerdmans, 1978.

Taylor, Richard, *Economics and the Gospel*. Philadelphia: United Church Press, 1973.

Tumin, Melvin, "Rewards and Task-Orientations," *American Sociological Review*, Vol. 20 (Aug.), p. 421, 1955. "On Equality," *American Sociological Review*, Vol, 28: 1, 1963.

Wilson, Everett, *Sociology*, Rev.ed. Homewood, IL: Dorsey Press, 1971.

Yinger, J. Milton, *The Scientific Study of Religion*. New York, Macmillan, 1970.

CHAPTER 25

THE FUTURE: INTRODUCTION

Anyone who has even a very rudimentary knowledge of history is aware that 20th century America witnessed major social changes. As the curtain falls on this century, the stage is a very different setting from that of the 19th century. Within the past two hundred years, the United States has changed from a predominantly agricultural society into an industrial and then a postindustrial one. As we prepare to move into the 21st century we may be sure that change will continue. It is social change, especially the rapid change of the past century, that is at the base of the problems included in the chapters of this text.

As Professor Walker discusses in this final article, social change is inevitable. Some changes work for the good of the social order; others harm the system. The effects of most, however, are a blend of the positive and negative. Given its inevitability, it is important to consider the process of social change and its implication for the future. Without such thoughtful reflection, we would go blindly into the future, "muddling through" rather than actively shaping our social world. Christians need to be proactive, Walker suggests, as they assess the future in social problems terms.

Walker challenges Christians to move toward a "proleptic Christian future," by using the Word of God to anticipate the coming of God's kingdom. From the Scriptures we can know about a reality that is to come, and we can "act on that future ahead of time." He applies this approach to four issues dealing with the future: future shock, socialization and education, anticipatory democracy and Christian values. In this introduction we would like to take a somewhat different tack to complement the discussion found in this chapter. We would like to suggest the application of "proleptic eschatology" to three commonly identified sources of social change, namely, (1) *cultural innovation*, (2) *technology* (technique), and (3) *human action*.

There are three distinct sources of *innovation*: discovering an aspect of reality that already exists (e.g., discovering a new planet); using existing knowledge to produce something that did not exist before (e.g. inventing nuclear weapons), and diffusion or the spread of cultural elements from one society to another. Historically, organized religion has often been guarded about innovation, sometimes with good reason. Scripture tells us that the sin of Adam and Eve was in coveting the god-like knowledge that was to come from eating of the forbidden fruit (Genesis 3:5-6). Are there some discoveries that are best left unmade, some inventions that the world would be better off without, some diffusion that may cause havoc for other societies? There are many illustrations that could be used for discussion from articles in this text. Is it possible that we know too much about nuclear weaponry for the good of the human race? Does our knowledge of genetics coupled with advances in *in vitro fertilization* feed our desire to try to take control away from our Creator?

Technology, the practical applications of scientific or other knowledge, is often identified as another related catalyst of social change. The influence of technology seems so powerful that some sociologists have supported a theory of *technological determinism*, the idea that our culture has been shaped primarily by technological developments. While many of these developments have positive consequences, there is also no question that technology impacts each of the social problems we have chosen for inclusion in this text. Broadening this concept, however, may make it even more relevant for a Christian grappling with a proleptic eschatology.

The French Christian sociologist Jacques Ellul in discussing *The Technological Society* (Vintage Books: 1964) uses the word "technique" to assess a broader process of change in which technology is but a component. For Ellul, *technique* is "the totality of methods rationally arrived at and having absolute efficiency (for a given stage of development) in every field of human activity." The emphasis is on *rationality* and *efficiency*. Technology is thus but one part (albeit an important one) of a larger phenomena. He contends, "Technique is not an isolated fact in society (as the term technology would lead us to believe) but is related to every factor in the life of modern man . . . ."

Looking over the problems discussed in this text, one could reflect on the extent to which they have been the result of "efficiency" rather than love and justice, of "rationality" rather than seeking the will of God. Relying on technique has permitted us to achieve a technologically advanced world, but at what price? Ellul makes the following observation about the future:

> In our cities there is no more day or night or heat or cold. But there is overpopulation, thraldom to press and television, total absence of purpose. All men are constrained by means external to them to ends equally external. The further the technical mechanism develops which allows us to escape natural necessity, the more we are subjected to artificial technical necessities . . . . The artificial necessity of technique is not less harsh and implacable for being much less obviously menacing than natural necessity . . .(p. 429).

Most sociologists would concur that social change is not the result of some blind force we call "innovation" or "technique." Human action, both individual and collective, can and does affect social change. There is room in sociological theory for the Christian proactive response called for by Professor Walker's article.

Unfortunately many Christians have responded to social problems generated by social change in reactionary rather than visionary ways. Two responses have been especially common. One has been to proclaim that "Jesus is coming back very soon"; therefore, it is futile to worry about changes occurring in "the world." Another response has been to try to bring back the past, a time gone by that is thought to be more Christian than the present. Neither response is the visionary type we suggest appropriate for a proleptic eschatology.

Jesus' vision for His Father's kingdom is a radical one. It is a kingdom based on love rather than power. It reflects a world where leaders are servants, the last are first, and adults must become as children. The kingdom of God that is among us rests not on military power and economic resources, but on faith—a believing with certainty the things unseen. It is a kingdom that is not of this world, yet it is in us and among us. The question is whether Christians have Jesus' passion for the Father's kingdom—or whether we have simply a nostalgia for days gone by. Are we seeking the Holy Spirit, asking Him for a clear vision of this kingdom that we are called to help bring about in

462

the world in which we live? That is the challenge we hope Professor Walker's article on the future will impress on us all.

THE FUTURE AS A SOCIAL PROBLEM

J. Thomas Walker

INTRODUCTION

We are living in an unprecedented period of rapid social change that has in many ways left us cut off from a stable, traditional past. The ever accelerating rate of change in science and technology, ideas, values and our basic institutions has become problematic since it is not clear where this will lead us. This chapter deals with the need to be able to understand social change in order to anticipate alternative possible futures. Only in this way will we have a rational and moral choice in the construction of what we hope to be a desirable future. Without such insight and sensitivity we are more or less stuck with the consequences of what all too often are our own ill-thought-through devices. But there is hope. Christianity offers direction in the knowledge of the transforming power of the final future into the present moment.

PROBLEMATIC ASPECTS OF THE FUTURE

The Reality of Social Change

There are important differences to note between life in a traditional society as compared to life in a modern one. Unlike modern societies, traditional people experience such slow social change that it is hardly recognized. Thus, what change does exist is rendered negligible. Traditional norms, values, knowledge and institutional patterns are passed on from generation to generation, thus maintaining the status quo. In fact, behavior is chiefly routinized as a functional adaptation to conserve what have become the time-tested "best ways of doing things." Such tradition and routinization serve to link the past with both the present and the future. That is, past knowledge and behaviors provide the key to the present, and since the future is thought of as an indefinite extension of the present, routines tend to guarantee a foreseeable future. For such people the future carries few surprises.

Things are quite different, however, in a more modern society characterized by rapid social and technological change. Although there is significant continuity with the past, conceptions of the past, present and the future become quite distinct. In fact, intergenerational differences may give rise to different concepts of each. Unlike life in traditional society, the validity of past knowledge and behaviors becomes less functional as the forces of social change fashion the present and the future. Thus, the past, present and future become segmented or cut apart from each other.

While we use images and memories of the past as well as perceptions of current conditions to construct what we regard as the present, we recognize that past and present are not the same since intervening change has taken place. For the same reason we do not expect the future to be the same as the present. Actually, the present and future become interactive. Our conception of the future affects the way we behave in the present and conversely the decisions that we make in the present have consequences for the future. Nowhere is this more evident than in playing the stock market. Assuming the "buy low — sell high" strategy, whether one enters the market at a particular point in time depends on one's conception of the future of the market, or more specifically the future of the particular stock that one is contemplating purchasing. And conversely the decision that was made has effects at various future points in time. That is, the stock may rise, lower or remain the same, affecting one's future net worth accordingly.

At a societal level sometimes our choices and actions turn out to be positive and adaptive. Sometimes they turn out to be negative and problematic. But usually they have resulted in a mixed blessing bearing both certain advantages and certain disadvantages. (For example, nuclear generating plants provide greater electrical power but carry with them the dangers presented by nuclear waste or nuclear accidents, including the possibility of facility "meltdown.") This has led to the development of two major types of general characterizations about the future — those with an optimistic outlook and those with a pessimistic outlook.

Pessimists and Optimists

On the one hand, the pessimistic view raises serious questions about the future. Of concern is the possible negative consequences of both the rate as well as the direction of current change. What kind of a future is likely if we continue to waste our resources and pollute our environment? Will our resources sustain continued economic growth? Is continued economic growth really good? In our affluence will future Americans possess a strong work ethic? Just what is happening to religion, family and education as basic social institutions?

On the other hand, the optimistic view reflects the confidence that although problems exist, important headway is being made that will result in social improvement. On the whole, optimists believe than all of our current problems will be solved without much difficulty. To them, problems should be seen as challenges that we can and will solve. Or, in the optimistic words of Julian Simon and Herman Kahn, "solutions usually leave us better off than if the problem had never arisen; that is the great lesson to be learned from human history" (Simon and Kahn, 1981, p. 3).

But both the pessimists and the optimists are looking at the same object of study. How is it that they come to hold such divergent positions? The answer is that they focus on and emphasize quite different trends. And they have different opinions and degrees of faith in our ability to deal with our problems. But an underlying theme in both pessimistic and optimistic thinking about the future is that major problems exist. It becomes important, then, to look at the future in social problem terms.

THE FUTURE AS A SOCIAL PROBLEM

Although social problems are capable of being defined many different ways by different segments of the population, there are *three* basic criteria on which sociologists generally agree. *First*, social problems are structural or social in origin. That is, social problems at least in part, stem from either the way society is organized or the way that it functions. *Second*, social problems are of considerable social magnitude so as to affect large numbers of people or at least certain influential people in the society. And *third*, social problems lend themselves to viable alternatives or solutions that society can employ through collective social action (Montero and McDowell, 1986, pp. 4-7).

Although there are both positive and negative aspects to social change and its effects on the future, it is meaningful to think of social change and the future in social problem terms for at least *five* reasons. *First*, many of our current social problems, if not caused by, are at least intimately linked with social change. For example, the poor quality of American education can be linked to social change characterized by such factors as the growing demands placed on our schools, less stress placed on fundamental skills and the erosion of academic and behavioral standards (Caddy 1987, pp. 102-109). And widespread substance abuse can be linked to alienation and the pressures brought on by changing times (Eitzen, et.al., 1989, pp. 578-579).

Social change, of course, is not exactly new; what is new is its present occurrence at an alarming and almost incomprehensible rate. Since the Industrial Revolution of the 18th century the pace of change has steadily accelerated so that we can characterize the present as an era of *convulsive* change. Up through the first half of the 20th century technology changed rapidly but social arrangements remained relatively unaffected (Cornish, 1977, pp. 3-4). Trends since 1950 reveal that social arrangements have been remarkably affected, as reflected in modern values and lifestyles.

Second, Alvin Toffler coined the term "future shock" to describe what he recognized as "the shattering stress and disorientation that we induce in individuals by subjecting them to too much change in too short a time" (Toffler, 1970, p. 2). Toffler characterizes this condition as an affliction of which large numbers of people suffer. At the heart of the concept of "future shock" is the idea that technology has bombarded modern man with a bewildering diversity of decisions. The result has been a condition that Toffler terms "over choice." He further characterizes modern society by its *transience* (as seen in the temporariness of everyday life: throw away products, mobility and short-term human relationships), novelty (as seen in new developments in science and social and political arrangements) and *diversity* (as seen in new products and lifestyles). Essentially Toffler argues that "unless people quickly learn to deal with the rate of change in their personal affairs as well as society at large, a massive adaptational breakdown is inevitable" (Toffler, 1970, p. 2). Thus, social change can be problematic at a personal as well as at a societal level.

Third, as we attempt to solve the social problems confronting us we should recognize that seldom do our efforts achieve a "final solution" to any particular social problem. This is so chiefly because causality tends to be quite complex in sociocultural affairs which involve systemic relationships that require a holistic perspective. The intended solution of certain social problems can thus generate further problems. And sometimes the "solution" can be worse than the "condition" to be corrected. Not infrequently the far-reaching consequences of institutional change have been unintended, unanticipated and even undesirable (Jones, 1980, p. 1). That is, change produces further change. Change feeds on itself. Primary causes create effects called secondary effects, which may create further effects called tertiary effects, and on and on. The recognition of this further stresses the point that it is important to think of social change and the future in social problem terms.

A *fourth* reason to think of the future in social problem terms is because certain developments, such as the nuclear arms race and environmental pollution, threaten the continued existence of human life. Other developments such as the growing destruction of the rain forests and the ozone layer certainly have the potential to affect human adaptation to our planet in a drastically negative way. Indeed solutions to some such developments may be very complex and lie beyond our normal institutional means for dealing with them. The ozone layer belongs to everyone, especially to future generations, and environmental pollution goes beyond simple state boundaries, or even national boundaries for that matter.

Closely linked with this last point is the recognition that many of the current practices with which we approach the future are based on questionable if not faulty assumptions of the past. Is biggest really best? Can we have infinite growth? Can we continue to use our environment as a dump? These types of questions need to be raised, for much of such human behavior is simply not rational. Unless we reflect on issues such as these, we may unwittingly be bringing about our own extinction.

A fifth reason to think of the future in social problems terms is the recognition that changes in social norms and values tend to accompany (or perhaps follow from) the general forms of social change. This can be seen as cutting across all major institutions. Thus, there have been recent significant shifts in institutionalized values and we cannot be certain that they bode well for the future. Marriage and family are not what they used to be. Our society is becoming more secular and materialistic. Our schools are failing us and we frequently question just what ethical as well as substantive preparation our young are actually receiving for a life of meaningful achievement, self-fulfillment and service to others. Marvin Cetron and Owen Davies have noted that hardly any aspect of American life is free of ethical problems (Cetron and Davies, 1989, pp. 292-295). Thus, we need to consider just where these new values and trends are likely to lead us.

Although it is helpful to think of the future in social problems terms it is important to keep in mind that social change is not necessarily always problematic or socially disruptive. Social change certainly has many positive aspects. And in certain cases the absence or lack of change may be problematic, as exemplified by the unwillingness of certain individuals, groups and even institutions to lawfully uphold civil rights laws of the 1960s. But our present concern with social change and the future is ameliorative in nature. We therefore turn to an analysis of the concept *future* and the means whereby we can become proactive in it.

TOWARD A PROACTIVE FUTURE

Future Studies

Since the late 1940s a new area of inquiry has emerged — *future studies*. By definition, *future studies* is the study of the future with the purpose of being better able to anticipate, prepare for and influence future events. This is possible not only by anticipating the future in a forecasting sense, but also in an alternative future sense. That is, researchers of the future frequently construct alternative futures which enable them to identify key decision points that are likely to influence the probability that certain possible futures actually obtain. The perspective of future studies, then, provides us with the possibility of being better able to anticipate the future and thus the opportunity to exercise a degree of choice — to be *proactive* rather than *reactive* in life's events.

But as in any intellectual endeavor the way that we approach the subject of study is extremely important. The conclusions that we arrive at and the solutions that we derive rest on the basic premises of the perspective that we adopt. We now turn to the major premises of future studies.

Premises of Future Studies

The future is not predictable in any exact sense. This is so for several reasons. First, we have only fragmentary data on the past and present. Secondly, we have an incomplete understanding of the processes of change. Thirdly, we can not exactly anticipate the direction and influence of individual choices. Fourthly, we can not account for unanticipated events or "surprises" such as what the legal profession terms "acts of God." Also, the degree of uncertainty varies with the field being studied. In some fields, such as physical systems, uncertainty may be relatively low. But for complex social, political and economic systems the uncertainties are quite numerous (Amara, 1981, p. 25). Thus forecasts are usually qualified to be "surprise free."

We cannot know the future in a scientific sense because the future is prefactual. That is, science rests on facts or empirically verifiable events for its validation. Since future studies are prefactual they of necessity must deal with "surrogate knowledge." Those who study the future must create their object of study and subsequently characterize its reality. This, of course, is not science. But this does not mean that, if given a fairly solid knowledge base, we can not assign reasonably relative probabilities to the likelihood of the occurrence of certain subsequent events.

Change feeds on itself. That is, change has the effect of producing other changes which have the effect of producing yet other changes and on and on. Frequently these "chain effects" may be both unintended and unrecognized, but nonetheless causal. Cornish has well illustrated this point by suggesting that the automobile might contribute to the deterioration of one's community or even one's own marriage. With the coming of the automobile people are provided with a means of traveling rapidly, easily, cheaply, privately, door to door. Consequently, people patronize stores at greater distances from their homes — stores that are generally bigger, with larger clienteles. As a further consequence residents of a community do not meet each other as often and do not get to know each other so well. As a consequence of this, people become strangers to each other and find it difficult to unite and deal with common problems. They find themselves increasingly isolated and alienated from each other. Finding themselves isolated from their neighbors, family members come to depend more on each other for the satisfaction of most of their psychological needs. And when spouses are unable to meet the heavy psychological demands that each makes on the other, frustration occurs. This, then, may lead to divorce (Cornish, 1977, p. 8).

The future is to be understood as the result of holistically operating causal factors. If one is interested in looking at the future in terms beyond a very narrow scope, it is important to adopt a holistic approach because reality is systemic in nature. Harmon, for example, has noted that social systems behave like integrated, organic wholes (Harmon, 1979, p. 14). Events seldom occur in isolation so as to have no effect on other events, situations or sectors of the social system. In fact, the opposite is verified by experience. In the preceding example of the introduction of the automobile, many different types of factors needed to be considered — new technology, increased geographical mobility, altered social behavior in the community (greater social isolation, less social dependence), greater dependence on family for meeting psychological needs, inability of

468

spouses to meet heavy psychological demands imposed by their mates and subsequent personal frustration. The reality of the meaning of such a scenario is more than the effect of each isolated event. The chain of events as holistically perceived offers a profoundly more insightful analysis.

The future is not predetermined (Amara, 1981, p. 25). It is neither fixed nor inevitable. That is, there is no single future out there waiting to happen (Toffler, 1983, p. 182). Rather, the future consists of many possibilities and even probabilities. What eventually happens is a consequence of many complex factors acting holistically to produce what becomes "real." Especially important is the realization that a great deal of what happens in the future is the result of the decisions that we make and the actions that we take at key points in our history as we live out our lives.

Thus, future outcomes can be influenced by individual choices (Amara, 1981, p. 25). The excursions that researchers of the future take frequently do not so much result in forecasts of the future at some point in time so much as in the construction of alternative futures. A stress of the concept of alternative futures emphasizes the realization that we can exercise choice among alternative possibilities in the future. While we have no guarantee that our choices will always result in our particular desired or preferable future, the exercise of choice can be used to direct ourselves toward what we regard as preferable and away from what we regard as undesirable.

Methods of Studying the Future

Those who study the future do so by using various methods and techniques. Some approaches are highly formal, while others are quite intuitive. In any case each has its own assumptions, perspective, strengths and weaknesses. Therefore, the various methods and techniques should not necessarily be contrasted and regarded as mutually exclusive (Schwarz et.al., 1982, p. 11). Frequently they can supplement and complement each other, rendering a more insightful analysis. A brief description and summary of the major methods include 1) trend extrapolation, 2) the Delphi technique, 3) technology assessment, 4) cross-impact matrix, 5) models and simulations, and 6) scenario construction.

Trend extrapolation is probably the simplest and most commonly used forecasting technique. Essentially, it involves the characterization of the rate and direction of past trends followed by the projection of such trends to some point or points in the future. This method is called trend extrapolation precisely because it projects a known trend beyond the empirical data that support it. Frequently this involves simply plotting a variable on a graph over time so as to yield a curve which can be projected into the future.

The *Delphi technique*, developed by researchers at the RAND Corporation, is a method for polling experts so as to obtain the best possible results from consultation. It rests on the assumption that a number of informed people in a given field are more likely to make better judgments and forecasts than would be made by a single individual. The Delphi technique can be a very effective forecasting method when the subject under study does not lend itself to precise analytical techniques, but yet would benefit from collectively distilled subjective judgment.

Technology assessment refers to a wide variety of specific policy studies that examine the effects of technology on society in terms of its introduction, extension or modification. Such analyses tend to stress the unintended, indirect and delayed consequences of technology. Hence, options for the future are investigated (Porter et.al., 1986, pp. 208-213).

The *cross-impact matrix* enables forecasting which takes into account how one factor, situation or event may influence another to produce a certain outcome in the future. Unfortunately, most forecasting methods tend to produce only isolated extrapolations or forecasts. But the cross-impact matrix captures the interactions among variables as they causally operate on one another. By using a cross-impact matrix researchers can gain a holistic understanding of causality.

Models and simulations are similar in that they both are representations of a more complex reality. However, models are static while simulations are dynamic. By observing how models are organized or structured, researchers can learn how the structure influences behavior. Researchers can, by means of mathematical equations, build a computer model of such complex systems as the U.S. economy. By feeding in certain assumptions the economy can be dynamically simulated and researchers can learn a great deal about how a complex set of variables act on each other to produce particular results. By asking the computer certain "what if" questions, complex unanticipated and far-reaching ramifications are now able to be analyzed.

Scenario construction involves working out possible developments or paths into the future. Scenarios are hypothetical sequences of events that are constructed for the purpose of focusing in 1) causal processes and 2) decision points. Scenarios of the future can be constructed meaningfully so long as the researcher has a solid knowledge of the facts attendant to the scenario, an understanding of the causal processes at work and a creative imagination of the relationship between the two. The construction of scenarios typically involves asking two questions: 1) How might some hypothetical event come about, step by step? and 2) What alternatives are there for each actor at each step for preventing, diverting or perhaps facilitating the process? Scenarios are important in that they stress that future possibilities may well hinge on the decisions that we make in the present.

SOME MAJOR CONCERNS FOR THE FUTURE

Future Shock. As pointed out earlier, Alvin Toffler was concerned with the reality of future shock (Toffler, 1970). Change can occur so rapidly as to produce in individuals a bewildering stress and disorientation. Sociologically, future shock is similar to what social theorist Emile Durkheim called *anomie*, for it involves personal disorientation brought on by lack of order, predictability and stability in social life.

Socialization & Education. Upon surveying the modern world, Margaret Mead (1970) recognized that not only is the intensity of change important, but the nature of change is as well. According to Mead we have irreversibly shifted from a "postfigurative" culture to a "cofigurative" one. That is, due to rapid social and cultural change, a shift had occurred from a social reality in which both learn from their peers. Whereas a cofigurative culture is grounded in the present, a postfigurative culture is grounded in the past, rendering it inadequate to meet conditions of life imposed by the present.

Yet the older generation controls the power and resources needed by the youth to adapt and develop. Thus the older generation is trapped and the younger generation has no role models or established socialization experiences for assistance in addressing life. The youth cannot look to the past of their parents, since they regard it as a miserable failure. Hence both generations are isolated and lonely (Mead, 1970, pp. 63-97).

Having said this, Mead believes that we are in the process of developing a "prefigurative" culture where the old will learn from the young. Unlike the postfigurative culture that continues to replicate the past, in a prefigurative culture the future dominates the present.

Thus a prefigurative perspective would free the imagination from the past and put it where it belongs — in the future. With a continuing dialogue, the young will provide the older generation with access to "new experiential knowledge: without which a meaningful future cannot be constructed" (Mead, 1970, p. 94). Thus with direct participation of the young, a viable future can be built.

If the hope of the future is with our young, then it becomes important to consider the best educational means to prepare them for the task of dealing with a rapidly changing world. Clearly, our present system needs marked improvement. In many current curricula, concerns for the future are simply absent. In fact, in many cases we are training people for jobs that will not even exist in a few years.

Anticipatory Democracy. Alvin Toffler (1970, 1980, 1983) has expressed considerable concern about the ability of our society to govern itself adequately under the conditions imposed by rapid social change. Politicians tend to have limited time horizons which usually do not extend beyond the next election. While voters may occasionally be polled about specific issues, they are not asked to voice, or even think about, the general shape of a preferable future. Consequently, little thought and little effort are given to the long-term future (Toffler, 1970, pp. 483-484).

Toffler also views the technocratic methods of the present as being inadequate for the future. Technological plans frequently are reactive, piecemeal, and contradict and cancel one another since there is no clear vision or image of a preferred future to bring meaningful order out of the chaos of change. Technocratic administration is thus out of date, especially since it assumes a "top down" formulation of policy that fails to consider the crux of the matter — the need for a participatory democracy (Toffler, 1970, pp. 470-479). An anticipatory democracy is therefore needed. This would involve wide participation and influence based on decisions that are grounded in a long-term, conscious concern for the future rather than a short-term concern with the immediate (Dator, 1987, pp. 99-100).

Dominant Values. Whenever dealing with human social behavior, past, present or future, the issue of motivation arises. And closely connected to motivation is the structure of values that characterize social actors. Values are basically individual and collective definitions of what is socially desirable. They are important because as they become internalized during the socialization process they come to serve as the standards by which various social acts and goals are judged.

Over the past several decades numerous studies have been conducted to learn more about the changing character of American life and just what this might mean for the future. One such study, *The Lonely Crowd*, by David Riesman and associates (1950) distinguished between "inner directed" and "other directed" individuals. Inner directed people acquire from their parents while yet children an internalized set of norms and values. Such internalized principles serve as an "internal gyroscope" to guide them throughout life. The inner directed person of the 19th century had a personality that was driven by productive Protestant Ethic work values — serious attitudes toward purpose in life, work and leisure. However, other directed people of the present rely on the expectations and preferences of others for defining their beliefs and values. They are not anchored in solid and enduring values, but rather constantly tend to take on the values of others as they move from one social situation to another. They lack a fixed identity so that even in a crowd they are lonely and alone. Furthermore, inner directed individuals are seen as being replaced by other directed individuals, a change which affects all major institutions.

Similarly, Philip Slater's *The Pursuit of Loneliness* (1970) raised the question as to whether America would have a viable society since technological change and an individualistic ethics had cut the individual off from important social moorings such as family and community. The individual was left without a comfortable sense of self- and efforts at self-enhancement resulted in an even worsened state of affairs.

Daniel Bell's *The Cultural Contradictions of Capitalism* (1976) stressed a conflict in the changing values of capitalism. Due chiefly to the need to advertise and expand markets, capitalism promoted new values — to enjoy life, spend money and live hedonistically. These values, of course, fly in the face of the Protestant Ethic values upon which American capitalism was built — individuality, hard work, achievement, frugality and deferred gratification. But people must follow these older values if they are to be economically able to enjoy the newer values. Thus, the two sets of values contradict each other, and following the newer hedonism risks the very future of our capitalist way of life.

More recently, Christopher Lasch (1979) sees much of modern American society as characterized by a "culture of narcissism" that has its roots in an earlier competitive individualism. To Lasch a new emphasis on the search for self-fulfillment has resulted in a narcissistic self-absorption which removes individuals from social and political life. Lacking in self-esteem, they strive for approval from others. Uninterested in the past or future, they engage in narcissistic efforts toward self-preservation rather than self-improvement.

Perhaps the most recent major critique of American values was accomplished by Robert Bellah and his associates in a work entitled *Habits of the Heart* (1985). Like Bell and Lasch, they see self-fulfillment as a basic value of our day. But American individualism and rational self-interest erode the basis for traditional values. Where in the past institutions such as family, Church and local community held the self-oriented individual in check, this is no longer the case. People are becoming less committed to community and social life, and they are retreating into their own private lives. This raises one of the most pressing moral dilemmas of the day — the conflict between American individualism and the important need for community and commitment to each other. The survival of a free and democratic American society may well rest on an appropriate response to this issue.

These various studies all emphasize the need to take a close look at the values by which we live. While we cannot revert to the past, it is clear that we must in the future find ways to meet our need for community and commitment to each other.

TOWARD A PROLEPTIC CHRISTIAN FUTURE

A futurist perspective is valuable in that it provides a rational and meaningful orientation toward imaging the future. Such an ability is important if we are to adjust effectively to the world in which we live. Simply to be good stewards of the blessings and gifts of God requires such a consciousness and methodology. Such a perspective is also imperative if we are to extricate ourselves from all the harm that we have done to ourselves and our environment, God's creation, in the name of development and human progress.

But beyond this, the future can be viewed from two basic vantage points. We can begin by mastering history and learning to understand the present in order to be in position to forecast the future on the basis of identifiable trends. Or we can view it the other way around. We can begin with the finished world of God's plan and then look backward to the present. Taking these two perspectives together yields what theologian Ted Peters has termed "Proleptic eschatology" (Peters, 1980, p. 12). *Eschatology* refers to the study of last or final things — to the Christian hope for the future of all things. And *proleptic* refers to our anticipation of such a reality to come — to know and be able to act on that future ahead of time.

The concept *proleptic eschatology* essentially views God's creation as ongoing, with God creating from the future rather than from the past. God draws man toward His own purposes. Christ's resurrection is proleptic for He is the future made present. Our faith in God gives us new life with which we can come to know God's will for a consummate future. In Peters' words:

> Proleptic eschatology is realistic and dynamic. By projecting a vision of God's will for the ultimate future of all creation in the face of the approaching crisis, it provides us with an overall goal plus the confidence that with God's help we will get there. Instead of muddling through, a church that lives proleptically will be characterized by creative action and an ultimate sense of direction (Peters, 1980, p. 32).

The concept of a Christian proleptic eschatology offers considerable insight into how we might appropriately deal with the future, given the serious nature of the problems presented. From a Christian perspective we shall offer some suggestions to the four major issues raised earlier — the problem of dealing with "future shock," socialization and education for the future, the need for an "anticipatory democracy" and the need to be anchored in solid Christian values.

Future Shock

At a personal level the Christian can deal with future shock by recognizing that, although we are living in a period of rapid social change, there is stability in the Christian faith. The Christian message and the tenets of Christianity apply to all historical periods. While we may be subject to being bombarded by a bewildering range of decisions, and modern life may be known for its transience, novelty and diversity, we can be sensitive to a conscious awareness of our mundane reality and the need to keep this reality in a broader Christian perspective.

A broader Christian perspective suggests the stability of the Christian community and the deep and enduring relationships that believers share. Those who experience too much change in too short a time — who change jobs, move to a new part of the country, etc. — can share with one another for mutual support. Through prayer and meditation we can temporarily escape the world's accelerating pace and devote attention to things that really matter — Christ's kingdom and our role in it. And, in keeping our priorities properly ordered, we can be in a good position to act on our beliefs and values. Recognizing the enduring nature of the Christian perspective and the Christian hope for the future, we can generate and provide people with images and even experiences that they are likely to encounter in the future. Such images and experiences, of course, enable us to approach the future from a position of strength and firm conviction rather than fear and confusion.

Socialization and Education

It is not easy growing up in a complex and rapidly changing world. While the future belongs to the young, they have the least control and authority over the resources necessary to deal with it. Frequently, they are educated for a world which is no longer there, as though they were asked to live in the past. Christian concern demands a greater respect for the dignity of our youth that parallels how we are taught to respect our elders. The old adage that the young should be "seen and not heard" falls short in this regard. While it is important to bring the young up in the way of the Lord, it is also important to recognize that we can learn a great deal from our youth that is important to the future of us all, if we are only willing to listen. The young are educated on the "cutting edge" of new knowledge in science and technology. And, in general, they are more adaptable to change than are older people.

Any educational program for the future must be grounded in a concern for anticipated problems of the future by providing students with the requisite skills and fundamental values for thinking about and acting responsibly in a changing world. This should be carried out in a Christian environment of love and mutual respect for all generations, especially future ones, as we all work to the greater glory of God.

Anticipatory Democracy

If a democracy is to function adequately in a rapidly changing world it must be able to anticipate the future and engender broad participation among its constituents. Without these two prerequisites democracy can become elitist, out of touch with the real problems that it faces and essentially undemocratic. Specific issues reflected in current trends, such as environmental pollution, the wasteful use of our natural resources and the nuclear arms race, need to be studied in futurist terms and dealt with before the kinds of options that would be democratically desirable become closed to us.

Social policy must represent the interests and future well-being of all peoples. It is important that the Church take the lead here, both as an advocate for its own constituency as well as for those disenfranchised peoples whose voices are not heard. A Christian conception of social, economic and political justice demands as much.

Fortunately we can see progress being made along these lines. As early as 1975 we saw an addition to the House Rules of the United States House of Representatives requiring that congressional committees must consider the future on a continuing basis (Bezold, 1978 p. xxv). Since about that time significant interest has been expressed concerning the promotion of anticipatory democracy. Citizen *ad hoc* groups have been organized at the local, regional and state levels to forecast possible futures and define goals for public policy. Certain denominational and futuristically oriented "watchdog" groups regularly inform government about social policy. With greater education among people and participation in decision making, progress is being made, but much more is needed. Through faith in God's future, the Christian is called upon to work toward a new world of social justice, peace and love.

Dominant Values

We live in a world of conflicting social values and in this sense our rapidly changing culture is somewhat schizophrenic. Traditional values have become eroded and are being replaced by more modern, hedonistic — even narcissistic — ones. As suggested above, this has resulted in a social world in which community is lacking and service to others is becoming an empty phrase. Further, due to the materialistic nature of our modern world, social image tends to fashion our self-identities and conceptions of self-worth.

The serious Christian, however, possesses the ability to see beyond such shallow and fleeting values which yield only a shallow and fleeting life. Christianity anchors all believers in solid, deep and enduring Christian values that, being basic to God's plan, transcend time. St. Paul tells us to be not conformed of this world, but rather to be transformed that we may prove what is that good and acceptable and perfect will of God (Romans 12:2). We are to be filled with the Spirit (Ephesians 5:18) and are to grow in grace and the knowledge of Jesus Christ (II Peter 3:18). Armed with such knowledge and will, Christians can live and promote a positive image of the future — God's kingdom of justice, community, freedom, joy, peace and love.

Study and Discussion
Questions

1. Why is it meaningful to think of the future in social problem terms?

2. Why is the future to be thought of as a social problem in today's world as compared to the world of previous generations?

3. What are the major reasons for adopting a pessimistic view of the future? For an optimistic view of the future?

4. What evidence is there to support Toffler's thesis of the impending disastrous consequences of "future shock"?

5. What is meant by the newly emerging field of future studies? How does this approach enable us to become proactive in the future?

6. Upon what basic premises does the field of future studies rest?

7. Describe the major methods of studying the future.

8. What do you believe are the major concerns or social problems that we will have to face in the future?

9. What is meant by a Christian proleptic eschatology?

10. How can the concept of a Christian proleptic eschatology enable us to live a more Christlike life in the plan of God?

References

Amara, Roy, "The Future Field: Searching for Definitions and Boundaries." *The Futurist* 15: 25-29, 1981.

Bell, Daniel, *The Cultural Contradictions of Capitalism*. New York: Basic Books, Inc., 1976.

Bellah, Robert, and Richard Madsen, William N. Sullivan, Ann Swidler and Steven M. Tipton, *Habits of the Heart: Individualism and Commitment in American Life*. New York: Harper and Row, 1985.

Bezold, Clement (ed.), *Anticipatory Democracy: People in the Politics of the Future*. New York: Random House, 1978.

Caddy, Douglas, *Exploring America's Future*. College Station, TX: Texas A&M Press, 1987.

Cetron, Marvin and Owen Davies, *American Renaissance: Our Life at the Turn of the 21st Century*. New York: St. Martin's Press, 1989.

Cornish, Edward (ed.), *The Study of the Future: An Introduction to the Art and Science of Understanding and Shaping Tomorrow's World*. Bethesda, MD: World Future Society, 1977.

Council on Environmental Quality and the Department of State, *The Global 2000 Report to the President*. Vol. I, Washington, DC: U.S. Government Printing Office, 1982.

Dator, Jim, "Hawaii 2000, The World Futures Studies Federation, and Me: Thinking Locally and Acting Globally." Pp. 87-100 in Michael Marien and Lane Jennings, *What I Have Learned: Thinking About the Future Then and Now*. Westport, CT: Greenwood Press, 1987.

Eitzen, D. Stanley, and Maxine Baca Zinn, *Social Problems*. Boston: Allyn and Bacon, 1989.

Harmon, Willis W., *An Incomplete Guide to the Future*. New York: W. W. Norton and Company, 1979.

Jones, Thomas E., *Options for the Future: A Comparative Analysis of Policy Oriented Forecasts*. New York: Praeger Publishers, 1980.

Kauffman, Draper L., *Futurism and Future Studies*. Washington, DC: National Education Association, 1980.

Lasch, Christopher, *The Culture of Narcissism*. New York: W. W. Norton & Co., 1979.

Mead, Margaret, *Culture and Commitment*. Garden City, NY: Natural History Press/Doubleday and Co., Inc., 1970.

Montero, Darrel, and Judith McDowell, *Social Problems*. New York: John Wiley and Sons, 1986.

Peters, Ted, *Fear, Faith and the Future: Affirming Christian Hope in the Face of Doomsday Prophecies*. Minneapolis: Augsburg Publishing House, 1980.

Porter, Alan, "An Introduction to Technology Assessment and Impact Analysis." Pp. 208-213 in Albert H. Teich (eds.), *Technology and the Future*. New York: St. Martin's Press, 1986.

Reisman, David, Nathan Glaser and Reuel Denny, *The Lonely Crowd: A Study of the Changing American Character*. Garden City, NY: Doubleday Books, 1953.

Schwarz, Brita, and Uno Svedin, *Methods in Future Studies: Problems and Applications*. Boulder, CO: Westview, 1982.

Simon, Julian, and Herman Kahn (eds.), *The Resouceful Earth*. Oxford: Basil Blackwell, 1981.

Slater, Philip, *The Pursuit of Loneliness*. Boston: Beacon Press, 1970.

Toffler, Alvin, *Future Shock*. New York: Bantam Books, 1970.

Toffler, Alvin (ed.), *Learning for Tomorrow: The Role of the Future in Education*. New York: Vintage Books, 1974.

Toffler, Alvin, *Previews and Premises*. New York: William Morrow and Co., 1983.

Toffler, Alvin, *The Third Wave*. New York: Bantam Books, 1980.

Whaley, Charles E., *Future Studies: Personal and Global Possibilities*. New York: Trillium Press, 1984.

Vago, Steven, *Social Change*. Englewood Cliffs, NJ: Prentice-Hall, Inc., 1989.